VISCOUNT HALIFAX

EDWARD FREDERICK LINDLEY WOOD

FIRST BARON IRWIN, THIRD VISCOUNT HALIFAX

VISCOUNT HALIFAX

A BIOGRAPHY

ALAN CAMPBELL JOHNSON
author of "ANTHONY EDEN," etc.

ILLUSTRATED

IVES WASHBURN, INC.
NEW YORK

PRINTED IN THE UNITED STATES OF AMERICA

PREFACE

"So perhaps the book is intended to be popular rather than serious. The case for writing the biographies of living men is at best poor unless they offer their collaboration." Thus commented the *Times Literary Supplement* on a recent biography of Neville Chamberlain written while he was still Prime Minister, and it summarized what I suppose is the general verdict of literary and even political purists to books of this nature. But without challenging, although it is tempting to do so, the arbitrary distinction between seriousness and popularity, and while freely admitting the many obvious difficulties, even with the subject's active assistance, in the way of adequate and impartial analysis of a public career which is in active progress and necessarily screened from full public scrutiny, there is still, I believe, a margin of usefulness for the contemporary biography.

In undertaking this study of Viscount Halifax I had in mind that only a synthesis of the three distinct phases of his career contained in the three names by which he has been known could do justice to the inherent continuity and consistency of his life story, and that such a narrative was needed if balanced judgment was to be applied to the man and his work. Secondly, although for the past fifteen years he has been among the most powerful of British leaders, he remains a more than usually submerged personality. His way has been set in places of power and influence and he has never felt the need to court popular approval or attention, with the result that although quick to defend the causes he has advocated he has only rarely been stirred to justify himself as well and has suffered more than his fair share of misrepresentation. This book is in no sense an apologia, but it is an attempt to break down the barrier of anonymity that stands between Halifax and a critical estimate of the man; nor is it primarily a personal study, for I have been at pains to fill in the political background.

Both with the outbreak of war in September 1939 and

with his appointment as Ambassador to Washington in January 1941 his career reached a dividing line where it is convenient to pause and take stock of his past record in order to assess his potential impact upon a momentous future. In considering his interpretation of Britain to the people of the United States at this historic moment in Anglo-American relations or in envisaging his role at the next peace settlement, his previous record as Viceroy or Foreign Secretary, moralist or Cabinet Minister offers valuable and revealing precedents. My biography of Anthony Eden, published in 1938, was based on a similar assumption that Eden's resignation from the Foreign Secretaryship in February of that year was in fact a boundary line in his political fortunes where it was possible to link his achievements with his prospects.

The tendency of literary criticism to suggest that it is unseemly and inexpedient to write books about great men until they are buried and their private papers unearthed has, I believe, to be resisted, if only because in discouraging the concept of books about the living for the living we are in danger of separating biography from the mainstream of contemporary literature, leaving it as the mere adjunct of the historical text-book, pious obituary or not infrequent impious exposure. Also, from the political view-point, Democracy has already paid a heavy price for hiding its leading lights under the bushel of excessive reticence. Halifax's diffidence and modesty are such that he is quite willing, and indeed would probably prefer that if his career is considered to have any intrinsic interest posterity should weigh its merits and tell his story. But with all deference I believe the advantage rests with making the attempt even though the material is limited, the perspective close and incomplete and Halifax in the midst of the cataclysm in which everything he stands for is at stake, than to wait upon futurity which will in any case be better served.

If therefore this work is ephemeral, its facts and interpretations defective, its conclusions tentative or dogmatic, I hope that the principle of writing books about living contemporaries will not on that account be condemned. Lord Halifax is called to leadership at one of the great formative periods in his country's and the world's history, and my essential purpose is by sifting available material about his life to provide some clues to the quality of the man and his statesmanship. Such a purpose commends itself as worthwhile even if this biography has failed to achieve it.

. . . .

I have received much valuable help from many sources in the compilation of this book, but wish to place on record above all my appreciation of Lord Halifax's kindness and courtesy in allowing me to publish for the first time two of his private Indian Papers, the notes of his private Address delivered to the Princes in June 1927, and his important Note on Dominion Status written in November 1929 at the time of his historic Dominion Status Announcement. These documents throw new light on two vital aspects of his Indian policy.

I am also deeply indebted to Mr. Malcolm MacDonald for going to so much trouble both to enlist Lord Halifax's help and to give me several indispensable introductions to prominent men whom Lord Halifax had suggested I should see as being intimately acquainted with his work in India. These included Sir Herbert Emerson, Sir George Schuster and Professor John Coatman, all of whom gave me their invaluable advice and impressions.

I would like also to acknowledge the help I received from Mr. R. A. Wiseman of the Dominions Office in connection with the tour of the West Indies in 1921. Mr. Wiseman was seconded from the Colonial Office to accompany him on the tour, assisted in the compilation of the Wood Report and is in a unique position to recall that important phase in Lord Halifax's career. Needless to say, while strongly fortified by this distinguished and authoritative advice, I take full responsibility for all conclusions I have drawn from it.

In the preparation of Part I I would like to pay tribute to the comprehensive and unstinting help I have received from Mr. Harry Hodgkinson of the Liberal Publication Department, and to the material and advice given me by Mr. Neville Masterman. For the period covered by Part II I am grateful to Mr. A. K. Milne for a judicious summary of Press material. I owe much, too, to my wife's patience and accuracy in transcribing this bulky manuscript into type and helping to guide it through proof.

Of the many authorities on which I have unashamedly drawn for much of the detail of and background to Lord Halifax's career I must make special mention here of J. G. Lockhart's brilliant study of Lord Halifax's father, the second Viscount, in particular the second volume. For the Indian period I have derived much help from Professor Coatman's *Years of Destiny,* and from the selection of Lord Halifax's Viceregal speeches (including his great address to Toronto University in 1932) published under the title of *Indian Problems*; while for the period from 1934 to 1940 I have dipped deeply into the admirable collection of Lord Halifax's speeches edited by H. H. E. Craster and published by the Oxford University Press. I am much obliged to Sir Humphrey Milford for his kindness in supplying me in advance with a page proof of this book.

I have felt it inadvisable when quoting speeches available only in press reports to translate the passages from *oratio obliqua* into direct speech.

ALAN CAMPBELL JOHNSON.

April 1941.

CONTENTS

PART III

VISCOUNT HALIFAX

ILLUSTRATIONS

PART I

EDWARD WOOD

CHAPTER I

THE WOOD INHERITANCE

SOME are born great, some achieve greatness and some have greatness thrust upon them, but to Edward Frederick Lindley Wood, first Baron Irwin and third Viscount Halifax, belongs the rare prerogative of being great in all three respects. His achievements and capacities would have marked him out for distinction quite apart from the status of his family or the favours of fortune. But as in the case of so many of the leading British statesmen of our time, in order fully to understand the contribution of Edward Wood to our public life it is necessary first to assess his career by describing his ancestry. An account of his family origins and background provides a clue to much that would otherwise be obscure in the pattern of his political, social and even moral outlook.

An adequate analysis of our old nobility with some more objective aim than to discredit the peerage for the purposes of the Parliament Act[1] has yet to be written; it would be an invaluable corrective to many misconceptions that prevail, particularly abroad, where the ethics as well as the status of British aristocracy have been subjected to much mischievous and ill-informed comment. Setting aside healthy recriminations of Party politics and the natural bias of privilege, it remains generally true to say that if British noblemen are holding many positions to-day of power and influence, it is because they have shown themselves as a class capable in rulership, competent in administration. Political experience has taught the British that to temper Democracy with recognized aristocrats is to leaven the lump. When the aristocrat abuses his trust, great is the scandal and deep the popular heart-searching, but when there is a long tradition of honourable if unsensational service to the State the praises remain unsung. If the aristocrat, placed by birth above ordinary

[1] The primary object of a slim volume published in 1911 under the title of *Our Old Nobility*.

ambitions or necessities, takes his duties very much for granted, so also does the public assume his achievements.

It is doubtful whether one in a hundred of the British electorate is aware that its Foreign Secretary, and now Ambassador to Washington, Viscount Halifax, is none other than Lord Irwin, Viceroy of India, or whether one in a thousand could go a stage further and identify both with the Hon. Edward Wood, a President of the Board of Education and Minister of Agriculture in Mr. Baldwin's Governments. Such transitions in title are observed but not assimilated, and, like the natural order of things, are no more closely associated in the popular mind than is the chrysalis with the winged butterfly. If the man himself is not popularly pieced together, even less is he identified with the names and records of his forebears. But the ancestry of Edward Wood is no formal catalogue of dim nonentities. He is the great-grandson of Lord Grey of the Reform Bill, grandson of one of Queen Victoria's most trusted statesmen—a Chancellor of the Exchequer and a pioneer in legislation for India, a great-nephew of Lord Durham, whose renowned Report laid the foundation of modern Canada, though no doubt he is more popularly remembered for his saying that he supposed a man might jog along on £40,000 a year! Through his mother, Wood is a descendant of the illustrious house of Courtenay which provided three Emperors to the Eastern Empire. The Wood family can, of course, make no such pretension, although it is deep-rooted in the history of Yorkshire. Actually there was no single family in Yorkshire comparable, for instance, to the Stanleys in Lancashire, but a number of well-known Yorkshire families had intermarried and had thereby collectively increased their prestige. The Woods, too, were elevated only recently to the peerage; Edward Wood's grandfather being the first Viscount, while the baronetcy was created in 1784—the same year, incidentally, as it was conferred on the nearby Edens of Durham. It is interesting to note that Anthony Eden and Edward Wood, whose careers in recent years have been so closely interwoven, are through their mothers related, both claiming Lord Grey of the Reform Bill as a great-grandparent.

These northern families know the meaning of power. It is difficult for those who are bred in the south, and for the Londoner in particular, to realize that it is the north of

England which has in many ways the greater influence in the moulding of British political opinions. Yorkshire, too, is assured of solid strength through its trade—the old staple, wool, and its modern equivalent, steel and engineering. The Woods not only shared in Yorkshire's prosperity, but testified to the prevailing character of those whose life is set in the broad Ridings—which is indifference to social convention combined with stern devotion to religious symbols and unwavering belief in the moral order. In the West Riding country there are the Woods of Hollin Hall, of Conyngham Hall and of Hickleton. "That at some remote period there was a common ancestor is suggested by the appearance in one form or another, on their crest or on their arms or both, of a savage, woodman, or wild man of the woods."[1]

The Woods of Hickleton were descended from a Robert Wood or de Bosco who apparently concurred in a grant of land in Carlesmore to Egglestone Abbey. Another early member of the family who emerges in brief tragedy from the anonymous annals of Tudor England was Robert, Prior of Bridlington, who was attainted for High Treason and executed in 1537, "the year when the Pilgrimage of Grace came to its bloody end". It is only fitting perhaps that Edward Wood, with his High Churchmanship, his love of Anglo-Catholic ritual, and his father with his lifelong devotion to the cause of union with Rome, culminating in the conversations at Malines, can both claim direct descent from one who followed the banners of Robert Aske in the last and greatest challenge to English Reformation. It is not hard to believe that Edward and his father would have answered the call precisely as the Prior of Bridlington did, not simply to defend a Priory but to assure the continuity of the Catholic tradition which had impressed itself so deeply into the life and faith of the northern shires. We find, however, that the Woods, in common with most other houses which paid the extreme penalty for defying Henry VIII's tyrannous tight-rope conscience, in due course made their peace with the new order; for a direct ancestor of the Hickleton Woods was George of Monk Bretton near Barnsley, whose eldest son became a collector of revenue of the dissolved monastery of Bretton.

[1] J. G. Lockhart, *Charles Lindley Viscount Halifax* (in two volumes, Volume I 1838-1885, Volume II 1885-1934), Vol. I, page 3. This classic study of his father is an indispensable guide to Edward Wood's ancestry and early life and I quote freely from it throughout.

This son, also named George, succeeded on his father's death in 1589 to the lease of The Smithies, in due course "was a joint Lord of the Manor of Bretton and bought The Smithies outright from the Crown, thus becoming a landed proprietor".[1] On his death in 1638 he left The Smithies to his second son John, apparently disinheriting for some reason his eldest son Robert, of whom little is known save that he was baptized at Royston in 1589, died and was buried there in 1676, thus setting a precedent for longevity in the family.

There was another brother, Peter, who fought under Gustavus Adolphus in the German wars and was killed at the siege of Leipzig, but direct descent was through Henry Wood of Barnsley (1645-1720), a son of Robert, and through Francis, also of Barnsley (1696-1735) who was a J.P. and Deputy-Lieutenant of the County of Yorks, to Charles Wood, the third son of Francis. Charles, who was born in 1731, went to sea at the age of sixteen and fought in the Seven Years War and the War of American Independence. In September 1782 he was in command of the *Worcester*, of sixty-four guns, and took part in the action of Hughes' squadron against the French at Trincomalee. His ship, the rearmost, was attacked by two of the enemy and made a "most notable defence". The last shot in the engagement wounded Wood in both legs, tearing away one knee-cap and injuring the tendons of the other leg. He died at Madras on October 9th after some agonizing days, "probably a victim of the crude naval surgery of the day".

It was upon Charles' second brother, Francis Wood of Barnsley, that a baronetcy was conferred in 1784 with remainder to the issue male of his father. Thus it was that when Francis died in 1796 the baronetcy devolved on Francis Lindley Wood, the elder son of Captain Charles. The history of Francis Lindley (1771-1846) need not detain us. He had military and naval interests, though he did not achieve any outstanding distinction, most of his life being confined to the West Riding. It was his elder son Charles who, in a career loaded with honours, was to be raised to the peerage as First Viscount Halifax, and to lift the name of Wood from the respected obscurity of north country

[1] Lockhart, ibid. For the origins of the Wood family see also Foster, *Pedigrees of the County Families of Yorkshire*.

squires into national eminence and the exclusiveness of Court society.

. . . .

Charles Wood was born in 1800; at the age of eleven he went to a preparatory school at Everton, thence to Eton, where he was "the most promising young man in every respect they have had for some time". From Eton he went to Oriel College, Oxford, where he achieved a Double First and blazed an academic trail for his grandson Edward to emulate. His career at University over, he undertook with relish what was for those days a most unconventional version of the Grand Tour, through Germany, Switzerland and Italy. He reports that he had "a straw hat . . . a face burnt to the colour of a polished wainscot, a beard fit for a Bernese peasant, a black neckcloth twisted round my neck and the end tucked under a string on my shoulder which supported my coat rolled up on my back *à la* knapsack and fastened to the other shoulder by my handkerchief; waistcoat open, white trousers rolled up into short large breeches, dirty splashed stockings and large shoes, with a six foot pole armed with an iron spike. *Me voici!*"—an authentic if flamboyant portrait of an early, perhaps the first, British hiker! At Verona he saw Napoleon's Marie Louise, a forlorn forgotten celebrity, whom he described as "plain, middle-sized, and pale, and very uninteresting in manner and appearance". When he returned home his father disbursed the £4,000 necessary for him to become a Member of Parliament for Grimsby in 1826 in the Whig interest—just when the Whigs showed signs of emerging from their long eclipse.

On July 30th 1829 Charles made his "happy and brilliant" marriage to Mary Grey, daughter of Lord Grey, the Whig Leader. Mary, who died in 1884—a year before her husband—lived long enough for Edward and her other grandchildren to remember her as "a frail but very particular old lady, who had beautiful little white hands and always wore gloves in the house. When the butler brought her any change, it was carefully washed before being handed over; when she went to stay in a small hotel she would bring her own sheets; and when she visited her chiropodist she never went in her own carriage, but called a four-wheeler for reasons of delicacy."[1] The honeymoon was spent abroad,

[1] Lockhart, Vol. I, page 13.

but in the course of it Charles had an alarming illness—the precursor of fatal ill health in his family—and nearly died at Genoa. He made a quick recovery, however, and returned home to be re-elected for Grimsby and to reap the political first-fruits of his marriage by being appointed Secretary to his father-in-law, who was now Prime Minister.

During the next two years the struggle over the Reform Bill dominated all else in our public life and succeeded in rending family relationships asunder. As Grey's " shadow ", Wood was naturally deeply committed to it. He seems to have had considerable acumen—or inside information—about the Bill's hazardous journey through Parliament, for he is reported to have given the correct forecast of the majority of nine which it duly received after a last dramatic debate in the Lords. He sprang from his seat, shouting " We have won "—exuberance which provoked Lord Stanley into retorting angrily, " I could kill you." Lady Mary Meynell recalls in her *Memoirs* that when the Bill became law Charles Wood and John Grey " ran hatless and hallooing into the streets in the early hours of a June morning ". But in spite of these outward signs of enthusiasm his considered estimate of " the Bill, the whole Bill, and nothing but the Bill "—which, as one historian has aptly observed, turned out indeed to be nothing but the Bill—was shrewd enough. It was, he thought, " an efficient, substantial, anti-democratic, pro-property measure ". And as such, being an orthodox Whig, he approved it. For the Whiggery he advocated in frequent speeches in the early years of his political career was in its essence efficient, substantial, anti-democratic and pro-property, and it was not surprising therefore to find him, during the Second Peel administration for instance, only with difficulty accepting reforms of a radical character. He was not converted to the Repeal of the Corn Laws until 1844, and in company with John Bright strongly opposed restrictions on the labour of women and children in Ashley's Factory Act of the same year: Gladstone, too, had no enthusiasm for Ashley's measures, though he would have hardly avowed, as Wood did, that he " detested " them.

Like his grandson after him, Charles Wood made steady, conscientious, if unsensational progress through minor office. He lost his seat at Grimsby in 1831, then held Wareham for a year, but on 14th December 1832, in the first reformed Parliament, was returned for Halifax, which he represented for no less than thirty-two years. From 1832 to 1834 he was joint Secretary to the Treasury, then in 1835 he was appointed Secretary of Admiralty, but resigned from that office along with his brother-in-law, Lord Howick, four years later. His experience at the Treasury encouraged Lord John in 1846 to make him Chancellor of the Exchequer, and on his appointment to this high office he was sworn a member of the Privy Council. In the same year he succeeded to the baronetcy on his father's death. His administration of the Exchequer was successful without ever being brilliant. In 1848—the seething year of Revolution in Europe—he had actually to introduce three Budgets. Russell's proposal to increase Income Tax had to be dropped by him within a few weeks of its introduction. Wood, for his own part, was always a strenuous opponent of new expenditure or taxation. His administration was a curious blend of advanced and reactionary thinking. On the one hand he sponsored and obtained a Select Committee on financial distress, was induced to sponsor £5,000,000 railway loan to Canada—a momentous decision for the future of our Empire—and repealed the Window Tax; on the other, confronted with grievous distress in Ireland he had no remedy for the wretched inhabitants save for the excessive population to adjust itself by natural means. After having survived the Ministerial crisis of 1851 he resigned, unregretted, in the following year when the Ministry fell.

It is, however, with Indian administration at one of the most critical phases in all the chequered history of the British Raj that the name of Charles Wood, First Viscount Halifax, will be most readily identified. Well might Edward Wood on landing in India as Viceroy commend himself to Indians by recalling the achievements of his grandfather. His periods of office bestraddled the Indian Mutiny. Between 1852 and 1854, as member of the Aberdeen Administration, he was one of the last to hold office as President of the old Board of Control. During this period comes his great Charter Act of 1853, " one of the most notable Indian measures ever passed by Parliament. By it the system of Government in London, in Calcutta and in the provinces was improved and modernized. It removed nepotism; it established a separate legislative council for India; it gave provincial governments direct representation at the centre. No less significant was Wood's education policy. His historic despatch of 1854, which bears the impress of a powerful, sympathetic and imaginative mind, was the logical sequel to Macaulay's Minute, and created the beginnings of the educational system with which we are familiar."[1]

Between 1855 and 1859 his work on India was interrupted by a period of office in Palmerston's Cabinet as First Lord of Admiralty, which was chiefly remarkable for his success in inducing Parliament to maintain the number of men in the navy in a period of military exhaustion following the Crimean War. During this time the Queen conferred on him the G.C.B. It was not until 1859, therefore, that he resumed his great labours for India, this time as Secretary of State. He had prepared the way for the extinction of the East India Company's regime while operating through the Board of Control. Now he was called upon to work with the new India Office and to heal the hideous wounds of the Mutiny. It was an awe-inspiring task, but the extent of his success can be gauged from the catalogue of his measures over the next seven years. He passed Acts limiting the number of European troops to be employed in India, reorganizing the entire Indian army, amending conditions of Civil Service and regulating the Legislative Council and High Court. This last measure, known as the Indian Councils Act of 1861, is in many ways the Magna Carta in the history of India's journey towards self-government. Here is embodied in legislative form the essential principle that Indian people should have a voice in the supreme council of their country. It is logically and morally the precursor of the Morley-Minto Reforms, of the Montagu Declaration, and above all of Irwin's Viceroyalty.

Before the great structure of his grandson's achievement Charles Wood's measure may seem to be embryonic; for all that, it would be fairer to assert that Irwin merely extended in the light of modern experience an ideal of self-determination which his grandfather conceived at a time when bloody terror might well have inspired repressive and authoritarian policies. On the economic side he met the need for railway extensions and dealt drastically with India's disordered finances. At first he was obliged to sacrifice his

[1] Lockhart, Vol. I, page 20.

own precepts as Chancellor of the Exchequer and to borrow largely. The growth of Indian debt led to a grave dispute with the Government of India and culminated in the resignation of the Indian Finance Minister, for which Wood was severely though somewhat unfairly censured. He was vindicated by the Budgets of 1863, 1864 and 1865, all of which registered prosperity, enabling him to reduce expenditure and to extinguish the debt. His record was one which assures him of a high place among the makers of modern India.

In 1865 his Halifax constituency, after thirty-two years, rejected him and he was returned for Ripon, but no sooner was he elected than he met with a serious accident on the hunting field which obliged him to give up all arduous official work.

Following his resignation from the Indian Secretaryship he was raised to the peerage and took the apt title of Viscount Halifax of Monk Bretton. His only return to official life was between 1870 and 1874 when he served in the office of Lord Privy Seal, a post which Edward was to hold and which then, as now, involved no departmental responsibilities. In Gladstone's time, however, the Privy Seal was not so obviously a device with which to provide the Government of the day with some eminent man who could be seconded to undertake special duties, as, for instance, Edward was, to assist an overburdened Foreign Secretary and curb his initiative in Cabinet. For the First Lord Halifax the position was more a reward for past services than a repository of secret and informal influence.

During the course of his long life with its diverse interests he succeeded in securing for himself and for his family the confidence of Queen Victoria and the Court. Granville asserts that in 1857 he was " an object of great indignation " to Victoria and Albert, who apparently thought that he had in some way underrated the Queen's prerogative; but whatever the cause of the royal displeasure, it was only a passing cloud; in general he enjoyed the Queen's favour. Following his accident she wrote, " Alone, crushed, isolated, deprived of the help and advice of her beloved husband, the Queen clings strongly to all her old and true friends and advisers, and amongst them she has ever had reason to include Sir Charles Wood." In addition, she wanted Gladstone to include him in the 1868 Cabinet " in some office with but little work ".

When Charles Wood, First Viscount Halifax, died at the ripe age of eighty-five he could claim by solid merit to have established the greatness of his house and to have assured a place in the nation's affairs for any of his descendants who might care to claim it. In him we find one side of Edward's nature, a capacity to absorb political experience, and in so doing, to carry out reform which his instincts might at first have led him to reject. Our history is rich in public men who have outgrown old ideas or prejudices, and the development of the First Lord Halifax from old Whig to new Liberal should be included in the list. Like all growth, it was a subtle process difficult to detect at any given moment or attribute to any one motive. The same faculty has been given to his grandson. It means inevitably the shedding of narrow Party loyalties. Edward is by conviction as profound a Conservative as his grandfather was Whig, but their respect for the party they support rests in its collective capacity to grow along with them; otherwise, in the hour of trial they will be found leaving their party behind. Edward, like his grandfather before him, upholds sure belief in politics as the " art of the possible "; a political ideal that cannot be made to mould or fit facts is probably a faulty ideal. Common-sense and an open mind were the watchwords of the First Lord Halifax,[1] which made him at once cautious in the tactics, bold in the strategy of political action. Edward embodies this characteristic, but he adds to it a quality to which his grandfather never aspired—intense self-discipline, the sense of moral purpose, of life lived " under the Great Taskmaster's eye ", together with that dialectic relish that comes from the pursuit of theological problems, in short, the religious impulse. Herein Edward Wood is the son of his father.

[1] After a brief account of the life and achievements of the First Viscount Halifax the *Dictionary of National Biography* makes the following assessment: " Lord Halifax was a man of greater influence in the Governments of which he was a member than his contemporaries appreciated. He was sound in counsel, exceedingly widely and well informed, and an industrious, punctual and admirable man of business. He was thus both efficient as a departmental administrator and valuable as a cool and sound judge of policy "—an appreciation that may well be applied by posterity to his grandson.

CHAPTER II

"I LIKE MY CHOICE"

THE First Viscount left four sons and three daughters. Edward's father, the second Viscount, was born in 1839. If only for the great age he attained—he lived on, frail but active, until 1934, that is, until Edward was himself fifty-three and back from India—he was bound to exercise a great influence upon his family. But his personality was overpowering, one which Edward, even if he had wished to do so, would have found the utmost difficulty in resisting. As a young nobleman who had enjoyed the accustomed privileges of Eton and Christ Church, he came under the influence of the Oxford Movement and gained from Pusey the conception of Ecclesia Anglicana as being not so much the Church of England as the Church in England. "He shared to the full Pusey's conviction that the Church of England had not forfeited her Catholic heritage, which explained why there was never any real danger of him making his personal submission to Rome."[1] He never suffered from "Roman Fever", that "disease"—as Lockhart neatly puts it—"mounting at times to an epidemic, as prevalent among young Anglo-Catholics as measles, and much more frequently fatal".[2]

As the son of the First Viscount and Groom of the Bedchamber, companion on journeys and close personal friend of the Prince of Wales,[3] Halifax seemed fairly set to follow his father with a distinguished career in politics. But the work of a Catholic layman held greater attractions for him. He worked with a number of priests and nurses in the London cholera epidemic of 1866, and thought for some time of becoming a lay brother of a religious order which was being founded in the Church of England. Even as a

[1] Lockhart, Vol. I, page 93.
[2] Ibid.
[3] Afterwards King Edward VII.

schoolboy he confessed to detesting Puritans and Roundheads, " all my sympathies were with Charles I and Archbishop Laud, and I remember calling myself an Arminian, not that I in the least knew what an Arminian in theology was, but because it was a reproach which was brought against Charles I ". As early as 1862 he had spent a winter in Rome, making his first acquaintance with the hierarchy of the Vatican and of the various Orders. But his faith was closely in line with what may conveniently be termed the orthodox High Church argument against Roman Catholicism evolved by the great seventeenth century divines, especially Laud and Andrewes, and revived by the Tractarians, Keble, Pusey, and Newman in the period before Newman joined the Roman Church.

It is beyond the scope of this work to examine the High Church beliefs of the second Viscount Halifax in any detail, but in so far as Edward has proved to be a loyal disciple of his father, and shares much of his father's faith, a brief excursion into theological controversy will perhaps be excused. In general the High Church position adopted by Halifax and his son is that the dogmas of Christian Faith were adequately defined by the General Councils of bishops up to the Council of Nicaea. Following the break with the Eastern Church and further schisms after the Reformation it was argued that Rome had put forward claims for herself as a judge of doctrine contrary to the old traditions of the Councils, and that she had added to the necessary dogmas such articles of faith as the Immaculate Conception and Transubstantiation, ultimately pronouncing these doctrines as infallibly true and necessary for salvation. The English divines stoutly maintained, along with the Eastern Church, that only what had been fixed by the United Church in General Councils was absolutely true and necessary for salvation. The normal Roman argument in reply to Anglicanism is that Rome has always been a decisive factor in the dogma and government of the Church, that the Primacy of Peter inherited from Christ was the same as the powers the Pope enjoys to-day, that the dogmas the Popes propounded had in fact always been believed, and that the Roman Church and Roman doctrine had never changed.

Cardinal Newman sought compromise in the view that the Roman Church was a development from what was to be found only in embryo in the Primitive Church, and thus was unconsciously applying to Church history the prevailing theory of evolution. His works, it should be noted, were regarded with great suspicion by Rome, and they led directly into modernist heresy in which it was virtually argued that from a series of myths, which included the gospels and the various dogmas, there had arisen the great Catholic Church, more important even than Jesus Christ Himself. Rome, of course, condemned this movement, but the Anglican Church stood by its conservative view (to be shared, after Pius IX's declaration of Infallibility, by Döllinger and the old Catholics) in only believing what had been pronounced before the schisms by the General Councils. Thus we find Halifax saying that no doubt difficulties could be reconciled, but that in spite of the faults of the Church of England since the sixteenth century, "such matters are no real trouble to me". He felt his faith and practice secure on the basis of the Vincentian Canon "*quod semper, quod ubique, quod ab omnibus*"—"what was believed in always, everywhere, by all men"—before the schisms.

The real link between High Churchmen and Rome, however, was the High Church belief in the Visible Church and in the institution by Christ of a certain "order". The true sign of the Catholic Church was thus to be found in the maintenance of his order from St. Peter onwards by apostolic succession and the sacrament of ordination. Christ had laid hands on the Apostles, thereby implanting special gifts, the Apostles on others, and so on down to the present day. By this process of reasoning, only Rome, the Church of England, the Eastern Churches and perhaps some Scandinavian Churches were part of the "true Church". In addition, Christ was present only in the Bread and Wine consecrated by properly ordained priests. Rome always maintained that the true sign of the Catholic Church was to acknowledge the Primacy of Rome and to be in communion with her, but she granted legality to the order of Bishops and priests of the Eastern Church though in schism. Halifax strove to make Rome admit a similar validity for Anglican orders, but the Pope, largely as the result of pressure from English Roman Catholics and certain influences in Rome, condemned them. The Church of England, of course, is broad enough in its doctrinal structure to include not only the Protestant conception of the priest as a divinely inspired preacher called to convert the people by the word, and of the Bible as alone necessary for salvation, but also the Catholic view of the priest (to which Halifax continued to subscribe in spite of the Papal rebuff) as part of a continuous divinely appointed society receiving ordination and giving as a result certain spiritual gifts in Communion, Baptism and Confession which no one else outside the Visible Church had the right to give.

Both Halifax and his son have survived to see the steady growth of compromise, a process at once softening the dispute and narrowing the gulf between Roman and Anglo-Catholicism. Neither Church would probably now deny infallibility or inspiration to Scriptures and to certain Councils. Each sees the words of the Creeds as embodying absolute truths. But it is no presumption to suggest that Edward, brought up in the light of these modern influences, is in a position to see more clearly than his father did that even what had been held everywhere by everyone was not necessarily true, that some of the phrases of the creed could mean many things, and that religious language was symbolic and poetic rather than scientific. Neither historical criticism nor an understanding of religious symbolism were fully apparent in early Tractarian thought. As a result, the emphasis on dogma and membership of the Visible Church involved a one-sided ethic. It became more important to believe the right thing, to be in the right Church, to obey a strictly defined code such as the marriage law, than to lead the good life, to have real religious understanding, to do things from good motives and to look for a wider ethic involving for instance social reform, which was not directly sponsored by the Church. In some respects Halifax handed down to his son a more inherently mystical than Tractarian outlook, and he claimed that he learnt from the Prayer Book that the Body and Blood of Christ were the inward part of the Sacrament.[1] He always felt quite happy inside the Church of England, though was never angry when others were converted to Rome. Indeed he even believed the Roman Church was necessary for some temperaments, but he was equally clear in his own mind that his duty was to work where God had placed him, and he suspected that the

[1] See Lockhart, Vol. I, page 83.

motives of some converts was to get out of difficulties and give up the fight from inside the Church of England.

. . . .

In 1868, at the tender age of twenty-nine, Halifax became the second President of the English Church Union, an amalgamation of several earlier and unco-ordinated societies founded over the previous twenty years in various cities and towns. The general object of the new Union was to act in a sense as the guardian of the Oxford Movement. Specifically it was to defend and maintain unimpaired the doctrine and discipline of the Church of England in a sense favourable to High Church ideas, and to give counsel and protection to lay and clerical persons suffering from unjust persecutions or hindrance in spiritual matters. The origins of this movement were comparatively modest, but his acceptance of the Presidency was to prove an historic decision. In the first place he held the position until the end of the Great War, a period of fifty-one years without a break, and was then to be re-elected in 1934, in his ninetieth year, in order that he might preside over the amalgamation of the Union with the Anglo-Catholic Congress. His long tenure of the office was to be famous as much for his defence of the Catholic faith first against the Ritualist persecutions which preceded and accompanied Disraeli's Public Worship Regulations Act and then against the modernist onslaught on the doctrine of the Church, as for the long and patient preparation for the Union of Christendom culminating at Malines in the resumption of relations, albeit tentative and indirect, between Rome and Canterbury.

It is not surprising that so formidable a record in lay churchmanship meant the exclusion of other interests. In the same year that he became President he wrote to his father about his decision not to go into politics. The kernel of the matter, he explained, was that " at a moment when the idea of what the Christian Church is has wellnigh faded out of their minds, Parliament does not seem the battle-field ". The Liberal Party was anti-clerical, and in any case if Mr. Gladstone had failed to convert it to sound churchmanship how could he hope to succeed? The Conservatives were going to the wall, as the current of thought and opinion seemed then to be against them. " As a Liberal in Parliament," he added significantly, " I should be in a false position. As a Conservative, I should be false to all my traditions. . . . I see a future when under Liberal auspices and under the influence of modern ideas the Christian Church may develop its energies and influence the world in a manner which shall throw into the shade the triumphs of days gone by."

Liberalism, however, was not destined to carry out his expectations in Church policy, and it was to Conservatism that he ultimately turned, breaking with his father's party traditions and making new political associations for his heir to inherit. But it should be stressed that in matters in which Church doctrine or his own conscience was at stake he did not hesitate to oppose whatever Party or Court interest stood in his way. His decision to alter the family motto from "*Perseverando*" to "*I Like My Choice*" symbolizes his independent spirit, for, as he told Edward, the new motto was in allusion to his own choice between his work for the Church and his position in the household of the Prince of Wales. Disraeli's Act regulating Public Worship was primarily an anti-Ritualist measure. Anglo-Catholic priests were coming into contact with the law and the English Church Union was frankly urging them to resist it. Charles had no doubt where his duty lay, and in spite of all the ties of friendship with the Prince and even of the Queen's wishes, let it be known that he did not feel he could continue as Groom of the Bedchamber, a decision from which the Prince, after considerable private pressure on his part, was unable to deflect him. The same characteristic we shall find in Edward, who for all his Conservative philosophy was quite ready to vote with Socialists on an issue of high ecclesiastical policy.

In April 1869, within a year of linking his public life to the destinies of the English Church Union, Charles Wood married Lady Agnes Courtenay. It was, genealogically considered, an even more splendid match than his father's. Only the rotund grandiloquence of Gibbon can do full justice to the bride's ancestry, and we duly learn in the *Decline and Fall of the Roman Empire* that "the purple of three Emperors who have reigned at Constantinople will authorize or excuse a digression on the origin and singular fortunes of the House of Courtenay". The first known bearer of this famous name was Atho, a French knight with a castle at Courtenay, fifty-six miles from Paris. His grandson Joscelin took part in the First Crusade and became Count of Edessa, a territory straddling the Euphrates. He ultimately fell in battle against the Turks, and his son died in captivity in Aleppo. Another grandson of Atho, Reginald, had a daughter Elizabeth, who inherited the estates and married Peter, a younger son of Louis the Fat, who at once assumed the name and acres of his wife. This in itself gives some indication of the status of the Courtenays. Their eldest son Peter, through marriage with the sister of the Counts of Flanders, was crowned Emperor of Constantinople, but he never reached his capital. His two sons, Robert and Baldwin, succeeded in turn to the Empire, but were dethroned by the first of the Paleologi.

The Courtenays of Devonshire claim their descent from the above-mentioned grandson of Atho, Reginald, who is supposed to have migrated to England. Henry II, for services rendered, supplied him with *en secondes noces* an heiress "with wide estates in the West country". Their descendant Hugh was created Earl of Devon by Edward I. By service and marriage the Courtenays became one of the greatest families of feudal England. They had Plantagenet blood in them by royal marriage, and throughout the Wars of the Roses zealously supported the House of Lancaster. The last Earl was designated as a possible husband for Queen Elizabeth when she was still Princess, but he died unmarried, with suspicion of poison, at Padua. The earldom, "which then fell into abeyance, was revived in 1831 in favour of a younger line of Courtenays which had been living inconspicuously and irreproachably at Powderham Castle in Devonshire". Lady Agnes' father was the second Earl of the revival and the eleventh in titular succession. As a commoner he was for eight years Member of Parliament for South Devon. From 1852 to 1858 he was secretary to the Poor Law Board, subsequently its president. In the interval he was for a brief period Chancellor of the Duchy of Lancaster. His son-in-law used to say that "Lord Devon knew only two forms of happiness—reading the Holy Office and attending the Board of Guardians". The career of Edward's maternal grandfather is no doubt a far call from the Imperial duties of Constantinople; but for all that he upheld his ancestral dignity and was regarded by the people in Devon with the utmost respect and affection. "I don't know what Lord Devon du," said a man, proposing his health at a local dinner, " but all I du know is that if more would du as Lord Devon du du, there wouldn't be so many as du as they du du."[1]

Of Lady Agnes' character Lockhart gives a full and convincing account. It is clear that in their formative years her children—and she bore in all six, of whom Edward was the youngest—were dominated by her steady and powerful personality rather than by the more exciting though more spasmodic influence of their father. Perhaps it was from his mother and the Courtenays that Edward Wood derived a certain serene grandeur and an impersonal quality based upon an absolute self-assurance, itself derived from centuries of hereditary power and greatness. As for his mother, " she had a dignity and reserve which alarmed strangers and set them on their best behaviour. Even her children were a little frightened of her and scarcely got to know her properly until they were grown up. To them she represented discipline, whereas their father was the fun and adventure of life, the person who suddenly broke in on the routine of lessons, who told them the enchanting stories, and played the most amusing tricks, and took them for the most exciting excursions. But in any well-regulated household there must always be someone to say when it is bedtime, to administer the reproofs and ordain the punishments. That thankless but necessary function fell to Lady Agnes whose sense of duty was as strong as that of any Wood."[2]

Their first child, Charles Reginald Lindley Wood, was born on July 27th 1870; there were two girls, Alexandra Mary Elizabeth (born 1871) and Mary Agnes Emily (born 1877) as well as two more boys, Francis Hugh Lindley and Henry Paul Lindley, born in 1873 and 1879 respectively, before their sixth and youngest child Edward. At the time of his birth his chances of succeeding to the title with three elder brothers, the oldest of whom was only eleven years his senior, seemed remote enough. But before he had even reached his teens death had smitten this tragic family, leaving him the last surviving male heir to the accumulated lands and the hard-won privileges of the Viscounts Halifax of Monk Bretton. And his life must have seemed a slender enough thread. What reason was there to expect that the

[1] Lockhart, Vol. I, pages 159-161.
[2] Ibid., page 162.

catastrophe that struck down his brothers should miss him? The contrast between the photographs extant of the little chubby boy, serious but sure of himself, with cap and stiff collar and posed with his dog, and the drawn anxious face of the young Eton scholar needs no commentary. Inherent delicacy and sudden death had taken away in the interval the companionship of brothers and the laughter of carefree childhood.

CHAPTER III

"NOW THERE IS ONLY EDWARD LEFT"

"THE finest child you ever saw, quite enormous," was the verdict of his father on his youngest son, who was born on 16th April 1881. This radiant description, however, took no account of a serious physical defect—the boy had been born with an atrophied left arm. Such an affliction is a grim burden for a man to bear through life, and there is ample excuse for the compensations that it so often provokes in those whom nature has decreed shall not be as other men are. As often as not a withered arm has been the cause of furious and calamitous ambition, or, at the other end of the scale, sullen resentments and morbid introspection—in either case a cold resolve to avenge a cruel fate. The tragedy of the Kaiser is already a classic example, and increased medical and psychological knowledge may well lead posterity to hold him up as a figure to be judged more in sorrow than in anger. It argues much for the mental and physical poise of the subject of this biography that from childhood onwards throughout a long and exacting public career he has so carried himself that his affliction—in so far as it is noticed at all—serves only to add to the inherent dignity of his bearing and to enhance the detachment of his mind.

When the time for christening came we learn that the child's godfather favoured giving him the name of Pascal, but " that other counsels prevailed " and that he was finally christened Edward. Events that were first to disturb the even tenor of the child's life were the deaths of his grandparents, Viscountess Halifax on 16th July 1884 and the first Viscount just over a year later. Edward's father thus succeeded to the title and estates when Edward was no more than four years old. One result of the passing of the first Viscount was that Hickleton Hall had to be closed for a time. " Apart from sentiment, there was economy to be considered, for though the day of death-duties was not yet come, old

Lord Halifax had been over-spending his income for some years and, even before his death, there had been talk of the need for retrenchment. So the house was shut up, and Halifax went first to Garrowby, then to Howick, where he found his Grey uncle and aunt in very feeble health, and from there to the Moult, the little house in Devon, where he and his family took up their old life again."[1]

It was in one or other of these houses that the greater part of Edward's childhood was to be spent, and they provide the splendid domestic background which has tended to make his public life more a distraction and a duty to him than an outlet for ambitions unsatisfied and energies unused at home. Hickleton is six miles from Doncaster, was built by the Wentworth family between 1730 and 1750 and bought by Sir Francis Wood (the father of the First Viscount Halifax) in 1829. He moved there the following year, selling his home at the High Hall, Hemsworth, and establishing a ménage in which the place was virtually shared between himself and his son. It was not, however, too successful a venture. Between 1829 and 1832 many trees were planted and avenues laid out in the grounds, and in 1858 extensive alterations were made to the house itself. Although Hickleton had at the outset to be abandoned, Edward's father duly returned a year later and soon established himself there, and it was to be his headquarters during the last fifty years of his life, throughout which time he was constantly making minor improvements. The place was to be an " abiding interest " with him, so that " as late as 1930 his letters to his son are full of the little changes he is making and speculations as to the satisfaction they will give to the returning Viceroy ".[2] It was, however, to the church a hundred yards away from the house that he devoted the most intense attention, bringing its services into line with his doctrinal views. Mass duly replaced matins and the liturgy of the First Prayer Book of Edward VI was adopted with the special consent of the Archbishop of York.

In later years nearby coal-pits made the place rather grimy, and as soon as the guests for the Doncaster races had departed a move was usually made to the cleaner air of Garrowby, " raised a little above the plain of York with

[1] Lockhart, Vol. II, page 2.
[2] Ibid., page 92.

the wolds piling themselves up behind it ".[1] Halifax liked to eat his Michaelmas goose there, as " the stubble-fed geese of Garrowby were the best in the world " In the time of the first Viscount the place was " little more than a shooting-box lodging three or four people, and surrounded by some thousands of acres of wood, stubble and grassland ". Edward's father began enlarging it in 1892 and finished it the following year. Once again he indulged his mediaevalism with " a beautifully concealed priest's chamber ", " a big chest with a false bottom, through which a man may reach a secret passage and eventually reappear in another part of the house ", " hiding-places, cunningly concealed, and doors which are opened by the pressure of a spring, and spy-holes from hollow recesses in the walls, commanding views of some of the rooms ". Halifax assured the Clerk of Works that all this bamfoozlement was " to amuse the children ", but " it was all the greatest fun to plan ", and Lockhart shrewdly suspects that behind the fun " may have been a lurking hope that some day perhaps, with great good-fortune, he might find himself playing hide-and-seek in the house with the emissaries of Scotland Yard, pursuing him for some high ecclesiastical defiance ".[2]

Then there was Temple Newsam, situated a few miles out of Leeds, though within range of its smoke, which belonged originally to the Ingram family. The Woods became associated with it through the marriage of Emily Charlotte Wood, one of Edward's aunts, to the son of the house, Hugo Meynell Ingram. He was forty-two at the time and she twenty-three with a young man already courting her. But Hugo, who was rich and had splendid prospects, was able to outbid his more youthful though less lavish rival. When Hugo died in 1871 he left all his property to his wife Emily, who at her death in 1904 bequeathed Temple Newsam to her nephew Edward, though his father was to have the use of it for life.[3] In 1922 Edward presented this splendid Elizabethan house with its no less splendid grounds to the City of Leeds and it is now a museum.

[1] Lockhart, Vol. II, page 103.

[2] Ibid., pages 103-104.

[3] Emily, herself a formidable personality, was probably Halifax's favourite sister. He and his family spent much of their time at Hoar Cross, which she left to another brother, Frederick Wood, who took the name of Meynell. It was Emily who left Halifax the house at 88 Eaton Square, which was to become his and subsequently Edward's town residence.

Offering more intimate memories for Edward were the Moult and Bovey Tracey, both small houses in Devon to which the family migrated regularly in the summer months. The Moult, near Salcombe, was little more than a cottage and was lent to them by Lord Devon. Bovey Tracey was bequeathed to the family by Lady Halifax's uncle Canon Courtenay on his death in 1894, and Halifax visited it annually up to 1932. It held high place in his affections, for "there", as he confessed in a letter to Edward, "the past lives almost more for me than it does anywhere else". Here were ample opportunities for fine if sometimes perilous rambles over cliff and moor and all the vigorous experiences a young father may enjoy with a young family. "On fine days there was bathing, walking and riding, and when it rained there were ghost stories to freeze the children's marrows, and occasional dressings up in which he took as great a delight as any of them."

These ghost stories, carefully compiled and stored by his father up to his last years, were to be a major ingredient in Edward's mental and emotional pabulum as a child. Edward himself, in an introduction to *Lord Halifax's Ghost Book*, published after his father's death, has testified to the sensation these eerie and macabre stories produced and were no doubt intended to produce on the children, and to the underlying motive of his father's predilections for ghosts. "They appealed strongly", he writes, "to his natural sense of mystery and romance, which so largely dictated his scale of values in the appraisement of persons and things. Apart from the moralities, few charges in his eyes were more damaging to persons than that they should be judged devoid of imagination, and the actual framework of everyday life had value according as it corresponded to something more profound than itself, to be felt rather than seen, and to be apprehended only by some faculty more subtle than that of reason." Such a faculty is no doubt given to children, but not the compensating power of analysing it. What is a matter of quiet shrewd reflection for Viscount Halifax the mature statesman stimulated Edward Wood the child to almost unendurable tension.

His father would solemnly bring out the ghost book, to which he kept making additions in his own handwriting, at Christmas or some other festive occasion, "to read some of the favourites aloud before we all went to bed ". These included such blood-curdling themes as " the Renishaw Coffin ", " the Butler in the Corridor ", " the Grey Man of Wrotham ", " the Telephone at the Oratory ", " the Strangling Woman ", " Head of a Child ", " the Corpse Downstairs ", " the Vampire Cat "—and a galaxy of haunted rooms, prophetic dreams, and apparitions. With the certain exception of " Colonel P.'s Ghost Story ", which was deliberate invention on Halifax's part and obviously designed to meet the architectural peculiarities of Garrowby, most of the stories had been handed on to Halifax by friends and relations who knew his eager interest in supernatural experiences. Thus we find contributions from the Secretary of the English Church Union, from his nephews Everard Meynell and Charles Dundas,[1] or from Lord Hartington whose signature to his particular ghost story was duly witnessed by the King, the Duke of Devonshire and Lord Desborough. The ring of authenticity merely added to the thrill.

" Many is the time ", Edward confesses, " that after such an evening we children would hurry upstairs, feeling that the distance between the library and our nurseries, dimly lit by oil lamps and full of shadows, was a danger area where we would not willingly go alone, and where it was unsafe to dawdle." " Such treatment of young nerves," he continues, " even in those days, would not have been everybody's prescription; and I well recollect my mother protesting—though I believe almost invariably to no effect—against ' the children being frightened too much '. My father, however, used to justify the method as calculated to stimulate the imagination, and the victims themselves, fascinated and spell-bound by a sense of delicious terror, never failed to ask for more."

. . . .

One of the earliest references to Edward in Halifax's diary describes how Halifax draped an old gown belonging to his wife round his daughter Mary " and told Edward she was a fairy ". The Christmas of 1885 was spent at Hoar

[1] Halifax was connected with the Dundas family through his sister Alice, who married the Hon. John Charles Dundas, son of the First Earl of Zetland. Charles Dundas was their eldest son. Everard Meynell was the son of Halifax's brother, the Hon. Frederick Wood, who changed his name to Meynell on succeeding to the estate at Hoar Cross.

Cross with Mrs. Meynell Ingram. Removed from Hickleton, the ceremony was rather sad, although it was redeemed by "a family gathering, and the excitement of a meet of the Meynell at Hoar Cross, and the arrival of Silvertail for Edward to ride and games on Christmas night".

On his succession to the title pressure was once more brought to bear to induce Halifax to take up politics. Gladstone's majority was endangered by the revolt of the older Whigs and of the Radicals led by Joseph Chamberlain against the First Home Rule Bill. It was felt that the son of the old Lord Halifax would carry weight with recalcitrant Whigs. The accommodating Granville invited him to the Foreign Office, asked him whether he supported the Government and whether he would care for any part in it. He records in his diary that he promised general support, but refused office—"my Church work rather demanded that I should keep myself free".[1] His religious approach to life made it increasingly difficult for him to accept the tenets or discipline of either the Liberals or Conservatives. "The former are often so *wicked*, and the latter so blind as to the drift of things—in short, politics are a delusion and I am quite convinced that to have a vocation to be a monk is the happiest lot in life." A few days earlier Gladstone himself made a much more agreeable offer, that he should become an Ecclesiastical Commissioner, and this he readily accepted.

The deaths of his mother and father were to be for Halifax but the prelude to a series of bereavements. On May 29th 1886 he took his children to see the Trooping the Colour from the Admiralty stand. Henry Paul, the third son, the brother nearest in age to Edward, seems to have contracted a chill while waiting for the ceremony to start. Three days afterwards he was gravely ill with congestion of the lungs. He passed into a delirium "in which he kept repeating his prayers with painful intensity. Then he was distressed because he had been looking forward so much to watching an Ascension Day procession and had sent for some flowers with which to decorate the nursery." On June 6th the fitful struggle was over. His religious precocity—for he was only seven years old at his death—was shared, though not with quite the same fervour, by all the children, and had been carefully fostered by Halifax.

[1] Diary, October 30th 1885.

"Even in the chaff of the family he was 'the Cardinal', and by the child himself and by his brothers and sisters the idea of his dedication was accepted as something settled."[1] "He often said he meant to be a priest," Halifax wrote to Dean Liddon, the child's godfather, "and I think if he had lived he would have been a good one."

The summer of 1886 was spent at the Moult with the familiar round of bathing, walking and reading. Francis, it was noted, began to show ominous symptoms with a habit of sudden and disastrous bouts of sickness, while Edward, who was now just on five, was reported in his father's diary as being "obstreperous", but he was apparently given sixpence for "walking so well". The children's life has been described as amphibious—the children being in and out of the sea most of the day. Seashore caves had to be explored, and on one rather too ambitious expedition Halifax had to carry the little French holiday governess, Mlle Lublinska, who was the source of much family merriment in so far as "she could not hide her conviction that really the Woods did the most alarming things and that, in her opinion, Lord Halifax was the worst of them all".[2] The Christmas of 1886 was once again spent with Emily at Temple Newsam, and the following summer the family returned to the Moult. "Waverley" was read to the children; while their parents combined to entertain them with elaborate disguises. Lady Halifax, complete with wig, appearing on the scene as "Martha Jones, a nurse in charge of 'Jack Tar', to the complete flummoxing of Edward".[3]

In December of 1887 the family was at Garrowby, and Edward, the elder son of the Prince of Wales—the ill-fated Duke of Clarence—was a guest there. For some reason Lady Halifax was away—her husband in a letter to her reports modest high jinks by the children which might not have occurred if she had been present. "Agnes, in the middle of luncheon—though happily we at our table did not hear—asked if the Prince would be King after the Queen and the Prince of Wales, and thereupon announced that she would tell her children later on that she had had luncheon with her future sovereign. Then tremendous giggles from

[1] Lockhart, Vol. II, page 5.
[2] Ibid.
[3] Ibid., page 7.

her and Edward." The Christmas gathering was at Hoar Cross this time, and twenty-one sat down to dinner. There were elaborate tableaux. Edward with his cousin Francis Meynell impersonated the Princes in the Tower, while his sister Mary looked " very pretty as Lady Jane Grey "

Early in 1888 Halifax and his wife paid a sad and virtually farewell visit to the Moult to move their belongings from the place. The summer visit would have to be abandoned now that they had two large houses in Yorkshire on their hands, and although the place held the happiest memories for them, and their honeymoon had been spent there, it was only lent to them by Lord Devon, and Lord Devon's financial affairs as well as his health were giving rise to considerable anxiety. As a compensation Halifax took his wife for a summer holiday in the Black Forest; the children's activities, however, are not on record. In the November of 1888 Lord Devon died, old and full of cares, and the Christmas celebrations—the first to be held at Hickleton in five years, and perhaps the first of the series that Edward would remember—were " a little subdued with the gaps which had opened in the old circle. But there were the waits on Christmas morning, and cribbage with Aunt Georgiana in the evenings, and another crop of terrifying ghost stories." Indeed on this occasion they seem to have been too realistic and blood-curdling for Edward, as his father notes that he " had the prudence to go to bed 'for fear I should dream of ghosts' "

The holidays over, Edward's brothers returned to Eton, but anxiety over the health of the second son, Francis, increased. In addition to the sickness, there were signs during the previous spring of heart trouble, but he was finally allowed to go back to school after making a brief show of recovery. From Eton came the happy news of his promotion to the Fifth Form, to be followed by the dire report that he was unwell again. There followed anxious weeks during which Halifax journeyed constantly between London and Windsor, while Francis, whose right lung was congested, struggled fitfully. In London he was trying to grapple with all the legal and other business connected with the celebrated heresy trial of his friend, the saintly Dr. King, Bishop of Lincoln, a test of strength on matters of ritual in which the English Church Union was deeply engaged. On 12th March the trial began; within a week Francis was dead, and although Halifax was actually staying in Windsor Close he was too late to be with his boy at the end.

Charles, the eldest son, was now nearly nineteen, and although showing no special intellectual gifts had an easy and graceful character and was already a companion for his father. In October 1889 he went up to Christ Church, but within a fortnight was down with pleurisy. Halifax, " nearly dead with anxiety thinking of when I had gone to Francis ", hurried to Oxford. The crisis lasted for several weeks, but when it was over the boy was found to have tubercular trouble in the lungs set up by the pleurisy. It was imperative that he should spend the winter abroad. Madeira was the place chosen. It is interesting, though perhaps not surprising, to note that Halifax decided to take the whole family there. Edward's boyhood was spent within the fold of a family which was not only closely united by mutual affection but also regarded home life as something almost sacrosanct. The Woods were, in fact, a clan, and Edward, when his turn came to be head of a family, retained the clannish tradition with his own children. His father, living on among his own as a veritable Nestor, was, of course, a dominating influence in binding together yet another generation.

Thus it was that the Christmas of 1889 was spent at sea. In place of the Hickleton waits there were " some members of the Salvation Army singing ' Christians Awake ' ", while the cliffs of Funchal, which they saw on Boxing Day, " made us think of the beloved Moult ". In spite of the novelty of new surroundings, the growing anxiety of illness was ever present. " Lady Halifax herself was far from well, and Mary got chicken-pox, and later Charles, to cap his other troubles, developed jaundice."

In March 1890 came news of the death of Halifax's uncle, Francis Grey. In May Lady Halifax returned to present Mary at Court, and in the same month Charles had a further slight attack of pleurisy. On June 14th the rest of the family sailed for England, and went straight to Hickleton. There followed a short trip in Emily Ingram's yacht, *Ariadne*. For a time Charles seemed to gain in strength, but the doctor made it clear that there was no real hope, and four days after returning to Hickleton—on 6th September—" he slipped out of life without the least pain ". A. C. Benson described him as " the sweetest and dearest of characters, without the least touch of the hardness which so often accompanies high principles among boys ".

. . . .

"Now there is only Edward left," Halifax wrote in despair to his sister Emily.[1] It is not easy to convey a clear impression of the small boy aged nine who suddenly, as if by the Nemesis of Greek tragedy, had become sole heir to a great title. Henceforward upon him alone must have rested every hope that his parents had cherished for his three brothers as well as himself. It was indeed an oppressive and a solemn inheritance. All that emerges from the very scanty material about his early years now available to us is that he possessed a more robust temperament, a more vigorous mind, and above all a tougher body than had been vouchsafed to any of his hapless brothers. On the other hand he shared to the full their religious sensibilities. In March 1891 Dr. King, the Bishop of Lincoln, who had emerged triumphant from the trial at the Archbishop of Canterbury's Court, confirmed Edward's sister Agnes in his private chapel. Halifax, describing the ceremony to Emily, wrote, " his address was most touching, and Edward was so much moved that he said to someone who was there as he came out of the chapel, 'Was not the Bishop beautiful? Did he not look kind, and did he not say it beautifully? ' And then asked Agnes if she thought, if he was good, he might be confirmed some day like that too."

But Edward was never the stained-glass-window child. In August 1891 Halifax and his family were staying with Lady Beauchamp and her children at Roscoff in Brittany. The Abbé Portal, a member of the Society of St. Vincent de Paul, who was to exercise a great influence over Halifax and his son and to take a leading part in later years in the Malines conversations, had joined the party. Halifax had first met him when he took Charles and the family to Madeira, where

[1] For Halifax the sequence of death was not yet ended. Ten days after Charles' death, Liddon, the famous High Church Dean of St. Paul's who was both his confessor and his greatest friend, passed away. His last letter, composed the day before he died, was of condolence about Charles. " How I wish I could come to you! As it is, I can only pray for the increasing repose and light of Charles' dear soul, and that you and dear Lady Halifax may have that comfort which God only can give." Then followed the deaths in quick succession of his brother-in-law, Baldwin, who had only just succeeded to the Earldom of Devon, and of his greatest friend after Liddon, Lord Beauchamp, who had acted as Edward's godfather.

they had many rambles together and " much theological conversation ". On this occasion Portal was present at the station saying good-bye to the party. " I remember now ", Halifax wrote in his book *Leo XIII and Anglican Orders*, " his astonishment at the number of handbags and loose parcels we had with us, and the shade of something more than astonishment at the noise the children (Lady Agnes, Lady Maud Lygon, and my son Edward) made in the train." Perhaps it was that the children were letting off surplus energy, for during the Abbé's stay expeditions were cut down as he was complaining of " an unsubdued stomach "! None the less the picture emerges of a reasonably boisterous small boy not so lost in prayer and contemplation as to miss the joys of the open air.

The arrival of Silvertail was a great event, and almost as soon as he could walk we find Edward on horseback and being initiated into the rites of the hunting field to which his grandfather before him had devoted himself with such zeal. For Edward his school holidays meant the eager pursuit of Newbolt's " elements three "—to run, to ride, to swim—with emphasis always on riding. As for his father, enthusiasm for hunting was not quite so intense with him. Lockhart observes that hunting had an unshakable place in his picture of the compleat country gentleman, " and so he hunted ".

In the year following Charles' death Edward's mother fell gravely ill with typhoid, and although she recovered, her health was never robust afterwards, and regular trips abroad to such places as Monte Dore, Biarritz or Mentone had to be made for her benefit. Apart from the ever present menace of ill-health which brooded over the family, it was a spacious and well-established environment in which Edward grew to adolescence. The yearly round of Hickleton, Bovey Tracey, Eaton Square, the holiday abroad, the return for the Doncaster races and the accompanying house-parties, Garrowby, the endless stream of visits from friends old and new, the arrival and departure of distinguished guests who, as we have seen, included Royalty itself, Halifax's lavish old-world hospitality, all conjure up the vision of an undoubtedly privileged yet none the less delightful mode of living. What gave to it its peculiar quality and distinguished it from the average aristocratic round was the original and picturesque character of Edward's father. He may have shared the social prejudices of his time and class, but he was formidable not simply in the Victorian sense of the word; he added mystical piety to material well-being.

The unseen world to Halifax and to his son was thus no mere Sunday sermon platitude, but an urgent factor overriding the vanities of this life. If it was so, surely it intruded upon our senses and experience! Hence the serious undertone to his zeal for ghosts. Here was no idle search for sensation, but in essence an article of his faith. More than one of his friends who shared his religious outlook, including the brilliant if overwrought Robert Hugh Benson, found the same fascination in ghosts.[1] Halifax always hoped that he would actually see one, and Hickleton was reputed to boast a phantom housekeeper who had hanged herself and walked about the place at night. " No one ever credibly saw her, but Halifax never lost hope, and Edward, who, like the other children, had been brought up on the story, was heard to confess to a fear of meeting her in a dark passage."[2] The indomitable old man did, however, convince himself that he had seen a " blue woman " when staying at Temple Newsam in 1908, and at once let Edward know all about it. Even Lady Halifax found Temple Newsam, with its great historical associations, " a little too haunted to be comfortable ". The already uncanny atmosphere of Garrowby was rendered even more bizarre by a strange assortment of animals with which Halifax assiduously filled the park, where could be found various species of deer, yaks, emus, and kangaroos. These exotic beasts, unable to thrive in these unnatural surroundings, in due course died out, and we learn that after Garrowby had been handed over by Halifax to his son, " the remnants of the deer gradually and unobtrusively disappeared, to the sorrow of the former and the relief of the latter ".[3]

It was in 1894, and on the occasion of his father's and mother's silver wedding, that he was apparently first called

[1] " Since the Church in her motherly wisdom had placed a barrier across the road to Endor, Halifax condemned all the adventures and explorations of spiritualism. Ghost-hunting, however, was lawful, the more so as it might at any moment be thrust upon a man. The apparition might be the devil: but it might also be the working of a divine purpose, a message, a warning or a reassurance, which man was intended to receive and had no right to ignore."—Lockhart, Vol. II, pages 107-108.

[2] Ibid., page 105.

[3] Ibid., pages 108-109.

upon to officiate in public as son and heir. Hickleton tenants and Doncaster tradespeople were given a dance, but at the last moment Halifax was called away to Cardiff on Church business. However, " Edward, aged thirteen, filled his place most competently and 'danced with almost everybody', departing next morning, with tears, to Eton ".

CHAPTER IV

THE COMPLEAT SCHOLAR

In entering Eton Edward was following in the path of his father and two brothers before him. For the next five years, until the summer of 1899, his energies and ambitions were absorbed in the life of the great school. It does not seem that his sensitive, highly strung nature rebelled against the rigorous code of this unique forcing house of Britain's ruling class. The prerogatives and assumptions of Eton's way of life are in some ways sufficiently arrogant never seriously to be questioned by its pupils or masters. The effect of Eton's hallowed influence on Edward Wood was no doubt to dispel any latent self-consciousness about his rank while at the same time to give him insight into the implications of his social status.

He entered Mr. W. Durnford's House and was placed in Remove, and when he left was in First Hundred. His name is down as gaining only one school prize, when he was equal with de la Rue minor in the Head Master's Lower Boy French Prize. On the whole it is a record suggesting conscientious plodding rather than any precocious scholarship. Among his contemporaries and friends were the Earl of Dartmouth (who was then Lord Lewisham), Colonel Mark Crichton Maitland, of the Grenadier Guards, and the late Earl of Rosebery (then Lord Dalmeny).[1] In 1898-99 he passed the Oxford and Cambridge Examination, and when he left Eton for Christ Church, Oxford, his school career was regarded as creditable; he had gained the reputation for being a hard worker and a "good influence". The Head Master was the celebrated Dr. Warre, who did much to

[1] Major the Hon. Edward Cadogan, who was elected Conservative M.P. for Reading in 1922, appealing to Wood, then Minister for Education, for more educational facilities for those who could not afford it, asked his "right hon. Friend to remember the days of his youth, when he and I sat on the same bench, in the same class, in the same school, and doubtless gave the same amount of tribulation to the hon. Member for Windsor" (Mr. A. A. Somerville).

bring the classical traditions of Eton into line with new intellectual demands and social developments, and the background to this important transitional period in the school's history, which takes in Edward's time there, is set out with delicate insight in Percy Lubbock's *Shades of Eton.* While at school his zeal for hunting increased with his growing skill as a rider. When Edward was fifteen we find Halifax writing to his wife: "You cannot think how capitally Edward gets on with his riding. I believe he will take to it in good earnest. What a delightful companion he is! So pleasant and comfortable to talk to, and always so bright and merry and good-tempered."

Edward's transition from Eton to Oxford was smooth enough, and the calm, unruffled atmosphere of Christ Church, itself a university within the University, must have been congenial to his nature. Christ Church is not simply the largest of Oxford colleges, it is an institution set somewhat apart from the others. In a number of small ways it does not allow its essential pre-eminence to be forgotten. If midnight is the latest recognized hour by which the nocturnal undergraduate must be within the confines of his college, the Christ Church man is allowed until twenty past twelve. This small example may seem trivial enough in itself, but it is a significant symbol of the traditional status of Christ Church. The life of the undergraduate there is in a sense more individual and mature and less frankly gregarious than at most of the other colleges.

When Edward went up to Oxford the "golden age" of the Wadham triumvirate—F. E. Smith, C. B. Fry and John Simon, of Francis Hirst and J. S. Phillimore, of L. S. Amery, of Hilaire Belloc and the Republican Club, was officially over, but these scintillating figures often returned in graduate form and their influence was still felt. Edward's time at Oxford was marked by no undue political, religious or social ferment. Indeed his was a period of comparative intellectual calm between storms. Among his contemporaries were Arthur Salter, at Brasenose, who has always cherished a deep admiration for his political outlook and record, and John Buchan, also at Brasenose, his senior in years. Buchan in his posthumous autobiography confirms that in his time there were but few "militant fraternities" which have so often embittered and distracted undergraduate life. "We sought not allies in a cause," he writes, " but friendships for their own sake." But underlying the placidity there was evidence of profound change, and he observes that his time at Oxford was " one of those boundary periods, the meaning of which is missed at thc time, but is plain in the retrospect. The place was still monastic, but the clamour of the outer world was at its gates, and it was on the verge of losing many of its idioms." Thus it was that in the sartorial sphere Edward was to witness the arrival of the era of flannel " bags " and no hats; while phrases of Victorian and Regency origin disappeared never to emerge again. In more senses than one were Edward and his generation of Oxonians the last of the " bloods ".

While at Oxford he was to form intimate and enduring friendships, mostly among Christ Church men. He seems to have withstood the prevailing tendency for undergraduates of similarly favoured social position to congregate together and to monopolize the membership of extremely select clubs. On the other hand, the set to which he attached himself was remarkable and in some respects unique. A passion for hunting bound him to such men as Francis Baskerville and George Riddell and made them all indefatigable members of Loders. But whereas hunting at Oxford has been usually associated with undergraduates whose physical verve and social connections outshine their intellectual equipment, Wood and his friends were strange enlightened beings who all rode to hounds and secured Firsts. More than that, Loders under Wood's regime was no longer merely convivial, but developed into a society of moral improvement. Its dinners every other Sunday had about them the aura of a Young Men's Christian Association.

The impression Edward made lived after him. When he returned years later as a renowned statesman to receive from his old University an honorary D.C.L., the Public Orator saw fit to recall him as one who in his time at Oxford had been "*equitandi venandique studiosissimus*". His friendship with George Riddell was particularly intimate and formative. Up to Riddell's death in 1935 they were always in the closest contact with each other—enjoying all the free interchange of ideas which such a lifelong relationship brings with it. It was from Riddell that Edward's abiding interest in educational questions received much of its stimulus, and it was to Riddell that he turned when as President of the Board of Education he sought unofficial judgments on departmental problems. Among Edward's contemporaries at Christ Church who achieved distinction and who no doubt shared his companionship were H. L. Henderson, Truslove, Maurice Gwyer and Eric Maclagan.

Entering Christ Church as a Commoner he took what was then the comparatively unorthodox decision to read for Honours in Modern History. The History School was not at that time so overwhelmingly popular as it is now; no single personality had emerged at Oxford to give History the academic status that Acton and Seely had forged for it in Cambridge, although H. W. C. Davis, the great Mediaevalist, was then in his prime, and Hassall was at "the House" and, no doubt, one of Edward's tutors. For Edward history must have provided the most suitable medium through which to survey his father's religious beliefs and to analyse his own reaction to them; the whole theory of Anglican orders was based upon historical method and accuracy. The Oxford Movement had unearthed a new interpretation of the Middle Ages. The pursuit of history may well have helped Edward to reconcile the claims of politics with those of religion more easily than his father did.

It was at Oxford that he made first acquaintance with the philosophy of Edmund Burke—perhaps the profoundest of all British political thinkers—and from his works derived a respect for the origins and growth of the British Constitution which has sustained him throughout his career. If the study of history in general and of Burke in particular attracted him towards Conservatism, and away from his own Whig inheritance, at least it was a Conservatism of a more subtle and profound intellectual content than the prevailing brand that has secured his patient support both in opposition and power from 1910 onwards. Wood's historical background alone ensures that he has very little in common with the hard-faced *nouveau riche* industrialism which has dominated the councils of the Conservative Central Office in recent years. He could admire Mr. Baldwin without limiting himself to the restricted faith of Mr. Baldwin's rank-and-file followers. While at Oxford he seems to have abstained from the rhetorical delights of the Union, which is often regarded as a nursery of British statesmen.

Actually Oxford can boast almost as many statesmen who never even sat through a single debate in the Union as who aspired to become President, and among the leaders of our day neither Edward Wood nor Anthony Eden were reared within its precincts.

He was, however, still at the University when he appears to have made his first incursion into the fray of Church politics. In the nineties notoriety was gained by Mr. John Kensit, who until half a brick thrown at his head ended his earthly labours, organized gangs to enter ritualistic churches and interrupt the services by giving their opinions on Anglo-Catholicism in strong and even obscene terms. Naturally Halifax's own church at Hickleton was an obvious target, and the Kensitites duly appeared there in March 1900. They came by wagonette, but were prevented from speaking by the way in which the villagers banged old coal-scuttles and blew horns. "Whole thing most ludicrous. Edward and Agnes—indeed all of us—burning for a fight."[1]

In the winter or early spring he was to join his mother and father abroad, who took regular holidays in search of a cure for Lady Halifax's bronchitis or asthma. In April 1903 they hit upon Paraggi, near Santa Margherita, and Easter seems to have been spent there regularly afterwards. Friends would come to visit them at this "dream of beauty" and also to la Croix among the Montagnes des Maures. Dr. Lang, the Archbishop of Canterbury (then Bishop of Stepney), was among them, and he recalls the joyous expeditions Halifax would lead. "Among the hills at la Croix there was something almost cat-like in the swiftness and stealth with which he led the way through intricate paths, and his son Edward and I were hard put to keep pace with him."

. . . .

As the boy grew into manhood the relationship of father and son seemed to expand. Edward's career became an ever-increasing source of interest and pride to Halifax. In April 1902, with the traditional festivities, Edward came of age and the tenants of the Halifax estates duly gathered together to celebrate the great event. A few months before, Halifax had written to his sister Emily, "Edward is taller than ever, and though I say it as shouldn't, nicer and more

[1] Halifax's Diary, April 4th 1900.

delightful than ever. Coming out of church this morning I said to old Mrs. Clark of Barmbro', who is always there, 'Well, Mrs. Clark, he (Edward) don't grow any smaller!' 'Nay, that he don't. He puts you quite in the shade. But never mind—there's good stuff in small parcels.' Aren't our Yorkshire people delightful!" Edward was certainly no "small parcel", and by the time he had finished growing, had reached the substantial height of six feet five inches.

The correspondence between Halifax and his son has not yet, of course, been published in full, but for the better part of thirty-five years they wrote unstintingly to each other. They were often separated as Edward's career expanded, but their letters were far more than a formal link. J. G. Lockhart, at work among the Hickleton Papers, has seen most of them and can speak with unique authority. He observes that such was the relationship of Halifax with his son "that he could write with none of those half-conscious reserves that inhibit the letters of most men to most of their correspondents. He had a perfect assurance of being understood. He knew, for example, that when he declared, as he often did, that he would like to strangle somebody, Edward would know that he was merely voicing his irritation at something the man had said or done."[1]

When in April 1903 Edward returned to Oxford from Paraggi to complete his last summer term his father wrote to him with a real pathos. "It was with a heavy heart I wished you good-bye yesterday. It has been such a happy visit and it has ended so soon, and now everything we do here will remind us of our walks with you and we shall be feeling all the time, 'Oh, if only Edward were here!' And somehow the bloom will have gone and it will all be only a second best. Do you remember that first walk your Mama, you and I had together? . . . It cannot be like that again. But we shall, of course, enjoy ourselves, and I shall be making plans all the time to come back here again with you. . . ."[2]

In October Edward, having secured a safe First in Modern History, sat for his Fellowship at All Souls. Whatever the outcome of this supreme intellectual assault, his

[1] Lockhart, Vol. II, page 183.
[2] Dated April 24th 1903.

career was obviously approaching a decisive phase; his father accordingly had important advice for him. "I have also been thinking a good deal of your plans," he wrote. "It seems to me you have been working hard now for some time and that a good rest and change would be a good thing for you. After this next examination, whether you get the Fellowship or not, you will be free, and it is a freedom which will not occur again in so complete a way . . . County Councils, Yeomanry, etc., are all impediments to getting away; it might, perhaps, be a good thing not to get entangled with all these till after you had corrected and supplemented the knowledge got from books by the knowledge which comes from *seeing* men and things. How would it be for you to go abroad for a year—to visit South Africa, Australia, India, and perhaps America, with Japan thrown in? But I only throw this out as a suggestion for your consideration. . . . A great deal could be seen in a year or a little longer, and then with all this experience you might come home, energize on the London Council, prepare to come into Parliament, and begin the course which, if God pleases, is to enable you to do great things for Him and the Catholic Church, England and the world generally."[1]

Three weeks later came the splendid news of Edward's success at All Souls. "I cannot say what a pleasure it was ", wrote his father at once, "when, on coming home from my ride yesterday, I found three telegrams—from you, from Walter Riddell, and from F. Cunliffe, telling me that you were elected. It was just a feeling of true joy and happiness and gratitude. You will know how impatient I was for your mother s and Mary's return from York. . . . Your Mama arrived about 6.30. 'Is there a telegram?' 'Yes, three. Edward has got it.' And then such rejoicings and delight as never were. We were—we are so pleased. My dearest son, it is indeed delightful, and I do thank God for your success with all my heart. . . . This bit of your life completed, and so completed that there is nothing left to be desired. It remains all good, all finished, and an earnest, please God, of how it may be with each successive part till that end comes which shall set the seal upon the whole. I am indeed happy, happier than I deserve, for I never gave my father this pleasure. He was to his father what you are

[1] Dated 15th October 1903.

to me, a source of pride and delight, and I like to think that you are making up for my deficiencies and giving him the pleasure which he would have been so pleased and happy could he have had at my hands, but of which I never gave him one drop."[1]

Halifax might well be satisfied. Edward's Fellowship at All Souls meant not merely that he had crowned a highly successful academic career, but had gained admittance to one of the most privileged and select communities in the intellectual life of the nation. Here was a testimonial that would carry him through the preliminaries of any career he might care to take up. As a result of reforms in the Foundation in the middle of the nineteenth century, All Souls is devoted principally to the study of law and history. Various professors and dons of these Faculties are members of the College and the remaining Fellowships are thrown open to competition among former law and history students. The Fellowship lasts for seven years only. Thus a constant succession is assured of the most brilliant of each year's jurists and historians as well as students in the new Modern Greats School of political science, who are enabled to work in the closest collaboration with the leading exponents in their branch of study. It is safe to assert that the Fellow of All Souls is a man marked out for a position of authority in public life, and there is no surprise if he reaches the summit of power, but only disappointment if he falls short of the opportunities that are set out before him.

Edward, with all the connections of his family, had by means of his Fellowship made his future a subject of lively speculation among those who had patronage at their disposal. It is not, however, surprising that he pondered deeply over the mature advice of a father who cherished such an unbounded affection for him and who, for all his personal eccentricity, could put forward precepts with all the worldly wisdom of a Polonius, and that he duly fell in with the idea of a Grand Tour before settling down to the career expected of him. We have at our disposal only a few fragmentary and unrelated facts about the great journey he undertook during the years 1904 and 1905, but even they are sufficient to suggest its importance in the moulding of his political outlook. It is to be noted first of all that instead of confining

[1] Dated 4th November 1903.

himself to an orthodox visit to the various European capitals, he followed his father's advice in detail, went farther afield and made an excursion into the Empire.

His plans seem to have been arranged to coincide with those of his parents, who in the winter of 1904 and the summer of 1905 paid two visits to South Africa to see their elder daughter Mary and her husband Captain Sutton. They arrived in Capetown on 15th November 1904, and we learn that Edward joined them towards the end of the month. "They had planned going on after Christmas to Johannesburg and Rhodesia, and had originally had the idea—though it was the most ephemeral project—of sailing from Beira to India in February, and so to Ceylon in March." But this project dissolved with the news of the dangerous illness and then the death of Edward's aunt and Halifax's favourite sister, Emily of Temple Newsam. The party caught the next boat home.

In February 1905 we hear that Edward "resumed his interrupted journey" to India, and that in the following autumn, "coming from Australia" he again joined up with his parents and enjoyed the hospitality of the Suttons at Capetown. This time there was a "delicious" expedition into Basutoland, a journey by car to Kimberley, where a diamond mine was duly inspected, then on by train to Bulawayo and even farther north to the stupendous Victoria Falls, under the shadow of which Halifax bathed several times "regardless of crocodiles". They then returned to Bulawayo, making a pilgrimage to Cecil Rhodes' famous sepulchre in the Matopos: "It is like seeing Moses' grave—only no one ever did see it—on the top of Mount Nebo." Next they went to Ladysmith and made a tour of some of the Boer War battle-fields—a somewhat bleak essay in sight-seeing which may have encouraged Lady Halifax to the confession of "a *longing* to be started home". Edward, it seems, left them at Ladysmith, returning to England and thereby missing the "great excitement of their journey"—a trek across the Transkei in an ox wagon and Cape carts.[1]

. . . .

For a novice in Imperial politics Edward could hardly have undertaken his tour at a more propitious time. In Australia he was to find the great Federal experiment, to

[1] *Vide* Lockhart, Vol. II, pages 171-173.

which the various States had voluntarily subscribed on New Years' Day 1901, in its fourth year and flourishing in spite of the most gloomy prognostications. In India he could witness the first-fruits of Curzon's gigantic labours—and ponder over the splendour of his achievement as also over the limitations of what was, for all the fever of the Viceregal initiative, an imposed order. In South Africa there were perhaps the most exciting developments of all. We learn that Halifax lunched with Milner at Muizenberg, discussing politics with him. The meeting seems to have made a deep impression on Halifax, and from henceforth he was an unflinching champion of Milner and his work. For Edward the contact must have had a special interest in so far as Milner had gathered round him a group of brilliant young men dubbed somewhat unfairly as Milner's Kindergarten. The identification of Milner's somewhat harsh personality with Prussian influences has perhaps been heightened by the ruthless efficiency displayed by himself and his young disciples, who were for the most part the cream of Edward's contemporaries at Oxford.

This is not the place to enter on an assessment of the famous Kindergarten. It is sufficient simply to note that Edward, without ever fully identifying himself with them—and it is significant surely that young and unattached as he was, and coming upon them in the middle of their great mission of reconstruction after the Boer War, he was not there and then drawn into their midst—was to set a course in which their careers and outlook were to exercise a special influence upon him. From New College Milner had gathered round him Lionel Curtis, whose capacious intellect made him the unquestioned leader of the group, the Hon. Robert Brand, Lionel Hitchens, George Craik, Douglas Malcolm, Philip Kerr (afterwards Lord Lothian) and Edward Grigg. Balliol supplied Patrick Duncan, who, as Sir Patrick, was the first South African ever to hold the office of Governor-General in the Dominion of his birth. L. S. Amery, too, was in Africa as a newspaper correspondent—in sympathy with the movement without being actually attached to it. From Brasenose came John Buchan, and from Magdalen Geoffrey Robinson, better known to the world as Geoffrey Dawson and Editor of *The Times*. Curtis, Dawson, Amery, Brand and Malcolm had, like Edward, but recently been elected Fellows of All Souls. They all held key positions and it seemed they must carry everything before them. But for one reason or another, with their work accomplished in Africa their careers fell away. Some, no doubt, were content to exercise influence behind the scenes, but for the most part, considerable and indeed momentous as their influence was, it was not given to them to do more than that. The power and the glory went to the comparatively unambitious and easy-going Wood; the Kindergarten, with all its zealous talent, dissolved into personal frustration. None the less they lived to enjoy the triumph of their idea, which is embodied in what we now call the "British Commonwealth of Nations"

Edward had witnessed at first hand the genesis of this Commonwealth, and the experience undoubtedly impressed upon him an acute sense of the importance of constitutional forms and development. Essentially the Federation in Australia, the Curzon reforms, the strivings of the Milner Kindergarten were part of one and the same Imperial aspiration. In the atmosphere of political exhaustion after the Boer War there was a real danger that the Empire might simply disintegrate; this menace was met by the compelling demand for the better organization of the Empire. It was not enough that the Empire should be a splendid sentiment or even a glorious battle-field; it could only survive on the principle that what was best administered offered the longest and largest allegiance.

On their return to England Kerr and Grigg founded the *Round Table*, which embodied the bold and independent ideals of the Kindergarten and was to give searching scrutiny to many problems of Imperial Government both in the West Indies and India with which Wood was identified as a Minister or Viceroy; Curtis emerges again as a material contributor to the historic Montagu-Chelmsford Report, upon which the main structure of Wood's constitutional policy for India was based; while Kerr (as Lord Lothian) shared responsibility for the vast Government of India Act which superseded the Montagu-Chelmsford Reforms and brought Wood's work to its logical conclusion. Curtis we find again as adviser on Irish affairs in the Colonial Office during perhaps the most critical phase of all in Anglo-Irish relations—the period of the 1922 Treaty—when Churchill was Secretary of State and Wood undergoing his first experience of Office as Under-Secretary. When the time came to find a suitable successor as Viceroy to the illustrious Lord Reading, Dawson as Editor of *The Times* may well have played an integral part in bringing forward Wood's obscure name to the notice of the proper authorities at Court as well as in helping to persuade Stanley Baldwin to part with his friend and Minister of Agriculture.

In many respects the life work of this important group culminated in the Statute of Westminster of 1931, which formally sanctioned resolutions made at the Imperial Conferences of 1926 and 1930. After that we find them searching after wider if less tangible objectives. If Federation could knit together the British Commonwealth it could do the same for the world at large; perhaps the Federal formula was the only solution to the diplomatic anomaly of political and economic nationalism. Curtis and other members of the group gave impetus to the founding of the Royal Institute of International Affairs, which was designed to be a fact-finding treasure-house for the architects of the new world order. It was indeed fitting that Wood as Foreign Secretary should have chosen the annual dinner of the Royal Institute to deliver in the spring of 1939 his historic warning to the Powers which were preparing to engulf the civilized processes of reasoned collaboration; for he was addressing there men who, beyond most in our time, had delved into the conditions of constructive peace.

The group were to impinge yet again on Wood's career after the resignation of Anthony Eden, and there can be little doubt but that the support of Lothian, Geoffrey Dawson and Brand, all of whom had access to Cliveden House, helped to smooth the way to his appointment as Foreign Secretary.

CHAPTER V

BIOGRAPHY AND MARRIAGE

EDWARD returned from his world tour to find the England of 1905 absorbed in political debate. The great fiscal controversy was at its height. In Parliament Winston Churchill, brilliant young son of an illustrious father, was harrying the languid Balfour in his fastnesses and even endangering the Conservative Administration. It was a period of ferment auspicious for young men who saw visions to seize power from old men who merely dreamt dreams. Nothing would have been more natural than for us to find Edward Wood, a young man with an enviable record and reputation, fresh from his stimulating travels, rushing into the fray and emerging in the forefront of some great political renaissance. But instead he stood aside and resisted the temptations of easy and perhaps premature success. There were, no doubt, several motives urging him to caution. In the first place there was his Fellowship; he had the moral obligation to see that it was not simply a sinecure, and with each passing year the opportunities for quiet study would be less, and distracting responsibilities the more insistent. Then again, in an environment of almost frenzied partisanship, the impressions gathered from his journey must have drawn him away from the jargon of party arguments. The passions, for instance, aroused by the Liberals' exposure of the conditions of Chinese labour in South Africa can have evoked small sympathy from one who had just been there and was in a position to gauge it against the full magnitude of our task and achievement.

If he favoured the dominant plea for action he was not ready to advocate it at the price of a Liberal ticket. Alien and radical voices were being raised in the land; this new insistent Liberalism was altogether too far removed from the Whig tradition for the dutiful heir of a landed nobleman to subscribe to it. On the other hand he could not conscientiously champion the moribund Conservatism that was dragging on a weary rearguard action in Parliament and testified only to disunity in the country at large. As for Joseph Chamberlain's plea, the truth would seem to be that Edward, having reflected deeply upon the closely argued Free Trade versus Tariff Reform debate, had not come down decisively on one side or the other. Then again the political fate of his brother-in-law, George Lane Fox,[1] with whom he was on terms of the utmost intimacy, was hardly encouraging and could not be lightly ignored. Standing for a seemingly safe seat in the Conservative interest at a by-election in 1904 he had suffered a surprising reverse. This ominous result was duly confirmed when, along with the fine flower of Conservative England, he was handsomely defeated in the catastrophic election of 1906—at Ripon too, the constituency which Edward was to gain four years later and to hold for the rest of his Parliamentary career.

Perhaps Edward had not yet given up the idea of following in his father's footsteps and becoming a fully fledged ecclesiastical layman. At least he seems to have taken a hand in the great Education controversy in which Halifax and the English Church Union were deeply involved. The Liberals' Education Bill which was introduced by Augustine Birrell, President of the Board of Education, on 9th April 1906, was the direct sequel to a fierce Nonconformist agitation against the Balfour Act of 1902. This Act boldly attempted to bring the Voluntary Schools within the national system of education, and provided them with the financial assistance they had always wanted, in return for an unwelcome degree of control by the local education authorities. This provoked the passive resistance led by Dr. Clifford, and many Nonconformists preferred distraint on their household goods to paying an education rate for the support of Roman Catholic and Church of England schools. The Liberal Party took up their cause, and Birrell's Bill provided that the only recognized schools were to be those of local education authorities which were to be given powers to acquire existing voluntary schools. Facilities for de-

[1] George Lane Fox, afterwards Lord Bingley, married Edward's younger sister Agnes in September 1903. He was the nephew of George Fox, Halifax's contemporary and friend. Halifax described it as "altogether a delightful marriage. We have known him and his always. . . . There is no one I should have liked better."

nominational teaching were to be stiffly curtailed; but the Bill was so mauled in the Lords that the Government dropped it and the unhappy Birrell was transferred to the even less congenial atmosphere of the Irish Office. It is all dead controversy now, but at the time it threatened to provoke a grave religious schism in the country as well as to foster a dangerous contempt for law. Halifax naturally attacked with all the conviction of his fervent nature, and it was on the occasion of a mass meeting at Trafalgar Square that Edward, now aged twenty-five, delivered one of his first public speeches, a fiery baptism of which we have no detailed account. With typical modesty he wrote back to his mother. " Trafalgar Square did, I should think, pretty well. I was very much uplifted by the reception that those thousands of people gave to Papa; most moving. There were a great many people, and the greatest possible enthusiasm." Papa, it may be added, was himself so uplifted that he first broke his umbrella and then knocked off a policeman's helmet.

In the same year—1906—Halifax found further cause of friction with the triumphant Liberal Government when it insisted on censuring Milner for an incident during his period of rule in South Africa. He was furious with the resolution and its supporters. Winston Churchill incurred his particular wrath. " I could have strangled him with my own hands," he wrote to Edward, and without regard for the tactical consequences or Milner's wishes, forced a retaliatory resolution through the House of Lords asking their Lordships to record their high appreciation of Lord Milner's services, which they duly did by the handsome margin of 170 votes to 35. This incident only reinforces the impression that both Edward and his father, without ever fully entering into its administrative implications, found the Empire-building activity of Milner and his Kindergarten a refreshing antidote to the dullness of Conservatism and wellnigh heathen ambitions of the Liberals. By 1907 Halifax was describing the Administration with relish to Edward as " the most detestable Government that we have ever seen ".

For the next two years Edward turned aside, perhaps without undue regret, from political questions, and devoted himself once more to the pursuit of historical and religious themes suitably intermingled with the life of a young country gentleman of leisure. In April 1907 he went with his father to la Croix, and has recorded in a letter to his mother how on the Channel crossing they fell in with Dr. Paget, the Bishop of Oxford, and how " he and Papa, after a preliminary reconnoitring of each other from a distance, settled down and had a real good talk. Exactly like two dogs who are not sure whether they will fight or not and so walk round each other making up their minds on the subject, until they finally settle it is less trouble to be amicable."

. . . .

It was during this period that Edward made his first and only major excursion into authorship when he accepted an invitation to write a short biography of John Keble. The book was one of a series of lives of " Leaders of the Modern Church " published between 1905 and 1909 by A. R. Mowbray under the general editorship of G. W. E. Russell, who himself contributed studies of Pusey and of Liddon. D. C. Lathbury added two more volumes on Dean Church and on Mr. Gladstone, and there were also biographies of Bishop Westcott by Joseph Clayton, Bishop Wilberforce by R. G. Wilberforce, and Frederick Denison Maurice by C. F. G. Masterman. Russell, in a general preface describing the origin and scope of the series, explained that the publishers " had formed the opinion that Ecclesiastical Biography is apt to lose in attractiveness and interest by reason of the technical and professional spirit in which it is generally handled. Acting on this opinion they resolved to publish some short lives of ' Leaders of the Modern Church ' written exclusively by laymen. They conceived that a certain freshness might thus be imparted to subjects already more or less familiar, and that a class of readers, who are repelled by the details of Ecclesiasticism, might be attracted by a more human, and in some sense a more secular treatment of religious lives."

The selection of Wood, with his father's credentials, to have a share in this High Church enterprise was a sound enough decision, but it is doubtful whether the series as a whole came up to the publishers' expectations. The standard set by Masterman's brilliant and secular study of Maurice was not sustained; Wood's study of Keble was conscientious enough, but the desired lay influence does not emerge, and it might well have been written by an ecclesiastic for the benefit of those who were prepared to take an ardent interest in the Church controversies of the nineteenth century. He is very conservative and reverent in his attitude to Keble, does not give much of the background to the Oxford Movement and is careful to avoid allusion to any of those elements in it that aroused the ridicule of Lytton Strachey. For a first literary venture into the theological maze the book is surprisingly circumspect, only emphasizing those aspects of Keble's life which would not alienate the opinion of the day. He shows no particular interest in Newman's controversial personality and the Rome-ward urge, nor is he unduly excited by the violent stand made by the Oxford Movement against liberalism. He picks a dutiful and painstaking path through these forgotten feuds, but the impression prevails that he is not passionately interested in them. Although he is careful to rebuke the " liberals ", the reader is left with the feeling that he is not always quite comfortable about Keble's position.

In the sixties, when there was a proposal to increase the endowment of the Regius Professorship of Greek, the deep hostility of High Churchmen to Jowett for what they regarded as his unorthodox and indeed heretical outlook overflowed. " The dispute was tortuous and prolonged and it is needless to revive it," Wood tersely observes. Keble subsequently contributed £100 to a suggested prosecution of Jowett, and justified his action in a letter to *The Guardian*. " To some ", is Wood's significant comment, " these sentiments may seem intolerant, but if they are to be appraised correctly, due allowance must be made for their environment. In no case is it easy to be accurate in forming retrospective judgments. What one generation must resist, the next may not infrequently accept, from never having had the alternative submitted to it."[1] The true course, he declares, often lies between indifference and bigotry, and he quotes Archbishop Tait's dictum that " the Liberals are deficient in religion and the religious are deficient in liberality ".

In the concluding chapter Wood emerges briefly to put his own solution to the moral dilemma created by new knowledge. " In some minds the impression that survives a study, often somewhat cursory, of events contemporary with Keble's life, is that he and the party he represented were,

[1] *John Keble*, page 150.

through their insistence on the importance of a right belief, intolerant fanatics."[1] But "it is not altogether easy for the present generation to judge truly in these matters". The prevailing thought of 1900 represented a considerable departure from the ideas of the 1850's. "One feature of this change consists in the increased facility with which men nowadays have learnt to recognize conflicting rules of life, and to allot to each the control of a certain sphere of action. In this sense it is a reflection in the case of the individual, of the change that has been taking place in the relations of Church and State." Formerly a man "was accustomed to go through life more simply, yielding an undivided allegiance to a single principle. The theory of persecution . . . justified itself by the general acquiescence in the position that the right faith was everything." Toleration followed "primarily as a matter of political expediency", but reinforced "by the deeper consideration that truth is not objective only, but that it has a subjective side as well". This discovery or "revolution in opinion added enormously to the complexity of life. A man might cling to his old convictions as tenaciously as ever, but he could no longer ignore that other men with equal faculties and goodwill as himself were equally assured that his convictions were erroneous."[2]

"Hence, for convenience' sake, the faculty has been acquired of drawing distinctions between the principles which should govern different departments of life, and of separating between them. What is not possible for a man as a member of the Church is not impossible, nay may even be right, for him in his capacity as a citizen. The thought of the present day has been deeply influenced by this leavening process, and finds it easy to reconcile what might at first sight seem contradictory. It is permissible to think that the leaven has spread too far; it may be that the reaction from the wish to insist on a rigid uniformity has led to an undue loosening of the bands upon the other side. Each age is apt to think that, though an uncompromising course of action may have been necessary and good for its predecessor, and eminently to be desired of its successor, it is scarcely a policy to be recommended immediately for itself. Such an attitude demands a careful scrutiny. For, be it clearly said, those to

[1] *John Keble*, page 223.
[2] The full argument is to be found on pages 224-225.

EDWARD WOOD, 1909

whom their principles mean anything can never act as if they were non-existent, while it is only those who possess principles themselves, who are likely to comprehend the existence of the principles of other people."

"Real liberty is not licence. Rather is it the attainment, by a regulated following of law, of that vantage-ground from which the perspective of the lower plains may be discerned, and conflicting duties more easily harmonized."

"To the majority of human beings this frame of mind does not come naturally. Indeed its acquisition postulates a rigid self-restraint in matters of daily life. When man first realizes that he is called upon to play the part of fellow-worker with GOD, his natural instinct will be to dread the intrusion of the human within the pale of the Divine. But as this very intrusion is his privilege, he will perpetually remind himself that he is a man of unclean lips, mysteriously set upon the threshold of Heaven. Hence necessarily springs humility, well termed the only ladder which will reach to Heaven."[1]

This passage is quoted in full not only as revealing his powers of closely reasoned argument, his flair for "divine philosophy", but as indicating a mature and settled outlook on life in which all his subsequent experience seems only to have confirmed him. Here is summarized the whole essence of his belief in a personal inward religion and his firm refusal to follow the prevailing tide of automatic subscription to external dogmas such as scientific propositions. Here is the firm basis of toleration, implied throughout his life, but not perhaps so openly proclaimed. When discussing the attack made by Keble and Pusey on *Essays and Reviews*, a now wholly forgotten book, which in its time did make some effort to reconcile new scientific ideas with traditional Christianity, Wood emphasizes that they were attacking "the rationalistic temper" of the work, and he goes on to admit that different ages have to express unchanging truth in different ways.

For all his book's inevitable limitations he showed himself fully alive to the nature of the conflict between liberal rationalism and revealed Christianity, and he made a substantial effort to preserve a personal balance between the two. "The claim of reason to provide an exhaustive basis of thought and action, and the refusal to acknowledge the

[1] *John Keble*, pages 225-227.

existence of any philosophy outside her own, contain a wider and more threatening danger than lies in any one specific heresy. For unlike the ordinary heresy, the rationalistic spirit has no preference for one faith rather than another, but is impartially destructive of all faith alike."[1] The concluding paragraph of the whole book hints that the author feels he is fighting on issues that were safely past and did not belong to his age. " To each generation time and circumstance offer peculiar problems for the solution of which there is no golden rule "; and Keble's character is held up primarily as " an example of encouragement ".

Wood is always trying to bring out the element of moderation in Keble, almost to the extent of imposing his own sense of moderation upon him. There was actually a certain similarity between Keble and himself. Both were brought up from childhood in a Catholic tradition, and both relished their growth in such an environment. It is significant that Wood emphasized Keble's view that it is the duty of a man to stay in the position to which God has assigned him in spite of evil around him as long as he is free to protest and maintain his own belief, and that he should not look for escape elsewhere, for instance, by flying to Rome. Strong in his traditional heritage and outlook, Keble, unlike Newman, could survey undismayed the changes of which he disapproved, and Wood's faith is essentially the same. Then again the serene background of Keble's life, the atmosphere of the quiet country parish ruled for generations by squire and vicar, was all congenial to Wood, who could share with him a Christian unconsciousness of the darker and more difficult sides of life. It is characteristic, too, that Wood should quote with praise Keble's criticism of feeling being allowed to govern religious life, but that he should also be anxious to bring out the human side of Keble's character, stressing particularly his sense of humour.

In spite, however, of Edward's and his father's natural sympathy with Keble's concept of the Church as an independent organization defending itself against State interference and secularization, and of the mutual appeal of a sacramental faith, the general impression remains that the work was primarily a pious duty. Without ever being quite fair to the more liberal attitude, he adopts every now and then a

[1] *John Keble*, page 200.

slightly priggish tone, the outcome of special pleading and of the attempt to repress the discomfort it involves. If the work, therefore, is conscientious to the point of dullness and rather less "handy and readable" than the editor of the series desired, it displays real power of analysis and grasp of historical method, and it survives as a first work with which any author would have just reason to be satisfied and as ample confirmation of his right to a Fellowship.

. . . .

The life of Keble made its first appearance in September 1909,[1] at a moment of great personal excitement and rejoicing for Edward—for at the end of that month he was married to Lady Dorothy Evelyn Augusta Onslow, younger daughter of the fourth Earl of Onslow.[2] It is not surprising that in a brief preface to his book he expressed regret to all who had so readily assisted with suggestions and advice "that pressure of time should have prevented me from turning their kindness to more satisfactory account". The engagement seems to have been a whirlwind affair in comparison with his usual placid and slow-moving manner of life. We learn that he burst into his father's bedroom at half-past two one morning towards the end of July with the news. Halifax gave a diverting account of the proposal in a letter to his daughter Mary. "It happened last night at Lady Esther Smith's. Before it happened she (Lady Dorothy) and Edward were talking together, and she said, amongst other things, that she had been to a fortune-teller with some others, and she was sorry she had, as it had given her a shock. After the event, Edward having said he did not approve of fortune-

[1] A second edition of the book was published by Mowbray in September 1932 to coincide with the centenary of Keble's Assize Sermon, which is generally accepted as marking the official opening of the Oxford Movement.

[2] Her family has a long tradition of public service and can trace their descent from a Clerk to Parliament in Elizabeth's reign, and from Sir Thomas Foote who was Lord Mayor of London in 1649 and was an influential adviser of Oliver Cromwell. His grandson Richard, the first Baron Onslow, was Lord of the Admiralty and also Speaker of the House of Commons. The family was to produce another Speaker, Arthur Onslow, whose son George was created first Earl of Onslow in 1801. Lady Halifax's father, the fourth Earl, had a distinguished career, and was successively between 1887 and 1911 Under-Secretary for the Colonies (which was to be Edward's first Ministerial appointment), Parliamentary Secretary to the Board of Trade, Governor of New Zealand, Under-Secretary of State for India, President of the Board of Agriculture, and Chairman of Committees in the House of Lords. This last position has subsequently been held by his son, the fifth Earl. Lady Halifax's elder sister is the well-known Countess of Iveagh, one of the pioneer women M.P.s, and if she had seen fit to follow her sister's example Lady Halifax herself might well have met with similar success in politics.

tellers, asked her what the shock was; she said the fortune-teller had seen *his* name in her hand. There's for you! What do you say to that? Edward is, I believe, going to bring the young lady to see us to-day. Everyone says she is delightful"—a verdict, it may be added, upon Edward's bride which thirty years of married life has in full measure confirmed.

In line with his father and grandfather before him he had made a socially brilliant match, but, far more than that, he had allied himself to one who had the priceless faculty of growing with him as his career grew, supporting it without ever intruding. The British political leaders of our generation have been fortunate in their wives—but upon none has fallen a larger degree of responsibility for her husband's success than upon the present Lady Halifax. The supreme test of Viceregal entertainment found her more than equal to the demands made upon her. She emerged triumphant from perhaps the most critical social clique in the world; indeed she succeeded in imposing her own simplicity and charm upon an etiquette that had become almost menacing in its elaborate detail. There can be no doubt, too, but that her sure social sense has reinforced her husband in his tenure of the Foreign Office. Here the wife's duties, though less spectacular than the royal status of New Delhi, are no less exacting, and the successful entertainment of diplomats and their wives is a subtle and nerve-racking process. After eighteen years of uninterrupted public life and the rearing of a happy and gifted family, Lady Halifax puts at the disposal of her husband and his career the same quiet dignity and freshness of character that encouraged him to follow up the good auspices of the fortune-teller.

The marriage took place at Hickleton church, and considerable attention was given both to the form of the service and to the credentials of the guests invited. The case arose of a certain friend who had remarried after divorce. Wood, be it noted, in his book, had quoted Keble with something like approval for the view that the Church had a right to its own marriage laws different from those of the State—but the last word rested with his father. "It is very awkward, Edward," he observed. "I certainly should not have her at Hickleton, but I might send her a haunch of venison for Doncaster Races"—a nice distinction which no doubt relieved Edward's uneasy conscience! Thus to the accompaniment of the customary rejoicings and festivities of his father's tenants Edward had in feudal fashion consolidated his status and career by a judicious marriage.

Three months later the difficulties that had prevented him from taking part in the 1906 General Election disappeared in the all-consuming constitutional struggle arising out of Lloyd George's People's Budget, and in Asquith's first appeal to the country in January 1910 both he and his brother-in-law were elected with comfortable margins in the Conservative interest by Yorkshire constituencies—Lane Fox for Barkston Ash, and Edward for Ripon; but the Liberals retained their majority, and with the necessary assistance of Irish and Labour votes were ready to open the attack on the privileges of the House of Lords. Edward did not adopt an extreme attitude and seems to have held the balance between his father's advocacy of the House of Lords and his own natural loyalty to the faithful Commons.

His father's close friendship with Balfour's private secretary, the Right Hon. J. S. Sanders, must have been of great assistance to Edward in the early days of his Parliamentary career; but Halifax's fastidious independence made it equally possible for them to cultivate and entertain the rebellious Joseph Chamberlain. As an example of Halifax's elasticity of outlook on lay questions it should be noted that in his resolve to dish the Whigs after their Education Bill he advised Balfour, through Sanders, to put forward Old Age Pensions on the Unionist programme at the next election—a subversive suggestion which, fortunately for Lloyd George, Balfour politely brushed aside. It was the fate of the Education Bill that encouraged Halifax in the delusive belief that a firm policy on the part of the Lords would make the Government give way. Early in the year he discussed with Edward what was then the fashionable idea of a reformed Second Chamber and secured the formidable support of Lord Balfour of Burleigh for his own particular variation of the theme; but this and many other compromises vanished away and Edward for his part was not called upon to make any special contribution to the vexed question of the Veto.

Considering how well established he now was in Yorkshire—a lieutenant in the Yorkshire Dragoons, with considerable interest in the agricultural and general affairs of the county, maintaining both Temple Newsam and Park House in Harrogate—his début in Westminster was tentative and modest enough. Admittedly he was laid low with a slight attack of appendicitis in March and took a six weeks vacation to recover, but when at last late on the evening of 15th June 1910 he rose to make his maiden speech to a half-empty and inattentive House, the occasion and his contribution to it can hardly have appeared even to the most discerning Parliamentary prophet as an event of any special significance.

CHAPTER VI

THE MEMBER FOR RIPON

A MAIDEN SPEECH in the House of Commons, although it is invested with traditional courtesies, is always an ordeal for the new member, and as often as not, factors beyond his control—the almost casual inconsequence of our Parliamentary life and procedure—dictate whether his début will cast before him a shadow of future greatness or be consigned to immediate oblivion. Stanley Baldwin's first speech was about coal, and was so undistinguished that for some time even the meticulous Hansard confused him with his father, to whose constituency of Bewdley he had quietly succeeded; Neville Chamberlain's name attracted attention for his maiden speech, but otherwise he made no particular impression. In Wood's case, he was told by the Chief Whip to keep alive a debate on Egypt until Balfour was ready to make the concluding speech for the Opposition. He has himself confessed that he was given an hour's notice to prepare the speech, and that it was on a subject of which he was completely ignorant.

Earlier in the year the Egyptian Prime Minister, Boutras Pasha, had been murdered, and Sir Eldon Gorst, the British Consul-General in Cairo, fixed the crime on the Nationalist Party, which largely depended on the support of Egyptian students. A cynical Egyptian comment of the time was that it had taken Britain twenty-eight years to teach the Egyptians how to shoot their Prime Minister! More edifying were the observations of Theodore Roosevelt, who, when presented with the Freedom of the City of London at the Guildhall on 31st May, used the murder of Boutras Pasha for a homily on British rule in Egypt. " In Egypt," he solemnly observed, " you are not only the guardians of your own interests; you are also the guardians of the interests of civilization; and the present condition of affairs in Egypt is a grave menace to both your Empire and to civilization. . . . In such a situation as yours in Egypt, weakness, timidity and sentimentality may cause even more far-reaching harm than violence and injustice. Of all broken reeds, sentimentality is the most broken reed on which righteousness can lean." All this was fervently approved by the Conservatives, who, in raising the Egyptian problem a fortnight later, complained that the Prime Minister's murder should have been dealt with "promptly" so as not to allow time for him to become a national martyr.

Such was the background to Wood's maiden speech. The very fact that he was asked merely to kill time and allowed no opportunity for careful preparation gives his ideas a perhaps more genuine ring than if he had been enabled to elaborate a brief. A few salient passages from the speech will show effectively how far he has advanced in statesmanship from his first dim and tentative reactions to the Imperial theme. Yet underlying the orthodox Tory jingoism to be found in his bland reference to the Egyptians as a "black people" and in his observations upon "superior" and "subordinate races"—which suggest that he is not the only British leader who has managed to rid his system of Nazi claptrap before assuming public responsibility or coming to years of political discretion—can be detected an effort to give expression to a more humane and tolerant view-point, a certain sense of strife in this off the record harangue between what he really thinks and what he is expected to say.

"One often hears," he declared, "that when a white nation is dealing with a black nation it is practically governing by force. I think that even in those conditions government remains what it always is—government by consent. Anybody who has lived or who has passed his time among those conditions among black people must recognize that government in that case is also government by consent—by which I mean that the black people are prepared to be governed by the white people—or your government is not worth a day's purchase. If that is true, as I think it is, surely the argument that under all conditions and at all times all men are equal is one of the most flimsy and one of the most academic that could possibly be brought forward. It is no more true to say that all men are equal at all times than to say that all men have red hair or false teeth. And while we on our side most emphatically disclaim any attempt permanently to hold down the black races, we do at the same time insist that if our position in those countries is to be maintained, it can only be as it is at the present moment, by maintaining the position and fulfilling the functions of a superior race. . . ."

In this connection some Government members had expressed suspicion of the use of the word "prestige"—"I am, I confess, set to wondering whether they and I mean the same thing when we use the word 'prestige'. I think in the minds of some hon. Members there is the idea, when the word is used, that it means right or wrong—the white man will be upheld and supported and that the black man will be downtrodden, and will have extremely scanty opportunities of justice. That is not my meaning when I use the word 'prestige'. My meaning is that the subordinate race should by all means be fairly treated, and that there should be no sense of injustice. But given that condition, surely you are in a position to insist that the black race must and can only be treated as subordinate to the race charged with the government of their country for the time being. The time may come, and I hope it will come, when those races with whose government we are now charged may be in a position to assume the control of their own fortunes, and may be able to work out their own destiny. When that time is reached, I am sure that all parties in this country will be prepared to assist them when they make the attempt." To encourage them in any such ideas of self-government, however, when they were still "in the condition of political children" was not only to court disaster for those engaged in the government of the country, but "it is to court disaster in one of the most valued possessions of this country and bring into most serious jeopardy the white races wherever they are in contact with the black races". These random comments were not over modestly described as "one or two considerations which must govern our dealings in Egypt to-day".

In contrasting Edward's subsequent record with this Prologue of Blood and Iron it is perhaps relevant to point out that the great Gladstone himself made his début in Parliament with a defence of the slave trade, and to suggest that there is a time-honoured tradition of apostasy in our public life, whereby the mental horizon of the young true-blue reactionary seems steadily to expand and his outlook broaden down from precedent to precedent, while on the other hand the arteries of the dashing young progressive harden with the passing of the years, and disillusionment with the processes of reform leads him to place an ever-increasing reliance upon the *status quo*. Political experience belies outward appearances, and the journey from revolutionary fervour to ultramontanism, from diehardism to reforming zeal can easily be spanned in the course of a single public career; and indeed under a political system where the sovereignty of discussion is recognized, such odysseys are likely to be the rule rather than the exception. Not too much should be made, therefore, of Wood's reactionary débût; he grew in a political environment that encourages growth. As for the Egyptian debate, even Grey, winding up for the Government, saw fit to placate the Conservatives by giving an assurance that the occupation of Egypt would continue, and by adding a threat that agitation against it would lead to " more assertion of our authority ". Roosevelt's speech had not embarrassed him and he had listened to it " with the greatest enjoyment "!

The only other noteworthy contribution which Wood made to the brief 1910 Parliament was in the debate on the Accession Declaration Bill. This was a measure devised by the Government, and drafted by Asquith and the Archbishop of Canterbury, both masters in the art of embodying compromise in a formula, to remedy a situation against which Halifax had agitated ever since the death of Queen Victoria. On his accession the Sovereign is required to make a Declaration of his intention to uphold Protestantism. It had originally been framed in 1678 in the atmosphere of panic aroused by the Popish Plot, and it contained phrases about Transubstantiation highly offensive to the King's twelve million Catholic subjects, and much resented by many High Churchmen, including Halifax. In 1901 he made a strenuous effort to get it amended, and went to see Queen Alexandra on the subject, who confessed to him that she hated it; but Lord Salisbury's Declaration Bill succeeded only in stirring up the Protestants without appeasing the Catholics. " Whatever securities Parliament chooses to take ", Halifax wrote to his wife, " that the King shall not be a Roman Catholic, the method of picking out particular doctrines and making men deny them is not the way to do it." The Salisbury Bill soon died an inglorious death, and Edward VII was thus the last King to make the old offensive Declaration.

By 1910 there was general agreement that the grievance should be finally redressed. Asquith had the support of Balfour[1] and most of the Opposition; only a few back-benchers from Ulster led a minor revolt against Transubstantiation, the Mass and the Virgin. Halifax told the English Church Union that he was in favour of abolishing the Declaration altogether, and he found the new wording "odious". The King was now to declare himself "a faithful Protestant", and Halifax was sure that in popular estimation this would still mean "a profession of Protestantism versus Catholicism which I for one cannot stomach. I shall therefore come to London, make a speech for the freedom of my own soul and vote against all amendments which are worse than what the Government propose." However, he finally gave his approval to the Bill, having duly said his say in favour of abolition.

Edward, in the somewhat stodgy debate in the Commons on 27th July, took the opportunity faithfully to reflect the family view-point not merely on the Declaration but on the status of the Church as well. As for the Declaration, he argued that the Protestant succession was amply safeguarded not only by the Act of Settlement and the Bill of Rights, but also by the fact that the Monarch took Holy Communion by Church of England rites which he thought no Catholic would do. But on the wider issue he objected to the description of the Church of England as "the Protestant and Reformed Church". "There is a sense in which the Church of England is Protestant and Reformed," he observed with true filial piety, "but we do not regard that as the true constitutional or historical description of the Church to which we belong"; however, he conceded Hilaire Belloc's point, made later in the debate, that "we owe a duty even in the House of Commons, to reality", and voted for the new Declaration without further demur.

. . . .

[1] It was Balfour who, with delicious irony, described the old Declaration as condemning certain Catholic doctrines "in language which, I believe, Roman Catholics think theologically inadequate".

Four days after this debate Edward became a father, for on 31st July Lady Dorothy gave birth to twin daughters, one of whom, Anne Dorothy,[1] survived.

The death of King Edward had brought about a truce in the constitutional struggle, but the autumn saw the two Houses returning to the fray more irreconcilable than before. The Government was by now resolved to settle the right of Veto once and for all, and the composition or reform of the Lords was considered only as a means of securing legislative sovereignty for the Commons. In December Asquith asked for a further mandate from the people to redress the balance of the Constitution. The people's verdict left the Parties in much the same condition as before, and both Edward and his brother-in-law were returned with similar majorities. The Parliament Bill of 1911 compelled Edward and his father to take difficult decisions. The King's reported promise to create a sufficient number of peers to ensure that the Bill passed the Lords filled Halifax with dismay, and his immediate reaction, as he told Lansdowne, was that he preferred "the Bill by itself to the Bill plus the peers". A group, however, led by Halsbury and Willoughby de Broke, was formed to resist any surrender, and became known as the "Ditchers", in contrast to the "Hedgers", who hoped to the bitter end that their abstention would help to bring about some compromise. As it was, the "Ditchers" grew in number and influence and threatened to defeat the Bill, and with the Government obdurate, it became clear that abstention would not be enough, and ultimately Halifax in a two-minute speech came out on the side of the Diehards.

For Edward the dilemma was even more acute; the Conservatives were naturally bound by the closest ties of blood and interest to the Lords, and he himself was the heir to a title, but at the same time as a Member of Parliament in opposition, he could not afford to be accused of being less sensitive to the status of the Commons than the Liberals were. Wood's efforts to reconcile these conflicting loyalties, without carrying any deep conviction or displaying any particular originality, show him in the process of developing technique in the tactics and strategy of Parliamentary debate. He intervened twice in the Committee stage of the Parliament

[1] She is now the Countess of Feversham.

Bill in support of two cleverly contrived Conservative Amendments. The first proposed that where the Lords refused unamended passage of a Money Bill, Royal assent should only follow a further debate in the Commons. The Bill as it stood provided that when the Commons had passed a Money Bill, the Lords had to pass it without amendment within a month; otherwise it became law. On 17th April (the fourth day in Committee) Asquith opposed this Amendment on the ground that it involved " a Fourth Reading in this House. That is an entirely novel proposition and one which goes beyond the constitutional powers of this House." Except for " one or two regrettable and wholly exceptional departures ", the Lords had invariably accepted Money Bills for generations past, and the Clause was merely a " reaffirmation and a constitutional recognition of a long-established practice ".

Wood supported the Amendment, saying that he thought it touched the field of machinery, not of principle. " All that this Amendment would do," he pleaded, " would be to transfer some of the power and a portion of the position which are at present held by the Second House to this House. . . . There might well be a discussion in the House of Lords, or in any Second Chamber, which might turn upon quite different points to those which had been raised in this House, and the points which emerged there might be quite different to those which emerged from the discussion here. If you had an obstinate Government who were conscious of a weak case it might well be that they might snap their fingers at what had been found to be the most effective criticism in another place, and would hold that, having run the gauntlet of criticism in this House they should withdraw their Bill from discussion at once and pass their Act in the way contemplated by this Bill ".

The Government, with Home Rule no less than the Budget in mind, had provided that a non-Money Bill rejected by the Lords in three successive Sessions should become law. The Conservatives felt themselves to be on safer ground in resisting this proposal, and on 26th April (the tenth day in Committee) they moved an Amendment that after a third rejection a Referendum should be held. The Liberals were implacably opposed to any such suggestion, although not all went quite so far as Winston Churchill, then Home Secretary, who asserted that when once the Referendum was adopted, "Parliamentary and representative institutions which have been the historic glory of these islands would be swept away, and, in their places, we would have the worst forms of Jacobinism, Caesarism, and Anarchy". The Government case, as stated by Herbert Samuel, was briefly that the Referendum would play havoc with legislation for social reform, and that it applied to every Liberal Bill (except Money Bills) to which the Lords took exception. "There is no machinery of any kind," he added acidly, "by which equal measure can be meted out to Conservative legislation."

A Labour Member had asked why, if they were to have a Referendum, the Tories wanted the Lords as well. "The answer is simple," was Wood's reply. "We want the Referendum to take the place in this remodelled constitution of the check hitherto supplied by that Second Chamber—a check which, under this Bill, is to be removed from us." Perhaps the answer was not so simple, for this was really no answer at all. However, "We know that the real objection to the Referendum, under whatever guise it may be . . . is that the Government and their supporters wish to make the House of Commons to-day not only supreme as between the two Houses, but sovereign over any Parliament and over any possible wish of the people outside." Of the previous adventures of the Lords he said: "We have hitherto had the power of insisting at certain times that the House of Commons shall be brought into touch and into line with public opinion, and the check or guarantee we have had up to this time being removed, we are bound to insist upon another."[1]

It must be admitted that the period from the passing of the Parliament Act up to the outbreak of war in August 1914 was bleak and unpromising for a young Conservative, especially one of Edward Wood's cast of mind. The influence of his father still dominated his political outlook and in a sense circumscribed his activity, for, as Lockhart observes,

[1] Chiozza Money, who followed, claimed with some justice that Wood had hardly faced the fundamental objection to a Referendum. "You can only obtain a clear issue," he pointed out, "when the Government decides not to stand or fall by the result of the Referendum. . . . What then follows? The Government refers a measure to the country, it decides not to stand or fall by the result. What is the consequence? Ministerial responsibility ceases and you have got the beginning of the end of the Parliamentary system."

the Parliament Act took the heart out of politics for Halifax. " He would continue to do his duty, to vote and speak occasionally, when the service of Church or State summoned him; but the Constitution had been broken and there had been a betrayal. He had turned the last page of a worthy and dignified volume, in which in 1831 his father had helped to write the first chapter." The very fact that " the whole business of politics had become uncongenial " to Halifax, " not by the act of one unscrupulous Government so much as by a slow process of deterioration ", undoubtedly had an enervating and depressing effect upon Edward's political ambitions. In one respect, however, Edward was enabled to put aside the prevailing gloom in Conservative politics, for in the autumn of 1912 his eldest son was born. Following the usual family discussion the child was christened Charles Ingram Courtenay after his grandfather, grandmother and the previous owners of Temple Newsam.

In Parliament he continued to put occasional questions to Ministers—one to Asquith, for instance, asking what steps the Government proposed to take for the relief of distress if the coal strike continued, suggests that the physical and social implications of labour unrest were not wholly lost upon the Member for Ripon. But his only sustained intervention was to oppose with much of his father's vehemence and vigour the Disestablishment of the Welsh Church. Both Halifax and Edward strove with unflagging zeal in Parliament and the country at large to keep this highly contentious though no less wearisome measure off the statute book. Both feared, not without some reason, that the Conservative leaders might be persuaded to sacrifice the Welsh Church as the price of some concession from the Government over Home Rule, and though neither relished the even more far-reaching attack on Union with Ireland, doctrinal conviction deflected them from the main stream of Conservative enthusiasm for Ulster. " The Orangemen ", wrote Halifax, " are the most senseless and bigoted faction on the face of this earth, and the sooner the Conservative and Unionist party can get rid of them the better for that party."

It may be safely asserted that Edward's determined opposition to Welsh Disestablishment sprang as much from his character as from his upbringing, and he attracted attention in so far as he relied on something more than orthodox

Party arguments. The logic of his case soon found him developing a thesis to which even his father might have hesitated to subscribe. In combating the doctrine that a man should be split up into taxpayer and Churchman, he exclaimed, " What we need to learn is that every citizen is individually responsible for any other citizen, and that there is a real social membership in the State. I am quite sure that the Labour Party will agree with that, and I submit that you can only establish that on a moral basis. It is obvious that the State cannot do so itself." Such an appeal to Labour at such a time from a Conservative back-bencher argued unusual conviction and courage. The importance, then, of his prolonged journey through the undergrowth of Welsh Disestablishment is that he emerged not simply as his father's voice, but as a Christian in his own right. " Religion," he asserted in 1914, " and the religious instinct is the real underpinning foundation of society, and is the basis upon which society as a whole must always rest." Here was his credo, the standard to which he has ever since aspired, put forward at the outset of his public career and without reservation.

He may not have shown any particular brilliance in these pre-war years, but he established himself with his fellow Members of Parliament as a man whose sincerity could not be questioned and whose motives were above reproach. In doing so, he became one to whom—when the Conservatives had once more seized the helm—office could be safely entrusted. His religious preoccupations thus enhanced the one attribute which above all conformed with aristocratic convention and ensured his success with the Conservative hierarchy—namely, a readiness to accept political promotion without appearing to be unduly ambitious for it. Politics is by no means a self-evident career for the son and heir of a landed nobleman. Edward's religion helped him to regard politics within the Conservative fold as a form of social duty, a task to which he must, if required, dedicate himself.

. . . .

But August 1914 put an end to thoughts of political advancement and raised more imperative obligations. He at once mobilized with his regiment, the Yorkshire Dragoons, but was not called up, and anxious to volunteer for active service, sought his father's advice. " No one can decide for another what such things involve," Halifax replied, " so I

EDWARD WOOD, 1914

can only say that whatever your decision may be, and whatever the consequences which it may involve, I shall feel from my heart that you have made the right decision. Your mother—we have talked much together—bids me say that I am speaking for her as well as for myself. One thing only I know—whether you go or stay, we shall be equally in God's hands."

That he should have sought guidance from his father on so intimate a problem reveals a significant trait in his character—personal decisions did not come easily to him, his conscience made him almost overscrupulous in estimating the effect of his own actions upon those who were near and dear to him. His father and mother had left him free to choose, and he resolved to go, but in April 1915 he was still in England, although awaiting orders at any moment.

In the meanwhile, Temple Newsam was converted into a military hospital, in the capable charge of Lady Dorothy, whose efficiency, we learn, was highly praised by Sir Michael Sadler, then Vice-Chancellor of Leeds University. In July Halifax was writing to him of a visit to Garrowby, full of praise of the garden, which was "in the greatest beauty". Lady Dorothy's new border in the corner behind the chapel received special mention, but, less happily, the observant old man detected a new policy being adopted towards the egregious Japanese deer in the park—"Dearest Edward, don't get rid of the deer for the sake of the cattle and the sheep." But for once "Dearest Edward" was adamant.

A few days after he had received his orders and had left with his regiment without being given time even to say good-bye to his parents—"so we have given up thinking of it and shall think of you as we were that last Sunday at Garrowby, and shall go to church here on Saturday morning instead, which will bring you and us very near together and in the best and most real way. It will be better so in all respects and we shall pray God to-day and every day to have you in His keeping and bring you safe back to us all."[1]

While Edward was in France his children stayed frequently with their grandparents, and the indefatigable Halifax would send him frequent reports of their progress. Scott's novels were being read aloud to them. "Charles", he wrote in September 1915, "wants coping with. He has

[1] Halifax to Edward July 29th 1915.

a strong will of his own—a very good thing to have too. But this morning he and your Mama had a pitched battle in which, however, she came off victorious."[1]

In the following year a second son was born, and his parents elected to christen him Francis Hugh Peter Courtenay. Peter was chosen, being the name by which Edward's great friend, Hugh Dawnay, was intimately known, but it did not meet with Halifax's approval, who let it be known that "I could not endure Peter". In the first place it was not a family name, and the only Peter Wood he could discover had been ill-advised enough to fight for Gustavus Adolphus in the Thirty Years War. If anything happened to Charles ("which God avert!") could the prospect of a Peter, Viscount Halifax be faced with equanimity? Once again, however, Edward stood firm, and the child was duly named Peter, though his grandfather refused for many years to call him anything but Francis.[2]

The lack of decent drink during the war greatly perturbed Halifax. "I shall not give up my beer" became one of his many battle-cries, and when he presented his two small grandsons with silver mugs he wrote most feelingly to their father: "I so trust those boys will never be teetotallers!"[3]

[1] Halifax to Edward, September 9th 1915.
[2] *Vide* Lockhart, Vol. II, page 240.
[3] A bucolic sentiment in much the same vein as when he confessed to Edward that the Liberal Licensing Bill made him begin to think that drunkenness was a virtue!

CHAPTER VII

THE GREAT OPPORTUNITY

EDWARD WOOD'S war record both at the Front and in the few appearances he made in Parliament should help to dispose of those catchpenny clichés that have typified him as a saintly quietist, ill-adapted to the ruthless demands of modern war, or an innocent apostle of appeasement. Instead of a mild country gentleman somewhat wistfully "doing his bit", we find a militant Major Wood commanding his regiment in the thick of the terrible 1916-1917 battles, mentioned in despatches, returning during brief spells of leave to demand of the Government more vigorous leadership. Nor were his demands based on vague dissatisfaction. He knew what he wanted and laid his finger with unerring precision upon the political defects in our war effort at that time.

Early in 1916 he was pleading forcibly for a smaller War Cabinet. "A Cabinet," he protested, "even if it were a Cabinet of archangels, is not an ideal body for administering a great war in which you require prompt decisions and, above all, men to be at liberty to think without being immersed in departmental work." To-day such an argument might seem to be a platitude, but at the time when it was put forward it was startling and novel and altogether too drastic to convince the Prime Minister. Yet if Asquith had been roused to adopt Wood's advice when it was given, he might well have been able to repair the military fortunes of the nation as well as to restore his own rapidly waning political prestige.

Similarly unacceptable was Wood's attitude to military service. In the same debate he followed Sir John Simon, who was then concentrating his unrivalled gifts for special pleading in an attack upon conscription. Wood had the temerity to resist his conclusions with a special emphasis. "I think," he asserted, "that in after years it will be thought a somewhat extraordinary thing that in the twentieth month of the war we should still have been having one delay after another, that we should still up to the last moment have been making frenzied efforts in the cause of straightforward voluntary recruiting, and that we should have been having one recruiting statement after another." Such had been the stimulus of the massacres of Flanders upon this modest young layman, who hitherto had confined himself to a reverent pursuit of his father's High Church principles, that he was now ready to help in breaking up the uneasy 1916 Coalition and combine with any party—and he deliberately included Labour—which was "prepared to carry on the war, as I conceive, with more vigour".

His urgent interest in the problem of manpower led him to accept the offer of an appointment in the Ministry of National Service. Its first Director had been the then comparatively obscure Neville Chamberlain, whom Lloyd George had impulsively snatched from his duties as Lord Mayor of Birmingham, but Chamberlain resigned in August and Wood came in under his successor, Auckland Geddes, and it thus seems unlikely that Wood ever made contact with his future chief on national service work. Certainly it would have been a most unhappy enterprise over which to meet or form a first appreciation of their respective talents. Wood may have been drawn in, as others were, by the compelling glow of Lloyd George's personality.

The principle of setting up a Department to deal with the problem of National Service had been approved by the Asquith Cabinet, but its execution coincided with the emergence of the Lloyd George regime. The original experiment broke down for several reasons which the new Prime Minister, in all the frantic hustle of his newly won power, seems to have overlooked. The functions and powers of the new Department were never adequately defined; it was called upon to prepare the ground for compulsion while emphasizing only voluntary recruitment; its relations with the older departments and with Labour were never smooth; if its duties had been purely administrative Chamberlain might have succeeded, but the primary need was for publicity and propaganda, for which he had no interest or aptitude. "Constant efforts were made by me", wrote Lloyd George in his *War Memoirs*, "and by others to infuse a new spirit into the Department by the introduction of men of more suitable type into the work, especially on the publicity side. Mr. Chamberlain regarded these suggestions as involving an aspersion on the men he had chosen for the purpose—all able men for other tasks. He stubbornly resisted every proposal made to him for improving and strengthening the Department in certain directions where it was patently deficient."

By August 1917 both Chamberlain and a Parliamentary Select Committee came to the same conclusion: that there was not much object in the Department's continued existence. It had cost the taxpayer just on £200,000, in return for which it had placed 35,000 men and women and distributed 70,000 soldiers and civilians on the land—a disappointing return.

When Auckland Geddes took over, he and his colleagues had the inestimable advantages of being more openly Lloyd George's men and therefore enjoying more of his confidence, but in addition a much clearer agreement was reached as to their status and duties. Relations with the Ministry of Labour were precisely defined and an overlapping of functions ruled out. The result was that Wood was able to share in far more impressive achievement than had been possible under Chamberlain. Moreover, whereas Chamberlain had had to cope with an almost exhausted voluntary effort, Auckland Geddes was to be allowed to administer the conscription Wood had so frankly demanded. It was a great relief to his parents to have him back after two years at the Front, but it is clear that he entered on his new work in no spirit of civilian complacency. The fate of Neville Chamberlain gave point to his complaint at the end of 1917 that " it is mainly political co-ordination that we lack ".

Perhaps, too, it was exasperation at the difficulties inherent in his labours for National Service that caused him in December 1917 to enliven a debate on the Registration of the People Bill, which disqualified conscientious objectors from voting at Parliamentary elections during and for five years after the war, with an unusual outburst. " I feel . . . absolutely no sympathy," he exclaimed, " with the real conscientious objector. . . . I am told that in the United States they do not waste time about passing special laws and legislation as to conscientious objectors, but that if they are quite sure they have got the right people they compel them to wear scarlet uniform and walk the streets." His mind was clearly set upon the complete military overthrow of Germany. The Lansdowne letter, which made for deep heart-searchings among Liberals and Conservatives alike, struck no chord of sympathy in him, and he replied almost frigidly to Lord Beauchamp, a friend of the family, who as Chairman of the Lansdowne Committee had sought his support.

While the war was drawing towards its delusive end, and amid the " flimsy rejoicings " of armistice, Wood sought relief in ranging his mind over broader vistas of public policy than he had hitherto contemplated, with the result that, although never swerving in his essential Conservatism, he became more independent, articulate and progressive in outlook.

It is often held against him that he put his signature to the notorious Lowther Petition which, it is alleged, compelled Lloyd George to adopt a more intransigent attitude at Versailles than he would otherwise have done. These critics, in branding Wood as a fierce Diehard, somewhat compromise their colleagues who find him wanting on the grounds of excessive gentility, but in any case they probably overlabour their point. The motives of the promoters of the Lowther Petition may not have been high, but they were not for that matter profound. Many of the Members who signed it probably did so out of a genuine belief that Lloyd George was throwing away at the Peace Conference the fruits of a military victory that had not been pressed home; but whatever the particular reason for Edward Wood associating himself with this deplorable Round Robin, it is much more likely that his real attitude was summed up in a letter which his father wrote to *The Times* on the " Hang the Kaiser " theme. Such an action, he claimed, was wrong in principle, because it was an assumption of Divine justice, and, in policy, because it would invest the victim with the halo of martyrdom. It is difficult to believe that Edward would have contradicted this thesis either on grounds of principle or policy.

Ireland provides one example of the moderation and sweet reason he applied to the manifold problems of peace-making, and, incidentally, it brought him into some measure of sympathy with Lloyd George. In the dark days of December 1916 he did all in his power to support the new

Prime Minister in his efforts to remove Anglo-Irish misunderstanding "which has for centuries been a source of misery to the one and of embarrassment and weakness to the other". In a debate on 21st December he urged the Government to take its courage in both hands and advise the Crown to make a generous departure on new lines, which would enlist the services of all representative Irishmen and would give the Irish leaders an opportunity of proving the sincerity of what they had said they were willing to do by way of assurances and guarantees to Ulster. As for the Ulstermen, while they had deserved well of the Empire in the past, they would earn a nobler title still to fame if they would now freely accept the invitation to make a great venture of faith, without which no such experiment would be possible. In the spirit of these constructive sentiments he is to be found in May 1918 accompanying his father to 10 Downing Street and lunching with the Prime Minister in order to back up a proposal from Halifax that Lloyd George should ask the King to cross over to Ireland and make a personal appeal to his Irish subjects to join the army. "Mr. Lloyd George thought the suggestion very interesting, but after consideration decided against it, probably wisely."[1] This did not deter Halifax from writing a letter of appreciation to the Prime Minister, shortly after the Armistice, praising him for "possessing the best of all God's good gifts—the gift of imagination". Thus were old feuds forgotten in the first flush of victory.

Two other problems of policy which were linked up with peacetime reconstruction and which were of deep interest and close concern to Wood were agricultural economy and relations with the Empire. Upon agriculture he could speak with some authority. He voiced unreservedly, but without the usual narrowness of vision, the views of the producer. As early as February 1918, during a Debate on the Address on the subject of Food Supplies, he asked that the cost of food to the consumer should be based on the cost of production. If that would fix it too high to do justice to the consumer, then as a temporary war measure subsidies should be given to place the food on the market "without turning off the tap of production by making it impossible for the producer to grow it at a profit". This policy he argued

[1] Lockhart, Vol. II, pages 245-246.

would keep the price of food within the reach of the poorer classes. These were sentiments calculated to warm the hearts of Yorkshire farmers, even if in the last resort it meant a policy of hush money to the distributors.

More ambitious and elaborate was a scheme for Federal Devolution which he set out as a Motion and formally moved on 4th June 1919, and which, on a free vote of the House and with the somewhat mystified support of Walter Long for the Government, was carried by 187 votes to 34. As a result, the House was of opinion that " the time has come for the creation of subordinate legislatures within the United Kingdom ".

. . . .

His motives for bringing forward this complex and seemingly academic measure at a moment when Parliament and the nation were preoccupied with all the vexing details of Peacemaking, were set out in a 25,000 word pamphlet he wrote during the summer in collaboration with Sir George Lloyd. Significantly enough they called their work *The Great Opportunity*—and explained that " the purpose of this pamphlet is not to present a complete political policy, but it is rather prompted by the conviction that, when so much seems shifting and uncertain, there is a wide demand for some coherent statement of first principles by which the professions of parties may be tried ".[1] Into this framework Federal Devolution fitted. The continuous session of Parliament had reacted unfavourably on the work of Ministers, Members, and Civil Servants. Ministers had to give too much of their time to answering Parliamentary questions, Members were unable to keep in touch with their constituents, while Civil Servants were without the respite which the autumn was designed to afford them. " The result has been an excessive strain upon the whole machine of Government, a deterioration in the quality of administration, and damage to the public position of the House of Commons." Only extensive constitutional changes would overcome these serious evils, which would be gravely aggravated after the war. But " the difficulty that confronts any Government, and most of all a Government staggering under the responsibility of a world-war, is that the country generally is not conscious of the causes of the evils we have referred to, but

[1] *The Great Opportunity*, page 3.

only of the evils themselves ". Of necessity it must put victory before constitutional reform, and was likely to show impatience and irritation at being invited to consider important proposals affecting the Constitution. " None the less we believe that it is the duty of the Government to deal with this question and to anticipate a situation of which the difficulties will be only accentuated by delay."[1]

In brief, the solution Wood and Lloyd favoured was to devolve to England, Scotland, Wales and Ireland certain powers now vested in the United Kingdom Parliament at Westminster. Conservative opinion was opposed to the proposal as being an attempt to short-circuit the Irish Home Rule question, but Wood and Lloyd put forward various safeguards to meet the likely objection of their political colleagues. As far as Ireland was concerned public opinion would refuse to sanction any proposals so repugnant to the Ulster population as to require force to bring them into operation. Parliament at Westminster was to devolve only local powers to the suggested local legislatures. Responsibility for justice, defence, foreign affairs, the central administration of economic policy and finance, as well as for industrial legislation, would remain as before at the centre. The benefits arising from Federal Devolution would be to give more adequate time and study at Westminster for the consideration of matters affecting the collective destinies of these islands and the Empire; while the local assemblies would gain a more intimate and efficient control of affairs which were especially their own. This scheme and the arguments adduced in its favour are cited at length as evidence of what in general the authors meant by " the Great Opportunity ".

Keeping in mind the background of tense military crisis in which the pamphlet was written and of unreadiness and exhaustion in which it was published, Wood deserves to be remembered for his collaboration in promoting during 1919 the unpopular theme of a planned reconstruction of Britain rather than for his share in any ill-considered ultimatum to Versailles. The Conservatism set out in *The Great Opportunity* deserves to be contrasted with the sordid aims and personnel of the Tory rank and file who helped to make up the Khaki Coalition. It is not, of course, possible to assert

[1] *The Great Opportunity*, page 37.

with any confidence where Lloyd begins or Wood leaves off in the actual composition of the book, but as a whole the somewhat laborious style, the emphasis upon agriculture, education, and above all upon the Christian pattern of society suggest that Wood provided most of the material and thought. Actually before the book even appeared Lloyd had left Parliament to enter on his brilliant if controversial career of Imperial administration.

Collaboration with Lloyd might suggest to some, who have not read the book or are unacquainted with Lloyd's record, an essay in Diehardism, but the reverse is the truth; the real significance of Wood's friendship with the man who had already worked with and earned the praise of the great T. E. Lawrence on the Arabian Bureau, was in its emancipation from the orthodox party opinions. In his brief career in the House of Commons Lloyd had never been afraid of challenging the advice of the Whips. He was a Diehard, it was once shrewdly observed, only in the Baldwinian sense of the term—namely, through sticking to his principles for more than three months at a time. He is essentially the administrator with much the same zeal for Imperial authority and reform as was typified in the ideals of the Milner Kindergarten. In spite of profound differences in temperament and subsequent disagreements over great issues of policy, Wood and Lloyd have never strained their friendship for each other. Both are fired with a burning belief in the inherent goodness of the British way of life—belief that amounts almost to fanaticism; but whereas Lloyd is mercurial, restless, brimming over with self-confident energy, Wood is slow-moving, calm, and actuated by a sense of reverent duty. Lawrence, while admitting that it would have been impossible for the Bureau to have done so much so soon without Lloyd, added that he was "avid rather to taste than to exhaust"—a criticism which could never have been levelled at Wood's powers of conscientious application. In short, their talents are complementary, the one gifted with what the other lacks.

It is not impossible that Wood wrote the main body of *The Great Opportunity* and that Lloyd, fresh from the Arabian epic, and disillusioned, as Lawrence was to be, with the sordid reality of the conquering Britain he had been proclaiming to the Arabs, found Wood's diagnosis right in line with his own half-formed thoughts, and wished to be associated with him in its publication by some more formal procedure than a few separate words of praise. This hypothesis may be doing Lloyd a grave injustice, but only in some such way can the intrusion on every page of Wood's idiom and ideas be satisfactorily explained.[1] If Lloyd had taken a greater share in it, there would surely be more distinct traces of his vivid personality—from beginning to end it is the gospel according to Wood.

Beyond the Federal solution mentioned above, no radical constitutional or social changes are advocated, but a number of home truths were restated which the Conservatives duly overlooked and which even Wood, when he attained Ministerial rank, was unable to apply. Here are some salient examples: "The nation must be convinced, and led to act on the conviction, that its interest in agriculture is more immediate than in that of any other industry, and that it is short-sighted folly to neglect it." "The question of religious teaching . . . is not one upon which the State, in our view, can afford to remain neutral." Then again, "Regard must be had to the extent to which the House of Commons is tending to become a legislative assembly registering the executive decrees of Government." The danger was attributed not merely to the war emergency but to the position of the Members themselves. Their salaries were, in effect, cancelled out by "the recurring burden of election expenses". "The inevitable result of this is to increase the power of the party machine in the House of Commons, by making it more difficult for Members to vote according to their own judgment against the declared party policy." The modern tendency of Governments to make all votes or Government business into votes of confidence, places Members "in the false position of being compelled to choose between recording their vote, against their better judgment in favour of the Government, or, on the other hand, voting

[1] There are many instances. On page 6 "the writers" think it is doubtful whether the principles of civilization, "of which the British are used to think they have been the particular guardians, would have been likely, apart from the Christian dispensation, to win the allegiance of the world". Or on page 84, in discussing Prohibition and Liberty: "After all, the pleasures of drink, rightly enjoyed, are perfectly moral and legitimate, and can claim the highest scriptural authority"—hardly Lloyd's language. Then again, there are references to the House of Lords, and Welsh Disestablishment, which take up the threads of debates with which Wood was specially concerned before the war.

against the Government with the knowledge that if they are successful in the division lobby, they are likely to expose themselves to the double liability of loss of salary, and what is in effect a financial fine in the shape of the expense of an election ". Apart from this, there were reasons for returning to the older constitutional practice of Free Votes which did not involve the fate of the administration. Only thus could the sovereignty of discussion be assured and the consequent improvement in legislation effected. " The present system is hostile to independence, and is perhaps, more than any other one thing, responsible for the diminished respect in which the House of Commons is coming to be held." The almost open barter of honours in return for substantial contributions to Party funds was denounced in this veritable Appeal from the New Whigs to the Old. Well might Burke have exclaimed, " Honours and rewards should be the well-merited expression of a nation's thanks to those who have served it well. Indiscriminate distribution of such things makes public scandal, and honours improperly gained or unworthily bestowed are no longer honourable."

Reconstruction on the economic side meant that it will be the duty of the State to take such measures, whether or not they involve resort to Tariff expedients, as will provide the widest markets for the sale of British products. The same measures were involved " in the no less exceptional circumstances of to-day " as were successfully adopted in the sixteenth century to meet " the aggression of the Hanseatic League ". Imperial Preference followed logically from this thesis. " Fiscal autonomy by each component unit of the Empire not only does not preclude, but indeed may be rightly supplemented by, some system which will enable the Empire to speak with a single voice in economic negotiations with Foreign Powers." There is no hedging as to the rights of labour or the status of the Trade Unions, merely an apt demand for reciprocal contributions to the principles of democratic government. " The complaints of trade unionists themselves that ballots are improperly conducted, either with insufficient voters or under some form of moral compulsion, are so numerous that there is probably some foundation for them."[1]

Some readers might be tempted to dismiss *The Great*

[1] *The Great Opportunity*, page 53.

Opportunity as a trite and ephemeral production, but for all its limitations—its attack on the pre-war Liberal Governments, for instance, is a travesty in partisanship, and mars the moderate and objective temper of the work—it finally absolves Wood and Lloyd of having submitted to the prevailing mood of exhaustion and complacency, of easy money and easier virtue which was to snatch from the Allied victory a world-wide defeat. Except for Neville Chamberlain's Housing Act—the principles of which Wood anticipates—the record of Conservative achievement can hardly be reckoned to have met either in the letter or the spirit the challenge of *The Great Opportunity.* "We have affirmed the responsibility of service which lies upon every individual; but for the more efficient discharge of his duty we have emphasized the obligation that lies upon the State to ensure that individuals may live their lives under conditions of reasonable security and content." Here was the dynamic of a new Conservatism which was in due course to rally round the leadership of Stanley Baldwin; but it perished for lack of the central purpose which Wood and Lloyd had called for and were themselves unable to contribute—Wood at the height of Baldwin's glory being absorbed in India and Lloyd in Egypt.

It should be noted that in largely confining his conception of "the Great Opportunity" to a programme of domestic reconstruction, Wood was not simply following convenience but a principle. Indeed his primary concern was with a practical nationalism which will "insist that as political and social physicians we show our capacity to heal ourselves before we attempt to heal others. If we achieve this we need not doubt that we shall be contributing effectively to the general betterment of world conditions. For this reason we believe that the attempt in some quarters to discredit national feeling, in order, as it is supposed, to gain strength for cosmopolitan internationalism, proceeds from a radical misunderstanding of human nature. . . . The nation is as truly the foundation of internationalism as the family is of the nation."[1]

This emphasis is unexceptionable in a war fought to vindicate nationality, but when he applied it to tariffs we detect the first germ of the fatal intellectual confusion in

[1] *The Great Opportunity*, page 8.

which the League of Nations ultimately made shipwreck. Tariffs are indispensable adjuncts to the national finance and trade of many nations, therefore " it would be fatal to the wide inclusion of nations to assert that tariffs are in themselves barriers to membership of a League of Nations ". Carrying the argument a stage further, " it is obvious that the United States would never allow, nor would anyone suggest, the interference on the part of any international authority in the political or fiscal relations existing between those domestic units—Georgia or California for example—that compose the Union. On an exactly similar analogy, therefore, we should deny that a League of Nations could exert any jurisdiction in regard to any domestic arrangements that might from time to time be agreed upon internally as between the several states that constitute the British Empire." But the analogy was not exactly similar. Georgia and California had abandoned the privilege of imposing tariffs against themselves and the outside world. Australia and Canada had done no such thing, as Britain found out to her cost at Ottawa.

Wood made the theme of the League his special subject in a number of his speeches just after the war. He was sincerely convinced that it was the one solid gain derived from the sufferings of the past four years and he looked beyond the halting formulae of the Covenant. " As I understand, the ultimate ideal of the League demands at least three things: it demands universal disarmament, it demands economic freedom, and it demands arbitration." Yet how was economic freedom to be reconciled with unbridled tariffs, or disarmament with the claims of political sovereignty? As for arbitration, Balfour, the Foreign Secretary, disparaged Wood's " noble and interesting idealism " with the chilling comment that " Nations which do not want to keep the peace will not be bound by these treaties of arbitration "—realism which Wood was not prepared to deny, but which for the present did nothing to shake him from his self-deception. Along with his political contemporaries and colleagues he persistently advocated the half-hearted and double-minded compromise between giving lip service to the ideal of internationalism and catching up with the facts of national power politics. The point to note is that this delusion was not fostered simply during the time of testing over Abyssinia, but was inherent in Wood's philosophy from the very birth of the League.

. . . .

On 22nd April 1919 his father and mother celebrated their golden wedding, though on a modest scale, chiefly because of the state of Lady Halifax's health. The war had been a severe trial to her, and, apart from the inevitable anxieties, it had ruled out the annual search for the warm climate of the Continent. She was now in her eighty-first year and had only just recovered from a serious illness. In May they paid their usual visit to Bovey Tracey, and on 7th June, Halifax's eightieth birthday, there was "a great excursion" with Edward, Lady Dorothy and their children to the beloved Moult. They returned to London towards the end of the month, and Lady Halifax underwent an operation which proved more serious than was at first anticipated. On 4th July Halifax was told there was no hope of her recovery. After she had received the Sacrament and Extreme Unction and bade farewell to her servants, her husband and three children were by her bedside. "You'll take care of him, won't you? " she said to her children. Soon afterwards she became unconscious and died peacefully. "For Papa it is the end of everything," wrote Edward's sister Mary. "I feel now he is only longing for the moment when his call will come to join her."

Indeed it seemed as though his work was done, for in February he had resigned the Presidency of the English Church Union. "I have grown deaf, my sight is failing, my memory is not what it was, and I am every day more conscious that I am not able to discharge the duties of President as they ought to be discharged." But to find a successor to one who had given his long life to upholding Catholic interests in the Church of England and who had delivered his first annual address to the Union in 1868 was no easy matter. To a new generation of clergy it spelt the end of a beneficent tyranny, and their demand was for more latitude. Halifax and the indefatigable secretary Hill, with and through whom he had ruled with such all-embracing efficiency, were looking for a young President who would maintain their standard of vigour and authority. Various names were put forward. Athelstan Riley, Lord Phillimore, Lord Hugh Cecil, and Lord Wolmer all refused or were found wanting for a thankless and exacting position. It was generally agreed that apart from Riley and possibly Phillimore, Edward was the only obvious candidate whose record was unexceptionable and whose name would probably have helped to reconcile the contending factions within the Union, but by now he was too deeply engrossed in politics to consider assuming the mantle of his father's life-work.

His refusal to step in and fill the void in the English Church Union caused by Halifax's resignation marks the opening of a new chapter, not so much in his career as in his intellectual and moral development. Up to this point his father's outlook towers over his, he is effective and forcible largely in so far as he reflects ideals already upheld by Halifax. He gave his own ponderous sincerity to Halifax's various ecclesiastical and lay convictions, but his capacity for reverence—a marked feature of his personality—led him to retain an almost adolescent acceptance of his father's initiative well on into manhood. When the Presidency of the Church Union passed to Sir Robert Newman it meant that Edward had in fact, following the precept of the family motto, made his choice. He would resume the course set by his illustrious grandfather.

CHAPTER VIII

WEST INDIES AND OFFICE

THROUGHOUT 1920, in the October of which year his third son Richard was born, he attended to his Parliamentary duties assiduously in spite of increasing family responsibilities. He took part in most of the big debates, and, as during the Irish crisis for instance, his voice was persistently raised in favour of progressive solutions and non-party policies. Such an independent attitude was likely to commend him sooner or later to Lloyd George, and it was no surprise when in April 1921, to his father's intense satisfaction be it said, he held his first Government office as Under-Secretary of State for the Colonies.

If through the hazards of war the promotion had been long deferred, he could now, at the age of forty, take satisfaction in an initial appointment of exceptional interest and importance. First it is to be noted that the Colonial Office was still, when he represented it in Parliament, responsible for the manifold interests of the whole Empire; there was as yet no separate Dominions Office, which was not created until July 1925. He had therefore to make himself acquainted with a wide range of subjects, but in British politics, the wider the range the better the apprenticeship for high office, the specialist is at a discount. Secondly his chief was Winston Churchill, who, as Secretary of State, had characteristically gathered round him a galaxy of talent for the vast task of Imperial regeneration after the war. Wood was thus not only to experience at close quarters and at the outset of his Ministerial career the dynamic influence of Churchill's leadership, but to be associated with a brilliant team of men called in to supplement the career Civil Servants.

It was at the Colonial Office that he came into contact, though he never reached terms of intimacy, with T. E. Lawrence, to whom Churchill gave the scope to repeat in peace his former triumphs among the Arabs. The piercing genius of this lonely man, with its blend of mediaeval, renaissance and modernist attributes, was to rouse Wood to produce in his memory one of the most powerful funeral orations of our time. To guide Churchill through the bogs and snares of Irish Settlement, the omniscient Lionel Curtis had been seconded as Irish adviser; while serving as Churchill's political private secretary and acting of necessity as an important liaison officer, was a young Scottish baronet, Sir Archibald Sinclair, who was later to gain distinction as a bold and eloquent spokesman of Liberal opposition to a Foreign Policy with which Wood was identified, but who never sacrificed on that account Wood's warm and lasting friendship.

Foreign observers find these intimate relationships between political adversaries difficult to appreciate. Is it possible for both the friendship and the opposition to be genuine, they ask. Not according to totalitarian standards. Admittedly in Wood's case animosity is not a dominant characteristic, but even Neville Chamberlain, who seemed to regard all party opposition as a personal affront, enjoyed the private esteem and goodwill of opponents who regarded his leadership and policies as little short of a national disaster. The secret is that the system is such that there is no need to carry the invective over into private life, and further than that, the vendetta is (as Sinclair once neatly reminded Chamberlain at the time of the Anglo-Italian Agreement) a word of foreign origin. The political scope of an Under-Secretary is usually limited to what Churchill, in a fit of youthful exuberance, once condemned as "mere detail"; but the Colonial Office in 1921 was an exception to this rule, first because the Imperial problems under its wing were far too numerous for the Secretary of State to attend to personally, and secondly because Churchill was wholly engrossed in the politics of Ireland and the strategy of the Near East—hence the need for Lawrence and for Curtis. Wood was thus left with a far wider initiative than he might normally expect.

In July he was called upon formally to move the Ministry's Vote of Supply, and in the same month came the interesting announcement that the Under-Secretary was to pay an official visit to the West Indies. It was important news for the West Indies in so far as there had been considerable agitation for the reinforcement of the whole constitutional, social and economic structure of the islands; new demands had arisen from the war, and Wood's visit was the first official British reaction to them. For Wood the visit was a political enterprise which would clearly test his powers to the utmost. There is some uncertainty as to who originated the idea of the tour, though it does not seem to have come from Churchill himself. Probably it was the outcome of consultation between high Departmental officials. What is certain is that there had been no such tour before. In fact no Secretary, Under-Secretary or even permanent Under-Secretary, had ever paid a personal visit while still in office or on the active list to any part of the Empire. Wood was thus playing the role of an explorer, and not the least significant indirect result of his tour was that it inaugurated in the years following a whole series of similar visits by Colonial Secretaries and Under-Secretaries.

When Wood set sail at the beginning of December in the *Valerian*, a ship lent by the Admiralty, he was accompanied by his friend, the Hon. W. G. A. Ormsby-Gore (now Lord Harlech) a Conservative M.P. of similar independent and progressive leanings to his own, and Mr. R. A. Wiseman of the Colonial Office. Upon Wiseman fell the primary duty of collecting material for the Report, while Ormsby-Gore was to help Wood with the innumerable speeches and ceremonies that were crowded into the next two hectic months. The ladies, including Lady Wood, did not join the party until the tour was under way and the party had reached Barbados; among the distinguished visitors present in the West Indies at the time was Lord Salisbury.

. . . .

The problem of the West Indies presented special difficulties to the would-be reformer. Peculiar to it, of course, was the influence of the American democratic outlook, and a policy of suppression or imposition would be courting disaster. There is thus no analogy between Wood's recommendations for the West Indies and his work in India. The West Indies had a tradition of constitutional government, but largely owing to the activities of nineteenth century prospectors it had been allowed to lapse. Wood was thus called upon to envisage a revival of old liberties, and not, as in India, the breaking of new ground. But there was no uniformity among the constitutions that had gone out of use or were still fitfully working. The Barbados' constitution, with its fully elected legislatures and nominated governments, was virtually identical with that of an American State at the time of the War of Independence. In Jamaica the constitution in fact centred round the veto of a minority in the Council which was known as " the Power of the Nine ". By the time Wood appeared on the scene the " Power of the Nine " had caused sufficient trouble to the Governor and unsettlement to the people to give Wood the pretext for recommending its abolition.

There are three distinct types of British Colonial Government. The most primitive is confined to a Council consisting of Heads of Departments; an advance on this is a Council of Heads of Departments and of a given number of nominated unofficial members as well; then thirdly there is the Council with official, nominated unofficial and elected members. The elected members may or may not be in the majority, but in any case the paramountcy of the Governor is clearly defined. This last type is the most common in the West Indies. The kernel of the constitutional problem was therefore whether, and if so, how far, the representative principle embodied in the elected members should be extended. This delicate problem was rendered more complex by the then popular idea, to which Ormsby-Gore originally subscribed, that the cure for all West Indian ills was to be found in wholesale Federation. On wider issues of the economic and social condition of the islands he was confronted with unnecessarily complicated and irritatingly vague material. Admittedly there was a census in 1921, but in general there were no good statistics. Population figures were unreliable, the acreage of this or that island was an unknown quantity, while the entire land tenure of Santa Lucia was based on an alleged Red Book which was rumoured to be somewhere in Paris. There was no real sense of fact or accurate statement to guide Wood and his colleagues through a veritable maze of unrelated detail.

The tour itself was almost like a royal progress. Certainly in the attempt to cover all the ground they carried out a programme that occupied nearly every waking hour and would have done credit to royalty. The itinerary mentions a long sequence of interviews with Parish Councils, but in the West Indies a parish is equivalent to a British county. At every stop long speeches had to be delivered and even longer ones listened to. Wood was, from the outset, extremely popular and seemed always to strike the right note. One particular story he told very often which never failed to please; it was of the rival sausage-makers who lived on opposite sides of the same street. One of them duly advertised his wares as " the best sausages in this street ", to which the other replied with " the best sausages in this country ", which the second capped with the announcement " sausage-maker to the King ". So the first sausage-maker, not to be outdone, immediately posted on his window " God save the King "! This story, be it noted, was used by Wood to illustrate the West Indians' reputation for personal loyalty to the Crown which dated back to the time of Queen Victoria's ascendancy. In this connection Wood was particularly pleased with the Admiralty's loan of the *Valerian*, which he felt would aptly symbolize to the West Indian mind not only the naval strength of the Empire but also the Empire's dependence upon Britain. Ormsby-Gore's attitude was slightly different, and his humour more caustic than Wood's. One instance will suffice to confirm this point. British Guiana had a hoary dispute with all comers over what constituted the British West Indies, and stoutly maintained that she was not a part of them. On the menu card of a dinner given at Georgetown in the visitors' honour appeared the inscription "British Guiana, B.W.I." Ormsby-Gore at once chaffed the organizers about it. Wood, for his part, would not have been so quick to seize on such a point.

It may be added that the local patriotism of British Guiana was only an example in a general refusal of the islands to consider Federation. The obstinate facts may have come as a shock to Ormsby-Gore, but Wood, thoroughly briefed as he was beforehand, was never committed to the Federal solution for the West Indies. At Jamaica they found the idea dismissed as monstrous. Even in the already federated Leeward Islands they discovered an active movement afoot in favour of defederation. It is typical of Wood's good sense, however, that having reached the broad conclusion that Federation was impracticable he was not on that account prepared to abandon it altogether, and for the educational and police services he expressly advises in his

Report in favour of Federal control. With regard to the police his first reactions had been towards defederation, but the local chief of police argued convincingly that it would be impossible to carry on if it were to be adopted. This was not the only time that Wood was persuaded by first-hand opinion. One reason for his own popularity and the force of his report was that he was always ready to profit by experience and advice; he was never high-handed and never rejected good counsel because it came from a subordinate source.

The party finally left Trinidad for home—not on the *Valerian* this time—on 14th February 1922. His Report was published in the following June as a Blue Book comprising over eighty closely printed pages. Keeping in mind all his other departmental duties, the production of his Report in so short a time is signal evidence of his powers of application. While Wiseman was setting out the material he would clamour for copy, both the phrasing and the recommendations were his and his alone, and moreover he subjected the Report to the most careful revision. He dealt comprehensively with the political aspirations of the West Indians, particularly the growing demand for direct representation in the Legislatures, and made the vital distinction between this aim and completely representative government which was neither desired nor desirable. He recommended that provision should be made for including a certain number of elected members in all the legislatures while preserving the control of the Secretary of State. They would be a direct link between people and Government, and the experience of Jamaica showed that they had the requisite sense of responsibility. He proposed for Jamaica itself that the elected members should actually have the majority in the Legislative Council, while the Government retained a " reserve power " for extreme urgency.

In addition to the constitutional problems the Report dealt comprehensively and under separate headings with economic, medical, educational and miscellaneous subjects, putting forward in every case concrete proposals. " It must be remembered ", he wrote, " that this tour was the first of its kind in the long history of the West Indies. The occasion was therefore regarded as a new departure by the Colonial Office, deliberately concerned with the object of promoting a closer touch between those responsible in the United Kingdom for the administration of the Colonies and their inhabitants." On the other hand, it was well in line with a long Liberal tradition within the Colonial Office itself. A study of Colonial Office documents over a given period would open the eyes of many glib critics of British Imperialism; few departments of State can boast a more sustained record of humane and progressive administration, and shortcomings can usually be traced to outside overriding influences such as the Treasury. Totalitarian propaganda flourishes on British reticence; tucked away in the archives of the Colonial Office is enough honest material to confound German colonial propaganda once and for all.

A deplorable example of this reticence must be cited in connection with the Wood Report itself. Its popularity was immediate and the Stationery Office ran out of the first edition within a few days of publication. A second edition was called for and as quickly consumed. From the beginning there was an intense demand in the West Indies, but no effort was ever made to satisfy it. The substitution of elected for nominated representatives was undoubtedly a big advance. Then again the tour had a much more urgent significance in that it was no Royal Commission with mere advisory powers. Wood was the Government's representative, and his recommendations, once made, were likely to be carried out forthwith. In fact the Report was accepted in full. Yet the West Indies were not given a reasonable chance to obtain this *locus classicus* of their subsequent constitutional and social advance. Wood's name is still remembered in the Indies by an older generation with a real affection, and Wood Town, a communal and banana growing settlement, bears witness to his fame, but it is fair to suggest that the influence of his Report would have been far more beneficent and far-reaching than it was but for the penny-wise stupidity of the Mandarins of His Majesty's Stationery Office.

As for Wood's own career, by successfully focusing general interest in a forgotten but loyal outpost of Empire he inevitably attracted attention to himself. He was, in fact, the author of what was recognized by Parliament, Press and public alike as a great State Paper. Such was his popularity with the House that when he again moved the Colonial

Office vote the Labour spokesman referred ecstatically to his " winged words of wisdom ". At a moment when there was at once a complete dearth and an urgent need of fresh blood in Conservative leadership, Edward Wood had made his presence felt; and in such a way as to bring him to the attention of a group of Conservatives which included the then unknown Stanley Baldwin and Bonar Law himself who, waiting for the pretext to bring down the Lloyd George dictatorship, had in mind to substitute for it a form of " Tory Democracy " sufficiently broad-bottomed in policy if not in personnel to appease the rising forces and the hungry demands of Labour.

Wood's absence from England during the sordid Party intrigues which brought about the downfall of the Coalition was good enough, his absorption with social reforms in the Empire which Socialists, Liberals and Conservatives alike could applaud was even better still. His hands were clean and he was without commitments, his friends indeed would not have been surprised if he had now left politics altogether. Here was a man for the watchful Stanley Baldwin, whose wont it was to sit through hour after hour of barren debate studying the psychology and the prospects of back-benchers, to cultivate and to encourage. From about this time onwards a personal friendship of momentous political implications steadily ripened between the Anglican aristocrat and the Nonconformist business man.

. . . .

Events soon conspired to put the Wood Report in the background and to confront its author, along with other Conservative members of the Coalition Government, with grave political decisions. Lloyd George's resolve to stand up to the new Kemalist Turkey following the Chanak crisis brought to a head the issue of loyalty to his leadership, which was finally resolved on 19th October at the historic Carlton Club meeting. The full story of that astonishing occasion has yet to be told; in its effect on subsequent world history it was probably the most decisive Party meeting in the whole history of British Party politics. As an inauguration of Tory Democracy, it was a mockery, and it is to be hoped that such unwholesome and arbitrary procedure will never again be allowed to mould the destinies of this and other nations, but as marking the introduction of Conservatives to the policy of appeasement it may perhaps be viewed in a more favourable light. Setting aside Party ambitions, it is probable that the Carlton Club Conservatives were right and Lloyd George wrong over our relations with the new Turkey.

In the period of trembling uncertainty before the meeting Wood showed himself to be well informed about possible developments; he released to his constituents the following Delphic indiscretion: "Don't let any follower of the Conservative leaders," he is reported as saying, "who have been working in coalition with Mr. Lloyd George, think that he can honourably repudiate his share of responsibility for the mistakes—if mistakes there have been—or for the general policy that has been pursued. I do not hold myself free to repudiate any share of responsibility for what has been done during the last three or four years,"[1] which was about as neat a way as can be imagined of drawing attention to the Government's sins, while remaining morally free to stand by Lloyd George if he weathered the storm and by the Conservatives if he did not.

After the Conservatives had prevailed in November, and his own integrity had once more been confirmed by the electors of Ripon, he was duly rewarded by Bonar Law with his first Cabinet post, and followed the renowned H. A. L. Fisher as President of the Board of Education. Education had always been his special subject, and his appointment was therefore both congenial to himself, welcome to his friends and generally approved as sound; but to succeed Fisher, whose great reforms had been one of the outstanding successes of the Coalition, in a Cabinet consisting mostly of Dukes and Marquesses, was to invite a damaging anticlimax.[2] Several of the most powerful leaders, such as Churchill, Birkenhead and Austen Chamberlain, either elected or were compelled to remain in the wilderness, which, of course, gave Wood his opportunity to attain Cabinet rank and to be sworn a member of the Privy Council rather earlier in his career than he might otherwise have expected; but the absence of these celebrities seriously weakened the Government both at Westminster and in the eyes of the country as a whole.

[1] *Yorkshire Post*, 7th October 1922.

[2] Two future colleagues, Neville Chamberlain and Thomas Inskip, were in the Bonar Law Government as Postmaster-General and Solicitor-General respectively, but not in the Cabinet.

The first Education Debate in the lifetime of the new Government was on 29th March, and Wood's defence of the Board as well as Sir John Simon's attack on it set the tone of all subsequent debate during his period as President. The subject was specially raised on the Adjournment by Simon, who at that time still preserved some of his earlier Liberal zeal for social reform and who had already crossed swords with Wood over conscription. He wished, he said, to call attention to the Board of Education's "action in directions that seem to me to retard rather than to promote public education and to justify some challenge and to call for some defence". The Fisher Act was, Simon claimed, the greatest educational advance of the last fifty years, but "it is common knowledge that important parts of it are in a state of suspended operation". "If, indeed, the betrayal of the ideals expressed in that Act were to take place, that would constitute the gravest of all the backslidings of the last four years. The position is this: the proposals of the Act of 1918, and still more the spirit in which those proposals were conceived, became involved in the general ruin which overtook elaborate schemes of all sorts when at length the extravagance and waste of recent years in every direction frightened the country into a fit of indiscriminate economy. . . . It appears sometimes as though in these latter days the Board of Education was acting merely as an outpost of the Treasury, cutting down and limiting educational standards, and putting forward, indeed, definitely retrograde proposals."

Simon offered examples. Before the war the Board had withheld £10,000 from the London County Council because its classes were too large. In co-operation with the Board the London County Council introduced a scheme, suspended during the war, for building new schools to reduce classes to a maximum of forty children each. Now the Board would not permit the London County Council to carry through the scheme. "That seems to me to be an illustration of a very serious change in outlook and temper." If forty was the fair maximum, half the classes in the country were too large; if fifty, more than a quarter of elementary school classes were above the limit. On the fifty principle free places in secondary schools were, at the minimum, twenty-five per cent of the total; now the Board had made that the maximum.

If Simon had followed the line of attack expected of him Wood's reply was also characteristic. "Minor economies," he observed, "are inevitably bound to be annoying. They are, as sometimes happens in private life, often regarded as ridiculous. We all laugh at one another's private economies, which really achieve nothing, such as a man writing his letters on the half sheets he tears off his dinner invitations, and things of that sort; but however critical we are in regard to the economies of somebody else, if we search our conscience closely enough, we shall find that we have one economy of our own. . . . It is totally misleading to assume that expenditure is identical with efficiency. There is a line that lies between both. As I conceive the duty of the Board of Education in these days it is to endeavour to pursue economy, having regard to the general exigencies of the public service in such a way that the system of public education is not impaired, and that when times become easier the original position can at once be resumed. It is inevitable that in these days we must be prepared to see a certain marking of time, a certain retardation of expansion (fortunately Simon's phrase!) However much we may deplore it, it is not primarily damaging the efficiency of the system if we preserve for ourselves and the country the power and capacity to jump off again as soon as the opportunity comes."

This sentence is the epitome of Wood's conception of his duty, namely, to assume the function of a refrigerator and put educational progress in cold storage in order to keep it fresh and sweet until such time as the country had the financial strength to enjoy it. With regard to twenty-five per cent free places scheme he pointed out that where a school had over this quota in the past it was allowed to keep it. And "as compared with before the war and now the number of places in secondary schools on the grant list is almost exactly double and . . . the free placers have had their almost mathematically accurate share".

In the course of this debate he put forward one peculiar plea which it is doubtful whether he would now support and which is hardly up to his usual scrupulous standards of controversy. He alleged that the complaint "that the youngest children require the best teachers is really not one that effectively stands examination and criticism". The explanation was curious. Teachers in charge of schools had considerable liberty and discretion in allotting staff to particular classes, and in 644 departments in Lancashire only 78 had the lowest classes taught by trained certificated teachers. "Therefore, the argument that the youngest children require the most highly trained teacher is one that does not, on examination, appear to be supported"—even by the teachers who advanced it. But before he could get fully into his educational stride he was to be called upon to play the part of a Solomon in Foreign Affairs.

CHAPTER IX

EDUCATION AND EXCURSIONS

IN the middle of all his duties at the Board of Education Wood was suddenly during April whisked away to represent Great Britain at a meeting of the Council of the League of Nations in Geneva. Curzon, the Foreign Secretary, was unable to attend owing to the prior claims of the Second Lausanne Conference which was so effectively to implement the Tory reconciliation with Turkey and by a diplomatic masterstroke to meet Kemal's demands while planting Turkish nationalism firmly in Asia. The Foreign Office was thus otherwise engaged, Bonar Law was still nominally Prime Minister but desperately ill, and Curzon was regarded as heir to the throne. Wood was thus casually dragged into the vortex of international affairs at a moment when there was a virtual interregnum in the Cabinet.

It is not impossible that the influence of Stanley Baldwin, who a month later, to Curzon's intense surprise and chagrin, was to succeed to the Premiership, may have decided that Wood should be sent to Geneva, but wherever the responsibility lay it argued unusual confidence in the Minister of Education's political prowess. No sooner had he reached Geneva than, as principal British delegate, he found himself called upon to preside over the Council, at which nineteen States were represented. At first the business ran smoothly, satisfactory accounts were received, and noted, of the progress in the restoration of Austrian finances; the frontier between Hungary and Czechoslovakia was demarcated; Lord Robert Cecil's Treaty of Mutual Guarantees was referred to Member States for comment. There was no public reference, however, to the Ruhr occupation, although it overshadowed the whole meeting. Wood had, in fact, been asked to preside over the League of Nations, the first-fruits of the Allied contribution to European order and goodwill, at the very moment when Anglo-French relations were at their worst and strained almost to breaking point.

In this tense atmosphere the vexed question of the Saar was raised. Under Articles 45 and 46 of the Versailles Treaty, France could exploit the coal mines in the Saar Valley in compensation for the French mines destroyed by the Germans during the war. She was not given, even temporarily, territorial possession. Government was placed in the hands of a Governing Commission to be appointed by the League. In 1923 the Commission consisted of a French president, a representative of the Saar citizens, a Belgian, a Dane and a Canadian. On 7th March a decree was promulgated by the Commission (although the Canadian representative, Waugh, dissented) under which gaol for five years and 10,000 francs fine were the maximum penalties for publicly casting discredit on the Treaty of Versailles, or for insulting or traducing the League of Nations, its members, or the State signatories of the Treaty of Versailles, or the Governing Commission of the Saar, or its members, organizations, or officials responsible for the conduct of its administration. Under the decree, meetings, processions and demonstrations might be prohibited if they were likely to lead to any of the above catholic selection of offences.

Wood's position was particularly delicate. The British Government deplored this decree, but was extremely anxious that there should be no pretext for any additional tension between Britain and France. Branting, the Swedish member, spoke in turn of strong disapproval with which Wood did not hesitate to agree. The President of the Commission then explained that the decree had been issued because of a strike of miners in the Saar in January, soon after the occupation of the Ruhr. The strike was really political, and the French could not exploit the mines unless some such regulations were in force. Again Wood did not hesitate to dissent from this plea; but by the time he had left Geneva no one had formally proposed the cancellation of the decree nor did the Council take action beyond setting up a Committee to make enquiries. Thus did he pass through his first test in reconciling French security with German rights. It was not a heroic début, but it was generally felt that he had managed to uphold moderation without unduly wounding French susceptibilities or deepening the German sense of grievance. There was, in fact, noticeably less friction at Geneva as the direct result of his resolute inaction.

But his ordeal was not over; an angry Liberal and Socialist Opposition at Westminster, still bitterly resenting the high-handed and unilateral action of France in occupying the Ruhr, did not feel bound to walk with the same wariness as the British Government or its hapless spokesman at Geneva. Liberty and Justice alike demanded that the decree should be denounced. Once again it was Sir John Simon who led the attack when on 10th May he moved the reduction of the Foreign Office Vote and proceeded to outline the constitutional position of the Saar. "The decree was put into operation, so far as I can see, illegally, because the Treaty of Versailles provides that before you change the law in the Valley of the Saar there must, at any rate, be consultation with a body supposed to represent the inhabitants, and the fact is that there has been no such consultation." Already a number of penalties had been imposed under the decree, and several newspapers had been suspended, one for six months. Simon asked what instructions Wood had received from his Government before going to Geneva, and recalled a letter written by the Allied and Associated Powers to Germany after the war regarding the Saar people: "The people will live under a government resident on the spot which will have no occupation and no interest except their welfare." The League Council could revoke at any time the appointment of any member of the Commission. There was, in view of the letter, a strong obligation on the British Government "to see that effective steps are taken to put a stop to what otherwise exposes the League of Nations itself to contempt and derision".

Wood's reply was in many respects his most important speech as a Member of Parliament. He explained that the Government first heard of the decree on 27th March, and that he was then given discretion to raise the matter before the Council. As Acting Chairman he thought it more courteous to allow Branting to proceed with his motion on the subject. He was advised that the decree was not beyond the legal powers of the Commission, but in reply to an interjection by Asquith, somewhat lamely admitted that this advice was not given by the Law Officers of the Crown. The decree was not brought before the Council for approval or disapproval, both of which were unnecessary. Even Branting did not propose its cancellation, but had "recorded the inevitable impression that it had created in his country, and which, I said, it would create in this country. He and I both questioned whether this was or was not the best method of dealing with the situation." The Chairman of the Commission had emphasized the dangers which would arise if the Saar Press, subsidized from Germany, was allowed to incite the people to an attitude of hostility to the Treaty of Versailles and the regime that it had established.

"In those circumstances," he went on, "I ask hon. Members to reflect what was to be the action of the Council. I ask them, if they can, to put themselves in the position of the Council, having no source of information as to what was happening in the Saar, but having before them the Chairman of the responsible instrument of government whom they had established. I do not think it was very likely that the Council, ignoring the considered opinion expressed by the spokesman of its own servant, on whose shoulders lay the entire responsibility of government and public order, would be willing, on that, to reject the advice deliberately tendered by its own servant, and to refuse to support those to whom, in the last resort, it was bound to look to carry on the government." The Government felt that the whole question of the administration of the Saar should be the subject of an impartial enquiry, and he had therefore been reluctant to press to an issue this smaller matter when more fundamental questions would have at an early date to receive consideration.

This was sufficient for Wood himself to escape the flood of invective that followed, and Asquith was careful to dissociate himself from any censure or criticism of Wood's action; indeed he "has not attempted to say one word in defence of this monstrous and ridiculous decree. One might ransack the annals of the Russian treatment of the question of Poland without finding a more monstrous specimen of despotic legislation, more suppressive of the elementary rights of free citizenship, than is here to be found; and this goes forth to the world with the authority of the League of Nations." The decree was a "flagrant illegality", and he wanted it to be "treated as of no effect until the ordinary securities of civil life and freedom are restored to the inhabitants of the Saar Valley". Lord Robert Cecil thought the decree an "outrage", "an action which really is worthy of Prussian militarism at its worst"; while Herbert Fisher dubbed it "not law, but *opéra bouffe*". For all that, Wood returned to the Board of Education with bigger Parliamentary reputation and prospects than when he first set out for Geneva.

. . . .

But there was no pause to reflect upon the measure of his success, for three weeks later he was presenting the Education Estimates for the year 1923-24. He had reached a crucial period in his development and he did not falter. In his speech on this occasion are to be found all the characteristics for which, as Irwin and as Halifax, he is justly renowned, the fairness, the lucidity, the ease and withal the patent sincerity which does not eschew the occasional personal bias, as when he put forward the belief that those who value religious teaching in schools "are the great majority of the citizens of this country" and "would express the most earnest hope" that they will try to find a settlement of existing difficulties. (For this last observation it may be noted he was warned by the Chairman that he was "getting a little near to going too far" as possible legislation could not be discussed in Committee of Supply!)

One passage in particular illustrates the poise and ballast of his Conservatism, the idea that there is something more important and nearer to truth than mere cleverness. In meeting attacks on "what it is common to call bureaucracy", and particularly "the permanent officials of my office, that is, of the Board", he invoked the story of an Oxford tutor who lectured his students on the possible fallacies of logic. "He used to tell the students the story of a young man who at the University on three successive nights got drunk. The first night he got drunk on whisky and soda, the second night on brandy and soda, and the third night on gin and soda, and, with a disregard of logic, he ascribed his downfall to the only constant factor, the soda, and accordingly decided to forswear soda for the rest of his life. In this case the permanent officials of the Board of Education fill the role of the soda and water, and my right hon. friend and I are the alcoholic concomitants at whose door the responsibility for the actions of the Board which excite public comment should be laid."

The Estimates were for £41,934,047, £3,341,000 less than

in 1922-23 and as much as £9,000,000 less than in 1921-22. The background to these statistics is to be found in the demand for retrenchment that set in after the war. The proposals of the Geddes Committee included the elimination of 34,000 teachers, saving £8,250,000 a year and increasing classes from about thirty-two to fifty children, and the sending of children to school at the age of six instead of five. Neither the Coalition nor any later Government accepted these proposals, and the task of Fisher and his successors was to retrench with the minimum of damage to the legislative fabric of the 1918 Act. Wood accurately summed up the position by saying that the country " has learned to value education, and has no intention of allowing it to suffer permanent or serious set-back; but no less does the country recognize that it is impossible immediately to move as fast as we could wish until by general improvement of conditions the taxpayer and the ratepayer are better fitted to bear an increased burden ". A jockey crossing heavy ground should not try to flog his horse to the same pace as though the going were easy. " It is quite true that the vision of 1918 may be still unfulfilled, but the framework of the 1919 Act stands on the Statute Book unimpaired, ready to carry the Bill as soon as building operations can be resumed."

There was thus " the necessity for treading the hard path of economy "; but " this year for the first time the Estimates provide for the retention of children at school up to the end of the term in which they reach fourteen . . . the pupils are entering these (secondary) schools earlier and staying later. It is also a fact that these schools contain a larger number proceeding from elementary schools, and there is also a larger number paying no fees." Then there was a great post-war scheme of higher education for those who fought in the war. School teachers had voluntarily accepted a five per cent abatement of salaries, which meant a saving of £2,400,000 a year. In one way retrenchment had been a blessing in disguise; thanks to the year or two's delay local authorities would be able to build schools much cheaper. Finally, he wanted to do more in the way of special schools, for the blind, the deaf, the physically and mentally defective, and paid tribute to the Workers' Educational Association, through which " there is a specific and disinterested study of the highest quality pursued by working men and working women which is the envy of other nations ".

Later in the debate H. A. L. Fisher himself intervened to pay a significant tribute to Wood and his work. " The Committee is greatly indebted to the President of the Board of Education," he said, " not only for the skill and lucidity with which he unfolded his story, but also for the fine spirit which clearly informs him in relation to the great responsibilities of his office." " We have this very solid fact," he continued, " and it is a fact which ought to be known all through the country, that during my right hon. friend's two administrations, not only have the number of scholars in secondary schools been doubled, but the number of free places have been doubled. That is a very remarkable achievement. There has been no such achievement in the field of secondary education since secondary education was introduced in this country." Praise from such an authority was praise indeed.

One further measure passed during his period of office deserves notice here, and that is the Universities Bill which he steered through Parliament in July 1923 and which established, " in accordance with the recommendations of the Royal Commission, two bodies of Commissioners, one for the University of Oxford (Viscount Chelmsford, Chairman), and one for the University of Cambridge (Viscount Ullswater, Chairman), who shall make statutes for the University, and for any emoluments, endowments, etc., rendered necessary by the recommendations of the Royal Commission as to grants ". In moving the Second Reading Wood pointed out that after Oxford and Cambridge had submitted statements on their financial position and their needs, a Commission was set up presided over by Asquith to conduct an enquiry into their financial resources, to see whether they could or could not, by their own resources, unaided, make " such provision as was necessary in the altered conditions of the day ". After dealing with the mechanics of the Bill he concluded: " It is because I know . . . that at the present time universities are handicapped by the lack of material resources in the conduct of their work, and it is because as a son of Oxford I am so sensible of the advantage of what Oxford gave to me, and because I regard this Bill as the essential preliminary to enabling these universities to continue and develop their work, that I confidently invite the House to give this Bill a Second Reading."

In Committee there were two stumbling-blocks. Among the proposed Commissioners for Cambridge was Edward Hugh John Neal Dalton, Doctor of Science, Cassel Reader in Commerce in the University of London. The vigorous Minister of Economic Warfare in Churchill's Coalition of 1940 was not so highly esteemed by Conservatives in 1923, and one Tory back-bencher opposed his appointment, expressing surprise that " the name of Dr. Dalton was to be added to this Commission by a Conservative Government, because he is a gentleman who has been standing for Cambridge University as a Socialist Member ". Wood's reply was firm. " When I inherited the original names of the Commissioners . . . it never occurred to me to enquire what the politics of any of them were, and I think it is a new suggestion that, in appointing academic bodies of this kind, it is necessary to have such a careful regard for the niceties of political representation and balance."

The Board of Education had the right to nominate one man and one woman Commissioner to each list. The Oxford appointments went through without challenge, but on the Cambridge list the name of Bertha Surtees Phillpotts appeared and was at once opposed by Major Sir Bertram Falle, who fulminated about women " who could chip in and go to a man's university " and who gave the House a lecture on farmyard selection. " Anybody who has bred horses will tell you that it is folly in the extreme to put colts and fillies together ", but an interruption by a Socialist to " keep it above that level " seems to have spoilt Sir Bertram's analogy, for without regard to his apparently wide knowledge of equine eugenics he concluded " once a woman gets on the Commission she will duplicate herself, if I may say so ". Wood was bland and assured: " Since the extension of the Franchise, I have voted on almost every occasion in my political life when the question arose, in favour of extending the rights of women. Once they secured suffrage, it seemed to me there was no logical ground where you could well stop." " It happens to be my own personal view," he added, " that the admission of women to full membership of Cambridge University is both inevitable and right. I hold strongly by the doctrine of the autonomy of universities, and

I also know that interference by Parliament in a matter of vital importance and controversy within the University, even from the women's point of view, is not unlikely to lead to undesirable results." He wanted Cambridge to be left to make its own reforms, and successfully resisted a Labour Amendment which would have compelled the Commissioners to carry out the Commission's recommendations on the position of women at Cambridge. The House should refrain from " any suspicion of interference with the internal autonomy of the universities ", and should " restore conditions in which this reform, if it be inevitable, will be carried out with the minimum difficulty, of friction, of ill feeling, and of discord ".

One of Wood's last contributions to enlightenment, before Baldwin swept his Government away by prematurely seeking a vote of confidence on Protection, was to give his and the Government's blessing to a Resolution of the League Assembly urging the Government of States-members to arrange that the children and youth in their countries should be made aware of the existence and aims of the League of Nations and the terms of its Covenant. " I gladly take this opportunity of recommending it to the favourable consideration of the authorities of the schools,"[1] he said in reply to a question from Lady Astor on January 17th 1924. By 22nd January the first Labour Government in British Parliamentary history had been formed.

Baldwin's decision to appeal to the country before it was ready for Tariffs was apparently taken at short notice, the outcome of a " hunch " rather than any close reasoning. We have noted Wood's predilection for Imperial Preference, but he must have shared the dismay of the Cabinet at having to fight such a precipitate and ill-prepared Election. Baldwin seems to have been under the impression that he was a mere stop-gap and he set his ambitions on the same scale as this lowly estimate of his prospects. " Well, having been Prime Minister will have been an interesting experience to have had " is the astonishing comment attributed to him at this

[1] The suggestion that they might consider making the League of Nations more familiar in the schools was duly issued to all local authorities over his name, and judging from his Socialist successor's comment that he thought of issuing a further memorandum on the subject it would seem that Wood was the pioneer in this matter. Its effects on the overwhelming Peace Ballot vote in favour of a League Policy eleven years later should not be overlooked.

time. It was a detachment Wood can hardly have appreciated. Although Ripon's electors remained faithful to him, a period of bleak opposition just when he was in the full flood of Ministerial activity and progress must have been, to say the least, exasperating. But it soon became evident that Ramsay MacDonald's Government, wholly dependent on the Liberals' vote and goodwill for its existence, was not likely to threaten the Conservatives with a prolonged exile, and within a year they were back in power again with Baldwin once more at the head and the Coalition Conservatives forgiven.

In the meanwhile Wood had put the Labour interregnum to good use, and it turned out to be a period of miscellaneous but constructive activity. In Parliament he did not confine himself to Education, but intervened in a wide range of topics, including agriculture, in which so much of his interest and experience lay. Indeed his contributions to agricultural debates created such a good impression on the House and on Baldwin that he may be definitely said to have staked a moral claim to the Ministry of Agriculture when next his leader had the disposal of that office. During this period, too, he strengthened his reputation for being a progressive. He welcomed the Labour Government's decision to carry out scientific research into animals' diseases by observing that " the fact of being an island, of having been fairly immune, has all tended to dull our sense of the necessity of acquiring, improving and developing our scientific knowledge ". A Labour Motion on 20th February calling for State pensions " adequate for the proper upbringing and maintenance of children " to be paid " to all widows with children, or mothers whose family breadwinner has become incapacitated " had his eloquent support. " A movement of national conscience " had insisted upon State liability towards " the victims of what I may call unmerited poverty ". It was increasingly the function of the State to recognize, and try to make provision for, " the casualties of modern industrial and economic life ". " I have often thought it is rather an astounding thing that the State should have made a move in other directions, such as old age, sickness, and so on, before attending to the matter. . . . We (the Tories) do not offer any opposition to a proposal that makes its appeal to our hearts no less than to the hearts of hon. Members opposite."

Similarly on 14th April he favoured the continuation of the scheme for Teachers' Pensions, since without it " they must be the victims of ordinary day-to-day anxiety. That anxiety breeds dissatisfaction and unrest, and a person in whose mind those influences are operating is not the right person to mould the character of the young generation." On the Ministry of Agriculture's Supply Day he drew attention to " a most astonishing disparity " between the number of Co-operative creameries in Denmark and in Great Britain. 1,650 in Denmark to a mere 38 in this country, and to our low consumption per head of milk, and " I am afraid, too often, its low grade of quality and cleanliness ". He called for a large development in the co-operative production of milk and believed that thereby we should not only be contributing to social health, but also working on sound economic lines. He asked for more co-operative milling and slaughtering. " At the present time the farmer has often to pay more for his offals than the miller pays him for his corn." The whole co-operative movement was being hampered by the lack of necessary capital for the farmers. The general problem was " a definite, steady, and regular shrinkage in the area of cultivated land in England ". His plea was " to reverse or even to retard the great movement of economic forces by which agriculture is at present threatened ".

. . . .

During the Easter recess he was called away to accompany his father on a mission the implications of which went far beyond the trivial round of Party politics. We left Lord Halifax in the summer of 1919 sadly bereaved and to all outward appearances at the end of his lifework, waiting only for release from the infirmities that were steadily gaining on him. But two years later he was transformed and revivified by the appeal of the Lambeth Conference for a Reunion of all Churches in which the Anglicans declared their willingness to accept from the authorities of other Communions " a form of commission or recognition which would commend our ministry to their congregations as having its part in the one family life ". The obstacle of the Bull *Apostolicae Curiae*, which condemned Anglican orders, was thus surmounted in the Anglicans' readiness to discuss the revision of their ordination. Portal urged that the opportunity now presented was too great to be missed and urged Halifax to make contact with Cardinal Mercier. Armed with letters of introduction from the Archbishops, Halifax met the Cardinal at Malines in October, when it was agreed that he should try to find "two dependable people" who might come back and continue the conversations. As the Archbishops took no official responsibility, the choice of colleagues rested entirely with Halifax, and after much discussion he finally took with him Dr. Frere, Superior of the Community of the Resurrection at Mirfield, a famous liturgiologist and believer in Reunion, and Dr. Armitage Robinson, the saintly Dean of Wells, who apart from his high Churchmanship had the advantage of being a close friend of Dr. Davidson, the Archbishop of Canterbury.

The first Malines Conversations in December 1921, as Halifax explained in copious letters to Edward, were concerned primarily in clearing away difficulties and preparing the ground for further negotiation. "We began", Edward was informed, "by going through my memorandum, which was generally approved of, and since that we have been going through the Lambeth Appeal for Unity. . . . The Abbé tells me that he thinks the Cardinal is pleased and that we shall succeed in our object." Dogma was avoided throughout, and while both parties looked forward to a sequel no further meeting was arranged. The death of Pope Benedict XV, together with the need for much preliminary work on both sides, including the attempt to get official recognition, made delay inevitable. This recognition was in part conceded, and at last, in March 1923, the same delegates met again at Malines to continue the discussion of "possible methods of a practical kind by which Reunion might be effected". The delay had given time for opposition to develop both in England and Rome. In England the English Roman Catholics were almost as disgruntled as the Protestants, while in the Vatican powerful influences were at work to modify the new Pope Pius XI's goodwill towards Mercier's efforts. Halifax was aware that time was working not only against himself, but also against the whole precious cause. The Archbishop of Canterbury's reserve exasperated him. York wrote sympathetically, "If, my dear old friend, you were a golfer, I would point out the danger of 'pressing', a fault which is very apt to spoil the game.

But indeed I know how natural it is for you, with the years shortening, to 'press'."

The Archbishop of Canterbury insisted that dogma should have priority at the next Conversations, and Bishop Gore and Dr. Kidd, Warden of Keble, for the Anglicans, and Battifol and Hemmer for the Roman Catholics were enlisted to dispute the fundamental question of the primacy of the Roman See. Preceded by a colloquy at Lambeth in which Anglican policy was laid down, the third Conversations, which took place in November 1923, were more formal and theological than the first two and were not so lightly explained away. The Archbishop of Canterbury attempted to incorporate a report of them in a Letter to the Metropolitans of the Anglican Communion as "an episode in the general movement towards Reunion started by the Lambeth Appeal". The form and implications of the Letter pleased no one, and but for Halifax's pertinacity the whole structure of the Malines Conversations would have collapsed. By April 1924 no date for further Conversations had been fixed, then the Archbishop wanted time for the controversy aroused by his Letter to die down, and it seemed unlikely that anything would be set in motion before the autumn.

In these circumstances Halifax arranged a purely private and unofficial visit to Malines at the end of April, the party consisting of himself, Portal, the redoubtable Lord Hugh Cecil and Edward. Halifax, now in his eighty-fifth year, explained that at his age he could not expect to make many more journeys to Malines and he was therefore anxious that Lord Hugh and his son, whom he liked to think would presently take over his task, should get to know Mercier. Edward was certainly well briefed, and there is no reason to doubt that he would have, if it had been necessary, assumed his father's responsibilities at Malines. It was on this visit that Mercier had the temerity to suggest that Halifax should make his personal submission to Rome. "*Au fond il ne comprend pas votre position,*" Portal commented when he was told of the incident, but Mercier was left in no uncertainty as to the firmness of his Anglican foundations.

It would be a mistake to regard Edward's visit to Malines as a mere holiday interlude in his political career; it might conceivably have overshadowed and altered the rest of his public life. As it was, Halifax outlived Mercier and Portal and survived to see the controversy Malines had aroused fade into historical perspective, while Edward, for his part, was never to meet the two Roman apostles of Reunion again. But should ever the great issue be taken up by Canterbury or Rome Edward Wood might well loom large in the role of entrepreneur, for which his father, by precept and example, had so lavishly prepared him. In him are the essential diplomatic gifts of patience, discretion and reserve which his father lacked; if his religious ardour does not burn so intensely the flame is steadier. Not for nothing did Mercier on his death-bed bequeath to Halifax the episcopal ring of gold set with a big amethyst and given to him by his family on becoming a bishop. "At last he said that if he was going to die, he wished Halifax to have the ring. 'I have always worn it.' Halifax made a gesture of protest. 'Yes, yes,' Portal interjected, 'for you and Edward.'"[1]

Up to his death Halifax wore it on a chain round his neck; when it became his, Edward had it set above the base of a chalice and presented it to York Minster for use at Mass on St. Peter's day and on the anniversaries of the deaths of his father and of Mercier. It aptly symbolizes Mercier's last message to the Archbishop of Canterbury: "*Ut unum sint*; it is the supreme wish of Christ, the wish of the Sovereign Pontiff; it is mine, it is yours. May it be realized in its fullness."

[1] Lockhart, Vol. II, page 327.

CHAPTER X

APOLOGY FOR AGRICULTURE

In June 1924 Wood was back again in the thick of the Party fray and dealing some shrewd blows at the Government's Agricultural Wages Bill, in the handling of which measure the Socialists showed an ominous stiffness towards the friendly criticisms of Liberals, whose sincere objections to somewhat rigid proposals were interpreted as intrigues with the Tories to break the Administration. It was the rapid development of this morbid suspicion that brought MacDonald and his men to ruin a few months later over the triviality of the Campbell Case.

Wood argued that to deal with wages alone narrowed the agricultural problem which Labour had promised to resolve with general prosperity, and pointed the usual moral between " professions suitable at an Election and the actual accomplishment in which promises are sought to be met ". " Put it on the gramophone! " cried an hon. Member. " I think it would be very valuable, even at the expense of broadcasting," Wood replied with ponderous sincerity, " if it had any hope at all of inducing reform in hon. Members opposite." The Co-operatives, he argued, could afford to pay good wages and run agriculture at a loss because they had a much more profitable business behind them out of which to finance their very unprofitable farming operations. The reason why the railway porter in rural districts, without working nearly as hard as the agricultural labourer, drew twice his salary was because the porter was dealing in a monopoly service which the public had got to have, and the public had to pay the price his union was able to put upon his labour. In the general scramble for higher wages and for subsidies to cover them he drew a picture of agriculture as the Cinderella left behind in the sacred name of Free Trade. He thought that the local committees set up by the Bill to fix minimum wage rates might be treated as so much wastepaper by " gentlemen in London who possess no local knowledge ", and that the Government had worked in deference to the notion that " the people in the country are all intellectual pigmies in comparison to the metropolitan Olympians ", views to which not a few Liberals subscribed.

One of his best Parliamentary efforts in this period of opposition was during the Board of Education's Supply Day on 22nd July. It was a speech in his best vein, mildly self-deprecatory but firmly justifying his own period at the Board and with an irony lighter and more unforced than usual. He began by saying that he could not claim, like Fisher, to have raised the Education estimates in two or three years from £15,000,000 to £45,000,000, or like C. P. Trevelyan, the Socialist President of the Board, to say that he had reduced the estimates by £25,000,000 and at the same time increased the educational service. Trevelyan had expressed surprise that there was no motion for the reduction of his salary, but " anybody who has ever enjoyed that salary will know that it is much too small to reduce ". There was, in fact, no real educational controversy dividing the parties. He demanded an increase in the number of secondary school free places, although " free secondary education for all " was not a wise catchword. The ideal should be that no child with ability should be debarred from the best education, right the way up, that the State could afford. Morgan Jones, the Parliamentary Secretary to the Board of Education, had condemned " the then Government—which was myself—for the serious restriction of the provision, if not the practical stoppage of the increase of adult education. . . . I have no objection to reasonable criticism, but, in point of fact, I felt the injury of this very much, because I thought that that was one of the good things I had done, and with regard to which I received warm letters of thanks from those connected with the organization of the Workers' Educational Association. . . . I have always thought that the development of adult education was one of the directions in which, with the least possible expenditure of money, you could get the greatest possible results. I think there is no field which produces so satisfactory or so rapid a result as this."

He was to make only one more intervention of note before the cataclysm of the Campbell Case and the forgery of the Zinoviev letter swept the Socialists from their uneasy tenure of office. On 2nd October the House was asked to approve the Labour solution to the vexed question of the Irish boundary, which was simply the technique of the Gordian knot or permission from Parliament for the British Government to appoint a Commissioner for Ulster if Ulster still refused to rectify the boundary with the Free State. This aroused deep Conservative instincts in him; Ulster was being forced into "compulsory arbitration", and whether her decision was right or wrong, was "exercising her plain rights". As a way out of the impasse he called for a form of moral strength which does not seem to have had any obvious connection with the wishes of Roman Catholics in Fermanagh and Tyrone to join the Catholics of the Irish Free State, but which, as a commentary in after years on the Munich Agreement and the policies that made Munich inevitable, has a stricter relevance. "I think it is the experience," he asserted, "of most hon. Members, whether in domestic or public life, that it is often much easier to acquiesce in a doubtful situation than to undertake the rather difficult job of disillusioning a person who is falling into error. Yet I hold it is a dangerous plan to go on acquiescing. You find that the difficulty grows greater with waiting and it is harder in the end to put it right than it would have been earlier."

. . . .

It is to his lasting credit that he did not seem to rely too heavily on the notorious "Red Letter" for his election to Parliament in November 1924. Although his increased majority suggests that the panic it aroused had seeped through to Ripon he sought more solid grounds for support, and on his return to Westminster was at once offered the substantial and expected reward of a place in Baldwin's new Cabinet as Minister of Agriculture. It was a key post in the strongest Conservative Ministry of our time. Zinoviev had succeeded in returning 415 Conservatives, in reducing the Labour Party from 191 to 152, and the Liberals from 155 to a mere 42. The Coalitionists were now Wood's colleagues: Austen Chamberlain at the Foreign Office, Birkenhead Secretary of State for India, Balfour Lord President of the Council, and his old chief, Winston Churchill, at the Treasury. Wood, at the age of forty-four, was the "baby", and in this Government of veterans the average age of the

Under-Secretaries suggests that a man could regard himself as precocious and specially favoured if he was given any office by Baldwin under the age of fifty.

Baldwin was undoubtedly relying on Wood to exploit to the full his special knowledge of the country and sympathy with its ways of life in order to produce some spectacular legislation that would enhance the Government's somewhat vague domestic programme. Thus encouraged, Wood was first off the Ministerial mark with a high-sounding Statement of Agricultural Policy published in the Press on 28th November. In this he declared that despite the good material to be found in previous reports, e.g. Lord Selborne's Committee on Agricultural Policy, it had hitherto not been possible to obtain agreement in the industry itself or by the country as a whole as to the main principles of a national and stable agricultural policy. But the Government now thought that another attempt should be made, the objective being " that the industry should be conducted in such a manner as will secure the maximum employment of labour at reasonable rates of wages together with the full use of the land for the production of food at the lowest possible prices consistent with a fair return to all those engaged in the industry ". So the Government had decided to call a conference of the three main interests, landowners, farmers, and workers, for " concerted discussion and enquiry " to hammer out a policy that would give " confidence and stability " to the industry, and would be " likely to be acceptable " to public opinion. The Conference agenda was then impressively amplified. Arable land should be increased if possible, being of " primary importance ". The Conference was to be asked how great a decline in arable acreage there would be if nothing was to be done, to indicate measures to counteract such a decline, and to make recommendations sufficient to add a million arable acres or about ten per cent of the existing total. Too much attention should not be given to wheat to the exclusion of other crops, although enough arable land should be in cultivation, enough skilled labour, implements, buildings and drainage ready for a switch over to wheat in an emergency. Development of the livestock industry was important, it already accounted for about seventy-five per cent of our agricultural production, but a further increase in its production did not so directly affect the Government's immediate concern to put more men on to the land. On the same day came the announcement that the Government had taken over the Labour Government's proposals for a ten year diminishing subsidy for sugar made in this country from home-grown beet together with a minimum price to growers in early years.

This pace, however, could not be maintained, and in spite of his immediate popularity with the farmers, the ambitious policy soon began to flag. He proposed inviting delegates to the Conference from the representative Farmers and Workers Unions and from the Landowners Association. Months passed, but there was no sign of his Conference materializing, and in March he was obliged to confess to the House that it could not take place as the Workmen's Unions had refused to co-operate. A few days later he announced publicly that he would interview the various interests separately, which proved to be an admission that the whole project was in fact still-born.

He was more successful with the Beet Subsidy and steered the Bill through its various stages with patient competence, but it was a poor substitute for the abortive Conference. He was at pains to describe the efforts made over a dozen years to establish the beet industry in this country and to point out that in all beet-producing countries some State assistance for it was always required at the outset; but exactly why the taxpayer was being called upon to finance this unprofitable and unnatural crop was not made clear, nor was the measure his own. Noel Buxton for the Labour Opposition was quick to shower compliments on the Government for showing that imitation was the sincerest form of flattery, and on the Minister of Agriculture for becoming " the stepfather, the generous stepfather of the offspring we produced ". Wood laid down originally that the State's assistance should be temporary and its commitments should be definite, but these good intentions were lost, and he was thus the unwilling sponsor of a dark and bottomless commitment.

If his policy fell short of the original expectations it had aroused and his Ministry shared in the increasing volume of criticism levelled against the Government for its general complacency and inaction, his personal reputation did not suffer unduly. He spoke with the authentic voice of the countryman, he could give articulate and constructive form to the farmer's historic "grievance", and the force of his opinions undoubtedly made a deep impression on Parliament and the country, which helped in some measure to bridge the gulf between his otherwise obscure and secondary achievement and the dazzling eminence to which he was suddenly called at the end of 1925.

Two examples of his agricultural oratory will suffice to illustrate his idiom and ideals. In March 1925 he gave his blessing to a Private Members' Bill authorizing the advancing of loans and the levying of rates for the purchase of allotments. The Bill was actually moved and seconded by the Members for Oxford and Cambridge, one of whom observed that the charge against the two places was that they were always in disagreement with one another. "The charge I have generally heard preferred against Oxford and Cambridge," Wood retorted, "was that in agreement with one another, they resisted everything that other people thought reasonable." It was therefore a peculiar pleasure to find them linked together in the cause of reform. "The allotment movement," he continued, "is, and always has been to my mind a kind of meeting point, where town meets country, and country meets town, the promontory over which one moves to meet the other, and on which they may both meet and shake hands, and understand one another better." A man who got bitten with the soil through an allotment might find his way to small-holding and thence to farming, "and, in so doing, to bring a new current of human material into the rather stable business of agriculture". The explanation was that "in all this you are really dealing with one of the primitive instincts of mankind. It is the call of the soil from which we spring, and to which we are, therefore, so to speak, permanently enchained in our instincts. I have known men who have been willing to go three, four and five miles out of town to their allotments, so strong was the call of the soil to the town dweller."

Within this speech is contained the kernel of what may perhaps be termed his land mysticism, and reverence for the soil is as inherent in his religion as cure of the soul. He is, in fact, the phenomenon of a landed magnate with acute sensibilities. Even more revealing was a speech delivered during the Third Reading of the Agricultural Returns Bill which was fathered by him and which gave the Government

WOOD FAMILY GROUP

With his wife and children, Ann, Charles, Richard and Peter in 1925, the year before his appointment as Viceroy of India

compulsory powers to collect agricultural statistics. It was, on the whole, a non-controversial measure; the system of voluntary returns had broken down, some of the farmers "were dilatory, while others forgot about the returns altogether". Lloyd George warmly welcomed the Bill. There was, he observed, no other country which could not give an accurate account of what was done with its land. Every man who owned or occupied land was a "trustee for the community and the community has a right to ask him for the account of his stewardship". During the Third Reading Sir Archibald Sinclair made an eloquent appeal to the Minister "in no hostile spirit, but with a view to increasing the amount of information to be obtained", to include within the Return not only arable land but also land "which is or has at any time been capable of being used as arable", and moved an Amendment to this effect. "I consider it necessary and urgent to take full stock of the whole agricultural resources, actual and potential," he said, and in this demand he was firmly backed by Noel Buxton and Lloyd George.

Statistics were never in themselves a source of inspiration to Wood, but Sinclair's Amendment had raised issues of high policy and roused him accordingly. "The Government welcomes any opportunity that this House may take of evincing its interest in what is the foundation problem of English national life." His "hon. friend" Sinclair was "one of the most persuasive members of a persuasive assembly", but even his powers of charm and persuasion were not enough to justify his Amendment. "What does the Amendment ask? It asks that we shall obtain a return of land which is, or has at any time been, capable of being used as arable. . . . I give full rein to my imagination in allowing myself to think what land, under that definition, could conceivably be excluded. Forty or fifty or seventy years ago I believe that those of our grandparents who lived in London and were fond of shooting might have shot snipe in Eaton Square. . . ." While in sympathy with the object of the Amendment to prevent depopulation and to effect the best possible cultivation of the land, he could not accept it because "obviously all the buildings of England were built upon land that was at some time capable of being used as arable". Nor could the problems it raised be tackled purely on a statistical basis of acreage. "The reason why that land is not cultivated is that competitive conditions do not allow of its cultivation, in the main. I know you may qualify that by saying that we have not applied education and science sufficiently to the problem. That is quite true. But I happen to live in the country, where I see derelict cottages also, away up on hills and hill-sides, and the reason for their condition is that that land has gone out of cultivation since the high prices on which it came into cultivation at the time of the Napoleonic wars. My own land went out of cultivation, or part of it, and houses ceased to be lived in when the Napoleonic war crisis came to an end. The right hon. gentleman (Lloyd George) says, 'You can grow a lot more of what you want to eat in England on your own soil.' I agree with him. It can be done, at a price. You may be able to improve your methods by this or that or the other improvement, but when you have done that it comes down to the question, 'Can you do it at the price?'"

Lloyd George must know well that this was a question on which "the great industrial population of the country has a final and decisive voice". When he preached the doctrine of more home-grown food, "what he is really doing is to invite the House and, through the House, the country, to reconsider the deliberate policy that it has pursued for sixty or seventy years past, a policy which, as he now sees, and indeed as all men now see, has brought agriculture and the men and women who live by agriculture, who live on the land, into a position of straitened circumstances. . . . May I ask one other question? What is your test of efficiency in farming? Most people say they want farming carried on efficiently. Is your object a system by which you can produce what you want to get out of the land as efficiently and cheaply as you can? If that be your object, you will go in for all sorts of machinery and for the development of labour-saving devices. The more you develop towards that ideal, the more you will find the population of the land going down. It is not my ideal. My ideal is a form of agriculture which, while being well carried on, will strike a balance, with the balance slightly tilted, or a good deal tilted, in favour of keeping on the land the maximum population which the land will support."

Here is Wood's philosophy in full with its seasoning of

Charles Lamb's quiet irony, as instanced by the snipe in Eaton Square. He has this pleasant faculty, only at times a rather ponderous propriety seems to warn him off it. From this speech with its half-contemptuous reference to " all sorts of machinery " and superficial glance at science as applied to the land, emerges the traditionalist, almost the reactionary. His concept of rural society is frankly dictated by faith rather than reason; for all his efforts to assimulate new social tendencies, he gives the impression of being out of his depth in modern technical civilization, almost afraid of it, which may be one explanation of his underlying sympathy with Gandhi. He proclaims a vision of a Merrie England with subsidies which as an ideal and a symbol is the British counterpart of Gandhi's spinning-wheel. But above all the speech brings out the man's essential honesty: Yes, you can have a flourishing agriculture if you are prepared to pay for it. Are you? Sixteen years after Wood's clear statement of the dilemma the challenge has still to be met.

During the summer of 1925 he was fully occupied grappling with the legislative intricacies of a Tithe Bill which warded off without appeasing the contending factions. As farmer and churchman he was well placed to arbitrate in the grand manner, but apart from a brief homily on its historic origins, always a welcome relief from the contemporary tangle, he refused to back a bold solution. The Allotments Bill had also to be steered through its remaining stages, and finally there was the annual *compte rendu* of Supply Day for his Department which " deals with fish and fertilizers, sugar and sheepscab, rats and reclamation, and, if I may add without offence to anyone, it deals with pigs and also with parsons ". He emphasized that the twin functions of the Ministry were protection and development, and " I put protection first because in agriculture, as in the field of international affairs, no development is possible without security, and at the present moment agriculture is suffering from a feeling of great insecurity ". There was to be a clean milk campaign to remove public distrust of the purity and keeping quality of British milk; although no specific grants were mentioned, research into animal and plant disease was to be further encouraged, in particular by means of practical demonstrations because " farmers learn much more quickly through the eye than through any other sense. I do not think in that respect they are peculiar. You might exhaust your breath—to give a homely illustration—in describing to a susceptible youth the beauties of the most ravishing lady. As long as you speak of her, he will listen no doubt with attention, but with the blood flowing calmly; but let the same youth but catch a glimpse of the whisk of her petticoats with the tail of his eye, and he will immediately surrender. That is an illustration of the importance of trying to promote research and the influence of demonstration through the eye." He called for well-organized co-operative marketing to eliminate fluctuating supplies and to supply agricultural markets "not as to-day according to what the farmer or supplier has in hand, but according to what the market wants", and emphasizes the need for a cultural and educational background to agriculture sufficiently attractive to reverse the drift to the towns; finally he conjured up the vision of country life at its best that would survive "long after the circulars of administrators, and even the speeches of politicians have all passed away into the limbo of forgotten things".

The Labour spokesman, A. V. Alexander, found it "a very pleasing speech", but regretted that there was not more specific indication of policy. The National Farmers Union, finding no Protection or subsidies forthcoming, shared those regrets but cut out the compliments. Throughout the summer a regular series of resolutions was pouring in from its Branches condemning the entire Government. But Wood was to be only one in a long succession of Ministers of Agriculture who, victims of retrenchment in the Treasury and of industrial bias in the Cabinet, could make no promises or could not implement them if they did. All Wood could say was that he proposed not to make any declaration of policy himself to a forthcoming meeting of the Council of Agriculture, but to listen to their policy and "incorporate that with the other elements in my own mind, as a foundation for advice" to the Prime Minister in the course of the next few months. "No policy," he added, "is going to do any good to agriculture that does not promise to be permanent, and that is liable to sharp reversals by other political parties. I would ten times sooner see the good that might be done by any agricultural policy left undone than see a policy which is liable to repeal in the third year, and to reconsideration in the fifth." He had, however, small profit from this pious sentiment, for at the Annual Conservative Conference at Brighton on 8th October a resolution was passed unanimously calling on the Government to make a definite statement, without delay, on their agricultural policy and " to carry such policy into effect forthwith ".

. . . .

The Ministry of Agriculture was, in fact, to be a death-trap for promising political careers, and Wood was only rescued from his growing Ministerial dilemma by the tremendous invitation to succeed the Marquess of Reading as Viceroy of India. How Edward Wood's name first came to be canvassed for such exalted duty is still largely a matter of conjecture. It is widely believed that the influence of Geoffrey Dawson and other members of *The Times*' editorial staff discovered him as an ideal Viceroy and whispered his name at the proper time both to the proper authorities in George V's entourage and at 10 Downing Street. But whoever made the initial move, even if it was Baldwin himself, certain factors worked decisively in his favour, overriding the obvious objections of his youth and his complete inexperience in the intricacies of Anglo-Indian administration. In the first place there was no obvious candidate, and certainly none to compete with Reading in status or prestige, in itself a situation encouraging a bold experiment. Secondly, Baldwin's mind seems to have been set in the direction of constitutional advance for India; if such a policy of fulfilment was to be carried through successfully it needed a man who shared his intimate confidence and his moderate outlook; Wood amply fulfilled both requirements. Then there were his religious preoccupations; the dangers of an ardent Christian ruling over no less ardent Hindus and Moslems were obvious, but it was equally arguable that he was going to a country where his sense of spiritual values would be most deeply appreciated.

Finally, as with the appointment of a bishop, so with the selection of a Viceroy, the operation is delicate. The King, and particularly a monarch with George V's scrupulous regard for constitutional prerogatives and proprieties, must give something more than his customary formal approval to one who is to represent him in such a personal capacity. The Prime Minister, therefore, had to be *persona grata* with the King and the candidate for Viceroy *persona grata* with them both. Ramsay MacDonald, for instance, had ideas about appointing a Labour successor to Wood, but he set about promoting his candidate without due regard for the King's status and susceptibilities in the matter. The result was that the King rejected his man out of hand, and without troubling to consult Downing Street further, shrewdly invited Lord Willingdon to be Viceroy. Baldwin's relations with the King were admirable and his access to him easy. While as for Edward, his father's connection with Edward VII's Royal Household and his grandfather's friendship with Queen Victoria must have been sufficient precedent or testimonial, if any such were needed, to commend him to George V. Actually Halifax entertained King George and Queen Mary at Hickleton shortly after their Accession, and it was from Hickleton, with Halifax sharing the responsibility of advising them to go, that they courageously visited a colliery which had been the scene but a few hours previously of a disastrous explosion.

The King's and Baldwin's problem whether to offer him the Viceroyalty was not, in a sense, so difficult as Wood's whether to accept it. To most men the response to such an honour would be self-evident, but it is clear from Lockhart's account that the personal upheavals and separations and the immensity of the tasks it involved weighed heavily upon him. He would have to leave the life he loved so well at Garrowby, his children and, of course, his father, who now, at the age of eighty-six, could hardly expect to be alive to welcome him back at the end of his term. With such considerations in mind it was a five years exile, but beyond that, he was aware that although Reading was leaving India comparatively undisturbed, the stillness was deceptive; there was a tension below the surface of events that might burst out at any moment and swallow up the best-laid constitutional plans. It was by no means certain that the mandate of appeasement which he was to embody would be adequate to meet the situation. Reading's own estimate was that his successor would enjoy about a further eighteen months of peace and quiet, after which the storm would assuredly break.

There was ample background for Edward's anxiety,

justification for his prayers. "The decision must depend", his father wrote to him on 10th October, with the resignation of the religious mind, "upon what, as far as you can judge, is God's will for you, and that again can only be ascertained by the light which comes to a conscience that is inspired by the single delight of doing, as far as one can, what is God's will for us in this life, and seeks that inspiration in much prayer and recourse to God Himself. When that is done, the matter is largely taken out of our own hands. . . ." Lockhart then describes the famous occasion when Edward went up to Hickleton to talk it over, "and after some discussion Halifax said, 'Never mind about the consequences. If you really try to discover what you ought to do, and then do it, you need never reproach yourself afterwards. What we must do is to say our prayers.' They went to Mass together on the day of St. Simon and St. Jude (28th October), and when they came out of church, Halifax said: 'Well, I think you ought to go.' 'So do I,' replied his son. 'Then that's settled, and don't let us talk about it any more.'"[1]

The immediate result of his acceptance was the conferment upon him of a Peerage, the end of his career in the Commons and of his long association with the faithful electors of Ripon. He thus gained the rare privilege of joining his father in the House of Lords. The title he chose was Baron Irwin of Kirby Underdale, which recalled the old Scottish Viscountcy of Irwin held by the Ingrams of Temple Newsam, but which, as far as the public was concerned, quietly buried the name and the memory of Edward Wood. The next three months were a hectic round of farewells and God-speeds which usually succeed in overwhelming the unhappy Viceroy long before he sets sail for India. His constituents paid him many generous tributes. In January he was presented with the honorary freedom of Harrogate, while in March the Ripon divisional Conservative Association gave him a set of Georgian gold dessert plates as a farewell offering. In a brief speech of thanks he referred to the House of Commons as "a great training ground" and in summing up great events from his fifteen years as Member said he would recall all his life Lord Grey's speech two days before the country went to war with Germany.

[1] Lockhart, Vol. II, pages 352-353.

Then there was a farewell dinner at Doncaster given by the Queen's Own Yorkshire Dragoons, which he then commanded as Lieutenant-Colonel. He was not, however, finally to sever his connection with the regiment and is now its Honorary Colonel. On this occasion he was presented with sleeve-links from N.C.O.s and men, and in thanking them he recalled how in the early days of the war, the fifth day after mobilization, they marched to York with rifles loaded, but how in sharp contrast was a march to Driffield some time later when they went out to meet the Germans—one of the alarms of that period having been raised—without rifles loaded. . . . Among the many reasons which made it difficult for him to decide to go to India, not the least was that of giving up the command of the Queen's Own Yorkshire Dragoons. " My service and my command of this regiment have been among the best times of my life," he said, and his sincerity need not be questioned.

On 8th February he was given a dinner by the members of his three Colleges, Eton, Christ Church and All Souls; the Bishop of Oxford presided and was supported by the Provost of Eton and the Warden of All Souls. A fortnight later the Prime Minister presided over a private and non-party dinner at the House of Commons, and there were lunches and dinners sponsored by such bodies as the East Indian Section of the London Chamber of Commerce, the Royal Colonial Institute and the British Indian Union.

On the whole, such formal festivities are not calculated to betray the Guest of Honour's deeper motives or inner thoughts, but such isolated phrases as " even more important is the development of Education, whereby intellectual isolation is overcome and people come to understand the limitations of their knowledge ", or again the " tenure of a Viceroy is but a drop in the great river of life of India, ever flowing from the hills of antiquity ", reveal clearly enough the moral calibre and background of the man to whom had been entrusted for the next five years the welfare of India's seething millions. He undertook the obligations, accepted the honours and entered on the vast adventure with a truly awe-inspiring steadiness of mind and humility of spirit.

PART II

LORD IRWIN

CHAPTER XI

INDIAN BACKGROUND

THE wearying though far from formal round of official farewells was over at last. The succession of toasts and presentations had revealed that the new Viceroy, if virtually unknown to the British public at large, was certainly sustained by a widespread and influential body of well-wishers. Church and State, the Services and the civilian testified alike to their belief in the qualities of Irwin's character and his capacity to meet the immense demands that would be made on him in India over the next five momentous years. For the send-off itself at Victoria station on March 17th it seemed as if the entire valour and intellect of the nation were assembled to do homage to Irwin. The two younger sons, Peter and Richard Wood, over whose education their parents decided to maintain personal supervision, had already embarked at Tilbury a week before. Otherwise the Viceregal Party was present in full force. It included Major C. O. Harvey, the military Secretary, and the three A.D.C.s, Captain Claude Waller, Captain John Herbert of the Royal Horse Guards and Lieutenant J. B. Gordon Duff, officials upon whose self-effacing technique the outward and visible success of the new regime would to no small extent depend. Lady Irwin's retinue was headed by Lady Mary Herbert, who, as a member of the House of Pembroke, was well within the inner ring of Court Society, and by Alexandra Lady Worsley, bearer of an honoured Yorkshire name.

The King was represented at the station by Lord Somers. Stanley Baldwin was present in person, as was the Archbishop of Canterbury to give his special blessing to a devout champion of the Anglican order. Birkenhead, who had naturally taken a prominent part in choosing Reading's successor, was there too, but whatever concept he may have had of his position at the India Office at the outset, the vision was fading rapidly. Whether in terms of intellect, political outlook or moral judgment the new Viceroy and his Secretary of State had very little in common. But Birkenhead was reinforced on that day by a splendid array of Conservative Imperialists. Salisbury, Londonderry, Douglas Hogg, Cunliffe Lister, Phillimore, Fitzalan, Elvedon, and the greatest of them all, Winston Churchill, somehow symbolized by their presence at Victoria station on that March afternoon a solemn reminder to Irwin of what was expected of him—ideals, yes, but not to the point of concession or dangerous innovation.

He was almost embarrassed by the splendour and size of the farewell. In a short and rather nervous little speech of appreciation he said that he and Lady Irwin were well aware that this splendid send-off was not on their account but was rather a spontaneous tribute to the place held by the Indian Empire. To the gallant old Lord Halifax, who had come from the North specially to see his son off, the occasion can have had no such symbolic meaning. He had written to him a few months before. "As for me, it would almost certainly be good-bye, but at my age that again is not a matter of any real importance either to you or to me." But it was not possible for him, after all his years of striving, to content himself now with sitting and waiting. According to *The Times*' reporter, Viscount Halifax, "in spite of his eighty-six years, is understood to be contemplating a visit to his son next winter". He comforted himself with the thought that if he went he might be able to get in some tiger-shooting.

In the meanwhile he resolved to write to Edward with the same weekly regularity that Edward set himself in his correspondence with Stanley Baldwin. Viceregal House has never had a more painstaking letter-writer; during all the exacting routine Irwin never failed to acknowledge and take detailed interest in his father's news, or to supply his political chief with a comprehensive private estimate of the situation over and above his official memoranda for the Secretary of State and the India Office. Finally, old Halifax made a solemn vow with himself, whatever might become of the visit to India, to keep alive until his son should finally return, and however much he might feel the break in what was a very deep relationship, he was also proud to have lived to see Edward taking over the supreme office in an India which his grandfather had done so much to mould.

Edward was the sixteenth Viceroy since the period of his grandfather's reforms, and although the basic problems of constitutional advance, communal and racial settlement, economic and social progress were still broadly the same, the development of the nationalist movement among the small minority of politically conscious Indians had set a new pace and demanded a more comprehensive and complex response from the British Raj. To some extent this response was still conditioned by the tragedy of the Indian Mutiny. What some writers call the " Mutiny complex " still tugged at the sleeves of those who would promulgate reform or those whose function it was to administer it, but it is fair to say that by Irwin's time no Viceroy could have set out for India with any intention, avowed or implied, of going back on the conception of self-government embodied in the renowned Montagu-Chelmsford Reforms. However great the provocation—and the last months of Reading's term of office were dark and threatening—no Viceroy could have hoped to survive a repudiation of the 1919 Act. Indeed the difference between Radicals and Diehards had now narrowed itself into a dispute as to when the next step forward should be taken.

Irwin, during the brief respite of his fortnight's voyage to Bombay on *The Mooltan*, must have reflected anxiously on the tasks awaiting him. At first sight the responsibility was intolerable, portentous powers seemed to be handed over to the Viceroy on a platter for him to carve up as he saw fit, but appearances in this instance are deceptive. The Viceroy, by the nature of his office, had to stand aloof from much of the fray. In as far as he represented the King-Emperor he could do no wrong, but his very status set a limit to the range of his initiative, and as the *persona* of so cautious and self-effacing a monarch as George V, the flamboyant autocracy of a Curzon was a memory but no longer a precedent. As the head executive officer of the Government of India, as the source of military commissions and civil honours, as the principal liaison between the British Government and the Princes, he was heir to what was still the greatest pro-consular office in the world; but what before the Reforms had been susceptible to direct action was now more a question of informal advice.

In some respects Irwin was bringing just the right equipment for his work, an open mind and no previous experience of India. There is little reason to believe that he had given the Indian problem any more thought than does the average back-bench Member of Parliament. He was not committed in advance to any theory, and it was difficult indeed for the experts to place him save under the general heading of a Baldwin man. Some felt that he would find it hard to match the administrative and intellectual range of his predecessors, who, from Curzon to Reading, had all been men of unusual personal distinction. Curzon, in particular, had set a record for almost superhuman Viceregal energy, but considering the colossal scope of his activities his achievement was strictly limited. He behaved like an enlightened despot, and did not visualize the Viceroy as having anything to do with a transition to responsible self-government.

. . . .

In his farewell speech to the Byculla Club Curzon had declared his " earnest hope that the Viceroy of India may never cease to be head of the Government of India in the fullest sense of the term. It is not one man rule, which may or may not be a good thing—that depends on the man—but it is one man supervision, which is the best form of government, presuming the man is competent." The only alternative that he could see for India was bureaucracy, " which is the most mechanized and lifeless of all forms of administration ". Curzon's response to this mechanical peril was a Durbar in 1903, the cost of which has been estimated at no less than £5,000,000. His was a splendour which, if he had known, the Orient did not understand and did not need. He was ruthless in his attack on incompetence wherever he found it, and was contemptuous of the frothy sentiments of the new Indian nationalism. " My own belief ", he had written to the Secretary of State in London, " is that Congress is tottering to its fall, and one of my great ambitions while in India is to assist it to a peaceful demise." But in spite of this misunderstanding of the material he was trying to mould, in spite of the controversy he stirred up by such action as the partition of Bengal, his term of office had aroused the educated Indians to a new awareness of political questions and to a consciousness of India's place in the world.

His successor, Lord Minto, nominated by the Conservatives, had hardly arrived in India before he found himself the representative of the powerful Liberal administration of Campbell-Bannerman. He was thus the spokesman for a government which had attained power on a reaction against adventures, commitments and the aggressive imperialism of the Boer War period. Superficially, history repeated itself when Irwin, the Conservative, worked in conjunction with the Second Labour Government, but there is a deeper affinity between Irwin and this period. The news of the great Liberal victory came as a trumpet-call to the Indian nationalists. In view of the Liberals' election pledges, they anticipated an orgy of reform and enlightenment. John Morley, the new Secretary of State, however, was more a Whig than a Radical and his positivist beliefs left him wholly out of sympathy with the mysticism of the East. " The real truth ", he wrote, " is that I am an Occidental, not an Oriental. . . . I think I like Indian Mohammedans, but I cannot go much further in an Easterly direction." Minto, a soldier without party or philosophical commitments, was probably more alive to the claims of the resurgent nationalists. At least he was ready to admit that the Government of India would not suffer unduly by the admission of Indians to a share of it.

But although Morley and Minto were soon at work on their reforms, the lack of any previous plan, as well as the outstanding military successes of that other backward agricultural country Japan, only intensified the bitterness and disillusionment of political India. From henceforth an influential section of opinion favoured direct action for the attainment of constitutional power, and from 1907 onwards India was the scene of increasingly grave acts of lawlessness. The Viceroy, however, was not to be discouraged, and when at last after two years the Morley-Minto Reforms were sanctioned by Parliament they received a surprisingly warm reception. For the proposals were cautious enough. The Imperial Legislative Council—or Legislature of the Central Government—was enlarged from twenty-one to sixty, while the membership of the Provincial Councils was doubled. This did not mean any addition to the powers of these bodies. They still were allowed no effective control over the Executive, namely the Governor-General, or Viceroy in Council. It was merely that the volume of criticism was officially increased, and the only substantial concession was the introduction for the first time of an Indian, Sir Satyendra (afterwards Lord) Sinha, as Law Member, into the inner sanctum of the Viceroy's Council. It may be pointed out that even this innovation was violently opposed by the other members of the Council and by such enlightened and Liberal Viceroys as Lord Elgin and Lord Ripon.

Minto had gone so far as to suggest that he could do without an official majority in the Imperial Legislature, but Morley would have nothing to do with any such experiment in democratic control. In an oft-quoted speech in the House of Lords explaining the Reforms, he declared, " If I were attempting to set up a Parliamentary system in India, or, if it could be said that this chapter of reforms led directly or necessarily up to the establishment of a Parliamentary system in India, I, for one, would have nothing at all to do with it." Instead, the Reforms gave statutory recognition to the lamentable facts of communal conflict. Certain minorities, in particular the Mohammedans, had reserved to them a certain specified representation. Here was the origin of all the subsequent dispute on the relative merits of joint and separate electorates which overshadowed so much of Irwin's Viceroyalty, and became the symbol for the Hindu and Moslem communities alike of vast incompatible religious pretensions and political programmes.

Lord Hardinge's Viceroyalty had seen the spread of Moslem discontents and the growth of organized communal politics through such movements as the Hindu Mahasabha and the Moslem League which cut across the simple conflict between Indian nationalism and the British Raj. There were occasions when all the interests could unite momentarily, as, for instance, in the struggle for the rights of Indians overseas. It was from this struggle in South Africa that Gandhi had built up his unrivalled reputation as an Indian leader of Indians, and had forged his unique weapon of satyagraha or soul resistance. It fell to Lord Hardinge's lot to express the unanimous sentiment of India when, giving his blessing in November 1913 to the mission of Mr. Gokhale, Gandhi's distinguished predecessor in the leadership of Indian nationalism, he voiced " the sympathy of India deep and burning and not only of India but of all lovers of India like myself for their compatriots in South Africa in their resistance to invidious and unjust laws ".

Lord Hardinge's tenure had not been easy. On his way to lay the foundation-stone of the Government building at New Delhi he had been wounded by the terrorist's bomb and lamed for the rest of his life. Yet he had managed to bring a united India into the war for freedom and democracy; it was a great achievement, and his insistence that India's service should be on equal terms with other parts of the Empire has been well described as a magnificent act of statesmanship, which the subsequent disillusionment was all too soon to overshadow. The first rapture could not be sustained. Moslems found themselves facing a divided allegiance, the sound of the *muezzin* could be heard in Turkish trenches calling the faithful to prayer, nor was their splendid heroism of avail against the scandal and disaster of the Mesopotamian campaign.

By the time Lord Chelmsford had succeeded Hardinge in 1916, a situation not far removed from political revolt was prevailing. The Hindu extremist, Tilak, emerging from his retirement, spread, with the aid of Mrs. Annie Besant, the militant doctrine of Home Rule, and came to terms with the Moslems. The Lucknow Congress of 1916 saw the final defeat of the Moderates in that body, and once again the Government chose an atmosphere of increasing violence and tension to institute a series of complicated and carefully balanced reforms. Edwin Montagu, Lloyd George's mercurial Secretary of State for India, made his historic declaration to the House of Commons on 20th August 1917. The object of British policy he then defined as being " not only the increasing association of Indians in every branch of the administration, but also the granting of self-governing institutions with a view to the progressive realization of responsible government in India as an integral part of the British Empire ".

This declaration was to be Irwin's Magna Carta, but although the so-called Montagu-Chelmsford Report, ultimately embodied in the Government of India Act of 1919, was much more progressive and drastic than the Morley-Minto Reforms, the hostile reaction to it in India showed how far during the intervening ten years Indian sentiment had moved away from British policy. Congress, which had welcomed the 1907 proposals " with deep and general satisfaction ", now indignantly rejected the Montagu-Chelmsford

Reforms. Their main provisions, which did not finally come into operation until Lord Reading's time, were, a further considerable increase in the membership of the Legislative Council (from now on termed the Legislative Assembly), and the formation of a Second Chamber, known as the Council of State, for the Imperial Government, and consisting of sixty members, just over half of whom were elected. In addition, they established the Chamber of Princes, which brought the Native States into something like an organized relationship with British India, and which, in Irwin's time, was to be a formative factor in the otherwise haphazard growth of Federation.

But perhaps the most important feature of the Reforms was the evolution of what, on the somewhat misleading analogy of Antonine Rome, has been known as the policy of Diarchy. Certain subjects were "transferred" to the control of Indian Ministers, themselves responsible to the Legislative Councils, which now consisted of large elected majorities. This transfer system only applied to the Provinces. The Central Imperial Government was still safeguarded from the encroachments of Democracy. In addition, the Viceroy was left with a theoretically limitless power of certifying any legislation which he felt was necessary and which the legislatures had failed to pass. All this, however, was satisfactory enough if the Reforms could have been separated from their environment.

We are up against an almost tragic time lag in considering Irwin's political inheritance. It was in 1915 that Mr. Asquith had promised to view Indian questions from "a different angle of vision". Two years had been allowed to lapse before that promise was implemented. Then there was to be a further twenty months delay between Montagu's Indian visit and the passing of the Act. Montagu, who had been Under-Secretary during the Morley regime, passed across India with the fleeting splendour of April sunshine against a background of storm, was garlanded by Tilak and was actually invited to address Congress. "Dash down to the Congress", he records in his diary, "and make them a great oration. It might save the whole situation." Unhappily, gestures were not enough. He returned to an England locked in a life-and-death struggle with Germany, indifferent to everything Indian. During those twenty months after his visit events occurred which, in the words of the historian, " left an imprint on Indo-British relations comparable with the after-effects of the Mutiny ". The Government was ill advised enough to set up the Rowlatt Committee in order to supplement existing Defence and Press Acts. Its recommendations coincided with the Reforms. Thus it came about that the Indians nursed from the outset a sense of grievance, a belief that there was a catch in British democracy when it was applied to those who were not Britons.

By the time Irwin had come on the scene this concept of British duplicity had hardened into a dogma, but it has its roots in the misunderstandings and mistimings at the end of the war. It was not a happy period; there was an after-victory arrogance in British rule; a resolve to restore pre-war conditions. The Punjab, from where the overwhelming majority of India's native army had been recruited, became the centre of acute disturbance, which culminated in the massacre at Amritsar. The memory of General Dyer was still a disturbing factor in Irwin's time, but a far deeper cause of distress was the appalling influenza plague which swept across the country and wiped out between thirteen and fourteen million Indians.

From this welter of suffering and discontent the figure of Gandhi emerged proclaiming his nationalism in the dialect of Hindu religious practice. Satyagraha, ahimsa or the doctrine of harmlessness, hartal or day of fasting, became symbols of moral and physical resistance to the entire British system of government. It was Gandhi's purpose to raise his political controversies on to the plane of moral conduct. This was at times to involve both himself and the British Government in confusion and compromise. From Gandhi's point of view Congress was often a defective vessel. The outcome of an historic controversy between Tilak and Gokhale had been that Congress definitely rejected truth as the objective of its propaganda. Exploiting propaganda solely as a weapon of war, it made immense strides among an ignorant and imaginative population, but at the expense of its integrity. For this Gandhi was to suffer, but by his peculiar emphasis he was attacking the British Raj on its blind spot. However mistaken and unimaginative British administration might be, it was unaccustomed to being dubbed " satanic ". The strong line taken by Irwin's friend, Sir George Lloyd, who, as Governor of Bombay, had helped to make up Lord Chelmsford's hesitating mind by arresting Gandhi and clapping him in gaol, was really no solution. The success of this measure could not be judged by the absence of any upheaval after it.

By the end of Lord Reading's term Gandhi had retired from the scene after illness and further imprisonment, to all outward appearances a symbol of renunciation, defeated and indifferent. For our purposes it is important to realize that he had not, officially at least, gone beyond the demand he made when he launched his Non-Co-operation campaign in 1920, which was for a Round Table Conference, " a real Conference ", as he told the Ahmedabad Congress the following year, " where only equals are to sit and there is not a single beggar ".

It had not been possible for Lord Reading to do much more than mark time. The very provision in the Montagu-Chelmsford Reforms that they should be renewed within ten years by a Statutory Commission was regarded as proof of their experimental and impermanent character. Congress, now dominated by new leaders such as C. R. Das and the Pandit Motilal Nehru, formed a Swaraj Party and entered the legislatures for the express purpose of obstructing the Government by constitutional methods. After the second elections under the Reforms they controlled two of the Provincial Councils and had a solid block of forty-five members in the Legislative Assembly. Their entrance was in some respects an unwitting tribute to the achievement of the first Assembly. Some useful social legislation had been passed (including the repeal of the Rowlatt Act), precedents and conventions were being established.

On the other hand it was evident that Lord Reading was leaving behind him unsolved problems of the first magnitude. The financial structure of the new Constitution had been subjected to excessive strain from the start, which was in part due to such diverse causes as the failure of the life-giving monsoon, the Afghan war, and the slump of 1920. The Provinces had been allotted certain sources of revenue, but under what was known as the Meston Award, were liable to make a scale of payments to the Central Government. This in itself was a fruitful source of controversy in the future. The Central Government had to make the maximum demands at a time when the Provincial Governments, also heavily hit by the slump, were least able to contribute; the stability of the rupee was soon in danger, and an unfavourable balance of trade developed. Severe retrenchment became the order of the day, and political agitation centred round such pecuniary problems as the currency question, direct taxation, fiscal policy, and the problem of military expenditure. In 1923 Sir Basil Blackett, the brilliant Finance Minister who was to bring his labours to a triumphant conclusion during Irwin's Viceroyalty, proposed as a remedy the doubling of the hated Salt Tax. Like the gabelle of French Revolution fame, the Salt Tax was more a symbolic than an actual grievance. It applied to all and had become a mark of servitude. The Assembly defeated the proposal, and Lord Reading was reduced to choosing between another Budget deficit or reliance on his powers of certification under the 1919 Act. He decided to certify the tax, and the outcry following his action was a warning to Irwin of the limitations under the new Constitution of the Viceroy's prerogative.

But as Lord Reading's term at Viceregal House drew to its close there was a relaxing of political tension and even interest. India was given over to Commissions and Enquiries, the first of which, under Sir Alexander Muddiman, prepared the ground for the Statutory Commission which was due to be summoned by 1929 at the latest, or any time before as the Viceroy might see fit to advise. It had been called together by the ephemeral Labour Government, and reported when Mr. Baldwin and Lord Birkenhead were firmly in the saddle. A Majority Report had no important alternatives to suggest, but a Minority of four Indians, including the most influential Liberal leader, Sir Tej Bahadur Sapru, frankly condemned Diarchy.

By the time *The Mooltan* was on its way to Bombay it seemed that all interests were united in rejecting Montagu's great experiment. From the Swarajists and Congress leaders to Lord Birkenhead himself, who described Diarchy as " the kind of pedantic hidebound constitution to which Anglo-Saxon countries had not generally responded ", there was no one prepared to defend it, and the Moderates who had tried to work the Constitution were particularly disillusioned. Congress, in the meanwhile, kept one stage ahead of facts by developing " a national demand " as soon as Commissions seemed likely to open the door to a Round Table Conference.

. . . .

Such in briefest outline was the trend of public events under the rule of Irwin's distinguished predecessors. It had not fallen to their lot to see the ordered and steady development of Anglo-Indian relations. Rather, progress had been spasmodic, the set-backs persistently coincided with advances, promises which aroused excessive hopes seemed always delayed until, when they were translated into action, they evoked excessive disappointment. Political forbearance or belief in compromise are not essentially oriental attributes. When Irwin took over, there was a sense, then, of frustration, foreboding and of suppressed excitement before a tremendous climax. To the layman the full immensity of his mission may well have been overlooked or dismissed with the same impatience as the Irish question. But if Indian affairs are baffling in their complexity, it is as well to recall that by India is meant a continent with a diversity of cultures and density of population with which in comparison Europe is almost an elementary exercise.

As Viceroy of British India, and excluding his special relationship with the six hundred Native States and their eighty million subjects which compromise a third of India in area and a quarter in population, he presided over the destinies of 270,000,000 of her peoples. Of the nine Governors' Provinces, Burma was larger than France, Madras and Bombay larger than Italy, the Punjab, United Provinces and Central Provinces larger than Great Britain. Madras, United Provinces and Bengal all had bigger populations than Britain, France or Italy. It was a British Raj and there were 160,000 Europeans to support it, but for every one European there were a thousand caste Hindus. The Moslem minority problem embodied a population of 80,000,000. Hindu Untouchables who, to quote the Simon Report, " for all other Hindus cause pollution by touch, and defile food and water ", reach the gigantic total of 75,000,000. Of these teeming hordes over ninety per cent struggled as their fathers before them with the parched land and were gathered into India's half million villages, which, for the most part, were little more than a collection of mud huts.

Mortgage and debt dominated their lives. Eighty-six per cent of India's people could neither read nor write. It was a land of over two hundred and twenty languages, nearly all of which were mutually unintelligible. English was the official language, and a mere two and a half million Indians understood it. These categories could be almost endlessly set out. There was Hinduism comprising about half of the British Empire's and an eighth of the world's population, with its elaborate caste system involving no less than 2,300 castes.

The bare recital of these figures acts as a corrective to all who try to summarize the Indian problem in all-embracing formulae, and when we come face to face with such phrases as "Indian opinion" or "united India" we are bound to admit that we refer to a tiny if very articulate fraction of the people. Montagu had been moved by "the pathetic contentment" of the dumb millions; as a challenge to their unfathomable silence and their age-long endurance, the whole history of British rule is but a fleeting unknown incident.

CHAPTER XII

INITIATIONS

The Mooltan dropped anchor at Bombay on April 1st. All was ready for the customary pageantry of a Viceregal reception, but it so happened that April 1st 1926 was Good Friday, and Irwin at once directed that the civil ceremonial should be postponed. Actually he landed, but simply in order to attend the three-hour service at the little church on Malabar Hill. Afterwards he returned to the boat and his official arrival took place the next day. It is difficult to over-estimate the importance of this episode; the story of it spread across India with lightning speed. Most Indians had reached the regrettable conclusion that an Englishman's religion was either a mere formality or part of the apparatus of his power. The Viceroy's Sunday church parades were evidence more of a procedure militant and here on earth than of spiritual exercise. The Eastern mind found it hard to sympathize with religious practice which had little more to it than the routine etiquette of a social occasion. When Reading—a Jew—was sent to govern Hindus and Mohammedans there was widespread speculation over possible reactions, but when it was found that His Excellency was sufficiently accommodating as regularly to attend Divine Services at Simla and elsewhere, it was difficult for Indians to appreciate the value of his Jewish traditions or his Christian belief.

Irwin by this simple act of devotion could not with any amount of conscious effort have made a more favourable first impression. From the outset India was aware of the presence of an Englishman for whom his religion was an integral part of his life. From the outset he set a precedent which he never allowed himself to break. Whenever Sunday came and he was on his travels, the Viceregal train would be specially stopped in order that Irwin might attend the nearest wayside church. In his first letters to friends in Yorkshire he slipped in an appeal for funds for an Anglican

Church in New Delhi. That his arrival should have coincided with Easter only served to concentrate the attention of a people peculiarly susceptible to symbolic values on the arresting personality of the new Viceroy, and to show him for what he was, an enthusiastic practising Christian who, when he entered a church, put aside the trammels of earthly greatness, refused the special places reserved for him and, as a fellow worshipper, quietly joined himself with the rest of the congregation.

On the Saturday he submitted to the formal splendours of the greeting at the Apollo Bundar. In the decorous language of *The Times* Own Correspondent, " the hot weather is beginning, but it is not yet too hot for the enjoyment of the brilliant ceremony which marked his arrival at the Gateway of India ". India in all its variety and contrast was there to welcome him, from the Princes in their coats of many colours to Patel in his khaddar or homespun, the symbol of Gandhi's resistance to the Raj. Patel, whose venerable appearance belied his impish temperament, acted as President of the Legislative Assembly, and Congress's spearhead in the policy of obstruction. Behind a screen of neutrality he was soon to be engaged in a personal clash with Irwin and to be thwarted in his tactics by an even firmer resolve than his own. Sir Henry Lawrence, Acting Governor of Bombay, received Irwin officially, while according to *The Times* the subsequent procession " was decidedly successful, and popular interest and enthusiasm was unmistakably aroused ", which was no doubt the formula to cover the welcome to all new Viceroys. What was certain, however, was that from the moment he set foot on Indian soil he would be involved in an exhausting and closely packed round of official engagements from which there was to be no respite. Within forty-eight hours of his arrival he had inspected reclamation works, replied to an address of welcome from the Bombay Chamber of Commerce, received the Princes, met officials at a Government House dinner and been sworn in by Sir Norman McLeod, the Chief Justice of the Bombay High Court.

On Sunday night he left Bombay, and on the morning of Tuesday, April 6th, entered Delhi, his capital, to take up residence at Viceregal Lodge. He and Lady Irwin seem to have responded to this last ordeal to the utmost satisfaction of the social columnists. The hot weather was already several weeks overdue, and they drove through the troop-lined streets of Delhi with Viceregal escort of cavalry on a dustless morning in a climate deliciously cool and clear. Their children were sent on to Dehra Dun and the ceremony at the station was confined to meeting a small number of high officials. The main reception was awaiting them in the grounds of their new home. The cavalcade made a gallant picture, as, greeted by a fanfare from the Viceregal trumpeters, it slowly trotted along the winding red paths into the grounds of Viceregal Lodge. Irwin inspected the Guard of Honour formed by the 2nd Battalion of the Royal Warwicks and the formidable Frontier Force Rifles which had given him a Royal salute. Lady Irwin, it was noted, wore a champagne-coloured dress and a green hat, while his Excellency was in a grey morning-suit and white topee. They were having their first experience of the ceremonial tortures that have to be endured in the name of constitutional monarchy. "The whole of the remainder of the Company filed past and their Excellencies shook hands with everyone." Then to the accompaniment of the National Anthem they took possession of their new home.

But while Bombay and Delhi were given over to hunting and garden-parties in honour of the new Viceroy there was a very different welcome in the crowded bazaars of Calcutta. At the very moment that Irwin was being sworn in, the police and military were engaged in a desperate effort to suppress what *The Times* Calcutta Correspondent described as " the most serious outbreak of communal rioting for many years ". The riots actually started on the Good Friday when a Hindu procession with band playing stopped outside a Moslem church and refused to move on. The northern part of the city was soon full of rioters. During the next few days of terror over seventy-five fires were started, at least forty persons killed and three hundred injured. A serious situation was only brought under control by the most severe regulations. All gatherings in the streets of more than five persons were declared illegal and at once broken up. This Calcutta riot was the signal for a whole series of massacres—no less than forty during the first year of Irwin's Viceroyalty. Thus before he had had time even to look round and take his bearings Irwin was brought face to face with the most obstinate and persistent of all the many problems that distract the progress of India in its struggle for nationhood.

The outward and visible signs of conflict, which for the most part centre round such comparative trivialities as the so-called cow-music controversy, are no real guide to the deeper influences intensifying it. If it were simply the difficulties connected with the Moslem slaughter and the Hindu worship of cows, or the Hindus disturbing Moslem prayers with their noisy processions, a *modus vivendi* would not be beyond reach. But as soon as the Provincial authorities intervened, the cry of " religion endangered " was raised or the more sinister interpretation put forward that the British were fomenting disorders simply to have the pretext of suppressing Hindus and Moslems alike. For religious, social and economic motives were hopelessly intermingled. " Only to a small extent ", assert Edward Thompson and G. T. Garratt in their brilliant work *The Rise and Fulfilment of British Rule in India*, " is this enmity based on race or religion. It may be better regarded as the revolt of emancipated lower caste Indians against the social and financial domination of the higher castes." They point out that less than a sixth of the Moslems are of a different race to the Hindus, and that the great bulk of Moslems are descendants of converts from the lower caste Hindus. By becoming Moslems they at once assumed a new social consciousness. Then again the economic grievance is deep-rooted. Often the Hindu is the moneylender or petty employer and the Moslem the indebted peasant or the labourer, or, as in Bombay, the hated strike breaker.

Ironically enough, with the promise of self-government and the spread of such democratic ideas as party representation, the castes have discovered the potentialities of organized political agitation. Although the 1919 Act retains the communal electorates set up under the Morley-Minto Reforms in response to the Moslems' demand and with the formal approval of the Hindu leaders, the result has simply been to confine and distort the new constitution. Practically the only way to alter the *status quo* was by wholesale conversions, which of course intensified the activities and jealousies of Hindu and Moslem missions. The flames were further fanned by a cheap Press and such provocative publications as the notorious *Rangila Rasul*, which was a libellous attack on the Prophet. This particular book, involving protracted legal action and the ultimate murder of its author, was still a potent cause of friction in Irwin's time. Here was enough combustible material to baffle the best intentions and the strongest will. For thirty years Gandhi had wrestled with the problem only to confess failure. "I have admitted my incompetence," he confessed at Calcutta in May 1926, "I have admitted that I have been found wanting as a physician prescribing a cure for this malady. I do not find that either Hindus or Musulmans are ready to accept my cure and therefore I simply nowadays confine myself to a passing mention of this problem. . . ."

Such detachment was not possible for Irwin. His position and temperament alike demanded something more than formal Viceregal concern, but he made no immediate move. No sooner had he reached his "country house" at Dehra Dun after the ceremonies at Delhi, than he and his family were all taken ill with feverish chills and he had to cancel an engagement to open the headwork of the gigantic Sutlej Valley scheme which, at a cost of £15,000,000, was to irrigate 14,000 square miles of parched land. There was considerable disappointment in Lahore, the capital of the Punjab, but within a day or two he was reported to be making "satisfactory progress", and on 21st April he made his State arrival at his summer capital of Simla, high in the Himalayas. The procession climbed the narrow streets from the station to the Viceregal Lodge to an accompaniment of snow and thunder. In spite of the freak weather the crowds duly assembled and the trappings of sovereignty were duly brought out. "A gorgeous Royal umbrella was held over their heads in a carriage with postillions." In Simla he met the members of his Council who had left Delhi on their annual flight from the hot weather of the plains.

Actually the ill-fated New Delhi was still far from complete. *The Times* Correspondent, on a visit there in June, found the Viceregal Lodge at Raisina unfinished and uninhabitable, and forecast an uncomfortable three-year period of transition there for the official world, with personnel scattered over an area from twelve to twenty-five miles long, and supplies to the household held up owing to the distance of the new capital from the bazaars of the old city. Here were some considerations which must have caused Irwin and his family to feel more at home perched up in the heights of Simla, which had about it almost the atmosphere of one of those Swiss mountain resorts packed with the pride of British Society, with a background of natives sufficient to make it picturesque, and which seemed to be made more for perpetual holiday than for executive government.

. . . .

For a month or so Irwin remained quietly out of the news. There were no hints of a change of policy or indeed any policy at all. There were signs that the Viceroy was determined to eliminate some of the pomp which had been allowed to accumulate round his predecessors and abandon the elephant's howdah for more modest if less impressive transport. This simplicity in outlook and action soon made a deep impression upon all who came into contact with him, and when at last in July he felt impelled to intervene personally in the communal question, it was this simplicity, obviously based on deep religious experience, which made his appeal so arresting, and converted an ordinary after-dinner speech into a plea which forced every responsible element in the political and religious life of India to recognize the presence in their midst of a new and compelling moral leader. But Irwin displayed in addition a lively sense of tactics in the choice of occasion for his *tour de force*.

The dinner held on 17th July in Simla was under the auspices of the celebrated Chelmsford Club which, as its name suggests, was founded to symbolize the spirit of the Reforms, and welcomed membership from every community, British and Indian alike. It was thus in marked contrast to most of the Clubs Irwin might have addressed, which deliberately refused admission to Indians, and only accepted Britons under rigid rule of caste. When Irwin rose to speak at the Chelmsford Club it was fair to say that the distinguished company gathered from every part of India represented all communities. Among the guests were Mr. Patel, President of the Legislative Assembly; Mr. Ghuznavi, the leader of the Moslems in Bengal; Sir Tej Bahadur Sapru for the Liberals, and the influential Pandit Madan Mohan Malaviya, doyen of the orthodox Hindu Mahasabha; a prominent Congress personality. Sir Bhupendra Nath Mitra, the only Indian Member of the Viceroy's Executive Council, in proposing Irwin's health modestly did what was required of him by expressing his confidence that India under Irwin would make vast progress, " even in communal matters ".

Irwin is described in his reply as speaking " with deep earnestness, every word falling slowly and clearly and producing its full effect on the minds of his audience ". He did not hesitate to reply on the personal note. In refuting the suggestion that the Government welcomed the dissensions, he staked his first claim. " I do not believe," he declared, " that there is any general disposition to impugn the good faith of the British Government or their desire to achieve the progressive realization of responsible self-government in British India. . . . The most superficial analysis of this policy can lead to no other conclusion than that the British Government recognized from the outset that harmony between the two great communities was an essential condition of the attainment of their goal. And by harmony I do not mean the surrender by either community of its individuality. But I do mean the harmonious intercourse of daily life and the mutual acknowledgment of common rights and duties in all that goes to make up Indian citizenship. . . . For the success of our own policy, for the very credit of British statesmanship, we were bound to do and we have done everything in our power to promote such better understanding. If, indeed, the reality of communal antagonism should prove permanently more powerful than the hope of an all-India patriotism, it is obvious that the foundations upon which we had sought to build would be rudely shaken."

India has not often heard a more generous assertion of British objectives, a more magnanimous approach to her own peculiar difficulty. " India has given abundant proof," Irwin continued, " of her power to assimilate her multitudinous people. Shall she fail in this final task? In the evolution of political institutions, the British genius has never yet met defeat. Shall it be forced to admit defeat in India? It is to me unthinkable. I look forward to the day when India may be able through ordered progress to take her rightful place in the great fabric of civilization for which the British Empire stands." In the meanwhile he paid tribute to the devoted work of District Officers, British and Indian, upon whom the ultimate responsibility for checking communal disorder rested. He then dealt very firmly with suggestions that separate communal electorates were a cause of irritation.

"The time may come, and I greatly hope it will, when with general consent the necessity for such special representation will be no longer felt"; but for the present the Central Government and local authorities were bound to assure minorities of representation. As far as the Legislatures were concerned, "these arrangements were the result of a compact to which Indian opinion at the time of the introduction of the Reforms desired effect to be given. . . . All communities were thus enabled—and, indeed, the action could hardly be justified on any other grounds—freely to take part together in fashioning India's destiny, and opportunity was ensured by which no community should at the outset be impeded in making a joint contribution to a common task." To the suggestion that the Government might be induced by pressure from one side or the other to modify or enlarge these privileges—itself a factor making for communal unrest—Irwin returned a categorical assurance. Whatever the Royal Commission might decide, and without trying to anticipate it, "I wish," he said, "to state very plainly on behalf of the Government of India that in advance of that enquiry, while there is no intention of curtailing the special scope of these special statutory arrangements, there is equally no intention of extending them."

He then announced that he had anxiously weighed the possibilities of convening a Round Table Conference to consider the situation. "If I could think that there was a real likelihood or even a real chance of such action effecting improvement, I should not be deterred from adopting it by the inevitable risk of failure." He asked for bilateral undertakings from the leaders themselves, but before these could be given the lesson of the 1924 Conference should be learnt. "It failed in my judgment because it was not preceded by any adequate change of heart and feeling throughout the communities which were there represented."

And so, to his splendid peroration, which for its sustained fervour, for its texture of phrase and quality of argument, is among his finest achievements in oratory and proclaims a vision of statesmanship rarely excelled in the tumultuous history of modern India: "The more I ponder over the problem, the more clearly do I feel that the first work to be done is by the leaders of each individual community within their own ranks. It is upon them that the grave responsibility of the first vital step lies. I am convinced that on reflection they will see that the interests of their own community and the future of their country alike demand it. Let the leaders and thoughtful men in each community, the Hindu among the Hindus, and Moslem among the Moslems, throw themselves with ardour into a new form of communal work and into a nobler struggle, the fight for toleration. I do not believe that the task is beyond their powers. I see before me two ancient and highly organized societies with able and esteemed public men as their recognized leaders. I cannot conceive that a really sincere and sustained appeal by them to the rank and file of their co-religionists, supported by active propaganda of the new gospel of peace, would pass unheeded. In past centuries each community has made its great contribution to the annals of history and civilization in India. The place that she has filled in the world in past ages has been largely of their creating. I refuse to believe that they can make no contribution now to rescue the good name of India from the hurt which their present discords inflict upon it.

"In the name of Indian national life, in the name of religion, I appeal to all in each of the two communities who hold position, who represent them in the Press, who direct the education of the young, who possess influence, who command the esteem of their co-religionists, who lead them in politics or are honoured by them as divines. Let them begin each in their own community to work untiringly towards this end; boldly to repudiate feelings of hatred and intolerance, actively to condemn and suppress acts of violence and aggression, earnestly to strive to exorcize suspicions and misapprehensions and so to create a new atmosphere of trust.

"I appeal in the name of national life because communal tension is eating into it as a canker. It has suspended its activities. It has ranged its component parts into opposite and hostile camps.

"I appeal in the name of religion because I can appeal to nothing nobler, and because religion is the language of the soul, and it is a change of soul that India needs to-day. In all religion, I suppose, there must be present in the mind of the individual a sense of personal deficiency, a consciousness of failure to apprehend more than a fraction of life's mystery, which constantly impels him, with irresistible yearning, to reach out for higher and yet higher things. Whatever, indeed, be the creed that men profess, such creed is the attempt men make to know the Forces that lie beyond human vision, and learn the secret of how human nature may be defined, and in so doing realize the ultimate purpose of their existence. Achievement is hard and can only come through much patience and humility, which will in turn beget a wide tolerance of the deficiencies of others. But the reward is great, and there can surely be no greater tragedy than that religion, which thus should be the expression and the support of man's highest instincts, should be prostituted by an alliance with actions through which those instincts are distorted and disgraced.

" Such a development, if it were unchecked, could only end in the infliction of a mortal wound upon human character, upon India and upon the cause of that religion in whose guise it was allowed to masquerade."

This one speech confirmed Irwin in public estimation as being equal to his office. From henceforth what he had to say would be followed closely as much in the lobbies of Westminster as in India itself. Here was a man with a new approach to Indian questions; at a critical moment the British had sent out a Viceroy who was prepared to set aside formality and that slight but exasperating hint of patronage which undid so much of the goodwill and work of his predecessors. Instead, he substituted a profound sense of India's importance and a moral earnestness which raised controversies to a higher level and imposed on India's leaders a fresh responsibility.

Indian Press comment showed that Irwin had penetrated opinions firmly prejudiced against the British Raj. *The Bombay Chronicle*, organ of Congress, gladly acknowledged the sincerity of feeling inspiring the pronouncement which " in parts is all that could be desired ". The highly critical *Hindustan Times* also picked out Irwin's " rare sincerity "— " there is no bluster in the Viceroy's words ". In the House of Commons Josiah Wedgwood, an influential and outspoken Socialist, paid significant tribute to him as " a democrat " with " a rare vein of religious sincerity—an ideal man to have as Viceroy ", and *The Times* gave a leading article under the heading of "Lord Irwin's Appeal" which showed in no uncertain terms that Irwin's policy was appreciated and underwritten by Printing House Square. It spoke of a "direct and profoundly convincing statement". "It so happens that he has a strong personal qualification for dealing with that subtle essence of the Indian problem which few clearly realize but which does matter far more to most Indians than any details of political theory or political organization . . . In India the religious interest is the deepest of all. The goal of devotional endeavour is unity, salvation, release. To this profound instinct Lord Irwin earnestly appealed."

But in spite of the spontaneous and immediate enthusiasm among Moslems and Hindus in his audience, the influence of the Chelmsford Club speech was from beginning to end personal, nothing happened as a direct result of it to ease the situation. The riots continued in all their fury, and it was tragically clear that the communal leaders had only a limited authority over their followers. When a month later Irwin made his maiden speech to the Council of State and Legislative Assembly at the beginning of their session he adopted a rather sterner tone. He was still anxiously waiting for signs of "mutual tolerance which alone can put an end to discord. . . . Meanwhile we have obligations to law-abiding citizens." "The antagonism," he added, "which some members or sections of the communities concerned have recently displayed towards the observances of others appears to some extent to be based, not so much on traditional loyalty to any creed, as on new assertions of abstract rights, which it is sought to invest with the sanctity of ancient principles. This tendency has been more marked in the recent troubles than at any previous period in the British administration." The Government was not to be deterred by unreasonable claims, violence, or the threat of violence, from doing its clear duty. The debate which followed revealed that the major Hindu-Moslem strife spread out and infected the relationships of all the other communities, and the only contribution the Government was able to make was to underpin the law against seditious literature.

There was not enough evidence of a constructive will to settlement to justify the Viceroy taking for the present any further personal initiative. Besides, there were other problems to demand his attention and take up his time. He was soon, for instance, applying his special knowledge to India's greatest industry and his own special subject. During a visit to the Central Provinces, which he described as "the meeting point of three of the great crops of India—Wheat, Rice and Cotton", he received a deputation of farmers at Nagpur, the capital, and addressed them in terms they could understand and appreciate. "You may console yourselves," he said, "with the thought that it is the country population which is the backbone of any nation, and the foundation of its true prosperity. I am talking to-day as a farmer to farmers. I know that all of you are men who have interested yourselves, as I have, in modern agriculture, and have practical experience of your profession. You may be certain therefore that I will give my most sympathetic consideration to the various questions you have raised."

In his speech to the Combined Legislatures at Simla he was able to announce that the Royal Commission on Indian Agriculture, under the Presidency of Lord Linlithgow, with formidable personnel and wide terms of reference, would begin work within two months. The ground had already been prepared at a Conference of Ministers and Directors of Agriculture from the Provinces held in Simla during June, which occasion Irwin used to emphasize his special interest in the Commission's work for the welfare of the Indian agriculturist. "No system of administration could be justified which did not aim at making an improvement in his standard of life and his equipment to take a proper share in her (India's) future its first and chief concern." Constitutional reforms were placing the destinies of India increasingly in the hands of the rural elector, and Irwin was quick to recognize that the process of educating him in his new responsibilities was primarily the function of the Central Government; but in tackling the vast problem of India's agricultural depression both he and the Commission were engaged in long term work. Its completion they could not expect to see in their time, but that the foundations were so firmly laid was in no small measure due to Irwin's personal supervision and sustained enthusiasm.

. . . .

While the Commission was making a preliminary survey of the Provinces during the autumn, Irwin was inspecting the

Punjab and North West Frontier. The choice of this area for his first Grand Tour was particularly fortunate. Many of the districts had never before been visited by a Viceroy; while from the Punjab the overwhelming majority of India's army had been recruited. Here it was that the splendid Sikhs had helped to build up the " Punjab tradition " for martial efficiency and valour; here, too, that a rich land and a sturdy peasantry gave the lead to India's agricultural economy. The loyalty of the Punjab was an indispensable factor in the maintenance of British influence and authority.

Those who were at Lahore for Irwin's State arrival confirm the impression of his enormous popularity, which, in spite of subsequent political set-backs, never deserted him. The salaaming crowds in the streets during the drive to Government House, the lavish Durbar at the old Fort, better known to the devotees of Kipling as " Fort Amara ", would undoubtedly have warmed Kipling's heart, as would Irwin's homily on the Punjab as " a nursery of fighting men ". Naturally he was bound to lay emphasis on the military theme, to visit such centres of martial glory as Jhelum. They entertained him in the magical gardens of the Shalimar; they showed him the renowned Badshali mosque, they filled in every moment of his working hours with official routine and reception, but they could not prevent him from setting the stamp of his own ideas on the tour.

Without warning, he departed from the carefully arranged programme in order to visit two villages a few miles from Lahore, and see their life without ceremony or concealment. He examined specially the working of the local Co-operative Society. The co-operative movement is described in the Annual Survey for 1926-1927 as " unquestionably one of the most promising and important of the efforts now being made to improve the conditions of life in India ". The success of the experiment varied considerably with local conditions. In the Central Provinces where Irwin had already made a similar excursion he found a somewhat unsound capital structure. In the Punjab, however, the Co-operative Society had taken root and was making the most satisfactory progress. Under the guidance of an extremely prudent Governor, Sir Malcolm Hailey, a formidable financial organization was developed. Here was the spirit of enterprise with which Irwin was resolved to identify his Viceroyalty.

Two-thirds of his speech at the Lahore Durbar was devoted to agriculture—its progress and its philosophy. Some looking at the superb natural resources of the Punjab might be tempted to say " what I have is good enough ". " But nothing is good enough if it can be made a little better. The farmer is by nature a conservative. It is right that he should be so. He has inherited precious knowledge from those who have tilled the soil before him; and we do wrong if we hold the accumulated wisdom of our predecessors as of light account." The small man depending on fine margins was bound, above all, to tread the path of safety. It was for the leaders of agricultural enterprises to be the " pioneers of improvement ". " A spirit of enquiry," he continued, " is already abroad, but I think there may still be room for a greater spirit of adventure, and a more determined ambition to leave your land to your sons a little better than you found it. I was astonished to learn recently that from a single cotton plant given out for cultivation eighteen years ago as the result of scientific selection at the Lyallpur Farm, no less than 960,000 acres have been planted. That one fact alone is to me ample proof of the almost romantic results that may be attained by the application of scientific enquiry and analysis to agricultural problems." His mind was, in fact, well adjusted to India's diversity. His reverence for tradition, based on the historian's discriminating appreciation of the doctrines of Edmund Burke, combined with readiness to accept the boundless potentialities of scientific method, particularly fitted him for the task of leadership in a country where, in Morley's famous words, there is " a long slow march in uneven stages through all the centuries from the fifth to the twentieth ".

In his arduous tour of the North West Frontier Irwin was making contact with perilous and sombre lands where the influences of modern civilization had merely scratched the surface of tribal custom. Whether as traveller, historian or Viceroy he found himself face to face with compelling contrasts. His political sovereignty over these parts was dim, and as he made his way across the administrative border of the settled provinces into the mountainous regions of the so-called transborder, which in its turn is bounded by the Durand Line, political rule merged into military occupation. He had first of all to consider the Frontier from the view-point of India's external relations; in the words of the Survey, "The North West Frontier is still the solar plexus of the British power in Asia." But in this respect peace prevailed. There was no Napoleon on the scene to dream of emulating the triumphs of Alexander. There was no specific threat from Soviet Russia. Amanullah's little war in 1920 had ended with a frank renunciation of British control over Afghan foreign policy, and Amanullah was now fully engaged on his frantic search for dress clothes and top-hats with which to Westernize his bewildered tribesmen.

The most difficult problems of government were presented by the no-man's-land between the administrative border and the Durand Line, which was under the day-to-day jurisdiction of aptly named political officers. Irwin made a very thorough inspection of this area. His journey up the fateful Khyber Pass was described by a correspondent as "an interesting break in the round of desperately hard work involved in the present tour". Here he gathered the fruits of peace and received cordial greetings from the chieftains of the fierce Afridi and Shinwari tribes. He was able to widen the range of his visit by obtaining what was literally a bird's-eye view of the Frontier. "I can claim to have viewed the Frontier question," he told his audience at Peshawar, "from a different angle from any of my predecessors, as it has not been the good fortune of any previous Viceroy to view the Frontier from the air as I have to-day. Perhaps my most lively impression was the suddenness with which the rich and fertile plains of Peshawar merge into the barren hills of Independent territory. I felt that in that sharp contrast was typified the whole Frontier problem as it existed in the times of the Great Sikandar, of Mahmud of Ghazni, of the Mogul Emperors, and as it exists to-day."

But he could emphasize progress. Flying over the Peshawar Valley he looked down on "the cluster of buildings not far from the mouth of the Khyber Pass which form the Islamia College. It is both significant and appropriate that almost the first scene which strikes the eye of the traveller from Central Asia should be this tangible proof of the value that the North West Frontier Province ascribes to her higher education which she has thus pushed forward to the very gates of tribal territory." Islamia College was primarily for the sons of the frontier chiefs and represented an ambitious attack on the traditional lawlessness of the tribes. Just how formidable they were can be estimated when it is realized that they can boast the astonishingly high proportion of three-quarters of a million fighting men out of a total population of about three millions. In addition they must rank among the toughest fighters in the world, against whom, under cover of their own difficult country, only the most highly trained troops have any chance of survival. It was estimated in 1920 that at least 140,000 modern rifles were in tribal territory.

The tribes have close affinities as well as persistent feuds, and the quarrel of one with the British was as often as not the quarrel of all. The Sikhs did not hand over to the British any consistent policy, and for a long time there was controversy between the "forward" and "close border" schools of thought, between the advocates of penetration and of non-interference. As is customary with British policy, a compromise was reached in Curzon's great Frontier settlement by which the tribesmen were paid to keep order in their own country and regular troops were withdrawn. The idea of occupation was abandoned, but the tribes were given a vested interest in their own good behaviour. By Irwin's time this policy had reached an advanced stage, and the first elements of self-government were being brought to the most intractable territory of all, Waziristan.

After a successful visit to the outpost of Malakand, that other historic route into India down which Alexander's armies passed two thousand years ago, leaving roads that are still in use, Irwin made his way south until he reached Waziristan itself. Although no lover of ceremonial, he was not so prejudiced against it as not to recognize the right time and place for it. Nothing could have been better judged than his State entry into Razmak, or his reception of Mahsud jirgas or delegations. Seated on the balcony of the Razmak garrison he looked down on a hundred or so turbaned and bearded Mahsud leaders squatting before him, magnificent men for whom these few moments of direct and personal contact with the Viceroy were worth years of indirect and subordinate relationship. In his tour of the various frontier outposts—Idak, Miranshah, Razani—and in his speeches and inspections he was making something more than a formal contribution to probably the most hazardous experiment in British Frontier policy. For he was the first Viceroy ever to visit Waziristan; to the Waziris the fact that he should have chosen so early in his Viceroyalty to break the new ground was taken to be both a signal compliment to themselves and reassuring evidence that no reversal of Government policy would be countenanced.

Irwin, for his part, was able to travel along splendid high-roads driven through what he called "forbidding hills", to rely on the protection of the Khassadars or tribal police, by now almost in sole charge, to promise his "earnest consideration" of further Reforms, and his "personal sympathy" for improved irrigation. "I listened with much concern to your story of the difficulties with which the inhabitants of the Marwat Tehsil have to contend in obtaining a supply of drinking water. I can well realize the hardships which they must suffer in the pitiless heat of the summer." The whole tone and temper of Irwin's outlook as revealed by this remarkable Viceregal tour was a challenge alike to easygoing or reactionary ways of thought. There was far from unanimous support either among the Civil Service or the Army in India for encouraging tribal democracy, an excess of which, it was argued, was at the root of most disturbances. But Irwin at a critical stage in the policy's development determined to see for himself, and what he saw, he found good. Accordingly with an emphasis —based not on technique but on deep personal resolve— he put the whole weight of his authority behind the experiment in order to give it the greatest possible momentum for its ultimate success.

The same note was struck in his visit immediately afterwards to the Native State of Bahawalpur, where he inspected the vast Sutlej canal work, the official opening of which in April he had been unable through illness to attend. He promised then to see it at the earliest possible moment, and in keeping that promise proclaimed again his profound interest in all instruments bringing India the material benefits of the modern age. Control over the waters of the mighty Indus and Sutlej would bring new cultivation and enlightenment to vast areas of what has been described as "legend haunted desert dominated by feudal strongholds ". Enjoying, or perhaps more accurately undergoing, his first experience on the back of a camel, Irwin rode out to see a new canal colony village, and, it is reported, was duly regaled with the sight of a good winter crop and of unorthodox ploughing with teams of camels and buffaloes.

Contemporary accounts unite in emphasizing the value of Irwin's " personal touch " throughout the tour, and this was largely because it compromised not simply the status of the Viceroy but the forthright perception of the farmer. He was unstinting of time and energy; so full was the programme he had set himself that it was found necessary for Lady Irwin to undertake a miniature and highly successful tour of her own in order to complete it. The verdict which perhaps most effectively pays tribute to his achievement is the sober but none the less sincere statement of a journalist at the time, " the Frontier has met Lord Irwin and accepted him ".

CHAPTER XIII

THE PROBLEM OF THE PRINCES

In November we come upon another aspect of Irwin's vast hegemony when he delivered the first of his formal Addresses at the opening of a session of the Chamber of Princes. Literally speaking this was one of his few purely Viceregal functions. The Princes, jealous of their ill-defined prerogatives, are quick to distinguish between the Viceroy or representative of the King-Emperor, and the Governor-General, a title derived from the time of the East India Company, or head of the Government of India and president of an Executive Council the authority of which they in no way recognize. As Edward Thompson justly observes,[1] "That in practice the distinction is difficult to keep up, since Viceroy and Governor-General are one and the same person, makes no difference in their attitude." The extent of their rule is enormous, and however loudly Congress leaders might deplore their continued existence, it was evident that no constitutional advance was possible that did not take into full account their views and their power.

The Chamber of Princes, one of the principal innovations of the Montagu-Chelmsford Reforms, gave direct representation to one hundred and eight of the States, a further one hundred and twenty-seven were represented by twelve members; this left over three hundred petty States unrepresented in the new order and with little option but to sink back into their proper position as a feudal baronage. The one hundred and eight directly represented States cover half a million square miles and comprise nearly sixty million inhabitants, while the remaining one hundred and twenty-seven are contained in a mere six thousand miles with a population of less than a million. The Chamber of Princes was in itself little more than an advisory and consultative body more fitted for discussing grievances than for pressing

[1] *Reconstruction of India*, page 209.

them home. On the other hand it helped to develop among its heterogeneous membership the sense of a common interest.

When Irwin succeeded Reading he found the atmosphere somewhat embittered by the Berar dispute, which involved the prerogatives of the Premier Prince, the Nizam of Hyderabad. The Nizam was ruler of a State bigger in area than Great Britain, and in population and wealth than many European nations, one of the five chieftains entitled to a twenty-one gun salute, and himself not only reputed to be the richest man in the world, but also the enlightened advocate of social reform, and altogether a determined and forceful personality. Treaties were originally made with the Princes when Britain was one of several Paramount Powers and, it was claimed, were signed on a basis of equality as between two High Contracting Parties. The Nizam put this claim to the test when he demanded in September 1925 the return under treaty of the Province of Berar, which he asserted his father had bartered away overawed by the great genius of Lord Curzon and without understanding his position under existing treaties. He spoke of "two Governments that stand in the same plane without any limitations of subordination of one to the other". Lord Reading was undoubtedly disturbed by the request, but made no answer until the following March, a month before Irwin's arrival, when in a letter of insulting severity as from King-Emperor to a recalcitrant subject the Nizam was informed that the Berar matter could not be considered and that "the sovereignty of the British Crown is supreme in India and therefore no ruler of an Indian State can justifiably claim to negotiate with the British Government on an equal footing. Its supremacy is not based only upon treaties and engagements, but exists independently of them."

Such was the humiliating end of a request which summed up the secret aspirations of the vast majority of the Princes. The Nizam, in the role of the sulking Achilles, temporarily retired from the Chamber of Princes and was aggressively absent when Irwin made his first effort to heal the breach. The situation had not been improved by negotiations during the summer between the Nizam and the Government about the administration of Hyderabad, which the more sensational and not wholly disinterested Press interpreted as a further example of British determination to clip the Princes' wings. In addition there was a recent abduction scandal involving a favourite dancing-girl who had left a Maharajah to live with a Bombay merchant. The merchant was murdered while he and the girl were driving together in a car in Bombay. A Commission was set up under procedure which was recommended by the Montagu-Chelmsford Report, but which the Princes had already sharply criticized, to enquire into the Maharajah's alleged complicity. The Maharajah, however, refused the enquiry and chose to abdicate, adhering to the belief that " neither on the analogy of international law nor as a matter resting upon treaty is a Prince of my position liable to be tried "

Against such a background of controversy Irwin had no easy task in conciliating the suspicions of the Princes without repudiating the high-handed attitude of his predecessor. Once again he relied heavily on the personal touch. At the outset of what was one of his longest and most comprehensive speeches in India he invoked the memory of the first Lord Halifax. " I can claim indeed," he declared, " something in the nature of a hereditary interest in the Indian States, as one of the best remembered actions of my grandfather, as Secretary of State for India, was his approval of Lord Canning's proposals for the grant of the adoption *sanads* to the Rulers of the principal States." The reference was to a major act of statesmanship, formally revoking by means of *sanads* or Letters of Recognition to about one hundred and fifty States the British refusal to acknowledge the right of the Princes to adopt heirs, which refusal during the Mutiny aroused deep and dangerous enmities. Actually the Princes have never admitted that these *sanads* involved any right, not previously enjoyed, but Irwin was justified in recalling them in as far as they brought about a new era of goodwill between the Princes and the Paramount Power and symbolized the relationship he himself was seeking.

The whole emphasis in his speech was in contrast to the Reading approach. The States, as he pointed out, had their place in his philosophy of history and seemed " to stand astride the centuries ", but over and above that, he managed to convey to them his belief in the vital part they and British India alike had to play in " the world task of building a better and greater future than the past or present ". Here was perhaps his greatest contribution to Indian political thought. From his supreme position he saw India in a fresh perspective. He countered the arrogance that arises from a deep sense of inferiority, and the various internal dissensions by investing the sum total of Indian life with a new importance. He attacked its political and social introversions by ignoring them.

It was in this spirit of a greater unity that he asked the Princes to visualize themselves as "partners" in India, to waive their persistent claims to increased control over Customs revenues, to set up a Standing Committee to hold informal talks with him and his advisers, and to give more support to the Chiefs' Colleges and so to ensure the quality of their own and their nobles' education. In his appeal to them to lead a crusade against the traffic in opium he emphasized India's membership of the League of Nations. Abuse of opium was "a reproach cast on India in the eyes of the world". If it was necessary to reject their full demands over the status of Minority Administrations, "to offer advice" to absentee Rulers, and even to intervene in the internal government of the States "in extreme cases", the dominating impression left with the Princes—already confirmed by personal contacts—was of a discreet and God-fearing man who could be trusted in the exercise of admittedly ill-defined powers, and whose will to conciliation was the outcome of strength and not of weakness. There was about him a personal integrity which consistently attracted the Indian mind.

. . . .

That his popularity was genuine and already overflowing could be seen by the ovations he received in December during his first visits to Cawnpore, Allahabad and Calcutta. The official festivity of flags, fairy lights and fireworks could not alone have made these occasions live in the memory—it was the surging enthusiasm of the crowds. Calcutta, the scene of so much communal disturbance, with its industrial overcrowding and cheap labour, was naturally fertile soil for the political extremist. Actually when Irwin arrived the Swarajists were protesting vehemently against the imprisonment of their young leader and hero, the city's chief Executive Officer, Subhas Chandra Bose, and had organized a demonstration under the lyrical banner "Bengal's heart bleeds white while Subhas lies in Mandalay gaol". There was certainly no need to take action against the demonstrators, their efforts were swamped in the triumph of Irwin's ceremonial entry. He refused to take the customary short route and deliberately drove through a considerable part of North Calcutta where the rioting had occurred the previous Easter. During his stay he made several speeches, the background to which was intrusive nationalist agitation for the release of Bose and the other *détenus*; but Irwin picked upon the capital of Bengal, which of all the Provinces was most deeply engaged in professional agitation, to display his fundamental quality of detachment and develop his belief in the policies and principles that lie behind politics.

At the Bengal Club he invoked the doctrine of trusteeship as defined by Burke in his famous speech on Fox's India Bill. To-day it would be " a huge mistake " to suppose that " politics and the play of political forces " were the sum of the Government's contribution to India's future. Thus for the peaceful development of the North West Frontier, " we have not forced upon the tribes any exasperating regulations that would merely antagonize people who worship the individual but doubt the authority of the law. We trust rather for our influence to the name of British justice and to the personality of the British official, and I cannot speak too highly of the way in which they have justified that trust."

Then again to a gathering largely made up of British officials at the United Services Club he urged, " it may well be that we politicians have been accustomed to regard ourselves as specialists and to overrate the mysterious nature of our profession. But the truth is that men are more important than politics." He did not shirk the political issues, however, and significantly enough, addressing the influential European Association, he set out in detail his attitude to the insistent problem of constitutional advance. It is clear from this speech that Irwin's opinion on the vexed question of Dominion Status had taken shape by December 1926, and that he was already well aware of the volume and intensity of the opposition he might expect in due course from his Conservative friends at Westminster. " To them I would only say that whether Great Britain will ultimately be judged right or wrong in seeking to guide India along this path it was hardly possible that she should have acted differently.

The path of nations, as well as that of individuals, is greatly influenced by inherited character."

His criticism of the Reforms was "in the realm of principle". By this standard "power and responsibility ought to go hand in hand, and power is only safely exercised by those who have a sense of equivalent responsibility". Accordingly in the period of transition or training in responsibility through which India was now passing there was bound to be "some failure to reach the ideal adjustment of responsibility to power". "Speaking of central politics," he continued—and the passage should be noted carefully in the context of the approaching struggle—"so long as there is in the hands of the Governor-General reserve power by which in the last resort they can secure what they conceive to be essential, it is evidently possible for popular representatives to escape the sense of responsibility that ought to accompany the power, even though only partial, which they exercise. Again, so long as the Government of India is not fully responsible, in the strict sense of the word, it is impossible for parties or politicians to feel the salutary check of being compelled to replace in the task of government those who have been the targets of their criticism and attack. It therefore follows that one of the principal distinctions between the different Indian parties is apt to be the degree of vehemence with which they assail the policy of Government. The latter, necessarily in great degree inarticulate, is presented as the common opponent of patriotic citizens." These were real difficulties so long as it was necessary for the final power to be retained by a Government not directly or wholly responsible to popularly elected representatives.

How would Parliament act? It had no preconceived ideas, it would react sympathetically to India's own political developments. "But if Parliament is a well-wisher it is also a shrewd and competent judge, and Parliament will, I suspect, realize that at the root of the whole question lies the problem of what I may call the average political sense of a wide electorate. An educated electorate is the only sure basis of democracy. Without it politics are the possession of a small class of intelligentsia, and the leaders of political thought who must be pioneers of political development would be the first to realize that in these conditions the political system, instead of resting broad based on intelligent popular judgment, is insecurely poised on an inverted apex. We have unhappily witnessed in the last few months a deplorable exhibition of communal narrowness and animosity. Let there be nothing communal in the European outlook on Indian politics." From the emphasis in this speech he never departed, and those who expressed indignant surprise later on at Irwin's policy of conciliation and fulfilment had only themselves to blame—no new Viceroy could have done more to stress the trend of his thoughts. Admittedly, political developments during the coming year did little to assist Irwin, but he was abundantly justified in underlining from his own view-point and with his special authority the weaknesses of the Reforms.

It was not until November that Baldwin and Birkenhead announced the historic decision to send out the Simon Commission in terms that were unfortunately to stir up the very bitterness they were intended to allay. In the meanwhile a dangerous and delicate situation had arisen in India, the outcome of a complex variety of causes over which Irwin had very little direct control. In the first place Congress, after a period of comparative impotence, which had been largely produced by internal divisions and the persistent efforts of sectional interests to dominate its platform and which prompted G. T. Garratt to assert in 1925 that "Congress politically has shot its bolt", took on a new lease of life. In Central politics it identified itself with opposition to the Currency Commission and to Irwin's brilliant Finance Minister, Sir Basil Blackett, over the highly technical question of the stabilization of the rupee, and in doing so, gained the wholehearted support of the Hindu moneyed interests. In the Provinces, particularly in Bengal and the Punjab, Congress propaganda had much to do with a new outbreak of terrorist crime.

But over and above deliberate political campaigns there was considerable economic depression and industrial unrest in India at this time. American business men and Indian Nationalists from their different angles did not hesitate to attribute these calamities to the decadent or dominant but essentially "satanic" influence of Britain. During the year 1927-1928 no less that thirty million working days were lost in strikes, an immense increase on earlier figures, while for

POMP AND CIRCUMSTANCE

Attended by resplendent Viceregal bodyguard Lord and Lady Irwin walk down the steps of the Belvedere, Calcutta, to a farewell Garden Party, preceded by the Governor of Bengal, Sir Stanley Jackson, and Lady Jackson, December, 1930

the first time the harsh dialect of Marx was heard over the land and, to quote the historian, " added to the general confusion and insincerity of post-war Indian politics ".[1] All this upheaval was intensified by the unabated fury of the Communal riots. The Hindu Mahasabha and the Moslem League, still waxing in power and prestige, gave no lead to religious settlement in an atmosphere of impending political change. Both were to a large extent dominated in their attitude to Reforms by the growth under Diarchy of a regular system of spoils and patronage to which there was but limited access.

As if this spurious and bloodstained rivalry was not enough, India was subjected to a bout of hysteria with all its ugly manifestations of mutual hatred following the publication of Katherine Mayo's *Mother India.* Admittedly this volume was enough to provoke the most long-suffering of Indian Moderates. It assaulted the social and moral strongholds of Hinduism; it was a scornful indictment of a whole way of life written with the passion of a preacher but the status of a tourist. This last fact many Indians in their fury overlooked, and it was widely suggested that the British Government had sponsored it. If Miss Mayo gave American opinion a chance to sympathize with the daily routine of British rule, she made it all too embarrassingly clear that the Indians were congenitally incapable of governing themselves. The second implication undid all the good of the first. In the exacting task of remoulding India's constitution, to which Irwin had by now dedicated himself, this book was a distracting influence. Only Gandhi and Irwin, it seemed, remained aloof from the frenzy over *Mother India.* To the Mahatma it was " a drain inspector's report, a book for Englishmen to forget and Indians to remember ".[2] He was too devoted to truth to condemn it out of hand, but at that time his voice was not heard above the tumult.

Irwin, of course, from the nature of his Viceregal office could not devote himself exclusively to any one problem, and much of his time had to be given up to ceremonial duties. At the beginning of 1927 there were two such occasions which had a rather wider significance. First was the com-

[1] Thompson and Garratt, *Rise and Fulfilment of British Rule in India,* page 629.

[2] Glorney Bolton, *Tragedy of Gandhi,* page 195.

pletion of Sir Samuel Hoare's famous flight from London to Delhi. The journey took in all thirteen days, though the 6,300 miles were completed in sixty-three flying hours, which must have been quite long enough for Sir Samuel, his wife and their party to be cooped up in their primitive Hercules machine. The flight was a fine achievement, and Hoare was able to underline British interest in India's aerial development and the Government's desire to make India the centre of flying in the East, as well as to look forward to the then remarkable prospect of weekly services between the two countries. All this led the chronicler eagerly to anticipate flights from London to Delhi before many years were out, taking no longer than the railway journey from Peshawar to Madras. At the airport Lady Irwin christened the plane *City of Delhi* and, raised on a small platform under the shadow of its propeller, Irwin aptly described it as adding one more to the many roads which lead to Delhi. Shortly afterwards his comparison of Hoare's flight with that of the annual migration of the sand-grouse from Central Asia to Bikaner (where he was speaking) and his reference to Hoare and his wife as " those strange birds of the air " were not perhaps quite such happy efforts!

Hoare as Air Minister had his Departmental business to attend to, but the presence of a Cabinet Minister, who was subsequently to blossom forth in Parliament as the supreme exponent of Indian Reform, gave Irwin an invaluable opportunity to exchange views and information. Hoare was not the first Government visitor to put Irwin into direct contact with London. Winterton, Birkenhead's second in command and Government spokesman on Indian affairs in the House of Commons, had already undertaken a comprehensive six weeks tour during which there was, no doubt, ample discussion. Hoare's visit may well have confirmed that Birkenhead was ready to set up a Commission when Irwin should say the word, but was irritated by Non-Co-operation and in no mood to consider any Round Table Conference until Indians had shown their willingness and ability to unite in deeds as well as words. It was clear, however, that Birkenhead's restiveness was not as yet directed against Irwin.

The other ceremony, the State opening of Sir Herbert Baker's grandiose Council Chamber at New Delhi, had far more formal magnificence about it than the christening of an aeroplane, but it is certainly arguable that when Sir Samuel Hoare stepped out of his machine he was performing an act of greater symbolic meaning for future Anglo-Indian relations than when Irwin turned the golden key to open the Council House. The whole building testified to hopes that had not been fulfilled. When the Duke of Connaught laid the foundation-stone in 1921 and formally launched the Reforms he could dilate with justice on India's rebirth to higher destinies, but when Irwin was honoured with a command from the King-Emperor to say that " the new capital that has arisen enshrines new institutions and a new national life ", there was an air of unreality about the proceedings which not even Irwin's massive oratory, or his plea that in the earlier design of the new city such a building as this had found no place, could wholly dispel. After suitably stressing the architect's noble conception of Indian unity in building the Princes' Chamber and the Legislative Councils within one immense circle of pillars, he escaped into metaphysics. " The circle stands for something more than unity. From earliest times it has been also our emblem of permanence, and the poet has seen in the ring of light a true symbol of eternity." But the only truth was that words alone could not breathe life into New Delhi. Its architecture might endure, but as a national capital it was still-born.

. . . .

A week afterwards Irwin's good intentions were to be further frustrated. In his address on 24th January 1927, opening the Delhi Session of the Legislative Assembly, he covered, as he was bound to do, a wide range of topics, but the essential purpose of the speech was to prepare the ground for a Royal Commission. This duty he discharged in the guise of a liaison officer with an admirably frank discussion of the relation and attitude of Parliament to the general problem of India's constitutional advance. It was a timely reminder to extremists to face realities and to Parliament itself to remember its pledges, but unfortunately in a brief preliminary progress report he had confirmed rumours that Indian troops would be sent out to China to assist the hard-pressed and meagre British forces engaged in protecting British life and property from the ravages of a confusing but none the less violent and widespread civil war. From this struggle Chiang Kai Shek emerged the champion of yet another brand of Asiatic nationalism. Irwin did his best to put the whole matter into correct perspective and to point out that British policy in China was purely defensive and that India had agreed to co-operate simply because her forces were immediately available and nearest to the scene of action. But such simple reasons were not readily accepted as true, served merely to stimulate a fierce attack in Press and Assembly, and in fact did nothing to cover up a tactical blunder.

Indian opinion lost sight of Irwin's closely reasoned defence of Parliamentary responsibility for constitutional development in the outcry over these Indian reinforcements for British bondholders. The Indian Press at once took up the theme that Britain was planning a war of aggression in the Far East in order to destroy whatever prospect of effective Chinese unity there might be from the Southern Army's successes. Congress papers spoke of Indians being made unwilling instruments of the perpetuation of China's slavery. As Austen Chamberlain was undergoing attacks in similar vein from Lloyd George and others, Irwin would have been well advised to resist the request with greater vigour. If he had done so, it is improbable that the British Government would have insisted on Indian reinforcements. As it was, the day after Irwin's speech Mr. Srinivasa Iyengar, the Swaraj Congress leader, moved the adjournment of the House in order to question the Government's right to send the troops to China without first consulting the Assembly. Sir Alexander Muddiman, the Home Member, objected on the grounds that such a motion would be bound to raise discussion affecting the relations not only of the Indian but also of the British Government with Foreign Powers. Patel the President, however, ruled that the motion was in order and directed that it should be taken up for discussion later on the same day. But before this could happen Irwin was obliged to exercise his powers under the Reforms and to disallow the motion "as affecting the relations of His Majesty's Government or of the Governor-General in Council with any Foreign State". It was the first time Irwin had been compelled to act in this way, but, given Congress's instructions to its members in the Assembly and Irwin's original complacence at Whitehall's decision, it was virtually unavoidable.

There was further material for dissension between Viceroy and Congress in Irwin's first public reference to the Bengal *détenus*, which was an extremely polite but equally stern refusal to release them. This decision was heralded as " imprudent callousness " and as showing that Irwin was " becoming imbued with the bureaucratic tradition " and was " bankrupt of far-seeing statesmanship "; but the language loses some of its force when it is recalled that Bose had just lost a libel action he had brought out against *The Statesman* for calling him the " directing brain of the terrorist organization ", which was ruled to be fair comment. Irwin could hardly have overruled so clear a verdict without undermining all confidence in Bengal's judicial processes. But the atmosphere of recrimination created by these comparatively minor issues weakened Irwin's position in the preliminary trial of strength between Government and Congress over the Currency Bill as well as in the subsequent and far greater struggle over the Statutory Commission.

For the next few months Irwin's public duties consisted largely of State visits to the Princes. The exacting formalities were interspersed with some much-needed rest and sport or were enlivened by purely picturesque occasions, as at Jamma when he and his family were placed on " gorgeously caparisoned " State elephants. He bagged four tigers in Bhopal, and at Srinagar enjoyed some duck-shooting. It was while Irwin was on holiday at Srinagar that Birkenhead on 30th March, in a comprehensive review of Indian affairs, gave the first official hint that there would be no objection to accelerating the appointment of the Statutory Commission, but he at once proceeded to spoil the offer by adopting a somewhat arrogant and patronizing tone. The Indian electorate was told that it no longer supported Non-Co-operation, while the Swarajists heard that they had lost ground; nor was there widespread satisfaction at learning from Birkenhead, of all people, that his objection to Indian politics was that they were swayed by the personalities of leaders rather than by political principles.

It is significant to note here that *The Times* takes Birkenhead to task in much the same way as Irwin would have done by suggesting that hero worship of the Party leaders is not an unhealthy sign when a people is new to Party politics. Birkenhead had praised his Viceroy in no uncertain terms for his lead in preaching peace between Hindu and Moslem. He had, he said, exercised important influence on Indian opinion, and, " untrammelled by traditional etiquette, has established far closer touch with the Indian peasant than any of his recent predecessors ". But for all that one detects a deeper appreciation of Irwin's position in Printing House Square than at the India Office, a readiness in fact to defend the Viceroy if necessary from his critics at home. The same *Times* leader commenting on Birkenhead and the Statutory Commission suggested that the ideal body would consist of judicially minded men who were able to agree. It would be no use filling it up with extremists. It is interesting to speculate how far Geoffrey Dawson, the Editor, was again expressing Irwin's thoughts and whether a deliberate *ballon d'essai* was being put up in favour of Sir John Simon. Be that as it may, Indian reaction to Birkenhead's speech through the Nationalist Press was so hostile as to suggest that whatever choice Birkenhead made would be automatically unsuitable. Even the *Times of India* sharply pointed out that the question was not whether the Commission was ready for India, but vice versa.

The contempt and bitterness with which Birkenhead's hint was received was in many ways a severer blow for Irwin than for Birkenhead himself, who spoke as though he expected hostilities and accordingly made no particular effort to avoid them. For Irwin it meant a further period of informal and private discussion with the leaders of British India and the States with whom he had by now established excellent personal relations; in particular he had made headway with the Moderates or Liberals, who in their determination to work the Reforms had broken with the Nationalists and without any considerable popular backing had gained considerable prestige through the statesmanship of such leaders as Sir Tej Bahadur Sapru and Jayakar. Sapru, like Sir William Beveridge or Gilbert Murray, was a splendid conference man, a brilliant drafter of the formula that will reconcile contradictory views. He understood every phase and aspect of negotiation, and in a period in which the conference method so dominated India's political horizon Sapru's help was indispensable.

. . . .

In July Irwin held conference with the Political Officers from the States and the Frontier. Proceedings were so secret that not even a communiqué was issued, though this last omission was probably because the Princes disliked public discussion of their affairs within the precincts of British India. Though Irwin respected this susceptibility, the purpose of the meetings must have been to find out whether the scope of the Commission could be so widened as to bring them into its terms of reference. Indeed, he told the Chamber of Princes in February 1928 that "in the course of those conversations it became clear to me that, if and when larger proposals involving wide changes in the present relationship between British India and the States fell to be actively considered, it would be of real importance that many matters of immediate relevance should have been previously examined".

It was at one of these "frank and friendly discussions" that he gave several of the Princes a private address on "Administration and Government" which served to emphasize the need for them to pursue domestic policies of enlightenment and reform if they were to play a worthy part within the framework of any constitutional plan for India as a whole. But on this particular occasion he revealed also, with an Aristotelian clarity, his own approach to the broader problem of how to reconcile the ancestral autocracies of the Native States with the basic traditions of British Democracy. In view of the momentous struggle in which the British Commonwealth is engaged against the Nazi doctrines of the master race and the slave state, and in view also of many misconceptions about British aims in India, the brief Notes of his Address, bald and impersonal as they are, constitute a timely refutation of those critics who glibly assert that the British Raj maintains the Princes as feudal relics with callous indifference to the welfare of their subjects simply in order to rule India by keeping it divided. Perhaps the Princes would not have survived to this day without the backing of the Raj, but with that backing goes a volume of advice on the arts of responsible self-government which they can afford to ignore only at their peril.

Irwin's historic personal contribution to this advice, which he is now allowing to be published for the first time, represents a broad outline of policy by which I am authorized to say he stands firmly to-day. The Notes are set out in the following twelve points:

I. The function of Government may be described as the task, firstly, of ensuring to the individuals composing the society governed, the opportunity of developing themselves as human beings, and, secondly, of welding them into a compact and contented State. The discharge of this double function involves the necessity of finding and maintaining the due balance between the rights of the individual and those of the State to which he belongs.

II. Stated differently, the ordered life of a community depends upon being regulated, not by the arbitrary will of individuals, but by LAW, which should expressly or tacitly be based upon and represent the general will of the community.

This is equally true of Autocracy, Oligarchy, Democracy, and the efforts of rulers, therefore, whether they be One or Many, should be directed to the establishment of the REIGN OF LAW.

III. The application of these principles implies—among other needs—

(*a*) the protection of individual liberty, rights, property, etc.;

(*b*) the provision of adequate machinery for the adjustment of disputes between individuals;

(*c*) the provision of adequate machinery of justice, i.e. proper code of law, law courts, appeals, etc.;

(*d*) the recognition of the equality of all members of the State before the law.

IV. These things depend upon—

(i) an administration conducted in accordance with the law;

(ii) an efficient and uncorrupt police force;

(iii) an efficient judicial system, strong in *personnel* who are secure from arbitrary interference by the executive and are secure in the tenure of their office so long as they do their duty.

V. The fundamental purpose of Government stated in I implies that Government must follow definite principles in –

(*a*) the collection of revenue from its subjects;

(*b*) the expenditure of revenue so collected.

VI. REVENUE. Taxation should be –

(1) as light as possible;

(2) easy of collection; otherwise the annoyance caused to the Taxpayer is out of proportion to the benefit to the State;
(3) certain—i.e. the Taxpayer should be able to forecast his liability;
(4) proportionate to the means of the Taxpayer to pay.

VII. EXPENDITURE. From this it follows that the proportion of revenue allotted to the personal expenditure of the Ruler should be as moderate as will suffice to maintain his position and dignity, in order that as large a proportion as possible may be available for the development of the life of the community and of its individual citizens. The civil list of an enlightened modern Ruler is normally fixed at either a definite sum, or a definite percentage of the total income of the State.

VIII. Under the general head of development fall—

The creation and maintenance of roads and communications.
Education.
Health and other social services.
Agriculture.
Housing, etc.

The devolution of many such subjects to local bodies makes for good government.

IX. Government must be, by the nature of its task, *responsible*, not *irresponsible* in character.

In democracy, it is responsible to a wide electorate, but where this visible responsibility does not exist (as, e.g., in autocracy), its inherent responsibility to its own purpose as defined in I remains.

X. Every Government should have some machinery by which it can inform itself of the needs and desires of its subjects, and by which these can make their voice heard.

This machinery need not be strictly representative (or elective) in character, but its essential requisite is that it should maintain a close connection between Government and Governed.

XI. There are other matters, such as religious toleration, the encouragement of mutual confidence and harmony between employers and employed, in which Government may not be able to make effective use of law, but in which it is none the less bound to direct its influence towards the preservation of friendly and neighbourly relations between the different component parts of the single unity of the State.

XII. Perhaps the principal necessity for a personal Ruler is that he should be able to choose wise counsellors, and having chosen them that he should trust them, and encourage them to tell him the truth, whether or not this is always palatable.

There is much wisdom in the words of Bacon:

"Thinke it more Honour to direct in chiefe, than to be busie in all. Embrace, and invite Helps, and Advices, touching the Execution of thy Place; And doe not drive away such, as bring thee Information, as Medlers, but accept them in good part."

14.6.27

Herein were contained the minimum human rights which the Princes were called upon by the Viceroy to vouchsafe to their peoples if a wider collaboration with British India was to be undertaken. Beyond that, what precise form such collaboration might take Irwin may not as yet have closely considered.

CHAPTER XIV

PREPARATIONS FOR SIMON

"THE idea of an all-India Federation", according to Thompson and Garratt, "was introduced into Indian politics in the same casual manner as diarchy. It did not develop logically from previous constitutional experiments nor was it the fruit of long political agitation."[1] Yet in Irwin's negotiations, now officially taken over and sponsored by Birkenhead, we may perhaps detect one of the opening moves in a whole series of political thrusts and counter-thrusts which were to culminate in the general acceptance of a Federal solution. But for the present Irwin had to work along inner lines, and in August he returned to the theme of Hindu-Moslem rivalry in a last desperate effort to produce some semblance of united purpose before announcing the Statutory Commission. Once again the Communal leaders felt the full force of a mind trained in the pursuit of religious compromise and in the expression of moral values.

He spoke of Calcutta as "under the mastery of some evil spirit, which so gripped the minds of men that in their insanity they held themselves absolved from the most sacred restraints of human conduct". National self-government was impossible without the self-government and self-control of individuals and merely served to "disguise under an honourable title the continuance of something perilously akin to civil war". Great Britain and India were partners in the task of achieving self-government for India. "I cannot reconcile it," he added fervently, "with my conception of a real and effective partnership in this matter between Great Britain and India to confine the responsibility, either of myself or my Government, to a mere repression of disorder. Necessary as that is, the situation, as I see it to-day, demands a more constructive effort", which, being interpreted, was a willingness to mediate if called upon by re-

[1] *Rise and Fulfilment of British Rule in India*, page 625.

sponsible Hindu and Moslem leaders to do so. The initiative he had refused to take after the Chelmsford Club speech, however urgent now, was still as liable to political misinterpretation. Indeed the rumours of a Statutory Commission made the party leaders more than ever sensitive about their claims, and their response to the Viceroy's offer was even more suspicious and unhelpful than it probably would have been a year before. Well-informed observers at Simla noted that their immediate reaction was to harden their hearts because the Viceroy was encroaching on spheres of influence that belonged to Congress and the Legislative Assembly.

Irwin's argument merely had the effect of bringing to the surface the fundamental Congress aim of Independence which it was Irwin's primary objective to bury by a policy of Partnership through Commission and Conference. Even Conference was as yet hardly on the horizon of practical politics, and if in the meanwhile the Congress were to be provoked into making Independence its be-all and end-all a situation of the utmost gravity would be bound to develop. Nationalist Press comment on Irwin's appeal throws some light on the delicacy and dangers of his position. *Forward* recognized that India's salvation lay in freeing the country from the influence of bigoted fanatics and political self-seekers, but doubted whether *foreigners*[1] with the best intentions could be of any help. While *The Bombay Chronicle* went so far as to call the proposals disappointing and insulting. The Viceroy evidently had a low opinion of the mind and conscience of India if he imagined her people would accept his diagnosis of her present malady as fair and accurate. "The outstanding fact of the Indian situation is not communal tension, but the denial of freedom, and until Indians become complete masters in their own country they cannot remove communal tension or bring about other social reforms."

This approach was symptomatic. All parties were putting up their price, but the tragedy was that when India at last had a Viceroy who really believed in the Conference method, the Swarajists, under the influence of younger leaders such as the Pandit Jawaharlal Nehru and Subhas Chandra Bose, began to move away from their allegiance to it, which Congress had proclaimed ever since 1921, in

[1] The italics are mine.

favour of the doctrine of National Independence. The dilemma of Indian politics is that they are always once removed from reality. As soon as India had a Viceroy ready by temperament and conviction to translate co-operation from a phrase into a policy, Congress was attracting to itself fresh influences that were already rejecting interest in the Round Table Conference idea altogether.

. . . .

The next three years of Irwin's life is, in essence, the story of his gigantic attempt to resolve this endless frustration whereby British Reformers were always adopting the cause Indian Nationalists had just abandoned. For such sustained personal endeavour it is hard to find a parallel in the annals of British Viceroyalty. In a period when British leadership was for the most part dull and diffident, Irwin's lonely struggle for India's nationhood had about it an epic quality. Not the least remarkable feature in his final achievement was his initial defeat. For how else can be described the veritable holocaust of anger following his formal announcement of the personnel and terms of reference of the Simon Commission?

It is not so much a matter of apportioning blame as of recording that there was a clear lack of liaison between Whitehall and Viceregal House and a deplorable lack of tact in the handling of the Indian leaders. Expectations were aroused when it was known that Irwin had at last asked Gandhi to New Delhi. Eighteen months had passed, and he had consulted with the leaders of every shade of opinion except with the one man who more than all of them put together could claim to speak for India as a whole. There can be no doubt but that Irwin's religious emphasis had made a profound impression on the Mahatma, who was still officially in retirement. From the recesses of his famous Sabarmati Ashram he, too, was grappling with the problem of Communal dissension, but in retreat, and by simply adding to his disciples a few Moslems who were already prepared to take a national view of their duties. The leader of these Nationalists in the Congress was Dr. Ansari, the distinguished surgeon, but neither he nor even Gandhi himself were dominating Congress at this time. In fact Gandhi was so far removed from active politics in November 1927 that he was at first uncertain whether he should accept

Irwin's invitation. Overcoming his scruples he was ushered into the Viceregal presence along with Patel, Iyengar and Dr. Ansari, who was actually President Elect of the forthcoming Madras Congress. Altogether Irwin saw during the next few days four leaders of Congress, three of the Nationalist Party, three Moslem Leaguers, two Liberals and two Independents.

Then on 8th November this orgy of private negotiation was publicly explained by a lengthy Statement under Irwin's signature introducing the Simon Commission. Its laborious arguments and balanced phrases, however, merely underlined the painful fact that the purpose of Irwin's talks with the leaders was just to inform them that their collaboration and advice were no longer needed. The Commission had been chosen without either. Never had Indian leadership felt itself to be so affronted. It was reasonable to expect, in view of his unusual regard for the doctrines of self-government, that Irwin would not call leaders together unless he had some responsible status to offer them. But, as Edward Thompson pungently put it, "the good kind Government looked benevolently at these expectant children and then announced that it had a piece of interesting news—that seven English gentlemen were coming out to have a look round India, and then to give advice as to what should be done about India."[1] But it was not even news—all the details had been fully and accurately announced in the British and Indian Press four days in advance of the Viceroy's statement. "Yes, sir," replied Mr. Baldwin to the troublesome questioner in the House of Commons, "I have no information as to how that leakage has occurred. To the best of our belief, it occurred in India."

Undoubtedly the most distressing aspect to the Indian leaders of this lame and somewhat shabby procedure was that Irwin should have had any part in it. The statement was decisive evidence that Irwin had supported the exclusion of Indians from the Commission. "For myself," he had written, "I cannot doubt that the quickest and surest path of those who desire Indian progress is by the persuasion of Parliament that they can do this more certainly through members of both Houses of Parliament than in any other way. The Indian Nationalist has gained much if he can

[1] *The Reconstruction of India*, page 153.

convince Members of Parliament on the spot, and I would therefore go further and say that if those who speak for India have confidence in the case which they advance on her behalf, they ought to welcome such an opportunity being afforded to as many members of the British legislature as may be, thus to come into contact with the realities of Indian life and politics." That he put forward a good case made it none the less galling. A Commission with a substantial number of Indian representatives, he argued, would have to include British official members as well, yet neither could be expected " to reach conclusions unaffected by *a priori* reasoning ". Unless the Commission was unbiased, Parliament would inevitably approach consideration of its Report with " some element of mental reservation ".

More alarming than all this, however, for those who identified their own political hopes with Irwin's, was the blurred account he gave of the status of Simon and his colleagues, whether they were, in fact, inquisitors or *rapporteurs.* If it was to be an inquisition into India's fitness for self-government it mattered little that the Indian Party leaders would have full opportunity of laying their views before them or be allowed the right to challenge their findings by sending delegations to a Joint Select Committee of both Houses of Parliament, which was to take further evidence before Parliament reached its final decision—the whole conception of the original reforms was undermined from the outset. Instead of going forward from the spirit of the 1921 Act, the Commission might actually become a pretext for revoking it and returning to the Morley-Minto dispensation. Some such design may well have been at the back of Birkenhead's mind, although it is more likely that he agreed to advance the Commission two years ahead of statutory requirement to forestall a possible Labour Government in 1929, as well as to reinstate himself with a Conservative rank and file, intensely suspicious of his Coalition record, by means of a spectacular success in India. He could not fail to remember, however, that these self-same Conservatives had approved the clause in the Reforms setting up the Commission as a safeguard and check on a dangerous democratic experiment.

Although Irwin's attitude was in no way affected by Birkenhead's past or the Government's future, his Statement represents an uneasy compromise with these distracting influences. The Commission itself was an inoffensive body. In Sir John Simon as Chairman, India was assured of the services of Britain's most expensive lawyer, a Liberal from whose career most of the Party groups could derive some satisfaction. His colleagues were, to quote *The Times*, "second flight" men; the reason for this was that no man with any considerable political prospects was likely to exile himself from the Parliamentary scene at Westminster for two whole years, during which a General Election was scheduled to take place. They comprised two Peers, Lord Burnham and Lord Strathcona, neither of them with any Cabinet experience, four back-bench Members of Parliament, two Conservatives and two Socialists—one of the Socialists was the then wholly unknown Mr. Attlee, without influence in his Party and chosen, as Birkenhead frankly admitted, without the Secretary of State ever having met him. Of greater political and personal significance was the selection of Colonel George Lane Fox, Irwin's brother-in-law and intimate lifelong friend, with whom he had first set forth on his political career. Rumour at once asserted that Lane Fox was to be the entrepreneur between the Commission and the Viceroy and that his presence only went to show how deeply Irwin was involved in the whole idea and formation of the Commission.

If Irwin's primary purpose had been to promote some semblance of Indian unity, some general formula that would smooth the way for Simon and his colleagues and eliminate factious controversy, he was to be completely baffled. The next three months was a continuous babel of boycott resolutions, claim and counter-claim, from which one deplorable fact alone emerged, that India was divided against herself, and united only in a general hostility to the Simon Commission, the political value of which was effectively undermined before even it set foot on Indian soil. Gandhi at once returned to his Ashram, no doubt regretting that he had ever left it. He made it clear to his followers, however, that he liked the new Viceroy; "whatever the differences between Lord Irwin and myself," he was reported to have said, "the new Governor-General is a man I can trust to tell me what he thinks." Gandhi's immediate reaction to Irwin, his appraisement of the man behind the statesman, must not be

FAREWELL TO THE PRINCES

Irwin as retiring Viceroy shakes hands with rulers of the Native States before leaving Bombay for his homeward journey to England. April, 1931

overlooked. It was a far more impressive gesture than many of the somewhat theatrical attitudes adopted at this time.

Gandhi does not allow of any essential distinctions between political and moral judgment; for him personality is the mainspring of politics, and the quality of a man's actions is largely to be found in the quality of the man himself. It is a political philosophy which Gandhi has reinforced with an astonishing insight into human character. His vision in this respect is both an inborn talent and the outcome of intense religious application, and his favour is thus never a formal or barren compliment. Gandhi detected at once in Irwin the three great gifts of sincerity, simplicity and humility, saw that he, too, believed in character and tried to live up to his belief. The devout Christian and the devout Hindu had a bond of faith and an understanding of each other not shared by sceptics or dialectical materialists.

But the personal goodwill between Viceroy and Mahatma was as yet merely a latent force. The ambiguities underlying Irwin's statement of 8th November were far from providing Gandhi with a pretext to emerge from his Ashram and exert a moderating influence on Congress, which duly met at Madras, gleefully boycotted the Simon Commission and everything to do with it. It went further. Srinivasa Iyengar, urged on by Jawaharlal Nehru, successfully moved a Resolution declaring for complete Independence. Nehru's all-consuming energy had prevailed over the more limited desires of Gandhi and the older leaders, and had persuaded them that Dominion Status was not a clear enough challenge to the policy embodied in the Commission. All this was sufficiently dangerous, but the Moslems, traditional protégés of the British, were split in two on the issue of boycott. One half of the Moslem League met at Lahore under Sir Mohammed Shafi, a former member of the Viceroy's Executive Council, and offered qualified support, while the other half followed the lead of Ali Jinnah, who had been chiefly responsible for reviving the League in 1924, in insisting on the boycott of the Commission and in adopting in principle a Congress Resolution to promote Hindu-Moslem unity. All the Commission would do, Jinnah asserted, would be to patch up the Constitution, and that was useless.

But worse even than Moslem dissensions was Sir Tej Bahadur Sapru's blank refusal to co-operate. His decision must have come as a profound shock to Irwin, who undoubtedly assumed that his vast knowledge of constitutional questions would be at Sir John Simon's disposal from the outset. Instead Sapru, presiding over a meeting of the Liberal Party at Madras, demanded that it should repudiate not only the Commission but the entire spirit in which the question of India's further advance had been approached by Parliament. On the other hand, other Moderate leaders, including Jayakar and Dr. Moonje, while resenting the lack of Indian representation, were ready to bargain over a Joint Committee to sit alongside Simon's colleagues and under Simon's jurisdiction. The opposition of powerful elements in the Hindu Mahasabha was assured when the venerable Malaviya urged boycott. These decisions were not in every case final, nor did they necessarily represent the views of Provincial leaders and followers, but the violence of the controversy made judicial and impartial enquiry, to say the least, difficult.

The situation had not been improved by Birkenhead's elaborate apologia in the House of Lords. For some unknown reason he allowed a fortnight to elapse between his speech and Irwin's Statement. There might have been an advantage in this delay if he had been prepared to appease India's wounded self-esteem. Instead he used the occasion to throw down a further challenge. "I have twice," he asserted, "in the three years during which I have been Secretary of State, invited our critics in India to put forward their own suggestions for a Constitution, to indicate to us the form which in their judgment any reform of the Constitution should take. That offer is still open." Taken in conjunction with an even balder suggestion he made to the leaders that they should produce "an agreed scheme", it amounted to a taunt that they could hardly ignore. Birkenhead's ponderous insolence remained with him throughout his public life, but a technique that was pure gold to the Oxford Union or for a maiden speech in Parliament was tinsel when applied to the vast theme of India. "Lord Birkenhead", wrote Philip Guedalla, "has managed to acquire a passable command of grave Johnsonian polysyllables. But his diction always bears traces of the grease paint; the style seems to come straight from Clarkson's; and that eloquent jurist struts in it like a self-conscious modern in Georgian fancy-dress." It is not surprising that Birkenhead's affectations infuriated Indian leaders, moderate and extremist alike, or that his cleverness was instrumental in goading them out of pride to take a false decision—to accept the challenge and produce the " agreed scheme ".

. . . .

But in the meanwhile Irwin made further efforts to impose his own calm and reflection in an atmosphere of increasing hysteria, recognizing that the Moslems, as far as a vote in the Legislative Assembly was concerned, held the balance. He did his utmost to bring Jinnah back into the fold and made a substantial offer to him. But it was too late; although Jinnah had not come out on the side of boycott immediately, he did not delay any longer after the Birkenhead speech. Birkenhead, for his part, made it clear that " careful consultations " with the Viceroy had not left him in the least depressed or discouraged by the repercussions of Moslem opinion, but Viceregal Reports can hardly have justified optimism, even though Irwin was making the most intensive efforts to rally support.

It was a long-established custom that Viceroys should spend the Christmas season in a centre where they could make contact with official opinion, and Calcutta was usually chosen for this purpose. In 1927, however, Irwin decided to go to Bombay and the West of India. It was an astute and courageous move. Bombay, as much the symbol of Indian as Calcutta of British financial resource, had been particularly affected by the great currency struggle. Its business leaders were deeply engaged in politics, were shrewd and persistent opponents of Government policy, and at the end of 1927 were in a dangerous mood and ready to sustain a boycott movement with their indispensable funds. Irwin's visit was therefore at a critical moment and a full round of public and private engagements was prepared. His justly renowned personal touch might well have won over to cooperation many influential elements—especially the Moslems—who were wavering, but it was not to be put to the test, for no sooner had he arrived in Bombay than he was struck down with a severe attack of malarial fever. It has been justly called a disastrous illness. It meant simply that he was unable to make any further effective intervention until his address to the Combined Legislatures on 2nd

February, only a day before the Commission landed at Bombay, and within a fortnight of the Assembly's momentous debate and vote on the issue of co-operation. The occasion demanded the clearest assertion of Irwin's personal attitude; much anxious thought had been given to the statement of 8th November, but it was not enough in itself; it had failed to create sufficient confidence or to produce a safe margin of support.

Irwin was alive to the full danger of the situation. Jinnah's defection threatened a defeat in the Assembly, the result of which would be, in terms of Constitution building, the virtual abdication of the Legislative Councils set up under the Reforms, in favour of the various sectional interests which would at once be in a position to assume an importance unwarranted by their real political status. As accompaniment to his words were feverish preparations for a *hartal*—or day of mourning, which was little less than a general strike in religious disguise—to greet Simon and his colleagues on their arrival. There was a real danger, which Irwin fully recognized, that the boycott movement would become predominantly Hindu, for the various organized minorities began to rally to the Commission as the natural protector of the weak community against the strong.

The drama of Irwin's last appeal for co-operation will not be quickly forgotten by those who witnessed the crowded scene in the Assembly Chamber at Delhi on that brilliant February morning. It has all been admirably recalled in Professor Coatman's *Years of Destiny*. "From the scarlet, gold-embroidered throne on the President's dais", he writes, "Lord Irwin looked down on his audience, and as they looked up at the tall figure reading the measured words with grave emphasis, their eyes could not have missed a row of bright metal plaques on the panelling of the Chamber above and on both sides of the throne—those plaques were the heraldic devices of India and the other Dominions of the great Commonwealth of Nations. And below them Lord Irwin was pointing out to India's representatives the road for India to take for her to find herself an accepted and acceptable member, resting in that Commonwealth as her device rests among theirs on the walls of her Parliament Chamber."

India, he asserted, was offered the prospect of real collaboration; to dispute this was to mistake shadows for reality. The Commission's work in India, he argued, was from the outset meant to be in close association with the Select Committees of the Central and Provincial Legislatures. "In due time the Commission will have completed its task and the matter will pass into other hands. At this moment, as the Commission moves from the stage, the Central Legislature has, if it so desires, through chosen representatives of its own, perhaps the greatest and most powerful means of influencing the further current of events. It is at this juncture invited through some of its members to sit with Parliament itself, acting in its turn through its own Joint Select Committee." It could not, in Irwin's view, be seriously maintained that these Indian representatives actively collaborating with Parliament in a Committee Room at Westminster were only to play the role of witnesses. "Any such impression is as strangely at variance with the intentions of Parliament as it is with any such picture as I have sought to draw of the process in operation."

So much for the assurances on formal procedure; he now turned to what he clearly regarded as the core of his argument. The strength of India's position would depend almost entirely on the quality of men she chose to represent her. "Constitutional forms are nothing but instruments in the hands of men. . . . And as men are greater than the instruments they use, we gravely err if we suppose that complaint, however loud, of the tools which circumstances have placed in our hands will suffice to induce posterity to hold us guiltless, if in the result our workmanship, whether through lack of will or of capacity, is found wanting. Whatever men may be tempted to think at the present moment, I dare predict that the searching inquest of history will not fail to return judgment against those who sought to use their power to hinder when it was in their power to help." He then rebutted, with a candour India has all too seldom heard from a Viceroy, the grave charge that the exclusion of Indians from the Commission was a deliberate affront. Not all the leaders, of course, were sincere in stressing it, but behind that particular charge lay whole eras of political ambiguity and racial discrimination.

Irwin's challenge at the eleventh hour was in words which were the reverse of patronizing and which by their very indignation testified to his belief in the responsibility as well as the status of India's leaders. "Let me make it very plain," he declared with special emphasis, "that I expect Indians, as I would myself, to be sensitive of their honour. None can afford to be otherwise, for honour and self-respect lie at the foundations of all racial life. But honour and self-respect are not enhanced by creating affronts in our imagination, where none in fact exist. . . . In the present case British statesmen of all parties have stated in terms admitting of no misconception that the appointment of a Parliamentary Commission was in no way intended as any affront to India. Time and again this assertion has been repeated, and I would ask in all sincerity by what right do leaders of Indian opinion, who are all as jealous as I am of their good faith, and would resent as sharply as I any refusal to believe their word, impugn the good faith and disbelieve the plain words of others? I would deny to no man the right to state freely and frankly his honest opinion, to condemn—if he wishes—the action of His Majesty's Government in this regard, or to say that they acted unwisely or in misapprehension of the true feeling that exists in India. That, again, is a matter of opinion. But what no man is entitled to say—for it is quite simply not true—is that His Majesty's Government sought to offer a deliberate affront to Indian honour and Indian pride."

Finally, "I have during the time that I have been in India been careful to avoid saying anything to magnify differences that must inevitably exist and have never invited any man to forgo principles to which he felt in conscience bound to subscribe. But let nobody suppose that he is assisting the realization of his ideals by reluctance to look on facts as they are." These were simply that the Commission had been established with the assent and co-operation of all British parties. "They will carry through their enquiry with, it is hoped, the generous assistance of all shades of Indian opinion. But whether such assistance is offered or withheld, the enquiry will proceed and a report will be presented to Parliament on which Parliament will take whatever action it deems appropriate."

It speaks volumes for the strength of Irwin's position that he was able to express himself in such direct personal terms. At a critical moment in Anglo-Indian relations he had made a profound appeal for reconciliation. If magnanimity had prevailed, this speech would have been decisive. But as Irwin spoke, the leaders remained impassive. Motilal Nehru, with his Congress followers ranked behind him, was thinking of other things, of collaboration with his Brahmin cousin, the Liberal Sir Tej Bahadur Sapru, in framing a constitution that would secure India's unity over and above the Commission and in spite of Lord Birkenhead. No sign came from Malaviya and the Nationalists or from the Moslems—they were waiting upon to-morrow's arrival of the Commission, and momentarily attention turned from the Viceroy and the Assemblies to Sir John Simon and his colleagues.

CHAPTER XV

BOYCOTT

THE reception prepared for the Simon Commission at Bombay by organizers of the *hartal* and supporters alike was marred by a torrential downpour of rain which made an unexpected appearance five months ahead of the monsoon. There were some garlands and messages of welcome together with black flags and the monotonous refrain of " Simon go back " that was to greet them at nearly every wayside station during their laborious trek. On the whole it was a flat and dismal affair which offered but little encouragement to either side. " If the boycott really represents the degree of political judgment in India the Commission need hardly go beyond Bombay," declared *The Times*, but the real evidence as to their future usefulness was in Delhi, for which the Commission at once set out. They stayed at the Western Hostel, which is Government owned and houses a great many members of the Legislatures during the Delhi session. It was hoped that the Commission would have the chance of making valuable contacts with the leaders, as the hostel was full of legislators when they arrived, but the situation was not improved by the Congress and Nationalist members carrying their opposition to the extreme of a complete social boycott. All the same Simon was able to convey that he had a major offer to make which was to turn the Commission into a Joint Conference. There was to be added to the seven British Commissioners a corresponding body of representatives to be chosen by the Indian Legislatures.

He set out the offer in detail in a formal letter to Irwin published on 7th February, and its general design could hardly have been more reasonable and conciliatory. When Provincial matters were under consideration the Provinces concerned were to be invited to collaborate by adding their own selected members to the Conference. There are good grounds for believing that if Irwin had recommended and

Parliament adopted this procedure from the outset much of the hostility to the Commission, particularly that of the Hindu and Moslem Moderates, would have disappeared, and that before leaving India Irwin himself regretfully concurred in this view.

Simon is a master in compromise and this letter was no exception, but it failed in its purpose on account of two reservations. First there could be no Joint Report. The Indian Committee could either submit its views to its own Legislature or arrangements could be made for them to be included in an annexe to the British Report. If Simon had conceded more, he would have given the Commission the very status Irwin and Birkenhead had so elaborately rejected, but here was a pretext for dissent which was at once seized upon by the extremists. Even greater offence was taken at the passage in Simon's letter insisting that " it is quite clear to us that each side of the Conference will require from time to time to meet by itself ". Sir John left it to himself to say why and when separate testimony should be received, hoping that all would rely on his sense of fairness. " I imagine that the Indian side may find occasion when they would think it well to act in the same way." He was quite mistaken, and the scheme had ultimately to be withdrawn after pressure from Sir Sankaran Nair, who was to become Chairman of the Indian wing, and from the Punjab Council, the first of the eight Provincial Councils in India that agreed to co-operate with the Commission. But by making the point at all Simon had roused the deepest suspicions that the Commission had ulterior motives for wanting to see special interests in secret conclave. There was always a catch, it seemed, in British goodwill.

The reaction was immediate. Within three hours of receiving the letter the boycott leaders replied, " We have most carefully considered the line of procedure indicated in the statement of Sir John Simon issued to-day. But our objections to the Commission as constituted and the scheme as announced are based on principles which remain unaffected by it. In the circumstances we must adhere to our decision that we cannot have anything to do with the Commission at any stage or in any form." Among the signatories were Iyengar for Congress, Malaviya and Jayakar for the Nationalists, Jinnah and Sir Purshotandas Thakurdas, who led the formidable opposition in the currency crisis, for the Independents. Beyond a mild offer to put himself at the Commission's disposal there was no further public initiative Irwin could take; he could merely follow anxiously along with the rest of India the course of the proceedings in the Assembly.

Lala Lajpat Rai, the Hindu Nationalist, had moved the fateful resolution in favour of complete boycott and inaugurated a debate which reached a standard worthy of the occasion. Perhaps the most notable speech of all came from the Rao Bahadur M. C. Rajah, a member nominated by the Government to represent the Depressed Classes. His outcast community, he declared, would go before the Commission confident that it would receive justice at its hands. It required unusual courage for an Untouchable to challenge in this way the serried ranks of Brahmins and other high-caste Hindus. He was defying the relentless code of slavery imposed upon him and his kind over countless generations, and in doing so he evoked the intense enthusiasm of the Moslems, whose religion, like Christianity, recognized neither caste nor class. Sir Basil Blackett used all his powers of quiet invective and banter to discredit Jinnah and his cross-bench followers of Moslems and Hindus who were still clinging obstinately to boycott, but they were of no avail against the discipline and resentment of the opposition, and the policy of collaboration received its initial defeat. The voting, however, was close enough—sixty-eight to sixty-two in favour of boycott in the second biggest division in the Legislature's history—to raise the hope that it was not a completely final or negative verdict.

Once again Birkenhead had breathed defiance at the critical moment. On the very day the debate opened he made a speech at Doncaster severely warning the boycott leaders that their policy would merely persuade Parliament that India had already gone too far on the road to self-government and that nothing would stop Parliament from doing its duty. *The Times*, again underwriting the Viceroy, stressed the criticism that this Doncaster homily was bound to arouse. Even Birkenhead's friends conceded that although what he said was the truth, he had chosen the wrong time to restate it. It was to be his last decisive intervention.

The remainder of 1928 is given over to ever-increasing disunity. The Boycott Committee had won its first and greatest victory, but it was a hollow triumph based solely on a negative, impelling India towards the paths of sectarianism and disintegration. By the end of the year, in spite of prolonged negotiation, the Moslems had closed their ranks against settlement with the Hindus, but it was soon found that it was easier to refuse Irwin's offer of help than to find anyone else with his personal prestige or influence to take his place as mediator. The communal breach was not confined to religion; the failure of the various unity conferences reacted unfavourably on the boycott leaders' efforts to draw up an "agreed" Constitution for India to outdistance anything the Simon Commission might produce. They had to fall back on the familiar question-begging device of sub-committee, and ingenious as the Sapru and Nehru Report was, its very complexity gave weight to Irwin's warnings. "It was in essentials", says Edward Thompson, "the old wretched battle between Hindus and Moslems for division of seats and jobs."

The Report was published in August while the Simon Commission were in England preparing to return to India in the autumn, and it was further evidence, if such was needed, of the impenetrable difficulties awaiting them. It is not impossible that Irwin had already abandoned hope for its success, and was looking tentatively towards the bigger objective of the Round Table Conference which, of course, necessitated co-operation between British India and the Princes.

His wisdom in preparing the ground with the Princes during the previous summer was soon to be confirmed during the course of debates on two Bills in the Legislative Assembly, both of which showed the dangerous forms of nationalism that might emerge from India if the urge to union was not adequately directed. The first, introduced by S. N. Haji, was a Coastal Reservation Bill which virtually eliminated European interests from India's coastal traffic. The relations between non-official Europeans and Indians had greatly improved in recent years, and their common understanding was an important factor in future constitutional progress. The effect of the Haji Bill was to undermine goodwill and encourage in British business and financial circles intense distrust in Indian Home Rule; for the disquieting factor in the uproar over the Bill was the ease with which Hindu and Moslem could sink their communal differences when racial prejudice was involved. The Member for Commerce, Sir George Rainy, was able to prove that the proposals would actually injure Indian ports and shipping, but the lure of economic nationalism when reinforced by racial instincts was too strong, and the Indian vote was almost unanimous for the Bill Irwin from the outset was well aware of its implications, and in a vain attempt to bring about a compromise actually intervened to the extent of holding meetings at Viceregal House between himself, Sir George Rainy and the representatives of the Indian and European interests concerned.

Even more serious was the reaction to the Public Safety and the Trade Disputes Bills, formally introduced by the Government in the autumn of 1928, which were designed to meet the growing and not wholly unallied dangers of Communism and industrial unrest in India. The law as it existed only covered offences by foreign Communists; the new Bill was introduced to combat the activities of Communist agents who were British subjects. Irwin's arrival in India coincided with moves by the Kremlin oligarchy to carry out decisions reached at the Third International in 1924 for large scale operations in India, and the appointment of a number of young British organizers financed from Moscow soon sharpened the edge of extremist politics. Social and economic conditions alike were considered to favour the spread of Communist cells, and it was felt that, as with China, the addition of European agitators would produce impressive results. Congress, it seemed, provided a ready-made machine, control of which was rapidly passing into the hands of younger and more violent men. The Communists allowed themselves to be absorbed into this convenient anti-British Party. The Communist menace in 1928 was an altogether more formidable bogey than the hyper-cautious Stalinism of to-day, and Irwin was only taking elementary precautions in his determination to eliminate Communism from India, and, while pursuing this root-and-branch policy, to offer the Nationalists of whatever creed or party a political prospect sufficiently attractive to make them disavow Communist programmes and colleagues. There were in India, as Irwin well knew, a whole variety of interests for whom Communism was either an attractive or at least a desperate expedient, and this Communist activity cannot have been a wholly negligible influence in Irwin's advocacy of a Round Table and Dominion Status policy.

. . . .

The arrival of the agitators was soon followed by a sinister increase of strikes and union disputes. Over half a million workers were involved in strikes during 1928-1929, nearly five times as many as in the previous year, and in the great general strike at the Bombay textile mills, which lasted throughout the summer of 1928, there was a loss of no less than twenty-two million working days. In many respects the Communist scare was only a symptom of deeper disorder. India, it seemed, was descending rapidly into depths of chaos and futility. The brutal murder in December 1928 of a young British police officer at Lahore by Bhagat Singh, who was only arrested six mouths later after throwing a bomb in the midst of the Legislative Assembly, was the signal for an orgy of terrorist violence during which, as a matter of mere routine, trains were wrecked and buildings razed.

In politics the same spirit of destruction prevailed. Patel, the President of the Legislative Assembly, became involved in a furious dispute with the Government, in the course of which the opposition dressed him up as a martyr to British intrigues. Actually the reverse was far nearer the truth. Patel gave expression to his extreme Nationalist beliefs by studying the Constitution and elaborating during his ample leisure time a whole series of devices whereby, under the disguise of a neutral chairman, he virtually brought the procedure of Government in the Legislature to a standstill, and certainly made it appear ridiculous to members and public alike. Most Moderates in the Assembly sided with the Government in resenting his activities, which brought them all into disrepute. It was recalled that Patel's predecessor, Sir Frederick Whyte, had managed to invest the office with a profound dignity and to give members pride in themselves and their work, and there were not lacking Government officials who urged Irwin to take the necessary constitutional action to remove Patel from the Chair. When he refrained from following this advice and was content to carry on with Viceregal interventions they were resentful, and alleged that he was favouring this recalcitrant Nationalist at the expense of his own Home Minister, who was a much busier man than Patel and had to bear the brunt of Patel's attacks.

But Irwin, even if he lost some of their sympathy and understanding during the vital months ahead, was more far-seeing than his officials. If he had tried summarily to dismiss Patel he would undoubtedly have deprived himself of his last shred of influence with the boycott leaders. They would have regarded such a step as final proof of British insincerity, and of Irwin's hypocrisy and resolve to crush any real Indian opposition if it was effective enough to be embarrassing. Actually no Government motion condemning Patel would ever have passed the Assembly, and Irwin had no authority under the Constitution to nominate a President over its head. It was still possible for Irwin to keep in touch with Sapru and Motilal Nehru, Jayakar and Jinnah. But Simon and the British Government were having to struggle on without those contacts. Irwin's ultimate success was largely due to his persistence in maintaining a life-line between himself and the boycott leaders. It is not surprising that the lesson he drew from Patel's antics, as from nearly every manifestation of dissent in the Assembly, was that an irresponsible executive and an elected legislature were in fact what they seemed to be, irreconcilable—necessary perhaps for an interim period, but impossible in any enduring form of government.

There were other and graver warnings. The Calcutta Congress in December 1928 heralded the momentous return of Gandhi to politics. Although he was about to enter the period of his greatest personal ascendancy the immediate situation was one which threatened to defy all leadership. The Nehru Report had been put up for adoption by Congress, but by no means satisfied the extremists. Subhas Chandra Bose moved an amendment in favour of Independence which was only lost by 1,350 votes to 973, and Gandhi was left with the unenviable task of finding a formula to satisfy the rival factions under Motilal Nehru, who was responsible for the Report, and Iyengar, who was sponsored by the younger men. The compromise finally reached, whereby the British Government was given twelve months to accept the Nehru Report, which in itself was unacceptable to nearly every section of Indian opinion, while Congress at the same time familiarized its public with the goal of Independence, was satisfactory to no one.

Both Irwin and Gandhi from their different view-points were only too well aware that Congress had taken the easy way of blank denial and had lost touch with reality. Jawaharlal Nehru and Bose lacked the intellectual stability necessary for constructive statesmanship, and almost by instinct ran away from responsibility. Gandhi tried in vain to double the time limit to two years. "Our Congress role to-day," he cried, "is nothing but a bogus affair. Let us face facts. It is worth nothing. We want a living register of the Congress." He called the issue of Dominion Status *versus* Independence a bogey Congress should dismiss from their minds. He warned them of "the struggle within our ranks more bitter than the struggle with the environment which is outside of ourselves". It was a timely statement, for the effect of Congress bravado was merely to provoke each Party to retire into splendid isolation and restate its maximum demands. The Princes were quick to reaffirm their determination to stand by the British connection. The All-India Moslem Conference, under the Presidency of the Aga Khan, put forward the most far-reaching communal claims, the bold clarity of which were in striking contrast to the cautious subtleties of the Nehru Report. They came out decisively for a Federal Constitution in which the separate election of Moslems was "essential in order to bring into existence a really representative democratic government".

What were Irwin's reactions towards this babel of conflicting political aims which for the rest of his time in India was so effectively to drown the sound of all other major problems of government, whether social or cultural, financial or economic, and to turn them "into mere incidents or phases of the great political hurly-burly"?[1] The Parties had been gathering for their annual assemblies in Calcutta, and it was Calcutta in the midst of these preparations and anxieties that he chose for giving an impressive indication of the trend of his thoughts. With Indian politics lost in a frenzy of partisanship, with the Conservative Government

[1] *Years of Destiny*, page 234.

at Westminster dying of mere inertia, Irwin refused to succumb to the prevailing mood of despair. His words during those last dark days of 1928 have about them the hallmark of high statesmanship—detachment of mind, grasp of principle, distrust of dogma. " A constitution," Motilal Nehru and his colleagues were reminded, " must be made to fit the facts and is not a thing to be laid down *a priori* in the hope that the facts will somehow or other fit themselves in behind." Of the Congress extremists, " I make bold to say that the most bitter and confirmed reactionary would never have it in his power to inflict one-tenth of the damage upon India's cause that it is likely to suffer at the hands of its false friends, who would guide it towards the morass of independence ".

Quietly and persuasively he emphasized India's unifying influences, first in terms of geography and the community of economic interest enclosed within it, and then of the deeper loyalty to the Throne and Person of the King-Emperor. " During these latter days," he added, " we have been able to measure the affection which binds the King-Emperor to the hearts of all his people, as from every quarter of his dominions thoughts have turned together in sympathy, anxiety and prayer to his long struggle with an exhausting illness." The reference was apt. The spontaneous gratitude at the news of George V's steady recovery after his life had hung in the balance made explicit what until then had been no more than a latent sentiment of Imperial solidarity. From henceforth there was a new sense of personal relationship between the Sovereign and his peoples which duly affected Indian opinion and worked in favour of Irwin both as Viceroy and as political mediator.

The time was not yet ripe " to examine the precise implications " of Dominion Status, but he made it abundantly clear that Parliament would not default from its expressed intentions; " the political genius of the British race has learnt to express itself in the form of free institutions, and it cannot easily lend its best efforts to any other form of political evolution."[1] On the other hand, those who were supporting Dominion Status for India at the earliest possible moment would find the ground cut from their feet if British opinion were allowed to reach the conclusion that it was valued by

[1] Calcutta Club dinner, December 27th, 1928.

India only as a stepping-stone to complete Independence.[1] As for Communist activities, he characteristically chose to meet them on philosophic grounds rather than to trot out the usual Tory clichés of treason and conspiracy.

It was Irwin's strength in a country deeply influenced by dialectic that he was not afraid of ideas. Communism, he argued, ignored the fundamental harmony, the just balance and proportion between the claims of the individual and of the society of which he was a component part. "We shall very certainly fail if we permit ourselves to forget that individual personality is the strongest and most securely rooted element in all human nature." On the material side, the Communist denial of the right of property stultified the natural expression of personality and ran counter to the first human principle. Spiritually it stood in bleak opposition to "principles by which the best of human life is guided and inspired. For in the gospel of hatred which Communism finds itself in practice compelled to preach, there can be little room for generosity, or charity, or self-sacrifice, or, finally, for religion itself." The implications of its philosophy on India were not remote, for India, "perhaps more than any country in the world, has constructed her life upon the framework of property and social custom and distinction". A more enlightened opinion was seeking, and would more and more insist upon, Reform. "But reform is one thing and revolution another, and let no man be under any delusion as to the price India would pay in her inherited and traditional life for such a revolution if it were ever unhappily effected within her boundaries." The philosophical approach, however, did not go far enough in itself to meet an increasingly dangerous situation.

For the next four months Irwin's attention was largely absorbed with finding administrative remedies to meet the perils of political terrorism and industrial strife. Controversy was to centre round the detailed debates in the Assembly over the two comparatively defensive Government measures on those subjects, and to be complicated both by the Government's ill-omened determination to gather support for its policy by sponsoring a Communist conspiracy trial, the notorious Meerut Case, and by Irwin's wearisome disputes and accommodations with Patel. In his formal

[1] *Vide* address European Association, Calcutta, December 17th 1928.

address opening the new session of the Assembly in January 1929 he took a firm line with the recalcitrant Congress majority which had helped to throw out during the previous session the Government's original Public Safety Bill. "The anticipations," he declared, "on which my Government then acted have been justified." It is important to note that he explicitly linked up the spreading of Communist ideas and methods with the labour unsettlement in Bombay and the indefinitely prolonged strike in Calcutta, and included in the new measure powers to forfeit and control Communist funds from abroad which had helped Communists in India "to promote and prolong for their own ends these industrial troubles", but, as *The Times* pointed out, neither Communism nor even Non-Co-operation could fully explain the labour problem.

A more fertile source of discontent than Russia was the extreme poverty of Indian working classes and the filthy slums in which they lived, and it is to Irwin's credit that he recognized that the mechanism of the Trade Disputes Act with its Courts of Enquiry and Boards of Conciliation were not enough. "I have long felt," he said, "that the best way to secure the advantage both of employers and employed is for the Government to undertake a review of the conditions under which labour works." So he announced the appointment of yet another Royal Commission, this time under the Chairmanship of Mr. Whitley, Socialist Speaker of the House of Commons, of Housing Act and Whitley Council fame, to begin work in the autumn. Whitley's record and reputation was one to which even Congress opposition found it hard to object, unless on the somewhat highly coloured pretext that his enquiry was "foreign interference". On the whole, however, the Whitley Commission was a victory for Irwin, and strengthened his hold over those elements who were ready to extend the scope of the boycott. In particular was there satisfaction when Irwin a fortnight afterwards sharply reminded the Princes of their peculiar obligations in sustaining India's industrial welfare. Certain capitalists were trying to evade factory regulations in British India by setting up factories and mills in the Indian States where hours were longer and suitable accommodation for factory hands was not obligatory. Their Highnesses were warned against the short-sighted policy of granting too ready a permission to employers to adopt for their own benefit unprogressive methods in the treatment of labour.

All the same, the debates in the Assembly dragged on with increasing vehemence and with neither Government nor Opposition prepared to grant an inch of ground. Patel left no one in doubt but that his Presidential powers were at the disposal of the Opposition, which he allowed the fullest scope to exploit delaying tactics. Although the tension must have been almost unbearable for the Government spokesmen, who had to bear the brunt of the oratorical storms, the fundamental responsibility for Government policy rested with Irwin, and it is one of the most notable of his personal achievements that when he left for England in June on his momentous short leave there was no final breach either between Government and Opposition or even between Patel and himself. Irwin had the perspicacity to realize that the entire Opposition was desperately anxious for a pretext to walk out and leave the Government as a mere rump in an otherwise empty Assembly. The full potentialities of such action can only be measured if taken in conjunction with the seething discontent which the Public Safety and Trade Disputes Acts were modest attempts to meet.

It is no exaggeration to suggest that the price of Irwin's failure at this time would have been revolution on an unprecedented scale. Recognizing Patel's pivotal position, he refused to allow himself to be provoked by him, but instead went out of his way to be accessible, with the result that President and Viceroy were soon engaged in a whole series of informal talks. Such was Irwin's personal charm and sincerity that Patel did not hesitate to pour out his Presidential troubles to him.

During February there was considerable speculation in political circles when Patel gave a tea-party at which Irwin, Gandhi, Jinnah, Motilal Nehru, Malaviya, the Maharajahs of Bikaner and Kashmir and Sir Abdul Qaiyum were all present. Although reporters were forced to agree that a tea-party was not a cover under which political conversations were likely to take place, and that the Viceroy was not meeting the leaders on this occasion with any such end in view, it was duly noted that this was not the first time that Irwin had honoured Patel by being his guest. Perhaps the real significance of the tea-party was that it symbolized a reaction from the extremism of Indian politics. Patel had become the unofficial leader of Congress in the Assembly, and his influence was now definitely cast against any exodus on their part.

As the winter session wore on Irwin's list of private callers steadily grew until it seemed that the whole Government's centre of gravity had passed from the Council Chambers to his private study. Apart from his sincere belief in the efficacy of personal contacts, he was carefully preparing the ground for his Grand Design, which was nothing less than to break up the boycott movement and take the necessary action to unite the whole of political India behind a constructive policy of collaboration. He cast his net wide enough to include Congress, or at least a section of it. In his speech to the Assembly he had already vehemently reaffirmed the 1917 Declaration. "As actions are commonly held more powerful than words, I will add that I should not be standing before you here to-day as Governor-General if I believed that the British people had withdrawn their hand from that solemn covenant."

In addition he had described his status as involving a double duty, on the one hand of seeing that the King's Government in India was carried on, and on the other as standing as intermediary between India and Great Britain. Authoritarians at Westminster and harassed officials in remote outposts were equally glad to hear from the Viceroy that "those who can guide public opinion in this country are doing no service to India if they accustom her to think lightly of disobedience and constituted authority, whatever the title by which such disobedience may be described". But no less reassuring to India's sensitive leadership was his conception of himself interpreting "as faithfully as he may the hopes, the feelings, the desires of the Indian people to those who may from time to time compose His Majesty's Government in Great Britain" and begging the Government "ever to place the most favourable construction on all their proceedings".

Here was an unmistakable advance on pre-Reform ideas about Viceregal status and duties, and when on 19th March it was formally announced that Mr. Wedgwood Benn, Secretary of State for India in the newly elected Labour Government, had invited Irwin to return to England in June for private consultations with him, Indian hopes rose high. It was felt that this strange Conservative Viceroy would at last be able to give real effect to his progressive aims now that Socialism was in the saddle at Westminster. The sense of expectancy had been further stimulated by Ramsay MacDonald, the new Prime Minister, in a fulsome speech delivered during the previous July to the British Commonwealth Labour Conference. "I hope that within a period of months rather than years"—and a good prospect of power in the near future lent added significance to his words —"there will be a new Dominion added to the Commonwealth of our Nations, a Dominion of another race, a Dominion which will find self-respect as an equal within the Commonwealth. I refer to India."

Once again Indian opinion was rushing ahead of realities, once again it was to be pulled back abruptly. Within a week of the announcement of his short leave Irwin was compelled to issue a ukase to the Assembly disallowing any discussion of policy behind the Government action in making arrests and house searches for Communist agents. Motilal Nehru had suggested the discussion, had been supported both by Iyengar and Malaviya, and of course ruled in order by Patel, who, fortified by a close study of British constitutional history, had begun to see himself in the heroic role of a Stuart Speaker of the House of Commons defending Parliamentary liberties from Royal prerogatives. But Irwin's plea that such discussion was "detrimental to public safety" was to receive within the next fortnight terrible vindication.

For while Patel on 8th April was in process of obstructing the Public Safety Bill with subtle argument, two Bengal extremists—one of them Bhagat Singh, the uncaptured murderer of Mr. Saunders—tried to obliterate it and its authors altogether by throwing two bombs into the middle of the Assembly, and firing at the members two or three rounds from an automatic pistol. One of the bombs pitched very near to Sir George Schuster, and it was the luckiest of chances that he was only slightly wounded in the arm and not killed outright. The force of the explosion was tremendous, and but for the particular form of bomb, which burst into large fragments not into scattering splinters, the loss of life would have been calamitous. As it was, only one member was seriously wounded, but with Sir John Simon in the President's gallery, a witness of the scene, India and the world reacted deeply not so much to the outrage that had been actually committed as to the tragedy that had been so narrowly avoided. Irwin at once called Patel to discuss with him the prorogation or at least adjournment of the Assembly, but Congress was so intent on pursuing its other vendetta with the Government that it was ready to condone even the fanaticism of the *soi-disant* "Hindustan Socialist Republican Army". Patel and his Party were not ready to listen to reason; instead they forced on the deadlock when on April 11th Patel ruled the Public Safety Bill out of order.

Irwin acted promptly and with a decisive vigour that confounded those critics who had doubted his capacity to meet the challenge of violence. In the first place he suspended further consideration of the Public Safety Bill and instead used his powers under the Constitution to give effect to it by means of an Ordinance. He then summoned both Houses of the Legislature and risked all his patient conciliation in one stern and courageous warning. He did not hesitate to lay considerable responsibility for the terrorist activities at the door of those who advocated law, order and the practice of non-violence, but who at the same time limited their advocacy to endless attacks on the executive authority. If there was to be reprobation of the crime let it be unqualified. "To condemn a crime in one breath and in the next to seek excuse for it by laying blame on those against whom it is directed, is no true condemnation."

As for Patel's ruling, it was contrary to the original purpose of the Reforms and debarred the Government from seeking or the Legislature from considering special powers. There must in future be no similar interruption in the normal legislative procedure. The impression that Sir James Crerar had been, in a sense, let down by his Viceroy could not withstand this crushing rejection of Patel's claim. On the other hand, Patel's respect for Irwin (one distinguished administrator has described it to me as amounting almost to personal devotion) was such that he was ready to waive all his private ambitions to become President of the next All-India National Congress and to put himself after his own fashion at the service of Irwin's policy. Yet Irwin's action had destroyed all his pretensions, and naturally he did not give way without a struggle. He set out in a formal letter his " great pain and surprised sorrow " at Irwin's unconstitutional procedure and re-emphasized all his original contentions that the Chair was the sole and final authority on points of order and that legally only the Assembly could criticize its President. Having won the major action, Irwin's reply—through his private secretary—was typical. He disclaimed any intention of criticizing Patel's ruling and so sugared the pill that Patel was ultimately able to read out the correspondence to the Assembly and regard the incident as closed to his own satisfaction. Irwin had, in fact, been making a close study of the psychology of India's leadership; his religious emphasis, his aptitude for political philosophy which led him always to translate the particular into the general, had brought him into closer sympathy with the Eastern mind than his critics at Westminster realized.

He was not given to self-advertisement, but when at the end of June he left Bombay on the *Rawalpindi* (now of glorious memory) to begin his period of leave, he could claim to have attained by intense application a real mastery over the intricacies of the situation. After all this mature reflection and detailed analysis he reached a major decision. The deadlock with Patel had only been resolved by an arbitrary device which no Viceroy could safely regard as a precedent. The controversy had shown how slender were the threads of political goodwill and racial sympathy by which the entire constitutional experiment was hanging. The passions aroused by the Meerut conspiracy trials, the increasing prestige and intransigence of the Moslem community, the spread of political violence, in stark opposition to Gandhi's doctrine of satyagraha but unavoidably identified with his return to political activity, all these factors combined to suggest to Irwin the need for nothing less than a re-orientation of British policy and restatement of aim.

The change of government at Westminster must have influenced him in this direction quite as much as events and opinion in India itself. The Second Labour Government was admittedly a minority administration, but the resounding defeat of Baldwin and of the significant slogan " Safety First " upon which he had obstinately relied, had not failed to raise Indian hopes. The Moderates were further encouraged by MacDonald's astute decision to appoint Wedgwood Benn as Labour's Secretary of State for India. Benn was a former Liberal with a fine war record, an experienced Parliamentarian, by training and disposition a staunch advocate of Constitutional processes. In Benn Irwin found a sympathetic colleague who, if lacking Birkenhead's histrionic gifts and intellectual equipment, yet had a bigger vision of his job; indeed the India Office was about to experience a Secretary of State more ardent for large scale reform than any since its previous Liberal chief, Edwin Montagu.

The relationship between Viceroy and Secretary of State is never easy. Almost inevitably one or other gains a personal ascendancy, contact is formal at a distance of six thousand miles, and whatever the leaders may propose, the disposal rests with two groups of officials, one at Whitehall and the other at Delhi, who, in a delicately adjusted Constitution, do not readily appreciate each other's status or problems. Further, while the Viceroy almost invariably submits his policy speeches to the Secretary of State, the Secretary of State is not required to return the compliment. It was fortunate for India that Benn and Irwin were able to meet in the summer of 1929. For after three months of close consultation they had established so sure an understanding that Benn never flinched from bearing the burden of the criticism Irwin's initiative had provoked.

Irwin's first visit on arrival was, of course, to Garrowby, where the reunion of father and son was only the joyful climax to frequent and intimate correspondence. The break had been somewhat shortened by Lady Irwin's stay in England throughout the summer of 1928. And with Irwin back again, Halifax, now in his ninety-second year, soon resumed the old relationship. Irwin remained his youngest boy; few would have guessed that a Viceroy was on holiday at Garrowby or Hickleton. The story is told of one of Halifax's ecclesiastical friends invited up to Hickleton, while Irwin was there, for consultation on some particular church matter in which the old man was interested. The guest naturally had tea with father and son, but after the tea things had been cleared away, Halifax turned to Irwin, who, quite apart from his great position, was himself approaching the ripe age of fifty, with the bland yet peremptory command usually addressed by fond parents to children of five and under, " Now toddle away, Edward, go into the garden. My friend and I want to have a talk." Edward, so it is reported, took his leave without protest and toddled away.

Although he was officially on leave and badly in need of rest, he was soon, within three days after landing in fact, immersed in a series of conferences which, if private and informal, were none the less exacting. Indeed he was to be hard at work throughout his holiday and was to take a more momentous personal initiative while in England than he had yet been called upon to do in India itself.

CHAPTER XVI

DOMINION STATUS

IRWIN had come home in possession of the prospective main recommendations of the Simon Commission a year in advance of their publication and several months before its Report had been drafted. The Commission was still industriously sifting its evidence and paying tribute to the magnitude of the constitutional problem by pondering over a lengthy if somewhat sententious factual preface. But Irwin knew by the time he had reached England and conferred with Benn that Simon was going to refuse the fences without which the Commission could not logically complete the course it had set itself. Diarchy was to be condemned, no doubt, but Provincial Autonomy was to be so safeguarded as to be virtually meaningless and Federation to be postponed *sine die*. Simon was anxious to go further in the direction of Reform, but he was unable to carry Lord Burnham with him, and he was even more anxious to produce a unanimous Report. Thus not for the first time in the annals of Royal Commissions was the tail wagging the dog, but Irwin realized at once that the Report when finally published would not only destroy all his patient mediation with the Moderates and more tractable Congress groups, but also play into the hands of the extremists who were hoping to exploit Gandhi's return to politics by developing boycott into something like revolt and civil war. The bitterness aroused by the exclusion of Indians from the Commission's personnel would be as nothing compared with the fury when it was known the Commission's recommendations offered no substantial redress.

Irwin accordingly put before Benn two major proposals. First, the whole question of India's constitutional future should at once be the subject of a Conference to be attended by representative delegates from Parliament, the Indian States and British India. This proposal was, of course, calculated to bring the whole era of Commissions to an end and to concede on a grand scale this vital principle of Indian participation against which Irwin had so doggedly set himself when Simon's terms of reference were originally discussed. Whatever he may by now have thought of his thesis of October 1927 he was now ready and anxious to reverse it. This statesmanlike resolve was backed by the full support of the political parties and leaders at Westminster and was further reinforced by Simon himself who, as the Report was to show, frankly admitted that to confine constitutional action to British India was not enough and that a satisfactory solution of India's political problems must embody the Native States as well. The proposal pleased Gandhi, while Reading could see no objection to it.

The workings of Irwin's mind were not wholly unknown in India, and even before he left Bombay, the *Times of India* was speaking of a "fateful mission", assuring Irwin of the confidence of the people of India and actually foreshadowing a Round Table Conference as the principal outcome of his deliberations. "Indian co-operation", the paper asserted, "is forthcoming if asked for in such a Conference." Irwin's holiday roughly coincided with the publication of the Report of the Butler Commission upon which he had placed such high hopes when he first commended it to the Chamber of Princes. Set up originally to consider the questions of the sovereignty and rights of the States, the Commission produced a sound enough document, but its modest and inconclusive proposals were telling evidence in favour of a more ambitious approach to the problems it raised. There was, then, the most widespread support for the Conference. In these protracted discussions at the India Office the first Round Table Conference took shape, and emerged as a substantial plan of action.

But Irwin had a second proposal to make which to all outward appearances was no more than the reiteration of an avowed aim, the repetition of a well-worn phrase. He proposed that the Conference should be heralded by a solemn Government statement that Dominion Status and nothing less was the goal of India's political progress. To Irwin such a statement embodied no secondary policy to be considered apart from the Conference. It was rather an essential supplement without which in his judgment the Conference itself would be from the outset condemned to failure. If the Conference idea was a big innovation in terms of British policy, there was nothing new about it to Indian thought. Already the word was a Congress cliché with a more advanced meaning than the Whitehall version. Congress envisaged a Conference which would be nothing less than a Constituent Assembly with full powers to draw up an Indian Constitution the basis of which was unqualified Dominion Status. Irwin never admitted that any such sweeping demand should be met, but he was deeply impressed with the dangers that would arise if, after the necessary safeguards had been accepted, no formula was found publicly to identify India's aspirations with Britain's policy. His analysis was calculated to break the political boycott movement in India, but it did not take full account of the British reaction.

He at once found himself up against Lord Reading, whose counsel was sought, and whose precise and logical mind would have nothing to do with vague or intangible objectives. The demands of psychology and self-esteem did not make Dominion Status appear any more honest or practicable to him unless it meant some clearly defined programme of action to be realized within a given time and under given conditions. In this opinion he carried Lloyd George, who, on behalf of the Liberal Party, accepted his judgment on Indian affairs. Admittedly the Labour Government depended on the Liberals for its majority, but Benn was ready to take the risk of a Parliamentary storm and to approve a Viceregal statement to be made on Irwin's return to India.

Irwin, for his part, was confident that Stanley Baldwin, his old chief, would not press home the opposition. He had done so much to imbue Baldwin with his own views on India, and after long talks it seemed that he was ready to defend Dominion Status in Parliament. Given Baldwin's backing he felt that the growing uneasiness in powerful Conservative circles, focusing round Lord Salisbury in the Lords and Winston Churchill in the Commons, would be duly allayed. The strength of his personal position must also have encouraged him and the Government to go boldly ahead with their double policy. *The Times* was able suitably to stress Irwin's popularity by publishing a series of letters urging that his term of office should be extended for one or two years so as to allow him time to complete his policy of reforms. This in itself would not have been specially noteworthy—the argument that five years is not long enough has been applied by friends and relations to nearly every Viceroy—but in the case of Irwin the majority of the correspondents were prominent Indians of different schools of thought and included Yakub, Deputy-President, and subsequent President, of the Legislative Assembly.

By the beginning of October the deliberations were completed and the decisions taken, but beyond a general impression that Irwin had interpreted in a liberal spirit his promise to present Indian opinion to the British Government no immediate action was expected. The secret was well kept. On October 10th Irwin left for Marseilles, where he embarked again on the *Rawalpindi* and arrived in Bombay on the 25th. *The Times* confined itself to a brief report that he would consult members of his Council before announcing what the result of his mission to England had been, and that he would take up his residence in the new Government House on 23rd December. *The Times*' reserve was partly to be explained by a sensational letter from Birkenhead which appeared the previous day in the *Daily Telegraph* after Geoffrey Dawson had refused to publish it. Birkenhead described the purpose of his intrusion as being " to point out the danger of any intervention by Government in a matter which, by the consent of all Parties, has been committed to a Commission representative of all those parties ". " It is immaterial in this connection," he added, " whether views extraneous to the Commission are published in this country or India. Such a publication is equally improper and perilous in either case. The decision of the Commission must not in any respect be affected by outside comments or explanations." If Birkenhead's real objective was to prepare the ground for a political crisis in Britain his letter was an effective contribution, but if he had in mind to stop Irwin from proclaiming his policy he was soon to be disappointed. But the sense of expectancy could not be wholly suppressed and the Indian leaders were gathering in Delhi and Bombay.

. . . .

Within a week, on 31st October, Irwin, wholly undeterred, had published his momentous Statement in a

Gazette Extraordinary. In it he formally announced a Conference " in which His Majesty's Government should meet representatives both of British India and the States for the purpose of seeking the greatest possible measure of agreement for the final proposals which it would later be the duty of His Majesty's Government to submit to Parliament ". The Conference was represented as being Simon's idea, and Irwin was careful to point out that Simon's original proposal in his letter of 6th February 1928, setting up a Joint Parliamentary Committee, " would still be appropriate for the examination of the Bill when it is subsequently placed before Parliament, but would, in the opinion of the Commission, obviously have to be preceded by some such Conference as they have suggested ".

But if Irwin deliberately presented the Conference as part of the accepted order of things (and indeed the first half of the Statement was little more than an elaboration of points already set out in letters exchanged between Simon and Ramsay MacDonald and published in London along with it) he was equally at pains to reintroduce Dominion Status without any such protective covering. " In view of the doubts ", ran the decisive paragraph, " which have been expressed both in Great Britain and India regarding the interpretation to be placed on the intentions of the British Government in enacting the Statute of 1919, I am authorized on behalf of His Majesty's Government to state clearly that in their judgment it is implicit in the declaration of 1917 that the natural issue of India's constitutional progress, as there contemplated, is the attainment of Dominion Status."

With these few bold phrases Irwin had performed an historic act and had quite unwittingly made a formidable début on the stage of world politics. The effect on Indian opinion was, to quote Sir George Schuster, who was Irwin's Finance Member at that time, " electrifying ". " At a stroke," asserts Professor Coatman, " it transformed the entire situation." Nothing less would have done so. Before Irwin's voice was raised, all seemed to turn on the Congress ultimatum. The year which at Calcutta they had allowed for the unconditional acceptance of their Constitution by the Government was rapidly coming to an end. One of the murderers of Mr. Saunders had died after a hunger strike, and as his body was passed from Lahore to Calcutta there were scenes of fervour and devotion.

Irwin indeed had returned to find political India bordering on a state of alarm, with the parties holding each other off at a distance and mobilizing their own resources for conflict. The blessed words Dominion Status, combined with Irwin's avowed intention of breaking through the webs of mistrust, offered a new hope to all who in their hearts desired peace and an end to a wearying and confused struggle. The response was immediate and impressive. Liberals and Moslems and the political Princes all gave the Statement the warmest of welcomes. Even more significant was the reaction of the powerful European Associations of Bombay and Calcutta embodied in a formal Resolution: "We the Council of the European Association desire you to convey to His Majesty's Government our firm support of the Viceroy's recent declaration. We consider such a declaration not ill timed, and it clarifies the issue to all competent observers. We consider that the Statutory Commission has not suffered in prestige, but by its work alone has made possible the contemplated Conference." In some respects this resolution was Irwin's final vindication. India's industrial community—British, American, Native—had unhesitatingly recognized the need for a new dispensation and endorsed the Viceroy's approach to it. By tradition and interest alike these Associations were citadels of the established order. Their recognition of the need for change was a damaging riposte to the Diehards at Westminster.

The Congress leaders, too, were deeply impressed. At Delhi on the day after the publication of the Statement, Gandhi, Motilal Nehru and Jawaharlal Nehru were in conclave with the Mahasabha leaders, Malaviya and Moonje, and the Liberals, Sapru and Ramaswamy Aiyar. Another representative gathering of leaders at Bombay, which included Jinnah, Jayakar and Mrs. Naidu, had promptly issued an almost unanimous manifesto welcoming Irwin's initiative, and Gandhi was known to be enthusiastic. At first it seemed that the Delhi meeting would also convey its unconditional acceptance, but at this point Jawaharlal Nehru emerged to oppose Irwin with a blank and sullen refusal. Normally his suspicious attitude would not have been decisive. He was under a deep personal obligation to

Gandhi, to whom also was largely due his political status, but unfortunately the Lahore Congress was only six weeks away, Jawaharlal was to be its President and Gandhi was talking glibly about "the year of youth's awakening". Jawaharlal saw himself in a splendid role unfurling the flag of independence—and here was the Viceroy, the symbol of alien supremacy, obstructing his heroic vision with some niggardly formula for a Round Table Conference! To make matters worse Gandhi argued for its acceptance on the grounds of the Viceroy's personal sincerity.

Credit must be given to Jawaharlal for realizing at once that Irwin had at one stroke altered the balance of Indian politics; the offer of a comprehensive settlement from the British Raj not only seized the initiative from the Congress extremists but also compelled them if they refused the outstretched hand to make good their defiance. Even Jawaharlal was astute enough to realize that his reliance on flamboyant gestures could not outweigh the Viceroy's constructive resource, and in his revealing *Autobiography* he makes an attempt to hide his naïve vexation at being forestalled by Irwin. He describes in oracular terms how as the Lahore Congress drew near he felt that "events were marching step by step, inevitably pushed onward, so it seemed, by some motive force of their own. . . . Hoping, perhaps, to check this onward march of destiny, the British Government took a forward step and the Viceroy Lord Irwin made an announcement about a forthcoming Round Table Conference. It was an ingeniously worded announcement which could mean much or very little, and it seemed to many of us obvious that the latter was the more likely contingency. And in any event, even if there was more in the announcement, it could not be anywhere near what we wanted." The Conference taking place as it did a few hours after the Announcement, he speaks of the "almost indecent haste with which it was called together". Gandhi and the other leaders wrestled with him, and not until late the following evening did they obtain his signature for a joint manifesto. "As was not unusual with me," he confesses, "I allowed myself to be talked into signing."

The manifesto, while accepting Irwin's invitation to attend the Conference, recommended for the consideration of His Majesty's Government that the Conference should be empowered to draw up a scheme for immediate Dominion Status, that the majority of delegates should be chosen from the Congress Party and that all political prisoners should be forthwith released. Like all documents in which Gandhi has had a hand, it was cautiously worded. Jawaharlal might argue—as indeed he did—in terms of conditions, but the manifesto spoke of " should " not of " must ", the saving clauses were no more than recommendations. There was, of course, at once an outcry both in India and England that extremists had won a great victory and led both Irwin and the Moderates into an impossible position. Not that Jawaharlal ever saw it in such a favourable light; for him it was " a come down ". Yet after the Press in both countries, from their different standpoints, had duly analysed Irwin's Announcement, political critics whose prejudices and interests had not wholly blurred their vision began to revise their judgment.

The reality of Irwin's triumph could not be overlooked. Whatever excuses Congress leaders might afterwards make, their signatures on the manifesto were an early recognition from the most powerful political party in India that the Viceroy's solution could not be safely rejected. Whether their provisos were recommendations or conditions, their readiness to attend a Round Table Conference and discuss Dominion Status at all was a major reversal of policy, a move away from the left and towards compromise. At one stroke Irwin had immeasurably strengthened the position of the Moderates. They were only too well aware that the Congress organization had its roots deep in popular support, while there was practically no body of opinion to support their leadership. On the one hand they were ready to travel a long way with Congress in order to enjoy their patronage at the Conference, and on the other they were resolved to give substance to Irwin's hopes by making the Conference a success. They saw the Conference as their supreme opportunity for the full exercise of their intellectual power, and from henceforth they were Irwin's faithful allies.

But it was not only in terms of political manœuvre that Irwin had gained the day. The overwhelming response to his Announcement implied a more enduring conquest—the people, as apart from the politicians, recognized the meaning of his policy, welcomed him as their friend, and provided him with an Indian following enjoyed by no Viceroy since the spacious days of Elgin. Had Parliament reflected his magnanimity, the misunderstandings of an era might have been swept away and a splendid future of constructive collaboration assured. In his efforts to foster goodwill he had exceeded all expectations.

. . . .

India now waited anxiously for Parliament to endorse his Announcement, but Parliament interpreted its functions as the Grand Inquest of the Nation to conduct a prolonged and unhelpful post-mortem. In the House of Lords, Lord Reading, while welcoming the proposed Conference, developed in detail the reasons for his unwavering opposition to the Dominion Status Announcement. First he thought it highly improper for such a statement to be made without the formal assent of the Simon Commission, whose authority and prestige were likely to be undermined by it. Secondly it was idle to use phrases which would not convey a clear meaning to India and to everyone in this country. The only way to counteract misconception and misinterpretation was "to state in plain unequivocal terms what was meant and what was intended by the Government". Finally, the use of the phrase Dominion Status would lead Indian politicians to press for concessions the Government would be unable to make. Reading's speech was lengthy and carefully prepared. His arguments were well marshalled. Weight was added to it by his great personal prestige, and by his status as spokesman in the Lords for the Liberal Party, which was still identified in the Indian mind with traditions of Gladstone and Ripon and the defence of the downtrodden. Unfortunately his words reached India in such an abbreviated form that the very misconceptions and misunderstandings he was hoping to eliminate were merely intensified.

Lord Parmoor and Lord Passfield, speaking for the Government, did their best to underline Irwin's thesis. The Announcement was, they argued, in no sense an attempt to forestall the Simon Report but rather to prepare a good atmosphere for its reception; at the same time, however, in the reports that reached India, they did not succeed in suggesting that the reference to Dominion Status was much more than a polite formality; their emphasis, so it seemed, was all upon reservations. Then Birkenhead, on behalf of the Conservatives, pompously requested the Simon Commission " to treat that which the Government have instructed or authorized the Viceroy to do so as irrelevance ". Irwin's Announcement, he argued, was made merely to appease extremist elements, but we could only discharge our obligations to India by a firm refusal ever to submit to threats. The language and temper of this Debate gravely prejudiced Irwin's position. The old suspicions returned—was this the substance of his offer?

Worse was to follow. The Commons, two days later, when they debated India, made it clear beyond all doubt that Party orthodoxy was the overriding consideration. Stanley Baldwin, of whose support Irwin had no doubt felt confident, led off with a powerful homily the hard essence of which was that on his personal responsibility while on holiday in France he had approved of the reference to Dominion Status, but on his return, discovering that Simon washed his hands of it and that his Party disliked it, he was bound now to go back on his word. The exaggerations of Lord Rothermere gave him his alibi. With unusual ferocity he denounced the *Daily Mail* for daring to assert that he had committed his Party to Dominion Status, and in a wealth of righteous indignation he managed to hide the humiliation of a statesman whose personal judgment at that time counted for so little with his followers that he was forced to come to heel at the first crack of his Party whip.

The truth was that Baldwin's whole leadership was in peril. The Conservatives, weary after five years of power, had just lost an election based largely on his personality and on the slogan of his choice " Safety First ". There was some heart-searching among Conservatives whether Mr. Baldwin's pipe and stonewalling were good enough, and they were on the look out for any issue of policy upon which they might challenge his authority. The activities of his friend and protégé the Viceroy offered a splendid occasion for a trial of strength. This personal motive should not be overlooked in the increasingly vehement opposition of the Diehard Conservatives which, though aimed principally at his chief, was no less a source of embarrassment to Irwin himself for the remainder of his term.

But if Baldwin unblushingly abandoned Irwin the Reformer, he dealt with typical resource a shrewd if indirect blow at his Conservative critics in his vigorous defence of Irwin the Man. The hapless *Daily Mail* had insinuated that Baldwin would be hard put to it to explain to his followers his responsibility in ever recommending him as Viceroy. "Let me tell the House," was Baldwin's emphatic reply, "that when it became my duty to submit a name to His Majesty for the Viceroyalty of India, Lord Birkenhead, then Secretary of State for India, and I discussed that matter at length, and passed in review many names. It is a most anxious and grave responsibility when any Prime Minister has to find a Viceroy of India. It was only when we had considered many names, that he suggested the name of Mr. Edward Wood. My first answer was, 'I cannot spare him.' He is one of my most intimate friends, not only politically but personally, a man whose ideals and views in political life approximate mostly to my own, a colleague to whom I can always tell my inmost thoughts. On reflection I felt that India must have the best that we could send. That was the reason why I agreed. I asked him if I might submit his name. I had great difficulty in persuading him. He was interested in his work, which he was performing admirably. He did not want to leave his home and only took up that office with the high sense of duty that we all expect of him. I will only add that if ever the day comes when the Party which I lead ceases to attract to itself men of the calibre of Edward Wood, then I have finished with my Party." There is no need to doubt the sincerety of this remarkable tribute, but the very fervour of his words only helped to emphasize their warning to those who hoped to press home the attack on his leadership by further resistance to Irwin's policy.

There is no more powerful testimony to the strength of Irwin's character, with its rare blend of candour and detachment, than his success during this difficult phase in the history of the Conservative Party in maintaining his friendships and prestige with those whose dislike of Baldwin was second only to their objections to the Dominion Status Announcement. Among the critics, for instance, was Lord Lloyd, but recently exiled from Egypt by the Labour Government, who felt the deepest disquiet at Irwin's policy and grappled with his old friend to dissuade him from the course he was resolved to pursue, but when once he realized that his arguments and pleas were of no avail there was no bitterness left over to spoil their relationship and mutual regard. With equal sincerity Lord Lloyd could have proclaimed his admiration for the Viceroy. If the issue could have been confined to one of personal chivalry the damage could no doubt have been undone, but political suspicion could not be quelled.

The rest of Baldwin's speech was wrapped round in ponderous rhetoric, simple thoughts, and resounding generalities—the sum total of which was sufficiently a Parliamentary *tour de force* to earn high praise from no less an authority than Balfour, but bore little or no relation to Irwin's problems or India's expectations. Lloyd George followed and repeated Reading's arguments with his own Celtic emphasis. The man who had so brusquely dismissed Montagu was still in no mood to appreciate gestures. The Indian leaders, he argued, are clever men, far more clever, it seemed, than their British protagonists. Their price for collaboration in the Round Table Conference was rising hourly—did Irwin's Declaration imply a change of policy to meet demands? But Wedgwood Benn, in spite of provocations and sharp verbal exchanges—during which Lloyd George conjured up a vision of him as a " pocket edition of Moses " smashing the tables of the Covenant—courageously stood his ground. The Viceroy's personal position should have been kept out of the debate, but it had been dragged in and, he added, " although my acquaintance with Indian affairs is recent and scanty, yet I am in touch with Indian opinion from day to day, and the Viceroy occupies in India by his character a position of respect and affection which is a real pillar of Empire ". The declaration, he asserted, was a " restatement and an interpretation of the Montagu policy. Lord Irwin's statement must stand as it was drafted and no gloss must be put upon it. . . . The Montagu policy stands as a cardinal article of faith in British policy towards India."

He gave as the first reason why the Government decided to authorize the declaration that they were advised to do so by the Viceroy. " I should like," he continued, " to exalt the Viceroy in this matter, because he came to England as an ambassador of peace, and he has gone back to India as a messenger of appeasement "—which last capacity in those far-off halcyon days implied abject surrender in the eyes of orthodox Conservatives but was sublime heroism to

Socialists. "We do not shelter behind the Viceroy. He offered advice and we were free to reject it. We did not reject it because it agreed with our own convictions." He reiterated Irwin's reasons in favour of making the declaration at this time, first, to rid India of all doubts that British policy was changing, of the suspicion, be it noted, that it was going not beyond the Montagu policy but back upon it; and secondly, to secure a background of goodwill for the Simon Report. For Indians who appreciated the full significance of Irwin's policy and Parliament's responsibility for breathing life into it, Benn's speech was the one ray of hope in this unprofitable Debate. Simon gracefully declared his neutrality and concealed the chagrin he must have felt at being forestalled; while Ramsay MacDonald was brief and perfunctory—" the Government have reached a decision on advice and that is the end of the matter ", was the tone he adopted, which satisfied neither India nor the House.

Actually the immediate result of the Debates was greatly to strengthen Irwin's position. The measure of Indian disappointment in Parliament was the measure of its recognition that Irwin had taken great risks on India's behalf. " The policy on which he was now embarked was so patently his own, and he had fought for it with such skill and knowledge and determination, that he could never, with even the shadow of plausibility, be accused of being the mere mouthpiece of the Government or any other political body in England. He had done a great thing."[1]

. . . .

The value of Irwin's achievement is enhanced when it is realized that the facts at his disposal and the impressions he had formed about the situation could not be fully disclosed at the time. He and Benn had to take their decision knowing in advance that it would not be feasible for them to reveal in public their underlying motives, hence the sense of grievance at Lloyd George's persistent questioning as to whether the reference to Dominion Status indicated any change in tone or substance in previous policy. Irwin had gone out of his way to consult Lloyd George with other leaders and it is inconceivable that he should not have given them all in private the fullest explanation.

I have received permission to include a hitherto un-

[1] *Years of Destiny*, page 268.

published "Note on 'Dominion Status' as understood in Great Britain and India" written by Irwin himself during November 1929. The importance of the document can hardly be overstressed. It summarizes an approach to the problem, the fruit of his unique experience and profound reflection which was overlooked both in the Debates and in much of the controversy then and afterwards. As with the Notes on Administration and Government given privately to the Princes, I have authority for saying that in this Note he summarizes his considered views on Dominion Status at the time and that he stands by every word of it to-day. It runs as follows:

"In considering the public discussion to which the phrase 'Dominion Status' is now being subjected it is important to appreciate what seems to be a fundamental distinction between the general political thought of Great Britain and of India, for I believe the failure to do so is responsible for not a little misunderstanding.

"To the English conception, Dominion Status now connotes, as indeed the word itself implies, an *achieved* constitutional position, of complete freedom and immunity from interference, by His Majesty's Government in London. This conception has taken very much more definite shape as a result of the 1926 Imperial Conference, though I am not sufficiently well informed to say whether any Dominion could have been said, or was ever said, to be enjoying Dominion Status, while His Majesty's Government in London still exerted (except in formal matters) the right of active interference with its affairs. I doubt it. But anyhow, however dynamic and fluid a term Dominion Status may be in the sense that its implications may possibly be still further expanded and developed, there is now no question but that when an Englishman speaks of Dominion Status, he means a constitutional state enjoyed within the Empire by a political entity over which His Majesty's Government retain no right of supervisory interference.

"The Indian seems generally to mean something different. I should say that very few of the responsible sort who speak about immediate Dominion Status for India ignore the fact that complete Dominion Status in the sense outlined above is not possible for at least some time to come.

But they seem to me to be thinking on different lines from those followed by British thought. Whatever he may feel it necessary to say in public, the Indian is not so much concerned with the *achieved constitutional state*, in the British sense, as he is with what he would consider *the indefeasible assurance of such achievement*. In all the constitutional discussions of the last two years, the underlying element in much of Indian political thought seems to have been the desire that, by free conference between Great Britain and India, a constitution should be fashioned which may contain within itself the seed of full Dominion Status, growing naturally to its full development in accordance with the particular circumstances of India, without the necessity—the implications of which the Indian mind resents—of further periodic enquiries by way of Commission. What is to the Englishman an accomplished process, is to the Indian rather a *declaration of right,* from which future and complete enjoyment of Dominion privilege will spring. Thus to the Englishman it is a contradiction in terms to speak, as Indians habitually do, of *Dominion Status with reservations,* but to the Indian for whom the phrase 'Dominion Status' is rather the hall-mark of constitutional direction or constitutional quality, the 'status' is not necessarily unreal because it has not as yet attained full completeness. The Leaders' Statement issued in Delhi on my announcement of October 31st talks of the Conference framing a Dominion constitution 'suited to India's needs'. The idea seems to be the same. Mr. Gandhi, writing in *Young India* of November 14th 1929 says:

"'I can wait for the Dominion Status constitution, if I can get the real Dominion Status in action, if, that is to say, there is a real change of heart, a real desire on the part of the British people to see India a free and self-respecting nation, and on the part of the officials in India a true spirit of service.'

"When, therefore, the Indian is told categorically by British speakers that he cannot expect to attain Dominion Status within the present century, he (using the phrase himself subconsciously in quite a different sense) is left with a general impression that Great Britain does not mean business.

"It is difficult to get the distinction clear, and it is

perhaps possible to elucidate it by way of simile, from the spheres of family and business. In the first, the full enjoyment of family rights may serve as the counterpart of Dominion Status in the constitutional field. A member of the family may have grown up, come of age, and attained full enjoyment of all his family rights. Or, he may still be a minor, enjoying certain rights at present, and the certitude of his full rights when he comes of age. To English thought, translating the simile into constitutional terms, the first has reached Dominion Status, the second has not. But to Indian thought, I fancy, the distinction would not be so much between the member of the family who is of full age, and the minor who is still under some measure of control, for in essence the rights of each are identical whether or not both have at any given time attained to their full enjoyment, and the difference here is only one of time. To Indian thought the real distinction is that between the member of a family (whether a minor or of full age) who enjoys or will enjoy full rights in family property, and a subordinate member of the family who has some rights but no title to share in the family property.

" Or again in business, all partners have as partners the same quality of status. But though the status may thus be the same, a senior partner may in fact have larger rights than a junior partner. But the partnership status of the latter assures him of the promise of full rights in time to come. In either simile, I think that Indian thought, when claiming Dominion Status, demands that it should be secured the status, though not immediately the full rights, of membership of the family or of partnership in the business. And this is perhaps not very different from English thought.

" No doubt there is the further difficulty of reconciling the constitutional responsibility of Parliament with the self-determination claims of the most extreme nationalist Indian thought. Gandhi said to me not long ago: ' If Great Britain could once give us liberty to order our own future, she would be surprised at our diffidence in undertaking responsibilities, and in the degree to which we should ask for her help.' But here it is evident that the only course possible is to afford every opportunity to Indian opinion to express itself by the way of Conference as proposed, with the assurance that any such expression must carry great weight with Parliament, and that the greater the unanimity of Indian opinion, the greater will be the weight attaching to its expression."—*November* 1929.

Irwin's critics, for all their ingenuity and conviction, have never squarely met Irwin's thesis as set out in this Note. An intangible barrier was dividing India from Britain, and in order to remove it Irwin was not demanding a new policy, such as the actual achievement of Dominion Status before India was ready to enjoy or Britain to concede it, but simply " the indefeasible assurance of such achievement ". However self-evident this assurance might seem to Lloyd George and the Conservatives, an era of disappointments and frustration had intervened between Montagu and Simon during which the gravest doubts about the sincerity of Britain's word had taken shape in the Indian mind, nor was it only a matter of reason. The hostility was essentially emotional.

In a letter to *The Times* on 6th November Sir Stanley Reed had urged that " the passion for equality is a dominating force in India; and if it is to be for ever denied, India will be driven out of the Empire ". Irwin's analysis was right. India was craving Dominion Status as a Declaration of Right, the influence of which, he might have added, rests on solemn reiteration. Nor was India's plea any less intense for being incoherent. Of particular interest are Irwin's references to Gandhi. In public he asks for " a change of heart ", but privately he hankers after " liberty to order our own future ". Gandhi's ambiguity is significant, as is Irwin's obvious recognition of the problems it presented.

Ironically enough, it was Irwin who, by his initiative, was directing the limelight on Gandhi, and from henceforth the development of his policy was increasingly caught up in the bewildering actions and reactions of the little mystic; indeed the logical conclusion of Irwin's concept of Dominion Status was, after the ordeal of Civil Disobedience, to be found in the Delhi Pact. What began as a broad vision of policy for India as a whole was converted first by conflict and then by compromise into the triumph of two tremendous personalities. Such was Irwin's and Gandhi's ascendancy during these next fifteen months that they were able to embody in themselves vast aspirations of race and creed.

CHAPTER XVII

THE DESTRUCTIVE ELEMENT

THERE is no need to pursue the steady growth of Conservative opposition to Irwinism in England. It fell to Wedgwood Benn's lot to meet the full force of this formidable onslaught, and tribute is due to him for the steady loyalty and gratifying success with which he backed his Conservative Viceroy throughout all the controversies of the coming months. In India the leaders who had signed the Delhi manifesto met at Allahabad to reconsider it in the light of the debates at Westminster, and after considerable heart-searching and discussion re-issued the manifesto without amendment. This decision confirmed the confidence felt in Irwin, and marked the firm resolve of the Liberals, the Hindu Mahasabha and the moderate Congressmen not to be led into the wilderness by Jawaharlal Nehru, who had not hesitated to draw the blackest moral from the proceedings in Parliament and thereby to discredit the Viceroy's Declaration. But although he was thus officially overruled, there were disquieting signs that both his father and Gandhi were now more receptive to his arguments.

The shadow of the Lahore Congress loomed ever larger. Motilal hated Jawaharlal's ideas about Communism and a Peasants' Republic, but he was proud of his son as the potential leader of India's youth and as President Elect of the forthcoming Congress. In addition, Motilal was aware that his own influence with the Viceroy was not as powerful as that of his kinsman Sapru. The Indian Liberals were attaining a greater tactical control of the situation than their power in the country warranted. Gandhi's misgivings went deeper. The implacable opposition of Liberals as well as Conservatives during the Debates had revealed the inherent weakness of the Labour Government's position, and he was beginning to wonder whether any action short of Civil Disobedience would redress the balance. He was, it seems, persuaded that in any case revolution was at hand and that only the self-discipline of satyagraha could save the country from widespread bloodshed, only his moral leadership raise the conflict from a narrow struggle with the Government of India to the supreme trial of strength with the Government and people of Britain.

With these far-reaching ideas at the back of his mind Gandhi began to grope his way towards compromise, which was in effect nothing less than to turn the recommendations of the Delhi manifesto into the conditions of Congress's attendance at a Round Table Conference. There was thus solid foundation for the rumour that Gandhi was toying with the idea of an ultimatum, and it was perhaps unfortunate that on 17th November Irwin left Bombay for a tour of South India. Divorced from the gathering crisis he left behind him he enjoyed a triumphal progress, but it meant that he had lost touch with the Congress leaders at the moment when his personal intervention might have tempered their suspicions.

He went first to Kolhapur, where he rode in a "highly ornamented caravan drawn by a pair of elephants with painted faces and red coats" and where the Maharajah complimented a Viceroy who had included the States in his vision of a united India; then to Kakanhote, where an elephant drive was organized in his honour from which, as he expressed preference to see the animals rather than shoot them, the party returned without firing a shot. At the beginning of December he entered Cochin State, which no Viceroy had visited since Curzon in 1900. In Hyderabad and Travancore, indeed everywhere he went, it was clear that his popularity and prestige were in the ascendant. From Madras to Trivandrum, at the southernmost extremity of India, he was acknowledged with the fervour usually reserved for conquerors or Congressmen. The warmth of his reception may have been a factor in rousing him to steal Gandhi's thunder at Madras, where in the boldest terms he denounced Hindu untouchability.

The tour was, in fact, an unqualified success, but when on 20th December he left Secunderabad he was returning to face a crisis of unknown dimensions. During his journey four of the political leaders who had signed the Delhi manifesto had conveyed a wish to discuss with him at the earliest opportunity matters arising from it, and arrangements had been made for Irwin to meet Gandhi, Motilal Nehru, Jinnah, Sapru and Patel on the 23rd—the day of his formal occupation of the Government House at New Delhi. Nehru and Gandhi were on their way to the Lahore Congress, and Irwin does not seem to have been fully advised as to the depths of their misgivings. There was a widespread impression that the two men were ready to go to London. Nehru was discussing with friends the prospects of the Conference; Gandhi was singing the Viceroy's praises. *The Times* was careful to stress that no negotiations were involved.

Gandhi, also coming up from the South, arrived at Delhi on 22nd December, having travelled deliberately in a crowded third-class carriage. His journey through the Central Provinces had been marked by scenes of hysterical enthusiasm. He refused to discuss political questions with the assembled correspondents save to observe that the meeting was at least a happy indication of a more conciliatory spirit all round. "At such a moment," he added, "silence is golden. To talk would only be to complicate matters." He had, he said, only read the Reports of the Parliamentary Debates "perfunctorily". An official statement announced that the Round Table Conference was to be discussed at the meeting. "Within a week", commented *The Times*, "the world will know whether Congress will come to the Conference or not." It is fair to suggest that as late as the evening of 22nd December an atmosphere of courteous optimism prevailed. But the answer was not a week in coming. Within twenty-four hours the news was flashed across the world of an attempt to assassinate the Viceroy, his policy of appeasement was in ruins, and there remained only the bleak prospect of deadlock and further violence.

. . . .

23rd December 1929 was to be a fateful day not only in the lives of Irwin and of Gandhi but also in the history of India and the Empire. The first reports wired through to London in the early hours of the morning were dramatic enough but inaccurate. The cable printed in the late edition of *The Times* described how Delhi had been shocked by an attempt to assassinate Lord Irwin within one mile of the new capital's station. "A bomb was thrown through a window of the dining-car, which was empty. The explosion was heard by people at the station, who thought it was a fog signal. The dining-car was wrecked, the floors being blown up. His Excellency's compartment was only three away. One servant was hurt." Another agency added to the confusion by publishing the wholly false statement that "Lord Irwin was safely in his residence when the outrage occurred".

Not until the following day was the full and true story available, when it was revealed that a heavy bomb had been fixed between the rails under a sleeper at a point where the track was single, about three miles from New Delhi station. The assassins were apparently lying in wait in an old tenth century fortress—Purana Kila—about two hundred yards away from the line. A length of insulated wire, buried about two inches below ground, ran from the bomb to a bastion at the corner of the fort walls, where it was connected to a battery which was duly discovered by the police. This was no desperate gesture of the crazed fanatic, but a cold and calculated crime, the outcome of scientfic terrorism.

Punctually at 7.40 a.m. the white carriages of the Viceroy's train, travelling at about thirty-five miles an hour, appeared out of heavy mists that shrouded the country and protected the conspirators. As the train passed them the button was pressed and the bomb exploded under the passage connecting the second and third coaches, in other words between the dining-car and the stenographer's office. So violent was the explosion that the floor of the passage was bent upwards in an arch, the steel work twisted and planks splintered. Heavy plate-glass windows in the second and third carriages were shattered to fragments. The fourth carriage, which contained Irwin's staff, was undamaged, while the fifth—the Viceroy's coach—was so little affected that Irwin had no idea what was happening until he was informed by his military secretary. Even then the news did not prevent him from quietly finishing his breakfast. To his staff in the fourth carriage the sound of the explosion came with no more violence than that of a fog signal. A moment later there was a severe jolt, but not until the fumes of smoke penetrated the compartment was it realized that anything was wrong. An Indian bearer clearing up in the dining-car was slightly injured, but no one else was hurt. It was soon discovered that the bomb had actually blown away a section of the rail two feet long and that the remaining coaches had miraculously jumped this gap without leaving the line. If the train had been derailed it would have inevitably rolled down a thirty-foot embankment.

This "miracle" was subsequently explained in a letter to *The Times* from a man who had formerly been Superintendent of Rolling Stock to the East Indian Railway. He pointed out that designs for a new Royal Train for the King and Queen's visit in 1905 were closely considered and that Curzon gave his final approval to a new type of six-wheeled bogey specially made to resist derailment which would certainly have little difficulty in crossing a two-foot gap. So what might have been disaster was in itself no more than an incident. Within a few minutes the train had reached the station, and Irwin, wholly unperturbed, smilingly greeted officials and entered his car for the drive to the new Viceregal House. Did he pause to think that he was taking formal possession of his capital almost exactly seventeen years after the day on which its foundation had been marred by the assassin's bomb? Then, as now, violence and frustration brooded over New Delhi and its Viceroy.

The immediate question, of course, was whether the meeting with the leaders arranged for the afternoon would now take place, but Irwin soon made it clear that he would not hear of a postponement. Although the attempt on Irwin's life starkly revealed the dangers in the pretensions of Congress, the fires beneath the thin surface of goodwill towards the Viceroy, it did not in itself materially alter political dispositions already taken. It was noted that although the leaders at once expressed their regret and abhorrence, Jawaharlal Nehru did not withdraw a passionate appeal issued under his name in *The Tribune* for funds to aid the defence of the men charged with the murder of Mr. Saunders at Lahore. "Donors," he asserted, "will be serving the cause of justice and humanity."

The vital interview undoubtedly began with Patel expecting that a settlement would be reached, and with Jinnah and Sapru anticipating that Gandhi would be making reasonable proposals for Congress participation in the Round Table Conference, while Gandhi's biographer quotes "a generally accepted belief" that when Irwin entered the room "he had in his pocket a list of the political prisoners whom he proposed to release ".[1] While there is no reason to doubt this surmise, it was never put to the test, for after two and a half hours of barren discussion the question of such an amnesty was never even touched upon. Gandhi, after briefly congratulating the Viceroy on his close escape from death, proceeded to develop what was obviously a carefully prepared thesis. Congress, he declared, would have nothing to do with the Conference unless Irwin would give a pledge that its sole function should be to work out a form of government for India equivalent to full and immediate Dominion Status.

Gandhi was in a particularly difficult mood, petulant and profuse. Everyone present realized that he was demanding far more than it was in the power of the Viceroy to concede, and not only was he destroying at one blow the corner-stone of Irwin's policy—which was, the assurance of Congress collaboration in India's constitutional development—but he was also effectively isolating Congress from the other great Indian parties. All Irwin could do was quietly to remonstrate that he was unable to prejudge or commit the Conference at all to any particular line and to dismiss the meeting with the heavy sense that he had been almost personally betrayed. His initial Declaration had been an act of faith which had now failed to evoke the trust of those for whom it was expressly intended. " The meeting was a waste of time, except in so far as it convinced all who desired peace that, if peace did not come, it would not be due to anything left undone by the courageous and selfless man at the head of India's Government."[2]

Gandhi had, it seemed, deliberately chosen the technique —which was soon to prevail over all Europe—of negotiating by ultimatum, and in doing so had not challenged Irwin alone. When he set forth his terms, it is reported that a deep silence fell on the other leaders. Patel had not been informed in advance of Gandhi's and Nehru's attitude and failed to appreciate it. Sapru and Jinnah, who had done most to organize the meeting, were deeply disillusioned. Sapru saw only the deliberate rejection of an immense opportunity. Jinnah sensed the symptoms of a political

[1] Glorney Bolton, *Tragedy of Gandhi*, page 215.
[2] Edward Thompson, *The Reconstruction of India*, page 168.

onslaught on the Moslems. The man who had risked so much to ally himself with the Moslems in the days of the Khilafatist agitation was now going out of his way to provoke Moslem animosities.

. . . .

The implications of the struggle ahead were fully revealed within a few days, when the anxiously awaited Lahore Congress was solemnly opened with Pandit Jawaharlal Nehru riding through the streets on a white charger. He was followed by a flock of elephants and surrounded by a bodyguard of Subhas Chandra Bose's League of Youth, who were all dressed in khaki and were a body openly preaching warlike action. But Nehru's pantomime was no triumphal procession. The choice of the capital of the Punjab for the Annual session of the Congress that was to proclaim India's "Independence", was, to say the least, provocative. Three thousand fully armed Sikhs were on the march. Some of the most formidable fighters in the world were moving on Lahore to throw down a challenge to Gandhi's leadership, and only the tact of a few British officers, who managed to divert the rival contingents, prevented a head-on collision between them in the streets of Lahore. The Moslems had vowed that they would take violent action to break up the Assembly. The Punjab Hindus were not behind Gandhi, while the Depressed Classes there were ready to take a hand in any disturbance that was going on. It is not surprising that Irwin gave close consideration to banning the Congress, with its city of tents, altogether. Finally, with troops brought to reinforce the local police, he decided not to intervene.

The Lahore Congress was dramatic and was therefore news. It was swamped by special correspondents not simply from Britain and India but from America and every part of the world. The story covered by them was concerned with the glaring highlights—the hoisting of the flag of Independence, the mass adulation of Gandhi, the parades and the jostling crowds; the Lahore Congress was, in short, a splendid jamboree which could be magnified into the Renaissance of India or the Death Scene of the British Raj by any lively scribe who confined himself to the surface of things. Behind the scenes, in the so-called Subjects Committee, there was a prolonged struggle over Gandhi's decision to boycott the Conference and over his leadership in general which wholly belied the enthusiastic unanimity displayed in the public Session.

Actually the structure of Congress is such that the Subjects Committee, which consists of the most influential leaders and ex-leaders, is an all-powerful executive. The longer this body deliberated the more evident it became that Gandhi was fighting a rearguard action and that Irwin had powerful allies within the arcana of Congress. Malaviya and Kelkar, speaking yet again for the formidable Mahasabha, Dr. Ansari, representing the Moslem Nationalists and leader of the group carefully nurtured by Gandhi, the brilliant and influential Mrs. Sarajini Naidu, poetess and an ex-President of Congress, all resisted to the utmost the resolution of the Nehrus, which finally endorsed the rejection of Irwin's offer. They did not hesitate to stress privately and in public the imprudence of this action. They were sincerely convinced that their leader had made a fundamental and disastrous mistake.

There is no doubt but that in his decision to let the Lahore Congress take place Irwin was dominating its feverish proceedings as effectively as if he had been there himself. Irwin's offer, Irwin's escape were alike the focal points for controversy, and Gandhi, before he unfurled the flag of Independence, had found himself assailed from both sides—attacking the Viceroy's policy in order to maintain his position against the Moderates, while defending the Viceroy's person from the ferocity of the extremists. Recrimination degenerated into farce when a formal resolution was submitted to the delegates that the Congress "congratulates the Viceroy and Lady Irwin and their party, including the poor servants, on their fortunate narrow escape", and was passed by 935 to 897 votes. "Let us be sure", observes Edward Thompson, "that Lord Irwin's sense of humour will value the knowledge that 897 of the Congress gentlemen think it a pity he was not blown to bits, while 935 think otherwise."[1]

Nor was this all. Gandhi had pleaded earnestly that "it will be a good beginning if you pass this resolution unanimously," to which the only response was an hour and a half's uproarious discussion, the waving of red flags and the

[1] *The Reconstruction of India*, page 169.

demand by a delegate for a recount on the disquieting but wholly understandable ground that several hundred votes had been unaccounted for. Upon this the tumult was so great that the recount was postponed to the end of the proceedings, when it was discovered as a fitting climax that the original figures were too many and not too few, but that the majority in favour of Irwin alive was about forty more than before! Another resolution mildly approving Irwin's services was actually defeated, after Jawaharlal Nehru had sarcastically dismissed his "well-meant" goodwill and cumbrous phrases which were a poor substitute for hard facts.

Far more significant than all this, and a real source of encouragement to Irwin, was the opposition of 77 to 114 which, in the Subjects Committee, Malaviya was able to muster to the Independence resolution, and even those figures did not represent the closeness of the struggle, for the more responsible and influential elements were contained in that opposition. All the same, Gandhi had prevailed and Congress finally decided that "nothing is to be gained in the existing circumstances" by its representation at the proposed Round Table Conference, and that "this Conference therefore, in pursuance of the resolution passed at its session at Calcutta last year, declares that the word 'swaraj' in article one of the Congress constitution shall mean complete independence". Finally, "this Congress appeals to the nation zealously to prosecute the constructive programme of the Congress"—which, if the Resolution's terms were meant for a guide, implied chiefly boycott, abstention, and resignation—"and authorizes the All-India Congress Committee, whenever it deems fit, to launch upon a programme of civil disobedience, including non-payment of taxes, whether in selected areas or otherwise, and under such safeguards as it may consider necessary".

This virtual declaration of war, it may be added, was sufficiently lukewarm for Iyengar and Bose to detect reactionary tendencies, and to secede and form a Congress Democratic Party; but quite apart from this failure to hold the extremists, Gandhi's immediate reaction to his victory did not suggest that he was fully satisfied with it. The foreign journalists, sensing a major crisis in the magic formula of Civil Disobedience, at once crowded round its only begetter. When would he give the order, was not the year of grace at an end? But Gandhi had no answer for them. He was for the moment disillusioned. India, he announced, is not yet ripe for Civil Disobedience.

CHAPTER XVIII

GANDHI GOES TO WAR

IRWIN opened the New Year of 1930 by thanking Indians for their spontaneous condemnation of the bomb outrage, and indeed the volume of congratulations, which had swollen with many gifts of money, belied the niggardly response of Congress. His personal prestige in India was still immense. In Madras a great gathering of representative Moderates, under the auspices of the All-India Liberal Federation, which coincided with the Lahore Congress, had declared decisively in favour of supporting him and preparing for the Conference. A timely tour of Bombay, the great centre of Congress influence, was, in spite of the need for increased precautions, a surprising success. While on this important visit he received a deputation from the Moslem Federation which not merely condemned the attempt on his life but pledged support for the Conference, and there were encouraging signs that the Moslems were about to close their ranks against any extremist developments.

But if there was then ample evidence that the country was steadily rallying to the Round Table Conference, the forces released by Gandhi at Lahore were gathering momentum. While Irwin was enjoying the Maharajah's hospitality at Baroda, Gandhi, no more than a hundred miles away, was making an experiment with Civil Disobedience at Malia in the Bardoli area of Gujerat. He was merely taking up an old local controversy involving non-payment of land revenue to the Government with which Vallabhai Patel, the brother of the President of the Legislative Assembly, was closely identified. The agrarian agitation in the United Provinces, organized into local areas of resistance, had already, through the tough obstinacy of the peasants there, met with considerable success and was particularly potent material for a trial of strength with the British authorities.

Irwin had been bitterly criticized for his failure to crush

the Bardoli agitation from the outset, but many of the strictures were effective as oratory merely because they ignored the persistent and special difficulties in the way of dealing with it. It is sufficient to point out that at that time the United Provinces was enjoying the rule of Sir Malcolm Hailey, who was probably the greatest of Irwin's Governors. If Irwin delayed in taking a strong line he did so on the soundest of first-hand advice. The relationship between the Viceroy and his Governors is comparatively formal, a regular series of memoranda pass to and fro between them. In the three Presidencies, Bengal, Madras and the Punjab, the Governors are in direct contact with the Secretary of State, and thus have a special status which Lord Lloyd, as Governor of Bengal, did not hesitate to exploit to the full when he wished to take stronger action against Gandhi's first Civil Disobedience campaign than the Viceroy Lord Reading was at first prepared to approve. Sir Malcolm Hailey, however, was in close sympathy with Irwin's policy of reconciliation, had played no small part in the small circle of the Viceroy's closest advisers in formulating it, and was fully alive to its strategic implications.

The supreme objective was to avoid a clash with Gandhi which would wreck the Round Table Conference before ever it assembled in London; in other words, to save it from those same preliminaries of suspicion and boycott which so effectively undermined the prospects of the Simon Commission. Hailey accordingly refused to be unduly provoked by the tactics of Vallabhai Patel; on the other hand, in his address to the Legislative Assembly Irwin, while patiently reiterating the motives for his Dominion Status Announcement, laid down clearly and sternly the conditions under which the Round Table Conference would be held and its success enhanced. His speech was ignored by the Nationalist Press, nor did it receive due attention in Britain. In it he declared bluntly that the Conference would be held whether boycotted by Congress or not. "The fact that some decline to take any part in deliberations so closely affecting their country's future only throws greater responsibility upon, and, I would add, gives wider opportunities to, those who are prepared to face and solve difficulties in a constructive spirit." In addition he put out a solemn warning that such doctrines as repudiation of allegiance to the British Crown, refusal to recognize India's financial obligations and other symptoms of Civil Disobedience would not find cover behind the Government's hitherto generous definition of seditious speech.

While he was on the brink of his final decision Gandhi had written: " Civil Disobedience alone can save the country from impending lawlessness and secret crime, since there is a party of violence in the country which will not listen to speeches, resolutions or conferences, but believes only in direct action." But Irwin was neither impressed nor deceived by this inverted logic, and his reply was emphatic: " Although the very authors of the present policy deprecate, some on grounds of principle and some on grounds of expediency, resort to violence, they can hardly be so lacking in either imagination or recollection of past events in India as not to be able to picture the results which must follow, as they have always followed, from the adoption of the policy they recommend." But in spite of well-chosen words that brooked no misinterpretation the speech did nothing to deflect Gandhi from his grave purpose. The House had been full save for a block of twenty out of the thirty-eight Congress seats, and the measure of Irwin's success, as he well realized, would be at the least to maintain this attendance and to prevent the boycott from spreading.

Almost at once there was a fresh and unexpected threat. It did not come from Gujerat but from within the precincts of the Assembly itself, not from Vallabhai Patel but from his brother the President. The bomb outrage in the Assembly in April had, it will be recalled, momentarily saved the Government from an awkward predicament by silencing the President just when he was about to deliver a verdict that would have precipitated a major crisis. The questions then at stake were resolved by the Viceroy's prompt use of his powers under Ordinance, but it was asking too much to expect that Patel would maintain his silence. If the bombs had destroyed one quarrel, they now provided the pretext for another. The protection of the Assembly had naturally enough become a question of deep interest to all its members. The Government saw no reason to alter existing police arrangements, but Patel found increasing support for an agitation to appoint a special protective staff under his own control. The Assembly appointed a committee, under the chairmanship of Sir James Crerar, the Home Member, to consider the question. Crerar, who soon found himself alone in his advocacy of the old order, refused to give way, and Patel, when the winter session began, seeing the police as usual in the gallery, at once ordered the public out, and the session was continued for some time *in camera*.

Irwin had been away from Delhi while all this trouble was brewing, but had sent a special message to Patel on the subject. Unfortunately, through a series of misunderstandings, Crerar failed to transmit it, and whispered rumours soon developed into a campaign of open assertion that the omission was not accidental. Crerar's personality was not wholly suited for coping with *agents provocateurs*, and it was not long before Patel succeeded in widening the whole scope of the dispute. All the Opposition save for the Moslems—and their abstention merely added fuel to the flames—ranged itself behind the President in his grievance, all the old suspicions seemed to come to the surface. Admittedly Congress had laid down that none of their members should attend the Assembly and the order had been largely disobeyed, but those who were present, and in particular the Hindu Mahasabha members, were in an uneasy and dangerous mood. Only a small incident was needed for them to be lost to Irwin's influence altogether.

As a background to Patel's intrigues there was the distracting knowledge that Gandhi was on the eve of his momentous decision to defy the Government, as well as the constant clamour of Congress propaganda that the Opposition rump in the Assembly should join the front line fighters for India's freedom. In addition, evidence was pouring in to the Viceroy of organized terrorist activity on such a scale as to suggest the symptoms of revolution. Bomb factories were discovered in Calcutta and bomb carriers were being arrested throughout India, plans to instigate a general strike and so to paralyse industrial life and military movement had apparently reached an advanced stage, and all the while Gujerati agitation was making headway. Yet in spite of all this tension Irwin's personal influence still dominated the scene.

Returning to Delhi he at once conferred with Malaviya, whose goodwill in the problem of police protection for the

Assembly's inner precincts was essential if a workable solution was to be reached, and quickly effected the necessary compromise between his Government and Crerar on the one hand and Patel and his backers on the other. The speed with which he disposed of what in itself was only a trifling question occasioned some resentment among members of the Civil Service, who felt that Sir James Crerar had received summary treatment from the Viceroy, whose prime duty, so it was argued, was to protect his Ministers from public criticism. But Irwin was not the kind of man to let Crerar's *amour-propre* stand in the way of settling a dispute which was threatening to poison the entire political atmosphere.

Important officials who worked closely with him at this time, while freely admitting his great human qualities, his simplicity, his ready sense of humour, yet could not fail to detect an olympian detachment, a concentration on higher strategy, which in a sense raised him above them and their problems. Whereas most leaders imply to their various subordinates that each one of them is indispensable to him, Irwin, quite apart from his principles in the matter, gave the impression of being altogether too preoccupied to engage in any such personal etiquette. But his remoteness was one minor factor in a veritable tornado of criticism that gathered round him for his refusal to forestall Civil Disobedience by arresting its leaders. Winston Churchill brought out his biggest guns from his oratorical armoury, while Lord Lloyd never wearied of invoking his own wholesome, if forcible, remedies for satyagraha. Undoubtedly distance lent an enchantment to the view of those who advocated a strong line, which was wholly lacking for the unhappy Viceroy, who was in the middle of the fray and only too well aware that the muzzling of Gandhi in advance of any actual offence on his part raised many more problems than it solved. Such an act would automatically bring down the Moderate Hindus, disgruntled but still undecided and personally in sympathy with Irwin, on the side of Congress and against the Conference.

Just how delicate was the situation can be seen in the reaction of Malaviya when the Government, provoked once too often, at last arrested Vallabhai Patel for his part in the Bardoli agitation. Malaviya, as leader of the Nationalist Party in the Assembly, at once moved the adjournment of the House as a censure on the Government's action. Throughout the subsequent debate he was obviously in deep distress, and when one speaker rashly referred to the possibility of Gandhi's imminent arrest and its effect on the Conference he was moved to interrupt angrily, "Who would go to the Round Table Conference if Mahatma Gandhi were in prison?" And if Malaviya went over to Civil Disobedience it was safe to say that he would be taking the rest of the Assembly Opposition with him. But for the moment Gandhi avoided the irrevocable decision, and although the disturbances increased and the Government's prestige declined, Irwin was content to wait upon events and indeed was determined to do so. At the end of February he addressed the Chamber of Princes and was greeted with special warmth. Never, they declared, had there been a Viceroy more respected, beloved or popular. He was India's truest friend. Here at least were powerful allies ready to entertain constructive, far-reaching ideas on collaboration with British India, if for no other reason than to counteract Gandhi's influence in their territories.

On 3rd March he flew with Lady Irwin to Meerut to watch some polo matches, but flew back to Delhi after tea. Early the next morning Reginald Reynolds, a young English Quaker who had joined the Sabarmati Ashram, arrived at Viceregal House. As Reynolds, incongruously clad in khaddar and topee, strode past the mounted guards at the entrance to the House, Gandhi was no doubt relying on the impression this symbol of British support for his cause would make. As far as Irwin was concerned the response was disappointing; Reynolds was given the status solely of a postman, and returned to his master with nothing more than a formal acknowledgment of receipt from the Viceroy's private secretary. Gandhi's message was characteristic in the subtlety of its politics and the honesty of its convictions. Irwin addressed as "Dear Friend" was blandly informed that Gandhi had decided on the date Civil Disobedience should begin and the form it should take. On 12th March he would solemnly begin a pilgrimage to defy the salt laws. "The party of violence", he wrote, "is gaining ground and making itself felt. Having an unquestioning and immovable faith in the efficacy of non-violence it would be sinful on my part to wait longer. This non-violence will be expressed through Civil Disobedience, which for the moment will be confined to the inmates of the Satyagraha Ashram but is ultimately designed to cover all those who choose to join the movement."

In a previous communication with the Viceroy at the end of January he had set out a series of conditions on which he was ready to call off Civil Disobedience which were almost as incongruous a catalogue of grievances and aspirations as those which were gathered together in the Pilgrimage of Grace under the banner of the five wounds of Christ. Total Prohibition and the 1s. 4d. rupee, the reservation of coastal shipping and the reduction by half in the land tax and in all military expenditure, a general anmesty for political prisoners and a free licence for firearms, smaller salaries for Service officials and protection for textiles, along with the demand for the abolition of the Salt Tax, were lumped together as social and economic reforms which the Government must concede. If Gandhi seriously believed in this patchwork programme he can hardly have understood the implications of responsible power in India or the nature of the Viceroy's authority. The first thing, for instance, the rulers of an Independent India would have to do would be to increase taxation, civil and military, if they were to offer to the people the necessary minimum of social and economic security and cultural development. The tariffs he advocated would have entrenched the very industrialism his philosophy abhorred. But quite apart from the desirability or relevance of his terms or the motives behind his emphasis upon them, Gandhi seems to have ignored that they were not within Irwin's discretion to grant even if he had been willing to do so. "He is talking," commented Edward Thompson, "as if he thought he were dealing with Akbar or Aurungzebe." Certain it is that Irwin gave him very little excuse for any such misapprehension; without underestimating its violent consequences he refused to take his challenge tragically, and once again replied through his private secretary. "Dear Mr. Gandhi, His Excellency the Viceroy desires me to acknowledge your letter of March 2. He regrets to learn that you contemplate a course of action which is clearly bound to involve a violation of the law and a danger to public peace." But as earnest of Irwin's readiness to act as well, came the announcement on the same day as the delivery of this letter that Vallabhai Patel had been arrested and sentenced to three months imprisonment.

. . . .

Gandhi had shown considerable acumen if some inconsistency in selecting the Salt Tax from his list of grievances. It had always been a particularly unpopular monopoly, and in order to raise it Reading had been compelled to rely on his powers of certification, and the memory of that particular controversy was still embarrassingly alive. The peasants' food is of such a meagre quality that it is usually unpalatable if it is not seasoned. Salt is therefore not a luxury but the barest necessity to the poverty-stricken millions of India. The perfectly legitimate thesis that Irwin and the Government had officially agreed that the Salt Tax should be brought before the powerful Tariff Board was not calculated to carry weight against Gandhi's more emotional plea that it was an impost on the poorest of the poor. Nor would India bother to recall the dietetic asceticism of Gandhi's Ashram where salt was banned in the interests of self-control; the spectacle of the frail Mahatma marching with his disciples to the beach at Dandi on the Gujerat coast, there to dip a bucket into the sea, boil the water and display the illicit sediment, was one which those who were liable to the tax would understand, approve and all too easily imitate.

But even this splendid procession, which started for Ahmedabad at dawn on 12th March, with the garlands and little children, with the pony presented by a well-wisher for Gandhi to use when he was tired of walking, and the joyous company of journalists, did not provoke Irwin from his policy of watchful patience. On the night before the Ashram set out on its adventure there was the keenest speculation about the possibility of Gandhi's arrest. The inmates listened for the police car that never came. Instead the journalists were given every facility to mock the Mahatma with such headlines as "Gandhi as Godiva", and in due course as the story lost its news value, to disappear from the scene. In the meantime Congress leaders were gathering at Bombay, worried at the flat reaction to their leader's historic revolt against the Raj.

When at last on 6th April Gandhi waded into the sea to the cry from Mrs. Naidu of "Hail, Deliverer!" he no doubt hoped to be rescued from absurdity by a spectacular arrest.

But once more he was to be disappointed. "A satyagrahi overcomes his adversary with love; the Government of India was crippling its rebel with inexhaustible patience and kindness."[1] Gandhi was reduced to returning to Bombay by train. Here he found the revolution he had inaugurated functioning in earnest, the monster he had created was already out of control. In truth Irwin's attention was directed elsewhere than to the non-commercial and non-violent manufacture of salt by a prophet in search of publicity. The Congress leaders soon left behind them the gentle precepts of their master and were in the thick of the most far-reaching disturbances in the whole history of the British Raj. Not only were these violent attacks on Government and private property and isolated murders of officials, British and Indian, but also a vast commercial boycott covering all India.

In April two events in particular startled the world; the dramatic raid on the Chittagong armoury during which six Government servants were killed and a large store of ammunition seized and taken away into the jungles, and the grim riots in Peshawar where, through the inertia of the local administration and in spite of the proximity of considerable military force, the mob gained control of the city for several days and looted the bazaars. Peshawar is the key to the North West Frontier, and trouble there, in itself formidable enough, spells unrest among the mighty warriors of the hills. There can be no doubt but that the rapid spread of Civil Disobedience, the measure of success attending it, the efficiency of Congress technique involving such new and sinister elements as the boycott of British goods with the connivance of wealthy and influential Indian interests, the fervent support of women who were actually leaving their Purdahs to join in the fray, the refusal of the famous Garhwal rifles to face the mob at Peshawar, marked an advance on anything the Government had experienced in Gandhi's earlier campaign, and must have come as a genuine surprise to Irwin.

Ex post facto criticism is easy, and in his handling of this unprecedented situation he has been subjected to more than his fair share of it. Robert Bernays, for instance, in *Naked Fakir*, his vivid diary of a visit to India a few months

[1] Glorney Bolton, *Tragedy of Gandhi*, page 220.

later, which is otherwise extremely favourable to Irwin and his regime, sets out the familiar argument of his weakness in failing to check the spread of grave disorder between Congress's declaration of war at Lahore in December 1929 and the ultimate arrest of Gandhi in the following May, and in doing so no doubt reflected a view generally held in official circles. He argues that by delaying until May his decision to restrain the ringleaders he not only gave them time to prepare their campaign but also chose the moment when Civil Disobedience was most formidable to set about crushing it. This analysis, however, is deceptive in its clear-cut simplicity and does not do full justice to the complexity of the problem confronting Irwin. It was not possible for him to survey Civil Disobedience solely in terms of military action. Indeed military considerations may well have been a factor urging Irwin to caution. The memory of Amritsar and General Dyer hung like a pall over the Higher Command of the Indian Army, and although the Commander-in-Chief, Sir Philip Chetwode, was a great leader convinced of the need for reforms and in closest sympathy and contact with Irwin, there was none the less a deep reluctance in the Army as a whole to put down Civil Disobedience unless underwritten in every particular, great and small, by the Central Government. The same lack of confidence operated in the Civil Service.

But over and above the reservations of his Executive Irwin had to keep in mind the lonely and precarious position of his Government. Its whole existence was based upon the loyalty of a handful of police who were compelled to work under most difficult conditions. Civil Disobedience was calculated to undermine their patience, and the provocation of highly organized passive resistance was bound to lead to harsh retaliation which the Government could not approve but dared not disavow. As a counterweight to the criticism retailed by Bernays it is worth recording the considered estimate of Negley Farson, the American journalist, in his remarkable autobiography *The Way of a Transgressor*. He was in India throughout the summer of 1930, and he was only one among many of his fellow-countrymen who cabled outspoken criticisms of the British Raj to America, where, to quote the historian, " Imperial relations are still viewed in terms of the Boston Tea Party ".

Farson describes receiving an invitation to lunch at Vice-regal House the day after he had reached Simla, and on the basis of an understanding that he would report nothing of what was said Irwin led him off for " a long talk on the whole Gandhi business ". " Irwin . . . has been criticized (and was being violently attacked both in England and India at that moment by Diehards) for what was claimed too soft a hand in handling Indian affairs. All I can say is that out in India I had one big Indian after another assure me that if it had not been for Irwin's character there would have been bloodshed all round. The Indians, particularly the Hindus, can understand and appreciate a saintly character. And if Gandhi was a holy man, Lord Irwin certainly was a saint. I think he is the finest Englishman I have ever met —with perhaps the exception of honest George Lansbury. It was the fact that lots of the Indians believed in Lord Irwin's sincerity that kept them quiet. 'They are saying down in the Plains,' said that tall figure, looking down into the Himalayas, 'that " you cannot govern India from the Hills! " Well, perhaps the Plains are too far from the Hills for the people to understand what is being done up here. Here are two more Ordinances that I am, very reluctantly, going to have to invoke to-morrow. You can have the first news of them to send them to your paper, if you like.' "[1]

Nor can Irwin be accused of not having acquainted himself with the facts of the disturbed situation. Only a few days before the Peshawar riots, he had completed a careful survey of the North West Frontier, and then, when it was obvious that the trouble had spread beyond the bounds of local remedy, he did not waver. By a series of stern but well-timed blows he succeeded within the course of a few hectic weeks in breaking the back of Civil Disobedience and transforming a movement that was leading straight to revolution into a retreating conspiracy. A mere recital of the action taken by him during this time belies once for all the legend that he was a weak Viceroy. Those who were responsible for executing his orders testify that his religious convictions seemed to reinforce the very ruthlessness of his policy of suppression, even if it was inevitable that the same conviction should equally impel him to forgive his enemies after he had vanquished them.

[1] *The Way of a Transgressor*, page 608.

There was, of course, in Irwin's time no Provincial autonomy. The Viceroy laid down the general line of policy in the Provinces and was also responsible for law and order there. Thus in defeating Civil Disobedience Irwin did not confine himself to seeking special powers, but also actively encouraged reluctant Provincial Governors to carry out the various Ordinances, and if necessary enforced discipline over their heads. He was the first to take action after the failure of the local authorities to suppress the Peshawar revolt. His immediate response to the Chittagong outrage was to promulgate by Ordinance expiring sections of the Bengal Criminal Law Amendment Act. President Patel's last gesture of defiance was to proffer his resignation; Irwin caused " a profound sensation " by accepting it at once. In doing so he abandoned all semblance of polite belief in Patel's impartiality with a sharp reference to " you and those with whom you are once again to be associated ", and bitterly upbraided him for inciting his countrymen to violate the law. On the same day he revived the Press Act of 1910, repealed in 1922, which involved far stricter censorship.

Then on 5th May Gandhi was quietly and smoothly removed from the Bombay Express and taken off to Poona gaol in a fast car. An astonished multitude of his fellow passengers and countrymen, Hindus and Moslems alike, were helpless witnesses of a drama in which the apostle of non-violence was quietly submitting to a technique of force that was to say the least non-violent. The symbolic significance of this moment might have been suppressed altogether —as no doubt Irwin hoped it would be—had not Negley Farson and a colleague, Ashmead Bartlett of the *Daily Telegraph*, following up a " strong hunch ", driven to the scene and secured the greatest news scoops in their careers. Owing to the world's curve Farson was able to supply America from San Francisco to Chicago with the headline " Gandhi arrested at Borivli six o'clock this morning "—by the same afternoon. By the next morning Bartlett's story, with Gandhi's exclusive comments, were in the *Daily Telegraph*. The seething excitement in the bazaars of Bombay had thus reached the British breakfast-table with the speed of light. But if this leakage was unwelcome Irwin was not wholly unprepared for it. There was to be no follow up with a dramatic trial, and Gandhi recapturing the world's imagination with another confession of sin and plea for punishment. He was arrested, this time under a Bombay Ordinance introduced a hundred and three years before, which enabled the Government to imprison him without trial as " a menace to public order ".

Irwin knew more about the nature of the spiritual force behind Civil Disobedience than the furious Diehards who so confidently breathed slaughter from the deep recesses of their London clubs. Equally distorted was the impression conveyed by Congress propaganda, now being cyclostyled and not printed in order to evade the newly revived Press Censorship Act, of a " good old pious Irwin " sitting in Simla and viewing the situation with " unctuous unconcern, in all Christian charity, and with a smile of supreme contentment that the law's authority was being maintained ". Irwin's appraisal of Gandhi's leadership was the outcome neither of defeatism nor indifference. Farson, with all the shrewd perception of a great news reporter, had soon extracted the essential strength of Gandhi's campaign—the subtlety of which seemed to be lost as much upon the Bengal terrorists as upon the Anglo-Indian Colonels. Gandhi, he argued, " longed to hold the British up as wife-beaters before a shocked world. The spirituality of his Civil Disobedience movement rested upon a masochistic base."[1]

Not for nothing did Irwin return Gandhi to the Yeravda as a *détenu* rather than as a convict. Farson describes asking Irwin what he really thought of Gandhi. " The first time I saw Gandhi ", was the reply, " I was tremendously impressed by his holiness. The second time I was tremendously impressed by his legal astuteness. The third time I was sure of it." " ' Of which, your Excellency? ' Lord Irwin merely smiled and looked down into the Himalayas. ' That is for you to decide,' he said." Farson confesses he could never make up his mind, and it is probable that Irwin himself has never succeeded in resolving the riddle to his final satisfaction. " All I know ", Farson concludes, " is that I have never for one moment doubted his absolute sincerity "—nor did Irwin, who could appreciate his great protagonist on a higher plane than that of political expediency. " Most religious men ", Gandhi once observed in a moment of acute self-analysis, " are politicians in disguise; I, how-

[1] *The Way of a Transgressor*, page 595.

ever, who wear the guise of a politician, am at heart a religious man." It was an estimate that could have been applied with equal justice to Irwin himself, and at least it ensured that neither of them would allow the discord of events to make a future reconciliation utterly impossible.

. . . .

In the meanwhile, as the disorders worked steadily towards their climax in July, Irwin did his duty relentlessly. Jawaharlal Nehru, Abbas Tyebji who succeeded Gandhi as temporary President of Congress, and Mrs. Naidu who succeeded him, were soon rounded up, and although officially the continuity of Congress leadership was always maintained, all those who had any weight in the movement were imprisoned. At one time the "weak" Viceroy had filled the gaols with no less than sixty thousand political offenders, yet in spite of his preoccupations with suppression and ordinances his primary concern was still the Round Table Conference, he was still persistently wooing the Moderate Nationalists. The arrest of Gandhi had undoubtedly disturbed the Hindu Mahasabha, and some even of its Right Wing leaders who had disassociated themselves from Civil Disobedience had publicly withdrawn their support for the Conference. There were sinister signs that the communal situation, which had been comparatively quiet, was boiling up to another crisis, and that the necessary minimum of unity for fruitful discussion would not be maintained.

Accordingly a week after Gandhi's arrest, Irwin published an important statement as well as correspondence between himself and the Prime Minister. The statement solemnly affirmed that Civil Disobedience had in no way deflected the Government from its policy of constitutional reform announced during the previous autumn. Although Congress had refused to participate in it, the Round Table Conference would be held in London as arranged. Proceedings would start towards the end of October, immediately after the Imperial Conference. Characteristically Irwin ended his statement by invoking Luke xi. 52 as testimony against Congress—"Ye have taken away the key of knowledge: ye entered not in yourselves, and them that were entering in ye hindered." The correspondence between himself and MacDonald was interesting chiefly because it answered at some length the question of how the personnel of the Conference would be chosen; briefly, invitations were to be left solely to his discretion. These definite announcements undoubtedly helped to reassure Moderate opinion and were a stimulus to a notable All-Parties Conference held in Bombay under the chairmanship of Sir A. P. Patro, the famous leader of the Madras Justice Party. The Europeans were strongly represented, but the total result of Patro's praiseworthy efforts at conciliation was simply to re-emphasize the old dissensions; the delegates were soon split up into two groups, the Hindus, who wanted the question of unity to be reserved for the calmer atmosphere of St. James's Palace, and the Minorities, who were not prepared to postpone their demands for safeguards.

If the Unity Conference raised more difficulties for Irwin than it solved, worse was to follow during June with the publication in two monumental volumes of the Simon Report. The first volume industriously and with a wealth of scholarship set out the results of a vast fact-finding survey. This survey was intended primarily for British politicians and public, but unhappily it was read and discussed chiefly by Indians, who were in no mood to be dissected, however sympathetic or methodical the process might be. Emphasis was carefully laid upon India's diversity, and the communal question was analysed at immense length. On the other hand, in discussing recent unrest the strength of Nationalist sentiment was dangerously underestimated. The second volume contained the concrete proposals. They were of " a conservative character and such innovations as they contained had already been discounted by moderate opinion both in England and India ".[1] Diarchy was to make way for Provincial Autonomy, but an elaborate system of safeguards by means of special powers for the Governor and authority left with the Central Government, made the concession into little more than a verbal manœuvre. There was to be no major modification of the Central Executive until the Native States were ready to join in a Federation and the country was strong enough to defend itself, " two provisos which were taken as clearly deferring any transfer of authority for a generation or more. Indian Nationalists could not be expected to consider such proposals seriously. Their status was left unchanged, and their future would

[1] Garratt and Thompson, *British Rule in India*, page 635.

have been dependent upon two factors, neither of which was under their control."[1]

The Report was in a sense progressive, the concept of popular control over law and order in the Provinces was conceded, Burma's claim to autonomy recognized, there was to be no putting back of the administrative clock, but its origins as an imposed British enquiry, the large measure of agreement among the Party representatives on the Commission (the skill with which Simon retained Burnham without losing Attlee and Hartshorn was to prove a Pyrrhic victory) came as a great disappointment to many Indians who had been expecting advanced minority opinions, and merely confirmed " the idea that all Englishmen, once they are in office, take the same view about India ". Much of the chorus of bitter invective which greeted the Report was ill-considered and no doubt prearranged. Irwin's Dominion Status Announcement and offer of a Conference may well have killed whatever small chance it had of receiving serious attention, but taken all in all his original fears on first hearing the draft recommendations of the Report were amply justified. If he had been content just to wait on the prospect of a favourable reaction to the Simon Report, knowing its terms in advance as he did, he would have incurred a far greater responsibility for India's dissensions than ever he did by taking the initiative. Sifting the reasoned and disinterested criticism from the purely factious abuse, it is quite clear that the Simon Report failed to approach the demands of even moderate Indian opinion, while many responsible Europeans argued that quite apart from the dissatisfaction of nationalist sentiment the form of government proposed would prove extremely cumbrous and difficult to work. Although Provincial Autonomy was widely welcomed, the Moslems were far from happy about safeguards, and the Sikhs were loud in their complaints at the small percentage of seats allowed them in the Central Legislature.

It should not be forgotten that Irwin took the drastic step of postponing in the previous year the General Election that was due to be held at the end of 1929. His only motive for making such an extreme use of his powers was to give the Report a fair chance, for the Congress Party and other elements had announced their intention of fighting the elec-

[1] *British Rule in India*, page 636.

tion on the simple cry of "boycott the Simon Report". Such a struggle would have had fatal consequences not only for the Report but also for the entire constitutional future of India. Apart from a few Moslems and the Madras Justice Party, the Assembly and the Provincial Councils would have been packed with overwhelming majorities pledged in advance to have nothing to do with the Report. Thus, far from undermining the Report, Irwin more than anyone else tried to create the necessary conditions for it to succeed on its own merits; his failure was the outcome both of the contents of the Report itself and of new circumstances beyond his control.

CHAPTER XIX

KNIGHT OF THE ROUND TABLE

As the time drew near for the Simla session of the Legislature there were the most ominous rumours not only of the Government's ability ultimately to control the situation but also of the usefulness of the Conference—would it not be yet another instrument for Britain to impose her will on India? Would not the delegates have to confront " reactionary " Liberal and Conservative M.P.s in addition to the well-disposed Government representatives? Once again Irwin was called upon to strengthen the weak and rally the faltering. Once again in his address to the Combined Legislatures he rose to the critical situation. Once again the inherent strength of his attitude was not in any new statement of policy but in his clear approach to the pressing problems of Civil Disobedience and the Conference and the wider perspective into which he fitted them. No provocations or disappointments, it seemed, could undermine his faith in the greatness of his mission.

He firmly rejected Gandhi's thesis that Civil Disobedience was " a perfectly legitimate form of political agitation, to which resort is had only under pressure of regrettable necessity. I cannot take that view. In my judgment it is a deliberate attempt to coerce established authority by mass action, and for this reason, as also because of its natural and inevitable developments, it must be regarded as unconstitutional and dangerously subversive." Against such mass action the Government were bound either to resist or abdicate. " The present movement is exactly analogous to a general strike in an industrial country which has for its purpose the coercion of Government by mass pressure as opposed to argument, and which a British Government recently found it necessary to mobilize all its resources to resist." This was, by the way, the first and only occasion on which Irwin ever committed himself in public to an opinion upon the General Strike; and such a mild reference four years after the event can hardly be said to classify his attitude to a controversy which split asunder most of the essential compromises of British public life and branded the reputations of so many of his Conservative friends and colleagues.

To those Moderates who had never believed in Civil Disobedience and to many more who had attached themselves to it but who were beginning to doubt its ethic and usefulness, Irwin, whose sincerity even at the height of the struggle was never questioned by anyone, offered fresh hope. " The gravity of the present movement," he asserted, " does not deflect my judgment on the question of constitutional reform by a hair's breadth to the right or left. I am not fighting Civil Disobedience because I lack sympathy with the genuine Nationalist feelings of India." Then again, " so far from desiring to secure so-called victory over a Nationalist movement constitutionally pursued, I desire nothing more than to be able to help India so far as I can to translate her aspirations into reality ". That he was not confining himself merely to vague aspirations was obvious from his clear and far-reaching definition of the scope and function of the Round Table Conference. It was not right to prescribe for it any terms more limited than in the Dominion Status Announcement. Agreement reached at the Conference " will form the basis of the proposals which His Majesty's Government will later submit to Parliament ". It was thus not " a mere meeting for discussion and debate ", but " a joint assembly of representatives of both countries, on whose agreement precise proposals to Parliament may be founded ". The Conference would thus be free to approach its task " greatly assisted indeed but with liberty unimpaired by the Simon Report ".

In his peroration he spoke as a friend rather than as a Viceroy or Governor-General. " India is a country the scale of whose history and physical features alike condemn those who would take small views. The monuments with which her land is enriched attest the faith and perseverance of her master craftsmen, and reprove those who would believe that any other qualities can serve the constitution builder, who builds not for himself but for futurity." He stressed the utter tragedy that Congress should have refused the hand of friendship extended last November and thrown aside the finest opportunity that India has ever had. "I would hope that it might yet not be too late for wiser counsels to prevail. . . . Thus two roads to-day lie open, one leading us, I think, to turmoil, disunity, disappointment and shattered hopes; the other guiding those who follow it to the India of our dreams, a proud partner in a free Commonwealth of Nations, lending and gaining strength by such honourable association. India to-day has to make her choice. I pray God she may be moved to choose aright."

The British reactions to this courageous speech were not helpful. A few hours before its publication Birkenhead plucked up courage to issue "a tremendous warning"; but, as *The Times*' leading article pointed out, the text hardly justified these gloomy forebodings. In spite of Birkenhead's encyclical there was, it asserted, "no disparagement of the Simon Report, no proposal that we are to empty the gaols of lawbreakers in order to equip the Round Table with witnesses". But in some respects this very defence of Irwin by *The Times* was in itself a warning and a criticism. The Dominion Status Announcement had undoubtedly disturbed Geoffrey Dawson even if it did not destroy his confidence in the Viceroy's policy or his loyalty to the man. *The Times* was still his staunch champion in all the welter of criticism to which he was subjected in Press and Parliament. But Dawson, perhaps more keenly alive to the formidable potentialities of Conservative opposition to appeasement in India than Irwin, saw fit to "write down" Dominion Status. When Irwin released his historic Announcement the "Thunderer's" defence was merely that it was the repetition of a policy solemnly proclaimed at least seven times in the previous twelve years. Dawson was now thankful that there was no incursion into this "peculiarly barren field of controversy", and was obviously urging Irwin to pursue the Round Table Conference with rather less valour and more discretion than he had shown over Dominion Status. The speech seemed to imply a willingness on Irwin's part to make another approach to Congress in order to make his list of invitations complete, the Congress Press had been quick to take up this point, and the temptation should be resisted. Thus we find *The Times* somewhat blatantly pronouncing that there was no obligation to honour an agreement made between one political party in England and another, however predominant, in India, but that this was not in Irwin's mind. Certainly it was not, but what was in Dawson's?

For once a *Times* leading article came straight to the point. Although the Ministers in England were right to let Irwin take measures for defence and not interfere with him in that field *The Times* thought they were leaving too much responsibility with him for shaping future policy. It went on to suggest a number of men who might advise the Viceroy and give him " some indication of the best opinion in England "; the names mentioned were Ramsay MacDonald, Simon, his two Socialist Commissioners Attlee and Vernon Hartshorn, Reading, Austen Chamberlain, Peel, Winterton, Zetland and Goschen. It is difficult to believe that Irwin can have found this friendly proposal other than embarrassing or to understand how these eminent exponents of the " best opinion " could have lightened his burden. Was he to be answerable to their recommendations or was their advice to be simply informal? In either case was it right or feasible that the Viceroy should be distracted by the influence of men six thousand miles from the scene of action in dealing with a complex and swiftly moving situation that demanded above all a wide personal discretion? In some respects even the stark opposition of Churchill or Rothermere was preferable to such protection. Actually *The Times* was soon joining issue again with Churchill for making a tactless outburst in which he had asserted that no responsible person could suppose for a moment that the forthcoming Conference could produce Dominion Status for India or that Dominion Status " is likely to be obtained for India within the lifetime of anyone now living ".

It was perhaps fortunate for Irwin that he was altogether too preoccupied with developments in India to worry himself unduly about British reactions. The period between his speech to the Legislatures in July and the opening of the Round Table Conference in London in October was one in which his Herculean capacity for work was tested to the uttermost. Not only did the whole future of the Conference depend upon the team of delegates he succeeded in collecting, but also he and his Executive Council were engaged in drafting a full length Despatch giving the Government of

India's considered views upon the recommendations of the Simon Report, the basic purpose of which was to supply the delegates with a draft from which they could reach ultimate agreement. The Socialists were obviously disappointed with the Simon Report and no effort was made, in spite of Conservative pressure, to find a special place at the Conference for Simon and his colleagues in their capacity as Commissioners. It was left to Irwin then to profit in three months from the failure of Simon over three years.

With regard to personnel for the Conference the two Liberal leaders, Sapru and Jayakar, at once interpreted the generous language of Irwin's speech as opening the way to their mediation between him and the leaders of Civil Disobedience, and on 13th July they addressed a letter to Irwin seeking permission from him to visit Gandhi, Motilal and Jawaharlal Nehru in their prisons " so that we may put our point of view before them and urge them in the interests of the country to respond to our appeal, to enable the big issue of Constitutional advance to be solved in a calm atmosphere. We desire to make it plain that in going to them, we shall be going on our own behalf, and we do not profess to represent either the Government or any party in taking this step. If we fail in our attempt, the responsibility will be ours." Irwin readily gave his assent to these proposals; the stake was far too great for him to reject any effort, however faint the prospect of success; but in thus encouraging Sapru and Jayakar, he inevitably gave these two leaders a special status.

The negotiations were delicate and prolonged, they had ready access to him and enjoyed his confidence, while he on his part voluntarily submitted himself to consideration of their detailed advice and impressions. Arising out of these contacts Sapru did not hesitate to express his fervent belief that Irwin was the greatest friend India had ever had, but even this manifestation of devotion did not set at rest the fears of Irwin's official advisers, some of whom felt that behind Jayakar's and Sapru's idea of mediation was an excessive sympathy with the Congress view-point. They were alarmed whenever Sapru was in Irwin's company, which, since the negotiations dragged on until the beginning of September, was often. The Indian Liberals and Moderates were not held in high esteem by British officials in India, and were regarded as lacking followers, convictions or courage. Although this damaging estimate may have been generally accurate, it could not be fairly applied to Sapru or Jayakar, whose inexhaustible energy and resource was an important factor in the final vindication of Irwin's policy.

If Irwin's Executive Council failed to appreciate Sapru's motives, Gandhi and the Nehrus were equally suspicious; Jawaharlal records " we talked and argued in a circle, hardly understanding each other's language or thought, so great was the difference in political outlook ".[1] Irwin's permission was obtained for the Nehrus to be transferred to the Yeravda gaol where Gandhi was housed, but they were much irritated that they were only allowed to see their leader in Sapru's presence. In the various interviews during July and August Gandhi was unwilling to consider any modification of his original " eleven point " ultimatum. Indeed in a letter which summarized the Yeravda negotiations, and which was composed for Irwin's benefit, their price had, if anything, gone up. No solution, they now declared, would be satisfactory unless it " recognized the right of India to secede from the British Empire . . . and also gave the right to refer, if necessary, to an independent tribunal such British claims and concessions, including the public debt of India, as seemed unjust ".

The tone of the document as well as the terms themselves made it very difficult for Irwin to continue the negotiations at all, but he was not to be provoked into closing the door or into barren recrimination. While deploring the blank refusal of the Nationalist leaders to recognize the grave injury being done to the country by Civil Disobedience he quietly reasserted his readiness to revoke the Ordinances as soon as the movement was called off. Until then no useful purpose could be served in discussing the leaders' proposals in detail. Although unable to give an assurance that all political prisoners not guilty of actual violence should be released, he said he would recommend the local Governments concerned sympathetically to consider all cases on their merits. He also stated that he was ready to give Congress adequate as distinct from majority representation at the Conference. But there was to be no response to these offers. Sapru and Jayakar hurried once

[1] *Autobiography*, page 228.

again to the prison with the text of Irwin's letter. Motilal Nehru, who was desperately ill, asked the peacemakers to convey to Gandhi his general disappointment with the tone of the Viceroy's reply, which merely confirmed Gandhi in his *non possumus* attitude. The whole of this interesting episode ended informally in failure with a letter from Gandhi and his colleagues on 5th September stating that they saw no meeting ground between the Government and Congress.

Three days later Motilal Nehru was released, his sentence remitted, but he did not survive to see peace at Delhi and died before the negotiations had begun. Motilal was the first of the Nationalist leaders to be disillusioned by Civil Disobedience, and in spite of all political differences always had the highest regard for Irwin and his motives. During the height of repression, he was heard once to confess with complete sincerity, " I do wish it had not to be Lord Irwin " —a sentiment which Gandhi could appreciate even if his son Jawaharlal could not; but his influence over them both was very powerful, and towards the end was setting in favour of compromise. But for a deplorable blunder Motilal might have taken a powerful initiative in effecting a settlement; as it was, local officialdom put him under lock and key on a charge of conspiracy while he was actually on his way to discuss the whole Congress position with Gandhi, and Irwin unhappily for once gave way to Civil Service pedantry in allowing his arrest. This action, together with his fatal illness, removed from the scene when the situation was perhaps more critical than at any time since " Clemency " Canning, the only Indian with sufficient authority and experience to have deflected Gandhi from the tragedy of Civil Disobedience.

. . . .

The negotiations, it must be confessed, had not been helped by the issue of two more Ordinances. Between the middle of April and the end of December Irwin had powers through no less than ten Ordinances—an unprecedented number representing a sum total of arbitrary rule which had been wielded by no previous Viceroy. These Ordinances were well designed to meet the various forms of Civil Disobedience. The movement, like Gandhi's eleven points, was a response to a complex variety of grievances which took different shapes in different Provinces and cities. Ordinances were readily adapted to meet local crises. Thus we find Irwin invoking in Bengal a Criminal Amendment Ordinance to meet the particular threat from the gunmen and bomb-throwers of East India. The Sholapur Martial Law Ordinances, which made it illegal for more than four people to gather together in the street, was a drastic challenge to the communal disturbance in that city. Unlawful Instigation Ordinances were directed against the agrarian unrest in Bombay and the United Provinces. A Martial Law Ordinance hammered out order in the stricken bazaar of Peshawar and among the wild Afridi tribesmen. There were special Ordinances to deal with picketing, the non-payment of taxes, intimidation, to arrest a plotter while he was in another part of India from where he planned to hatch his plot. To get round the Press Censorship, Congress bulletins were, as we have seen, being cyclostyled and not printed. In July Irwin duly issued an Ordinance to include cyclostyle bulletins within the scope of the Press Act. But even then Congress publicity still poured out until in October he invoked an anti-propaganda Ordinance of the utmost severity to which he felt constrained to attach over his signature a long explanatory memorandum. It rendered all Congress party premises liable to seizure, made certain offences non-bailable and allowed no appeal after sentence.

This catalogue of absolutism is surely a final refutation of the charge of weakness so persistently levelled against Irwin. He wanted peace with Gandhi, he was ready to take action to get it, but he never consented to tamper with law and order in the process. Thus at the end of August reports of very secret conversations between Sapru, Jayakar and himself, with suitable observations on his "marvellous patience", coincided with the stark announcement that Patel, Ansari and the venerable Malaviya were among further members of the Congress Working Committee who had been arrested and sentenced to six months imprisonment. Then again, one of Gandhi's demands had been that the public debt of India should be referred to an independent tribunal along with other British claims and concessions; Irwin, in thanking Sapru and Jayakar for their gallant efforts for peace, did not hesitate to upbraid them for making open references to confidential conversations to the effect that the Government might agree to a partial repudiation of debts and took the opportunity to issue a categorical denial. He revealed in a public speech[1] a few days later that no sooner had Sapru and Jayakar begun their mediation than there was the suggestion that private assurances to supplement an open statement of Government policy would be acceptable. "I do not doubt that assurances on certain points very material to the speedier restoration of peace might have been received, if I on my part had been ready to give assurances on the constitutional issues in private that I was not prepared to give in public."

In as far as Irwin was deeply committed to a much criticized policy of appeasement at the time, and was later to experience at the hands of Adolf Hitler tactics and demands not dissimilar from those of Congress, his decisive reaction to secret diplomacy is particularly noteworthy. "That method is not one that ever has, or ever will, make any appeal to me," he declared. From the view-point of immediate developments it would have undermined the whole idea of a Free Conference and given undue weight to the pretensions of an important but none the less single political party. "To have given any such private engagement, in order to buy off the Civil Disobedience movement, would have been not less than a betrayal of all other parties in India, and, above all, of those who throughout these last troubled months have supported Government. . . . I hope my severest critic here or elsewhere will never be able to charge me with having spoken with a different voice in private from that which I have employed in public utterances."

In this catch-as-catch-can era Irwin has always set himself a particularly high standard of public conduct, and in doing so laid himself open to criticism which less scrupulous statesmen tend to avoid. The moralist in politics makes the search for compromise particularly arduous in that he demands from his adversary an acceptance of values roughly equivalent to his own. Here we may detect Irwin's underlying sympathy with Gandhi—at least his attitude to violence was religious even if confused. The full force of his wrath was directed against "those holding important positions in the Congress organization who are not ashamed

[1] Punjab Government Farewell, Simla, September 29th 1930.

openly to confess that the question whether or not to adopt a policy of violence is one of mere expediency and not of principle, that the issue is one to be judged not on moral but on practical grounds, and that, if the way of violence is to be rejected it is only because it promises no substantial results ".

By the autumn Irwin's attack on Civil Disobedience had borne fruit and the peak period of crisis had been safely passed. The original force had spent itself and deputy leaders were relying on fresh expedients, such as belated attempts to set up a parallel government which were making no appreciable headway. The struggle had settled down into a war of attrition; the boycott of British goods and the refusal to pay rents and taxes were reinforced by the application of social sanctions, but on the whole Congress propaganda had extended over a wider area only at the price of achieving less intensive results in particular localities. District Officers had, in general, mastered the no-revenue campaign, and the persecution of Civil Servants by now was an inconvenience rather than a cause for alarm. However, it was clear that although thousands of small Indian traders were ruined by the commercial paralysis produced by the Congress campaign, the Hindu trading class was still firmly, if less enthusiastically, in sympathy with the movement.

On the economic side, as Irwin himself implied in his address to the Associated Chambers of Commerce in December, the movement was but an aggravating incident in the spread of a world slump. Irwin was never very strong on economics and he was lucky in the calibre of his successive finance Ministers, Sir Basil Blackett and Sir George Schuster, but even he was alive to the consequences of effective boycott against the catastrophic background of a world-wide fall in the prices of wholesale commodities. Brutal facts would teach Gandhi and his colleagues a lesson here which no amount of Viceregal warning could achieve. During Elections, Congress sponsored demonstrations against the Round Table Conference, but although the platforms were adorned with the presence of Jawaharlal Nehru, Patel, Bose, Sen Gupta and others on the expiring of their sentences, Irwin could take comfort from their failure to provoke any noticeable animosity against what was still his supreme project and the cornerstone of all his hopes. The mediation of the Moderates had failed, but Sapru never lost faith in Irwin and pledged himself and his colleagues to do everything in their power for the success of the Conference.

When at last the eighty delegates sailed from Bombay Irwin could look with pride on the high status and representative character of the leaders he had secured from British India and the States alike; their combined presence in London was almost wholly the result of his own ceaseless labours necessarily carried on behind the scenes. Indeed it is no exaggeration to claim that if the dramatic success of the Conference from which emerged a clear new vision of Indian unity was of any one man's making that man was Irwin. His creative will dominated the momentous proceedings at St. James's Palace as surely as though he had been there himself to draft the resolutions and mould the speeches. At the outset publicity for the Conference was somewhat limited. In India Congress papers reduced boycott to absurdity by trying to ignore its existence; while in Britain certain Press Lords, with greater subtlety but with an equal intolerance, refused to feature India or Indians on the tacit but deplorable assumption that to do so was inherently unpatriotic. But the British Press as a whole was equal to a great occasion and helped to build up an atmosphere of restraint and responsibility which must have come as a refreshing if unusual experience for the delegates. Moreover, the Conference came at a moment when there was a comparative lull in British politics, and it suggested, in spite of the sober European dress of the delegates, a colourful, almost glamorous distraction for the British public from the humdrum inactivity of a dim Socialist Government which for all its good intentions failed to hold popular imagination. Indeed the Conference was as much an opportunity for British as for Indian statesmanship to find itself. On the whole, the procedure and publicity were such that Irwin's pervasive influence was consciously or unconsciously ignored by the Press of both countries. There was almost a conspiracy of silence which in as far as his personal contribution was concerned Irwin himself did nothing to dissolve. But his achievement was not any the less remarkable for being suppressed and anonymous.

He had deliberately brought to an end the era of Royal

Commission and imposed inquests; but in substituting Conferences for them, apart from the psychological gain in self-respect, the hard core of the problem, the political union of All-India, remained. Nor was the larger union feasible unless British India emerged ready to co-operate as an entity with the Indian States. Even when technically achieved, All-India would not come to life until its status in the British Commonwealth was established. The only hope of making headway where the Simon Commission had been held up, rested in the preparations and informal discussions before ever the delegates sat round the table. The magic formula was Federation, but it would work magic only if the Princes were ready to invoke it. To the astonishment of the Government and officials in London the Princes did not hesitate but at once declared their willingness to join in a Federation on the basis of responsible self-government. Thereupon the spokesmen of the different interests and communities all took up the same theme and even the representatives of the Conservative European Community gave its guarded approval. From that moment the decisive victory had been gained.

. . . .

How far did the news come as a surprise to Irwin? He provided part of the answer in the course of his farewell address to the Chamber of Princes.[1] After asserting that "few of us, I imagine, had anticipated or foreseen the dramatic announcement" made after the delegates' arrival in London, he went on to reveal that "I had, of course, from time to time, and even as late as last July, when I conferred with certain of Your Highnesses in Simla, had the opportunity of discussing with some of you the advantages which a federal system in this country would clearly offer, and the mutual benefits likely to accrue from some form of financial and economic union between the States and British India. But I had no certain indication that the States would as yet be willing, by surrender of the necessary powers, to make a system of Federation a reality." It would seem, however, that the decisive information first reached him while the ship which carried the delegates to the Conference was still on its way to England. A member of his Council cabled him from Aden that two of the most powerful spokesmen

[1] March 1931.

from the States, Sir Akbar Hydari, Prime Minister of Hyderabad and representing the Nizam, and Sir Mirza Ismail, for the Dewan of Mysore, had evolved a detailed Federal solution to which Sapru had in general terms given his weighty approval.

It is not too much to suggest that Irwin had already helped to direct their thoughts, together with those of the progressive Princes such as the Maharajah of Bikaner, the Nawab of Bhopal and the Chancellor of the Chamber of the Princes himself, the Maharajah of Patiala, towards the desired Federal solution. There had been strong and not ill-founded rumour that certain delegates had in mind to force a crisis by standing out for Dominion Status as the basis upon which all the subsequent proceedings of the Conference should rest, and that only a few minor safeguards should perhaps be conceded. To thwart this danger Irwin was only too willing to let his Dominion Status Announcement be swamped along with the Simon Report by the new demand for Federation.

His efforts, however, did not stop at general preparation or advice. No sooner had the Simon Report been published than he set out, as we have seen, on the immense task of formulating in detail with his Executive Council the opinions of the Government of India upon the recommendations made in it. The outcome of these labours, which involved almost daily meetings over many weeks, reaching their climax and conclusion towards the end of September, was the famous confidential Despatch the contents of which were duly forwarded to London but not to be disclosed until the opening day of the Conference. As with the Wood Report, he took a large measure of personal responsibility for the text of the Despatch, hammering it into shape with Haig, his Home Minister, but now he was up against a new factor which had not hampered him when the West Indies was his theme—the need to obtain the unanimous agreement to his proposals from conservative and cautious colleagues. It was in this particular work of unanimity that the Simon Report had been shipwrecked. It will be recalled how the Simon Report began on a big scale only to tail away. It implied a Federal solution which it lacked courage to advocate.

In spite of the staggering achievement of producing with

so many distractions and anxieties, with so little available time for quiet reflection, a weighty critique which was in effect an advance on the Simon Report, the Government of India Despatch on examination failed to sustain the expectations it had aroused. Professor Coatman has dubbed it "inadequate and timorous", and adds significantly, "Lord Irwin's own policy was undoubtedly directed towards much wider immediate objectives than those contained in the Despatch, and one naturally asks the reason why a State Paper of this importance emanating from his Government did not bear more clearly the impress and show more practically the influence of the views of the head of the Government. The student of Indian politics can only suppose that unexpected strength to oppose more liberal proposals developed inside the Council, which is naturally, on the whole, a very conservative body, and that the Despatch represents the maximum amount of common agreement obtainable."

It would not be fair, however, to dismiss the proposals in the Despatch as negligible because they did not give the delegates the lead they had hoped or even because moderate opinion in India rejected it. As with the Simon Report, hard facts moved too fast for it; but taken from its all-absorbing context it can be more easily recognized as a great State Paper. Briefly, Irwin succeeded in establishing through it Responsibility with Safeguards, the thesis that was ultimately to be enshrined in the Government of India Act of 1935. "We have endeavoured to point the way to action that may need to be taken to place upon the constitution the first, but definite, impress of Dominion Status. . . . The Government of India would no longer merely be the agent of the Secretary of State. For the first time it would possess a distinct individuality. . . . It is the essence of our proposals that control should be of such a nature as to establish partnership in place of subordination."

Unhappily for their prophetic reputation the authors of the Despatch committed themselves to the view that "the time has not yet come when the general body of Indian States would be prepared to take a step so far-reaching in its character as to enter into any formal federal relations with British India". On the other hand, the general thesis that there should be overriding powers for the Viceroy on certain subjects for all purposes and on all subjects for certain purposes, could only be approved by the exponents of safeguards, while the proposal that three members of the Viceroy's Council should be chosen from among the elected members of the Indian Legislature was a welcome concession to the champions of popular representation. The detailed proposals on the rival Minority claims were less acceptable, but his failure here in the light of the persistent deadlock at the Conference over this intractable subject must not be held against him, and the Despatch as a whole bears the hall-mark of a mature mind that had mastered the intricacies of probably the most complex administrative and constitutional problem of the modern world.

As we have seen, however, the constructive attitude of the Princes prevailed over all doubts and half-measures, and by the time the plenary Conference had split up into its component parts there was added to the list a large and powerful Federal structure Sub-Committee presided over by Lord Sankey. Before the Conference adjourned this Sub-Committee had succeeded in building the framework of a division of powers between the Federation and the various units composing it. So much attention was naturally attracted to the Federal structure Sub-Committee that the work of the eight other Sub-committees dealing with such diverse yet vital issues as Franchise, Defence, the separation of Burma from India, of Sind from Bombay, the future Government of the North West Frontier, and Imperial Services were forgotten. The Conference was identified in the public mind with Federation and with nothing else. This was not the only popular misapprehension. It was soon rumoured that there was considerable coolness between the British Conservative delegates and some of the Indians, and that the Indians for their part were confining contact to the spokesmen of the Labour and Liberal interests.

Actually there was no such breach, nor had Irwin any reason to be dissatisfied either with the team selected from among his Conservative friends or with the political balance of power which left the final decision with the Liberals, who, apart from their key position, enjoyed the exceptional leadership of Reading. The Conservatives, Zetland (Ronaldshay of Curzon fame), Peel, Sir Samuel Hoare and Oliver Stanley, were all far from reactionary in outlook, and Hoare, who was now making his first detailed acquaintance with Indian constitutional questions, was to emerge as the principal author of the Government of India Act and its great defender in a dramatic struggle with Churchill. Indeed, so infected had he become with " Irwinism " that Reading was rumoured to have confessed in a moment of indiscreet alarm that " Sam Hoare, you know, is too much the Radical for me! " But of course when the moment of crisis came and everything depended upon the official line taken up by the Liberals, there was nothing wrong with Reading's Radicalism.

A detailed appraisal of the Conference is not relevant to a narrative of Irwin's career and it is only necessary to note that there was a long period of depression during which Moslem and Hindu spokesmen, following their instructions to the letter, stood adamantly by their extreme demands in the Minorities Committee. Prolonged and barren discussions during the Conference had the effect only of intensifying communal differences and of leaving Irwin to reconcile groups that had become if possible even more intransigent than they were before their journey to London. Communalism admittedly had wrecked Civil Disobedience, but it almost succeeded in breaking up the Round Table Conference as well. Not until the beginning of January were the high hopes which Irwin had placed upon it triumphantly revived by means of three great speeches. The first was from Sapru, who, addressing the delegates for the better part of a day, expanded a detailed scheme, with suitable safeguards, of responsible self-government for an All-India Federation. His statement was a masterly analysis faithfully reflecting the temper of Irwin's mind not only in its passionate sincerity but also in its subtle and constructive search for an enduring compromise.

Two days later Reading, fully conscious that all eyes were upon him and with judicial gravity, pronounced the Liberal verdict in favour of Sapru's thesis. He approved the setting up of a Cabinet consisting of seven or eight Ministers in charge of the various Departments and undertaking collective responsibility. He looked forward to a time when opposition would disappear as between Cabinet and Viceroy, Viceroy and Legislature, and when the Ministry would use its best endeavours to represent the view of the Legislature.

In such circumstances many of the safeguards upon which there was now so much emphasis would probably never come into force. The enthusiasm of the delegates knew no bounds, and Jayakar exclaimed, "If only all my countrymen could have heard every word that Lord Reading said there would be complete confidence in India from now onwards."

Of Indians, only Srinivasa Sastri held back; he was too much of an idealist to avoid showing his disappointment at Reading's emphasis on safeguards. It was Sastri, "India's Ambassador", "the golden-voiced orator", Privy-Councillor and Companion of Honour, whom Irwin had been wise enough to send on special mission to South Africa, the scene of Gandhi's fight for depressed Indians thirty years before. Sastri had done much to raise the prestige of Indian statesmanship while in Africa and his co-operation at the Conference was something which Irwin could ill afford to lose. Fortunately, although Sastri was disappointed, he did not come out into open opposition. Indeed, as he reflected on the solid material gains at the Conference, he played his part in maintaining a united front when the time came for the delegates to seek the support of the Indian people for their handiwork. Then again, Sir Samuel Hoare speaking for the Conservatives, while frankly refusing to underwrite Reading's pronouncement, achieved considerable popularity by proclaiming an open mind and a readiness to wait upon events. He asserted that the Conservative answer would be deeply influenced by the full proposals coming from a united India, and in doing so encouraged the forces making for union. Many were to take up the torch, not least Sir Mohammed Shafi on behalf of the Moslems.

The way was clear for Ramsay MacDonald in effect to ratify the implied agreement, which he did with all due solemnity on 19th January in a powerful speech adjourning the Conference. He accepted the principle that with the specified safeguards the responsibility for the Government of India should be placed upon the Central and Provincial Legislatures. "With a Legislature constituted on a federal basis, His Majesty's Government will be prepared to recognize the principle of the responsibility of the Executive to the Legislature." The delegates had risked much in setting out for London in the middle of Civil Disobedience and they could not afford to return without visible result, but the Prime Minister's epilogue meant that they were going back to India with the first victory in the campaign for Federation.

India and the world at large were deeply impressed, and assessments were made as to whom the main credit belonged. Irwin could not expect perhaps to be included in the list, but, as Coatman has justly pointed out, in the success of the First Round Table Conference he saw his policy, " for which he had worked so hard and endured so much, accepted and acclaimed by the vast majority of Indians and vindicated by his own countrymen, amongst whom was his immediate predecessor ".

CHAPTER XX

THE DECLINE OF DISOBEDIENCE

It was obvious that the goodwill engendered in London could not be maintained nor the optimism justified unless the background of Civil Disobedience was removed and the active collaboration of Congress as the most powerful political organization in India secured. At the end of 1930 the prospects of Irwin taking any initiative to bring about this great consummation were no doubt considered to be as remote as the chances of success even if he did make one last attempt. His period of office had only about three more months to run. The usual procedure was for a Viceroy to avoid entering upon controversial commitments at the end of his reign and to leave the political balance-sheet clear for his successor.

No Viceroy in living memory had evoked such bitter dissensions. Ever since the outbreak of Civil Disobedience Rothermere had been personally conducting in the *Daily Mail* a "Save India" campaign. His articles were subsequently reprinted as a pamphlet and had undoubtedly helped to whip up an atmosphere of the finest journalistic frenzy from which major political crises are calculated to emerge. Irwin, of course, did not escape this invective, which was directed as much at his party colleagues as at the hated and unhappy Socialists. A good example of Rothermere's philippics appeared in the *Daily Mail* of 18th January 1931, only one day before the triumphant conclusion of the Conference. "There is a conspiracy", screamed the Mikado of Carmelite House, "to overthrow the beneficent authority which Britain has exercised in India for nearly two centuries. At its head stands the Viceroy himself, Lord Irwin. The appointment of this weak, sentimental and obstinate man to a post of such supreme Imperial importance for which he was totally unfitted by temperament and experience is one of the most glaring examples in British history of how personal friendship can warp judgment. Lord Irwin's policy from the first has been one of surrender to the King's enemies. He has humiliated himself and lowered the prestige of his country on which British rule in India entirely depends." Behind Rothermere stood powerful interests, and if Irwin had borne the slightest resemblance to this caricature of himself he would no doubt have surrendered to his British critics as well, and taken easy refuge in a final bout of repression. Winston Churchill was relentlessly exploiting his influence and prestige to rally the Conservative Party in favour of a strong line over India.

Baldwin, as Irwin's protector, had only just emerged from one dangerous conflict with the Press Barons at the price of a Referendum pledge, and he cannot have been anxious gratuitously to enter into another. Empire Free Trade had been a stiff enough struggle, but it would be as nothing compared with " Indian Surrender ". It is unlikely, then, that Baldwin favoured any repetition of the Dominion Status wrangle. As for Ramsay MacDonald, he was satisfied and relieved that the Conference had passed off so well, but like Baldwin he was not anxious to join issue with Conservatives on India even if the immediate result might be a schism in their ranks. If Irwin's only consideration had been the British political line-up he would probably have played for safety, trusting that the Federal idea would find fertile soil and that the weary struggle with Congress would die away of its own accord, but it was not to be. His primary concern was the situation in India itself. The Conference was largely of his making. It was his duty, as he interpreted it, to study its implications and pursue to the end his general policy wherever it might lead. Nor was he the man to alter his course for the sake either of ease or popularity.

There were signs that the Civil Disobedience movement had passed its zenith. The Congress leaders had failed to take advantage of the Conference and provide any effective counterblast to it; their organized demonstrations were declining in attendance as well as excitement; terrorist outrages, though necessarily serious, were more sporadic. Worse, from Gandhi's point of view, the support of the boycott by Indian business was encouraging forms of industrial exploitation particularly undesirable to the apostle of the hand-loom. The cotton mills at Ahmedabad, which overlooked and darkened the prospect of his Ashram, were actually thriving as the result of Civil Disobedience, and at the expense not so much of the British as of their Indian rivals in Bombay. Then again, the ever latent communal question threatened to undermine the best laid plans. At the Conference the Hindu Moderates, for all their constructive zeal, were well aware that they were not carrying even the higher caste Hindus with them in what should have been a common cause, and the proceedings of the Minorities Committee in London were followed with increasing exasperation which culminated in savage communal riots. In short, British and Indians were from very different motives moving towards a position in which they both were ready to call off the Civil Disobedience struggle. " The English were sick of warfare, and perhaps, in the final analysis, Mr. Gandhi was right: suffering had made his countrymen worthy of freedom."[1]

The first public sign that Irwin was not averse to making a fresh approach to Congress was during his last official visit to Calcutta in December. It must be confessed that the details of his stay there were not encouraging symbols of peace or goodwill. His reception at the station platform was restricted to a few high officials, and it was noted with relief that there was no untoward demonstration. A visit to the Scottish churches was cancelled at the request of the Principal because an attempt was likely to be made to " mar the harmony of the proceedings ". Arrangements for his reception at Serampore College had to be hurriedly abandoned, while a big garden-party was cancelled because police protection was impossible. *The Times* Correspondent reported that a very strong guard was necessary wherever he went. It may be added that the engagements on his official agenda were obviously restricted to those at which bombs are not carried—an old Etonian Dinner, a Horse Show, a ball given by Lady Irwin and a reception by the Yorkshire Society.

Perhaps the greatest alarm was caused by the abandonment, " owing to heavy rain ", of a Proclamation Parade to mark his departure from Calcutta. Much had been made of the fact that this farewell would be in public and preceded by a long drive through the streets; large numbers of troops

[1] Glorney Bolton, *The Tragedy of Gandhi*, page 227.

had already arrived on the parade ground as well as thousands of spectators. The official version was that at the last moment (actually after the Governor's party and escort had left Government House) it had been decided not to risk the Viceroy's lumbago in the rain. The lumbago was genuine, but the decision concealed perhaps excessive anxiety on the part of the Bengal Government. *The Times* went so far as to suggest that there had been one or two untoward and unreported incidents, but if that was so it did not in any way deter Irwin; whenever he had the chance to defy formality he did so. For instance, the story is told of a secret visit to the slum quarter of Calcutta. To the intense alarm of the police he left his carriage. Inhabitants duly called his attention to horrible defects in their houses. There was almost no sanitation, piles of refuse and filth blocked his path. So successful was he that an English lodger in one of the hovels was enabled to greet him with the complaint, " You have no business down here. Places like this aren't for the likes of you."

Civil Disobedience had been raging with special violence in Bengal, and Government policy had aroused some discontent among the British community there. It was alleged that the Government as a whole was lacking in strength and that the Viceroy in particular was driving it forward too fast while failing adequately to defend the interests of his commercial friends from the onslaughts of his terrorist enemies. Irwin, they said in the Clubs, was well meaning but did not apprehend the seriousness of the situation in Bengal. Such whispers demanded a frank answer and received it. In a powerful speech to the Calcutta branch of the European Association, he welcomed criticism provided the critics had constructive suggestions, but most of the advocates of strong government were " often more unanimous in their denunciation of Government than in describing in exact terms the matters in which Executive action falls short of their ideal ". In the attack on Civil Disobedience the Central Government had necessarily worked in close collaboration with the local administrators, and on no single occasion had there been difference of opinion on any point of substance affecting the special powers. He went on to deal roundly with the critics, who were " firm believers in what I may call the practicability of short cuts ".

But it was not enough to cry with the Queen in *Alice in Wonderland,* "Off with his head!" without even looking round; the gradual force of public opinion was a more powerful solvent than a drastic executive.

"The conditions, for example," he continued, "of prosperous and friendly commercial intercourse will always depend far more upon public opinion than upon Government action and, however emphatically we may condemn the Civil Disobedience movement—and nobody can feel more strongly than I do the harm that it has done, and is doing the cause of India—whatever powers we may find it necessary to take to combat it, so long as it persists, we should, I am satisfied, make a profound mistake if we underestimate the genuine and powerful feeling of nationalism that is to-day animating much of Indian thought. And for this no simple, complete or permanent cure ever has been or ever will be found in strong action by Government.

"Before this movement started, I formed the definite view, which everything that has happened since has only reinforced, that it would no doubt be possible to apply a far more ruthless policy of repression than anyone has yet suggested, and after a space of time, be it short or long, to create a desert and call it peace. . . . I do not believe that any man can doubt that, so far from facilitating the accomplishment of the principal purpose of Great Britain, which is to lead India to self-government and to retain her as an equal and contented member of the Imperial family of nations, such action, even if otherwise feasible, would, on the contrary, aggravate your task quite indefinitely, and probably destroy any hope of bringing it to a successful issue. The British people, more than any other, ought to know that in so far as the matter is one affecting the forces that we call nationalism, it cannot permanently be dealt with on such lines."

This speech put an end at once to complaints among Calcutta's European community about Irwin's weakness, but it aroused considerable if uneasy speculation as to his future plans. The denouement when it came a month later exceeded all hopes and fears. In his address to the newly elected and crowded Assembly—there were only twenty absentees out of the hundred and forty members—he deliberately took up the theme of Gandhi, his motives and ideals, a subject he had as deliberately left alone or referred to only with vague phrases on all previous State occasions. Now the emphasis was upon "the spiritual force which impels Mr. Gandhi to count no sacrifice too great in the cause, as he believes, of the India that he loves", upon Gandhi's willingness to believe that "men of my race who are to-day responsible for Government in India were sincere in their attempts to serve her", upon "ultimate purposes that have perhaps differed little, if at all", and upon assistance in accomplishing a "common end". All of which culminated in a direct appeal, "Is it not now possible, I would ask, for those responsible for this policy to try another course, which in the light, on the one hand, of sinister events in India, and on the other of the encouragement offered to India by the progress of the Conference in England, would seem to be the more excellent way?"

It should be noted that this appeal was launched two days before Ramsay MacDonald held out his olive-branch inviting Congress to the Round Table Conference, and also that both speeches were delivered following the announcement that Lord Willingdon was to be Irwin's successor as Viceroy, and that Irwin would be staying on until 17th April to suit Willingdon's convenience. Willingdon was admittedly Liberal in his political origins, but his appointment was by no means in accord with the plans made by the Prime Minister, who had injudiciously put forward a Socialist successor to Irwin. The name of General Smuts had also been widely canvassed, but Willingdon, the King's nominee, experienced though he was in Imperial governorship, was essentially a "safe" choice. If a dramatic initiative was to be taken it was evident that it would somehow have to be brought to fruition in the short time left to the retiring Viceroy. In spite of these Royal thunderbolts, perhaps even because of them, the liaison between Irwin and the British Cabinet was never closer than at this critical time when the delicate operation was in progress of transferring the Conference technique from Britain to India. It may be added that the plans were carefully laid and that Irwin's prestige and influence carried the day both with the Cabinet at 10 Downing Street and with the Executive Council in New Delhi. With the latter he had, no doubt, a considerable tussle.

The stark questions were how could Congress accept the invitation to co-operate while still in gaol, and how could the Government release Congress while Civil Disobedience lasted? Neither the Executive Council nor the Civil Service as a whole relished the answer he was pressing upon them. The Executive Council, with the notable exceptions of Sir Philip Chetwode the Commander-in-Chief, who both from friendship and conviction was heroically translating Irwin's general policy into terms of army reforms, and Sir George Schuster, the Finance Member, was never really in sympathy with Irwin. He did not, on his side, go out of his way to cajole them, and never found it easy to share the burdens of high policy with them. Collectively they were, to quote Robert Bernays, "an indifferent team". They fought hard against the reference to Gandhi in Irwin's Assembly address; they now struggled, but in vain, against the inevitable sequel —the unconditional release of Gandhi and his friends.

. . . .

That Irwin had prevailed over his advisers was revealed in an official announcement which roughly coincided with the reception by telegram in New Delhi of MacDonald's historic speech. The decision was simply that the Government of India, "in consultation with Local Governments", was to allow members of the Congress Working Committee full liberty of discussion between themselves and those who had acted as members of the Committee since 1st January 1930. Accordingly "notifications declaring the Committee to be an unlawful association . . . will be withdrawn . . . and action will be taken for the release of Mr. Gandhi and others. . . . My Government will impose no conditions on these releases, because we feel that the best hope of the restoration of peaceful conditions lies in discussions being conducted by those concerned under terms of unconditional liberty. . . . I am content to trust those who will be affected by our decision to act in the same spirit as inspires it. . . ."

The immediate reactions were not wholly unexpected. Squatting on the platform at Bombay station Gandhi resumed contact with world opinion. "I have come out of gaol," he said, "with an absolutely open mind, unfettered by enmity and unbiased in argument. I am prepared to study the whole situation from every point of view and to discuss the Prime Minister's statement with the other Round Table delegates." It was, perhaps, Gandhi's supreme moment; not even the prolonged drama of secret negotiation with the Viceroy quite equalled the first rapture of his release, the overwhelming welcome at the Maidan, "probably the largest crowd ever assembled to meet one man", the huge headlines of the world's Press.

The measure of this victory for non-violence was the measure of disapproval from the throng of Irwin's critics. "No amnesty", wired the European Association from Calcutta, while Churchill was full of scorn and pity in the precincts of the Free Trade Hall, Manchester, that if the Viceroy and the Socialist Government had wished to foment disorder instead of hoping to quell it they could hardly have acted otherwise than they had done. "The reason why, in my judgment, Lord Irwin, for all his virtues and courage, has not succeeded in India as he deserved to, is because he has been proceeding upon a wrong mental theme. His attitude towards India has been an apology."

During a great Debate in the House of Commons the day following Gandhi's release, Churchill succeeded only in emphasizing the isolation of his splendour. Isaac Foot laid his finger on the dilemma when he raised again the issue that had vexed the House when the future of the American Colonies was at stake. "The question is, not whether this spirit deserves praise or blame, but what in the name of God are we to do with it?" Churchill was lavish with his blame, but when pressed for a remedy had nothing more constructive than the recommendations of the Simon Report imposed by British will-power. Had he availed himself of the opportunity of exchanging views with the distinguished delegates while they were in London? He had not, and Irwin, it may be confidently asserted, was in no way to be held to account for Churchill's obstinate reluctance to meet Indians. Indeed he had good reason to regret Churchill's prejudice in this matter, and did his utmost to remedy it, though without avail. Apart from Churchill, however, the tone of the Debate in the Commons for once bore some relation to the needs of the moment in India. Although Irwin's decision to release Gandhi had been announced forty-eight hours previously, there were but few provocative references to it; hon. Members kept strictly to the matter in hand, a consideration of the Conference Blue Book, and as a whole their lead was followed.

The way was left comparatively clear for Gandhi and Irwin to adapt themselves to the new situation. But at the beginning of February 1931, a mere fortnight before the historic Gandhi-Irwin negotiations began, it was by no means inevitable that contacts between Congress and the Government of India would take the form of personal and private parleys between Viceroy and Mahatma, or indeed that there would be any contacts at all. Irwin had gone to the utmost limit in releasing the Congress leaders without condition; the next move obviously would have to come from them, and there were several factors influencing them to reject compromise. If Irwin was being urged to carry on the struggle against Civil Disobedience for two more months on the grounds that its financial and other resources were dwindling so rapidly that the police would by then be able to destroy the movement, Congress enthusiasts were no less confident that the same period would suffice to bring the Government of India to heel and to eliminate the distracting influence of the Conference delegates. Jawaharlal Nehru, in particular, was urging Gandhi to stand by all the demands of December 1929 and to raise his terms as the price of a truce.

These rival contentions were only resolved when Gandhi at last wrote to Irwin asking to see him " not as a Viceroy but as a man ": there were no other conditions to this historic request. In all the welter of discussion that followed, a significant similarity emerges between the reactions of Geoffrey Dawson and of Jawaharlal Nehru to Gandhi's special emphasis. According to *The Times* it was no more possible to regard the interview as a personal matter than it was to imagine the Commanders-in-Chief of two opposing armies meeting in the middle of no-man's-land simply to exchange war reminiscences. Jawaharlal, while paying tribute to Gandhi's unique psychological insight and force of personality, and admitting that therefore he would naturally always welcome a meeting with those who disagreed with him, felt bound to add that it was one thing " to deal with individuals on personal or minor issues; it was quite another matter to come up against an impersonal thing like the British Government, representing triumphant imperialism ".

Fortunately Gandhi thought otherwise. In the first place he realized, even if he did not admit it in so many words, that Irwin's action in releasing the Congress leaders was a sure token that a real reversal of British policy was taking place and that the Conference method was to be pursued to its logical conclusion. He realized also that if Congress was not ready to reap the benefits of this New Deal, the Conference Delegates who had risked so much by going to London in the first place assuredly were. They had, in fact, already issued a spirited manifesto which, even if it was in fact the outcome of hard verbal bargaining, left no doubt as to the progress made at the Conference. Did Congress offer a more inviting prospect? The politician in Gandhi knew no really satisfactory answer to that challenge. The moralist in him took note that if satyagraha had purified the poorer disciples it had certainly corrupted the richer ones. Gandhi's conviction, therefore, was set in favour of peace. He was spiritually uneasy of a struggle which could not be sustained without his inspiration.

. . . .

But before his letter could be delivered, a perilous period of uncertainty and sharp crisis ensued; Gandhi's desire for a " heart-to-heart talk " with Irwin the man sprang up only after many misgivings and much manœuvre. On 2nd February there was an interim statement to the effect that he and his colleagues had decided against the immediate cessation of Civil Disobedience. Irwin must have expected this and was obviously well aware that the real decision would be taken at Allahabad, where the leading Conference delegates as well as the Congress Working Committee were assembling to thrash out the policy of Congress. For Gandhi these prolonged and exacting conversations were overcast by the passing of Motilal Nehru. He, too, had come to Allahabad, but he was by now too feeble to take his share in the labours to which he had given so much of his energy and talent. He lay dying in the house next to that in which the Working Committee met, but Jawaharlal was too distraught to take any effective part in the meetings, and for Gandhi it meant the end of perhaps the most intimate political friendship of his life. In the funeral oration Gandhi described their last words together. " We shall surely win swaraj," he said, " if you survive this crisis ", to which Motilal Nehru had replied, " Why, you have already won it." Gandhi, as he confessed in the oration, believed that was true; but his problem at Allahabad was to carry the Working Committee with him.

The same spectre of repudiation haunted Gandhi and Irwin alike throughout these negotiations. Irwin was probably taking greater risks in view of his official status, but Gandhi's informal authority was more closely scrutinized by disciples and camp followers. Sapru, Sastri, Jayakar, and even the Nawab of Bhopal all reinforced the plea that the Conference method promised the best results for the future of Indian Nationalism. Gandhi made no serious effort to contradict their thesis, but with characteristic subtlety tried in one move to divert attention from Congress's failure to recognize it, to rally his younger extremists and to recapture the support of the Press—especially his old ally, American Press, which was by now loud in its praises for Irwin, the Round Table Conference and " the New Imperialism ". He simply wrote to Irwin demanding an enquiry into police outrages. The ever-increasing intervention of women in Congress agitations had added enormously to the embarrassing difficulties of the police in combating the technique of non-violence. Indian constables did not feel bound by the same standards of chivalry as are assumed by journalists to belong to the Western world. The European sergeants, provoked and overworked, did not always seem inclined to restrain their men.

Gandhi accordingly made much of an incident in his native Gujerat, where harmless women had been " forcibly dispersed " and " seized by their hair and kicked with boots ". There were, of course, many others, and if Irwin had conceded to this request he would have been compelled to initiate an enquiry that would have soon bogged itself and the wider issue of peace in a morass of legal pedantry and political invective. But in any case Gandhi had again picked upon the one controversy on which it was utterly impossible for Irwin to compromise. Quite apart from the ethics of the matter, no Viceroy could hope to strike a political bargain at the price of sacrificing the Indian police force. It was a proposition designed to remove the cornerstone from the structure of the British Raj. The decision might be difficult for Irwin in so far as it seemed to jeopardize the last chance of bringing Congress into line with his policy, but it can never have been in doubt. His reply was an out-of-hand rejection, but it was couched in mild terms. He implied that there might be individual cases of excessive zeal, but he was satisfied that the general conduct of the police in face of the most exacting duties had been admirable. He frankly appealed to Gandhi to let bygones be bygones.

In taking this conciliatory line Irwin had by no means shelved the police question, and as far as immediate settlement was concerned it was to remain the primary problem, but he had at least managed to see to it that the moral responsibility for refusing to negotiate remained with Congress. The real object of Gandhi's move was thus defeated. He showed his vexation at Irwin's reply in an interview he gave immediately afterwards to Robert Bernays. Bernays has described the scene in *Naked Fakir,* which as the diary of an ambitious young journalist and politician seeing India for the first time, contains many vivid pen-portraits of Irwin at this supreme moment in his career as Viceroy. The book covers the first four months of 1931, and the author's initial ignorance of Indian affairs has its compensation in an open mind, good contacts and a lively awareness of the great Imperial and human drama being played out to its precarious climax before him. Bernays' first-hand account of Irwin and his work has therefore a special vitality and value as a contemporary assessment. He was covering the "story" for the *News Chronicle,* and his interview with Gandhi was thus not simply to add spice for his reminiscences, but an urgent job of work for immediate publication.

He found the Mahatma in semi-state, quaint but pontifical. Much of the dialectic he exploited on this occasion was to be delivered and expanded in the talks with Irwin, but for the present the very idea of talks was pushed into the background. "I have unimpeachable evidence," he complained, "of the barbaric methods of the police. I have asked the Viceroy for an impartial enquiry, and he has refused. . . . I cannot say that I have found the Viceroy any more responsive than his predecessors. He is very stiff and frigid. I am very disappointed in him. I do not say that if the enquiry were granted I would co-operate. It is only one of the essentials. But I would regard it as a ray of hope. At present I see none." Bernays was left believing that only a miracle could break the deadlock. He was not to know his interview was little more than a pretext to heighten the sense of crisis that was, in fact, to be turned off like a tap. Behind the scenes the Conference Delegates were patient and made headway in spite of Jawaharlal, who was described by one correspondent as " bitter, ruthless and intractable as ever " and as likely to carry on the war with his Youth League even if Gandhi called off Civil Disobedience. But Mrs. Naidu, for one, was fully alive to the dangers of Gandhi succumbing to the extremists if discussions were unduly prolonged, and it seems probable that to her belongs the chief credit for switching Gandhi's mind from formal negotiations to what he described in his letter to the Viceroy as a " heart-to-heart talk with Lord Irwin—the man ".

The young and progressive Nawab of Bhopal, who arrived towards the end of the proceedings and who, for all his Western sophistication, readily appreciated the Congress view-point and was a personal friend of Gandhi, also exercised a decisive influence. He had been in constant communication with Viceregal House and made it clear to Gandhi that Irwin was ready, indeed anxious, to meet him, but that he (Gandhi) must make the initial request for the interview. It was not easy to argue with Gandhi. On one occasion Sapru summed up this apparent obstinacy to Bernays. " Our difficulty is," he confessed, " that we cannot get him to discuss real political problems. He is all the time putting to us moral and social conundrums." But when at last Gandhi was prevailed upon to write his letter, its style and substance represented a signal victory for the Moderates; there was no reference whatever in it to the police enquiry, and even more important it implied a willingness on Gandhi's part to come down from the position adopted at the Lahore Congress. The letter meant that Gandhi was now ready to discuss some alternative constitution for India to the Congress Declaration of Independence. The mainspring of Civil Disobedience was thus removed. Irwin's personal part in smoothing the way for this letter's composition and delivery is still a matter for conjecture, but it is clear that there was ample preparation and that Viceregal House was well informed of every development at Allahabad.

Outwardly at least the Viceroy's time was fully occupied with his ceremonial duties. On 10th February he solemnly inaugurated New Delhi, but it was a flat and disappointing occasion. *The Times* Correspondent was forced to admit that it would be idle to pretend that the ceremony had any popular support. All the approaches to this capital of " the New India " were blocked by police, and Irwin's brief speech was non-controversial to the point of being completely inaudible. The next day he attended the People's Fête in the old city, but once again there was little or no popular enthusiasm. The incident which was most favourably received as a symbol of better things to come was the appearance of a brilliant rainbow in the sky at the very moment that he stepped out on to the ramparts and lifted his hat in acknowledgment of the royal salute!

CHAPTER XXI

PEACE WITH GANDHI

On receipt of Gandhi's letter Irwin acted quickly; after a long conversation with the two arch-mediators, Sapru and Jayakar, his first meeting with them since their return from London, he sent back a cordial expression of willingness to meet Gandhi the next day, 17th February, at 2.20 p.m. So the stage was set for the most dramatic personal encounter between a Viceroy and an Indian leader in the whole seething history of the British Raj. What was there about these meetings that held the world's attention, that made people who had hardly given five minutes thought in their lives to the vast complexity of the Indian problem, follow every development—real or fictitious—with an eagerness usually associated with Test Matches and Cup Finals? The official communiqués were meagre enough, but the wires were soon buzzing with an endless flow of anecdotes and surmises. The Press were not manufacturing " a story ", the intense public interest was obviously genuine, the huge supply of newsprint was the outcome of overwhelming demand. One explanation is that ignorance and notoriety combined to provoke passionate reactions. Pride was wounded and prejudice reinforced by what Churchill, as the sublime reactionary, described as " the nauseating and humiliating spectacle of this one-time Inner Temple lawyer, now seditious fakir, striding half-naked up the steps of the Viceroy's Palace, there to negotiate and to parley on equal terms with the representative of the King-Emperor ". But above and beyond the polemic there was a widespread awareness that the contact between two strong personalities, embodying in their outlook, manners and religious beliefs much that was good and typical in their countrymen, was not only courageous politics but also apt symbolism. Here was an imaginative act which kindled the imagination of the masses.

Here also was a brilliant company of special correspondents to behold and report the swelling scene.

As for Irwin's own position on the eve of the talks, its peril as well as its glory might well have unnerved the most resolute of his contemporaries. The whole of his laborious policy of political and communal appeasement for India was now whittled down to a test of his own character and personality. It was difficult to believe that so tremendous a political responsibility could rest upon the shoulders of two men. Yet Irwin was well equipped to meet the demands made upon him. At this crisis in his career his aristocratic origins were an incalculable source of strength, they removed the terrors of personal failure, the lure of private ambition. If everything he had stood for crashed in ruins around him he could, like Cincinnatus, return to his estates without any regret provided he was satisfied in his own conscience that the action he had taken offered the best hope of peace and prosperity for India. In several respects the attributes of the devout British aristocrat run contrary to the spirit of the age, but in the crisis that confronted Irwin on the eve of his talk with Gandhi they were amply vindicated. The sense of moral purpose that his religion brought him, and the detachment that comes from an essentially humble and unself-conscious acceptance of his high degree combined to invest him with a greatness that made him equal to his gigantic task.

"No thoughtful person on either side was hopeful," Bernays observes, "but those who knew Gandhi admitted that if Lord Irwin failed with him no other Englishman would succeed." The simple truth was that experience and upbringing had taught Irwin and Gandhi much the same lessons. For both metaphysics and mysticism were something deeper than word juggling; both were quickened by the sense of sin and were acutely sensitive to the outward signs of poverty and social injustice. For both conscience pointed to self-denial, self-denial to the stoic's philosophy of life. There is something in Gandhi's ethic which is not far removed from Old Etonian. His personal integrity is to be seen in the strict secrecy he has maintained to this day over his talks with Irwin; their value was derived from an unwritten understanding that they should remain confidential, and Gandhi has resisted any advantage that might come from revelation. It is as inconceivable that he will raise the curtain without Irwin's express consent as that Irwin would do so without his. Then again Gandhi's reliance on character rather than intellect also implies an affinity with the standard of values surrounding Irwin from his childhood. When these men met they could enjoy a deeper understanding than they could easily translate into words. What began as a hard bargain tended to emerge as a common problem.

. . . .

On 17th February punctually at 2.20 Gandhi, huddled in a blanket, climbed the steps of the Viceroy's House in New Delhi which Irwin was now occupying for the first time. His drive along the stately Viceregal avenue offered a compelling contrast to the State procession of the previous week. There were no outriders and scarlet uniforms now. Gandhi's shawl and loin-cloth had superseded that spectacle of Empire, and the spectators, many of them Indian Civil Service clerks, who lined the paths must have been wondering which symbol would prevail. For if ever a man was negotiating in the guise of a sovereign power it was Gandhi on that February afternoon. The talk itself dragged on until well past six o'clock. It was to be the first of eight, involving in all little less than twenty-four hours of solid discussion. When Gandhi emerged, obviously weary and worried, he had nothing to say to the eager reporters. His excuse to them was that if he did not eat before sunset he would have to fast until to-morrow. All that emerged was quiet optimism in official circles and clear indication that the conversations were confined to the problem of bringing Civil Disobedience to an end and had not touched upon the fundamental proposals of the Round Table Conference.

The next day Irwin saw Gandhi again. This time their talk lasted from 2 to 5 p.m. A blank communiqué announcing that it was understood " that various matters emerging from the discussions are now under consideration and it is possible that some days may elapse before a further stage in the discussions is reached ", thinly concealed inconclusive results and a somewhat chilly atmosphere. Actually, there was a further half-hour interview on the next day—February 19th—which again stressed the possibility of delay before " a further stage " in the discussions was reached. This helped to scotch alarming rumours that the negotiations had completely broken down. The brief interview with Gandhi on the 19th was followed by a protracted discussion between Irwin and his Executive and by intense activity on the part of Jayakar, Sapru and Sastri, who were in almost hourly contact with both Viceroy and Mahatma. The self-imposed mission of these three brilliant men was, in its very informality, delicate. Over Irwin, of course, they exercised the most powerful influence, and he recognized the debt he owed them for upholding his policy in London and for enhancing its prestige, but it was remarkable how cordial and frank were their relations with Gandhi also. However bleak the prospects at Viceregal House, they stuck resolutely to their task of keeping the negotiations afloat.

There were limits beyond which Irwin and Gandhi unaided could not go. However much they might talk heart to heart or as man to man they were still essentially party leaders. Bernays gives a vivid account of the difficulties during the first part of the negotiations. He confirms that Irwin firmly refused to parley over the constitutional future of India, but at the outset put to Gandhi the bald question, "Do you accept the principle of the safeguards? If not, it is useless for us to continue our talks." Significantly enough Gandhi accepted the principle without reserve, and in doing so, as Bernays justly observes, finally disposed of the dangerous suggestion that Irwin was bargaining away the Empire. The conversations were thus narrowed down to a consideration of armistice conditions. Irwin argued that no lasting settlement was possible until the suspicions and hatreds of Civil Disobedience were out of the way. Gandhi raised three demands which were in effect his conditions for calling off the movement. First, the enquiry into the conduct of the police; secondly, the abolition of the Salt Tax; and thirdly, the legalization of "peaceful picketing" of liquor shops and foreign cloth merchants. The police question was undoubtedly the most important and the least susceptible to compromise.

Linked up with it was the problem of releasing political prisoners, which was also the subject of prolonged argument. Here Irwin was able to make the substantial offer that persons arrested during Civil Disobedience and not convicted of any violent crime would soon be released, while at the same time standing firm in his refusal to consider the reprieve of those who had been guilty of violence. Gandhi could not let the talks break down on that issue, indeed he could not do other than approve a policy which outwardly reflected his own ideals. On the other hand, many of his followers, the rank and file of Congress imprisoned under far more rigorous conditions than their leader, were unable to view his susceptibilities for satyagraha with his detachment. Their very devotion to him and his responsibility to them made it the more necessary for him to press for the police enquiry. It became, in fact, a kind of compensation for acquiescence in the punishment of his more unruly followers.

The details of this particular struggle need not detain us. Irwin could only reiterate his absolute refusal to consider any enquiry in any form. The conditions had not changed since the exchange of letters before the talks. He had been ready to pay the price of "No Enquiry—no Talks"; if, with the talks under way, the Congress Working Committee had not modified its views on this subject, then Irwin was equally ready to face the dire consequences of "No Enquiry—no Pact". Arguments that must have influenced Irwin in his decision to stand firm are to be found in the Government of India's Annual Report, where it is pointed out that the police had, in face of persistent efforts to subvert their loyalty, shown the most admirable restraint. Local Governments had the power to examine particular excesses and had not hesitated to use them, but these instances only served to heighten the impression that "the services of the police in face of exceptional difficulties has been of an extremely high order. It was therefore considered that in demanding a general enquiry into their conduct the Congress was not only attempting to shift on to others' shoulders responsibility for events which was primarily its own, but was in effect endeavouring to undermine the allegiance of the force to the Government in yet another respect; for if the Viceroy and his Council could be induced to concede this point in order to secure a cessation of Civil Disobedience, the morale of the police would in all probability be so shaken as to render them far less likely, henceforward, to constitute an effective obstacle to Congress activities." In his decision to stand firm Irwin was protected on a flank which Gandhi might reasonably have anticipated would be exposed. The

Socialists never wavered in upholding Irwin's defence of the Indian police. Wedgwood Benn's radical common-sense prevailed over Socialist sentiments about imperialist repression.

The other subjects up for discussion were not of such fundamental importance, but they were all equally vexatious and particularly well adapted to Gandhi's weaving logic. In his appeal for the abolition of the Salt Tax he was still holding out for victory in the symbolic struggle begun on the beaches at Dandi almost exactly a year before. His emphasis on peaceful picketing was as much mysticism as shrewd politics. If alcohol was the lie in the soul it was also Government revenue. The spinning-wheel might offer a return to Saturnalian conditions; it was also a direct challenge to Lancashire. It is significant that as soon as Irwin had adjourned the talks to allow himself time to communicate with London, Gandhi went straight to the palatial residence of Birla, the great Indian banker and millowner who was probably the most generous of all subscribers to Congress funds. Birla's formidable influence and interests were on the side of peace, and his arguments may well have had a more potent effect on Gandhi than the Viceroy's. All the same, Gandhi described Irwin as speaking to him " in the friendliest possible manner and with much sweetness ", and in an interview he gave to Bernays he said the situation " is not hopeless. At any rate it is not as hopeless as when I saw you in Allahabad." " I have found the Viceroy," he added, " friendly and courteous and frank. Perhaps I ought to add that for having described him to you last time as stiff and frigid. But the police repressions still go on."

Gandhi may still have hoped to make some headway by accumulating instances of police atrocities, but Irwin does not seem to have left much room for encouragement; according to one account his reply to these charges was to launch a healthy counter-attack on Congress violence. " I agree," he is reported as saying, " that the policemen may have hit the wrong people on the head, but if I had been one of them I should certainly have hit more of them." It is clear that Irwin's firmness on this issue was reinforced by the attitude of his Governors. Sir Frederick Sykes, who as a comparatively mild Governor of Bombay had endured more than his share of Congress attacks, threatened to resign if a police enquiry was conceded, and seven other Governors straightaway followed his lead.

On 27th February the talks were resumed in an atmosphere of gloom which was perhaps heightened by the reticence of Government circles, for their silence gave indefatigable Congress propagandists a clear field. The only official Government reaction was a formal and final announcement that there would be no enquiry into police excesses. The crisis was obviously deepening, and after three hours in which Irwin and Gandhi had once again negotiated alone it became known that Gandhi had set out his terms and that Irwin had refused them. There was thus a complete deadlock which Gandhi was apparently unwilling to resolve in any single detail. The next day the Congress Working Committee met and decided in favour of carrying on the war. It now seemed that only the funeral obsequies remained to be proclaimed.

. . . .

Gandhi had arranged to hand in the Working Committee's decision at half-past two on the afternoon of Sunday, 1st March. The tense progress of events on that fateful day have been fully recaptured by Bernays in his diary.[1] He describes writing out a five hundred word message for his paper after lunch beginning with " the prospects of peace, never really hopeful, have collapsed altogether this afternoon ". The first sign he had of unexpected developments was when he sought a statement from Sapru that would at least damp down alarming rumours that the Moderates were losing their courage and convictions and throwing in their lot with Congress. Gandhi's " final " interview was only expected to last for half an hour at the outside. Bernays sent his message to Sapru at four o'clock. At 4.30 Sapru's reply came back stating Gandhi had not yet returned from Viceregal House and that he could give no message until he had heard what Gandhi had to say. It transpired that the talks were still going on at 5.30.

Finally Bernays heard that Irwin had hurriedly summoned a meeting of the Executive Council at 7.30, that the conversations were to continue that night, that peace was once more on the map, and that Gandhi had arrived in an unexpectedly accommodating mood. But although the

[1] *Vide Naked Fakir*, pages 165-170.

exact details must remain a tantalizing mystery until Gandhi sees fit to publish his diary or Irwin to raise the curtain of aristocratic reticence that has so effectively covered his public life from the public gaze, enough was revealed at the time to suggest that the inspiration for Gandhi's *volte-face* came from Irwin, and Irwin alone. He had tried first of all to clear up verbal misunderstandings and to make minor concessions. Peaceful picketing, he argued, had been illegal, but could Gandhi honestly assert that the picketing Congress had indulged in for the past year was peaceful? Gandhi was free to call safeguards " adjustments " provided he accepted them. As for the police enquiry, he offered to have particular cases of alleged repression examined on the spot by the local authorities. Gandhi wanted the " suspension " of Civil Disobedience embodied in the text of an agreement. It was, he argued, the only weapon of the people, no word expressing finality would be acceptable; so after prolonged bargaining " discontinued " was used as meeting the requirements of Congress and His Majesty's Government.

Behind the pedantry of this procedure real progress was made; the very fact of negotiation in detail, even if Irwin was offering the shadow to retain the substance, was no small concession to Gandhi's prestige; but when it became clear beyond all doubt that small change could not buy the kind of peace Irwin envisaged—a settlement that would bring Congress into the fold of the Conference—he staked all on the personal appeal. Gandhi had asked for a heart-to-heart talk—well, he would have it. According to Bernays, the gist of Irwin's argument was " Forget all about your theoretic rights to demand a police enquiry; I admit that you have got the right to demand an enquiry. Of course you have. I appeal to you to forgo them. You must realize that nothing could result from a police enquiry but mutual recrimination. Cannot we let bygones be bygones? I appeal to you to come in on the side of peace." Less than five minutes of imaginative insight had achieved triumph after twenty hours of closely knit controversy had failed. Here was the " change of heart " to which Gandhi could testify and respond, here the true end of Irwin's political and moral policy.

At the decisive moment his analysis of Gandhi's aspiration was vindicated, and Gandhi's aspiration was India's.

Once again the key to the problem was psychological. The actual prosecution of a police enquiry was as nothing to Gandhi when compared with Irwin's admission of the right to it. Sapru, who had been urging Irwin all the time to try the emotional plea, was reported as saying, "You English can get far more out of Gandhi than you can out of me if you go about it the right way. Gandhi is a sentimentalist." But there was more to it than that, as both Irwin and Gandhi realized; Indian Nationalism was not merely a matter of sentiment, but of symbolic values for which formal diplomacy was no substitute.

While Irwin was in conclave with his Executive Council Gandhi was busy explaining his conversion to the Working Committee. Jawaharlal Nehru for one was not impressed, and for all his immense prestige Gandhi was confronted with the possibility of schism. Having walked by himself the five miles from Dr. Ansari's house, Gandhi arrived at 9.30 p.m. for further conversations with Irwin, which lasted until past midnight. No final agreement was reached, but Irwin, who was by then extremely tired, suggested a further meeting. "Good night, Mr. Gandhi," were his parting words as the incredible little man, shawl on shoulder and staff in hand, set out again on foot for his five mile journey home. "Good night, Mr. Gandhi, and my prayers go with you." With this final message of Christian goodwill ringing in his ears Gandhi must have been fortified in his resolve to save peace and at the same time underwrite the sincerity and earnestness of a Viceroy who had with him looked into India's future unafraid.

No sooner had he reached Dr. Ansari's house again than he aroused the Working Committee from its well-earned slumbers and grappled with it between half-past two and five in the morning. Against such daemonic energy the frail objections of mere mortal politicians could not for long prevail. Bernays, in company no doubt with many another journalist, was hurriedly revising the text of his message; there were "startling changes"—"The situation is more favourable to peace than at any time during the conversations."

But the rapture could not be maintained. Before the Delhi Pact was safely signed on the morning of 5th March there were to be some fearful alarms and excursions which almost reduced the unhappy Irwin to the point of mental and physical collapse. Monday, 2nd March, was Gandhi's day of silence, which held up the talks but allowed Sapru to pursue his vital duties as interpreter. Thc journalists were satisfied that the political barometer was still rising. On the next day, Tuesday, came the first report of agreement; after further prolonged discussion Irwin had called in his acute Finance Member, George Schuster, to discuss the Salt Tax with Gandhi, and a compromise had apparently been found. The police question had arisen again—this time Gandhi was complaining about the inhabitants being made to bear the expense of the punitive police, that is, of the extra drafts sent to reinforce the local force in an area where disturbances had taken place. This was not a major issue holding up the general settlement, but its selection was indicative not only of Gandhi's own mercurial disposition but also of the Working Committee's desire to carry on the fight.

On 4th March the world's Press splashed in huge headlines an official announcement of the Irwin-Gandhi Pact. Leading articles at once emphasized the personal triumph for Irwin. "He will end his term of Office", *The Times* Correspondent proclaimed, "with such a victory as has seldom been vouchsafed to a Viceroy"; but while the newspapers and public were celebrating and handing out bouquets the whole settlement was once more imperilled. While the final terms were being drafted Gandhi began to show signs of renewed uneasiness and to dispute every phrase. He told Irwin that he was unhappy, but could not at first offer any concrete reason. By the early evening, when Irwin was due to put in an appearance at a farewell garden-party, complete deadlock had been reached. When he arrived late on what should have been a scene of rejoicing it was noticed that his face was drawn and haggard. He was overheard saying to Sapru, "Gandhi is in my study still; I can do nothing with him; go along and see what you can do."

What new factor of contention could possibly emerge to cause such a storm at such a time? It was nothing other than the Gujerati rent agitation writ large and still sponsored by Vallabhai Patel, who, as President-elect of the forthcoming Karachi Congress at which the Pact would have to be ratified, was more formidable than ever. The particular point at issue was the return of lands confiscated for non-payment of land revenue. It seemed innocuous enough. Irwin and Gandhi had agreed on the general principle that confiscated lands should be restored, but where land had passed to a third party the original owner's forfeiture should be deemed permanent. The acceptance of this modest clause, however, meant the final defeat of Patel's campaign which, in its organization and leadership, was probably the most threatening of all Congress efforts at rent boycott. The basis of Patel's success was that he had been able to persuade so many of his followers to force the confiscation of their lands by holding out the promise that with the restoration of peace they would be wholly restored, whoever had purchased them in the meanwhile.

Once again Sir Frederick Sykes, who had led the Governors in their resistance to a police enquiry and who had borne the full brunt of Patel's activities, prevailed on Irwin to stand firm. He summoned his Executive Council, while Gandhi conferred again with the Working Committee. Both were adamant. Yet to all outward appearances there was no danger at all; beyond the parties concerned, only Sapru and a handful of officials were aware of the seething struggle beneath the surface. To heighten the depression, the night was engulfed in tropical rainstorms. But by the morning the storm and the crisis disappeared as suddenly as they had arisen.

. . . .

After an early breakfast and in streaming sunshine Irwin met Gandhi for the last time at Viceregal House to sign with him their Delhi Pact. Not until two o'clock in the morning had Irwin and Sapru hit upon a formula of peace, and curiously enough it had about it the inevitable casuistry which, if examined apart from its environment and context, might be said to typify the whole document. Land was not to be restored when once it had passed to a third party, but as a postscript Gandhi's objections to the clause were to be inserted.

The bald and overwhelming fact is that not one of the eleven points which were Gandhi's pretexts for launching Civil Disobedience and his conditions for ending it are to be found in their original shape in the Pact. An examination of the text soon persuaded Irwin's critics that Gandhi's only gains were consolation prizes and that Irwin's only surrender was in agreeing to enter into negotiation at all. First and foremost, the effective discontinuance of Civil Disobedience meant peace; the participation of Congress representatives in the Round Table Conference secured the immediate objective of Irwin's policy; but the bigger vision of India's partnership within the Empire, without which all his effort was of no avail, and a war of attrition as worth while a prospect as a laborious peace, was no less clearly retained.

Irwin, it will be recalled, had raised the question of safeguards at the outset, and Gandhi, still playing with phrases, had with surprising readiness agreed to his demand; and so it is that in Clause 2 of the Pact we find the hard core of Irwin's achievement. Congress would collaborate with the Conference on the vital condition that in the political future of India " Federation is an essential part; so also are Indian responsibility, and reservations or safeguards in the interests of India for such matters as, for instance, defence; external affairs; the position of minorities; the financial credit of India, and the discharge of obligations ". For some reason or other Gandhi does not seem to have revealed this clause to his followers if a somewhat cryptic passage in Jawaharlal Nehru's *Autobiography* is to be believed. " We saw the draft ", he writes. " I knew most of the clauses, for they had been often discussed, but at the very top, Clause 2 with its reference to safeguards, etc., gave me a tremendous shock. I was wholly unprepared for it." But he had no illusions about its implications. It blocked the way to Independence or a peasants' republic. " Was it for this that our people had behaved so gallantly for a year? Were all our brave words and deeds to end in this? The Independence resolution of the Congress, the pledge of January 26th so often repeated? So I lay and pondered on that March night, and in my heart there was a great emptiness as of something precious gone, almost beyond recall."

Perhaps Gandhi had more than a shrewd idea how Nehru and his friends would react to this clause, and endeavoured to distract their attention as well as Irwin's by emphasizing more spectacular but also more soluble problems. For instance, the question of peaceful picketing and the boycott of foreign goods had been the subject of prolonged and at times passionate debate, Irwin insisting that the economic security of the country as a whole should not be exploited by a single political party for its own ends. Gandhi determined that Congress should retain some control over its newest and perhaps sharpest weapon. The Pact blandly announced that the boycott of British goods as a political weapon was to cease, but picketing was to be allowed " within the limits of the ordinary law ". This formula was no absolute insurance against the future—" political boycott " and " peaceful picketing " are double-edged definitions—but in spite of Press criticisms it was sound common-sense. In any case Irwin could hardly press moral or economic objections to a swadeshi campaign " designed to improve the material condition of India " just when " Buy British " was emerging as an example for the world to follow.

As for the Salt Tax, Irwin was able successfully to resist Gandhi's sweeping demand that the people of India should be allowed to manufacture salt freely. But Gandhi could argue that the march to Dandi had not been fruitless. Administrative provisions already operating in certain areas for the free manufacture of salt by the local inhabitants were to be extended so as to bring relief to the poorer classes. There was enough material in the concession for Gandhi to point the moral and adorn the tale. British Press opinion, which had been somewhat obsessed with the outcome of the Salt Tax negotiations, was on the whole satisfied. As *The Times* pointed out, the concession was not new; it merely recognized an existing position dating from the Great War.

But the most intense speculation still centred round the police enquiry, and had Irwin made any material concession it would have been regarded on all sides as an unmitigated surrender. " Mr. Gandhi ", the world was solemnly informed, " has drawn the attention of the Government to specific allegations against the conduct of the police and represented the desirability of a public enquiry into them. In present circumstances the Government see great difficulty in this course and feel that it must inevitably lead to charges and counter-charges, and so militate against the re-establishment of peace. Having regard to these considerations, Mr. Gandhi agreed not to press the matter." It is hard not to admire the verbal finesse of this and succeeding clauses which embodied the Government's " reciprocal action "—the withdrawal of the special Ordinances, the release of political prisoners who had not been guilty of violent crimes, the remission of certain fines not yet collected—and which confirms the thesis that sainthood and subtlety are twin attributes, and that not in vain did Aquinas balance angels on the points of pins. It is sufficient to observe that the above solution marked in effect the decent burial of the police enquiry.

. . . .

Once the formulae were down on paper the mountains were soon seen to have been molehills all the time, which may in part account for the excessive jubilation among Indians to be followed by an equally excessive disillusion. These reactions were never justified by the cold facts underlying the settlement—the precarious background of disorders and conflicting sectional interest, the barrage of uncompromising opinions from Churchill to Nehru. Regarded purely as a political settlement the Delhi Pact raised more questions than ever it answered and was in the nature of an interim report. Admittedly on the practical details Irwin's victory was about as complete as it well could be, but the real gains were psychological and, as we have stressed before, in the realm of symbols. It was the triumph of the Dominion Status Announcement carried a stage further. On 1st November 1929 Irwin's insight into the psychology of Indian politics saved the self-esteem and secured the collaboration of the Moderates. On 5th March 1931 the same great gift of statesmanship performed the infinitely more delicate operation of bringing in Congress.

There are those who have urged that Irwin's five years in India saw the ruin of his policy and the triumph of his personality, but the paradox cancels itself out. Irwin's policy prevailed because of his personal ascendancy. " The truth is ", observes Coatman in his appraisal of the Pact, " that Indian politics are more a matter of psychology than are politics in most other countries. As long as Indians feel that they are being treated not only fairly, but as equals, they are not difficult people to deal with, and Lord Irwin's unprecedented action had given the Indian public the strongest possible proof that he, at any rate, was not going to allow any false notions of prestige to stand in the way of his dealing with any of their leaders on terms which they could accept without any possible feeling of resentment."

It is not surprising, therefore, that this historic meeting produced a crop of human stories which of themselves did almost as much to cement the good understanding as the formal articles of the Covenant. For the anecdotes—whether literally or symbolically true—have one feature in common: they bring out the underlying humanity without which the whole perilous fabric of Anglo-Indian relations must have been destroyed long before these two great representatives of East and West were called upon to meet and to embody in themselves the historic controversy. In their spontaneous good-humour was their common victory. No angry words passed between them, but while the unofficial though undoubted leader of India's millions showed deference and addressed Irwin throughout as " Your Excellency ", Irwin was quick to respond to his appeal for " man to man " talks by dropping the prefix " Mr." and referring to him simply as " Gandhi ".

Gandhi, for his part, was able to joke freely with Irwin about his imprisonment at Yeravda, while Irwin was just as ready to share in merriment over Churchill's lurid accounts of the meeting. For Churchill it was first and foremost the " humiliating spectacle " of the " half-naked fakir ". Irwin could afford to draw attention to Gandhi's meagre shawl more magnanimously and in better taste. After one prolonged conversation Gandhi had apparently forgotten the shawl. Irwin at once picked it up, remarking with a gentle smile, " Gandhi, you haven't so much on, you know, that you can afford to leave this behind! " Irwin's austere appearance and ascetic characteristics belie his fundamental kindliness. Gandhi can testify that his grave expression would easily enough dissolve into a smile. He is ponderous at times no doubt, but not at the expense of a keen and quick wit.

After Gandhi's defences and reserves had at last broken down before the personal appeal, Irwin suggested that they should drink each other's health in tea. Gandhi willingly agreed, but asked that his own part of the toast should be with water, lemon and a pinch of salt. This last ingredient was, of course, the official origin of all the troubles, and Irwin in his moment of triumph could not resist a delicious apology. " I am afraid," he said solemnly, " all I can offer you is *excise* salt." Gandhi was reported as saying immediately after signing the Pact that Lord Irwin had put him at his ease and disarmed his suspicions and that if there was any victory it belonged to both parties—a just estimate.

Those who had been prepared to face a prolonged resort to civil war or who had expected a formal agreement to seal up immediately and automatically deep political passions and processes, were alike disappointed with the Pact. Churchill, in the inevitable Parliamentary post-mortem, offset Baldwin's eulogies describing Irwin's Viceroyalty as a kind of rake's progress in seven stages. Yet, after all, Irwin had only applied to India Churchill's precepts for Ireland, and India was only Ireland writ large. If Irwin had failed to draw the moral of the Irish settlement from his apprenticeship under Churchill, he might plead that his master's voice was at times easier to hear than to follow. But the philippics of Churchill and his followers were lost in the general chorus of praise. American Press reaction did not hesitate to show surprise verging on incredulity at the Diehards' failure to prevent a compromise. "One wonders", commented the *Baltimore Sun* in a typical leading article, "how even Mr. Churchill could have been sincere in preferring bloodletting on the grand scale with the almost certain loss of India in the distance. . . . You can get agreement out of the apparently impossible when the negotiators are men of character and worthy purpose."

Perhaps the most enduring result of the Pact was in its salutary effect upon American opinion, for so long monopolized by Congress propaganda. It was now borne in upon Americans that a hitherto unquestioned conception of the underlying brutality and hypocrisy of the British Raj was not the whole story. Irwin gave to the vocabulary of the New World the word Imperialism in its pristine and unchallenged sense. Those who had denounced it as little more than a racket saw it now as a great political experiment, a democratic process with which all British-speaking peoples could proudly identify themselves. American surprise was well-founded, for in his determination to see the Conference method through to its logical conclusion Irwin had, in fact, broken with a long tradition of British policy. The immediate exigencies of the situation undoubtedly justified his action, and although within a year the whole policy seemed to be in ruin with Gandhi back again in gaol, the responsibility cannot be ascribed to Irwin. The failure was due principally to the irresponsibility of the Congress leadership and to world causes, culminating in the formation of the "National" Coalition in England.

In some respects the Pact demanded of Gandhi a statesmanship that it was not in him to sustain, but it is surely exaggerating to suggest that Irwin was aware of this from the start and was merely leading on the Mahatma with the object of humiliating him. If Irwin was at fault it was in overestimating Gandhi's personal control over his party. His conception that the Conference was overburdened with minority interests and could not survive without Congress reinforcement was sound enough; his policy was more open to question in relying upon Gandhi's influence alone to supply it. In addition, he may not have given full weight to what has been termed "the purely racial basis of Congress politics".[1]

Yet in spite of these criticisms, the immediate tributes of a personal friend and public opponent have stood the test of time and are accepted appraisals. "His qualities alone", observed an old Conservative colleague of his, "have stood between India and chaos"; while from the *Hindustan Times*, organ of Congress opinion, came the astonishing eulogy that "if Lord Irwin has earned an immortal place in the history of India, it is not only for showing himself a strong Viceroy, although even there he has had few rivals among his predecessors, but for having shown outstanding capacity for statesmanship and having saved India for the Empire".

[1] *The Rise and Fulfilment of British Rule in India*, page 640.

CHAPTER XXII

" SO MAY INDIA BE GREAT "

IRWIN might have hoped, as indeed he deserved, to be vouchsafed a quiet epilogue of honour and glory. Even his adversaries were bound to concede that he had joined the select band of " the great Viceroys ", but the peril from which he had rescued India at the last minute had been too intense, its causes too deep and complex, for Irwin to enjoy the luxury of an apotheosis. His career in India draws to its official close against a background of gathering storm. The hidden fire of communal passion burst out again in a hideous massacre at Cawnpore which threatened to destroy the whole structure of peace in its all-consuming flames. The sinister influence of Bhagat Singh was to threaten the Delhi Pact up to the moment of his execution and even beyond the grave.

These untoward developments conspired to distract Gandhi and Irwin from their efforts to confirm and follow up their peace. Gandhi's task at the Karachi Congress was rendered more delicate, while Irwin was confounded in his efforts to bring the next Round Table Conference to India. Just how far Irwin was committed to this last proposal, or at least to the idea that British delegates should avail themselves of an opportunity to visit India before another Conference in London, it is as yet difficult to assess. Undoubtedly he favoured the idea as representing a logical development of the " man to man " negotiations enshrined in the Pact, and there was a formal " exchange of views " between Viceroy and India Office on the subject. When, however, Churchill, reinforced by the *Daily Mail,* attempted to interpret the Conservatives' delayed refusal to have anything to do with a Conference in India as a defeat for Baldwin, Irwin for one was not to be provoked into accepting any public challenge. In private he did not hesitate to show annoyance at reports reaching Viceregal House of Baldwin's elaborate efforts to secure a show of agreement among his quarrelling supporters and in doing so to conceal his own convictions in a wealth of ambiguity.

Up to the last the speeches of the statesmen at Westminster seemed to interrupt rather than fortify Irwin in his healing work. Towards the end of March yet another crisis was provoked, this time by Lord Sankey, whose tact and discretion in presiding over the First Round Table Conference had won universal admiration; he had, it seemed, implied in a speech in the House of Lords that the safeguards referred to in the vital second clause of the Delhi Pact must be regarded as inviolable. It was an unhappy reference, for it not only suggested hidden differences of opinion between Viceroy and Government from which Irwin emerged to the left of his Socialist chiefs, but also provided Gandhi with a genuine grievance which he did not hesitate to exploit. He was already at work on "purna swaraj", weaving into that attractively deceptive phrase a mystical content which made "safeguards" seem but a meagre obstacle to full self-government. It is probable that nothing less would have enabled Gandhi to carry his followers with him or secure their acceptance of Mrs. Naidu's proposal that he should attend the Conference in London as the sole representative of Congress. As it was, his meetings were being broken up. Increasingly powerful Communist elements who had attached themselves to a "Red Shirt" movement somewhat incongruously identified with the tribal politics of the North West Frontier and led by a lithe and bearded man of the hills, Abdul Ghaffa Khan, added to the general confusion. Propaganda made out Abdul Ghaffa Khan and his Red Shirts to be more fearsome than the facts warranted, but their agitations were a source of some anxiety to Irwin. While for Gandhi the Red Shirt leader's startling progress—he was particularly in vogue at the Karachi Congress—was yet another sign that new and alien influences were rising up to challenge the authority of the old master.

The Sankey speech gave Gandhi the pretext he needed for writing to Irwin on the subject of safeguards and for attaching to it the question of Bhagat Singh's reprieve. The letter was accompanied by judicious rumours to the effect that the Mahatma was flatly refusing to attend the Conference, and was bringing into play from his armoury of spiritual resistance yet another weapon which he called a

"Soul movement". Irwin was not perturbed, however, and the inflexible will-power and the acute sense of proportion that had made the agreement possible were not lacking to confirm it during the last anxious days of his Viceroyalty. Irwin has been accused of sitting back and letting events take their course during the six weeks between the signing of the Pact and his departure for home. It is an unwarranted charge. It was absolutely essential to allow Congress opinion to come to a head, no initiative by Irwin could materially relieve Gandhi of his burden, which was to fulfil his part of the bargain by securing Congress ratification of his signature to the Pact. Nothing Irwin could do could prevent Congress seeking emotional relief for the loss of the police enquiry and other concessions and behaving badly in the process. Whatever expectations he may have had that the Congress would rise to new responsibilities were disappointed at Karachi. A series of feverish and ill-considered resolutions showed that India's Nationalists had learnt and forgotten very little indeed. The main resolution in favour of "purna swaraj", for instance, was nothing less than an open infringement of the Delhi Pact.

Through all these indiscretions at Westminster and Karachi Irwin picked his way with an almost Olympian detachment and perseverance. He admitted Gandhi's grievance on the question of safeguards, and he ignored the "purna swaraj" resolution. On the other hand, he remained adamant over Bhagat Singh. In vain Gandhi pleaded for reprieve; nothing shows more conclusively Irwin's understanding of the Indian mind and his authority with Gandhi than his handling of the Bhagat Singh case. Sir Herbert Emerson, the Home Member, who was called upon to play a prominent role in the Delhi negotiations, records listening with amazement to Irwin and Gandhi, after agreement had been reached by them that Bhagat Singh must be executed, engage in a prolonged discussion not as between two statesmen on the political implications of terrorism, but as between two saints on the sanctity of human life.

Shortly afterwards Irwin, in one of his impressive farewell addresses,[1] gave frank expression to his thoughts and motives. "As I listened the other day to Mr. Gandhi putting the case for commutation forcibly before me, I reflected,

[1] To the Chelmsford Club, Delhi.

first, of what significance it surely was that the apostle of non-violence should so earnestly be pleading the cause of a creed so fundamentally opposite to his own. I reflected also upon the quality of responsibility that falls on those in whose hands it lies and whose duty it is to decide finally whether their fellow men should live or die. And I am free to confess that I should frankly regard that responsibility as an intolerable one to any man to support unless he guided his conduct by adherence to certain very clear and definite principles." He had to satisfy himself that there were no facts in the case which were not before the sentencing tribunals and which might suggest a possible miscarriage of justice. No petition for Bhagat Singh and his confederate had tried to deny their guilt, and "I should regard it as wholly wrong to allow my judgment on these matters to be influenced or deflected by purely political considerations". As for the argument that it was undesirable for the executions to take place on the eve of Karachi, Irwin's answer was that the only alternative was "the wholly indefensible proceeding" of holding out the hope to Congress that there might be a reprieve, "whereas I should have in my own mind been clear that the sentence must be carried out as soon as the Congress had concluded". "I am quite prepared to think that it would have made the immediate atmosphere at Karachi easier, but only at the cost of enabling Congress to say with justice that it had been treated by the Viceroy and by the Government with complete lack of candour."

Where did the political advantage come in then? It followed naturally from the frank moral emphasis. It is incredible but true that in spite of his refusal to grant the reprieve Irwin was able to extract a pledge from Gandhi that he would specifically condemn acts of terrorism at the next meeting of Congress, and that Gandhi for his part kept his word and in all the orgy of tears over the murderer roundly denounced political crime. There could be no more compelling evidence of the trust that bound Viceroy and Mahatma to each other and made their relationship unique in the annals of British India. But the deadly influence of Bhagat Singh was not so easily removed and soon wreaked a terrible vengeance. On the day after his execution Congress declared *hartal,* and in doing so helped Irwin's Viceroyalty to end as it had begun, in the bloodshed of communal strife.

. . . .

Fighting broke out at Cawnpore between Hindu Congressmen and Moslems, whose only offence was that they did not wish to close their shops, which a *hartal* necessitated. The affray soon developed into one of the most violent communal riots ever known, into a second and perhaps even more hideous—for the full facts of the terror are still as dark as its origins—massacre of Cawnpore. It was a terrible blow to Irwin's patient hopes. It must have seemed to him, as the grim news trickled in, that the whole of his labours were in vain, that five years in Viceregal House as the temporary leader of a Raj that was itself but a small incident in India's gigantic saga, could not stem the tide of countless centuries of religious oppression. Of what avail were the devout genuflexions of an Anglo-Catholic, Old-Etonian squire against the persistent struggle of two mighty religions for the faith of a continent and the allegiance of a fifth of the human race?

Perhaps the strength of his influence lay in the very humility of his claims. He reminded the members of the Chelmsford Club how when addressing them five years ago at Simla he had made a very earnest appeal to the leaders of religious communities to throw all their weight on the side of religious and communal peace. "That appeal, with the news of Cawnpore still staring us in the face, I repeat to-day. Governments can here do comparatively little to remove root causes. They cannot change a people's soul. . . . I shall no doubt receive messages of farewell from many good friends I have made in India. But no message could so cheer me before or after I leave India as the news that a real settlement of Hindu-Moslem differences has been effected." Nothing less, he fully realized, would suffice if India was "to have any hope of building for herself a balanced national order in which all men may live and move and have their being".

For Gandhi, too, the news of Cawnpore was something far more than a reverse on the constitutional field; it struck at the roots of his pretensions to moral leadership of all Indians, irrespective of creed. Gandhi's "soul storm" over safeguards had died down—Irwin had conceded the vital principle that they were subjects for discussion at the forthcoming Conference—now he relapsed into depression. At first efforts were made to keep the news from the main body of the Congress delegates at Karachi. Then he threatened that he would hunger-strike to death if Hindu-Moslem differences continued to divide India. Then when his turn came to address the vast arena he challenged the centuries. "You may murder me," he cried, "you may cut my throat, but even if you kill Gandhi you will never kill Gandhism." But he emerged from Karachi triumphant; in fact his victory was too complete.

Congress in handing to Gandhi dictatorial powers, in appointing him sole delegate to the Conference, and in refusing to give him any instructions on the great issue of Federation over which it had completely failed to make up its collective mind, was sowing the seeds of future strife. Indeed this decision to send Gandhi to London alone and without a precise mandate may be regarded as the primary cause of the failure of the Delhi Pact. "Congress threw its future organization and the shaping of its policy into the hands of a man who had never succeeded as a disciplinarian. The process of disillusionment began at once."[1]

But it was not only on the Congress side that Irwin was confronted with disruptive developments threatening the future of the Conference. The Delhi session of the Chamber of Princes showed a strong movement among the smaller Princes away from Federation, and Patiala, for what seemed to be some personal motive, was far less enthusiastic than he had been in London. In his last address to the Princes, in which he reaffirmed the precepts of good government laid down in his private Note to them five years before, Irwin wisely reassured them that the federal constitution of All-India would not affect their internal autonomy in non-federal matters. On the other hand, he left them in no doubt as to his own attitude, and in his very frankness may well have brought the doubtful elements to heel. "The time is ripe for the change," he declared, "and, believe me, I welcome it. I welcome the enlargement of vision which sees beyond territorial boundaries and embraces in one wide sweep the identity of interests and solidarity of British India and the Indian States. But let us not forget that, as you acquire a

[1] *Rise and Fulfilment of British Rule in India*, page 640.

share in the control of common subjects, and as your internal affairs become of increasing interest to public opinion in India, there will come to you more and more responsibility for bringing your administrations to the level demanded of all modern Governments."

If the Princes needed this stern encouragement the Moslems looked equally for a lead and showed signs of succumbing to the prevailing disenchantment. An All-India Conference met over the Easter, a fortnight before Irwin was due to sail, and there was the usual communal wrangle. Shaukat Ali denounced joint electorates, and behind the scenes there were moves to bring the Moslems into contact with Churchill's group in London. That this perilous intrigue developed into nothing more than tea-time gossip in the lounge of Maidens Hotel may well have been due to Irwin's bold decision to take part personally in the negotiations. Any attempt on the part of the Moslems to identify their interest with the Conservatives would have been bound to draw the Liberal and Labour parties towards Hindus—with disastrous results for the future of Indian federation. It argues much for the strength of Irwin's position that he could, without any serious risk of compromising himself, step down from his throne to deliberate with one of the contending factions.

As the days drew on towards his final departure and the slow round of official farewells drew to its close, there was something more than the formal undertone of regret at his leaving. There was a growing desire, which found persistent expression, that precedents should be set aside and that he should be asked to stay on. There might be an endless sequence of set-backs; six precious weeks had passed since the signing of the Delhi Pact, with no proposals from London as to the date or procedure of the Round Table Conference; Gandhi was gnawing at the communal problem with almost monomaniac intensity and threatening dire consequences if his will did not prevail; Nationalist Moslems were gathering together in high dudgeon at Lucknow; there was another "senseless outrage" with the murder of the district magistrate of Midnapore; but against them all could be set a steady flow of tributes to and sympathy with the achievements and aspirations of the retiring Viceroy.

. . . .

No man could have done less than Irwin to court the popularity and affection which he so surely inspired, and which came from just those sections of the Anglo-Indian community whose goodwill he must have needed and coveted most of all. Irwin had given head to a new spirit among the British community. There was, for instance, no hostility, as might have been expected, among business men at the Delhi Pact. In spite of the jeremiads of the *Daily Mail,* industrialists were delighted and had nothing but praise for Irwin and his works. At the height of Civil Disobedience the President of the Bombay Chamber of Commerce had asserted that Englishmen favoured India's national aspirations and only demanded to trade under fair conditions—sentiments underlined by Irwin whenever he referred to Gandhi's swadeshi campaign. Even more impressive, however, was the enthusiasm he evoked among the younger men. Just before he left, over a hundred young Englishmen, banding themselves together as being all under the age of thirty-five, addressed a memorable Farewell letter to Irwin. " The burden which your patient statecraft places upon our shoulders ", they wrote, " is one no adventurous Englishman would wish to cast down. Whatever seeming loss there may be in privilege and prestige, there is no loss in the opportunities of personal service and individual influence. . . . Even if your policy had not been marked by the success that is now apparent to every impartial observer, we should yet feel compelled to acknowledge the inspiration of your example; for you have withstood the most unfair criticism that has been levelled at any Viceroy, and when you were charged with weakness, you ignored the charge with the quiet dignity of which strong men alone are capable."

With such a tribute Irwin could leave confident in the knowledge that his work was based on sure foundations; that his dream of constitutional progress had inspired those to whose lot it would fall to give it administrative substance. Then again it was perhaps no mere accident that Irwin's last Viceregal Ball, with its formal pomp and circumstance, was sparsely attended, whereas a special Garden Party he gave for Indian Clerks in Government offices was a huge success. Bernays describes a scene of almost pathetic enthusiasm. The guests arrived at 1.30 for a party that was due to begin at three. By 4.30 they had wolfed up all the food on the tables. Irwin, called out by his A.D.C.s a little earlier than expected, received a terrific ovation and was followed round the gardens by a solid phalanx of admiring Indians. Finally, when prevailed on to make a short speech, the whole assembly gave voice to delighted cheers—an unusual proceeding for Indians, who were often content to greet even their beloved Mahatma in stolid silence or with handclapping that would hardly embarrass a Mayfair drawing-room. For in truth Irwin had found his way to the heart of Indians as it has been given to few Englishmen and fewer Viceroys to do. Here at this garden-party bun-fight was the symbol of a deep thankfulness; for to a new Indian bureaucracy was given an ever-increasing opportunity both for service and for the glittering prizes if Irwin's scheme of things bore fruit.

Irwin's last days in India were at once hectic and poignant. Official ceremonies and private leave-takings did not allow him much time to reflect on the perils which he had overcome but which he must inevitably bequeath to his experienced successor, Willingdon. No doubt he regretted that he could not stay on and see the job through, but as he reminded the Combined Legislatures in his formal farewell to them, "though to a Viceroy five years of office must always appear as an outstanding epoch of his life, the historian of the future will be likely to mark the passage of events by tendencies rather than by persons who for a period were privileged to play their part upon this great stage". For his last Easter Sunday service he went quietly to join the congregation at Old Delhi Church. On 11th April he sent a message of welcome to Willingdon on his arrival at Aden. The following day he held an informal meeting with the delegates of the first Round Table Conference to discuss the still vague plans for the next one. Gandhi was there as an ordinary delegate. Two days later he left New Delhi for the last time amid the usual scenes of splendour and was given a magnificent send-off. During these moments of abdication he must yet have known the full majesty of power. In the enthusiasm and devotion for his person was a real reward for the reproaches and calumnies he had had to face in carrying out in five years the duties of a lifetime. If this simple upright man had indeed betrayed India Lord Rothermere would have done well to study his popularity before holding him up to contempt in the *Daily Mail.*

On 15th April he arrived with his wife and daughter, Anne, at Bombay, where he had his last heart-to-heart talk on Indian soil with Gandhi. While the Mahatma returned again and again to the communal theme, Irwin was able once more to extract a substantial concession, as he revealed later. He obtained " a specific and precise assurance that no discrimination would be used in practice against British goods as such ", and thus gave special point to Bombay Chamber of Commerce's praise of " his singleness of purpose ". Up to the end, therefore, he demonstrated his uncanny capacity to extract concessions from the little man who to everyone else has always seemed the most perverse of negotiators, but who to Irwin was pliable and conciliatory. On the same day he tactfully received a Moslem deputation and comforted them with the assertion that in his view it was up to the majority community to make the first move and give assurances about the position of the minority; with this, his political responsibilities came to an end. Willingdon disembarked the same evening.

In his address to the Byculla Club, the oldest club in India, which always claimed the privilege of entertaining departing Viceroys, he struck a subdued note, wishing no doubt to leave the way clear for any statement Willingdon might wish to make. On the 18th the quayside was prepared for the *Viceroy of India,* which had brought Willingdon out, to take Irwin home. It was a memorable and moving scene. His last farewell in its shining sincerity left an impression which seemed to transcend even the occasion of his leaving. He was more visibly affected, wrote one commentator, " than those who have been near him these anxious years have seen him, and he spoke in a voice which was audible only to the people close to the dais ".

But this short, indistinct speech was no less than a summary of all that India meant to him, an enduring apology for his patient policy and fervent ideals. " But one thing I have never doubted, and if my memory serves me I have more than once affirmed, that the only way of achieving the end which I believe we all desire, was by a synthesis of the best statesmanship of East and West, by the collaboration of two parties working side by side, not in any huckstering

DUTY DONE

Lord and Lady Irwin outside their London house in Eaton Square on their return from India. May, 1931

spirit as to who would get the best of a hard bargain, not with a view to this or that individual or this or that community gaining an advantage or victory over a rival, but with the sole purpose of creating and perpetuating a prosperous, strong and contented India embracing both British India and the States as an honoured member of the British Commonwealth of Nations. The end of that task is not yet. Though much has been accomplished, the stiffest part of the hill is to come. To none of us is it given to cast a true horoscope of the future or to foresee clearly the final shape of the great design on which for a while we are set to labour. The work of any man, or of any generation of men, is a small factor in the evolution of a nation, and we shall surely be weighed in larger balances."

Then after commending his successor to India and to Providence he reached his unforgettable climax. "In part of the Viceroy's House in New Delhi stands a column, presented by the late Maharajah of Jaipur, on which are inscribed the words:

> In Thought Faith,
> In Word Wisdom,
> In Deed Courage,
> In Life Service,
> So may India be great.

I can wish India nothing better, and so I would say to you and to all those in this country that I have tried to serve, 'In your thinking, in your speaking, and in your doing, God be with you.'" With these words of inspiration a Viceroy, who was above all else their friend, took leave of the valour and intellect of India assembled at the Apollo Bundar to bid him a last farewell. As his tall, lean figure vanished into the tropical haze there was general grief and even dismay that they would have to face the dark future without Irwin. There is no doubt but that Indians had come to rely upon him, to take his temperate influence for granted to such an extent that his automatic and inevitable retirement came as a shock. There was a strong undercurrent of opinion that he would somehow or other—the implications of the idea were not elaborated—carry on. The impression was perhaps deepened by the crescendo of events during the last weeks. It seemed unnatural that a year of Civil Disobedience should have been brought to a close by a Viceroy who within six weeks was due to leave for good.

. . . .

The authorities are agreed that his personality probably left a deeper mark on Indian life and thought than that of any Viceroy since Ripon. What was the secret of his extraordinary power? Here again the authorities have agreed on the answer by emphasizing his moral austerity, from which in large measure flows his political self-discipline and his capacity for intense application. During the last weeks, indeed throughout all the periods of crisis, he thought nothing of a sequence of a sixteen hour days' work. In one respect this sign of his sense of duty argued a failing, the inability to delegate detail. However urgent the business, his successor Willingdon would not allow his afternoon rest to be interfered with, and there is no evidence that he was any the worse Viceroy for taking a more general and less particular survey of his office. On the other hand, the constant reiteration of Irwin's ascetic and saintlike qualities is not the full story, and might well give a misleading impression of the Viceregal regime. Simplicity was the keynote of the social life Irwin encouraged. He and his family imposed on Viceregal House the homely ways of the Yorkshire squirearchy, the atmosphere of the country house party in which charades took the place of bridge.

Those who gained his intimate acquaintance or had access to him beyond official routine no doubt carried away the idea of a very human, warm-hearted man, more at ease in a tweed jacket and a pipe in his mouth, and evoking much the same choice mellow relationship as the University Don, with his well-stored mind, has to offer. On these occasions it would have been as out of place for a visitor to address him as " Your Excellency " as for an undergraduate to say " Sir " to the don. Not that he had any false diffidence as to his position. He might simplify ceremonial, for the seven bowings of Reading's time substitute but three, replace the howdah and robes of State with car and morning-clothes, but there were strict limits to his complacence, and woe betide those who overstepped the mark!

Bernays describes an occasion when at an investiture in the throne room of the Viceroy's House there was a great deal of chatter during the ceremony. There was a swift and devastating rebuke for the offenders. "Lord Irwin wishes it to be understood at once that when he is acting directly as the King's representative the etiquette must be as rigorous as in Buckingham Palace."[1] As one to the manner born he did not find it difficult to play the role of royalty. Indeed his outlook and mode of life were not dissimilar from those of the Sovereign he represented; their popularity, equally mystifying to them both, sprang from the same deep roots of God-fearing character. If George V could have ruled personally as Emperor of India there are good grounds for suggesting that he would have acted in nearly every detail, great and small, as Irwin did on his behalf. Irwin translated into terms of the British Raj, more literally perhaps than any other Viceroy during his reign, George V's interpretation of the constitutional monarch.

By training as well as inclination, education and agriculture held a high place in Irwin's calendar of duties; together they were subjects upon which the whole health, wealth and happiness of India depended, and they gave him closer access to the life of the people than if his special interest and experience lay in other directions. As it was, his knowledge of the more inherently "British" spheres of defence and finance did not go beyond the necessary minimum. Nor did he make any pretence of holding strong opinions on matters for which he had no particular aptitude. The fact that the military and commercial worlds did not loom large in his Viceregal career may well have heightened the misgivings of those who were in any case naturally disposed to misinterpret his policy.

In both these departments he was fortunate in his advisers. It can hardly have fallen to the lot of many Viceroys to have successively at his disposal during his period of office two such formidable Finance Members as Sir Basil Blackett and Sir George Schuster, or two such Commanders-in-Chief as Field-Marshal Sir William (now Lord) Birdwood and Field-Marshal Sir Philip Chetwode. Blackett and Schuster between them took off his shoulders the burden of the complex currency question and in a series of remarkable Budgets gave India the financial reserve to enjoy her share of prosperity between 1926 and 1929 and to weather the economic blizzard of the early '30s—it is a major achievement in

[1] *Naked Fakir*, page 127.

Imperial finance to which full credit has not perhaps been given. Irwin did not interfere with this healing work and he gave similar latitude to Birdwood's and Chetwode's well-considered army reforms. His close friendship with and profound confidence in Chetwode during the difficult days of Civil Disobedience ensured the support of the Indian Army not merely for the necessary military measures but its acquiescence in the political climax of the Delhi Pact. Chetwode gave the Pact his blessing, took the larger view, and thus laid finally to rest a certain tradition of hostility between Viceroy and Commander-in-Chief inherited from the notorious clash between Kitchener and Curzon.

On subjects which he had not made his own he allowed his lieutenants a latitude which gave the appearance almost of indifference to them and the details of their work. On the other hand, those who administered his "hobbies" found themselves under almost daily supervision. In the domain of agriculture the Linlithgow Commission's Report provided ample material for the exercise of Irwin's tireless energy, but it was to the theme of Education that he was able to direct his most mature thought. His series of addresses to the various Universities, Colleges and Institutes, the convocations and speech days which he so willingly adorned, gave him scope to cover a wide range of subjects congenial to his reflective disposition. On these occasions he could and did indulge to the full his taste for political philosophy, his precepts for the full life, his catholic yet discriminating delight in literature. These speeches alone testify to a well-stored mind; here are to be found homilies on the Art of Reading, on the Meaning of Scholarship, on Patriotism, on the Value of Education.

In an address to the Convocation of the Delhi University he gave some revealing quotations of passages in English literature which had made a life-long impression upon him. For the spirit of heroism he selects Shakespeare's Henry V's speech at Agincourt, and with more subtlety Exeter's description of the death of York and Suffolk. He gives full credit to the pathos of Exeter's vain effort to stop his tears.

> But I had not so much of man in me,
> And all my mother came into mine eyes,
> And gave me up to tears.

"Or let us turn," Irwin continues, "to Sir Walter Scott, for preference I think *Rob Roy*, and, though I believe true Scott lovers don't agree with me, *Ivanhoe*. Or the descriptions that I can still never read without profound emotion by Mr. Masefield of all the transports in the last war setting out with their human freight from Mudros to effect the landing at Gallipoli." If the reader's mood led him to the study of nature then Irwin chose a passage from "that great unfinished fragment of Stevenson's *Weir of Hermiston* or from Kinglake's description of the Dead Sea in *Eothen*". All his selected passages, he observed, showed the merit of simplicity, of economy in words, "for the monosyllable is the mightiest of all", and he went on to defend a cause which Churchill as Prime Minister has made so much his own. "Official letters would lose some of their terror and oratory would gain in force by being direct."

Irwin's interest in India's educational welfare, ranging from his fervent advocacy of a College for the sons of Princes to his anxiety over the cultural fate of the depressed classes, heralded a period of reform and development which was all part of his wider ideal of training India in the art of self-government and making smooth the way to it. Only thus, he knew, could the growing spirit of revolution, fanned as it was more by the alien influence of Communism than by natural domestic discontents, be finally exorcized. The process which Irwin was fostering, however, for all its potential insurance value against the future, involved the final condemnation of the old order. The older members of the Indian Civil Service knew well enough that five years of Irwin meant that there would be none of the terms of service, or rather feudal overlordship, for their sons that they had known. The social order immortalized by Kipling had vanished. Irwin saw to it that it would never return.

It was an irony that a man of such deep conservative principles should have identified himself with a liberal order of things, whereas his successor Willingdon, Liberal in party and conviction, was compelled to work within a framework of reaction. On the whole, Willingdon's policy was inevitable; whatever line Irwin had taken he would have necessarily left his successor with a situation demanding a "firm hand". Irwin by negotiating with Gandhi took the long term view, but if he had stayed on there is little doubt but that he would have acted very much as Willingdon did. Therefore for the sake of his reputation with Indians it is probably as well that he did not stay on. When he signed the Delhi Pact his task in India was in its essentials complete. The view at the time among those in high Government circles of differing views but in a good position to judge, was that Irwin's historic decision to negotiate with Gandhi was a move which had to be made and in the long run did immense good; that in a sense he succeeded in penetrating Gandhi's political and moral defences and in doing so permanently affected his relationship with Viceroys. The verdict of history will no doubt be to confirm this thesis and to prove that the assertion that he should not have negotiated at all was the narrow view.

So it was that the man who left for India five years before politically a minor luminary, unknown to the larger British or Indian publics, returned at the end of his time an illustrious statesman and one of the few Englishmen to make a really big impression on India. Perhaps no one in living memory had enjoyed such legendary fame with the masses. He did not earn this reputation for any special administrative genius; he was good on the large issues, but on questions he regarded as secondary—and they were many—he was comparatively ineffective, and he could not, for instance, challenge comparison with Curzon in all that pertains to executive capacity. Yet in spite of the grandeur and permanence of his work, Curzon by his very nature imposed his system on India, whereas Irwin, for all his shortcomings, for all the repressions during Civil Disobedience, remained and was in the last resort recognized as a Sophoclean, plastic character.

His greatness as Viceroy was in his simple humanity, his unassuming sense of humour. His was not the faculty of command and imposition, but of influence, persuasion, permeation. It is a greatness that will endure, and it is no idle guesswork to suggest that in fifty years time his name in India will stand out from among his contemporaries.

CHAPTER XXIII

INDIAN AFTERMATH

THREE days before leaving India Irwin celebrated his fiftieth birthday, and there was an exchange of telegrams between himself and the King. The intense strain of five remorseless years had aged him, there were deeper lines in his serious face, and his expression, always meditative, assumed an aspect of weary resignation. When he left it seemed only natural to stress his youthful promise, now he was returning to England an elder statesman before his time. A smooth and leisurely voyage, during which they called at Cairo, Port Said and Malta, was something of a rest cure. While on board both he and Lady Irwin took part in the ship's sports, which were under the efficient direction of General Sir Charles Harington, of Chanak fame. On arrival at Victoria where an enthusiastic welcome awaited them, marred only by a few unfriendly cries, and distinguished by the number of Anglican and other religious leaders present, it was observed how bronzed and well they looked.

They went immediately to Windsor Castle, where they lunched with the King and Queen; and where the King, as a signal mark of royal favour, made him a Knight of the Garter, the foremost in a whole procession of honours and eulogies to be conferred upon him. Irwin was already the recipient of the two highest awards for Indian service, the Grand Cross of the Star of India and the Grand Cross of the Indian Empire; his admission to a stall among the select Knights of the supreme order of Chivalry implied that his work in India had the special approval of the Sovereign whom he had represented. Thereby his reputation had been in a sense placed beyond the reach of harm from party controversies. Universities vied with each other during the next few months in showering honorary degrees upon one whom the Vice-Chancellor of Oxford in conferring an Hon. D.C.L. addressed as *vir sagacissime*. Especially gratifying must have been the spontaneity with which Yorkshire institutions joined in the general chorus of praise to honour a distinguished son. Part of his philosophy which he never ceased to stress was that only through local patriotism can larger loyalties emerge, and to whatever other spheres of greatness he was raised, he was first and foremost a great Yorkshireman.

He was able to apply the theme at a complimentary dinner given to him by the members of the Society of Yorkshiremen living in London when he attributed to Yorkshiremen the discovery of one of the " secrets at the root of life ", that life was always the product of a series of concentric loyalties finding its expression in the wider service to the State and to humanity. When he was in India, he added, he used to look forward with great eagerness week by week to the mail which brought the six copies of the *Yorkshire Post*, and Lady Irwin, who was not born a Yorkshire woman, used to be astonished to find him reading the *Yorkshire Post* before he read *The Times*. In one of his first political speeches on his return he defended himself against Press criticism and gave special praise to the *Yorkshire Post*, wishing, as he said, to bear public testimony to the value of its restrained and wise comments on Indian affairs. Sheffield's University gave him an honorary degree, Harrogate a civic welcome, while Doncaster conferred the Freedom of its City after having been among the earliest to offer him an official welcome. He revealed that the first political speech he ever made was on a Doncaster platform in support of Sir Frederick Fison. He had every reason to believe it was a very bad speech, but also to remember the complete generosity of a Doncaster audience. Also, as a boy, he recalled constantly coming back from school for holidays and his first enquiries always being for Doncaster butterscotch. He felt, he said, rather like a boy home for the holidays now after a rather strenuous schooltime.

Then, of course, there was the most delectable welcome of all at Hickleton from the villagers, the tenants, and from his father who, now in his ninety-third year, had kept his vow to remain alive for his son's homecoming. When Irwin's car reached the gateway of Hickleton it was stopped by some young men from the estate who attached ropes to it and dragged it triumphantly along the drive. An eye-witness has described the memorable scene of the old man smilingly waiting to greet his son at the entrance. "I still remember his white hair, and the way he straightened his back as the great moment of welcome arrived, and his clear, ringing voice as he said: 'I think that with God's help my son has been able to do a good work in India for his King and country, and for that other great country that has so many claims on his affection and interest.'"

Among the multitude of tributes and assessments in the Press and elsewhere *The Times* had its judicial last word and maintained its steady championship of the man and his works. In its leading article on 2nd May it assured him that he need have no illusion about the gratitude of his countrymen. He had been criticized both as the author of the blackest repression since the Mutiny and for carrying out a policy of "spinelessness and surrender", a charge made during the notorious St. George's by-election. He was attacked by journalists, the "Thunderer" maintained, because they could neither bully nor buy him. It quoted approvingly the *Statesman's* reference to the "cool strength" of his government. The best of the leaders of Indian politics had been brought together and had lived in close contact for five years with an Englishman whose character had impressed them with a new respect for all Englishmen. To sum up: "Lord Irwin has not solved the Indian problem, but he has pointed the way by which courage and faith and patience like his own will solve it in the end." Praise in similar terms was voiced by the Archbishop of Canterbury during an address at the Albert Hall. In April Lord Grey, paying tribute to the retiring Viceroy on behalf of Liberals, gave it as his opinion that there had been more cordial co-operation between Irwin and the Labour Government than between him and the Conservative Government.

Labour's term of office had coincided with Civil Disobedience, and MacDonald's Cabinet certainly showed remarkable loyalty in face of the criticisms levelled against a Conservative Viceroy as much during the period of repression as when he was negotiating a peace; but perhaps they were encouraged in their support for Irwin in that the most vociferous and sustained attacks came not from a disgruntled left wing of their own party but from Churchill and a group of diehard Conservatives whose policy was as great an embarrassment to Baldwin and the official Conservative Opposition as it was to the Government itself. Churchill was not long in resuming his offensive now that the author of the " great betrayal " himself was back among them, free from official responsibility and answerable at last to the strictures of Parliament and Party. Irwin for his part was ready to accept the challenge.

Within a fortnight of his arrival Churchill publicly proclaimed the Delhi Pact to be " a great disaster " and a " humiliation and negation to this country ", but on the selfsame day Irwin, addressing the British Indian Union, frankly declared in the presence of his predecessor that a " strong arm " policy was no good in India. The trend was towards self-government within the Empire, why ignore this, when it showed itself on all sides in India. Towards the end of June, with characteristic openness of purpose, he put forward an elaborate defence of his policy to a meeting of the self-appointed Conservative Party Indian Committee, and for three-quarters of an hour submitted to a barrage of questions concerned principally with the implications of the Agreement with Gandhi and with the boycott of Lancashire cotton goods. Wardlaw Milne was in the chair, while Churchill and Lloyd were there to heckle on behalf of the diehards, and Samuel Hoare to hold a watching brief for the moderates. A strong appeal was made to close the Conservative ranks and show a united front on India, but although Churchill thanked Irwin for coming, he insisted that there were still at stake points of high policy with which he could not agree. There for the time being the controversy rested.

Attention was now centred upon the Second Round Table Conference, which, with the vital addition of Congress in the person of Gandhi to its deliberations, would, it was felt, either vindicate or destroy Irwin's actions and arguments. But events of even greater moment were to relegate the importance of the Conference and its works. The crash of the money markets in America, the collapse of the Credit Anstalt Bank in Vienna heralded economic crisis in the strongholds of the City of London; it was as if the nation was in the grip of some mysterious death-dealing disease whereby the whole fabric of monetary, economic and therefore social security must inevitably dissolve. This same sense of doom was to be experienced in the United States, though there, where the tangible evidence of disaster was greater than in Britain, the response was far bolder. In her hour of crisis America was to throw up Franklin Roosevelt and the New Deal; Britain merely relapsed into disguised Conservatism and the rule of the old order. Among the first to appreciate the change in the balance of political forces involved in MacDonald's first National Government and the " Doctor's Mandate " Election of November 1931 were the Indian delegates, who realized that they would have from now onwards to deal increasingly with the Conservative point of view.

As for Gandhi, his intervention in the Conference was a tragic failure, while his impact with British opinion was unfortunate, and the impression of comic eccentricity prevailed. Worst of all, he was unable to resume the intimate and private talks initiated by Irwin, at which he was a far more effective figure than at big formal committees. By the time the Election was fought, what six months before would have seemed incredible now came to pass—India was no longer an issue. Such was the ebb of public interest that, in the words of Gandhi's biographer Glorney Bolton, " if Gandhi dropped dead at Bow the newspapers would relegate the announcement to a back page ". Amid all the panic and disillusion the one man who, it was felt, might save both Gandhi and the Round Table Conference remained in retirement at Garrowby, and while slump struck the world's money markets, and Japanese troops marched stealthily towards Tsitsihar, threatening with overthrow and bloodshed more than Manchuria's future or India's constitution, Irwin prepared for a season's hunting. Bernays had spoken the bare truth when he declared that Irwin should never let Gandhi out of his sight; but although Gandhi spent the better part of one September morning with him at his house in Eaton Square, absenting himself from the Round Table Conference for the first time in order to make the visit, it must have become obvious to him, if it was not before he went, that there was now little that Irwin could do to rescue him from his plight. At Delhi the initiative and the power rested with Irwin, at Garrowby he was simply a country gentleman. He could give advice and encouragement, but the leadership was no longer his. Further, he had a clear duty to do or say nothing, as Bolton justly points out, that would embarrass his successor in Delhi; rather it behoved Gandhi " to dominate the Conference and rescue Irwin from ill-deserved contempt ".

There is certainly no reason to doubt the sincerity of either Gandhi's or Irwin's desire to help each other; together they had fathomed the meaning of renewed hostilities. In the middle of November, within two days of each other, Irwin and Gandhi addressed the boys of Westminster School. Both speeches were acts of courtesy, although Gandhi had made a special point of bringing himself into contact with young people, particularly those from whom a new generation of the Indian Civil Service was likely to be selected; but it is unlikely that he would have come to Westminster School at such short notice but for the news that Irwin had just been there, and those who were privileged to hear them in such proximity were given special insight into the compelling appeal they made upon each other. Irwin made it clear that if he could have had five more years, he could have kept and consolidated the peace with Congress, and one member at least of his audience detected an undertone of regret that the opportunity was not vouchsafed to him. Gandhi, for his part, while defending Civil Disobedience by non-resistance as a " policy never before known in the world ", admitted that there were dangerous factors in it: " I admit I have performed rash acts of which I am ashamed ", but Irwin was " a great man who loosed the prison gates to us ", and was working wholeheartedly for India's national entity, responsibility and self-consciousness.

The tragic sequel to this testimony was that, less than two months afterwards, Gandhi, unable to redeem himself or Irwin in London or to control the disruptive forces at work in India, returned home, only to be arrested under the old regime of ordinance and incipient civil war. During his last few moments of freedom he wrote out a farewell message to Irwin which his secretary was instructed to cable to London. " Pray believe me," it read, " I have tried my best but failed. Nevertheless, I do not lose hope, and, God willing, I shall retain the spirit which you believed actuated me during that sacred week in Delhi. I shall not belie your certificate." Such was his confession of failure, and although he had a bitter journey to travel, through hunger strike to the very boundaries of death itself, Irwin never wholly forgot this *cri du cœur*, and in the coming years, in face of intense discouragement and powerful opposition, he played a notable part in launching the great constitutional experiment which he had striven so hard to create.

. . . .

The factor of chance inevitably moulds public careers often to convey false impressions, but with Irwin chance has with unusual consistency decreed that he should emerge unscathed from the political crises that have divided men and wounded reputations, by simply being absent when the plots were hatched or the decisions taken. Thus it will be recalled that at the watershed of 1906 he was not yet ready to emerge into politics, in 1921 when the Coalition squabbles were boiling over he was safely in the West Indies, while in 1926 he just reached India in time to miss the bitter feuds aroused by the General Strike; now with the parting of the ways in 1931 he was able to approve the formation of a National Government without having any responsibility for the procedure that brought it into existence. From one point of view it argues the strength of his position that he should have gained such rapid promotion at the price of so little intrigue, but from another it has given him a certain spiritual freedom from political controversy and moral superiority to the dictates of party convenience. His policy for India was one to which most Moderates could subscribe; only in the domain of foreign policy was he to be embroiled with the fierce partisanships arising from appeasement, but even here, as we shall see, his role was secondary, and it can with justice be claimed that few British statesmen in our time have been enabled to cross so many Rubicons with integrity and independence so intact. Throughout the critical months of October, November and December 1931 the only Press references to him were that another honorary degree had been conferred upon him, this time by St. Andrews University, and that he had become President of the Yorkshire Agricultural Society, but there is no account of any political speech from him, not even on his own subject of India.

Not until the end of January 1932 did he break his silence, when at a women's Conservative meeting in Leeds he gave his public answer to Gandhi's cable in a speech which was in effect a dignified retreat from Delhi. " After making every effort on the information before me to judge the events of the last month, I cannot doubt that the responsibility for the recent upheaval lies with the Congress Party, and their position is both unnecessary and unjustified." He had very little doubt that Gandhi did not desire that position, but he also had very little doubt that while Gandhi was in this country some of his lieutenants in India were creating a situation that, on his return, was scarcely within his power to control. The suggestion that the Government of India had gone back on the policy it had pursued when he was Viceroy represented " a complete misrepresentation of the facts ". They disliked the application of the present policy as much as anyone else, and there was nothing vindictive about their action. " In any agreement with Mr. Gandhi at Delhi, I expressly reserved to the Government the right to take any action that they thought necessary. I do not suppose that if I had been in India to-day I would have acted any differently from the way Lord Willingdon has done." Then followed an apology which he repeated a score of times in the coming months and which throws some light on his attitude to Anglo-German relations in general and to the Munich Agreement in particular. " The late Government and I have been criticized for having gone so far as we did in the direction of a solution. I do not regret it. I think that in the circumstances of a year ago it was clearly right, and I have very little doubt that it has been a demonstration to India and to the world that the British Government has steadfastly pursued its policy of peace. It has had the effect of making it quite plain to the world on whom lies the responsibility for rejecting the way of peace. A firm Government of itself will never solve the political question once the sentiments and passions of human beings are involved."

The reaction in India to these well-timed words was profound and immediate. At one blow the thesis that had been steadily built up by the Nationalist Press, that if only Irwin had been Viceroy he would have received Gandhi and not arrested him, was shattered. The *Hindustan Times* ruefully announced to its astonished readers " Irwin would have done the same ", and explained the ugly fact away by asserting that he, together with the British public, had been led astray by doctored reports from Government censors and

Diehard special correspondents. But the general effect of Irwin so sternly laying the blame for the rupture on Congress was to provide a healthy corrective to the sentimental legends with which interested parties were linking his name; while by associating himself so frankly with Willingdon he was undoubtedly moulding the political opinion of the vast majority of Moderates who still, as *The Times* Correspondent pointed out, " have implicit trust not only in Lord Irwin's soundness of judgment but in his great-hearted sympathy for Indian aspirations ".

Apart from this, his contributions both to the Indian and to the wider crises were non-controversial, and he was in much demand at this time as a lecturer and after-dinner speaker. In February he proposed the toast of Worcestershire at the annual dinner of the Worcester Association, over which Baldwin, as President, presided. His tribute to Baldwin was linked up with a characteristic anecdote; he said he was reminded of a letter he received when in India, which read: " My Lord, the biggest fool in England appointed you to your present position, and you reciprocated by making yourself the biggest fool in India. You are a traitor to your King and country, and I pray you will soon be recalled. I sign myself a pained watcher of your —— stupidities." " I feel," he continued, " some comfort in being associated so intimately with the President of this Association," and added significantly that he believed no man had done more for the cause of clean politics than Mr. Baldwin in the last ten or fifteen years.

But by far the most important of these various addresses took place when he accepted an invitation to visit Canada in April and deliver the inaugural lecture of the Massey Foundation at Toronto University. The subject he chose, " Some aspects of the Indian problem ", reflected his most mature thoughts on India, his deepest response to the questions, " what are we trying to do? " " why are we trying to do it? " He traced the origins of Hindu-Moslem rivalry, of an Islam the first duty of whose sons " was once to spread the true faith by evangelization, or if necessary by the sword ", and of a Hinduism " driven back upon itself, seeking in the development of its distinctive thought and practice a defensive armour against the strong proselytizing enemy within its gates ". Then followed Akbar's " catholic sympathy" for the many peoples under him and religious tolerance far in advance of the spirit of his age, but the struggle was to be renewed when Aurangzeb, his great-grandson, set out to impose Islam upon the fighting Hindu clans of Central India already roused against foreign domination by the great Mahratta leader, Shivaji. But Moghul power declined, and "upon the Imperial capital of Delhi descended from the north the invading and massacring hosts of the Persian, Nadir Shah. From the south swept the Mahratta hordes, penetrating even to Calcutta, where the famous Mahratta ditch still records the high-watermark of their achievement." The Sikhs, under Ranjit Singh, girded themselves to throw off the Moslem yoke. "From such clash of armies, contending for the body of a stricken Empire, it fell to the British to win peace, and in doing so to find themselves obliged to accept more and more of the direct responsibility of government." Our work in the restoration of law and order belonged to history and we had no reason to be ashamed of it.

To-day, "we are trying within the British Empire to foster the creation of a united India, sufficiently at one within herself in respect of those fundamentals on which every nation-state must rest, that we may devolve upon her people the power for the control of their own affairs, and the ordering of their own political life". India's course must be through unity to Imperial partnership; but he asks, "were it not wiser to play for greater safety by adhering as closely as may be to the old ways, and refrain from perilous incursions into the unknown? This question goes to the root of the whole matter, and drives us for reply to search out deeper causes than appear upon the surface of events. At times we talk of government and only imperfectly remember that, where political consciousness exists, government is never an abstraction, impersonal and detached, but ultimately must depend upon its power to command the allegiance of men and women, who will see in it a true embodiment of their own political thought, and adjudge it capable of giving concrete form to their political aspirations."

The long process of constitutional development had been hastened by the spread of English education and Western thought in India. Irwin's view on the historic controversy over the use of the English language, of which Macaulay was the great protagonist, was that it would be useless to expend regret upon what was past and what was probably inevitable. The English language had given to India a rich storehouse of experience, science and learning. "It has also given her a common medium without which that degree of national unity which exists to-day would have been impossible. Above all, English literature is the literature of freedom, and India has drunk her fill of this life-giving stream." The political implications were the same now as a hundred years ago when Sir Thomas Munro, the famous Governor of Madras, laid down that "the improvement of the character of a people, and the keeping of them at the same time in the lowest state of dependence on foreign rulers to which they can be seduced by conquest, are matters quite incompatible with one another".

He then went on to deal in detail with the obstacles in the way of India's union and progress. First there were the Indian States, comprising, with British India, "a curious and, I suppose, unrivalled piece of mosaic inherited from the past"; there were the difficulties and jealousies in the way of Federation; then there was the eternal communal problem; "to a cynic, indeed, Indian politics might sometimes recall Grote's comment on the Greeks: 'In respect of political sovereignty complete disunion was amongst their most cherished principles'; certainly the vital essence of unity in thought and purpose has yet to be distilled." The economic problem was ever present, "tempting or driving Indian youth in growing numbers to insure themselves, as they suppose, by education against the low standard of life that otherwise appears for most to be the only certain future. Too often—for Indian education has far outstripped her technical and industrial development—great sacrifices are made for no result; and bitter disillusionment becomes the recruiting sergeant for the revolutionary ranks." Finally India was puzzled by herself, by her contradictions and diversity. But new and untried forces were at work. Women were emerging from their agelong retirement and youth was on the march. From all the ferment, shared as it was by other Eastern countries, arose the strength of the Nationalist movement, of which Irwin gave masterly appraisal.

"We deceive ourselves unless we recognize that Indian nationalism is strong and will grow stronger." Gandhi, as far as any one man could be, was the symbol of this struggle. "He appeals to deep forces in Hinduism of which we know little, and he leads his followers into realms of thought where we can hardly follow. His onslaught upon Western materialism strikes a responsive chord in Hindu hearts, even though the hum of his spinning-wheel sounds faintly against the reverberation of the mill", but partly through temperament and "often, perhaps, through circumstances, Mr. Gandhi has repeatedly disappointed many of his warmest friends by his failure hitherto to evolve, and win support for, a considered and constructive policy. Here is one of the major tragedies of the Indian situation."

Britain's contribution to and responsibility for India's unity and security could not be gainsaid. "'Justice', says the Persian sage and poet, Sadi, 'is the adornment of Royalty', and the British Crown has brought to India justice, and secured it to her by its Imperial officers and Courts of Law." From this background of mutual interest "will it be possible for East and West in India to evolve a true partnership in action? We cannot tell; but we can not the less surely say that this is the biggest thing in all our history that we have tried to do, and that the penalty of failure would be exacted far beyond our own times or territories." His own conclusion was that "we can now feel tolerably certain that the most inclusive, balanced and logical method of advance lies in some form of federation of All-India, within the polity of the British Commonwealth, no longer on terms of subordination, but on a mutually accepted footing of equal partnership. In spite of the manifest obstacles in our path, whether from an intractable Congress, or from doubts which dismay many of our own friends, it is to this high purpose that we must consecrate our best endeavour."

. . . .

This great lecture was to prove to be, in more senses than one, his last word on the broader aspects of the Indian problem: for in July he was suddenly invited to join the National Government in his old post as President of the Board of Education. The vacancy occurred through the tragic and wholly unexpected death of Sir Donald Maclean, the brilliant Liberal leader. In terms of his personal prestige and advancement it was a modest offer, although it should be noted that there is a somewhat humiliating tradition of unemployment for Viceroys, and even the great Curzon had to wait ten years after his return from India before gaining access to the Cabinet as Lord Privy Seal. From Irwin's point of view his readiness to go back to a junior position in the Government was proof of his disinterested desire to put himself at the disposal of the Administration in a national emergency, but it was also the prelude to eight years of uninterrupted office and accumulating power.

India was the label against his name, and it is highly suggestive of how quickly the agitation against him had died down that MacDonald and Baldwin felt strong enough to include him in the Government. Indeed, his return to the political arena at a time when India was likely to be increasingly on the agenda implied that he was being invited into it on special terms, and it was widely rumoured that instead of attending to the details of his official department, he was busily assisting Sir Samuel Hoare, now Secretary of State for India, in producing and drafting a communal settlement. *The Times*, for instance, emphasized that Irwin in active service again would be a " reassurance to Indians, who may have been persuaded or disposed to believe the contrary, that there has been no variation or vacillation of any kind in British policy towards their country. Nothing is more certain than that it would have been impossible for Lord Irwin to join the Cabinet had there in truth been any departure, in Whitehall or in India, from the basic policy of full collaboration in the Reforms, or any weakening in the cause with which he has been most closely identified." His return to office, it was added, could not be regarded as the sectional gain of a particular " machine " or of any one element in the following of the Ministry; " it is an assurance to all that the Government remains true to its title."

But for the cause of Indian reform the gain was undoubted and probably decisive. Before he joined the Government the pro-Indian group could be said to comprise Lothian, the Under-Secretary of State for India, J. H. Thomas, and Sankey, Samuel and Snowden. MacDonald and Hoare in the pivotal positions were also well-disposed. Irwin helped to direct their general goodwill into positive adoption of Lothian's Franchise Report, which recommended twelve separate electorates, and into acceptance of the Indian Liberal manifesto, which denounced Provincial Autonomy without Federation. The Communal award led to Gandhi's decision to fast unto death as his protest against the vivisection of Hinduism, while the manifesto was a direct challenge to the Government's own projected constitutional compromise.

Thus under Irwin's influence MacDonald and Hoare were led to risk the martyrdom of Gandhi on the one hand and the break-up of the National Government on the other: MacDonald may have been reconciled to both these contingencies on the fatalistic assumption that both were sooner or later inevitable, and that the Government might as well split over India as over any other issue; but beyond such considerations remains the steady will-power of Irwin in pursuit of the *via media* and Hoare's final conversion to his ideals. No doubt Hoare was pursuing, as has been alleged, his " twin policy of repression and reform without reference to Parliament or public opinion "; and taking immense risks in the process; nevertheless the continuity of " Irwinism " throughout these terrible months of disillusion and disaster, when all that it implied seemed on the surface to be irrevocably lost, was, in fact, through the vigilance of its author, assured and maintained. Federation was retrieved, the Government was not broken, and Gandhi survived to see the vindication of the Untouchables.

CHAPTER XXIV

CALLS TO DUTY

WHEN President of the Board of Education in 1922 Irwin had first gained a name for being a Conservative of progressive tendencies, and there was now widespread expectation that his return would herald the liberal dispensation that Sir Donald Maclean had not lived long enough to inaugurate. But in fact Irwin's record belied his reputation, for, as we have seen, necessity in 1922 compelled him to emphasize retrenchment. Now, ten years afterwards, as the member of a National Government pledged to restore financial stability by drastic cuts in the social services, he was more firmly bound than ever to the same negative objectives.

It was not long before he was confronted with a rising tide of discontent in the teaching profession, which, for a variety of reasons, regarded itself as being called upon to do more than its fair share in the Government drive for economy. All his powers of discreet circumspection had to be called into play. One of his first speeches, an address to the City of London Vacation Course in August, was a homily on making money go farther, the main burden of which was that it was not surprising that those who had no source of income except fitful dividends or business and commerce that had melted away should look with somewhat jealous eyes upon those with small fixed incomes. It was only fair to recognize that such jealousy and controversy existed, and it would be a bad day for education if public opinion generally ever came to the point of questioning the disinterested pursuit on the part of teachers of their professional ideals. The best answer that teachers as a class could give was to carry on with their daily jobs and leave no room for doubt that, although they were human like everybody else, they were as ready as any other section of the community to take their fair share in patriotic effort and sacrifice.

The tone of these remarks was not calculated to appease

a militant National Union of Teachers which in October duly came in a large representative deputation to lay its grievances before Irwin in person. " Equality of sacrifice ", claimed by the Government as an underlying principle of the Economy Act, should be followed by equality of restitution wherever possible; conditions of employment should not in future be settled by the Government over their heads; normal methods of negotiation between teachers and local authorities should be resumed through the Burnham Committee free from limitations imposed under Order in Council in October 1931. The Government were not free from responsibility towards teachers who only three years before had been encouraged to enter the service in order to prepare for the raising of the school-leaving age to fifteen. The Government had thus deliberately accelerated the rate of recruitment; it was inconceivable that these additional teachers should now be left utterly stranded. Irwin promised to give these matters his " serious consideration ", and making one of his rare contacts with an organized trade union agitation must have reflected ruefully upon the controversies he was called upon to inherit in the name of national emergency.

Towards the end of the month he was busily defending the Board's attempt to administer the law of diminishing returns which was contained in the notorious Circular 1421. The provisions of this Circular made deep inroads into the system of free places and low fees in secondary schools, and was in a sense the most reactionary document penned by the Board in the post-Fisher epoch. Irwin's defence was disarming enough: he was, he said, the last person to suggest or desire uniformity, and went a long way with those who wished to see the greatest possible latitude afforded to all engaged in local administration in order that they might be thereby preserved from what was " generally termed bureaucratic interference from Whitehall ". There were three elements in the present arrangements which were difficult to justify: the substantial gap between payments by parents and the average cost to the public funds, the number of children of comparatively well-to-do parents who were enjoying free places in our schools, and the surprising differentiation of fees and practice between adjacent and comparable districts. These were legitimate points to make; what was more in doubt was whether Circular 1421 constituted an equitable or desirable solution of the abuses he mentioned. To the core of the controversy Irwin does not seem ever to have addressed himself in public. Towards the end of December he conceded to a deputation representing the various Welsh educational authorities that they should proceed with their own arrangements for fees, special places, and income limits under the regulations, " on the understanding that a reasonable increase in fees income was assured, and also on the understanding that, if they found it advisable to do so, the authorities might disregard the suggested increase which had been placed before them for their guidance by the Board ".

In the meanwhile he had been called away from purely departmental dilemmas by his appointment to the Parliamentary Delegation of the third Indian Round Table Conference, which, although the Labour Party had refused to nominate representatives, was well balanced in favour of the Federal solution. For the next two years Irwin was to be absorbed in an epic of committee work which has no parallel in Parliamentary history. Between November 1932 and March 1933 he was engaged on the Round Table Conference and in drafting the White Paper which, in its turn, was submitted to the promised Joint Select Committee of the two Houses of Parliament. This Joint Select Committee, to which Irwin was duly appointed, was under the chairmanship of Lord Linlithgow, included representatives of all three parties, and had, also as promised, the collaboration of seven delegates from the States, twenty-seven from British India and twelve from Burma. It entered on its herculean labours in April 1933, a mere three weeks after the publication of the White Paper, and did not leave off until November 1934. By then having accumulated a vast mass of evidence, it produced its recommendations from which was drafted the Government of India Bill that, after taking up most of the 1935 Session of Parliament, finally emerged as the historic Government of India Act.

Some idea of the size of the task into which this network of deliberations fits can be gauged from John Gunther's assessment of the contribution made by Hoare, upon whom, of course, the main burden fell. " As Secretary of State for India, he wrote the India Bill, the largest in the history of British Parliament; with supernal industry he answered

15,000 questions about it, made 600 speeches, read 25,000 pages of reports, and participated in a debate which lasted seven and a half years and comprised 15,500,000 words in Hansard, which is equivalent to twenty books the size of the English Bible."[1] It is not possible here even to begin assessing Irwin's total contribution to this veritable orgy of work; it will be sufficient to note that he was inevitably in a key position, not only from his status in India and in the Government, but also from the intimate understanding that grew up between himself and Hoare. As the Conference and the Select Committee penetrated further into the constitutional recesses of the sub-continent Hoare came increasingly to rely upon the man whose earnest mind and ripe judgment had so fully mastered the perils that beset them.

In these circumstances it is hardly surprising that Irwin largely confined himself in his various Educational addresses to non-committal homilies. Indeed what is remarkable is that he was able to speak as often and as fully as he did. In these speeches the theme to which he constantly returns —and it is to be found throughout all his public utterances —is the Socratic doctrine that he knows most who knows that he knows nothing. Thus in a Presidential address at a North of England Educational Conference in January 1933 discussing education and democratic citizenship he claimed that an unprecedented responsibility was placed upon the average judgment of the average citizen which was the foundation of British democracy. Mass propaganda was no substitute for the gift of right judgment, the power to discuss truth and the power to distinguish in public affairs the genuine from the spurious; to be a good nationalist was not enough, there were problems of international appeasement,[2] disarmament, readjustment of the world's economic life, and lastly India, " a problem which I believe to be the biggest thing that our imperial citizenship has ever attempted to undertake ", there were no short cuts to the solution of any of them; " equally their solution will turn not only on some analysis of pure reason, which I believe is seldom the arbiter in human affairs, but upon our success

[1] *Inside Europe*, 15th Impression, page 275.

[2] Was this the first public use by a member of the National Government of this unhappy word, the verb of which, according to Chambers's Dictionary, means " to pacify by granting demands "?

in finding the right readjustment of a great clash of feelings."

If one wanted education which would build a sound citizenship it was plain that no purely intellectual result would give it. One must require intelligence informed and, if need were, directed by imagination, by much patience, by sympathy, by perspective and by understanding. In the sphere of moral values the restraints of authority, tradition and convention were all being relaxed . . . biology and heredity were not infrequently invoked to assure that moral responsibility no longer rested heavily, if at all, on the individual, but this new philosophy had very little to say to many of the deepest things of life, and these deepest things might be very near the heart of national character building. Then again later in the same month he spoke of it as a great mistake to think of education as some mechanical process akin to factory production which ran so many hours a day. Humanity could not be standardized, for to try to do so was to ignore "the intangible forces from which it takes its root. . . . Love, laughter, sorrow, anger, courage, sympathy—all of these that are the elemental things of human life are supra-rational; it is not the least of Education's purposes to teach human beings to be the masters and not the slaves of them . . . but until, as I believe, the majority of the nation is alive to the necessity of maintaining Christian teaching let us not be blind to the insidious attacks that are being made upon the whole Christian position. To meet this we must be prepared all to concentrate rather upon the things on which we can be united than upon those which still unhappily divide us. Thus only may we hope to repel the forces which are gathering against these defences of our national life."

. . . .

It was a timely warning, for a week later Adolf Hitler, the arch-exponent of the new philosophy, the apostle of mass propaganda for whom democratic values were no more than hypocritical jargon, had become Chancellor of the Third Reich and was from the balcony of the Chancellory watching his pagan legions pass beneath him, their torches a thin line of Nazi fire disappearing into the night. How did the Government react to those in Europe who were so wantonly and ominously exploiting Irwin's doctrines? Curiously enough MacDonald began at once where Neville Chamberlain was to end; he invoked the appeasement that Irwin had mentioned, and called upon the by now established and respectable dictator of Italy to introduce his new German colleague to France and evolve a Four Power security which could cover all grievances and adjustments. "If first indiscretions are to be believed," commented *L'Intransigeant* on 20th March, "Mr. MacDonald and M. Mussolini are contemplating the formation of a 'peace club' so as to restore order in Europe. This would be a very exclusive club consisting of only four members: England, Italy, France and Germany. The first two nations would strive for a rapprochement between the other two, and, this result once obtained, all four could direct European affairs according to their wishes." However, in spite of MacDonald's protests that the whole transaction was within the framework of the League, in that all the four Powers had permanent seats in the Council, Daladier in March 1933 was far from satisfied, and after some polite but desultory bargaining, Mussolini's Draft Treaty was quietly consigned to the archives of the Quai d'Orsay and the Wilhelmstrasse.

The only tangible precaution against Hitler was taken by the statesman most immediately concerned, Dr. Dollfuss, who with his Christian-Socialist Government insured Austria against the Nazis by aping their technique, but, as *The Economist* pointed out with considerable prevision, "We have to reckon with the possibility of Dr. Dollfuss having a Nazi successor. And what is to happen if this hypothetical personage proceeds to proclaim himself one of Herr Hitler's Reichs Kommissars in the Austrian *Land* of the German Reich?" It was a question which Irwin was to be called upon to answer in circumstances he could hardly have foreseen in all the dim uncertainties and prevarications of 1933. So ended the first phase in the British Government's prolonged effort to reconcile the Europe of the Covenant and collective security with Hitler's Germany.

The episode is of relevance to this biography as in due course Irwin was to be deflected from India to Foreign Affairs; the exact moment cannot be named, nor was it the outcome of any formal action or precise development, rather it was an almost imperceptible process. As MacDonald, Baldwin and the Foreign Secretary Simon became more engrossed in the complexities of the world situation, and foreign policy came to occupy more of the Cabinet's time, the sense that Irwin's Indian experience provided an analogy for Europe and that his success was a precedent grew steadily, and his advice was increasingly sought by those upon whom rested ultimate responsibility for British foreign policy. 1933 was then one of the most formative years in Irwin's life, and even if his voice did not yet reach as far as Berchtesgaden, his duties and discretion covered a wide field of social, imperial and foreign relations.

During March, however, in spite of the anxieties aroused by Hitler's arrival on the European scene, Irwin was chiefly concerned with the Indian White Paper which marked the completion of the Round Table Conference, the end of what he described in the House of Lords as "fluid conditions". "I wish to make it clear," he added, "that the Joint Select Committee will not be dealing with a Bill but with the full proposals which the Government propose to issue as a Command Paper and as material for a Bill when the time of legislation is reached." Speaking in Leeds a few days before the White Paper was published and its terms known, he did his best to defend it in advance from anticipated right wing criticism, hitting out rather harder than was his wont. There were those who said that there was no serious problem in India, that it was only confined to a mere educated minority which would yield and disappear before a few years' firm administration. "That view, so far as I know, is not shared by a single Governor of any Province in India, nor by any responsible official of the great British services, nor by representatives of great business houses in Calcutta. . . . We delude ourselves if we suppose that Indian nationalism to-day is not strong and will not become stronger. That is the problem." Churchill had momentarily dropped his guard in observing that India was being represented by politicians who had learned to speak English and hate England at the same time. "No one would deny," Irwin retorted with unwonted fervour, "that there are politicians in India whose ideas those words fit, but when you think of the hundreds and thousands of Indians who collaborate with our race in peace and war, then I am amazed that any statesman in this country should permit to pass his lips anything so injurious and so untrue. Let us by all means, according to the angle of our minds, have our fears, but for heaven's sake do not let them be such as to strangle our faith, because no great Imperial achievement has been done by this country except by faith."

But in some respects this vehement outburst was aimed in the wrong direction, the provisions of the White Paper were so cautious, the safeguards so comprehensive that the most powerful and disturbing criticism came from the Indian Liberals. The general opinion in the City was that the safeguards "were as complete as they could probably be made. Indian stocks were slightly higher on the day in sympathy with the rise in British funds." But the price of a gratified stock exchange was the ill-concealed hostility of Jayakar, Sapru and Sastri, who roundly declared that the choice before the Government was to placate the Tories at home or win the confidence of the people of India. Joshi, the Labour leader, Moonje for the orthodox Hindus, Dr. Ambedkar for the Untouchables, and Sir Mohammed Iqbal for the Moslems, were all equally opposed to the plan which promised Federation by Proclamation, but not until the rulers of States representing not less than half the aggregate population in the States and entitled to not less than half the seats to be allotted to the States in the Federal Upper Chamber signified their desire to accede to it and Parliament had authorized it. Without entering into the details of its provisions here, Irwin was justified in commending it as embodying the largest possible measure of agreement obtainable between the politicians of both races and between the rival Imperialist and Nationalist view-points.

The trouble was that the Federal idea which arose in 1930 as an inspired and all-embracing formula had by 1933 become a somewhat faded vision. The Liberals who might naturally have expected to enjoy a large share in the administration of the new order were all relatively elderly men who, as the Joint Select Committee entered on its labours, must have wondered whether they would ever live to see a Federal or any other constitution come into being. Then again so laborious a search for compromise made no appeal to the new generation of Indian Nationalists whose influence over the future Irwin rightly stressed. Their minds, while rejecting the domination of the West, were moving with the prevailing tide against constitutional politics altogether.

Beyond these political trends were vague though vast developments in India's religious thought. The example of the new Turkey was inspiring the Moslem leaders. "The truth is", wrote Sir Mohammed Iqbal, "that among the Moslem nations to-day Turkey alone has shaken off its dogmatic slumber and attained to self-consciousness. She alone has claimed the right of intellectual freedom, she alone has passed from the ideal to the real." The yearnings of a new Hinduism were no less intense and were not wholly met by the pedestrian processes implied in the White Paper. It was also unfortunate if inevitable that the power of veto should in effect rest with the more recalcitrant Princes. All the same, Irwin could take comfort from the knowledge that Congress had not committed itself against the idea of entering the projected new legislatures, and that as time went on more influential sections of opinion came to realize that a practicable scheme of self-government had been put before the country, and that to reject it out of hand was simply to abdicate to the Conservative right wing's opposition to any form of central authority.

With these crumbs of comfort the Select Committee embarked on its huge enterprise. Only occasionally was their patient progress interrupted or enlivened, as when in July Lord Lloyd asserted that the Government were concealing a great deal of highly important information which, if disclosed, would show that communist and terrorist activities were not confined to Bengal but were spreading gradually, even rapidly, all over India. Reading raised the matter in the Lords, and Irwin for the Government sharply reminded Lloyd that if he had seen his way to assume responsibility of serving on the Joint Select Committee he would then have seen that no question more concerned the Committee than that of terrorism. The noble Lord would then have heard of and contributed much. . . . He then pointedly congratulated all in India for so successfully preserving order. Lloyd rather weakened his case by basing much of his evidence on an address given the previous autumn by Sir Charles Tegart, who at the time was speaking in this country as far away from the scene of action as Lloyd himself.

In October came Hitler's dramatic rebuff to Britain's patient efforts to reconcile the German claim for arms equality with the French refusal to disarm. On the very day that Simon produced his draft convention which was to effect disarmament by degrees, Hitler entered formally on his career of staccato hammer blows and announced Germany's withdrawal from the League and the Disarmament Conference. The novelty of his action after an era of conference, this substitution of brutal sudden death for respectable lingering illness, bewildered British opinion steeped for a dozen years in League procedure; it was in this atmosphere of confusion, with the Government setting out to damp down dismay and restore confidence, that Irwin made his début as a spokesman of Cabinet policy on Foreign Affairs. He spoke as an oracle. "I do not believe," he asserted, "that there is any danger at the present or for many years to come of war, but I do believe Europe to-day and for many years to come, if she is fortunate, will be at the cross-roads, in the sense that if Europe decides wrongly upon matters that will not lead immediately to war to-day she may very well unconsciously be sowing the teeth of the dragon that will for another generation turn into a harvest of war." He then turned on the critics of Locarno. "If it were scrapped to-morrow and we told France that whatever happened she could not count on our help, what," he asked, "would be the immediate effect upon the French talks on the question of disarmament? It would be good-bye to any hope of disarmament."

Irwin is not given to mouthing inconsistencies; the collector of political self-exposures will search in vain through his public speeches for major howlers, and his record is almost excessively blameless in this respect. When in March 1936 the circle narrowed and Locarno itself came on Hitler's list, Irwin significantly repeated almost word for word his "world at the cross-roads" thesis, and in spite of rumours to the contrary stood firmly behind the decision to implement our undertakings to France with Staff talks. *The Times* on Armistice Day summed up the position he maintained right up to the Czech crisis of 1938, when its leading article proclaimed that "despite the alarmists there is little risk of war in the near future, but there is great risk that the Powers disheartened by the recent turn of events may drift back into believing recurrent hostilities to be inevitable". From the outset he recognized and stressed that risk, was prepared to go a long way to eliminate it. Nothing should be done or left undone that would convert Germany's isolation from "a temporary misfortune into a permanent danger".

There is something of a contrast in this time between the expansion of his usefulness, prestige and influence as a free lance Cabinet Minister and the uninspiring and negative range of his departmental duties. Now he is moving the closing of redundant schools, now reiterating to the Burnham Committee Baldwin's reply to a deputation from the National Union of Teachers that the economy cut could not be restored to the teachers without a similar concession to all other civil servants, now rejecting the Archbishop of Canterbury's plea that he should look into the serious cuts in Teachers' Training Colleges. There is a hopelessness in his answer that with the non-realization of the raising of the school age and the numbers of schools declining there was likely to be unemployment in the teaching profession and not too many teachers must be trained. Wickham Steed has described putting up to him a scheme to create a German faculty attached to the University of London and costing the Government about £20,000 a year whereby German Professors of liberal mind, now exiled by Hitler, could give English students the benefit of their learning. "Such a faculty, I believed, would come to be a centre of sound and solid German culture at a time when free research and liberal teaching were being suppressed in German lands. . . . Lord Irwin disappointed me, his mind seemed to work too slowly to grasp all this idea might mean. He thought it a matter for the University Grants Committee—whereas I thought it a matter for a far-sighted statesman gifted with imagination. He may not then have understood the nature of Nazism." It is more likely that there were too many extraneous demands on his time and attention for him to improvise or initiate policy at the Board of Education.

. . . .

Two tributes were paid to his ever-growing prestige in the religious and cultural life of the nation when in July he presided over a great Anglo-Catholic Congress held at the Albert Hall to celebrate the centenary of the Oxford Movement, and in October a meeting of Conservative members of Convocation nominated him as candidate for the Chancellorship of Oxford University in succession to the late Lord Grey of Fallodon. The Anglo-Catholic Congress gave him a splendid chance to interpret reunion with perhaps greater detachment than his father could after a lifetime in the thick of the doctrinal fray. Irwin on this occasion repelled attempts to contrast the Evangelical Revival and the Oxford Movement, should they rather not be regarded as complementary? The Evangelical Revival had promoted changes in social conscience by reviving the appeal to the individual conscience. But there were deficiences, and it had been the privilege of the Oxford Movement to recall to men's minds "the splendour and power of a spiritual society resting upon a definite command, and living in the strength of corporate life maintained through the sacramental system". Differences were nearly all due to misunderstanding; these he hoped would be smoothed away by our generation, not through compromising with principles or suppressing faith but through a growing recognition on all sides that "'Catholic' is a title to which every member of the Church of England has a right, and of which every member of the Church of England ought to be humbly proud". The reunion of the Church of England with its own Mother Church, the great Church of the West, and the reunion here in England with those of their fellow Christians who left their Mother Church of England under the influence of causes and shortcomings, perhaps on both sides, which later years had done so much to remove, was the work to which their prayers and all their energies must be constantly devoted until it might be brought to fruition and accomplishment.

He reiterated his emphasis on reunion through social service in a letter to *The Times* in support of the Archbishops' campaign for slum clearance. "In the crusade against the slums such an opportunity is now offered for all working together to remove a stain unworthy of a country which still calls itself Christian." His father too clinched the argument when, making his last contribution to the cause of unity, he succeeded in effecting the amalgamation of the Anglo-Catholic Congress, Maurice Child's newer organization, with his own English Church Union. For some time it seemed as though the attempt would fail, and there was a long period of inconclusive bargaining which was only resolved in October by Halifax appealing over the heads of the governing body of the English Church Union to the rank and file, a successful procedure which to his great delight caused his son to accuse him of imitating the latest methods of Herr Hitler.

No less gratifying from the personal view-point was his formal election as Chancellor of Oxford University. There are no strictly administrative duties involved in this historic office which lasts for life, but neither is it merely honorary nor confined in scope to such ceremonies as Encaenia; it involves almost a spiritual overlordship over the living community of Oxford men past and present throughout the world. It was no easy task to find the right man to take the place of a Chancellor who just before his death had launched the Oxford Society, which was intended to give new substance to the ideal of banding together a far-flung Oxford community. But Irwin, with all his gifts of veneration, his earnest eloquence, reinforcing a genuine love of all that Oxford stands for, was a worthy successor to a company of Chancellors that had included Wellington and, in our time, Curzon and Grey himself. As Chancellor of the University he also shared *ex officio* control over All Souls with the Archbishop of Canterbury. Here indeed was a congenial consummation to his public labours, to enjoy at the early age of fifty-two and for the rest of his days an unchallengeable sovereignty over a university and college which held within its walls so much of the fabric of his philosophy.

On 7th December, following his formal election " in default of other candidates ", he was installed as Chancellor at a special Convocation held in the Sheldonian Theatre. The ceremony was conducted throughout in latin with all the solemn pomp and circumstance of antique procedure that springs direct from the scholastic custom of the Middle Ages. The procession of the Vice-Chancellor, Proctors, Heads of Houses, and Doctors duly met the new Chancellor at the Great Gate of the Schools and escorted him to the Divinity School, where he remained behind while they proceeded to the Theatre. Then with traditional latin ritual, the Vice-Chancellor, Dr. F. J. Lys, Provost of Worcester, after formally opening Convocation, directed the Bedells in these words: " *Ite, bedelli, petite Dominum Cancellarium.*" They returned, ushering in Irwin dressed in his black robes of ceremony embroidered with gold, the train of which was carried by his son and heir Charles who was then an undergraduate at Christ Church. When he was seated on the right of the Vice-Chancellor the Registrar was instructed to read the Instrument of Election, whereupon the insignia of office were brought forward and laid before the Chancellor. These were the Book of Statutes, the Common Seal of the University, the Sign Manual of the Chancellor brought by the Proctors, together with maces and staves of the Bedells, the Instrument of Election, and the Diploma of the Doctor of Civil Law. There then followed two latin orations in which the Public Orator, Cyril Bailey, eulogized Irwin, distinguished "*et mentis eruditione et morum suavitate*", and Irwin eulogized Grey and referred to their common descent from Grey of the Reform Bill. Only through Lord Grey's illustrious example could we escape that headlong and unbridled licence usurping the name of liberty which left liberty herself in danger of perishing beneath the feet of the dictator or at the hand of the revolutionary. At the end of his oration Irwin returned the insignia to the Vice-Chancellor and directed him to dissolve the Convocation. The procession left the Theatre and the historic ceremony was at an end.[1]

Shortly afterwards he followed Grey as President of the Oxford Society, and this helped to stabilize an ambitious experiment and set a precedent for a Chancellor always to hold this office as well. As he publicly testified: "My admiration and friendship for the late Chancellor unite therefore with my belief in the great potentialities of the Society in making it both a pleasure and a duty to do whatever lies in my power to foster the Society's growth."

Two days after the Installation came the alarming news that Irwin had been badly injured while hunting at Yapham in Yorkshire. He was thrown heavily when his horse ran into some wire, and received cuts on the head and arm. In the previous year he had achieved a great ambition when he was chosen Master of the Middleton Hunt.[2] This was to be his only serious fall, and two months afterwards, inde-

[1] A foreign visitor who was present and had also witnessed the rather more boisterous proceedings of a degree day was overheard describing the Installation as " much better, very nice "!

[2] He held this office until 1938, when the pressure of his duties forced him to resign and his son Charles took on the Mastership.

fatigable, he had returned to the field. It was difficult for anyone who is not intimate with the intricate pleasures of hunting to assess the part it has played in Irwin's life. Like cricket hunting has ethical and æsthetic qualities incomprehensible to the uninitiated, although it is far more open to obvious criticisms. Only once during the leg theory controversies did imaginative scribes apply to cricket the epithets usually reserved for blood sports, nor is it such a catholic and democratic form of outdoor exercise as cricket. Hunting is largely run for and by the " upper ten thousand ", and its etiquette is in line with the traditions of a feudal aristocracy; the London social round otherwise rigid and uncompromising none the less yields to the imperious demands of the hunt; the ebb and flow of the London Season is in strict ratio to activity in the shires.

Hunting then is part of the apparatus of the landed nobleman, but Irwin has imparted to it some of his own earnest purpose. For all his respect for traditions he is not the man to do a thing simply because it is done, he hunts with relish because he is good at it and finds it good. In India Congressmen and other " mild Hindus " were rather shocked and mystified at the assiduity with which this Christian Viceroy relished or overlooked the apparent cruelties of the chase, for until Civil Disobedience deprived him of the last vestiges of relaxation he hunted regularly with the Delhi Hounds. Just how much hunting meant to him can be judged from his candid confession, made in all sincerity, that if given the choice he would far prefer to be Master of the Bramham than Prime Minister! Irwin's sons maintain the family tradition and are no less enthusiastic than their father, and while at Oxford both Charles and Peter Wood distinguished themselves with the Christ Church pack. Their knowledge of hunting lore is quite sufficient for them if they so wished to contribute learned monographs on the subject.

Towards the end of 1932 old Lord Halifax in his ninety-fourth year had a happy thought. " Think of this," he wrote to Irwin. " Lawn meet of Hounds, November—Try Preserve[1]—Lord Irwin in red coat—Lord Halifax in red coat —Charles in red coat. Three members of the family all at once. Thing never known before this *must* be arranged." It was, and the scene was recaptured in a portrait by Norman

[1] A Garrowby covert, see Lockhart, Vol. II, pages 365-366.

Edwards of the three generations, Halifax riding a pony, Irwin and Charles Wood in their red coats, on the brow of Garrowby Hill over which the old man had ridden so many times in distant days. For all his wonderful resilience his time was drawing to a close. In October 1933 Charles came of age and the customary festivities which had marked Irwin's own majority were held. To the delight of the neighbours and tenants assembled in the stableyard at Hickleton, over a thousand in all, he made a little speech without relying on any notes. Charles also spoke, according to Halifax, " an admirable speech—not too long and not too short ", but for himself it was to be his last. His children (including Irwin who was by now almost fully recovered from his accident) and grandchildren gathered round him for one more happy Christmas celebration at Hickleton.

Then early in the new year he left for Garrowby, where on 8th January he was very unwell. On the 18th he insisted on being taken out of doors in a chair " to see the sea " again; his mind was wandering back to the far-off days at the Moult. He tried to walk, but returned to bed very exhausted. That night he was still conscious and received his last communion. When Irwin and Lady Bingley came to bid him good night he whispered to her, " I am worrying about my sins." He then lost consciousness, fell into a deep sleep, and at half-past seven the next evening he died peacefully. On 23rd January, the eighth anniversary of Mercier's death, there were two Requiems, the second immediately before the burial, and although the congregation was confined to neighbours and a few old friends the little church at Hickleton was crowded with mourners. His body was laid to rest in the south aisle.

As if by a miracle he had been spared to see his one surviving son fulfil all his early promise, far advanced on a career of glory to the family and honour to himself. But for Irwin it was the end of a unique relationship, the passing of a master spirit to whom he could turn to seek the strength and the guidance for which, as the scope of his life-work enlarged, he was more than ever in need; the removal of a buttress to his mind and character which, the longer it was there to support him, became the more indispensable element of his strength. Thus in mid-career had come the long-delayed farewell, a void he could not hope to fill.

PART III

VISCOUNT HALIFAX

CHAPTER XXV

ROVING COMMISSIONS

THE remainder of this narrative in essence describes how Edward Wood has succeeded in attracting to the name of Halifax, which meant a new beginning for him in the public estimation, a fame not far removed from, and in certain respects significantly parallel to, that of the renowned Marquis who steered the State through the perils of 1688. There is, as we have seen, no family relationship between Halifax and the great " Trimmer ", but who among our contemporaries, in his patient search for moderation both in the spheres of public policy and philosophic principle, more closely approximates to the architect of the Glorious Revolution?

His first public appearance as Viscount Halifax was to represent the Government in a vast all Party rally at the Albert Hall held under the auspices of the League of Nations Union. The Union was at this time approaching the zenith of its influence, and no political leader could, even if he wanted to, ignore the trend of its policy. This particular meeting was proclaimed as the first step in a campaign " to make Britain prepare to pay the price of peace ", and it was estimated that nearly seven thousand people were present. Halifax's special qualification to represent the Government was that he was a member of the informal Disarmament Committee of the Cabinet and was thus closely identified with the burning question of the hour—the fate of disarmament following the German resolve to rearm. He moved the main resolution of the evening to the effect that the meeting recorded its profound conviction that only through the collective system embodied in the League of Nations could war be averted and civilization saved, and showed some courage in doing so as the British Memorandum, which had been published the week before and contained the Government's revised views on Disarmament, was far from popular in Union circles.

Part of his speech was relayed after the news bulletin on a special record; thus the anonymous millions of British listeners gained their first impression of the new Viscount Halifax as a " League of Nations " man. Isolationists were suitably rebuked: " Those who preach the gospel of behaviour like that of Diogenes," he asserted, " retiring into his tub and disinteresting himself from the affairs of the world outside, are living in a dreamland of their own creation." Nor was there any antagonism between Empire and League. Life, to repeat a thesis that went back to *The Great Opportunity* and beyond, was built upon a series of mutually supporting loyalties each of which tended to be stunted and atrophied if it was content to be merely self-regarding. These broad assertions were well received, but when he came to discuss Disarmament he was on more delicate ground.

The British Memorandum, in the preparation of which he had a hand, after piously deploring the attainment of arms equality by the rearmament of Germany instead of the disarmament of the more heavily armed Powers, advocated the permanent and automatic supervision and control of arms, proposed that Germany should acquire an air force unless an acceptable control scheme had been evolved within two years, and should provide her army with a formidable equipment of hitherto forbidden tanks and guns three times heavier than before, and finally laid down that the German Army should be limited to 200,000 men. This last figure was the real *raison d'être* of the document. Simon had just returned from conversations with Mussolini and the French Government, and it had seemed that the British desire to keep Disarmament alive would be realized, but immediately afterwards hopes were dashed when the Germans sent a " final " demand to France for a short service army of 300,000 men and adequate defensive weapons.

The Draft Convention was no longer a practicable compromise. " I readily admit," said Halifax, " that if the British Government had only their own views to consider they might in some respects have framed the suggestion they made differently, but our business is to secure agreement—and I cannot myself doubt that if a substantial advance could be made by agreement, even if it were less than many of us would have hoped to see, yet that advance would operate as a real reassurance to a distracted world and would be eloquent of the world's determination to tread the paths of peace." "Even if the League was less securely founded upon practical necessity," he concluded, "and was predominantly idealistic, that would not be a reason for failing to support and strengthen it." The inconsistency between practice and precept is in part explained by Halifax's unreadiness to believe the worst as to German aims as well as by the lack of any decisive response within the Cabinet itself to a rapidly changing situation.

On 6th February, only the day before Halifax's decorous début, the grave unrest in France as a result of the Stavisky scandals broke out into fierce street-fighting, blood flowed in the Place de la Concorde, the Daladier Government collapsed to be superseded by a National administration under Gaston Doumergue of a far more right wing complexion than its British counterpart. Only with difficulty was it able to put out the flames of incipient revolution, and Louis Barthou, the new Foreign Secretary, who once had regarded the Versailles Treaty as too lenient, was not the man, with France in danger from within, to gamble on German goodwill. To meet this growing tension MacDonald and Baldwin hit upon a characteristic compromise. They appointed as Lord Privy Seal the young and promising Under-Secretary for Foreign Affairs, Captain Anthony Eden, and thus deliberately linked that free-lance office with the active conduct of foreign affairs, thereby setting up a virtual diarchy which was not effectively abandoned until four years later, when Eden disappeared from the scene, and Halifax, who had shared with him some of its hazards, took his place as Foreign Secretary. The attempt to hold the balance between Germany and France by dividing our foreign policy between a Minister with a slightly pro-German bias and one whose faith and reputation centred round the League and collective resistance to aggression was a good example of Baldwinian "duplicity", the doctrine of making the best of Teutonic and Latin feuds to which, it must be confessed, Halifax seems whole-heartedly to have subscribed.

The same compelling tide of events that had brought promotion to Eden was attracting Halifax into the flood of foreign policy. He had no practical experience in European affairs beyond his one brief excursion to Geneva eleven years before; he was, in fact, a complete novice. Eden, on the other hand, was already, at the tender age of thirty-seven, a recognized specialist who had served a long apprenticeship which went back to the days of Locarno and Parliamentary Private Secretaryship to Austen Chamberlain; it was Eden, too, who by his skilful pleading at the Disarmament Conference had done signal service for the Cabinet in gaining several minor victories on matters of secondary but none the less exacting detail. But for all that, as the situation rapidly grew in complexity, Halifax's grasp of high policy, fortified as it was by his immense achievements in the mysterious arts of reconciliation, caused Baldwin and MacDonald to lean more and more heavily upon his judgment.

The scope for informal advice was widened by the growing distrust for Simon, the Foreign Secretary, both on the part of high officials in the Foreign Office and of the country at large. No man in our time with such intellectual gifts has striven so hard for popularity and obtained such a meagre reward as Sir John Simon, but it was to be a tragic irony that for India and Europe alike his faculty for analysis and detail and his clarity of mind were to be wholly offset by a fatal incapacity for frank decision. India in 1927, Europe in 1934 cried aloud for a clear lead from Britain; in spite of the dynamics of a resurgent National Socialism, the general situation at the beginning of 1934 was still sufficiently malleable for a British craftsman of vision to mould it to his own peaceful purposes; but while the British Government, in the role of Janus facing both ways at once, was lost in uncertainty, Europe was being remorselessly hammered into the shape of the Swastika.

A variety of means was exploited to achieve the same end, which was the deliberate destruction of the League system and the Anglo-French unity that inevitably sustained it. Thus in 1933 Hitler capitulated to Pilsudski's demands in order to attract Poland from the orbit of League diplomacy, and in 1934 he was ready to destroy Austria on the assumption that in this instance the well-timed use of force was best calculated to defeat the aims of Geneva. Ironically enough it was Mussolini operating outside the framework of League procedure who provoked the Polish crisis and solved the Austrian one. His references to Treaty revision during the abortive negotiations for the Four Power Pact had stirred

Pilsudski to invite the French to march along with him and settle the Hitler menace once and for all. France, even more nervous than Britain of translating her legal and diplomatic supremacy into terms of force, refused the invitation, and, in the opinion of the shrewd Alexander of Jugoslavia, lost her last chance of retaining the allegiance of Eastern Europe at a price she could afford to pay. By 1934 Hitler had entered on his stupendous rearmament programme and the Austrian coup was only frustrated by Mussolini rushing a quarter of a million men to the Brenner; it was to be the Duce's last substantial intervention in Europe, from henceforth, for all his braggadocio, he is a secondary figure who is rescued only by the excessive if deliberate deference of Berlin, Paris and London.

But Hitler's plans were further advanced by the last death agonies of Disarmament. The object of the British Memorandum had been, as Halifax avowed, to produce agreement; in order to reinforce our thesis Eden was sent on his first Grand Tour, but except for the gain to his own personal prestige he reaped a barren harvest. Mussolini for his own reasons urged that Hitler's word should be trusted; Hitler also for his own sinister reasons spoke soothingly about disbandment of semi-military formations which included Roehm's S.A. battalions; the French began to raise the question of *garanties d'exécution* in order to conceal a grave division of opinion as to whether the British guarantees were in themselves adequate. Barthou, deeply suspicious of German aims, favoured accepting them without question, but Doumergue disagreed and was backed both by Tardieu and Daladier; the outcome, after a short Cabinet crisis, was that on 17th April Barthou handed a note to the British Chargé d'Affaires which concluded that France " regrets that the action of a third party should abruptly have rendered vain the negotiations undertaken by the two countries with equal goodwill and good faith ".

Thus did France incur the fatal odium of seeming to be responsible in British eyes for the break up of Disarmament at the very moment when Hitler was launching the greatest armaments race in history. " France ", observes Konrad Heiden in his brilliant study, *One Man Against Europe*, " had the unpleasant task of telling the English that she could not now disarm and explaining her reasons. Germany went on arming without a word. No less than three times the same thing happened in succeeding years: Germany quietly proceeded to act, while France was involved in troublesome and alienating discussions with England. No less than three times was Hitler to exploit the unique situation resulting from the fact that France's whole continental policy was based on the erroneous assumption of Britain's dominant world position as a peacemaker, a position Britain has never occupied throughout her history. Hitler saw this basic truth in each new disguise it assumed."[1] Britain was, in fact, groping her way from security resting on preponderance to security resting on balance, and in this process Simon's warning on the very night of the riots in the Place de la Concorde that " it is not the Anglo-Saxon habit to make defined engagements for undefined circumstances " represented the hard core of Halifax's more generous phraseology at the Albert Hall.

During the summer, Hitler's growing power was reflected internally in the murders of June 30th, the " night of the long knives ", and externally in the brutal assassination of Dollfuss a month later. The June 30th massacres had aroused *The Times* into comparing Hitler's rule with " oriental despotism " and " mediaeval tyranny ". Halifax, speaking just after the abortive Austrian putsch, denounced those powerful elements in Europe that accepted the philosophy of the once famous historical pamphlet, *Killing no Murder*. But both *The Times* and Halifax failed to press their indignation home. Although Britain had subscribed in February to a Three Power Declaration which underlined " the necessity to maintain the independence and territorial integrity of Austria in accordance with the existing treaties ", the prevailing political reaction in Government circles was that killing should not be called murder nor mediaeval tyranny be regarded as handicap if Germany could only be persuaded to rejoin the Comity of Nations at Geneva. Here France was expounding the doctrines of an Eastern Locarno, and Red Russia being heralded with all solemnity into the League Council. The politician in Halifax therefore spoke soft words, how tempers cannot be changed overnight, how recent events were " not helpful ", and how every foreign nation knows that Britain was

[1] *One Man Against Europe*, pages 126-127.

never likely to be animated by any desire other than that of peace; but the moralist and philosopher in him knew better.

In September, in an impressive address on "The World and Democracy", he saw clearly the underlying menace of totalitarian orders "in which the judgment of the common folk is completely surrendered and is placed in commission". "In general," he declared, "the revolutionary changes on the Continent may be said to have been due to causes that in greater or less degree seem to threaten democracy everywhere—the development of social conscience, the belief in short cuts due to the effect of war experience, the readiness to accept quack remedies, impatience with and distrust of old leadership, and the intolerance of those who disagree with one's own views." For the present, however, he was not called upon to put forward more than occasional random reflections on the European situation, and apart from the Albert Hall speech he made no further policy statement for the Government between the beginning of 1934 and May 1935. During this difficult period he was intensely active on the routine procedure of Government, which is the real test of a man's political capacity, and in the exacting round from the Board of Education to the Cabinet, from the Cabinet to the Joint Select Committee, Halifax's powers as a committee man were tested to the full. In India he was not subjected to quite the same give and take of argument and advice. In a sense his promotion to Viceroy meant that he had missed a stage in his administrative experience; he was now completing the apprenticeship, which had been cut short by his Indian career, in sharing Ministerial responsibility.

. . . .

By December 1934 he had discharged his final duty to the cause of Indian Reform, when amid cheers he moved in the House of Lords the historic resolution that "this House accepts the recommendations of the Joint Select Committee on Indian Reforms as the basis of the revision of the Indian Constitution and considers it expedient that a Bill should be introduced on the general lines of the Report". In a long and "deeply moving" speech he made his last major contribution to the cause to which he had dedicated so much of his energy and talent. The House of Lords, aptly defined in *The Times* as "the traditional reservoir of great proconsuls", gave close attention to Halifax who, in his most impressive proconsular vein, demolished the Fabian defences of the Diehards centred round Lord Salisbury's Amendment that the House should express its inability to give general approval to the Select Committee's Report until its precise recommendations were embodied in a Bill. He also uncompromisingly refused to admit Salisbury's further disruptive demand that the administration of the police should be " reserved ". The advocates of the strong arm felt the full force of this " weak " Viceroy's authority when leave to pass a general Bill on the lines of the Report was passed by the impressive majority of 410 to 127 votes. Salisbury maintained his pressure when the Bill was presented, and the remainder of the 1935 Session of Parliament was largely given over to debating its provisions.

When the great Act with its 470 sections and 16 schedules was finally passed, the main principle of India's unity through Federation had been won. " A new nation," Halifax declared, " is being brought to birth by the Mother of Parliaments herself. And this offspring is as legitimate as her other children . . . Canada, Australia, New Zealand and South Africa." In addition, the Provinces retained autonomy under native Indian Cabinets with certain powers reserved to the Governor who was himself responsible to the Viceroy. Given no undue interference by Viceroy or Governor, Halifax's assertion that India would be " unfrozen " by this provision was amply justified. It was these native Cabinets that were to control the police, hence Salisbury's alarm and emphasis on police reservation. " We cannot say, for example, how Cabinets will be formed," Halifax added, but that they would be formed and that their membership would be Indian was " inevitable ". Thirdly, the All-India Federal Government was made autonomous under a native Indian Federal Cabinet, although Defence and Foreign Affairs were reserved to the Viceroy together with certain special powers. The Communal Award was strong security against any stampede of the new and increased electorates.

" The hearing has been long, the decision is liberal. Whatever intransigents may say," wrote Sir Stanley Reed at the time, " the best brains in the Congress will strive for election, and if invited, will accept office. Through these means India will be kept within the orbit of faith in constitutionalism ", which article of faith was in line with Halifax's one and only formal prediction, that the new Constitution "will be found invested with a magnetic force strong enough to make it impossible for responsible men in India to stand aside". Halifax's contribution to the Bill's success in the Lords was nothing like as great as Hoare's in the Commons, nor was Salisbury's dialectic and oratory comparable to Churchill's, but the remorseless logic that sustained Hoare was shared by and in no small measure derived from Halifax. In the last resort, Hoare's mastery of detail, combined with Halifax's experience, out-distanced Churchill's more spectacular though less knowledgeable thesis. At last Churchill indirectly confessed defeat on the merits of the case when he appealed to the Committee of Privileges in a vain effort to challenge Hoare's integrity. The attack was triumphantly rebutted, and with it collapsed the last potential threat to Indian Federation. Churchill later, with typical generosity, acknowledged his defeat after full public discussion, and with profound democratic insight bowed to the sovereignty of Parliament.

In the meanwhile Halifax's long term as President of the Board of Education was drawing to a close. Here he could not claim the same degree of success as had marked his Indian labours; in part his failure was due, as we have seen, to the distracting demands made upon him by a harassed Cabinet, a grateful country, and an unwieldy estate. His interest in Education never wavered, and his shortcomings should be viewed only in terms of the high standard he set himself; he had been given, it seemed, an unrivalled opportunity to impress his educational ideals upon the country, but his best intentions were beaten down by economic storm and political stress. Accepting as he did the Government's overriding policy of Recovery through Retrenchment, he could only turn away from all educational reform demanding any large expenditure of public money. To the vexed question of the school-leaving age he accordingly returned no clear answer. In debate he argued that keeping children on a year to fifteen would not have nearly so great an effect on juvenile unemployment as was imagined. It would take, if introduced now (in 1934), to 1938 to feel the effects when the fourteen to seventeen age group would be declining. The other alternative to unemployment was juvenile instruction centres, but he had lamely to confess that Parliamentary time and the large need for new buildings were " some of the difficulties " in the way of developing the good work they were doing. The longer the controversy over teachers' salaries dragged on, the less credit it reflected either on the Government or on the teachers. The argument finally narrowed down to an interpretation of a stray remark made by the Chancellor of the Exchequer in his Budget statement for 1934. " I do not myself interpret that understanding," he had said, " so literally as to feel compelled to put everything back exactly where it was before 1931." However, Halifax was able to produce a five per cent restoration and the remaining five per cent was for the present lost in an unedifying dispute as to whether the National Union of Teachers had or had not accused the Government of a deliberate breach of faith.

On the whole he will probably be longest remembered as an Education Minister who gave notable expression to the broad principles on which British educational policy should be based. He said nothing new or startling, but he gave fresh polish to old truths, and in a period when an enthusiasm to save money constituted a positive threat to our social services, he helped the nation to retain its sense of educational values. He sturdily maintained the old reliance upon free judgment and firm character as against bulging intellect and the new and specious brands of educational dilettantism which arrogantly assumed the monopoly of progressive ideas on the subject. Welcoming delegates to a World Educational Conference at Oxford in the summer of 1935, he reached the core of his philosophy when he described those concerned with education, whether administrators or teachers, as " comrades in arms in the great cause of fashioning personality, which is true education ".

In a farewell article which he contributed to *Politics in Review*[1] under the title " Thirty Years of Educational Progress ", he emphasized as the chief landmark in the post war period the issue in 1926 of the Hadow Report, the intention of which had been to secure separate education for children over and under eleven years of age. On the issue of Church schools he was able to point to some progress, for by the time he had left the Board something like fifty-three per cent of the children over eleven were in reorganized departments.

[1] Published by the National Union of Conservative Unionist Associations.

The next step for the Government to take was designed to ease the transition into industry, " but the problem is much wider than this, and we shall be wise if we envisage it as part of the whole problem of dealing with adolescence—that difficult period between fourteen and eighteen when the immature boy or girl is acutely in need of all the help and guidance we can give ". Much remained to be done in developing technical education, " and the next step will be a comprehensive survey of the existing provision in the way of buildings and equipment with a view to bringing it up to date and enabling the work of the schools to meet the requirements of a fiercely competitive age. The supreme task to be faced—on national, not party, lines—is to ensure to every boy and girl that opportunity of a full development of talents and character which is at once the birthright of every Englishman and the aim of sound democracy."

. . . .

Parallel with his educational activities and perhaps even more congenial were his new obligations to Oxford. Nearly the whole of June 1934 was given over to functions and speeches in his capacity as Chancellor. On the 3rd he opened part of the extensions to the famous Ashmolean, which, as he pointed out, is the oldest museum in England and one of the oldest in Europe, founded two hundred and fifty years ago by Elias Ashmole, " a many-sided scholar and man of affairs, astrologer and quack doctor, financier, soldier, one of the earliest Freemasons, antiquary and author "; the next day he was presiding over the annual meeting of the Oxford Preservation Trust, dilating on the theme that in a civilized community there would be no need of such a society, but pausing to pay tribute to the efforts of those who had already saved from the builders part of Shotover Hill, some of the meadows of the Cherwell bank, the northern and southern slopes of Boars Hill and a green expanse in Headington. As H. A. L. Fisher, who had played a gallant part in the Trust's fight against ribbon development, pointed out, the struggle to girdle the growing city in its belt of green was likely to be long and the issue not beyond question, for Oxford's industrial population was growing by leaps and bounds and had to be housed. Halifax's backing was assured, however, for any useful initiative that might be taken. Towards the end of the month he was opening the East Quadrangle of Somerville, recalling the rapid growth of this women's college and its modest origin when "twelve students met in a room over a baker's shop in Walton Street". Now it was to be reckoned as equal in stature and achievement to colleges ten times its age. Three days later he presided over a meeting of the Oxford Society which met at the Foreign Office and paid unstinting tribute to the work of his lifelong friend Riddell, now Master of Pembroke, for his work in promoting it.[1]

But the most impressive occasion was the ambitious broadcast on 7th June, arranged by the Oxford Society, which gave an intimate and popular account of University life. Halifax, speaking in all for forty minutes, acted as guide throughout the programme, aiding his non-Oxford audience by contributing judicious snatches of history and legend. At the outset he spoke to Oxford men and women throughout the Empire words which have an almost nostalgic potency for those who, either by distance of time or of place, felt very far away from Oxford's haunting influence. "For all of us it was a time of new experience, when everything seemed worth while; a time of realization of wide liberty; of comradeship deepening into friendships that were to stand the strain and stress of an unknown future; for some, an opportunity to grasp knowledge with eager hands; for others a growing apprehension that the things of the mind could exercise a strange power and charm; and that through all this manifold process we were gradually being brought to find something that was in a true sense to be ourselves."

Some might be able to attribute to a particular individual the credit for awakening in them powers of appreciation and judgment hitherto dormant and unperceived; "others will recall, as they find themselves to-night again in Oxford, the magic spell cast upon them by the sheer beauty and grandeur of their surroundings. For myself I have only to close my eyes to see once again the sweep of the High Street from Magdalen Bridge to Carfax; with St. Mary's Church, and the great dome of the Radcliffe; or Tom Quad and Tom Tower in Christ Church standing up against the moonlight, and recapture something of the reverence and

[1] Riddell died in 1935 and *The Times* obituary is reputed to have been written by Halifax.

love that seemed to grow from looking on the work that nature and the hand of man had wrought together. In such environment, and with such background, Oxford has through the centuries prepared her members to play their parts upon the great stage of life; and she has no cause to be ashamed of their performance. Her task is not finished. Indeed, at no time in her history has there been greater need than to-day of the sort of service that it is in her power to render." And so to the sequence from Oxford's daily life—a Psalm during Evensong at New College, Great Tom's curfew, a pistol shot and the cheering of Eights Week, a fragment from Gilbert Murray's lecture on Prometheus, an excerpt from a Union Debate, the May morning hymn from Magdalen Tower, rehearsal of the Bach Choir. Memorable as was the total effect of this Oxford symphony, for many near and far it was the deep rich tones of the Chancellor's voice, the vibrant sincerity of his words and outlook that left the most abiding impression.

On 20th June his first Encaenia took place, coinciding almost to the day with the hundredth anniversary of Wellington's. The splendour of the pageant was completed by Halifax's choice of the *viginti viri* to be recipients of honorary degrees, all of whom were present in person to adorn the swelling scene. For the Church there was the Archbishop of York, politics were represented by Arthur Henderson, Walter Runciman and Sir Samuel Hoare, and the Services by Admiral Chatfield. From the Public Services came the Speaker of the House of Commons, Lords Derby and Tyrrell, Sir Maurice Hankey and Sir George Hill, and academic distinction was honoured in the persons of the Warden of All Souls, Sir Henry Miers the great Cambridge physiologist, Professor A. V. Hill and Professor J. W. Mackail. The arts were graced by Sir Edward Lutyens, Arnold Bax, André Maurois and John Buchan, while Geoffrey Dawson of *The Times* completed this list of Halifax's elect. The entry of the Chancellor, once more with his son as train-bearer, was described as truly magnificent, though there was something of an anti-climax when he had to stand waiting for nearly ten minutes while the great men were shepherded to their respective places. It was noted that the closely packed audience gave the greatest applause to Arthur Henderson and Maurois. Honours continued to be showered upon the Chancellor himself, including degrees from Dublin and London Universities and ranging from Patronage of the Halifax Building Society to Vice-Presidency of the Society for Promoting Christian Knowledge.

As Halifax's Indian labours drew to their close and the responsibility for the future fell on other shoulders, in particular on the new Viceroy-elect Linlithgow, there were persistent rumours that Halifax intended to slip out of public life altogether, and that he might use the probable retirement of Ramsay MacDonald from the Premiership to effect this transition. MacDonald returned from an illness to find growing opposition to his leadership, particularly among influential Conservative elements in the Coalition. These, however, did not include Baldwin, who was keenly alive to the advantages of his position behind the scenes as the National Government "Manager", but who, if MacDonald went, knew that he would have to emerge as the only personality who could command sufficient confidence to maintain the "National" façade. Halifax made one of his rare appearances in February 1935 on a purely party platform in order to defend the Prime Minister from his critics. MacDonald addressed a Demonstration in the Doncaster Corn Exchange in support of the Government, and Halifax, who accompanied him, spoke pointedly of him as "the principal architect of national unity", saying that he had often made great personal sacrifices and had never been afraid to tell the country the truth. He recalled MacDonald's wise counsel and firm support when he was Viceroy. He then significantly advised the audience not to think of an election until the National Government had got further through with its tasks, and openly rebuked Conservatives who ill-informedly criticized the Prime Minister—the whole country owed a great debt to him. But even this *ballon d'essai* failed to divert the pressure of party dissatisfaction.

By June the inevitable reshuffle had taken place and the unwanted election was left over until unforeseen events should cast the Administration in a rather more favourable light. There was, however, a constitutional limit to the postponement, and Baldwin experienced some difficulty in finding Ministers for posts they might have soon to vacate. There were also at this time gloomy forebodings about an inevitable swing of the pendulum. Lloyd George was in process of launching his " New Deal ", which he calculated would rally the discontented millions of Moderates who saw no hope either in the Government or the emaciated Labour minority. Accordingly *The Times,* under the heading of " Mr. Baldwin's Problem ", described how " Lord Halifax (another Minister for whom office has no attraction) has been persuaded to go to the War Office for the term of the present Parliament ". " It would have been disastrous ", the paper added, " to let him retire at this moment when the India Bill is just entering the House of Lords and any future Government will be the weaker for dispensing with his disinterested services."

If he was in fact only a half-time Minister of Education, his appointment as Secretary of State for War was little more than honorary, a token transfer that was not intended to produce any important developments either in manpower or military material. As we have seen, most of his first month as War Minister was spent at Oxford, and July was largely given up to India. But his brief spell at the War Office is a far from negligible phase; it gave him shattering insight into the state of our defences, for which up till then he had no direct responsibility, at the very time when Mussolini was planning his Abyssinian aggression and Europe was digesting the consequences of Hitler's conscription coup. The result was that while Baldwin resolved on his own confession to give his word that there would be no great armaments in order to avoid defeat at the General Election, Halifax, with no such doubtful preoccupations, openly preached the gospel of a strong Britain.

At the very moment when Anthony Eden at Geneva was straining the League to its supreme effort, urging the Committee of Eighteen " to prompt action " in Sanctions, Halifax, whose voice was lost in the prevailing excitement, told the world no less frankly that " so long as our defence forces are deficient we are open to the charge that we are in a position of trying to get from others that which we are not in a position to give to them, that we are trying to get ' security on the cheap ' ".[1] At Plymouth shortly afterwards he asserted that there was no single European man, woman or child on the Continent to-day who would not sleep more happily if he or she had the knowledge that Great Britain

[1] Speech at the 307th Cutlers' Feast at Sheffield, October 10th 1935.

was strong enough to make the policy of peace prevail over the world.

But for all that, the slumbers of the British electorate were not unduly disturbed. They were soothed by the opium in Baldwin's pipe. It was George Canning who first introduced Foreign Affairs to the public, but he had been very careful to prepare it in advance for the required decisions. Baldwin reversed the process, interpreting the function of Government as being to follow public opinion without informing it. This perversion of democratic leadership produced a satisfactory dividend when the country was asked to identify its surging enthusiasm for international law and order and a firm line against aggressors with support for a decade of National Conservatism. If Lord Cecil, by producing the Peace Ballot with its twelve million votes and ninety per cent majority in favour of the League, had fathered the greatest private poll in history, Samuel Hoare by his famous speech at Geneva, promising Britain's backing for collective resistance against all acts of aggression, had become its foster-parent for the purposes of a General Election. Lord Cecil's sheep were gently guided by Tory shepherds into the " National " pen. It was slick party politics and secured another five years of Conservative domination, but as an essay in national statesmanship it met in less than five weeks with the nemesis it deserved.

Halifax had no hand in this " Collective Security " illusion, but confined his Election campaign to some random if orthodox broadsides at the more verbose Socialist extremists whose doctrines, as he was no doubt aware, were as distasteful to the mandarins of Transport House as to himself. He conjured up the fearful vision of a House of Lords swamped with Socialist peers, of a Socialist House of Commons passing Orders in Council " much as is done in Russia ", of regional commissioners taking over local government ensuring that it worked in harmony with the policy of the Socialist hierarchy at the centre, and he solemnly warned the electors against such maniacs who would be able to concentrate all the power in their hands.

CHAPTER XXVI

RETREAT FROM GENEVA

WITH Baldwin's position assured, Halifax had now to make his final decision as to whether he would retire from the political arena; it was clear that if he elected to remain in the Government there was likely to be no further opportunity for retreat to Garrowby.[1] Baldwin was offering him the office of Lord Privy Seal together with the Leadership of the House of Lords, the implications of which were that without burdensome departmental commitments his influence and attention could gravitate towards whatever problem, foreign or domestic, that the Cabinet required. The original scope of his duties seemed to be almost as wide as the Prime Minister's, and Baldwin may have had in mind that Halifax, who as Leader in the Lords re-enacted his role in the Upper House, should in fact act as his deputy. MacDonald's defeat at Seaham left a gap; Neville Chamberlain beyond dispute was heir to the throne, but his preoccupations with the Exchequer ruled him out for such a part; whatever Baldwin may have had in mind, and whether or no Halifax was impelled to accept his promotion to these wider responsibilities on the basis of some special relationship with the Prime Minister, Hoare's disgrace and Eden's premature succession to the Foreign Secretaryship brought his work more and more within the orbit of the Foreign Office. Indeed in all the changes and chances, dismissals, resignations, promotions and retirements that have marked the personal conduct of British diplomacy between

[1] The many rumours of his wish to retire from political life caused his name to be associated with the various celebrities who, it was reported, were being offered the posts of (*a*) Provost and (*b*) Headmaster of Eton. It was no doubt a tribute to the importance assigned to his old School that Halifax in his prime should have been considered for these posts. Actually his lifelong friend Lord Hugh Cecil (now Lord Quickswood), who had accompanied him to Malines in 1924, succeeded the famous Dr. M. R. James as Provost, while as for the prospect of headmastership Halifax was supposed to have turned it down with the comment, " No, I would rather be Viceroy of India again! "

January 1935 and the outbreak of war in September 1939 the undisturbed and increasing influence of Halifax is almost the only constant factor; the November 1935 Election and Hoare's downfall were in a sense only incidents in his inexorable rise to power. He never sought the position, indeed it was the conflicting ambitions and view-points of his colleagues that heightened the value of his own moral purpose and intellectual detachment.

He did not, however, approach the task of European settlement wholly uncommitted, and in the period of alarms and excursions following the breakdown of disarmament he had reached the broad political conclusion about Nazi Germany to which most non-German Governments subscribed. In brief this attitude was, to quote Heiden: "Let Germany do as she likes at home. We will not hinder her in anything she is justified in doing as a sovereign State. If in the process she violates treaties we will protest. We will not intervene in Germany, but only arm and defend ourselves. So far as it is necessary in our own interests we will make alliances among ourselves, and form of the different parts of Europe a unity which no individual State can threaten."[1] For a very brief period during the summer of 1934 there were favourable signs that this policy might produce enduring results. Bolshevist Russia had been prevailed upon to enter the bourgeois League, Barthou, having assumed responsibility for the final demise of disarmament, produced his project of an Eastern Locarno.

Halifax seems to have been one of those in the British Cabinet who, while approving the agreement by which Russia assumed towards France the obligations of Locarno, insisted that if Locarno was to be invoked at all for Eastern Europe it should be so in full, and that if Russia should ever attack Germany, Germany could expect the aid of France. Germany's refusal to take part in this logically perfect network of mutual guarantees was an important factor in undermining British support for the Franco-Soviet Pact. France, keenly anxious for Britain to underwrite her continental commitments, was no less disillusioned by comparing the reality of Franco-Soviet collaboration with the vision of what it might have been. Hitler, however, had no illusions, and the force of his restless energy was bent upon destroy-

[1] *One Man Against Europe*, page 157.

ing the fabric of the Pact which, for the absence of a wider security, may be said to have preserved the peace of Europe without France or Britain fully realizing it. In 1934, too, Mussolini, fresh from his Brenner victory, was delighted that France and Britain were ready to share with him the burden of maintaining Austrian independence. "Thus two ideas met, two forms of national life seemed to coincide. French diplomacy represented the conception of the duties of the nations one towards the other, Italian Fascism the idea of their rights, history had reached a point where the two theories practically coincided."[1] But neither of these theories as applied by France or Italy fitted in with the hard facts that Hitler was resolved to forge. First came the test case of the Saar plebiscite; much capital was made of triumphant self-determination and of a precedent for an international police force, but in truth France, presupposing defeat, had already contracted out with Germany by negotiations in Rome once more outside the scope of the League. So vanished into the all-consuming rule of the Reich what Heiden has aptly called the "Vatican City of the League" —"the little strip of earthly sovereignty of a world-wide idea", and from its surrender Hitler could gauge the full limitations of the League Powers' support for the League's hegemony. Fundamentally Hitler and the League Powers were at one. They would fight only for their own sovereignties; Hitler to extend his, the League Powers to defend theirs.

Following the retreat from the Saar the League Powers reinforced their system of Pacts. Among the most important of these was the Franco-Italian understanding, reached a week before the Saar plebiscite, in which Laval gave Mussolini a free hand in Abyssinia while Italy renounced her claim on Tunis and reaffirmed Austrian independence in an impressive *procès verbal* which was to add Austria's other neighbours, Poland and Rumania, to the list of guarantors. This was followed by the famous Anglo-French communiqué of 3rd February 1935, which represents Britain's last formal invitation to Germany to subscribe to Security by Regional Pact. Nazi ambitions and French distrust were to be dissolved through "equality of rights in a system of security", as bait to secure German co-operation. The can-

[1] *One Man Against Europe.*

cellation of the armaments restrictions laid down at Versailles was envisaged. Finally, with a realism that Hitler could not ignore, a British proposal was added to the communiqué suggesting that the five Western Locarno Powers should " undertake immediately to give the assistance of their air forces to whichever of them might be the victim of unprovoked aerial aggression by one of the contracting parties ". With a technique which Bismarck himself would have admired, Hitler deflected this embarrassing attempt to clip the wings of his growing air power by inviting Simon and Eden to Berlin to talk things over with him, and then exploited the British acceptance both to increase French suspicions of British motives and to probe the psychological support of the British Government and people for unlimited rearmament.

The Government's *naïveté* in suddenly confronting at this particular moment a wholly unprepared public and Opposition with the first of its White Papers on Defence demanding of the nation the utmost military effort, played into Hitler's hand and provided him with abundant evidence of the latent pro-German and anti-French sentiment in Parliament and the country. The outcry in Parliament and the country compelled the Government quietly to shelve its defence proposals, and enabled Hitler suddenly to take what was till then the biggest political decision of his career, namely to promulgate general conscription and frankly announce the existence of the German Luftwaffe. Nominally the excuse given for Hitler's *détente* was Flandin's modest and technical decision to lengthen, a year before schedule, French army service to two years. Once again Hitler had got his way and at the same time succeeded in driving a wedge between Britain and France. Laval protested indignantly to the League while Simon meekly asked whether it was still in order for him to visit Berlin.

The Berlin conversations were officially described by Simon as " a disappointment ", but in fact what Hitler had to say in his inflated mood was little short of an ultimatum to Europe. He smashed the Eastern Locarno by a blunt refusal to have anything to do with a Pact with Soviet Russia. He was the defender of European culture against the Bolshevik virus. He promised not to assist any aggressor, but any attempts at security without Germany would be resisted. Simon went with an invitation to Germany to rejoin the League; he came back with a German demand for the return of colonies, as Germany could not return to the League as a nation with inferior rights. Hitler could not even promise non-interference over Austria as Austria was German land. On the project of an Air Locarno he spoke in menacing terms about the need for an air force perhaps stronger than the British and French in case Soviet air developments should " necessitate a revision of the figures ". Hitler also coolly informed his visitors that the German air force was already larger than the British, and only in the sphere of navies were his demands seemingly modest. Eden continued the tour. Stalin gloomily put forward his view that war was more likely than in 1914 as there were now three potential aggressors instead of one. Pilsudski was even more hostile to the Eastern Locarno than Hitler had been; only Benes was constructive, but he needed more help than he could give.

Stresa followed, but by now the British leadership was so alarmed that the very thought of a commitment made it turn pale; MacDonald and Simon had no sooner reached Isola Bella than Neville Chamberlain, on behalf of his colleagues left behind in London, let fall a calculated indiscretion to the effect that Britain was not to undertake any fresh obligations on the Continent. It was a needless precaution which merely threw doubt on MacDonald's and Simon's authority. " The result of the Conference ", Mussolini had ironically announced beforehand in the *Popolo d'Italia*, " will be a communiqué ", which was the truth, but not the whole truth. For overshadowing Stresa was Mussolini's resolve to profit from the European tension and seize his Abyssinian heritage. Three days afterwards the League formally condemned Germany for having " failed in the obligations which lies upon all the members of the international community to respect the undertaking which they have contracted ", and a committee was set up to ward off unilateral repudiation of treaties and watch over the peace of Europe. When Litvinov asked what if peace were broken in another continent, implying, of course, Abyssinia, Simon hurriedly suggested that the Council should deal with a practical question in a practical spirit. Realism prevailed, Mussolini despatched his army to Africa, the Eastern Locarno was quietly buried, and France was left with the prospect of a bare alliance with Russia.

The circle was complete; the situation had been brought about which Halifax for one was above all anxious to forestall, the alignment of Europe against one possible aggressor, Germany. " Was England to allow herself to be drawn into war because France had alliances in Eastern Europe? Was she to give Mussolini a free pass to Addis Ababa merely to prevent Hitler marching on Vienna? " Questions similar to these were undoubtedly posed by Halifax in Cabinet. His own friends, in particular Lothian and Geoffrey Dawson of *The Times*, had for some time been promoting Anglo-German fellowship with rather more fervour than the Foreign Office. In January 1935 Lothian had a long conversation with Hitler, and Hitler was reputed to have proposed an alliance between England, Germany and the United States which would in effect give Germany a free hand on the Continent, in return for which he had promised not to make Germany " a world power " or attempt to compete with the British Navy. *The Times* consistently opposed the Eastern Locarno and backed Hitler's non-aggression alternative. Two days before the Berlin talks, for instance, it advocated that they should include territorial changes, and in particular the question of Memel; while on the day they began its leading article suggested that " if Herr Hitler can persuade his British visitors, and through them the rest of the world, that his enlarged army is really designed to give them equality of status and equality of negotiation with other countries, and is not to be trained for aggressive purposes, then Europe may be on the threshold of an era in which changes can be made without the use of force, and a potential aggressor may be deterred by the certain prospect of having to face overwhelming opposition ".

How far *The Times* and Lothian were arguing and negotiating on the Government's behalf is still not clear, but that Halifax was intimately acquainted with the trend of this argument is probable. Simon seems to have returned from Berlin so deeply impressed with the German urge to domination as to have reached the conclusion that England would have to take sides for or against her, no middle course being any longer feasible. But Halifax was not reconciled to any such clear-cut view, his interest in Lothian's activities was simply in so far as they provided a possible way out of such stark alternatives. In any case Simon's days at the Foreign Office were numbered, and he was constitutionally incapable of following up his own conclusions. On 2nd May Laval somewhat grudgingly ratified the attenuated Franco-Soviet Pact, and Simon's forebodings seemed to be justified.

. . . .

It was into this vacuum that Hitler, on 21st May, in a speech to the Reichstag, poured his famous counter-proposals. The ideal of a united Europe he now finally rejected; instead, "We are ready to make a non-aggression pact which will exclude the use of force and strengthen in every neighbouring European State that feeling of security which will also be to our own advantage as the other party." He would have nothing to do with "obligations to render assistance which are philosophically, politically and objectively intolerable to us—the obligation to peace, yes!" He then proceeded to elaborate a thirteen-point programme. The second point formally declared that Germany, in its attitude to the Versailles Treaty, was only concerned with attacking those parts of it which "discriminate morally and objectively against the German people. The German Government will therefore unreservedly respect the other articles dealing with the common life of the nations, including the territorial points, and will make the revisions which in the course of time become unavoidable, only by way of peaceful understanding." In diplomatic language, here was a solemn promise from the head of the German Government never to change any frontier by force. He was ready, too, to stand by Locarno "so long as the others on their part adhere to this Pact". He was ready to join in discussions for an "Air Locarno", together with the abolition of heavy artillery, bombing planes and heavy tanks. Finally he repeated his offer to limit the German Fleet once and for all to thirty-five per cent of the British Fleet; "Germany has neither the intention, nor the need, nor the resources, to engage in any naval competition." The naval programme was the most specific suggestion, the Air Locarno the most important. The formula he adopted was that "the limitation of the German air arm to a condition of parity with the various other Western Great Powers renders possible at any time the fixing of a maximum which Germany will then undertake to observe scrupulously ".

On the day afterwards the House of Lords duly debated a motion in Lord Lloyd's name calling attention to the state of Britain's Imperial defence, in particular by air; that this debate should have synchronized with Hitler's speech was accidental, but it gave special significance to Halifax's reply for the Government. Hitler's primary object was to soothe British opinion and involve the British Government in sterile negotiation while securing as long a start as possible in air-rearmament. As an essay in the camouflage of ultimate ends the speech was a masterpiece, and Halifax was its first victim. " I am quite free to admit," he declared, " that that speech is perhaps the most important speech that has been made in Europe for many months, if not years ", and he at once defined it as " a notable response " to an appeal made by MacDonald a fortnight before. " Therefore, I have no hesitation in saying, on behalf of His Majesty's Government, that that speech, all it contains, and its implications, will most certainly receive, as it deserves, full and sympathetic and careful consideration at their hands."

Halifax played his part in allaying the very doubts that Hitler hoped would be allayed. " I would like to record my own judgment, which is also, I have no doubt, the judgment of everyone in His Majesty's Government, that there is very little hope of progress in Europe to-day if every time an effort is made by a responsible leader in another country, at once those elsewhere are tempted to give free rein to all the suspicions that the least worthy among their fellow countrymen would be tempted to hold." If he was stern with the cynics, his defence of rearmament was *sotto voce*. The Government had two dominant duties, to promote the dual policy of peace and defence, " and it is, I think, wholly misleading to suggest that these are incompatible, or to say that parity has nothing to do with peace and that we should only follow a conciliatory policy ". Arms limitation must be on figures acceptable to each nation for its own security. " It is exactly the same for Herr Hitler as for us. He has not yet limited his air force, and we have not yet limited our air force . . . but I profoundly agree that the best way to reach a lower level is to let it be known to the world that you are able and willing to maintain yourselves at a level wherever in default of agreement that level may be put."

The fate of the air pact is significant; a draft was handed to the British Foreign Office a week after the speech, but negotiations were held up in the first place because of Laval's insistence that any air pact discussions must be part of a wider settlement. After some preliminary generalities had been exchanged the British Chargé d'Affaires was told that Hitler " could not define his attitude on a question of such intricacy until after the holidays ". By the autumn the Abyssinian crisis had intervened, and when in December Hoare raised the question again, Hitler was reported as being unwilling to negotiate until the Abyssinian question had been liquidated. It took the British Ambassador ten days to arrange an interview with the Führer, who then asserted that the Franco-Soviet military alliance, directed against Germany, had rendered any air pact out of the question, " for the bringing into the picture of Russia had completely upset the balance of power in Europe. . . . Berlin might easily in a few hours be reduced to a heap of ashes by a Russian air attack." The Reich had gained a nine months' start in the air race.

Similarly delusive was the naval settlement. Here at last, it seemed, was a tangible proposition, and the British Government at once consulted its Admiralty experts, who reported favourably. Ribbentrop, Hitler's special envoy, arrived in London in the beginning of June, and within three days general agreement had been reached. France and Italy were not informed until 12th June. Once again the wedge was firmly adjusted between Britain and France, and when the terms of the Agreement came to be examined it was found that Germany had gained a vital concession, the ratio of 100 to 35 was not to apply to submarines. Hitler had claimed and gained the right to possess a submarine tonnage equal to the submarine tonnage possessed by the British Commonwealth of Nations. Less than three weeks after the Agreement had been signed Germany announced her intention of building two 26,000 ton battleships, two cruisers, sixteen destroyers and twenty-eight submarines. This programme was considerably older than the Agreement. By October Halifax and his colleagues learnt that twenty-five of the submarines had already been launched—it was a technical impossibility for them to have been built within the four months since the Naval Agreement.

The significance of the deception, however, was absorbed in the turmoil created by Mussolini's Abyssinian adventure. Abyssinia had disturbed the equilibrium of the Stresa Conversations, and Mussolini's war cries had been the accompaniment to the Cabinet reshuffle which, as well as sending Halifax to the War Office, had promoted the hero of the India Act, Sir Samuel Hoare, to the Foreign Secretaryship, brought Eden into the Cabinet without Portfolio but in the guise of " Minister of League of Nations Affairs ", and shunted Simon into the comparative seclusion of the Home Office. The combination of Hoare's thoroughness and mastery of detail with Eden's diplomatic experience and resource may have lulled the rest of the Cabinet into thinking that all could be safely left to them alone. The full implications of League resistance to Italian ambitions do not seem to have dawned upon the Cabinet collectively. Ever since the war it had been assumed that Italy was a diplomatic satellite of Britain revolving in the orbit of the Imperial system, that she was too exposed to British sea power to be anything else. But the growth of air power and the swelling ambition of the Duce, Kemal's " bloated bull-frog of the Pontine Marshes ", had challenged traditional ways of thinking. " Those responsible for British policy ", Heiden observes, " did not seem to realize how much conditions had changed to their disadvantage until the last moment, when they could not draw back, and found themselves drifting towards a diplomatic defeat on a flood from the lock-gate they themselves had opened."

But in fact both Hoare and Eden had been actively engaged in appeasing Italy, Eden before the war began and Hoare the very day before his historic Geneva speech. One of Simon's last acts as Foreign Secretary had been to send Eden to explain the Anglo-German Naval Agreement to Laval and to offer Mussolini a portion of the Ogaden, which was the nominal *casus belli*. It was a humiliating expedition, and Eden returned full of wrath against Mussolini and his works. The Duce had been no less explosive, and this disastrous interview was undoubtedly the origin of the two men's antipathy, which was in due course destined to affect Halifax's career. Hoare's discussion with Laval on 10th

LORD PRESIDENT OF THE COUNCIL

1937

September, the day of Mussolini's fantastic mass mobilization of the Italian people, virtually sealed Abyssinia's doom; for as Laval maliciously revealed at the end of December "in free discussion on an equal footing", Anglo-French policy ruled out "everything that might lead to war". Eden was present, and he raised no public voice against the proceedings. The experts were, in fact, deeply committed to settlement, and when Halifax declared at Sheffield on 10th October that, however precious Britain's old friendships with Italy were, they could not discharge this country from an honourable bond that she had undertaken, he was, to use Parliamentary language, "misinformed".

. . . .

By the beginning of November Mr. Peterson, the Foreign Office expert on Abyssinia, was in Paris discussing not oil but a peace formula. After about a fortnight deadlock had been reached. It was then that Hoare, on his way to Switzerland, on doctor's orders, in urgent need of rest after his unprecedented bout of overwork, was inveigled into breaking his journey at Paris and concluding the Hoare-Laval Pact. British public opinion, roused to a real sense of moral obligation over Sanctions, was outraged. Was this the sum total of the nation's pledge which Halifax, for one, before the Election had termed "its whole support to the Covenant to which we are bound by honour and by duty that we owe to our own people here and to the world at large"? The furore took the Government completely by surprise; Baldwin, who with justice prided himself on his insight into the trends of popular emotion, was for once deceived. He was completely unable to feel his way out of the political and moral cul-de-sac into which he had led himself, the Government and the nation. For, as Churchill observed with devastating clarity, "First, the Prime Minister decided that Sanctions meant war; secondly, he was resolved that there must be no war; and, thirdly, he decided upon Sanctions. It was obviously impossible to comply with these three conditions." Just how gravely the Government was imperilled has been revealed in Sir Austen Chamberlain's memoirs. Hoare's dignified resignation statement was sympathetically received; his thesis that his only aim had been to save not Italy but the League from defeat was widely accepted; but we now know what was previously just a conjecture, that only Attlee's tactical blunder in challenging Baldwin's honour after the Prime Minister's abject apology prevented Austen Chamberlain, by now the most powerful private member in the House, from leading a revolt against the Government. Chamberlain believed that if he had done so, he could have brought the Government down. As it was, Attlee's tirade brought him rushing to the aid of his stricken Chief.

In the Lords Halifax's task was no less delicate than Baldwin's. He was bound to Hoare by ties of friendship and respect. Hoare had been essentially Halifax's pupil over India; as a younger man he had earned the approbation of Halifax's father for his intelligence and pleasant personality. For himself Halifax had, by implication, to explain away his opening statement as Leader of the Lords, in which he had promised that the Government would " adhere to their policy, for which they have the overwhelming support of the mass of the people in the country ". But where Baldwin collapsed Halifax gained new strength. In a speech of great dialectical power he actually succeeded in launching a counter-offensive against the embattled champions of the League, arrayed in all their shining moral armour to do battle with a somewhat decadent Government dragon. Halifax, with a shrewd mixture of casuistry, common sense, close reasoning and fervour, undermined this vision and substituted the conception of Socratic statesmanship grappling with a conflict between personal and public loyalties.

" It was, let me remind your Lordships, by the League that the French Government and ourselves were charged with a moral mandate for that business of conciliation." Therefore, " I have never been one of those . . . who have thought that it was any part in this dispute of the League to try to stop a war in Africa by starting a war in Europe." The risks arising out of League membership were tolerable only if they were collectively met. " If I know the people of this country at all, they would never stand for membership in a League of Nations that was liable to land them into a single-handed war." Finally, " The League of Nations itself had never denied that there was a case to be met from the Italian side." That was " the framework against which the thought of those concerned in conciliation had to be set ". He went on to describe how there was nothing pre-designed in Hoare's visit. He did not go there to discuss terms of conciliation, and therefore was without instructions on the subject. Only Laval's insistence made him agree to stay and take a personal part with him; " in that, indeed, I think he could hardly help himself ". They completed their task, but before the details reached London the communiqué had been published in Paris bearing Laval's authority, to be followed by a pretty full publication of the so-called terms of peace in the French Press. " I want the House to observe the dilemma in which at that point His Majesty's Government were placed. I make no secret of the fact that when they read the terms they did not like them, though I am bound to add, in justice. that the terms in my judgment are not so bad as . . . public opinion outside has represented them to be. If it were relevant and the time permitted, I do not think it would be at all an impossible task to show, in one or two material directions at least, how these terms are definitely better, from the League of Nations point of view, than were the proposals of the Committee of Five." What was not irrelevant as a measure of the Plan's merits was that they were considerably less than Mussolini's official demands and that Italy did not regard them as unduly generous.

" It was quite clear that the Government could never refuse assent on that Monday night at the price of repudiating their Foreign Secretary, a colleague who was absent and who would have been unheard "; on the other hand, a decision could not be delayed because of the premature publication of the terms in Paris. " If we erred, as we did, in giving approval under such conditions to these proposals, I venture to think that we erred for motives that will be appreciated by all who know how close are the bonds of trust that bind colleagues, and how essentially those bonds of comradeship are the foundation of all that is best in the political life of a free nation. I am quite prepared to admit that we made a mistake—not the mistake that is commonly imputed to us, but the mistake of not appreciating the damage that, rightly or wrongly, these terms would be held by public opinion to inflict upon the cause that we were pledged to serve. Accordingly we share to the full the responsibility for the mistake that was made "—but, he might have added, we remain in office and do not regard it as the *prima facie* duty of a Government to commit suicide.

The moral he drew from this "tragic episode" is significant. First, though not foremost, he stressed the danger that may attach to direct meetings between responsible Foreign Ministers other than at Geneva, and the embarrassment that it must often cause to the individuals themselves—a warning here, perhaps, for Eden, whose appointment as Hoare's successor was imminent and expected. Much more significant was the rallying of opinion throughout the Empire to the cause of the League, but with large nations outside and other nations inside it not prepared to fight for any cause beyond their own national interest, "it really does behove all men of common sense to recognize both the risks and the limitations that are involved in pursuit of League ideas". While admitting the risks, he repudiated the logic of isolationists who hoped to eliminate risk by retiring behind national barriers; "nor does salvation come from the other kind of isolationists who would be prepared to see one nation alone pursue its ideals irrespective of the action of others. . . . Therefore you are forced back upon the best and greatest measure of collective action that you can obtain, and that will not serve the cause of peace unless in the last resort those who profess loyalty to it are both prepared and ready—I emphasize those words 'prepared and ready'—to use their strength in the cause of peace to which they pay lip service."

It was generally conceded that the quality of Halifax's speech raised the whole standard of the Lords debate above that in the Commons, although he had not absolved the Government from grave error in ever having endorsed the Plan at all. The Cabinet was, in fact, as much at fault in its deference to the French Press as in its misreading of British opinion; but for all that, Halifax had done the Government a great service in an hour of dire need. What was more important, though not so noticeable at the time, he had already covered his moral retreat from the League. Eden, whose popularity had reached giddy and dangerous proportions in the last few months, took no such precaution. He was thus not so well-equipped to meet the ambiguities of the situation. His elevation was not popular with powerful elements in the Conservative Party; he had been foisted upon them by Baldwin, and Baldwin, who had inaugurated diarchy in the conduct of our foreign policy to protect himself from popular criticism, had now to keep it in being to appease his party. Under these circumstances the obvious and acceptable guardian for "young" Eden was Halifax; imperceptibly, inevitably, this new role was assigned to him. In less than three months Europe had reached the parting of the ways, and Halifax was in the thick of the decisive Rhineland crisis.

. . . .

During this brief period it fell to his lot to deliver no less than three funeral orations, two in his capacity as Leader of the House of Lords, to mark the death of King George V, and of his predecessor in India, Lord Reading, the third as Chancellor of Oxford, when he unveiled in St. Paul's Cathedral a memorial tablet to T. E. Lawrence. His tributes to the late King and to Reading did not rise above the commonplace, but the memory of Lawrence inspired him to an eloquence that deserves comparison even with the matchless Churchill. The funeral oration is not a national characteristic, it is a Gallic art which, in our reticence, we have failed to cultivate. Halifax on Lawrence, however, must be classed as one of the rare exceptions in our time. He had never enjoyed Lawrence's close friendship or presumed to any special insight, but there was something in the fascination of Lawrence's personality which evoked a special response from him. Lawrence's "mastery over life", mysterious even to himself, was that not the aspiration behind much of Halifax's own religious exercise? "While, like all men, he owed much to the influence of heredity and environment, he, more than most men, had, or acquired, the capacity to mould life instead of lending himself to be moulded by it. Here lay the secret of his command over affairs, over others, and last but not least, over himself. . . . I cannot doubt some deep religious impulse moved him; not, I suppose, that which for others is interpreted through systems of belief and practice, but rather some craving for the perfect synthesis of thought and action which alone could satisfy his test of ultimate truth and his conception of life's purpose."

His vision of Lawrence "when he lay in the uncharted land between life and death, and saw his life no longer in part, but whole before him", recalls in the perfection of its technique Lytton Strachey's impression of Queen Victoria's last abiding memories or Arthur Bryant's evocation of Charles II's death-bed reverie. Halifax has more than a passing interest in the texture of language, but the sheer bulk of his political speeches tends to make him rely on sound second best; not for him the faculty of the flashing phrase, he is most articulate when far removed from politics. Although his political sense is acute and strongly developed, politics has had the effect of cramping his powers of expression, of almost stifling a poetic strain in him, and when much of the passion of political debate, in which he was constantly called upon to define and to defend great causes, has died away, it is not improbable that his reputation as an orator will be linked up with fragmentary asides, not the least of which was the valediction to Lawrence of Arabia.

"Once more, it may be, he visited the Norman castles which first, in boyhood, had excited his romantic sense, or walked again amid the ancient works of Palestine. Or there came back to him the vision of the endless desert, rocking in the mirage of the fierce heat of noontide, and once more he trod the dusty ways of Akaba, Azrah and the city of the Caliphs, and last of all, of his beloved Damascus, with her green gardens by the river, these fading in turn before the places of his spiritual heritage, Henlow, Bovington, Cranwell and the Air Force stations of India—Peshawar, Miramshah, Karachi. And before the end came, I like to think that he saw again the spires of Oxford, unearthly in their beauty, set in the misty blue of early May, until at last he reached no earthly city, but that city of his vision where he might see no longer as in a glass darkly, and know at length as he was known."

CHAPTER XXVII

RHINELAND WATCH AND WARD

KING GEORGE'S funeral was not unnaturally the occasion for some important and informal political contacts. Hitler, who had been carefully watching the complexities and embarrassments in Anglo-Italian, Anglo-French and Franco-Italian relations, had reached the broad conclusion that the hour of strategic decision was at hand and that the Rhineland, the key to France's system of Eastern European alliances, was ready for peaceful penetration; but with native caution he resolved to confirm his instinctive impressions. Against a background of newly discovered indignation at the incompatibility of the Franco-Soviet Pact with Locarno, Neurath while in London pointedly hinted to Eden that the German Government fully intended to respect Locarno provided that others should observe it in the spirit as well as in the letter. Eden, fully alive to the limitations imposed on him by public opinion and Cabinet mandate, answered with extreme reserve that he was glad to hear the German Foreign Minister say that. But Eden's very lack of candour told Hitler all he wanted to know.

In France Laval, after making one last effort to bring Germany into the French security system, fell from power and was succeeded by Sarraut, with Flandin as his Foreign Minister and Paul Boncour as French delegate to the League. In effect this meant that France was ready to make her choice as between Italy and Britain. First, however, Flandin, in view of the condition of virtual isolation into which France had allowed herself to sink, decided that the French Chamber should be asked to ratify the alliance with Russia—for such little store had Laval put on his diplomatic coup that from the moment he left Moscow he quietly shelved it. The disorderly and half-hearted reaction of the members of the French Chamber who gave the Pact only a three to two majority was yet a further indication for Hitler that French intransigence was being upheld more in the letter than the spirit.

On the same day, 20th February, that France ratified her alliance with Russia, Mussolini's forces captured Mount Amba Alagi, the main strategic position in Abyssinia. On 2nd March Eden at Geneva urged that hostilities should cease, but added that if not, the oil embargo would be applied. This was his demand to the League Powers, this the apparent price of Anglo-French understanding. Flandin let it be known that he might be prepared to pay it, and simply by keeping the question open broke the last strands of Laval's "Italianate" policy. But rumours about German designs on the Rhineland were now widespread and France had only Locarno left to lean on—the Russian Pact being still in French eyes morally an annexe to Locarno. Flandin asked the British Government to turn her general undertaking of support into a precise military agreement. A meeting of the two General Staffs was thus to be the price of the oil sanction. Eden, for his part, was ready to consider this tremendous proposition. By 4th March Hitler could read for himself in the newspapers that France had asked Britain for a military alliance and was ready to join in the oil sanction even at the risk of sacrificing Italy's Locarno guarantee. On 5th March Eden returned to London and reported to the Cabinet, which was now called upon to take potentially the most critical and formative decision in all the history of its relations with Hitler.

The decision was critical and formative, too, for the men who had to take and shape it. It was widely believed, however, that the Government had already made up its collective mind both against the oil sanction and assisting the French. At a private dinner-party given by Baldwin to which Eden and Flandin were invited, Flandin had asked outright what the British attitude would be in face of a violation of the Locarno Pact by the Reich — which Eden had merely countered by asking what the French Government would do. Flandin returned to France, and after some heart-searching the Ministerial Council authorized him to inform the British Government that France was ready to act if Germany carried out her coup. Eden was enabled to give this information to the Cabinet. However, influential Frenchmen were saying in Germany, even to Hitler personally, that there was no serious risk of France resisting, and of this also the Cabinet was doubtless not wholly unaware.

As early as 21st February a Havas telegram described the attitude of British official circles as being that no outside interference could possibly stop the Germans from reoccupying the Rhineland. The telegram added that the most that could be expected was that the British Government might view with favour an appeal to the League. By 25th von Hoesch, the German Ambassador, was apparently convinced that the British Government would do nothing, and expressed the view " that this was practically the same as tacitly giving permission to the Germans to remilitarize the Rhine zone, and he added that he had scored the most brilliant success in his career ".[1] Eden at the Cabinet on 5th March urged that if Rome failed to respond to the League's appeal for peace the oil sanction should be forced through the League's Committee of Eighteen. After prolonged discussion it appeared that the majority had declared itself against the military alliance. It was not a formal decision, the question was still open, and Eden was to discuss it further with Flandin at Geneva on 10th March.

In this brief hiatus, when France was without an effective ally, Italy's fate in the balance, and Britain poised between a decision hostile to Germany and no decision, Hitler struck. The march into the Rhineland, as all the world now knows, was a blind improvisation; a couple of French divisions could probably have arrested the entire confused force. The attitude of mind in which Hitler embarked on what was undoubtedly his biggest gamble is best summed up in his own confession later in the year that he had reckoned with only a five per cent margin of success. " If I fail," he told the doubting generals, " I shall commit suicide." We have seen that Eden was overruled in Cabinet while the Nazi steed was safely in the stable; now that it had safely bolted, the dominant reaction of those of his colleagues, and Halifax must be numbered among them, who had refused the eager young " Minister for the League ", seems to have been one of relief at their own foresight.

Halifax had probably reached the broad conclusion that the oil sanction was an unhappy necessity, not because he was convinced either of its effectiveness or ethic, but because

[1] Genevieve Tabouis, *Blackmail or War*, page 122.

the mandate of public opinion was so clear. It could not prevent war, for the conquest of Abyssinia was virtually complete; it would probably start a new one. All his conviction, his yearnings for religious unity, his historical upbringing, his sense of political and strategic values urged him to caution in our relations with Fascist Italy, but what was out of the question in his scheme of things was that we should assume a new and specific military commitment directed against Germany, which in fact offered us the certainty of one ally but the prospect of two wars. It was no longer the unacceptable prospect of stopping a war in Africa by starting one in Europe, but the even more bloodshot vision of supporting conflict in the Mediterranean by an expedition to the Rhine.

Halifax's friends, particularly Londonderry, Lothian and Dawson, were insisting, both in public and privately, on the inherent if rough justice of Germany's position. "The Locarno Agreement", *The Times* declared with almost malicious relish while the body was still warm, "was in some ways ahead of its time." The next day Londonderry, Halifax's immediate predecessor as Lord Privy Seal and Leader of the Lords, who had just returned from a round of friendly visits to the Nazi chiefs, pleaded for the patient consideration of Germany's case. "One would imagine," he wrote, "from reading what is reported in the newspapers, that Herr Hitler's action is looked upon as a challenge to the world. In my judgment it is nothing of the kind. The occupation of the demilitarized zone is a logical sequence to recent events." These were not necessarily Halifax's sentiments, but they were one influence among many urging him to recognize that Germany's grievance was of no less account because Hitler had picked upon the wrong way to redress it. He sensed that if popular opinion was braced to take action for the League against Italy it was no less resolved to do nothing for France against Germany. After all, said Bernard Shaw, it was only as though the British had reoccupied Portsmouth.

. . . .

Hitler, when he summoned the Reichstag on the morning of his coup after denouncing Locarno, offered to create a new system of security on the basis of a twenty-five-year non-aggression pact between Germany, France and Belgium, of a comprehensive air agreement which, it may be added was already under discussion between Eden and von Hoesch, and of rejoining the League without conditions. His proposals were at once embodied in a Memorandum delivered to the Locarno Powers at the same time as his speech. " And because Herr Hitler is talking peace even though he commits at the same time what is half-way to an act of war and the French seem to boggle at it, this country is definitely more pro-German than pro-French. The passion for peace can never have been as strong in this country."[1] Although unemployment had reached what seemed to be a permanent two million level, it was proving quite impossible to recruit the army up to strength. These hard, intractable facts could not be wished away. Baldwin moved instinctively towards the formula of peace, and in his quietism he had in particular the backing of Ramsay MacDonald and of Halifax. The attitude of Neville Chamberlain, the other Minister chiefly concerned at this time in the control of British policy, was more in doubt. How would Eden react? There were not wanting those who forecast and almost relished the prospect of a Cabinet crisis.

The Foreign Secretary had begun by bluntly warning von Hoesch on the morning of 7th March that the British Government were bound to take a most serious view of Germany's action, and in a severe statement to the House he gave great satisfaction to Paris and Brussels by making it clear that the Government considered themselves still bound by their obligations under Locarno so far as France and Belgium were concerned. Flandin, too, seemed ready to move. The only visible divergence was that the British Government wished to examine Hitler's Memorandum " clear-sightedly and objectively with a view to finding out to what extent they represent the means by which the shaken structure of peace can again be strengthened ", while for France it was wholly unacceptable, and to propose a new Pact having shamefully violated an old one was adding insult to injury. Flandin was clearing the decks for action. Baldwin's emphasis, however, was significantly different from Eden's. " In Europe," he declared in the Commons on the same afternoon as Eden's statement, " we have no more desire than to keep calm, to keep our heads, and to

[1] From " A Spectator's Notebook ", in *The Spectator*, 27th March 1936.

continue to try to bring France and Germany together in a friendship with ourselves." In other words, Baldwin was asserting that Britain should be not simply a guarantor but a mediator as well.

As if to reinforce this contention Eden had announced that he would be accompanied by Halifax in the conversations in Paris between the Locarno Powers which had been arranged for the following day. What had before been only whispers about Cabinet dissension became now the subject of open speculation in the Press, Clubs and other "well-informed circles". Madame Tabouis succinctly and without reservation seconds these suspicions when in *Blackmail or War* she asserts "Lord Halifax had been appointed to second Mr. Eden, who, the British Cabinet feared, might act recklessly if left to himself". *The Times* Political Correspondent, however, was at pains to stifle any such disruptive suggestions. "It is understood", he wrote, "that the suggestion that Lord Halifax should take part in the conversations with the representatives of France, Belgium and Italy in Paris to-day and thereafter in Geneva came from Mr. Eden himself, and was warmly approved by his Ministerial colleagues. There was a tendency among the critics of the Government at Westminster last night to suggest that the Lord Privy Seal was being sent as a restraining influence on his colleague, but the fact is that the Foreign Secretary was anxious to have Lord Halifax at his side in the difficult task on which he is engaged." It was Baldwin, the author of the doctrine that our frontier was on the Rhine, who stressed the "many-sidedness of truth", and in the case of the partnership of Eden and Halifax from the Rhineland crisis onwards it is probable that both Tabouis and *The Times* were right.

The Cabinet wanted to restrain Eden, Eden wanted to share the risk of repudiation, but if the system of diarchy in our foreign policy was thus retained it was diarchy with a difference. Under Simon and Hoare, Eden, as the *Survey of International Affairs* observes, had been a junior Minister with a specific field of work, "whereas Lord Halifax was an older, more distinguished and more experienced statesman than the Foreign Secretary to whom he was lending his assistance, and his sphere of action was left formally undefined". Further, with the dreadful fate of Hoare fresh to memory, it was clear to Baldwin that Paris was not a safe place for a British Foreign Secretary, but the Prime Minister's mind was at rest with an arrangement whereby the political welfare of his young protégé, Anthony Eden, was being watched over by his old and trusted friend, Edward Halifax.

When the discussions of the Locarno Powers began at the Ouai d'Orsay the next morning, 10th March, it was soon made clear that the divergence between the British and French view-points was not a matter of surface appearance. Eden and Halifax were genuinely surprised by the fervour of the French reaction. Flandin recommended a programme in which Germany should be called on to withdraw all troops from the Rhineland; if they refused, sanctions should be applied. Not until the demilitarized zone had been evacuated was France ready to consider a new Pact within the framework of the League Covenant. In order to give effect to this resolve Flandin asked that Eden's statement that the Locarno guarantee still held good should be translated into a definite alliance. Van Zeeland, the Belgian Prime Minister, put out the warning that the pretext of the Franco-Soviet treaty which Hitler invoked as the reason for his coup could not apply to Belgium; he added that the demilitarized zone had constituted Belgium's chief guarantee of security and principal reason for abandoning her pre-war neutrality.

Before such a barrage Eden and Halifax were forced to admit that their own position was no longer tenable. Their original instructions had been merely to recommend procedure in which the League Council should once more condemn Germany's unilateral action, once more " reaffirm the principle of the sanctity of treaties ", thereby clearing the way to open negotiations with Hitler. France was even ready to take the necessary military action alone provided the Locarno Powers would authorize her to do so. Eden played desperately for time, urged Flandin to consider as a compromise a part withdrawal of the German troops before and during negotiations. Flandin treated the suggestion with reserve, not wishing to commit himself in advance of the next League meeting due to begin on 13th March at Geneva. Eden and Halifax then produced their plan to bring the League to London. The advantage from the

British view-point was that Germany would be more likely to come there than to Geneva, while the other key Ministers would be available to take any important decisions. Flandin, too, was anxious to persuade Baldwin and his colleagues personally of the force of the French case. The British plan was therefore adopted, and it was announced on the evening of the 10th that the next meeting of the Locarno Powers would be held in London on the 12th and that the League Council would be opened there the next day. To all intents and purposes the Locarno crisis had been sterilized by this decision.

Although the British attitude stiffened during the next few days, France, by her original appeal to the League and refusal to take the law into her own hands, had shown that there were limits to her estimate of the peril to her security. Unilateral mobilization had been seriously considered by Cabinet Council, and the possibility of it caused our Foreign Office grave concern; but with the appeal to the League some form of adjustment could no doubt be made. It was to be a painful and laborious process. The complexities of the parallel League and Locarno meetings did not produce results comparable with the effort expended on them. Halifax was in the thick of the discussions and intrigues, but not even the ultimate appearance on the scene of Hitler's confidence man Ribbentrop revived what was essentially a prolonged and heavy anti-climax. Ribbentrop on arrival at Croydon was greeted with loud cheers as a harbinger of peace, and if Eden and Halifax had been alarmed at the militancy of French opinion Flandin must have been no less disturbed by the passive and pro-German tendencies of the British Government and people.

The British Ministers were still embittered by the French prevarications over Abyssinia, and the Franco-Soviet Pact was far from popular, although the Government had committed itself to the view that it was legally compatible with Locarno. There were those, however, who, without sharing Hitler's anti-Bolshevik hysteria, felt that this latter decision had given some substance to his plea of encirclement. In the public mind the obligations of Locarno were secondary to those of the League, the ethic of resistance to the Rhineland occupation was not on the same plane as the defence of Abyssinia. However, there was an influential pro-French school of thought, championed, of course, in Parliament by the famous hero of Locarno, Austen Chamberlain. His influence, too, seems to have had considerable effect on the attitude in Cabinet of his devoted brother. Flandin spoke in the highest terms of Neville Chamberlain's sympathy and understanding for the French case, while when Eden, before the arrival of the French delegation, had pleaded with the Cabinet to draw nearer to the French arguments, only Neville Chamberlain was prepared to second him.

The impression persists that Halifax and Eden did not draw quite the same conclusions from their historic visit to Paris. Certain it is that when the French delegation met Baldwin and presented their case, Baldwin simply reminded them that until British rearmament was more advanced the Government could not incur the smallest risk of war. Although strongly backed by Russia and the Little Entente, for whom a demilitarized Rhineland was the key to French political and strategic initiative in Eastern Europe, Flandin realized that he would either have to act alone to secure French rights or construct a new alliance with Britain. As he himself put it, " I decided, alone and on my own responsibility, to transform the guarantees in the Locarno Pact, the odds of which were in favour of France alone, into a bilateral Franco-British guarantee which, at any other time, would have been termed a military defensive alliance. Thus would evidence be given that France was ready to defend those who would defend her." The consent of the British Cabinet was obtained on 18th March, and with the lights burning late at the Foreign Office the Agreement was drafted. Britain had thus undertaken her first formal commitment on the Continent since 1914. The General Staffs were to meet. Ironically enough, Flandin, whose reputation has since undergone many vicissitudes, deserves much of the credit in bringing about the alliance and in keeping the temper of the British Government sweet in the delicate process. For there had been much doubt and difficulty within the Cabinet before reaching this position, and a serious rift had only just been avoided. From all the prolonged Cabinet meetings which went on late into the night, the babel of Geneva at the Court of St. James's, the complexity of double-barrelled League and Locarno diplomacy, Halifax emerged triumphant. Not for nothing had he haggled with the Eastern mind. "When everyone else was exhausted," wrote a foreign observer, "he seemed still as fresh as at the outset of the deliberations. He never lost his quiet composure. His advice was the product of good sense and complete self-command."[1] Although this was essentially his début in European diplomacy, he seems to have made as deep an impression upon the galaxy of experienced foreign statesmen gathered in London during these critical days and weeks as upon his own colleagues. Not only was his prestige enhanced within the Government, he was from henceforth a figure of consequence in Europe.

. . . .

The Locarno Powers having, with the exception of Italy which was not ready to act until Sanctions were removed, confirmed their obligations to each other, the most acute phase of the crisis was over. The next problem was to secure a German contribution that would bring to an end the "interim period" and make possible negotiations for a new Locarno. Discussions with Ribbentrop about the detailed proposals that were to cover this interim period made it clear that Germany was in no mood to accept them as they stood. One suggestion that the Rhineland should be policed by an international force, including Italian troops, had been pilloried as much in Britain as in Germany, but Hitler was aware that the purpose of these proposals was both to secure concessions for France and counter-proposals from himself.

In this atmosphere of uncertainty while awaiting the German reply Halifax made his first public statement on the crisis in a speech at Bristol where he deputized for Eden. It was a balanced and sober analysis. The words might have been Eden's except perhaps for the form of his appeal to Hitler. "We want no encirclement of Germany. We want to build a partnership in European society in which Germany can freely join with us and play the part of good Europeans for European welfare. I have never concealed from myself that in asking what we did from Germany we asked a hard thing. Indeed I would have been prepared to say that just because it was so hard a contribution, it placed it within the power of Germany to do something that, more than anything else, would have restored European confidence and have placed her in the position of making the greatest

[1] K. H. Abshagen, *King, Lords and Gentlemen*, page 78.

contribution of us all to the future of European peace."

Hitler's immediate contribution was to reject the Locarno Powers' proposals and put up his own, which were not available until 1st April, having been delayed for one of the Nazis' totalitarian elections. Germany made much the same offer as in her original Memorandum of 7th March, although there were signs of a willingness to revive the project of an Eastern Locarno and not simply to limit the new Pact to the West, but no suggestions to remove the tension during the interim period emerged. The Locarno proposals of a police force and of an appeal to the Hague Court were ruled as wholly unacceptable and derogatory to German honour.

European confidence, it seemed, was down to zero again. Would the French Council of Ministers who, after the first impact of the crisis had rejected military intervention by a mere majority of one, now reverse the decision? It was soon evident that they would not, but instead, anxious to avoid the trap into which Barthou had fallen in April 1934 when he had allowed the onus of breaking off negotiations to fall on France, would contribute their own memorandum, and make a show of keeping the discussion alive. Eden had already informed the House that the German response was regarded as unsatisfactory, and that letters had been sent to France and Belgium setting out the action to be taken if the attempts for a new settlement should fail and expressing willingness to start the General Staff conversations forthwith. Eden was still putting up a brave show of strength. A week before he roused the House to great enthusiasm when he bluntly said he refused to be the first British Foreign Secretary to go back on a British signature.

On 8th April, two days after the receipt of the French proposals and on the eve of his departure to join Eden in Geneva, Halifax gave an impressive and comprehensive review of British foreign policy. He had spoken before of the world standing at the cross-roads; he repeated the phrase with the solemn addition that "a hundred years hence, if the world survives, we shall all be judged by the direction that we now take; for upon the choice that we make depends much more than the issue of our immediate difficulties, and the price of wrong judgment will be a very high one. Though the cross-roads have long been in sight, it is true to say that the world has been brought right up to them by the recent action of Germany and by the inevitable reactions from it." These words hit the headlines of the nation's Press; Goebbels, if he had not already done so, began to pay attention to this new force in British foreign policy. Perhaps this upright Christian Englishman would be susceptible to the latest Nazi propaganda drive, which sought to display Hitler as Europe's crusader against the Bolshevist infidel. He was clearly a prudent man who might be expected to react slowly to the lightning stroke. But if he was really being used to act as a brake upon Eden, it was difficult even for such self-confident experts as the Nazis to decide from his public utterances at what stage he would be prepared to apply decisive pressure. It was one thing to recognize that the cross-roads had been reached, another to decide what turning to take.

Halifax's mood as expressed in his speeches at this time was watchful and cautious. Committed only to the overriding thesis of Peace, he saw the old alliances and the new isolationism equally as incitement to war. Therefore he groped his way over uncharted ground towards the *via media* of regional agreements that would neither divide Britain from Europe nor Europe from itself. " I believe that these regional and specific guarantees," he asserted in the House of Lords on 18th April, " so far from weakening, supplement and reinforce the Covenant and help it with its main job, which I would like some of our warmongers constantly to remember is peace." But his particular application of the doctrine can have hardly been relished by the Germans. First, it justified " particular and antecedent obligations to support France and Belgium, and the Staff talks were in my judgment a contribution which it was quite essential to make ", but more important it challenged Germany's fundamental design in the whole Rhineland episode, which was to counteract French and thereafter British control over or interference in Central and Eastern Europe. German troops in the Rhineland undermined the military potentialities of the Franco-Czech alliance, isolated Austria, and withdrew Poland further from democratic influence. Would the British leaders acquiesce in Eastern Europe as Germany's exclusive sphere of interest? Short of forestalling French military action, that was the kernel of Germany's purpose.

Halifax's answer left Hitler guessing on this supreme issue. This attitude should not be interpreted to mean that " because we have assumed more specific obligations in the West which we were not prepared to repeat for the East of Europe, therefore we disinterested ourselves from all events and issues arising outside what perhaps I may call the Locarno area. In my view such an attitude would be quite impossible, partly because peace is indivisible, and it is very hard for me to imagine that if the East of Europe were really aflame you could feel any confidence that the flames would not spread across to the West; but also because of our obligations under the Covenant, which are obligations by which we abide and which we intend to implement to the utmost of our power." Neville Chamberlain, Eden and even Baldwin had all gone out of their way to deliver the same warning. Hitler would return to ask and to act again. Halifax's attitude gave little ground for satisfaction among those of his friends who hoped to inveigle him into a pro-German position either to defend us from the Communist menace or, more indirectly, to save our Colonies at the expense of Eastern Europe.

On arrival in Geneva he was soon to witness the general disintegration of European morale. He found Eden struggling to obtain some sort of agreement about condemning Italy for the use of poison gas in the Abyssinian campaign. The matter had been raised in the Lords the week before, and Halifax had then no doubt but that " the indignation and moral condemnation implicit in every speech during the debate would be shared by the whole civilized world ". In practice, after a prolonged and unedifying wrangle, a feeble appeal was at last sent to Italy and to Abyssinia as well to refrain from the use of gas. Mussolini's reply was his intention to exterminate Abyssinia. Halifax had arrived specifically for the resumed Locarno meeting, and here, although the divergence between the British and French Governments was being gradually reduced to one of procedure, with Eden he firmly resisted the French thesis that the negotiations had already broken down in view of the German failure to consider measures to meet the interim period, nor would they have anything to do either with Sanctions or even a joint Four Power *démarche.* In the end agreement was reached and set out in a communiqué that the representatives of the United Kingdom would seek " the elucidation of a certain number of points contained in the German Memorandum ". France was appeased with the promise that points from her own counter-proposals would be contained in the British enquiries, that her peace plan would be examined by the League, that the Staff conversations would begin on 18th April, and that any changes in the Rhineland situation would at once bring the Four Powers together again.

Here was the origin of Eden's ill-fated questionnaire. By the time it had been composed, the Sarraut Government had been swept from power. Blum and the Fronte Populaire were ready to take their place, but the paralysis of French policy in the period immediately before and after France's General Election was only one factor tending to relegate the Rhineland crisis; new and sinister shapes were forming in the European kaleidoscope. The dual attempt to denounce Italian barbarism in Africa and to secure Italian co-operation in Europe was doomed to humiliating failure. Halifax had been able to see for himself the increasing reserve of the Italian delegate to the Locarno talks. Mussolini had drawn his conclusions from the events of 7th March and had decided that the time had come to side with the victorious and resolute Hitler. Well might Halifax, in an appeal for the Royal Literary Fund, yearn for the time to enjoy good reading and regret that for the present he was enmeshed in that class of Government that he believed Lord Palmerston described as the art of getting out of one damned mess into another.

But if Mussolini's defiance was bad for the Cabinet as a whole it was worse for Eden. On every side he was assailed. The Italian Press singled him out for special abuse. During April the *Daily Mail* went so far as to suggest that his downfall was imminent and that Halifax would be his successor as Foreign Secretary. During May and early June events continued to move remorselessly against him. First there was the hurried flight of the Emperor of Abyssinia from Addis Ababa. No sooner had the comprehensive and polite questionnaire been put to Hitler than Aloisi, Mussolini's suave delegate to Geneva, walked out of the League Council. But the unkindest cut of all came when Neville Chamberlain, in a speech to the 1900 Club, coined his one memorable phrase in describing the continuation of Sanctions as "midsummer madness". When Baldwin was pressed in Parliament to explain the Chancellor of the Exchequer's unprovoked aggression on the Foreign Secretary he said simply that he "made no complaint of what Mr. Chamberlain said". Chamberlain, as he later confessed to Sir Nevile Henderson, undoubtedly believed in the calculated indiscretion, but it is not improbable that this particular example had behind it the tacit approval of Baldwin and Halifax. Mussolini had won his war; to continue the struggle would render inevitable the divided Europe which the Dictators no doubt wanted, but which the British Government was resolved they should not easily obtain. Conquered Abyssinia was on that reasoning certainly not the issue on which to engage in a political or moral trial of strength, and there were fresh complications which were calculated to put Abyssinia and the Rhineland among the regrettable but dead episodes.

The Opposition, with its monopoly over *ex post facto* criticism, might deplore these issues as lost opportunities, but for the Government it was essential to take stock of changing facts and adjust the broad principles of policy elaborated during the Rhineland crisis to a new set of political conditions in Europe. Eden had now the clear choice of resignation or capitulating in face of the Cabinet's attitude. He stayed on, partly because of Baldwin's underlying trust and goodwill for him, although there was certainly no personal bitterness in his relationship with Chamberlain or Halifax, partly too because he was fundamentally aware that Abyssinia was lost both in the conception and rejection of the Hoare-Laval Pact.

As the Rhineland crisis receded, Eden and his colleagues drew closer together in their attitude to the Franco-German problem, Eden toning down the French thesis, his colleagues more aware of German aims. Thus we find Eden, in his speech to the Commons, announcing the withdrawal of Sanctions, declaring that nothing less than a European settlement and appeasement should be our aim and that there were elements in the present situation which (given an answer to his questionnaire) would enable us to attempt to conclude a permanent settlement based on the disappearance of the demilitarized zone. Whatever Eden's motives, the immediate outcome of the Abyssinian fiasco, together with Germany's offer to return to the League, was to raise in an urgent form the perennial question of the reform of the Covenant. On 4th July the Assembly of the League invited States Members to send in proposals for reform. Hitler was, of course, provided with the pretext he badly needed further to postpone his answer to Eden's embarrassing questionnaire. He could hardly rejoin a League that was in process of discussing and even modifying its constitution. No reply could be expected from him until after the session of the League Assembly in the autumn.

Then in the middle of July came the sudden though not wholly unexpected revolt of the generals and the havoc of civil war in Spain. Hitler was less inclined than ever to tie himself to any Western Pact; instead he prepared the ground for Austria's capitulation by the Agreement of 11th July 1936 and ensured Italy's compliance by transferring her attention to the Spanish arena.

CHAPTER XXVIII

ABDICATION AND ABSOLUTISM

AMID these baffling and ominous developments, Halifax was called upon to assume increasing responsibility. At the beginning of July he was defending the volatile Duff Cooper, who as Secretary of State for War had given a somewhat too enthusiastic voice to his Francophile sentiments. Duff Cooper, he assured the Lords, had not transgressed the general lines of Government policy. Having read the full text of his " cultured and polished " oration, " I found no mention of alliances ". On 22nd July he was once more representing Britain with Eden in Locarno conversations in London; this time only three Powers, France, Belgium and Britain, were represented. Baldwin presided and notable progress was made, thanks largely to Blum's initiative. The interim period was silently buried. Hitler's Rhineland coup was now described as " the situation created by the German initiative of the 7th March ". The French, while continuing to stress the indivisibility of peace, were ready to negotiate first of all for a new Western Pact, leaving until a later stage " the widening of the area of the discussion . . . with the collaboration of the other interested Powers ". There can be little doubt but that Blum made a most favourable impression upon the British Ministers; Anglo-French collaboration received a fresh impetus, " and in some quarters in London ", according to the *Survey of International Affairs*, " the prospects of a new European settlement were considered to be more favourable in the last week of July than they had been for a long time ". But as the days turned into months the hopes for Five Power negotiations, much less a Pact, steadily receded. Blum had suggested that Russia, Poland and the Little Entente should be invited as well, but the idea was turned down as a result of British opposition. The problem of Soviet intervention in Europe thus crept quietly into the Cabinet Room of 10 Downing Street, there to remain as the most perplexing and persistent of all the diplomatic problems that were to confront Halifax in the coming years.

In the Lords a week later he applied himself to League Reform and advocated emphasis upon the League's preventive powers. The operation of Article XI should no longer hang on a crippling unanimity. The League lacked sufficient power to give effect to " peaceful change ". His mind was moving in the direction of " a middle course ", involving a variety of obligations whereby each nation would undertake precise commitments only in accordance with its national circumstances, such as its military and economic resources, geographical position and national interest. Somewhat inconsistently he asserted that this country could not give a lead in the matter of commitments in advance of general discussions at Geneva. Only on the one basic principle of the Government's policy was he insistent, " indeed I think on no point in Europe to-day is there greater agreement than on the opinion that to return to any system that invited or appeared to invite the establishment of armed camps ranged in opposition to one another would be to court disaster ". A study of Halifax's speeches disposes of the idea that the so-called " appeasement " policy was either a last minute improvisation or that it was originally based upon any concept of surrender. It began for Halifax as a challenge to the thesis that the only alternatives confronting Europe were submission to blackmail or resort to war, but by the end of 1936 hard facts were undermining the logic of his position. Essentially, too, it was at the outset a sincere attempt to preserve the democratic way of life and thought without intensifying totalitarian rearmament and ideological extremism—a subtle operation appealing to one who, like Halifax, had delved deep into the arts of compromise.

In the first formative period Halifax was the clearest exponent of this policy of " prudence and fulfilment ". Two examples of the trend of his influence at this time will suffice. In the critical first fortnight of August Eden was on holiday in Yorkshire, and Halifax was put in charge of the Foreign Office. His duties at once brought him face to face with the problem of the Spanish Civil War, now just a fortnight old. At first it seemed as though the Republicans, fighting with little more than their fists, would not last out a month, and the rebels were soon within thirty miles of Madrid, but by the beginning of August it was clear that the Republicans, badly armed as they were, would hold their ground, that Hitler and Mussolini were too deeply committed to withdraw, and that, although the Spanish Republican parties had no close relation with Russia, and where they had, were in far closer sympathy with Stalin's hated rivals, Trotsky and the Bolshevist old guard, the flames of an ideological war were being fanned which threatened to envelop the whole of Europe.

Out of the precept and practice of intervention Britain and France evolved non-intervention. As Heiden has pointed out, "propaganda against Bolshevism cloaks a much more simple, general and dangerous principle of foreign policy intervention, the claim to be allowed to interfere abroad in one's own interests. It is formulated thus: 'We will not allow a second Bolshevik Power to arise anywhere.'" So it was that in those early August days of 1936 Halifax was busily giving shape to the democratic reply to this revolutionary menace; both London and Paris agreed that an appeal to the League would not be profitable as it had no procedure to cover civil war. In the interests of the desire for indivisible peace and the British hatred of European *blocs* France took the initiative in attempting to win over all countries which were ready to take practical steps to localize the war. There were delicate questions of definition. Were civil aeroplanes munitions of war? Should Non-Intervention preclude the supply of money and propagandist material? But by the time Eden returned Halifax had steered the negotiations to the point of agreement. The determined Anglo-French attitude surprised the Dictators, and they agreed in principle to associate themselves with the new policy. Talleyrand once described non-intervention as "a diplomatic term of unknown meaning", but whatever interpretation might be put upon British and French policy the danger of an immediate crisis over Spain had been averted.

While Halifax was engaged in putting Spain in quarantine at the Foreign Office, Sir Robert Vansittart, the Permanent Under-Secretary, was in Berlin in an effort to sound Hitler's intentions about the proposed Five Power Conference. He returned with no substantial promise and most of his personal suspicions as to Nazi aims confirmed, but on 18th September the British Government saw fit to deliver a note issuing a formal invitation to the Powers recapitulating the joint Anglo-French statement of 23rd July. Two days afterwards Halifax joined Eden in Paris and went on with him to Geneva. Once again the ideological distractions threatened to mar the harmony of the Locarno democracies. *The Times* spoke significantly of London feeling the difficulty only less than Berlin, which the Franco-Soviet Pact might place in the way of the wider agreement, but with the increasing danger to France of Fascist encirclement arising from the developments in Spain, Blum was less ready than before to modify the understanding with Moscow. By the end of 1936 therefore, Halifax, in his attempt to avoid European *blocs* on the one hand, and secure regional commitments on the other, was moving steadily towards an anti-Soviet position.

More subtly dangerous, however, was his approach to rearmament; the criticisms of political friends or opponents had never deterred him from raising his voice on this vital subject, and he was not influenced in the way that some of his colleagues were by mere considerations of political tactics and party advantage; in no public utterance had he ever suggested that Britain would be an effective agent for Peace without the military strength to enforce her argument; but by November 1936 the German programme had reached a stage where the Government was faced with grave decisions. The Socialist Opposition was still demanding guarantees on policy before signing a cheque for arms, but Churchill and the Sinclair Liberals, with commendable realism, brought to the fore the question of a Ministry of Supply. If, they argued, it involves a period of transition, readjustment during which production might be slowed down, the risk should be taken now while there was still time, but Halifax was not ready to adopt what in a Lords debate he termed " such heroic remedies ". " What is quite certain is that in the process you would gravely dislocate trade, Budgets, general finance, and the general credit of the country. Are we in fact to judge the question so serious that everything has to give way to the military reconditioning of our Defence Forces? Such a conclusion, in fact, appears to me to rest upon premises, not only of the inevitability, but of a degree of certainty as to the early imminence of war, which I am not prepared to accept."

But underlying Halifax's cautious optimism on the prospects of peace may well have been a deeper foreboding. If the German armaments challenge were to be accepted, where would the race end? Ultimately our stronger staying power would produce its reward, but at what a cost! Heiden again lays his finger on the critical consideration that must have dominated a man of Halifax's outlook. He points out that if the great Democracies had wished to follow the German example and "to transform themselves in peace time into military camps bristling with arms they would have been compelled to mobilize the minds of their people after the German pattern; in other words, their democratic ways of life would have broken down under the new stress". Halifax was ready to go a very long way before condoning any such mobilization. All his political and moral judgment condemned such a price. It was no mere matter of conscription that was at stake, but the spiritual integrity of a people.

As the months passed and crisis deepened over Europe, Halifax became ever more deeply absorbed and involved in its sombre details, but the informality of his function in Foreign Affairs still remained and there were diversions both grave and gay; in addition, at the beginning of September there were great rejoicings at Hickleton when with the customary ritual he and Lady Halifax entertained the lessees and tenants in celebration of the marriages of his eldest son and his daughter, both of whom, from the social and political view-points, had made brilliant matches. Charles by his marriage to Ruth Primrose had wedded the great Lord Rosebery's favourite grandchild, and Anne became Countess of Feversham. The Wood-Primrose wedding took place with almost royal magnificence at St. Paul's and was one of the outstanding social events of the year. Lord Feversham, a half-brother of Mrs. Anthony Eden, was a young man with considerable political talent, who at the time was Under-Secretary for Agriculture, and these marriage alliances were in themselves evidence of Halifax's own status among the oligarchy described by Esher as "the men who count".

In his position as Leader of the House of Lords there were occasional lighter moments which Halifax certainly relished, as when Crawford moved that in the opinion of the House "the growing practice of reading speeches is to be deprecated as alien to the custom of this House, and injurious to the traditional conduct of debates". Halifax replied with considerable diffidence "as a comparatively new recruit to your Lordships' House and as one not endowed with any fraction of the natural eloquence that would enable me to introduce the Army Estimates without a note". Most of the classic orations, however, he said, must have been read from written speeches, and added that it was certainly the practice of Burke, Sheridan and Chesterfield. Lord Curzon had related that from the Gallery of the House of Commons while Gladstone was making his great speech on the Second Reading of the First Home Rule Bill he was able to see that Gladstone held in the palm of his hand the complete peroration of that memorable speech. The Gods distributed their gifts with whimsical inequality. For those who had not the gift of speech to behave as if they had, merely spelt disaster. "I remember," he added, "the advice Lord Balfour gave me when I first entered the House of Commons. He asked me how I liked it there, and I replied that I felt rather like a little boy who had just gone to school for the first time and was rather diffident. Lord Balfour answered: 'My dear fellow, there is no reason whatsoever for feeling frightened in this place. All you have to do is to speak as often as you can and as long as you can, and you rapidly acquire that contempt for your audience that every bore always has.'" But such opportunities for Halifax to indulge in anecdote and irony were few and far between.

. . . .

When Parliament adjourned for its summer recess there were ominous signs of an unprecedented constitutional crisis affecting the new King and his Ministers, for Edward VIII was letting it be known in no uncertain terms that he wished to make Mrs. Ernest Simpson, an American divorcée with two former husbands still living, his consort. The news, although it had been featured by the American Press for months, was stifled here until the last possible moment. This reticence was not, it would seem, King Edward's wish, for he always insisted that Mrs. Simpson's name should appear in the Court Circulars. When at length the story broke, it was muffled thunder; the otherwise obscure Bishop of Bradford at a Diocesan Conference was moved to criticize the King's religious awareness, but in an interview afterwards he said he had studiously taken care to say nothing with regard to the King's private life because he knew nothing about it. For all his care, however, the great taboo had been violated. Even as late as a week before the Abdication an almost ludicrous secrecy was maintained, and the *Daily Telegraph's* Political Correspondent was reduced to using such stilted phrases as " the Cabinet has been compelled to face a situation of extreme delicacy and difficulty in connection with the King's future domestic life, and the Government are sensible of the fact that statements published in American and some Dominion newspapers are being widely discussed in this country ". For all the indignation it aroused at the time, Low's famous cartoon, " Secretly by dead of night ", summed up the Government's policy.

Baldwin succeeded in carrying the nation and Parliament with him on the major issues of what he described as the " integrity of the Crown " and the morganatic marriage, but the very smoothness of the process left a sense of intrigue, of preparation for all contingencies, which his statement to Parliament following the King's decision to abdicate allayed temporarily only to arouse again on more mature reflection. With consummate skill Baldwin arrogated to himself the whole responsibility for the Government's handling of the crisis. It was estimated that in his abdication statement, which lasted forty-five minutes, the word " I " appeared no less than a hundred and fifty times —a fitting symbol of the burden he bore. He disarmed his critics by his apparent candour, but when more light is thrown upon this mysterious episode, will Baldwin's narrative be wholly confirmed either in its detail or even in the general impression it conveys? The biographer of Lord Halifax can as yet do no more than pose this question, but in the meanwhile it is fair to suggest that history may well adjudge that upon Halifax rested the ultimate responsibility not merely in his constitutional capacity as the Leader of the House of Lords and Lord Privy Seal, but as the all-powerful middleman between Church and State, between Lambeth

Palace and Downing Street, the trusted friend who gave shape and substance to Baldwin's advice to the King.

His constitutional position should not be overlooked. The House of Lords had in some respects an even greater stake than the Commons in the " safe " solution of the crisis; hereditary and feudal prerogatives of the Crown touched them closely and were the fountain-head of their own status. It was thus Halifax's constitutional right to tender advice to the Crown on behalf of the Peers just as much as for Baldwin to represent the Government and faithful Commons. Very early in the reign the King and the Archbishop experienced difficulties over the form of the Coronation service, and there are some grounds for believing that the Duke of York was called in by the King to undergo these preliminary rehearsals with him. Halifax, for whom the religious implications of the service were no less vital, must have been well aware of and have shared the Archbishop's disquiet. Divorce does not enter easily into Halifax's religious scheme of things; for him as for the Archbishop there can ultimately have been no other alternative for Edward than Abdication of the Throne or renunciation of Mrs. Simpson.

Was he ever able to convey his views to Edward personally? Baldwin asserts, " I felt that in the circumstances there was only one man who could speak to him and talk the matter over with him, and that man was the Prime Minister. . . . I consulted—I am ashamed to say it, and they have forgiven me—none of my colleagues." He then described how he was in the neighbourhood of Fort Belvedere " about the middle of October " and saw the King there on 20th October. He does not positively assert, however, that this was the first interview he had on the subject, and six days before, on 14th October, the King was reported as having received Baldwin and Halifax. Baldwin's language does not rule out the possibility that the King's marriage had already been on the agenda, that what Halifax had to say was unpalatable and that from henceforth Baldwin thought it expedient to carry on the negotiations " without consulting his colleagues ". The alternative is that the audience of 14th October passed off without Baldwin revealing the trend of his thoughts either to the King or to Halifax. But the former supposition gives more colour to King Edward's repeated declaration to Baldwin, " You and I must settle this matter together. I will not have anyone interfering." Certainly Halifax's scope for official interference began and ended on 14th October, for he had no further audience of the King. But certain it is, too, that Halifax and all that he represented, whether as a social, political or moral leader, was bleakly opposed to the new pretensions of the King and his Court. The resistance to King Edward's new order significantly came first of all from Yorkshire, and it was sustained throughout by the landed gentry of the shires, by High Churchmanship, and by the overwhelming mass of political "Moderates"—all embodied in the ideals and position of the third Viscount Halifax.

While the Commons was hearing from the Speaker the last words of King Edward's last message, Halifax rose in a tense and silent House of Lords. The Earl of Onslow, his brother-in-law and chairman of Committees, was on the Woolsack, the gangways were crammed with Peers who overflowed the benches, their heirs crowded round the steps of the throne, the bishops in their surplices and white lawn sleeves added solemnity to the crowded scene. In clear unhurried tones he pronounced the fateful words. "My Lords, I have received a message from His Majesty the King which it is my duty to read." He then handed the message to Onslow on the Woolsack and moved that the gracious message be taken into consideration. Nothing he said gave the slightest hint of his own part in the crisis; if it was, in a sense, a victory for his cause he did not proceed to throw it away as the Archbishop of Canterbury did by sententious regrets and rebukes. The only phrase that betrayed the underlying conflict was: "We knew and have valued all that His Majesty had it in his power to give by way of inspiration, encouragement and understanding, and it is with great sadness that we have learnt of the untimely withdrawal of these gifts from the service of the State."

For the rest he had no difficulty in deflecting the limelight from himself. The "responsible" Press was conscientious in stamping out the ashes of a nine days' wonder and the others missed their target. "We have now a sober and respectable Court," wrote Hannen Swaffer, "perhaps we might try and get a sober and respectable journalism—and yet a more critical one. As it is, we are many of us becoming imitation Hearsts, frank about the wrong things."

Wherever the fault and whatever the motive, Halifax was never credited with his proper share in this royal Revolution, but it was hardly less complete, if somewhat less glorious, than the Trimmer's role in the crisis of 1688. What Horace Walpole called the "left-handed marriage" had been disposed of, and Disraeli's "domestic principle" upheld.

. . . .

The Abdication crisis undoubtedly strengthened the position of the Government in the country, and helped to divert attention from the increasingly sinister developments abroad. By the end of 1936 there was very little to show for the Government's pious aspirations. The Italo-German rapprochement was fully fledged. "The vertical line between Rome and Berlin is not a mark of separation, it is rather an axis," declared Mussolini in a phrase which is history. In July, while submitting over Austria, the Duce had refused to carry his new friendship with Hitler to the point of underwriting the Führer's Bolshevik phobias, but by November he was ready to convert the Axis into a World Triangle and to be an anti-Semite and a "sword of Islam" in the cause of a new Roman Empire.

As a diplomatic offensive the Anti-Comintern Pact was a far shrewder blow at Anglo-French solidarity than ever it was at Stalin's cautious regime. Ribbentrop, Germany's new and truculent Ambassador to London, who had succeeded to the position following von Hoesch's sudden death, was quick to point the moral and adorn the tale. He painted a picture of the consequences of the Bolshevik infection spreading over Europe; in his enthusiasm he transcended the bounds of diplomatic etiquette by reciting his hymn of hate before he had even presented his credentials. The bait was daintily fixed to the hook. "Once these forces of disintegration are brought to naught," he told the Anglo-German Fellowship on 15th December, "existing divergences between the nations, which in comparison with the universal menace of world revolution might be called no more than family quarrels, will, I believe, without great difficulty be solved." Ribbentrop had a privileged position in the Nazi hierarchy: he was not merely the German Ambassador, he was the Führer's "expert" on Foreign Affairs; his status saved him from his indiscretions and he undoubtedly made more headway with his political intrigues in England than is commonly conceded. If his object was to drive a wedge between France and Britain, it was no less to undermine the influence of Goebbels' stage villain, Anthony Eden.

After his reverse over Sanctions Eden had slowly regained his prestige. In November he gave a classic definition of British policy which became known as the Leamington formula; then in January 1937 he suffered a slight set-back in public estimation by hurriedly negotiating the so-called Gentleman's Agreement with Mussolini. It was logically sound enough to attempt to liquidate outstanding differences with Italy in view of the potential threat to all our communications as long as an undefined state of tension prevailed in the Mediterranean, but this particular act of diplomacy lacked preparation, and Eden's defence of it was apologetic, with the result that he displeased the Government without satisfying the Opposition. Indeed Eden's position in the Cabinet was becoming increasingly difficult; during the Rhineland crisis he had enjoyed the support of Neville Chamberlain, the goodwill of Baldwin and the mild supervision of Halifax. Ramsay MacDonald's influence was fitful and liable to be deflected more by sentiment than by rigid analysis. Simon had been inactive. Now the situation was different. Simon's prestige and power were waxing again; as Home Secretary and a great lawyer he had played an important part in guiding the Cabinet through the constitutional intricacies of the Abdication, and Hoare was back in the Cabinet again, chastened by his experience and less inclined than ever to indulge his Radical fancies. The presence of two ex-Foreign Secretaries, both with a grievance, both seeing in Eden the tendencies they wished to check in British foreign policy, did not make for harmony. Neville Chamberlain was still largely dominated by his illustrious brother, but since the Rhineland days that influence had led him towards his *volte-face* over Sanctions, and had not Sir Austen already visited Austria to persuade Schuschnigg to come to terms with Hitler while the going was good? Baldwin, for his part, with his eye on the Coronation and his own retirement, exhausted by the Abdication crisis, was inclined more and more to let his colleagues fight it out among themselves.

In this Cabinet top-heavy with foreign policy experts,

Halifax was not so intellectually committed or politically compromised as some of his colleagues; he was Baldwin's man always, but his growing authority did little to weigh the scales in Eden's favour. There was thus sufficient foundation of rivalry and reserve for Ribbentrop's machinations to achieve results. Hoare and Simon paid special heed to the anti-Bolshevist argument. A trial of strength soon developed. Non-Intervention was foundering and Eden was anxious to take a stronger line over Spain; he was overruled. Hitler, in his annual address in celebration of his accession to power, referred to Eden in terms calculated to minimize his influence, and when Eden pointed out that economic collaboration involved political appeasement on Germany's part, German propaganda at once suggested that he was not speaking for the Cabinet. More specifically, however, Ribbentrop had succeeded in securing the recall from Berlin of the British Ambassador, Sir Eric Phipps, who was a Francophile with experience of Germany covering the origins both of the Nazis and the 1914 war. He went further and submitted a list of names, including prominent British supporters of the Nazis who were not career diplomatists but who the German Government would have liked to see at the British Embassy. Sir Nevile Henderson, who was finally chosen, was probably not on that list, but he represented the required view-point.

In the devious sequence of events that made possible Halifax's dramatic visit to Berlin and Berchtesgaden in the following November, the removal of Phipps from Berlin must be accounted as the first and perhaps the most decisive. If Phipps' departure was a big victory for Ribbentrop and his British friends, it was equally a reverse for Eden. At the beginning of February Eden removed himself from all these discouraging intrigues by taking a fortnight's holiday on the French Riviera. *The Times*, in announcing that the decision was entirely his own, dealt sternly with " ridiculous and mischievous rumours to the contrary ". Once again Halifax deputized for him at the Foreign Office, and a week later received Ribbentrop for an interview lasting nearly two hours " on various subjects of interest to the two Governments on which the Ambassador was able to indicate Herr Hitler's views ". Some indication was certainly needed, for they were taking new shape. In addition to his claim to protect Europe from Moscow, Hitler in his Reichstag speech had brought to the forefront his claim for colonies which would "ever and again be raised . . . as a matter of course". This was followed, the day before Ribbentrop's interview with Halifax, by a provocative statement from the German Colonial League which contained the phrase "we need our Colonies, and we are going to have them". By the beginning of March Ribbentrop, who led the double life of a diplomat in London and a politician in the Reich, developed his argument at Leipzig by describing the division of the nations into "haves" and the "have-nots". If a compromise was to be reached between these two groups it could be found in only two directions; first through "the solution of the problem of the restoration of the former German Colonies", and the other by means "of the German people's own strength".

Halifax's reaction to these growing German demands can be detected in two speeches he made at this time, one to the League of Nations Union at Southampton, the other in the House of Commons. At Southampton he spoke boldly that the essence of collective security was that we never wished to go back to a system of exclusive alliances between any one or two Powers against any other one or two Powers, "but that we seek to build our foreign policy on a plan more comprehensive than exclusive alliances or precarious balance of power, a plan which invites the co-operation of all nations who are willing to co-operate with us, without any line of exclusion anywhere, in the cause of a better understanding between the nations". Further, it was to be achieved on a basis so broad that no country, "however powerful or well-equipped, will venture to try to disturb or break the peace. I would not remain a member of any Government that had a policy smaller or less broad than that." When, however, the details of his "Grand Design" came to be more closely considered in Parliament a few days later his attitude was somewhat less heroic. It was clear that Ribbentrop's manœuvres had left their mark. Hitler's bland promise that the "era of surprises" was at an end was put forward without qualification as a "reassuring element in the present situation". Then in defending regional pacts he emphasized that "though we believe that the cause of peace is in fact one, it may well be that an approach to a general settlement may be advanced by the solution of particular questions, which can be treated separately although they must ultimately form part of a larger whole ".

This was promising enough from the German point of view, but it assumed even more significance when taken in conjunction with a later passage in the same speech. Lord Allen of Hurtwood had proposed " a more constructive approach " by way of " a small conference in which all questions of possible difference would be brought into the arena of free discussion ". " But, as he spoke, I said to myself: 'Who would be participating in such a conference? Russia? ' He would know well, presumably, the difficulties an invitation of that sort might encounter." However, there was still a margin of ambiguity which Hitler would have to whittle down before the next stage in his march of destiny, for while sharing the anxiety of those " who see indirect but grave danger to the West of Europe from possible complications in the East ", Halifax went on to reiterate that " unless you are prepared on the one hand to say, 'I will fight in any case on behalf of peace, which is one and indivisible,' or on the other hand to say, 'I will only fight when I am myself the victim of attack,' there is an inevitable no-man's-land of uncertainty lying between, which is quite incapable of antecedent definition ".

It followed therefore " that if we are unable to define beforehand what might be our attitude to a hypothetical complication in Central or Eastern Europe, that is not to say that we disinterest ourselves in the fate of those parts of Europe. We have repeatedly maintained our determination to carry out to the best of our ability our obligations under the Covenant, and, if those obligations are not capable of achievement with precise exactitude, that is a feature—and I venture to think not an accidental feature — of the Covenant itself." This was in some ways the clearest exposition from any member of the Government of Britain's inherent interest in Germany's potential *Lebensraum*, and the speech as a whole marked out Halifax for the Nazis' special attention. Another step had been taken in the direction of a visit to Berchtesgaden.

Throughout the spring and summer the situation steadily deteriorated. The unedifying wrangles of the Non-Intervention Committee did nothing to relax the political and strategic grip of the Axis Powers on Spain. As the flow of German and Italian volunteers increased, the price of their withdrawal went up; and was duly associated with the conferment of belligerent rights for Franco, who was now no longer a "rebel" but the "nationalist" leader. By the middle of April a patrol system had been evolved, though Eden refused to either side the right of blockade.

. . . .

The public mind was undoubtedly confused by the Spanish struggle and to some extent infected by the prevailing mental disease in Europe that threatened to summon all values into one hideous conflict between Fascism and Communism. That the two rival creeds were virtually identical made no difference, but brought additional fervour to the heresy hunt and sting to the hatreds. Europe had seen nothing like it since the Reformation and the gigantic struggle between Catholic and Protestant for the souls of men. To steer a middle course intellectually or politically involved reserves of will-power and spiritual insight. The way of the Christian humanist became increasingly difficult. It was perhaps fortunate that in the midst of this holocaust of propaganda and armed menace, the Coronation ceremony intervened to remind the distracted British public of the conception of a free and mighty Commonwealth.

At the Coronation itself, taking his place with those Peers whom the Court of Claims entrusted with the Regalia, Halifax bore St. Edward's staff. Shortly after the Coronation, according to custom, loyal addresses from the two Universities of Oxford and Cambridge were read by their respective Chancellors; for a moment it seemed that Baldwin was going to deliver his address first, but it is on record that before he could begin, Halifax, with a verve that all Oxonians will appreciate, literally brushed him aside and established beyond further dispute Oxford's seniority and precedence!

The ideological dilemma, together with the overhanging threat of war, had tended to obliterate the meaning of Britain's heritage and contribution to the civilized order, and nothing became Baldwin better than when in his farewell to politics he urged the people not to admit the totalitarian virus into the body politic of the Empire, but rather to uphold against all new-fangled absolutism the tolerance and decencies of the English way of life. During the summer Halifax, too, was able to turn aside from the remorseless grind of European power politics, to expound broader principles and survey wider horizons. The themes to which he addressed himself at this time, "Democracy", "The Responsibilities of Empire", and "The Christian Attitude to War", were in a special sense interrelated; they had all been brought to the fore by the pretensions of triumphant Dictatorship.[1]

The appeal of Halifax's approach rests not so much in any particularly profound or original thought as in his inherent sincerity and powers of balanced and detached reflection; consistency is the keynote, he remains true to his old convictions. In his estimate of the British system, he upholds it, as Baldwin did, in that "it appears to us more favourable than any other to that development of personality, without which man cannot achieve the ultimate purpose of his existence". Democracy itself, he asserts, must stand or fall by the same fundamental test; an educated people alone can combat the ceaseless propaganda whereby identical facts appear so different as to be almost unrecognizable, "and by educated I mean a people so trained that it can apply its knowledge in wisdom, for knowledge alone is not wisdom". But he was sensible of the shortcomings inherent in a popular system, and in particular he stressed that there was cause for some misgiving as to democracy's capacity to handle the delicate problems of international relations. "The tendency of which there are signs to-day to import into our judgments on the issues of foreign policy our likes and dislikes of forms of Government elsewhere is full of danger." He condemned ill-informed attempts "to cut knots that it is often the business of statesmanship pacifically to untie", and "I conceive that in nothing will democracy be more severely tested than by its ability to exercise the

[1] Halifax's address on "The Responsibilities of Empire" was the last of a series of broadcasts planned to coincide with the Imperial Conference in London which Halifax had attended as a British delegate. He spoke from Oxford on 25th June, on the day when as Chancellor of the University he had accompanied Queen Mary, who laid the foundation-stone of the Bodleian New Library building, and had presided over the ceremony. His address on "Democracy" was one of a series delivered at the Bonar Law Memorial College at Ashridge under the auspices of the Association for Education in Citizenship which were reprinted as a book under the title of "Constructive Democracy".

restraint that is essential if the country is to exercise its full influence abroad, by presenting in that field a united front ".

But it was his address delivered at a service of prayer for peace at St. Martins-in-the-Fields and broadcast to the nation that created the deepest impression. The cult of absolute pacifism was then at its height; to many it seemed the only possible Christian response to the turmoil of totalitarian militarism. On the one hand, war had become so destructive to man's body and soul that the mere waging of it must defeat any moral purpose which it might be presumed to represent; on the other, there was the decisive credo of that great Christian and matchless demagogue, Dick Sheppard. " The issue is a spiritual one ", he had written. " For myself my pacifism begins and ends with the Spirit of Jesus Christ. I cannot believe that He would authorize or permit me to kill my brother, therefore whatever it costs and whatever the consequences I must refuse to fight." Now, in Dick Sheppard's own pulpit, and to the same packed congregation that he used to attract, Halifax, for whom both religion and peace were no less than for Sheppard supreme purposes of life, stood up to refute the pacifist thesis. In essence, he argued, the problem was one of a comparison of evils. War was the product and symptom of evil, but clearly not its only manifestation. It might well be that the refusal to face war would have the consequence of encouraging in a worse form the evil of which war was the visible outcome. " I am therefore led to conclude that the pursuit of peace under all conceivable conditions might mean the acceptance of greater evils even than war, conducted with all the devilish resources of the twentieth century, and might therefore in itself be more reprehensible than war seriously and solemnly undertaken in defence of vital principles that would be denied and betrayed by a refusal to break the peace."

We have travelled a long distance since the summer of 1937, but those words and arguments created a great sensation at the time. Pacifism had become respectable; the influence of such books as *Cry Havoc* had penetrated even into the drawing-rooms of Hampstead. Sheppard's converts cut across all social barriers; a closely argued counter-attack from a political leader of Halifax's standing, based solely on moral and religious considerations, struck deep into the pacifist position. *The Times* produced the address in pamphlet form, and within a week a second imprint had to be made. As was only to be expected, there was bitter criticism; Pat McCormick, Dick Sheppard's popular successor, was accused of allowing St. Martins' pulpit to be used for Government propaganda and for the glorification of war, and he was obliged to state publicly in a letter to *The Times* that he had invited Halifax to speak at the Peace Service not as a member of the Government but as a well-known layman, "because I knew he could express the views of the great majority of Christian people of all denominations and all parties, and would do more to rouse the people to prayer and work for peace than I, as a parson, could". This suspicion that Halifax had been put up by the Government to promote the mobilization of the public mind to accept war persisted, but for all that the persuasive quality and moderate tone of his argument made a lasting impression.

Baldwin's retirement brought to an end for Halifax his longest and closest political association. For fifteen years they had been comrades in arms on all great public questions; they had seen eye to eye in the strategy and tactics of imperial, domestic and foreign affairs; they drew the same distinction between the ideal and the actual. Both were shrewd apostles of the *via media*, whether in their attitude to Socialism or to the Indian constitution, to educational reforms or Anglo-German relations. "I am opposed to Socialism," Baldwin once admitted, "but I have always endeavoured to make the Conservative Party face left in its anti-Socialism"—a confession that equally covers Halifax's approach to party politics. Although Edward VIII might not see it as such, the Abdication solution was essentially a compromise. Between them Baldwin and Halifax had evolved a new conception of Conservative Imperialism; Baldwin was departing before its mission had been fulfilled or its future assured, but only the outbreak of a second world war could seriously threaten the structure. Halifax was now left to meet these gathering storms alone, for there had never been any understanding between him and the new Prime Minister, Neville Chamberlain, comparable to that which he enjoyed with Baldwin. Halifax was Baldwin's political heir in a sense that Chamberlain never was. Chamberlain, with his business instincts and clear-cut outlook, failed to appreciate Baldwin's indolence, his sly but steady refusal to forestall a crisis; nor as a Unitarian had Chamberlain any interest in Halifax's religious preoccupations.

It was clear that Halifax, even if he had wished to, would no longer be able to hold the balance, as Baldwin had done, between Eden and his Cabinet critics. Chamberlain had originally been Eden's ally, but he had now reached the conclusion that the only way out of the dilemma which Baldwin had transmitted to him was to come to terms with the Dictators. Halifax preached the overriding urgency of peace, the danger of allowing private judgments to be carried over into the domain of public policy, British readiness to clear up misunderstandings. Chamberlain resolved to fill in these half-tones, to carry the process of reconciliation to its logical conclusion. The fact that his whole public career had centred round health, housing and finance, that he was a novice and an amateur in foreign policy, merely helped him to view the problems with less dismay than the specialists among whom Halifax could now count himself.

CHAPTER XXIX

HALIFAX AT BERCHTESGADEN

How did Halifax react to the new regime? Just before the Coronation the Chamberlains spent the week-end at Garrowby. That occasion was to be of no small consequence in the history of Europe, for as the result of it the old reserves broke down, the two men discovered qualities in each other they had not before appreciated. Halifax admired Chamberlain's methodical common-sense; Chamberlain saw Halifax as the one man who could give moral weight to his own materialism, who could bridge the gulf between Baldwin and himself. In the Cabinet reshuffle Halifax became Lord President of the Council, an office by traditional precedence second to that of the Prime Minister himself, although during recent years the Chancellor of the Exchequer had, without any constitutional justification, come to be regarded as the heir to the throne.[1] The Lord President's position, as with that of the Lord Privy Seal, involved no departmental duties, but it brought Halifax *ex officio* into closer contact with the King and Court.

In May Sir Nevile Henderson, the new British Ambassador to Berlin, exuberantly launched the policy of active appeasement with a speech to the Anglo-German Fellowship when he called on more people in England to lay stress on National Socialism as "a great social experiment" rather than as a dictatorship. He ended with the declaration, "Guarantee us peace and peaceful evolution in Europe, and Germany will find that she has no more sincere, and, I believe, more useful friend in the world than Great Britain." Chamberlain followed up this exhortation by instructing Henderson to invite the German Foreign Minister, von Neurath, to come to London. The specific object of the

[1] In the Churchill Government, for instance, the Chancellor, Sir Kingsley Wood, was not even a member of the Inner War Cabinet, although he was subsequently promoted to it.

visit was a discussion with the British Government of the problem of naval control for Spain. This experiment in Non-Intervention had broken down through Hitler's withdrawal from it following the attack on *The Deutschland* by Spanish Government bombers; the prospects of setting it up again had not been improved by Germany's unilateral and brutal reprisals on Almeria; but Chamberlain had in mind to survey the whole range of Anglo-German relations with Neurath.

After some hesitation on Neurath's part, a date was arranged for the end of June, but long before then, Ribbentrop, alarmed at the prospect of his handiwork in London coming under the moderate Neurath's scrutiny, had persuaded his Führer to veto the visit. The pretext was an alleged torpedoing of the German cruiser *Leipzig*. The crew had only mentioned one torpedo, but Hitler's feverish rhetoric soon increased the number to four. The incident, if it ever took place, was wrapped in mystery, but its consequences were clear enough. With pompous indignation Hitler finally withdrew his fleet from waters where it was the object of "Red target practice". No effort was made to preserve diplomatic nicety and to suggest, after the *Leipzig* affair had died down, another date for the Neurath visit. Chamberlain had gone so far in assuaging Nazi anger as to admire Hitler's "restraint which we all ought to recognize", in doing no more than withdraw his ships after *The Deutschland* and *Leipzig* incidents. On 8th July he referred to Neurath's "postponed visit" and added that he fully shared Eden's hope that "some other occasion will present itself for discussions which may lead to a better understanding of each other's point of view". At the same time he paid court to Mussolini, and much was made of an exchange of letters, each in their own handwriting, between Duce and Prime Minister.

These gestures did nothing, however, to allay the violent ambitions of the Fascist Powers. In the Far East Japan embarked again on a war of unparalleled atrocity with the resurgent Nationalist China of Chiang Kai Shek. In the Mediterranean, in spite of a hopeful British Plan, there was an alarming increase in the attacks on shipping by submarines that were obviously not of Spanish origin. When at last, after many British cargoes had been sunk, an Italian torpedo was fired at the destroyer *Havock*, the Government was roused to action. The result was the Nyon Convention, which was to be Eden's and Vansittart's last diplomatic victory. This success for "collective security" was, of course, hailed by Churchill and the Opposition, but there was little enthusiasm for it among the junta of senior colleagues who comprised, in addition to Chamberlain himself, Hoare, Simon and, it would seem, Halifax. Eden did not hesitate to underline the moral he drew from Nyon; after denouncing the "masked highwayman who does not stop short of even murder", he pointed out that a conference was necessary "to mark clearly the horror that must surely be felt by all civilized peoples at the barbarous methods employed in these submarine attacks. The size of the Mediterranean and the consequent extent of the problem made collective deliberation leading to swift collective action imperative." A police force had been set up to deal with "this gangster terrorism of the seas".

"We seem to be back in the days of Baldwin," commented one Italian newspaper bitterly, "when Eden was supreme master of foreign policy. As long as Eden is at the head of the Foreign Office we must be on our guard." But if Mussolini really believed what he said, Halifax hastened to reassure him when in a statement to the House of Lords on 21st October he threw out the suggestion that it might be possible "to clear up a great many misunderstandings that have arisen out of the difficulties of the Spanish problem . . . and I can myself look forward—I do not want to be unduly optimistic—to the gradual establishment of a new and healthier atmosphere in which it would be possible to reach the position where Anglo-Italian conversations might be held". The rift was further widened in Eden's famous Llandudno speech. His words were as much a rebuke to Halifax as to Hitler. "We have said more than once that we in this country have no concern with the forms of government of foreign states. . . . But such toleration must be general. . . . I am as anxious as anybody to remove disagreement with Germany and Italy or any other country, but we must make sure that in trying to improve the situation in one direction it does not deteriorate in another. . . . We are ready and eager to make new friends, but we will not do that by parting with old ones." Lloyd George gleefully contrasted the first-class chauffeur with "the assembly of nervous wrecks behind him always pulling at his elbow". Eden obviously knew his own mind, but "I have been watching the thing," said Lloyd George, "and I can see that he is not having his own way in the matter." The sentiments in the Llandudno speech were admirable, but Lloyd George wanted to know first what Eden meant and secondly what he meant to do.

The answer was supplied by Chamberlain; Eden was packed off to Brussels, while in his absence the final arrangements were made for Halifax to go to Berchtesgaden. The Conference at Brussels held under the Nine Power Treaty was a forlorn and farcical attempt to achieve collective action in the Far East, spelt the collapse of League arbitration, and represented a grave personal defeat for Eden. "I earnestly hope that Japan will see her way to be represented there," was Halifax's meek plea, but it really made little difference. After three weeks of humiliating and confused discussion it was agreed that suspension of hostilities in the Far East would be in the best interests not only of China and Japan but of all nations. The Brussels fiasco only confirmed Chamberlain in his resolve to release British interests from the palsied procedure of the League. Halifax had already condemned an outbreak of war resulting from some policy which could claim the support of the letter of the Covenant which had been "drawn up under conditions totally different from those which prevail to-day". In other words, a "Save China" policy was not on the Government's agenda.

But to Chamberlain's way of thinking it was no less reprehensible to lose the chance of furthering appeasement by rigidly invoking considerations of national prestige. Admittedly the Neurath visit had not materialized and the Axis was hardening; a grandiose demonstration of solidarity had just been staged in Berlin when Mussolini and Hitler proclaimed their blood brotherhood. In addition, the recently signed Anti-Comintern Pact linked up the problems of British strategy in the Mediterranean and Pacific. Against such dynamic *real politik* the formal and traditional channels of British diplomacy were no longer adequate; sterile Foreign Office technique would have to be brought into line with "realities". Thus the idea of a senior member of the British Cabinet bearding the Führer in his den and extracting from him the exact nature of his demands appealed to Chamberlain as the only way out of a vicious circle of suspicion breeding armed alliances, armed alliances more suspicion. Halifax was the obvious and indeed only choice; Simon had been "disappointed" before, while the memory of his Pact with Laval was still too fresh in the public mind to admit of Hoare. In Berchtesgaden Hitler was no less anxious to unravel the Delphic utterances Halifax had given out on Eastern Commitments and Western Pacts, and if the oracle himself was ready to explain, so much the better. Hitler, for all the misgivings of his General Staff, was not a gambler; with his plans for Austria and the Czechs maturing, he was as anxious to check up on British policy as Chamberlain was to sift German intentions.

. . . .

Although, therefore, careful preparations had been made and conditions were favourable for a dramatic Anglo-German peace offensive, the first the public heard of Halifax's projected visit was in an exclusive and indiscreet announcement in the *Evening Standard* of 10th November. This paper reported that he would have an interview with Hitler, that Anglo-German relations would be discussed, "but no negotiations or specific issues—such as the former German colonies now administered under League mandate by Britain—are contemplated. If the present plan is carried out, Lord Halifax will leave for Germany on Monday week." The same evening, in an effort to damp down the sensation this "scoop" had caused, a communiqué of almost sublime circumspection was released from the Privy Council. "Statements in an evening paper . . . probably arise from an invitation he received through the Editor of *The Field*, presumably in his capacity as Master of the Hounds, to visit the Hunting Exhibition which is now open in Berlin, and subsequently to join a shooting party organized in connection with the Exhibition. The whole question of the visit has not yet come to a final decision and the question of personal contacts with German Ministers cannot therefore arise until a decision has been reached as to whether it will in fact be possible for Lord Halifax to accept the invitation extended to him." Two days later, however, while Chamberlain was on his way to preach the gospel of appeasement in Edinburgh, Simon made the formal announcement in Parliament that Halifax had accepted. The fiction that he was visiting Berlin primarily as Master of the Middleton and only as an afterthought as Lord President of the Council was solemnly maintained. The visit would be " entirely private and unofficial, but Herr Hitler had intimated after enquiry that he would be glad to see him ".

The Government was in an obvious dilemma; on the one hand it would have been auspicious to herald this announcement with the full unmuted blast of official approval, but on the other it was not safe to encourage speculation on what form the conversations might take. There was a further motive for reserve; although the project of direct negotiation with Hitler had been in the air for some time, it had met with powerful opposition; now the actual decision had been taken while Halifax was again in charge of the Foreign Office during Eden's absence in Brussels and therefore seemingly without Eden's knowledge or approval. Indeed one American diplomatic correspondent in London cabled New York that even before leaving for Brussels Eden had offered his resignation to Chamberlain, and only after intense pressure been persuaded to retract. Although it is tempting to suggest that the visit was deliberately arranged behind Eden's back, it is most unlikely that Halifax would ever have been a party to any such intrigue.

Many influences must have been at work to give urgency to the project. " I think I may claim ", wrote Lord Londonderry to Ribbentrop in December, " to have been partly responsible for putting the idea into Halifax's head that he should go over to Germany and establish a definite contact with the Chancellor and others in your country." Just before his departure Londonderry saw Halifax again, and in stressing that there was no time to be lost, " as the situation seems to me to be rapidly deteriorating ", added the plea that he should be as firm as possible. " ' I should like to see the Germans categorically pinned down to their programme,' I said, ' and think you might be able to get this from them.' "[1] But the most likely explanation of the hurried decision is probably to be found in the despatches

[1] See Lord Londonderry's *Ourselves and Germany*, pages 130 and 132 (Penguin Edition).

reaching London just after Eden had left Germany giving details of Ribbentrop's mission to Rome.

The enterprising Diplomatic Correspondent of the *Evening Standard*—and his contacts were such that he was not merely guessing—reported that Ribbentrop had asked the Duce's consent to complete the expansion of Nazi influence in Austria; " the anti-Communist façade of the Italo-German pact now about to be signed in Rome is a convenient cover for political development in Europe ". Schuschnigg's position in Austria was rapidly weakening, and the withdrawal of the last semblance of Italian patronage would undermine the fragile structure of Austrian independence and substitute for the " Vienna risk " far more threatening and incalculable hazards. Before the abyss Chamberlain and Halifax took fright, and what had been a good idea became desperately earnest politics.

No sooner had the announcement been made than the *Evening Standard* took its deepest plunge of all into the vortex of Anglo-German diplomacy. Under the heading " Hitler ready for Truce " the Diplomatic Correspondent wrote with the self-assurance of one who knew he could not be gainsaid and who had no use for what Ramsay MacDonald once apostrophized as " tail out of the bag " diplomacy. " I am able ", he wrote, " to give certain indications of the attitude of both the German and British Governments towards the coming talks. The British Government have information from Berlin that Herr Hitler is ready, if he receives the slightest encouragement, to offer to Great Britain a ten-year ' truce ' on the Colonial issue. During the ' truce ' the question of Colonies for Germany would not be raised. In return for this agreement Herr Hitler would expect the British Government to leave him a free hand in Central Europe."

By a " free hand " was meant that Britain should not interfere if Germany pressed for a free vote or a plebiscite in Austria or presented demands to Czechoslovakia " for the immediate recognition of the right of the German minority in that country to administrative autonomy within the State and to cultural unity with the people of the German Reich ". " Herr Hitler believes ", the Correspondent continued, " that a free vote in Austria would mean a Nazi regime in Vienna, and that political autonomy for the Germans in Czecho-

HALIFAX MEETS HITLER

Climbing the hill to Berchtesgaden for his famous conversation with the Führer on November 19th, 1937. Left to right: Dr. Schmidt (official interpreter), Halifax, Hitler, Baron von Neurath (concealed by Hitler) and Brückner, Hitler's bodyguard

slovakia would paralyse Russian influences in Prague. He attaches most importance for the moment to the solution of the Austrian problem in a sense favourable to Germany." Hitler's offer of terms would be accompanied by a long explanation of his foreign policy as embodied in the Axis and the Anti-Comintern Pact. "That will furnish an occasion for Lord Halifax to probe the essential facts with regard to the true nature of the relations between Rome and Berlin. Herr Hitler will find that the British Government are anxious to discover the exact extent and nature of Germany's demands for a lasting settlement of pending issues. But he will also be told that the British Government are not prepared to give away things which are not at their disposal. At the same time Lord Halifax will explain to Herr Hitler: (1) the particularly close relationship in which this country finds itself to France; (2) the desire of the British Government for a swift completion of a new Western Pact as a guarantee for the security and *status quo* in that part of Europe, and (3) the belief in London that international problems concerning Europe are best discussed and settled within the framework of the Covenant of the League of Nations." In addition, the public was informed that Chamberlain had asked Eden to prepare for Halifax the Government's instructions; these were necessary in view of the news that Hitler wished to avail himself of an informal conversation with a member of the British Cabinet for discussing "Anglo-German relations as well as Germany's plans for Central Europe".

The reactions to this omniscient and all-embracing prophecy were so rapid and violent as to suggest that the information had been supplied by interested parties high up in the Axis hierarchy for the express purposes of repudiating it, of creating a situation comparable with that which frustrated the Neurath visit, and in general of providing a pretext for Hitler to raise his terms. For on the very same evening the official Nazi *Parteikorrespondenz* rushed out with a violent diatribe suggesting that the whole visit might have to be put off because of certain conjectures in the British Press. In particular the suggestion that Hitler was ready to offer a Colonial truce in return for a free hand in Central and Eastern Europe aroused Nazi fury; it was "an outrageous calumny", "a journalistic swindle", "an imputation of shady bargaining which cannot be too sharply repudiated ". The " calumny " and the " swindle ", be it noted, in the eyes of these unctuous Nazi propagandists were not directed at Halifax, although the article obviously implied that he was ready to sell out other nations' liberties in order to relieve the German pressure on British property, but at Hitler for assuming that the Führer would for one moment consider forgoing Germany's Colonial " rights " in order to further her rights in Europe.

The thunder died away in time for Halifax to leave, although there were ominous rumblings throughout the visit; but the episode suggested that the same extremist forces that had kept Neurath away from Downing Street still had access to the Führer; and that a sharp cleavage of opinion prevailed among the Nazi leaders. British concern at what *The Times* described as the *Evening Standard's* " artless suggestion " was reflected in the haste with which Eden assured Delbos at Brussels that the scope and purport of the Halifax visit was purely " exploratory "; Eden then hurried back and a long conference ensued between himself, Chamberlain and Halifax at which no doubt the " instructions " were drafted. In spite of all the bluster and sarcasm, the basic assertions of the *Evening Standard* résumé have never been denied, and in the absence of any contrary evidence they still hold the field—the very indignation of the German Press in itself suggests that the terms of reference, whether deliberately or otherwise, had been uncovered.

The British Press engaged in a spirited argument as to the authenticity of the *Evening Standard* revelation, in the course of which Halifax's reliable and well-favoured *Yorkshire Post* indignantly rebutted the *Daily Telegraph's* accusation that it was merely paraphrasing the *Evening Standard*. The *Yorkshire Post's* Political Correspondent had obtained similar information independently " from sources satisfactory to any reputable journal ". The *Manchester Guardian* also entered the lists with the assertion that there was more truth in the *Evening Standard* article than was generally supposed. But in spite of this feverish speculation, the visit itself, for all the printer's ink poured upon it, did not live up to the excitement and the hopes it had aroused. Halifax left on the afternoon of 10th November, a day earlier than was expected, to allow him more time to meet German leaders, and was seen off at the station by Ribbentrop.

On arrival in Berlin the next day he was met at the Friedrich Strasse station by Sir Nevile Henderson and Dr. Bulow Schwanti, chief of the Diplomatic Protocol, and drove straight to the British Embassy. After lunching with Baron and Baroness von Neurath, old acquaintances of his, he piously spent his first afternoon at the International Exhibition, of which, indeed, as Sir Nevile Henderson has neatly observed, " he was in German eyes one of the principal exhibits ". Accompanied by Oberjägermeister Scheiping and Herr Lobenberg, the technical director, as well as by Henderson, he received a very friendly welcome as he made his way through the dense throngs who jostled round him; the hall was particularly crowded as his visit there coincided with the Busstag or Protestant day of Repentance. The Exhibition had been arranged in 1936 by Goering in his capacity as Game Warden of the Reich. British participation in it had been effected at the last moment by Henderson, and Goering was much gratified; but for Hitler the whole Exhibition meant nothing as he had no interest in sport and disapproved of hunting. The only part of the Exhibition which Hitler appreciated and which Halifax could not fail to see, as it was with heavy-handed Nazi ostentation placed by the entrance, was the German Colonial Exhibition with its huge map of the " lost territories " prominently displayed. There was also a portrait on the wall of General Goering's father, who was one of the more brutal Governors of German South West Africa. A brief statement of appreciation issued by Halifax afterwards referred to the international value of the Exhibition in reminding " sportsmen the world over—and most men are sportsmen in some degree—of all the things they have in common with one another ". Halifax's interest in hunting earned him the apt German nickname of " Halalifax ", which combined the German word for " Hark Away " (Halali) with his own title.

The German Press comment was voluminous and confused, mixing threats with cajolery. On his arrival, the well-known political commentator of *Deutsche Allgemeine Zeitung* was at pains to point a favourable if elaborate contrast between Halifax in 1937 and Haldane in 1912. Now the naval threat no longer existed, it was not now so much a question of eliminating antagonisms as of defining the roles each country was to play, and finally he paid a gallant, almost Gallic, tribute. In 1912 Haldane had spoken of Germany in an unguarded moment as his " spiritual home ". " It seems to be particularly useful," commented Dr. Silex, " that in Lord Halifax a firmly rooted Englishman is coming to us and one who has his spiritual home in his own country." In contrast with this polite deference were the insolent and somewhat sinister diatribes of the official *Parteikorrespondenz.* Halifax was now presented to British newspaper readers, it observed, " in the guise of an explorer who is to discover in Germany things hitherto unknown. He is apparently—on the authority of English papers—to have ' explanatory conversations ' with the Führer. The Germany of Adolf Hitler calls for no examination. ' Expeditions ' could sooner be despatched into the jungle of England's own politics. Here, it seems to us, is better material for ' explanatory ' action. Yes; such an expedition should find itself on the way to discovering some of the present obscurities of European politics." So the discussions and uncertainties remained right up till the eve of Halifax's pilgrimage to the incredible though " only begetter " of them all.

. . . .

In England there was a feeling of quiet confidence that the man who had mastered the endless subtleties of Gandhi's mind was best equipped to elicit the sympathy of the no less complex personality of Adolf Hitler. Professor Toynbee, in the *Survey of International Affairs*,[1] gives a shrewd and witty summary of the British reaction to the Hitler-Halifax meeting. " In the minds of his countrymen, peers and colleagues ", he writes, " Lord Halifax was regarded at this time with a certain pride and awe, not unmingled with a spice of sceptical amusement as a characteristically English exponent of some simple but noble virtues who at the same time had the gift of charming the most outlandish, un-English ' wild men ' by the unconscious exercise of an intuitive art which was capable of surpassing the Machiavellian triumphs of cleverer and less scrupulous politicians." " To the average Englishman's eye," Professor Toynbee continues,

[1] For 1937; Vol. I, pages 338-339.

"Mr. Gandhi and Herr Hitler were two hardly distinguishable specimens of the same species of foreigner in virtue of their being, both of them, superlatively exotic, and the average member of a British Cabinet may have reasoned in November 1937 that the guileless tamer of Gandhi had at any rate 'a sporting chance' of taming Hitler likewise. Were not both these political 'mad mullahs' non-smokers, non-drinkers of alcohol, non-eaters of meat, non-riders on horseback, and non-practisers of blood-sports in their cranky private lives? And did not the German Führer, like the Indian Mahatma, have some bee in his bonnet about the importance of being 'Aryan'?"

But the comparison of Hitler with Gandhi was not the mere fantasy of the inmates of West End clubs or East End pubs; a distinguished Central European statesman, who had been entertained at Berchtesgaden, was once asked what impression the Führer made upon him. "He is like Gandhi in Prussian boots," was the reply. Mussolini, after their first disastrous meeting in 1934, contemptuously dubbed him "the garrulous monk". The late Lord Allen of Hurtwood, who had long conversations with Hitler, told me that he came away with the abiding impression of his ruthlessness but of his asceticism as well. In a sense, Berchtesgaden is Hitler's ashram, his attempt to escape from the processes of Western civilization of which he is a far more virulent enemy than Gandhi. Both proclaim the simple life, both evoke the allegiance of the little man. But for all that, Hitler is the destroyer and Gandhi the creator. The trust that Halifax could summon from Gandhi arose from a moral perception wholly lacking in Hitler. There are vast tracts of human experience, Dr. Gooch once observed, which Hitler is too uneducated to visualize or to understand, with the result that Halifax found himself face to face not with a genuine mystic and religious leader, but with a sly, self-conscious tribal deity, a socially unsatisfied pagan with a gift for subordinating all things, from Providence to petroleum, to the uses of power politics.

When Neurath and Halifax left Berlin on the night of Thursday, 18th November, they had already had a full exchange of views. Neurath was one of the few surviving Weimar statesmen, and was widely and with some justice regarded as a Moderate. In fact his usefulness to the Nazis was at an end and his days of effective power were numbered; Neurath's view-point and promises, therefore, had to be taken with reserve. On arrival the following morning, they drove to Obersalzberg. Henderson stayed behind in Berlin, and Halifax was accompanied by Kirkpatrick, the brilliant First Secretary to the British Embassy. Hitler sent his car, specially fitted for cross-country driving, to bring his guests up to the famous mountain retreat. On arrival he met Halifax on the steps of his house and greeted him in the most friendly fashion. The assembled photographers were able to flash to their papers the phenomenon of a smiling Führer. He then showed Halifax over his villa, which epitomized his architectural as well as his territorial yearnings, and conducted him into the study, from which Halifax enjoyed for a few minutes the glorious view of the snow-covered Watzmann massif and perhaps paused to consider the cumulative effect of such grandeur and such exile upon a neurotic Austrian Dictator of Germany. Here was a symbol of German unity which no amount of political discussion, formal or informal, could rectify.

The conversations upon which the world's attention was riveted began between 10 and 11 a.m., lasted for two and a half hours, and included an early lunch. Halifax was closeted *à quatre* with Hitler, Neurath, and Hitler's famous confidential interpreter, Dr. Schmidt. No authoritative report has ever seeped through of the form or substance of the conversation, although, with the astonishing pervasiveness of diplomatic impressions, it was soon firmly established that Hitler had been " difficult ", and had adopted his old technique of looking through his guest and ranting at him as if he were the Reichstag, and that Halifax had received as unpleasant a shock as Simon and Eden had experienced in 1935. Polite references to Austria were, it seems, greeted with the taunt that the fate of that State had already been settled and there was nothing that the British Government could do about it. Did Hitler pause to gauge the tone of Halifax's remonstrance? Whatever the well-chosen phrase, it was mild enough to seal Schuschnigg's fate when, three months later, his time came to climb the hill to Berchtesgaden. The details of a Czech settlement were slurred over in a flood of invective about Franco-Soviet intrigues in Prague.

buffalo and elk, the bird life which had been fostered by the erection of no less than 40,000 box nests, he returned to the British Embassy, where Henderson gave a big dinner-party in his honour at which he met "most of the other leading Nazi Ministers". These included Field-Marshal von Blomberg, whose dismissal two months later was to herald the victory of the extremists; Dr. Frick, the devious Minister of the Interior, who first forged Hitler's German nationality; Dr. Schacht, the darling of the City and the Bank of England, and Count Schwerin von Krosigk, the Finance Minister. On the whole, it was a hand-picked list of Moderates whose power was rapidly waning.

On Sunday, 21st November, while Hitler was at work on his Augsburg tirade, Halifax attended Holy Communion at the English Church, and at lunch met the French, Italian and American Ambassadors. In the afternoon Henderson introduced Goebbels to Halifax and acted as interpreter between them. The Press problems of the two countries were more fully and rationally discussed than at Berchtesgaden, with the result that for a short while Nazi polemics were called off. "Nor can I refrain from observing," Henderson adds, "that the reasonableness and logic which Dr. Goebbels always displayed in private seemed to make, in spite of his reputation, quite a good impression upon Lord Halifax."

That night, after five days into which with characteristic German thoroughness more had been crammed than had at first seemed possible, Halifax returned to London. At five o'clock the next afternoon, only a little more than an hour after his arrival, he called on Eden at the Foreign Office. Afterwards he accompanied Eden to Downing Street, where the discussion was resumed with Chamberlain. The outside world was given scant material upon which to base any impression. The communiqué after the conversation with Hitler said simply that they "had a long discussion on the problems of international politics of interest to Germany and Great Britain". All Halifax told the expectant journalists at Berlin was "if we have succeeded in opening the door now, I hope we will not let it be closed again". There had been some rumour that he had invited Neurath to make his postponed visit to London, but he denied it, adding that it was not his but the Government's business to do that. The final douche of cold water was applied by

Hitler's own paper, the *Völkischer Beobachter.* Lord Halifax's visit, it pronounced, " cannot result in disappointment, nor can it raise any untimely hopes. This for the simple reason that in Germany there could be no intention of linking with the visit, which sprang from English initiative, any immediate political result whatever. The announcements about a visit by Baron von Neurath to London are, therefore, only speculations. There is no urgent necessity at present for such a journey." The good effect in Germany of an extremely discreet Lords debate, in which speakers on all sides of the House had spoken in most conciliatory tones about the Colonial question, was somewhat offset by Chamberlain's " progress report " on the Anglo-American trade negotiations. The German Press at once saw it as an effort on Chamberlain's part to draw the United States out of its political isolation to the advantage of England.

It was difficult to escape the conclusion from what was said, and even more from what was left unsaid, that the Hitler-Halifax conversations had in themselves neither opened nor unlocked any door whatever. For all Hitler's intransigence, the political commentators were agreed that the scope of the talks had in fact covered the ground that the *Evening Standard's* Diplomatic Correspondent had forecast they would, and the *Manchester Guardian* reported them under six drastic clauses. Firstly, Germany was to rejoin the League of Nations if the Covenant was redrafted, the sting of Sanctions extracted and the League itself finally severed from Versailles and war guilt; Minority treaties, too, would have to be revised, and Italy's conquest of Abyssinia recognized. Secondly, Great Britain was asked to consent to a reorganization of the Czech State on the model of the Swiss Federal system, the Sudetenland to acquire a status similar to that of a Swiss canton. Thirdly, there was to be no British diplomatic, political or military assistance for the Austrian Government. In return, according to the same authority, Germany would shelve the Colonial issue for six years, restore peace in Spain after Great Britain had given *de jure* recognition to Franco, and finally mediate in the Far East.

Once more the tender Nazi conscience was provoked, and in England *The Times* entered solemnly on its task of protecting the Government from the public. A long and revealing leader on "The Way of Appeasement" denounced "militant peacemakers". A parting of the ways was always "journalistically acceptable". Perhaps Germany's use of the *coup de main* to some extent explained the jumpiness affecting some journalists, politicians and the City, but there was every reason why, after an interval for reflection, the timorous should find the visit to Berlin and Berchtesgaden "a 'bull point' rather than a 'bear point' on the international Exchange". The peace-minded could best serve peace for the moment by ceasing to agitate themselves and others with "morbid fancies about corrupt understandings, trampled Austrians and bartered Czechs, and other presumed triumphs of cynicism or realism—according to the point of view. It will be time enough to protest against the Government's crooked or criminal intentions when there is some evidence that they possess them." Altogether it was an unusual and unnatural role for the "Thunderer". The *Manchester Guardian's* Correspondent never claimed that either Hitler or Halifax committed themselves to this agenda; what the apostles of appeasement resented was so forthright, and, as the tragic sequence of subsequent history has proved, so reasonable an estimate of what the agenda was.

The lay mind was not yet educated to the full diplomatic implications of appeasement, and revelations like that of the *Manchester Guardian* only made for dissension and alarm. But anxieties were not confined to the Press; public attention had been diverted from the Hitler-Halifax conversation by the State visit of King Leopold of the Belgians, which coincided with it. While Leopold and his advisers were in England they took the opportunity to express their alarm at reports reaching them that Hitler had mentioned to Halifax the possibility of changes to the advantage of Germany in the administration of the Belgian Congo. Further assurances were forthcoming when Chamberlain, after informing a packed House of Commons that the Hitler-Halifax talks were confidential and therefore nothing could be said about them, announced that the French Premier and Foreign Minister, Chautemps and Delbos, had accepted an invitation to visit London on 30th November for an exchange of views on the international situation.

In the meanwhile Halifax reported fully both to the

King and to the Cabinet, and efforts on the part of the indefatigable Geoffrey Mander, M.P., to secure a denial of the Press speculation were frowned upon by the Speaker. German official commentators did their best to forestall the visit of the French Ministers by stressing that it would be good business for Britain frankly to recognize German predominance in Europe. The question was frankly posed whether it was not more advisable for Britain, with her world Empire, to make certain, through agreement with Germany, of peace in Europe than to support French interests in Prague. Goering asked Henderson bluntly whether Chamberlain " meant business ".

CHAPTER XXX

CHAMBERLAIN'S FOREIGN SECRETARY

CHAUTEMPS and Delbos listened carefully to Halifax's recapitulation of his interview with Hitler and were not unduly disquieted by its comprehensive character. There was no unwillingness to admit Germany's claim to " colonial equality ", but they were not ready to tamper with the territorial clauses of the Peace Treaty. Delbos realized that on the vigour of French support for Prague rested the only chance of keeping the already emaciated Pact with Soviet Russia alive. As long as Delbos was in office what the Germans called " the French difficulty " remained. Non-intervention, for all its leakages, was upheld as having justified itself, and the French did not show themselves to be unduly pessimistic about Austria, apparently expressing the view that Schuschnigg would be able to rely upon Mussolini as Dollfuss had done. No final view could be taken, however, on the French attitude to the Central European situation until Delbos had completed his tour of Poland and the Little Entente Powers which had been arranged for December some months before the Halifax visit was envisaged. Its purpose was not, as the Germans alleged, to complete the encirclement of the Reich, no such objective could succeed when Moscow, the capital of France's greatest ally, was deliberately left out of the itinerary, rather Delbos sought to find out the attitude of the Succession States to a settlement between the four great Western Powers. In reply to Attlee, Chamberlain cautiously affirmed that a general settlement was the British Government's ultimate objective.

But while Delbos was piecing together the shattered fragments of the League and the British Cabinet was pondering the implications of Halifax's visit, Italy finally left the League, departing, as Mussolini bombastically declared, " without one pang of regret, from the tottering temple in which they do not work for peace but prepare for war "

Hitler backed up the Duce with the bleak announcement that Germany would never return to Geneva and that the word *Völksbund* should from henceforth be banned from all German text-books. An article by Flandin in the *Sunday Times* on 18th December showed the trend of powerful influences in France, and asked pointedly whether it was in France's interest to " assume the honourable but dangerous duties of European policeman ". Significantly, only two days later Chamberlain invoked the same phrase in a House of Commons debate when he argued that for the British people to constitute themselves " policemen of the world " was a task beyond their strength even with the backing of the League, especially at a time when the League was " mutilated ".

The New Year opened with the apparently innocuous announcement that Sir Robert Vansittart had been awarded the G.C.B. in the New Year Honours and promoted from his position as Permanent Under-Secretary for Foreign Affairs to a new post as Chief Diplomatic Adviser to the Government. To well-informed observers, however, the move implied the tactful transfer of one whose counsel on British policy to the Dictators was not wholly acceptable to the new regime at Downing Street, for as the months went by, Chamberlain, who was taking an increasingly active part in the daily conduct of Foreign Affairs, was relying not so much upon trained Foreign Office experts as upon a small group of personal advisers such as Sir Joseph Ball and Sir Horace Wilson, men unknown to the general public, with no more experience of diplomacy than Chamberlain himself. Upon these men, in particular Sir Horace Wilson, were soon concentrated almost incredible powers and influence. The removal of Vansittart to a position in which, as Halifax later pointed out, he was not concerned with the current affairs of the Foreign Office but only advised on major questions of policy " remitted to him for that purpose ", marked a definite stage in Wilson's rise to power and in the subordination of the Foreign Office to the will of the Prime Minister.

But in Germany a much more trivial event involved even more momentous and dramatic political consequences. The middle-aged Field-Marshal von Blomberg eloped with and married his typist, thereby committing a grave breach in the social code of Potsdam and involving himself in a feud with other German army leaders. Blomberg had always been faithful to the Nazis and had assured Hitler's supremacy when he ordered the army to give allegiance to the Führer as Hindenberg's successor the day before Hindenberg was dead. Behind the present feud were unfixed prerogatives, divergences of view on strategical and political issues as between the German army chiefs and the Nazi leaders. On 4th February Hitler took the pretext of the squabble over Blomberg's marriage to settle all controversies by a sudden reconstruction of the army command, diplomatic service and the German Cabinet, whereby he assumed direct sovereignty over all three. His compromise was to rid himself of all moderate and critical elements; Neurath, Fritsch and Blomberg were relegated, the extremists, in particular Ribbentrop, who succeeded Neurath as Foreign Minister, and Himmler gained a complete and bloodless victory. What had been latent in the situation that Halifax had witnessed for himself during his visit in November had now been brought about, as was typical of all Hitler's actions, with brutal suddenness.

Europe did not have to wait long for the dire results of this reshuffle, the most drastic since the " blood bath " of June 30th 1934. On 12th February Schuschnigg was subjected to his fearful ordeal by interview with Hitler, but instead of summoning immediately afterwards the world's Press and giving them a story that would have roused democratic opinion and perhaps have given Hitler and his Generals grounds for pause, he kept the fateful information of the bestial treatment to which he had submitted strictly to himself. Even in private conversation with the British, French and Italian Ministers he provided no details of his humiliating experience, and it was not until then that he gave the lie to Guido Schmidt, his Foreign Minister, who had gained his trust and who had completely betrayed him, and openly affirmed that he had received an ultimatum and been advised by Hitler that no foreign assistance would be forthcoming. It was Schmidt's misleading account of the interview—he and Ribbentrop were only admitted to Hitler's study after the ultimatum had been delivered—that made it possible for Halifax on 17th February to speak in the House of Lords of " the recent agreement between Germany and Austria ". When during the next week-end differences between Eden and the Prime Minister reached their climax, the Austrian crisis had not fully matured, Hitler was weaving his way towards decision, but the final form it might take had not yet been evolved. Schuschnigg's reticence still left the impression that if Austria's future was desperate it was not as yet hopeless and that in substance the Berchtesgaden agreement had been freely reached by two sovereign German Powers. Eden had already told the Commons that he was not in a position to estimate its exact effects, to which Halifax added on 17th February that " I think a certain element of reserve is prudent in our judgments of these events at the present time ".

. . . .

Eden reached his point of resistance to Chamberlain on the specific problem of Anglo-Italian negotiations, but on his own admission wider issues were at stake, and the background of Austrian menace undoubtedly encouraged them both to stand by their diverging view-points. For Chamberlain and for Halifax as well the possible absorption of Austria by the Reich, for all the high-sounding totalitarian blandishments of the Axis propaganda, constituted a grave defeat for Mussolini's prestige and a threat to his security. Republican successes in Spain, in particular the recent capture of Teruel, made the Spanish imbroglio more than ever an embarrassment. Anglo-Italian accord might act as a brake on Hitler's policy in Austria, only thus could the Stresa Agreement be brought to life again. For Eden Mussolini's weakness was Britain's opportunity to be strong. Nyon showed the Italian reaction to genuine strength, and only substantial *garanties d'exécution* could give reality to any real commitments entered into with so shameless a cynic as Il Duce. It was not as if the terms at the end were attractive. Britain was to make the substantial concessions, and in the realm of symbols was not the recognition of Italy's " Empire " in Abyssinia something more than a token withdrawal of volunteers from Spain? Were we to pay for the privilege of not being reviled from one end of the Mediterranean to the other by venomous Fascist propaganda? " I am myself pledged to this House not to open conversations with Italy until this hostile propaganda ceases." As Eden, already through his experience an elder statesman in his early forties, passed temporarily from power

ARCHITECTS IN APPEASEMENT

Chamberlain, Prime Minister, and Halifax, Foreign Secretary, returning to 10 Downing Street after a lunch at the Foreign Office to resume important conversations with the French Premier and Foreign Minister, Daladier and Bonnet. April 29th, 1938

and office he solemnly warned Parliament and the nation of the dangers ahead. " We are in the presence of the progressive deterioration of respect for international obligations. It is quite impossible to judge these things in a vacuum. In the light—my judgment may well be wrong—of the present international situation this is a moment for this country to stand firm."

Eden's resignation was a blow from which the National Government never really recovered. There was just that element of doubt and mystery which profoundly disturbed opinion. Eden had alleged as a cause of his leaving the Government that blackmail crept into the arguments of Count Grandi, the Italian Ambassador. A blank denial from Chamberlain was not enough to obliterate the disquieting memory of Eden's words. " It is certainly never right," he had said, " to depart from the traditional methods of diplomacy because one party to the negotiations intimates that it is Now or Never. Agreements that are worth while are never made on the basis of a threat." In addition there was the unpalatable fact that the crisis had coincided with one of Hitler's longest and most sinister orations in which he had made contemptuous reference to Eden, as if to speed him on his way. The impression remained accordingly that Eden was the Dictators' *bête noire* and therefore their victim, and with the " martyred " Foreign Secretary went the sympathies of a powerful body of opinion which had been largely harnessed to the League of Nations Union by Lord Cecil, and which identified much of its hope for the future of " collective security " and " defence against aggression " on the personality and career of Anthony Eden. It should be noted also that while Chamberlain was ready to appease potential enemies abroad he was in no mood to conciliate his opponents at home, but both offended their susceptibilities and resented their criticisms.

Eden's resignation was the first in a crescendo of crises, and was in that respect the most intense, for as the year advanced Europe reeled from one peril to another and the people became in a sense case-hardened. With the prospect of so many dangers ahead Halifax alone had the prestige, the experience and the character to succeed Eden as Foreign Secretary; for quite apart from Eden's popularity, it was obvious that Chamberlain intended to assume even closer supervision than before over the details of British diplomacy. From henceforth the Foreign Secretary's function would, it seemed, be shadowy and submerged, eligible for the kicks but not the halfpence. These, however, were not considerations to deter Halifax, who was ready faithfully to carry through appeasement and by now fervently believed that it served the nation's highest interest. If the Prime Minister wished him to interpret that policy at the Foreign Office he was prepared to do so; but the respect that gave him pause was his unwillingness to take apparent advantage of Eden's downfall; he had strong personal regard and admiration for the younger man, and from the purely personal view-point it was distasteful to succeed him under such distressing circumstances. Chamberlain, for his part, was only too anxious to have Halifax at his side, and would have invited him without a moment's hesitation but for the representations that Attlee made on behalf of the Labour Opposition for a Foreign Secretary to be chosen from the House of Commons. He wanted time to see what strength and support this thesis had, but in order that there might be no delay a statement was issued from 10 Downing Street that Halifax would take temporary charge of the Foreign Office.

To show the brisk purposes of the new regime, Eden resigned on the Sunday evening, but by eleven o'clock on the Monday morning, even before Eden's resignation statement had been made, Halifax was negotiating with Grandi and the Anglo-Italian conversations were under way. Three days later, in a speech that rang with conviction no less than Eden's, he dismissed the immediate issue between Chamberlain and Eden as " secondary " and not important enough to outweigh the agreement existing on the larger questions of " broad policy " to which Eden had testified in his original willingness for conversations to take place; but his argument was rather more effective when he turned to the " broad policy " itself, and on the eve of assuming his gravest task since the Viceroyalty, he invoked the analogy of India's communal problem. " It was said then, you remember, ' Is not India riddled by communal division? ' The answer was clearly ' Yes '. It was then asked: ' Is that not therefore falling on very unfavourable ground for representative institutions? ' The answer was clearly ' Yes '. Then one was asked: ' Have you any reason to suppose that all that problem will be any less acute in five, ten, or fifteen years time? ' The answer to that was obviously 'No'. Then one realized that the real question one had to ask oneself was: 'Because of these unfavourable conditions are you prepared to see the political problem bank up against you for five, ten, twenty years without making any effort to solve it and making it more difficult at the end? ' It is exactly the same, as I see it, with this great political problem of approaching the further establishment of peace in Europe. Are you going on for months and years refusing to face facts, watching your relations steadily deteriorate or potential enemies perhaps become converted into real enemies, and something happens which launches the whole world into irretrievable disaster? "

The reaction in Parliament to Eden's resignation was nothing like as strong as in the country. All Churchill's blandishments at a big meeting of the Constitutional Club failed to produce the response his chairman, Sir Patrick Hannon—a typical pro-Chamberlain back-bencher—aroused when he called on members to close their ranks. W. S. Morrison, one of Baldwin's protégés, was given a chance to prove his mettle on Foreign Affairs when he wound up the big Eden debate for the Government, but he failed to pass the difficult test, and Parliamentary opinion was ripe for Halifax's appointment. In addition, Lothian, Geoffrey Dawson and Brand, who used to congregate at Cliveden House as the Astors' guests and earned the title of a " set ", to which, in spite of imaginative left wing propaganda they never aspired, urged Chamberlain at the decisive moment to have the courage of his convictions and place Halifax, even though he was a Peer, in the office to which his experience and record so richly entitled him. They argued forcibly that to have a Foreign Secretary safely removed from the heat of the House of Commons battle was just what was required to meet the delicate international situation. Further, it was impressed upon Chamberlain that it was never intended under the Parliament or any other Act that the best man should not be eligible for a Cabinet post simply because he was in the House of Lords. There was, in fact, no such " convention of the Constitution ", and if there was, it should be resisted.

Accordingly the day after the great Lords debate

came the expected news from 10 Downing Street that Halifax was to be Foreign Secretary, while R. A. Butler, a promising young Conservative who had served his ministerial apprenticeship on Indian affairs, was to be the Under-Secretary. The delay in announcing Halifax's appointment, together with Chamberlain's avowed intention of answering all important Foreign Affairs questions in the Commons, led to widespread rumours, which persisted, that Halifax had taken office on special terms; but such was not the case, he neither laid down nor submitted to any limiting conditions. Although the Labour Party carried through its resolve to challenge the appointment of a Foreign Secretary, as Attlee put it, " safely tucked away in the House of Lords ", the most noticeable features of all the varied comment in Parliament and Press was the unanimous appreciation of Halifax the man. Nothing showed more clearly how high was his personal prestige than the chorus of praise that greeted him from all quarters at a time when political nerves were on edge and party dissensions unleashed. Only in a moment of exasperation did Herbert Morrison describe him as a " weakling ", otherwise the Labour Party did not forget their historic collaboration with him over Indian reform. Perhaps the most significant commendation came from Churchill. " The new British Foreign Secretary Lord Halifax must not ", he wrote, " be dismissed as a pious devotee of ' peace at any price '. Hitherto he has wielded undue influence in the Cabinet as a vague sincere advocate of making friends with everybody. Now in the collar of a great Department he will be brought face to face with grim duties arising from the movement of events, and I for one shall not assume he will be found unworthy of them."

. . . .

When Labour moved the adjournment of the House to challenge Halifax's appointment it committed a tactical blunder; underlying the move was, of course, an attempt to attack the entire policy on which Halifax and Chamberlain were embarking, but their efforts to condemn appeasement by protecting the rights of the House of Commons while at the same time praising Halifax led only to their own confusion. Sinclair was unwilling to follow Attlee. What other member would you prefer to Halifax? he asked him. Chamberlain blandly admitted that all things being equal he would have preferred a Foreign Secretary from the House of Commons, but that all things were not equal. Attlee had vehemently protested that Halifax's merits had nothing to do with the case; they had everything to do with it, Chamberlain retorted; there was, he said, no man on the front bench or off it who was better qualified. But the *tour de force* came from Churchill who, after reaching the nadir of his political fortunes during the Abdication crisis when Beverley Baxter confidently predicted that he had fallen never to rise again, was showing a supremacy in policy debate as well as an insight into the designs of dictatorship which made him every day more formidable. His mastery of Parliamentary tactics was never seen to better advantage than in this debate on Halifax. Here was a perfect blend of irony and barbed criticism which was a lesson to the serious Socialists and a warning to the pedestrian Chamberlain.

First he argued that there was no serious constitutional issue involved—" the great men whom I met long years ago would never have been shocked by the idea of a Foreign Secretary in the House of Lords. They would have been very much shocked by a Foreign Secretary in the House of Commons." The only difference between then and now was a wider franchise, a Conservative Party suffering from " a superfluity of adipose strength ". " We must not have anything derogatory to the House of Commons, but when we have the Prime Minister here what is the good of worrying about a Foreign Secretary? What is the point of crying out for the moon when you have the sun, when you have that bright orb from whose effulgent beams the lesser luminaries derive their radiance? There is no good working up a grievance on that . . . I am not quite sure about the sun. I gather from the astronomers that there have been some spots on the sun which have entailed a great deal of unseasonable weather and some of those queer Northern lights which presage strange events." It was for Chamberlain to decide whether he could take the strain he was imposing upon himself, but if a man tried to do more than he possibly could the only result was that many important things got left undone. Then followed a devastating recital of the other possible candidates for Foreign Secretary among the Cabinet. Sir Samuel Hoare " once bitten twice shy ", Inskip " very impressive physically ", Kingsley Wood with his cherubic bland smile confronting scowling dictators. " In fact one only realized how good these Ministers were in their jobs when one began to think of them in some other job."

There was no doubt, in the unhappy circumstances which had arisen, that Halifax was the man to bear the burden. Having known him for years and served with him for two years in the same Department he was confident, though differing from him, that he would do justice to the facts of the events as they were presented to him. " He is a man not only of integrity and high character but force and courage which, if ultimately provoked, will be found at least as lasting and enduring as that of any man on either side of the House." A great experiment had been launched. Churchill thought it most unpromising, but he recognized that it had been launched with conviction and that those who had launched it had paid a considerable price both in their own political interests and in our interests in Europe. Surely it was essential that it should be conducted by hands which were apt and inclined to carry it through, and by the men who really believed in the policy they had adopted and on which they had to a large extent staked their reputations. A stream of interrogatory pin-pricks was no way to control and guide the foreign policy of a great country aspiring to lead in Europe. " The less the Foreign Secretary speaks the more he says." This was the most formidable and penetrating analysis of Halifax's status, tasks, and prospects the House was to hear, it remained only to see whether Churchill's sombre estimate would be borne out by the facts.

Halifax began his duties by a long consultation with Lord Perth, who had returned from Rome for instructions. Parallel with Anglo-Italian appeasement he made a vigorous effort to take up the negotiations with Germany where they had been left off after his inconclusive talk at Berchtesgaden. Henderson was instructed to expedite an interview with Hitler which had been designed for February but which had been postponed as a direct result of the upheavals of the previous month. Henderson has described the fiasco of his effort to talk reason with Hitler, " who was in a vile temper and made no effort to conceal it ". During all the time that Henderson expounded the most mild and conciliatory proposals, which included a British contribution to the Colonial question, " he remained crouching in his armchair with the most ferocious scowl on his face ". In Colonies he evinced no interest, but if Germans were oppressed anywhere he must and would intervene, and if he did he would act like lightning. Behind the bluster he was uneasily groping for the political pretext to give Schuschnigg the *coup de grâce.* Only fifteen per cent of the Austrian populace supported the Schuschnigg regime, he declared, and Austria must be allowed to vote.

Hitler's discomfiture was evidence that the Austrian coup had not even yet taken its final shape, and this impression was heightened when it was known that on 9th March Ribbentrop would be visiting England to present to the King his letters of recall as Ambassador. Ribbentrop had no sooner arrived, however, than Schuschnigg made his last desperate decision to call Hitler's bluff. Whatever its advantages in the wider strategy of branding Hitler as the aggressor, it was tactically a fatal manœuvre. Not the least of its consequences was its catastrophic effect on the political negotiations in London, for it seems to have taken Ribbentrop as much by surprise as Halifax. The German Foreign Minister's first reaction was to rush back to Berlin, but he apparently received a ukase from Hitler to stay where he was, and do everything in his power to pacify Chamberlain and Halifax. On the afternoon of the 10th he had a two and a half hour interview with Halifax in which he vehemently denounced Schuschnigg's " subterfuge " and maintained Hitler's rabid objection to British Press criticism. Halifax spoke in general terms about the threat to confidence but does not seem to have adopted a particularly forceful attitude. One reason for his diffidence may have been the embarrassing knowledge that France, which like Britain and Germany had not escaped a domestic convulsion, was at the moment of impending crisis without a Government. Perhaps he hoped until the last moment that Mussolini would intervene with some peaceful formula, but when Schuschnigg rang through urgently to the Duce's private residence there was no reply.

That evening Lord and Lady Halifax, along with most of the Cabinet, attended an elaborate farewell reception at the German Embassy, but it was a tense and uncomfortable occasion. The next day Hitler first demanded the postponement of the plebiscite. This was no sooner conceded than a second ultimatum with a time limit of a few hours was delivered, requiring President Miklas to replace Schuschnigg by the Nazi puppet Seyss-Inquart. It was against this ominous background that Ribbentrop was entertained to lunch at Downing Street. Afterwards Chamberlain spoke in stronger terms than Halifax had used on the deplorable effect on Anglo-German relations that precipitate action by Germany would be bound to have; but the sole result of these remonstrances was to increase Ribbentrop's self-assertiveness. What was taking place was a purely German concern, Britain had no right to interfere with the Führer who was going to the defence of the Austrian National Socialists who had been obliged to apply for his help against Schuschnigg. It was a chastening introduction to the efficacy of appeasement. As Nazi tanks rumbled over the Austrian frontier and Nazi planes droned over Vienna, Halifax, it is said, paced up and down his spacious room in the Foreign Office and murmured "Horrible! horrible! I never thought they would do it!" Was it to be his destiny simply to watch, as his kinsman Grey had done before him, the lamps go out all over Europe? "I do not fancy that any British policy short of war could have checked the events of the last ten days," he confessed in the House of Lords post-mortem on the Anschluss. "The world has been brought, therefore, face to face with the extremely ugly truth that neither treaty texts nor international law have any influence when dealing with power politics, and that in that sphere, force, and force alone, decides, I say that quite objectively and, I hope, without passion, merely as a statement of a plain fact."

There was to be no respite. The absorption of Austria at once brought Czechoslovakia to the forefront of the troubled international scene. Hitler's coup had turned the great national defences of the Hartz mountains, and in his turgid tirade of 20th February Hitler had declared himself the protector of the ten million Germans in "two of the States adjoining our frontiers". While Chamberlain at the time of Eden's resignation was warning Vienna and by implication Prague of the collapse of all League guarantees, Delbos solemnly renewed France's pledge to fulfil her obligations to the Czechs. The Nazis immediately after their Austrian coup gratuitously offered the Czechs three assurances.

Goering informed the Czech Minister in Berlin that German troops had been given strict orders to keep at least fifteen kilometres from the Czech border, while Neurath told him that Germany still considered herself bound by the German-Czechoslovak Arbitration Convention of October 1925 which was an annexe to Locarno. Finally Goering on two occasions, once on behalf of Hitler, gave his word that it would be the earnest endeavour of the German Government to improve German-Czech relations. Jan Masaryk, the Czech Minister in London, told me at the time that he gave some credence to Goering's assurances in as far as he had been careful to give his word of honour as a Prussian officer, no doubt being aware that Nazi protestations were by now at a discount.

As an interim measure Halifax at once let Hitler know that the British Government took note of these assurances and asked permission, which was given, to place Parliament in possession of their actual terms. " By these assurances solemnly given and more than once repeated we naturally expect the German Government to abide. And if indeed they desire to see European peace maintained, as I earnestly hope they do, there is no quarter of Europe in which it is more vital that undertakings should be scrupulously respected." That was his comment on 16th March; during the following week the Cabinet was absorbed in producing a definitive statement which was duly read out by Chamberlain and Halifax on 24th March and which was a cumbrous attempt to avoid definition in advance of events. All that emerged was that Britain's obligations under the Covenant " may have no less significance " than her " definite obligations to particular countries ", namely to France, Belgium, Portugal, Iraq and Egypt. The one decisive passage in which the Government refused to add Czechoslovakia to the list of countries covered by " prior guarantee " was the only one to provoke a roar of cheers from the serried ranks of Conservative back-benchers; but hardly less significant was the brusque rejection of the Soviet proposal, made on 17th March, for a conference of all interested Powers to see what could be done to prevent further aggression.

CHAPTER XXXI

APPEASEMENT AND "THE MAY CRISIS"

In April appeasement began to come out into the open and Halifax's silent labour to bear fruit. Firstly, on the 16th after weeks of the most intensive and intimate negotiation, the Anglo-Italian Agreement was duly signed in Rome by Perth and Ciano. Halifax had clearly set great store on the settlement with Italy—was he not identified in the public mind with a mandate to see it through? Purely in terms of the mechanism of diplomacy, it was with its twenty-two separate documents something of a masterpiece, and covered all contingencies from one end of the Mediterranean to the other, but as a political contribution to appeasement exactly the same conditions applied to it as had rendered the Gentlemen's Agreement of January 1937 null and void. It was not, as Government apologists asserted, simply a matter of preparation of public or even official opinion, everything depended on the spirit in which Mussolini either wished or, after the Anschluss, was in a position to interpret it. But the Agreement was unusual in form, as in addition to the annexes to the main Protocol there were six letters exchanged between Perth and Ciano which required no direct negotiation in themselves but which went to make up the Agreement as a whole. Two of these aroused intense controversy. On the one hand, the British Government insisted on "a settlement of the Spanish question as a prerequisite of the entry into force of the Agreement between the two Governments"; this implied apparently not the end of fighting in Spain but simply the withdrawal by Mussolini of all or some of his volunteers. In return Great Britain undertook to raise the question of Italian Ethiopia at Geneva by urging the League to release its members from the general pledge and leave the question of recognition to their individual discretion; whereupon Great Britain would at once accord recognition. Here was a residue of doubt and deception which was to cause Halifax grave embarrassment.

Perhaps the most immediate grounds for satisfaction was the impact the Agreement made upon France, where at the beginning of April there had been yet another change of Government, involving this time a significant swing to the right. Edouard Daladier and Georges Bonnet, the new Prime Minister and Foreign Secretary, not only embodied political forces acceptable to the all-powerful Senate Finance Committee but also sympathized with Chamberlain's and Halifax's approach to appeasement. Paul Boncour during his brief term at the Quai d'Orsay showed signs of being restive about Britain's plans for recognizing the Italian conquest of Abyssinia, but with Bonnet there were no difficulties at all. He was ready to fall in with any device Halifax might propose, but in addition steps were taken to liquidate Franco-Italian differences on the analogy of the Anglo-Italian Pact.

At the end of April Daladier and Bonnet visited London, and the whole scope of the Anglo-French alliance was reviewed. Although it was intended to cover all the ground of British and French interests from Spain to Shanghai, a particularly urgent context was given to the conversations as the result of a provocative speech delivered at Karlsbad by Konrad Henlein, the Sudeten German leader. With perfect timing and with the usual facility of a puppet Hitler he set out the famous Eight Points which comprised the current objectives of his party and which finally rebuffed the efforts of the Czech Prime Minister Hodza to evolve a Nationality Statute codifying and enlarging the existing rights of all minorities in Czechoslovakia. Henlein now claimed full equality of status for Sudeten Germans and Czechs, which meant the abandonment of the concept of a Czechoslovak State containing a German minority. He demanded that boundaries should be fixed for the territory settled by Germans, that there should be an autonomous German administration of this area together with guarantees for those living outside it. The last of the eight points was perhaps the most alarming in that it insisted on full liberty for Germans to proclaim their Germanism and their adhesion to the " ideology of Germans "—in other words what Hitler a few days later described as his programme of " blood, fire and personality " was to be allowed to trample on the delicate experiment of Czech democracy. But more alarming to the French and British Governments was an additional demand even more presumptuous than " the eight points ", for he insisted as well upon " a complete revision of Czechoslovak foreign policy ", including the abandonment of the alliances with France and Russia and, it may be assumed, the transference of Czech politics and economy into the German system. This last demand was obviously the voice of Hitler himself and it represented his most ambitious assault to date on the Franco-Soviet Pact.

What was Halifax's reaction to these manœuvres? Two Press " forecasts " of the Anglo-French talks provide significant clues to his and the Cabinet's attitude. " There is some reason to believe ", wrote the well-informed Diplomatic Correspondent of the *Sunday Times*, " that Lord Halifax would like to raise the question of the Franco-Soviet Pact. He is hardly likely to ask France to abandon her alliance, because that would be courting a blank refusal. Lord Halifax will, therefore, probably confine himself to suggesting that the alliance—of which Herr Hitler has made so much capital—should be kept in the background of French policy." Even more frank was his colleague on *The Times*, who commented that " on the British side it may be mentioned again during the talks with what little enthusiasm the Government regard the Franco-Soviet Pact, but there is no truth in suggestions that a request will be made for its discontinuance. It is a sleeping dog; let it lie." To all outward appearances, however, it was awake and growling, and Halifax gave no public sign that he wished to muzzle it. Daladier told the British Ministers emphatically that if there was a German invasion of Czechoslovakia France would honour her obligations to go to the Czechs' assistance. Bonnet developed the theme that there should be concerted Anglo-French economic help for Czechoslovakia and that any Nazi attempt to impose political demands on Prague by closing her frontiers with Germany should be met by ensuring Czechoslovakia's access to the sea by way of Poland; then Czech trade could pass through Gdynia instead of through Hamburg or Trieste. This project was referred to experts and duly shelved, but it should be noted as representing the first and last effort to secure Polish collaboration in preserving the fabric of the Czech State. In reply to Daladier's firm reassertion of the Czech alliance, Chamberlain and Halifax simply repeated the formula of 24th March, repudiating commitments in advance of the event, but there were no illusions on either side that an invasion of Czechoslovakia would almost certainly lead to general war involving France's integrity and therefore British intervention.

The Czechs were satisfied, they had never expected Halifax to go beyond Grey's traditional reserve, but in order to forestall war, the British thesis of diplomatic action gained the day. Even the decision to intensify Staff contacts was, from the political view-point, whittled down when Halifax specially invited the Italian and German Ambassadors to see him a few minutes after the French Ministers had left Downing Street and explained to them that the Staff talks were purely defensive and in direct descent from the Locarno Agreement of 19th March 1936. Henlein's Karlsbad demands were rejected as in themselves unacceptable but as providing the pretext for a joint Anglo-French intervention in Prague which duly took place on 7th May when the British and French Ministers told the Czech Foreign Minister Krofta of the willingness of their Governments to give all possible help to assure a peaceful solution of the Sudeten problem within the framework of the Czechoslovak constitution. They urged that there should be greater concessions than those contained in the proposed Nationality Statute which Hodza had originally proposed to put into force at the beginning of July. The principal although unforeseen effect of this initiative was simply to hold up the Czech Government in their efforts to produce a legislative programme that would secure the allegiance of the various party groups. It would have been wiser to allow the Nationality Statute to become law and to have advised the Czech Government to make further concessions afterwards. Benes and Hodza were complacent, however, as they were still confident of Anglo-French intentions and did not think it wise to reject advice from Paris or London.

The second promising feature of the London conversations was the apparent unwillingness of the Ministers to regard Herr Henlein as a free agent or to submit to the German argument that the Czech-German dispute was just a "family quarrel". On the other hand Halifax seems to have hoped that by informing Hitler of the British and French initiative in Prague he might be persuaded to follow suit, and that then the way would be open to resume negotiations for a comprehensive settlement. If he had such expectation it was soon to be disappointed. Hitler and Ribbentrop were in Italy enjoying Mussolini's flamboyant hospitality and aggressively testifying to Axis solidarity when Henderson paid his first visit to the German Foreign Office, but neither on that occasion nor when he finally saw Ribbentrop was he able to secure the desired reaction. Hitler, he was told, warmly welcomed the British *démarche* but continued to regard the Sudeten problem as a purely internal question for the Czechs to settle with Henlein. Henderson, if his book *Failure of a Mission* is a reliable guide, seems to have accepted this rebuff without undue remonstrance on the simple assumption that Hitler was in no great hurry. When ten days later Europe seemed to be trembling on the brink of war Henderson from his vantage-point was at pains to minimize the peril.

But before the crisis of 21st May took shape Halifax spent a gloomy week at Geneva which for all the buoyancy and assurance of his various speeches to the League Council could not conceal his own distress. During that week a tribe of Italian journalists returned to Geneva to watch Halifax pay his tribute to the gospel of Fascist force by inviting the League to remove from its midst Abyssinia as the victim of aggression, and by resisting the plea of the Spanish Government to relax the cramping provisions of non-intervention. A heavy price was paid for Britain's friendship with Italy during those bitter days; nothing less than the burial of the League of Nations as an instrument of peace, the formal abandonment of the system which twenty years before Halifax had called the one worth-while result of the last war. The secret procedure with its embittered and unedifying wrangle over credentials of Haile Selassie and his advisers was an ordeal which undoubtedly distressed him. There are several witnesses to confirm that the conclusions he drew, though of little comfort either for Abyssinia or the Spanish Government in their public and official form, did not represent the whole story. Halifax returned from the deserted halls of Peace, more emotionally and morally disturbed than at any time since the launching of appeasement, and on purely political grounds a long informal talk with Litvinov, the Soviet Foreign Minister, must have set at rest any lingering doubts as to Soviet intentions if Czechoslovakia took down the sword in self-defence. Much of his apologia to the Lords was devoted to the moral conflict in his own mind. "I do think," he asserted, "that in this matter it is true that two ideals—righteousness and peace—are in conflict, and you have to choose between the unpractical devotion to the high purpose that you know you cannot achieve except by a war you do not mean to have, and the practical victory for peace that you can achieve. I cannot hesitate between these two when both my conscience and my duty to my fellow men impel me directly in the direction of peace." The recognition of Italy's conquest was thus "a question of political judgment" and not of "eternal and immutable moralities". In Spain, however, he detected no such conflict; the sooner peace could be reached the more righteous it would be.

Our Agreement with Italy gave us a stake in Franco's victory, our friendship with France implied a solution acceptable to the Republicans. At the same time the essential corollary to the Anglo-Italian Agreement was a similar Pact between Italy and France: the balance of political forces was such that the mediation Halifax offered at this time can hardly have been weighted against either side. The weakness of the British position was that by sponsoring non-intervention from the outset, it lost all power of manœuvre, and when Halifax proclaimed that he was no less anxious than his critics to serve the interests of democracy, his tactics are open to question but not his sincerity. Hitler undoubtedly took the British offer of mediation seriously, and in order to forestall any such untoward development put pressure on Mussolini to keep the Spanish cauldron boiling. Mussolini obligingly responded, and speaking at Genoa on 14th May cast doubt on the possible success of Franco-Italian conversations which were then in progress "because in one extremely vital matter, the war in Spain, we stand on opposite sides of the barricades". But this typical example of the Duce's braggadocio caused no particular alarm in Paris, where an influential school of thought was carefully weighing up the advantages of a hostile as against a neutral Italy and arguing that Prague could be better defended in the plains of Lombardy than on the Rhine frontier.

A sinister meaning was given to this thesis by reports from London in themselves far more disturbing than anything Mussolini had to say and, it was noted, significantly coinciding with Halifax's absence in Geneva. In the first place it was strongly rumoured that there had been powerful support in the Cabinet for the view that if war broke out over the Sudeten question Britain should not intervene unless Italy joined Germany. But even more disturbing was the despatch published in the *Montreal Star* on 15th May from the well-known Canadian correspondent in London, Joseph Driscoll, who described himself as " now privileged to shed what can truly be called official light on the real British attitude ". Chamberlain bluntly refused to admit or deny that he was the source of Driscoll's drastic information. But Daladier, Hitler and Mussolini were no doubt satisfied from the outset that Driscoll was merely filling in background material supplied by the Prime Minister to himself and a number of other American journalists on 10th May at a luncheon arranged for the purpose by Lady Astor. While Halifax was having an encouraging exchange of views with Litvinov Driscoll was discovering that " nothing seems clearer than that the British do not expect to fight for Czechoslovakia and do not anticipate that Russia or France will either. That being so, the Czechs must accede to the German demands, if reasonable." Driscoll was actually inspired to suggest instead of cantonization with which German propaganda was playing at this time, frontier revision which " would entail moving the frontier back for some miles to divorce this outer fringe from Prague and marry it to Berlin. A smaller but sounder Czechoslovakia would result."

. . . .

It is not surprising that Halifax returned to the Foreign Office to find a diplomatic situation ominously similar to that which encouraged Hitler to make his Rhineland coup; in other words that the relations between Great Britain and Italy, Italy and France, France and Great Britain were all sufficiently ambiguous, incoherent and paralysed to admit of the lightning stroke which would involve no effective retaliation from the Western Powers. During the third week in May reports reached London through the British Intelligence Service of considerable troop concentrations moving in battle order through Saxony to the Czech frontier. On the afternoon of Friday, 20th May, Benes summoned a conference of the Supreme Defence Council and of the Cabinet and immediate mobilization was agreed upon, while the army demanded the calling up of five-year classes of reservists. On the same afternoon Halifax instructed Henderson to obtain assurances that there was no truth in the widespread reports about German troop movements. Aware that the formal denial of the Secretary of State, von Weizsacker, would probably not suffice in view of the urgency of Halifax's request and the unhappy memory of falsehoods handed out to the British military attachés during the Austrian coup, Henderson asked Weizsacker to telephone General Keitel on his behalf for an authoritative statement. This was forthcoming within an hour, together with assurances to the Czech Minister in Berlin and to the Czech Government in Prague. Halifax at once transmitted the information received to Benes, and it apparently arrived while the Cabinet and Defence Council were still sitting. The Army Chiefs, in view of the British initiative, limited the mobilization to a one-year class and picked technical troops, but within six hours an army of 400,000 men with tanks, armoured cars and heavy artillery was ready to defend the frontiers.

The tangled events of the next day are blurred over both in Henderson's book, *The Failure of a Mission*, and in the official Government statement which Chamberlain and Halifax read out in Parliament on 23rd May. Henderson, convinced that the conclusions drawn from the British show of strength at this time proved disastrous, seems to be putting forward the special plea that there was no show of strength at all, but such an apologia is neither necessary nor convincing. " In fairness to the Czechs ", he writes, " it must be realized that much abnormal military activity—judged by normal standards—was continually going on in Germany, and that unskilled agents and observers can easily be misled." Can this airy sentiment really be upheld against the grave decisions reached by President Benes, who throughout the whole Czech crisis behaved with the most cautious correctitude? Does his bland account of the two military attachés who were sent by him to scour Saxony and Silesia on 21st and who not unnaturally drew a blank, take away from Halifax's drastic action in sending him three times during that fateful day to remonstrate with Ribbentrop? During the first interview Ribbentrop spoke to Henderson in cannibalistic terms. Two Sudeten Germans had been murdered at Eger; in return the Czechs would "be exterminated, women and children and all". His mood was almost identical with the aggressive brutality he was to display in September 1938 and August 1939, and so unsatisfactory and sinister did it appear that Halifax told Henderson to see him again the same afternoon. This time the warning contained in the Government statement of 24th March was repeated, with suitable emphasis on the point that His Majesty's Government could not guarantee that they would not be forced by events to become themselves involved. "Ribbentrop, who had been highly excited in the morning, had become sullen in the afternoon." He was quite unwilling to advise Henlein to observe the moderation we were asking the Czech Government to show. "If a general war ensued, it would, he declared, be a war of aggression provoked by France, and Germany would fight as she had done in 1914."

Halifax was still not satisfied, and the lights burnt late at the Foreign Office on that Saturday night as he made one more effort to dissuade Ribbentrop from giving violent advice and Hitler from listening to it. Henderson confines himself to saying that he conveyed to Ribbentrop through the Secretary of State (Ribbentrop having already left for Berchtesgaden to report to Hitler) "a personal message from Lord Halifax drawing his attention to the risk of precipitate action leading to a general conflagration, the only result of which might prove to be the destruction of European civilization. So far as official action went, this ended the so-called May 21st incident at Berlin." It is doubtful whether the verdict of history will support this niggardly estimate, it will probably concur with the view of a distinguished American commentator who asserted that "war probably was nearer at this moment than it had been at any time since the Armistice".[1] Furthermore, when a full

[1] *When There Is No Peace* by Hamilton Fish Armstrong, page 32.

and balanced account can be given, Halifax's influence and initiative may well emerge as the paramount factor that made for peace and postponed the crisis, that the Cabinet satisfied itself with Keitel's assurance and that Henderson's subsequent interviews were undertaken on Halifax's sole responsibility. " I believe ", writes Wickham Steed, " that he was stroke of the Government boat just then; and I should not be surprised to learn that the 'appeasers' took care he should not stroke it again in the following summer and autumn."

Halifax has never revealed in any public speech the grounds for his anxiety nor has he drawn any moral from his action. G. E. R. Gedye, admittedly not an impartial witness, but for all his strong political convictions first and foremost a brilliant journalist with unrivalled access to information in Prague, gives it as his considered opinion that the German design during this mysterious week-end was " to make a lightning dash into an unprepared Czechoslovakia, rush to the 'language frontier' and declare the Sudeten land annexed ". Not until there is definite evidence to the contrary it would seem that some such reading of what was in Hitler's mind prompted Halifax and Benes to take the decisive steps they did. Eighteen months afterwards Halifax said simply " whatever may be the exact truth of those days, the immediate anxiety which was aroused was the measure of the extent to which, even then, the German Government had succeeded in destroying confidence ". It would, of course, be idle to suggest that he regarded the immediate assumption that the Democracies had gained a great victory or that the collective principle had been vindicated as other than dangerous and delusive. He had responded firmly and clearly to a particular set of conditions as presented to him and he was no more bluffing in his resolve to preserve peace by negotiation than Hitler was in his readiness, even desire, to secure his demands by war. Hitler was gravely offended at the jubilation of the Foreign Press and allowed himself the luxury of a " nerve storm " which culminated in his decision on 28th May to order gradual mobilization of the army and to initiate work on the vast Siegfried Line, and to order that the whole Czech dispute should be settled on his own terms by October 1st.

One incidental victory for Halifax's firmness was that it gave Hitler a limit to his immediate hopes of driving a wedge between London and Paris. Halifax had throughout maintained close contact with the Quai d'Orsay, and a timely speech at Leeds by Paul Reynaud, who also had a long interview with Halifax on 20th May at the Foreign Office, enhanced the appearance of solidarity. Actually the strong sentiments expressed by Reynaud only helped to strengthen Hitler in his determination to rid Prague once and for all of Franco-Soviet influences.

But during the next month there were all the outward appearances of *détente,* and public attention during June was switched over to a new and menacing feature of the Spanish situation, the deliberate and intensive bombing of British ships by Franco's war planes. " It is pre-Nyon piracy again ", declared *The Times*, " which requires Nyon methods of countering it." None were forthcoming, however, and the Government and the Anglo-Italian Agreement made increasingly heavy weather as the summer progressed. By the beginning of July, too, it was obvious that the Czech Government and the Sudeten German Party were no nearer agreement but drifting steadily towards deadlock.

. . . .

In order to forestall the imminent danger Halifax took his second decisive step in approaching Prague to find out whether a British adviser would be acceptable in the Sudeten dispute. Attached to the enquiry was the polite but firm intimation that if the offer was turned down, the fact that it had been made and rejected would be duly published. It is not as yet possible to assert confidently who originated the idea of sending Runciman to Prague, but for all practical purposes the detailed responsibility of commending him and his mission to Europe fell upon Halifax. The technique adopted was informal and secretive. During July the attention of the British public was riveted upon the State visit of the King and Queen to Paris, which, for all the protestations against European *blocs*, was the democratic counterblast to Hitler's Roman triumph; and it was under the shadow of all this elaborate ceremonial the Runciman Mission was safely launched—although " launching " was perhaps a euphemism from Runciman's point of view. " I quite understand," he remarked after Halifax had carefully explained his function, "you are setting me adrift in a small boat in mid-Atlantic." "That is exactly the position," Halifax replied, but, he might have added, "I have taken steps to provide you with chart and compass."

For the world was startled to learn that the day before leaving for Paris Halifax had been entertaining, not at the Foreign Office but at his home in Eaton Square, the mysterious Captain Wiedemann, Hitler's trusted A.D.C. and former commanding officer. *The Times* Diplomatic Correspondent gave a lengthy and tendentious report of this confidential interview. Wiedemann was on special mission to London to convey a message of goodwill to the British Government from the Chancellor. Hitler, it seemed, "sincerely wished relations between the two countries to be improved". There were "no fundamental differences" and "everything was capable of arrangement". The German Government was anxious for a peaceful solution of the Sudeten problem though it was disappointed that Henlein had not as yet received the draft of the revised Nationalities Statute. In this bowdlerized version of the talk Halifax was described as welcoming Hitler's renewed assurances and putting up the one solid proposal that the German Government should collaborate in the pressing problem of refugees.

But behind the façade was the familiar German technique. All the evidence reaching him suggested that the time was ripe to drive another Nazi wedge between Anglo-French understanding, and although he was anxious for British collaboration to wear down Czech resistance from within he was not sure that the Runciman project would help and not hinder his purposes. On the general issue of Anglo-French solidarity Halifax did not waver, and rebuffed Wiedemann by rejecting outright his proposal that Goering should visit London to settle all outstanding differences with the British Government. There could be no such negotiations, he asserted, until the Czech dispute had been peacefully settled. Nor did Halifax give Wiedemann any reason to hope that the British Government would countenance a solution devised by Runciman or anyone else that would affect the sovereignty or the foreign policy of the Czechs.

The great French journalist, Pertinax, in a powerful review of the situation as it appeared to him at the end of

July, emphasized that the time factor was Hitler's greatest preoccupation. " Is time working for or against a Germanic Central Europe? If the Führer delays until the autumn will he not become a prisoner of peace? And could his regime fit in with such a denouement? For all his readiness to conciliate, Halifax did not provide Wiedemann with the essential clues he had been sent by Hitler to gather. Rather the impression was gained in the Wilhelmstrasse that the Foreign Secretary might well prove recalcitrant. That he had not moved so far in the German direction as, for instance, Henderson, can be seen from the scant enthusiasm with which the Ambassador greeted the whole idea of mediation. He describes telegraphing to Halifax in July that since there was not the slightest prospect of the Sudeten Germans being willing to accept the agreed settlement " on the basis of the maintenance of the purely national character of the Czech State, I had little confidence in the likelihood of the efforts of an independent mediator proving more successful than diplomatic action. I accordingly put forward the suggestion that the Italian Government should be invited to join with His Majesty's Government in proposing to the French and German Governments a Four-Power Conference to settle the problem."

The general trend of British policy had undoubtedly caused concern at the Quai d'Orsay, and on 12th July prompted Daladier to reaffirm in the most solemn terms the French pledge to Prague and to write to Chamberlain about his misgivings; Chamberlain replied cordially that the Foreign Secretary would, during the Royal visit, explain everything personally. It must have been a somewhat embarrassing mission for Halifax, and the utmost secrecy was maintained. But when it was learnt that for his talks with Daladier and Bonnet no permanent officials from either Foreign Office were present, nor even a stenographer to keep the usual diplomatic record of what was said, it was impossible to suppress speculation. Further, in spite of the reticence, Halifax was no more successful in making Daladier sponsor Runciman than Henderson was with Ribbentrop; but whereas Henderson was subjected to truculence and bad temper Halifax met only with polite irony. The French Embassy, Daladier politely informed him, was capable of doing all that was required in the way of "parallel action". Quite apart from the natural resentment at being confronted by Halifax with a *fait accompli* (for Basil Newton, the British Minister, was instructed to see Benes the day before Halifax saw Daladier) the French Government did not feel justified in joining in the mediation in case their action should seem to cast doubt on their fidelity to the Czechs or their confidence in the British.

"Pertinax" brings out in his article two points of historical interest; first that in the middle of June the French Ministers had already discouraged a similar British initiative on the grounds that it would only encourage Henlein in his intransigence, and secondly that earlier in the same month the British Cabinet proposed the neutralization of Czechoslovakia but that this was also rejected by France. By sending Runciman to Prague Halifax shifted the centre of gravity of Britain's moral commitment to France, but its validity was in no way undermined. "It should be insisted here," wrote Pertinax, "the mediation of Lord Halifax does not at all suppress the assurances given to French policy, not only in the Anglo-French Conference of April 29th, but also later."

CHAPTER XXXII

MUNICH REARGUARD

WITH Runciman's arrival in Prague the Czech drama enters on its Second Act, and the remorseless sequence from Prague to Nuremberg, from Nuremberg to Berchtesgaden, from Berchtesgaden to Godesberg and from Godesberg to Munich has already evoked a small library of revelation and criticism. In the generally accepted list of dramatis personae Halifax emerges as a secondary character, a mere Horatio to Chamberlain's Hamlet, nor is it allowed that he exercised any influence over the Prime Minister comparable to that of Bonnet over Daladier. A full assessment of his role lies in the future; for the present the part he played seems muffled, disguised and inconclusive, but this much may be said, when his policy and influence have been duly weighed, and when all his public utterances have been taken into account, the more ephemeral sifted from the deeper arguments, he does not seem to take his place among the most fervent or formative of the " men of Munich ".

Throughout August the situation rapidly deteriorated and was based upon anxious surmise about the terms of Hitler's forthcoming speech to the Nazi rally at Nuremberg: Halifax, however, showed no inclination to repudiate the firm procedure of 21st May. By the middle of the month there was widespread alarm over the vast scale of German military manœuvres, at the same time work on the Siegfried Line was being hurried forward at feverish speed—more than 400,000 men, it was estimated, being employed on Germany's Western wall. These developments were not allowed to pass without severe warning from Britain, and it should be noted that Henderson was ordered to deliver the memorandum over the signatures of Chamberlain and Halifax drawing the Führer's " earnest attention to the apprehensions caused in Europe by these measures " by way of

Lammers, the Head of Reichschancellory, for direct transmission to Hitler and thus leave out the obstructive Ribbentrop. The only result of this manœuvre was to arouse Ribbentrop's wrath, and it was he and not Hitler who finally replied with typical arrogance that the German Government could not discuss measures of internal concern with other Governments, adding that British efforts in Prague " had only served to increase Czech intransigence ". On the 24th Halifax gave his formal approval to Runciman's interim proposal that the Sudeten Germans should be granted cantonal self-government. The French could have no substantial grounds for complaint in this. In commending Runciman to Parliament Halifax had made much of the analogy between the Czech problem and the evolution of the British Commonwealth which had come about by means of " the principle of partnership in self-administration ". Runciman's desperate effort, however, to stem the rising tide of violence was of no avail, and on 27th August Henderson was recalled for consultation.

The questions before the Government were how to meet the crisis that Hitler's Nuremberg speech must inevitably provoke, how to assuage his fury beforehand and how to continue the negotiations afterwards. Henderson's advice for both dilemmas carried the day. In the first place Chamberlain's speech of 28th September summarizing the events leading up to Munich, describes how His Majesty's Government desired " to impress the seriousness of the situation upon the German Government without risking a further aggravation of the situation by any formal representations which might have been interpreted by the German Government as a public rebuff, as had been the case in regard to the representations on 21st May ". In other words the Cabinet no longer placed reliance on Halifax's diplomatic offensive, but he did not give in without a struggle and, it was rumoured, registered his disapproval by refusing to give a much publicized Government speech of warning which, in order to conform to the Cabinet's mandate, had now to be a muted trumpet sounding an inaudible alarm. The expected pronouncements came not from Halifax but from Simon in the course of an otherwise routine address at Lanark. In itself the speech was no more than an indecisive reiteration of the Government statement of 24th

March, but it is important not simply for giving encouragement to the Nazi extremists but for marking a change in the balance of power within the British Government.

From henceforward an Inner Cabinet emerges, consisting of Simon and Hoare in addition to Chamberlain and Halifax, with day to day control over the crisis. For all practical purposes this Quadrumvirate was answerable neither to Parliament nor the rest of the Cabinet, and consisting as it did of a Prime Minister who acted as his own Foreign Secretary in the Commons and two ambitious ex-Foreign Secretaries, it involved an unprecedented subordination of the Foreign Office and its political chief. It may well be asked why Halifax ever consented to such a status for himself and his department. First, although he might differ over means, there was no fundamental breach over the end, which was Peace by negotiation. Then again, he had no wish to embarrass Chamberlain, whose courage and initiative in assuming such a heavy personal burden he deeply admired and was anxious only to underwrite; for Hoare also he had a deep personal respect bred out of their collaboration over India. His relationship with Simon, however, was not so close, their careers and opinions had clashed. Halifax had no particular sympathy for Simon's cold and cautious calculations or his legal subtleties, while Simon for his part could not fail to regard his labours on the Indian Commission as having been forestalled and undermined by a pious but obstinate Viceroy. Simon, too, had ambitions to succeed Chamberlain, and Halifax, for all his detachment, could only be regarded as a formidable rival to the throne when the time came for the Conservatives to produce their own leader to baffle the pretensions of the National Liberals. In such a quartet Halifax might reasonably expect that his influence with Chamberlain and Hoare would be as great, if not greater, than Simon's. The real clash was not so much between the Ministers as between the officials, Wilson and Vansittart, and Halifax must take his share of the blame in ever allowing Wilson, who had about as much technical equipment for conducting Foreign Affairs in a crisis as Vansittart for handling a wages dispute, to gain his incredible ascendancy.

Two further decisions were taken well in advance of the Nuremberg speech which bear the mark more of Halifax's acquiescence than his initiative. First, we have it from Henderson that while he was still in London the idea of actual personal contact between Chamberlain and Hitler "took concrete shape".[1] Secondly, Runciman, having evolved the cantonal compromise with Benes and unable to secure any response from Henlein, decided to send a message to Henlein's master at Berchtesgaden—thereby converting British policy from its original purpose of mediation between two groups of Czechs to that of an award between Czechoslovakia and Germany. It is generally conceded that Runciman did not take this step unprompted by London, and that Hitler regarded it as further evidence of British surrender. His immediate demand was for the Karlsbad Points in full. On the strength of a further specific pledge, this time by Bonnet, that France would remain faithful to her pacts and treaties which she had concluded, and after renewed pressure from Runciman and Newton, Benes replied by presenting his "last word" offer to the Sudeten Germans, the intricate "Fourth Plan". In Runciman's opinion, Chamberlain declared, "this plan embodied almost all the requirements of the eight Karlsbad points" and formed "a very favourable basis for the resumption of negotiations".

The primary responsibility for wrecking what Chamberlain termed "not unpromising prospects" of a peaceful solution of the Sudeten problem on the basis of autonomy within the Czech State rests squarely with Hitler, who had now ordered Henlein to manufacture the necessary grievances and hold off negotiation until after he had spoken at Nuremberg; but that there were forces at work in Britain ready to anticipate Hitler's wishes with almost the same enthusiasm as Henlein himself was revealed by the sensational leading article in *The Times* of 7th September which gratuitously proposed that the Czech Government should allow the secession "of that fringe of alien populations who are contiguous to the nation with which they are united by race". The word "fringe" significantly made its first appearance in this Sudeten context in Driscoll's despatch. Perhaps Messrs. Dawson and Barrington Ward composed

[1] Henderson somewhat cryptically backs up the decision with Chamberlain's and Halifax's memorandum to Hitler which he says "in an indirect sense paved the way for the personal contact between the Prime Minister and Hitler which came later".

their indiscretion at the same time and from the same inspiration as Driscoll and held it back until they themselves deemed or were advised that the situation was sufficiently dangerous to warrant this drastic intervention. *The Times' ballon d'essai* is explicable only on the assumption that its authors regarded it as the one possible escape from a virtual declaration of war by Hitler at Nuremberg.

Printing House Square was not alone in seeing the red light; Mussolini on 8th September was steering Italy towards neutrality with a significant announcement that although Italy favoured autonomy she had never suggested that the Sudetens should not continue to be part of the Czech State. Henlein for his part had not waited to receive the Fourth Plan, but had rushed off to Nuremberg, where he remained as Hitler's guest. In London it was announced that Halifax had cancelled his scheduled trip to Geneva and that a full meeting of the Cabinet would take place on 12th September, a few hours before Hitler's speech. How did Halifax react to *The Times*' proposal? He probably concurred with the opinion of his beloved *Yorkshire Post,* which condemned it as " a singularly maladroit suggestion ", and there were strong rumours of a Cabinet split. Aided and abetted by Vansittart, Halifax was said to favour a public statement that with the publication of the Fourth Plan the Czechs had gone far enough in concession. Chamberlain and Simon, however, were doggedly in favour of watchful inaction.

Twice during the next fortnight at desperate moments in the crisis, this dissension revealed itself in the issue of contradictory statements from the Foreign Office and from Downing Street. On the eve of the Nuremberg speech foreign journalists in London were invited to the Foreign Office to receive an " authoritative " statement of British policy. After referring to the statement of 24th March and to Simon's Lanark speech the statement ran, " In the opinion of His Majesty's Government it should be impossible for the terms of these pronouncements to be mistaken. . . . It was clear from the first statement that they (the British Government) contemplated the possibility not only of other countries but also of this country being involved and that Great Britain could not stand aside from a general conflict in which the integrity of France might be menaced."[1]

[1] Associated Press-despatch.

But Chamberlain at the same time was receiving representatives of the British Press and giving them a less decisive interpretation of the Government's view-point.[1] The inconsistency was soon resolved when the foreign journalists were urgently requested not to mention the Foreign Office as their source of inspiration. They were to say simply that the expression of view came from a " responsible source ".

In this unsuccessful Foreign Office revolt it is tempting to suggest that the influence of Anthony Eden was at work. On that afternoon he had an interview lasting over an hour with Halifax, and the next morning there was a short sharp letter from him in *The Times* underwriting the Foreign Office statement, and while urging settlement by conciliation, re-emphasizing that Britain would be at France's side in any emergency threatening her security. " It would be the gravest tragedy," he added firmly, " if from a misunderstanding of the mind of the British people the world was once again to be plunged into conflict." Furthermore the Diplomatic Correspondent of the *Daily Telegraph,* Victor Gordon Lennox, who enjoyed Eden's confidence, definitely described the statement the next morning as an authoritative reiteration of Britain's position. But while conceding that Vansittart probably composed the statement in the first place and that Eden and Gordon Lennox duly promoted it, the ultimate responsibility for it must rest with Halifax. The Halifax regime at the Foreign Office was, for all the Christian mildness and humility of the Secretary of State, one of almost totalitarian strictness. For the statement of 1st September and the even more dramatic announcement on the 26th to have been produced against Halifax's wishes or behind his back is to misread both Foreign Office procedure and the Foreign Secretary's personality.

The immediate reaction in France, in spite of the reservations and ambiguities, was encouraging; then came the Nuremberg speech with its frantic assertions that " if these tortured creatures cannot obtain rights and assistance by themselves they can obtain both from us " and the well-founded hope that " foreign statesmen will be convinced

[1] " On 11th September I made a statement to the Press, which received widespread publicity, stressing in particular the close ties uniting Great Britain and France and the probability in certain eventualities of this country going to the assistance of France."—Chamberlain in his House of Commons statement on 28th September 1938.

that these are not mere words ". Hitler had for the first time openly demanded that the Sudetens be given the right of self-determination, but the Nuremberg speech was not in itself a declaration of war, nor even a formal ultimatum. That came two days later when Chamberlain made his famous journey to Berchtesgaden. In the meanwhile there were grave disorders in Sudeten territory, and Henlein pronounced that the situation had gone too far for the Karlsbad points to be any longer a basis of negotiation, but even more serious was what Alexander Werth has called the " terrifying dégonflage " of the French Cabinet. While the Inner Cabinet in London was in conclave with the Defence Ministers and Chiefs of Staff with a view to forestalling another Nazi coup, Daladier, on learning that negotiations between the Czech Government and the Sudeten Party had been broken off, was unable to make up his mind between Bonnet and the majority of the Cabinet who favoured further retreat and Reynaud, Mandel and the General Staff who counselled strong diplomatic action. In despair he appealed to Chamberlain either to urge Runciman to find a new basis of negotiation or to make direct contact with Hitler himself. This was essentially the most abject and decisive surrender of all in the Munich crisis; Czechoslovakia was France's ally not Britain's, yet Daladier was begging Chamberlain to take diplomatic action with Hitler on the Czechs' behalf which he was not ready to take himself. Hitler's intransigence at Berchtesgaden was in strict proportion to French inertia. " I have little doubt ", wrote Werth three days before Godesberg, " that the Berchtesgaden meeting would have been very different if during that time France had been making a show of strength."

. . . .

Halifax never seems to have made an issue of Chamberlain going on his journeys to Germany without either his Foreign Secretary or his Chief Diplomatic Adviser. For his own part it was not in his nature to put himself forward as indispensable to any Prime Minister, particularly one of such tough and determined character as Chamberlain, and as we have seen, it had been agreed beforehand that Chamberlain should go alone as a last resort. To all outward appearances this last resort had been reached, frontier clashes made Czech mobilization and German invasion hourly possibilities; this was no time to stand on personal niceties. On the other hand, although there was the utmost tension, Chamberlain and Halifax were undoubtedly of the opinion that the agenda at Berchtesgaden would be no more than a friendly discussion about a possible compromise. Only when Chamberlain returned and at once laid before Halifax the full extent of Hitler's demands did the full implications of the French defection strike home. Hitler had insisted on the return of the Sudeten Germans to the Reich under the magic formula of self-determination. There was to be no delay; rather than wait, he told Chamberlain, he would be prepared to risk a world war. But if the British Government would only accept the formula, he was ready to discuss the details arising out of it and to refrain from military action, unless unduly provoked in the meanwhile, until Chamberlain had discussed the position with his colleagues.

The hectic period between Berchtesgaden and Godesberg does not reflect much credit upon Halifax and must be accounted an inglorious episode in British foreign policy; but in spite of adding the weight of his authority to the deplorable diplomatic pressure upon Benes to accept the Anglo-French Plan and of allowing the publication of a White Book which gave an incomplete account and therefore misleading impression of British action, he continued to plead within the Cabinet, and during informal discussions with Daladier and Bonnet on the 18th, against the unconditional surrender. In Cabinet he grappled with the thesis of Simon and Hoare that British commitments should not extend beyond the Rhine, and while still placing the demands of peace above those of compromise none the less urged that the new partitioned Czech State should enjoy as just compensation for her sacrifice a more effective guarantee from Britain than for instance was ever applied to Austria. In addition, backed by Malcolm MacDonald, the Colonial Secretary, and Duff Cooper, First Lord of the Admiralty, he at first resisted the transfer to the Reich of Czech minorities with the German minorities as morally indefensible.

His arguments and pleas were undermined, however, by other influences which made stronger impact on Chamberlain and the Cabinet. First there was the discreet advice of Runciman, who while closely concerned with the local rights of the Germans left in Czechoslovakia, no doubt deliberately ignored the fate of the unhappy Czechs who were to be submerged aliens in the great Nazi blood brotherhood, and was careful to propose only flabby and ambiguous guarantees to be undertaken by the principal powers. Then there was the persistent defeatism of Georges Bonnet, which was far more sustained than Daladier's fits of defiance. Although he had positive assurances from Litvinov personally of Soviet aid in the event of France fulfilling her obligations, Bonnet saw fit both to withhold and to distort this vital information. Behind Bonnet was ranged the majority of the French Cabinet, and their watchword was by now Peace with or without Czechoslovak consent. In Rome Mussolini, conscious that destiny had dealt him a strong suit, had now committed himself more openly to Hitler's cause; while last but by no means least, Hitler's preoccupation with " our Germans " in the Sudetenland encouraged no less insistent claims from Warsaw on behalf of oppressed Poles in Teschen, and Hungarian revisionists were equally active. Polish ambitions were the more dangerous and included a large-scale plot with the federalists in Bratislava to foment revolution against the Central Government in Prague, and bring Slovakia and even Hungary under Warsaw's political influence. Hitler at once exploited and thwarted Poland's last attempt to become a Great Power, but not before the Poles themselves had broken what Heiden has called " the inner powers of resistance of the Czechoslovak State ". During these desperate days, Halifax did his best to damp down Polish pretensions, but without avail. The Anglo-French proposals bore witness to all these distracting and disturbing elements, and as a result the Czech Government was brutally informed that European peace and Czech vital interests alike coincided in demanding that the " districts mainly inhabited by Sudeten Deutsch " must now be transferred to the Reich.

Both the form of the guarantee and scale of the transfer represented a defeat for Halifax's view-point. One of the principal conditions of the proposed guarantee to the new Czech State against unprovoked aggression was that it should take the place of existing treaties " which involve reciprocal obligations of a military character ". In other words, the virtual abandonment of protection from Russia, the one state that could give immediate effect to its pledges, was to be the price the Czechs were to pay for provisional British commitment. *The Times,* with its endless resource in soothing understatement, blandly commented, " the general character of the terms submitted to the Czechoslovak Government for their consideration cannot in the nature of things be expected to make a strong *prima facie* appeal to them "! After a two hour session the British Cabinet gave its general approval to a set of proposals which, it was justly observed, brought an end to the whole system of security built up in the post-war treaties. By 11 p.m. on Tuesday the 20th the British and French Governments were in possession of the Czech reply. With impressive dignity it elaborated the difficulties of accepting or rejecting the Anglo-French Plan outright, and called for arbitration under the German-Czechoslovak Arbitration Treaty of 1925 which Neurath had expressly invoked after the Austrian coup and Halifax confirmed. As postscript to the Anglo-French proposals was the urgent reminder that Chamberlain must resume conversations with Herr Hitler not later than Wednesday—" We therefore feel we must ask for your reply at the earliest possible moment ", which was as near to an ultimatum to Czechoslovakia as France and Britain were prepared to approach in public. The Czech reply not only played for time, it also raised a moral dilemma.

In this emergency Bonnet resorted to subterfuge, and on his own initiative and without, it seems, consulting his colleagues instructed the French Minister in Prague to see Benes in the early hours of Wednesday morning to inform him without any polite circumlocution the consequences of rejecting the Anglo-French Plan. Halifax was invited to associate Great Britain with this dark procedure; he gave his assent, and in his name as Foreign Secretary a telegram was delivered to Newton in Prague of which, as Wickham Steed has put it, " no Englishman can be proud ". The Czech Government was given to understand that if it did not unconditionally accept the Anglo-French Plan it would stand before the world as solely responsible for the ensuing war, would be responsible for undermining Anglo-French solidarity because under no condition would Great Britain move if France went to Czechoslovakia's aid. Finally, if the refusal provoked war France gave official notification that she could no longer fulfil her treaty obligations. There has been much controversy about the exact nature of the British instructions sent to Newton.[1] The above account, based on a summary circulated by Professor Seton Watson, was dubbed by Hoare on 2nd October " as in almost every respect a totally inaccurate description ". But he did not see fit to offer any particular correction nor Seton Watson to withdraw his statement, and when Butler on the 5th October read out a text of the instructions in Parliament, the basic ultimatum was undisturbed. Halifax had directed Newton to point out that the Czech reply " in no way meets the critical situation ", and to press the Czech Government " to consider urgently and seriously before producing a situation for which we could take no responsibility ". Benes made an effort to have the demand put into writing, but this plea was brusquely set aside.

The instructions given to the French Minister have not yet been published, but when they are, it will probably be found that the gruesome details of the consequences of Czech intransigence were elaborated by him, and that Newton did " little more than underline British policy in the light of the decisions enunciated by his French colleague ".[2] Whatever Bonnet's motives for taking the steps he did, the conclusion cannot be resisted that the primary responsibility for the Hradschin ultimatum belongs to France and that, although confined to a verbal threat, it constituted a unilateral repudiation of solemn obligations, affirmed and reaffirmed by Bonnet until the beginning of September, upon which the whole structure of Czech foreign policy had been based. For the rest, until all the evidence is assembled, the last word rests with Rudyard Kipling:

> And that is called paying the Danegeld;
> But we've proved it again and again,
> That if once you have paid him the Danegeld
> You never get rid of the Dane.

. . . .

By 9 a.m. on Wednesday the Czech Government had capitulated, and under extraordinary pressure from the British and French Governments accepted their propositions

[1] *Vide* Hamilton Fish Armstrong, *When There Is No Peace*, pages 68-70.
[2] *Ibid*, page 69.

" on the assumption that the two Governments will do everything to apply them with every safeguard for the vital interests of Czechoslovak State ". A few hours later it had fallen, to be succeeded by a Government of National Concentration under General Syrovy, Inspector-General of the Forces and hero of the famous Czech anabasis of 1917. The same day Chamberlain reached Godesberg (this time the Foreign Office was more strongly represented, as Sir William Malkin reinforced Strang) only to find that the reward for his brokerage in handing the Czechs an ultimatum was to receive similar treatment himself. With shifty arrogance Hitler refused to have anything to do with guarantees for a new Czech State, showed no interest in the Anglo-French proposals, condemning them in much the same terms as the Allied Governments had rejected the Czech Government's reply of 20th September as a time-serving device. When he put forward his alternative memorandum a time limit of 1st October was named in it; none the less, after bitterly reproaching Hitler for this deception, Chamberlain promised to transmit the memorandum to the Czechs.

Chamberlain's report on the Godesberg proceedings seriously alarmed Halifax, who seems now to have persuaded himself that Hitler actually wanted to chastise the Czechs by a local war; accordingly his advice and the weight of his influence was for ensuring peace by proving to Hitler that if war was indeed his argument it could not be localized. Between Chamberlain's return from Godesberg and departure for Munich Halifax's flagging spirit of resistance revived. If Hitler was going to fight about procedure, there must be no flinching from the British side. After the Cabinet meeting to consider Chamberlain's report, Halifax duly delivered Hitler's ultimatum to Jan Masaryk, but he made no attempt this time to urge its acceptance. He did not apparently even go as far as Chamberlain did with Hitler and ask for a prompt reply. In view of the instructions he had given to Newton only three days before, and of his foreknowledge of Czech mobilization on the 23rd, his silence now was more than mere negative neutrality.

On the afternoon of the 25th, Daladier and Bonnet arrived after Goebbels had issued his proclamation that Hitler would deliver an " historic speech " the following evening and after Syrovy's Government had denounced

Hitler's Godesberg memorandum as " absolutely and unconditionally unacceptable ". Their meeting with Chamberlain and Halifax lasted until after midnight. The next morning the conference was resumed, and Gamelin was summoned. Although the results of these anxious deliberations were not officially disclosed, and although it was rumoured that more time had been spent on discussing ways and means of peace than preparations for war, an historic decision was taken. The French Ministers made one last show of strength and reiterated their resolve to stand by the Czechs in the event of German attack upon them; Chamberlain now responded to Halifax's counsel and as he revealed in the Commons on the 28th, " in reply we told them that if as a result of these obligations French forces became actively engaged in hostilities against Germany, we should feel obliged to support them ". He made no effort to embellish his dramatic declaration, in his narrative it appeared only as a fleeting incident. He undoubtedly attached greater importance to his own personal message to Hitler which Horace Wilson delivered just before the " historic speech " at the Berlin Sportpalast. According to Gordon Lennox,[1] only Daladier and Horace Wilson were acquainted with the exact terms of this letter, which Chamberlain wrote out in his own hand, and which, while referring to Hitler's " clear appreciation of the consequences which must follow the abandonment of negotiation and the substitution of force ", made no reference to Britain's new commitment.

Perhaps it would never have been made public at all but for another " authoritative statement " released by the Foreign Office early the same evening and printed in the British and American Press the next morning, the 27th. In one brief paragraph Halifax and the Foreign Office made their last attempt to call a halt to the dim depressing narrative of British retreat and surrender. " My claim to the Sudetens is irrevocable," Hitler had screamed, " Dr. Benes has to choose either peace or war." But beneath the bluster the experts detected a note of cautious uncertainty, of prevarication in the self-assertive Führer. Deliberately he narrowed down the conflict to one between himself and Benes and gave no hint to the bewildered German people that the stake might be world war or that the resistance of the Great Powers

[1] In the *Daily Telegraph* of 27th September 1938.

was stiffening. In order that Hitler and the world might be no longer in doubt, the Foreign Office solemnly informed both that " the German claim to the transfer of the Sudeten areas has already been conceded by the French, British and Czechoslovak Governments, but if in spite of all efforts made by the British Prime Minister a German attack is made upon Czechoslovakia, the immediate result must be that France will be bound to come to her assistance and Great Britain and Russia will certainly stand by France ".

The psychological and political importance of this document, its influence upon the ultimate preservation of peace, will no doubt be a subject for debate as long as the merits of Munich are discussed among men. Considered in conjunction with the guarantee to the French Ministers it is at least impressive evidence that Halifax did not waver in the moment of greatest danger. The nature of his achievement has been aptly summed up by Hamilton Fish Armstrong in his brilliant and impartial analysis of the crisis. " Halifax," he wrote, " in a divided Cabinet, had taken a step which Grey in the divided Cabinet of 1914 had not taken." It is surely idle to suggest that this commitment was undertaken only after it was known that France would not fulfil her obligations to the Czechs, for Great Britain's readiness to underwrite French engagements in itself created a new situation. If Poincaré or Viviani had been in charge of French policy in September 1938 the full meaning of Halifax's unprecedented initiative would have been brought home to Hitler. But by 1938, twenty years of disillusionment and misunderstanding following the comradeship of the trenches, pacifism, opportunism and political decadence had all played their part in undermining the vitality of the Entente.

No sooner had Wilson returned and given his alarming report of his meeting with Hitler to the " Inner Cabinet " than the doubts and the dualism returned. After hours of anxious discussion Chamberlain issued from 10 Downing Street a personal statement at 1 a.m. on 27th September in which he announced his continuing hope that Hitler would not reject his proposals for a Conference, to which he had already secured the Czech Government's assent. " It is evident," he added, " that the Chancellor has no faith that the promises made will be carried out." He now pointed out that these promises were made in the first instance not to Germany but to Great Britain and France. The British Government now pledged itself to see them carried out "with all reasonable promptitude" provided the German Government was prepared to settle "terms and conditions of transfer by discussion and not by force". This could in a sense be regarded as an alternative and complementary mode of persuasion, but Daladier and Bonnet and the French Press made no effort to preserve even the outward appearances of solidarity.

Instead of being grateful for what all his predecessors had striven in vain to achieve, Bonnet showed the utmost reserve. He was reported as replying to some deputies who asked him whether the authenticity of the Foreign Office statements could be guaranteed, that "we have not received any confirmation"; while Daladier two days after Chamberlain's declaration in Parliament was described as asserting that its origin was from "an official of no importance". *Le Matin*, as late as 2nd October, kept up the pretence, dismissing the "soi disant 'communiqué' of the Foreign Office" as "a clever lie". By the time Daladier revealed the facts to the Chamber of Deputies on 4th October Munich was history and the statement a matter of academic interest. None the less Eden, when Parliament debated Munich, did not hesitate to make "special reference" to it. "I believe," he declared, "that the historian of the future will give that statement an important place among the deterrents to war a week ago."

It was, of course, the mention of Russia that aroused the most intense speculation; was not the whole basis of Chamberlain's policy the elimination of Russia from the dispute, the return to Mussolini's classic concept of the Pact of Four? How was it that Halifax could give his assent for this taboo to be broken? It will be recalled that Halifax, when the crisis loomed large, cancelled going to Geneva as British delegate. Earl De la Warr, a junior member of the Cabinet and by no means an enthusiastic disciple of appeasement, took his place there. During the course of his stay he was able to make a first-hand study of the much-vaunted Soviet guarantees, and although Litvinov had expressed the utmost indignation at the pressure applied upon Prague to accept the Anglo-French Plan, De la Warr, after a long and comprehensive talk with him on the 23rd, was able to paint for Halifax a satisfactory picture of Russian intentions in the event of war. Rumania was showing surprising complacence towards the movement of Russian troops through her territory, while Litvinov confirmed his public declaration that although Russia would not feel herself bound to act unless France did, it did not follow that she would not come to Prague's aid either alone or through the League. In London there were different reports of Russian capacity to fulfil her obligations; in particular Colonel Lindbergh who, as the result of a short stay in Moscow presented himself as an expert on the Soviet military machine, had made his way into the drawing-rooms of the mighty and persuaded powerful interests already politically ripe for such advice that Russian aid, even if it was forthcoming, would be valueless. There can be little doubt but that the information reaching the Foreign Office from Geneva directly contradicted but did little to dispel the effects of a sinister and effective whispering campaign. Halifax, for his part, was far less anxious about the alleged deficiencies of the Soviet air fleet than about the terrifying and undeniable inadequacy of British defences. When an Opposition leader expostulated with him after Munich about the strategic disaster involved in the loss to the Allies of forty Czech divisions he apparently replied that he had been much more concerned about London's seven anti-aircraft guns.

. . . .

As the drama drew towards its incredible climax Halifax, in the eyes of the public, was more than ever the spectator of historic events. It was left to Sir Horace Wilson to give Hitler " at dictation speed " and in precise terms the British commitment to France on the morning of the 27th, to Duff Cooper to mobilize the Fleet, to Mussolini to dissuade Hitler from carrying out his threat to march at 2 p.m. on Wednesday the 28th, to Chamberlain to make the " last last effort for Peace ". All Halifax was called upon to do, it seemed, was to act as the messenger for Hitler's invitation to Chamberlain to go to Munich and so provide Chamberlain with the triumphant peroration to his sombre narrative to Parliament,[1] to be present at Heston Aerodrome to give the Prime Minister a hearty farewell cheer and bid him Godspeed for Munich, to join with the rest of the Cabinet in

[1] The first intimation of the impending denouement was when Halifax was seen to receive a message in the Peers' gallery and to hurry out.

the delirious welcome to the man whose obstinate resolve alone had stood between devastating war and the peace all longed for but none had dared to expect. But such surface appearances are deceptive; he had not been shelved by the Prime Minister, but on the contrary was constantly consulted by him in every phase of one of the most involved diplomatic struggles in modern history, no less complex in detail than the actual *casus belli* over Danzig a year later, and had on the whole held his own in the " Inner Cabinet ". Well might Chamberlain pay " an especial tribute of gratitude and praise to the man upon whom fell the first brunt of those decisions which had to be taken day by day, almost hour by hour. The calmness, patience and wisdom of the Foreign Secretary, and lofty conception of his duty not only to this country but to all humanity, were an example to us all and sustained us all through the trials through which we have been passing."

But beyond this well-deserved public acknowledgment of Halifax's collaboration in and responsibility for Munich, what is his real position? His statement to the Lords on 3rd October, which was simultaneous with Chamberlain's, is described as being " identical " with it, but actually Halifax's account bears full testimony and contains some significant variations in emphasis. He stressed first of all the two principles in conflict in the British mind; on the one hand the necessity " in the light of every political experiment our own people have made " of somehow meeting the Sudeten German claim, and on the other, " the feeling that, whatever might be said about this abstract claim, its determination by force was in the long run destructive of European order and of those relationships between nations on which alone security can rest ". In the effort to make just distinctions and to reconcile these conflicting claims " we were prepared to go to unusual lengths in placing pressure upon a friendly and independent Government to accept the Anglo-French proposals for full cession of Czech territory down to the majority German population line ". The Prime Minister's thesis did not admit going to " unusual lengths ", nor will there be found in Chamberlain's statement Halifax's emphasis upon the guarantee to the partitioned Czech State as a form of compensation for Benes' acceptance of the Anglo-French Plan. " We felt that if we were in conjunction with the French Government to press the Czechoslovak Government to accept proposals so drastic as those which we thought it right to lay before them in the Anglo-French Plan, in order to preserve Europe as a whole from war, we were bound ourselves to make a counter-contribution to balance the reduction of Czechoslovakia's defensive strength. In no other circumstances, I think, should we have felt morally justified in pressing her Government to go so far."

He did nothing to clear up the ambiguity of whether the guarantee would be "joint or several", but one phrase in which he referred to it as being "reinforced and buttressed" by Italian and German readiness to join in "when the other minority questions have been settled", suggests perhaps that he did not envisage it in his own mind as wholly conditional on Axis acquiescence. When six months later Hitler's legions marched on Prague and resolved all doubts, the question had still not been settled, and Halifax was compelled finally to declare the guarantee as null and void. But in his estimate of Munich he gave a far more forcible impression than any of his colleagues in the Government that Britain was under obligation to the Czechs, and only a departure from our accustomed non-committal attitude to Central Europe would be an adequate repayment.

Then again he gave a frank reply to the question why we had consented to the omission of Russia from Munich, a subject which Chamberlain pointedly ignored altogether, and repeated the substance of what he told Maisky while the Munich negotiations were actually in progress. "Five days ago it seemed to us vital, if war was to be avoided, somehow or other to get matters on to a basis of negotiation; but if we were to face the facts—and nothing was to be gained but rather everything was to be lost by not facing them—we were obliged to recognize that in the present circumstances the heads of the German and Italian Governments would almost certainly—at least without much preliminary discussion for which there was no time—be reluctant to sit in Conference with a Soviet representative. Accordingly if our principal purpose was to ensure negotiation we were bound to have regard to the practical conditions within which alone this purpose could be secured." But the impossibility of finding room for Stalin if Chamberlain and Daladier were to be allowed to talk to Hitler and Mussolini "in no way signified any weakening of the desire on our part . . . to preserve our understanding and relations with the Soviet Government ". Such an apology cannot have inspired Stalin with confidence in Halifax's political judgment, but the allegation that Halifax was a party to any appeasement intrigue to drive Stalin out of Europe can hardly be sustained. The very *naïveté* of his recapitulation of his message to Maisky is in itself testimony to its genuineness. As Foreign Secretary he more than any other member of Chamberlain's Government stood to lose by any deliberate action that drove Russia into the arms of Nazi Germany. Russia's absence from Munich, therefore, was " a regrettable necessity ", not a " consummation devoutly to be wished ". It is legitimate, indeed necessary, to criticize him for failing to foresee the consequences of discarding Moscow as an instrument of Peace, but until there is more evidence to prove his sinister motives it is best not to read more into his words than their *prima facie* meaning warrants.

He argued, as Chamberlain did, at great length and made a strong case to show that the agreement reached at Munich was in line with the Anglo-French Plan and a substantial retreat by Hitler from his Godesberg position. In the light of the evidence available to Halifax on 3rd October, and on the assumption that the International Commission set up at Munich would not from the outset be dominated and exploited by the Germans, his contentions were plausible, but he was pleading *in vacuo,* with the usual Nazi armoury of threats and chicanery Hitler had soon battered down the terms and intention of the Munich Agreement, had soon " persuaded " the Czech Government of the advisability to make a direct settlement and liquidate the last semblance of international supervision. When the International Commission set up to supervise the execution of Munich submitted to the German refusal to accept the Czech Government's 1930 census, and instead based its calculations on the archaic figures of the 1910 Austrian census which, apart from being out of date, had been notoriously rigged against Czech interests, Benes resigned. By this simple device Hitler had reached out beyond the Godesberg line and taken in his stride road junctions, aircraft factories and strategic apparatus. Thus was self-determination made the plaything of his military designs. The great bastion of democracy in Eastern Europe had fallen without a blow, and as Dr.

Chvalkousky, the new Czech Foreign Minister, hurried to Berlin, Prague's newspapers announced ominously " we have finished with the Western Powers ".

Halifax never claimed for Munich that it was " Peace in our time " or even that it was " Peace with Honour ". At best it was " an occasion on which it was found possible by discussion to effect real abatement in claims made " and, as he readily confessed to Parliament, " I may have had my share in decisions that can be held by some to be ill-judged. . . . There was indeed no clear way, but almost always a hideous choice of evils." In this vein he reminded the American people over the wireless in the first official apologia they had heard from a member of the British Government, there were " before us all the time two points which were unescapable ". First, if Germany had invaded Czechoslovakia nothing Britain, France or Russia could have done would have saved the Czechs from being overrun; while secondly he emphasized that the case of Czechoslovakia in 1938 was not analogous with that of Belgium in 1914, for even if war had come we should have embarked upon it knowing that no body of statesmen when it was over would have been able to redraw Czechoslovakia's boundaries on the scale of the Versailles Treaty.

It was not until fifteen months later, in a speech on the progress of the war at Leeds, that he publicly subscribed to Henderson's thesis elaborated in his *Failure of a Mission* that Hitler regarded himself not as having conquered at Munich but as having been cheated. Halifax now described the settlement as having given Germany all she immediately wanted, and admitted that in applying the Agreement every contentious point was decided in Germany's favour. Yet Hitler was profoundly dissatisfied. It became rapidly evident, Halifax asserted, that he " objected to the procedure of settlement by negotiation and that, if we may judge by all the evidence, he resented having been balked of a war over Czechoslovakia ". But when all allowances have been made perhaps Halifax's last word on Munich would be much the same as Sheridan's comment on the historically not dissimilar Treaty of Amiens, that it was " a peace which all men are glad of, but no man can be proud of ".

CHAPTER XXXIII

PARIS, ROME AND DISENCHANTMENT

In the twilight period between the Agreement of Munich and the occupation of Prague, there was no respite for Halifax. Although Parliament sanctioned the peace with a formidable majority and there were no signs of organized political revolt, British opinion was sharply divided over the effectiveness as well as the morality of Chamberlain's approach to the Dictators. Halifax and Chamberlain, however, were not allowed to complete their apology before Hitler had come to the rescue of their critics. A mere ten days after Munich, in a vindictive and deplorable speech at Saarbrucken he did his best to wreck two of the principal arguments for appeasement. In the first place he revealed that " at the beginning of the year " he had reached his " decision to lead back into the Reich 10,000,000 Germans who still stood outside " and thereby falsified his pledges to the Czechs and threw obvious doubt on the validity of his assertion that the Sudetenland was his last territorial claim in Europe. But beyond that, with an insolence unparalleled in the political interchange of Great Powers nominally at peace with each other he made the maintenance of good relations with Germany conditional upon the continuation in office of Britain's existing leadership. Should Churchill or Duff Cooper or Eden come into power the result would inevitably be war with the Reich.

Here were the same tactics that were employed successfully against Eden, but in a more open and arrogant form. Was Munich peace by negotiation? Not according to Goebbels, who derided the people " out West ", who on sensing that something was wrong sent " negotiators, mediators and debating societies ", but " did not appreciate that there was no chance for negotiations ". Was self-determination vindicated? Goebbels again had the answer when he spoke of Germany as fortunate in being able to call upon a principle dear to their opponents—self-determination—and as having

" hauled that principle out of the dark-room ". Then again there were well-authenticated reports that the Nazis were requiring as the price for their continued acquiescence in the ratio of the Anglo-German Naval Agreement a three to one preponderance in the Air. But terrible facts soon swamped even these sinister words when suddenly at a given signal the Nazis launched a monstrous anti-Jewish pogrom as an act of revenge for the murder of a minor German diplomatic official by a persecuted and distracted Jewish youth. In a flash the brutal meaning of Nazi culture was revealed to many who had hesitated and hoped against hope to bring a resurgent Germany into the comity of nations, now it was starkly evident that the man at the head of the German Government who after Munich stood out, to quote J. L. Garvin, as " the mightiest sovereign ruler since Napoleon and probably since Charlemagne " was leading a gigantic reaction and conspiracy against the Christian civilization of the West.

It might have been natural to expect that the response to these horrors would be a surge of democratic wrath drawing the Entente closer together than ever before, but such was not the case. Although the moral indignation in Britain was intense, France was too deeply absorbed in social and economic crises at home to react strongly to racial injustice across the Rhine. Neville Chamberlain had expressly dissociated general principles from policy. Munich had been the outcome of that distinction. But not the least disastrous result of Munich was the effect it had upon the principles and the policy underlying Anglo-French collaboration. With Munich safely surmounted, French opinion, though still lacking material for clear judgment, began to take stock, to realize the measure of France's defeat and danger, and in the process to look for scapegoats. Nothing was easier than to attribute the collapse of the Czech bastion to Britain's selfish initiative and no less selfish reticence. There was some resentment, too, at the Quai d'Orsay, which German influences did not hesitate to exploit, at Chamberlain's procedure in staying behind after Munich without first consulting the French Government in order to secure Hitler's signature to an Anglo-German declaration of friendship. Nor was British anxiety to follow up Mussolini's benevolent intervention at Munich by ratifying the Anglo-Italian treaty which had been in cold storage ever since April appreciated in France.

The price of such Anglo-Italian conciliation was " settlement " in Spain, where the war had now reached a critical stage for the Republicans, and where the granting of belligerent rights to Franco would clinch his victory and create a strategic situation that was causing grave concern to the French General Staff. When on 3rd November Halifax asked Parliament to agree that this was the moment to bring the Agreement into force the arguments he advanced can hardly have restored confidence in Paris. He side-tracked the obstacle of Spanish settlement by blandly alleging that the idea that the Agreement and the Spanish question were linked together was an assumption " without foundation ". " No doubt the situation will clear itself up as time goes on," Chamberlain cryptically observed in May when refusing to define what he meant by the settlement which Perth in his letter to Ciano regarded " as a prerequisite of the entry into force of the Agreement between our two Governments ". Halifax's denouement was a deplorable commentary on the whole structure of the British diplomatic approach to Fascist Italy. " I want to emphasize with all the force that I can summon," he said, " that it has never been true, and it is not true to say, that the Agreement had the lever value that some think to make Italy desist from supporting General Franco and his fortunes. Signor Mussolini has always made it plain from the time of the first conversations between His Majesty's Government and the Italian Government that, for reasons known to us all—whether we approve of them or not—he was not prepared to see General Franco defeated."

Here was the truth at last; a crisis of the magnitude of Munich with its resultant trough of uncritical relief was needed before Halifax saw fit to release it. Only under the shadow of world war averted at the eleventh hour was it safe to inform the public that a " settlement " in Spain meant nothing less than acquiescence in Mussolini's demand for Franco's victory. The secret of the delay in ratifying the Agreement was that the Republicans had been " an unconscionable time in dying ". For all Chamberlain's and Halifax's self-congratulation that but for the Agreement it would have been impossible for Great Britain to secure Mussolini's mediation at Munich, the facts remained that

British pressure had been no match for the obstinate fanaticism of the Spanish people locked in life and death struggle with themselves and with invaders; and that Halifax's persistent efforts to secure a firm foundation for Anglo-Italian friendship were from the outset frustrated; disillusionment over Mussolini's ultimate designs was no less inevitable and rapid than over Hitler's, only the process was perhaps more painful in that he placed a higher stake on the Duce's redemption. It was not enough to liquidate the problem of Spanish settlement by denying that it had ever existed. The Anglo-Italian Agreement could only come into effective force if there was a parallel understanding between Italy and France, but Mussolini showed no sign of extending to France the " indulgence " he had shown to Britain, while French policy, under the direction of the arch-appeaser Georges Bonnet, was wholly absorbed in securing an all-embracing settlement with the Reich in terms similar to the Anglo-German declaration which Chamberlain brought back with him from Munich.

Hitler gave encouragement to the French initiative; his mind had not as yet moved in the direction of a " deal " with Stalin, and his conception of a free hand in the East was still essentially at the expense of Russia. During December the new French Ambassador to Berlin, Coulondre, wrote in one of his brilliant despatches of how " the end seems to be well fixed. It is to create a greater Ukraine which would become Germany's granary. In order to achieve this Rumania must be subdued, Poland won over [the word used is " convaincre "], Russia dispossessed. . . . Many already talk of the advance to the Caucasus and Baku." To give substance to these dreams France must be kept complacent and the new element of suspicion between Whitehall and the Quai d'Orsay carefully fostered. The latest pretext for insidious Nazi suggestions was disquiet in France, now that the Eastern citadels had fallen, at Britain's unwillingness to underwrite French security with a large scale expeditionary force, but in addition France was in the throes of intense industrial and social unrest and facing economic and monetary chaos. The price of the Popular Front was not only the forty hour week and higher wages, but the flight of French gold reserves and a leap up in the cost of living. Paul Reynaud, the Finance Minister, had evolved a series of drastic decrees which in the effort to secure the elements of stability implied a final repudiation of Blum's New Deal, but the Daladier Government was endangered as much from the powerful elements to the Right and in the Army as from the highly organized Left.

. . . .

Against this background of turmoil and conflicting motives Chamberlain and Halifax, accompanied by their wives, paid a formal visit to Paris between November 23rd and 25th in a desperate attempt to apply appeasement to the Entente itself. Up to the last moment it had seemed that the visit would not materialize. Daladier had threatened the Finance Committee of the Chamber that if it did not approve the Government's finance proposals he would telegraph Chamberlain to postpone the visit, which was sufficient to secure him a small majority. After a stormy Channel crossing the British Ministers were greeted at the Gare du Nord by Daladier who managed to snatch a few moments from the growing struggle over the decrees. Half France was paralysed with strikes, the Government was on the verge of collapse. The presence of Chamberlain and Halifax at this moment provided the sorely tried Daladier with some badly needed prestige, but that public opinion was not so easily distracted was soon apparent in the mixed welcome awaiting the distinguished guests as they drove from the station to the British Embassy. Amid the cheers of greeting could be heard discordant shouts of " Down with Munich! ", " Down with the Decree Laws! " and " Vive Eden! "

Throughout the visit Axis manœuvres on the one hand and the industrial crisis on the other dominated the proceedings. On the 23rd the elaborate banquetings at the Quai d'Orsay were offset by the news that an agreement for closer cultural ties between Italy and Germany had been signed that day in Rome. The news on the 24th was taken up not with the prolonged discussion between the Ministers but with the statement from the German official news agency that Ribbentrop would be proceeding to Paris " within the next few days " to sign the much vaunted declaration of Franco-German neighbourliness. The talks were more than once interrupted while Daladier made vain efforts to deal with the rapidly deteriorating strike situation. During the day it was learned that the great Renault works, employing 33,000 men,

GRAND OPERA

Chamberlain, Mussolini, Halifax and Ciano attend a gala performance during the British statesmen's visit to pursue the policy of appeasement with Italy in January, 1939

had been occupied by the workers and only cleared after police had used tear gas. It was an ironical comment on the effectiveness of appeasement and of the Franco-German *détente* that almost the sole topic of Anglo-French negotiation within two months of Munich was the number of military divisions Britain was prepared to assign to France. The diplomatic situation, including Colonial claims and the Italian and Spanish dilemmas, received only summary treatment which gave substance to the verdict of the *Manchester Guardian's* Paris Correspondent, who described the talks as " useful in a negative sense " but as providing " no basis whatever for any constructive future policy ".

Problems of strategy were clearly not in Halifax's province, but this visit is noteworthy as marking the first occasion on which he accompanied Chamberlain on his travelling diplomacy. Admittedly Chamberlain was still exercising active and detailed control over foreign policy and Halifax held little more than a watching brief, but the presence both of Halifax and of Cadogan in Paris brought to an end the Berchtesgaden-Godesberg-Munich procedure. No longer was Chamberlain to enjoy a dictatorial discretion; from henceforth the Foreign Office resumes its normal functions and the Foreign Secretary's influence steadily grows. But this development was hardly noticed at the time, a British public satiated with political crises took a more lively interest in the news that Chamberlain and Halifax had called on the Duke and Duchess of Windsor at the Hotel Meurice, and the question of the hour was whether time had healed the breach and whether the Ministers, neither of whom had been formally presented to the Duchess before, had greeted her with the customary salutation due to Royalty. Reporters satisfied themselves that they did bow and address her as " Ma'am ", but the vexed question of her status in the Royal family remained. As long as she was only " Her Grace " and not " Her Royal Highness " the Duke, it seemed, was in no mood to return home, but political difficulties were smoothed over by this meeting.

In the public statement made after the Paris conversations there was the usual formula of " a complete identity of view on the general orientation of the policy of the two countries ". To Parliament Chamberlain was careful to stress that there had been no new commitments on defence and that the purpose of the visit had been " to exchange views rather than to take decisions "; while to the Press in Paris he spoke of being " greatly satisfied " with the Franco-German Declaration, the situation was constantly changing and " personal contact remains more desirable than ever". Three days after their return from Paris the Foreign Office followed up this last assertion by announcing that Chamberlain and Halifax would be paying a visit to Mussolini in Rome during the first half of January. It was stated that the idea had originated from a suggestion made by Mussolini at Munich. But two days after the Duce had declared that he would " in principle " welcome the visit, there was staged in the Italian Chamber with melodramatic effect that would have done credit to Goebbels a full-blooded campaign for the acquisition of French territories in the Mediterranean. Following a speech by Ciano explaining Italy's heroic role at Munich, the militant Farinacci, former Secretary of State of the Fascist Party, shouted out " Tunisia! Tunisia! "; his successor Starace then raised cry of " Corsica! " In the pandemonium that ensued " Nice " and " Savoy " could be heard; even the President of the Chamber, Ciano's father, joined in the demonstration. In the midst of this *mise en scène* Mussolini was described as sitting immobile, " staring straight ahead, his teeth clenched and his arms crossed over his chest ".

The next morning Ciano's paper, *Telegrafo,* asserted that this outburst was in the spirit of Munich; in other Italian papers Jibuti, Suez and Majorca were significantly singled out for democratic attention and probably represented the hard core of Mussolini's demands. But how were Chamberlain and Halifax to interpret a move which in its timing had all the appearance of crude blackmail? It was not difficult to link it up with Hitler's political and economic pretensions and to identify Mussolini as the Führer's accomplice in the all-important process of isolating Britain both from France and Eastern Europe, but there were also good grounds for asserting that Mussolini had in mind to bring himself as much to the notice of Germany as of the Democracies and was merely pointing out that his reward for his complacence over Austria and honest brokerage at Munich was by now overdue.

It was, however, a delicate operation for the British

Government to confirm the Rome visit without at the same time undermining the Daladier Government and adding to the general sense of suspicion and unreality in Paris which had undoubtedly disturbed Halifax. It seemed at first as if the dilemma had been gracefully sidestepped when on 3rd December Lord Perth paid two calls on Ciano, first to fix the dates of the visit, and then to draw attention to the terms of the Anglo-Italian Agreement about the *status quo* in the Mediterranean. Ciano was reported to have given the required assurances that Italy considered herself fully bound by the undertakings she had given, but to have added that he could not be responsible for " spontaneous demonstrations " during a carefully thought out speech. Chamberlain briskly accepted this glib assurance, and the next day Ribbentrop was smuggled into Paris. But Bonnet could not breathe life into his diplomatic masterpiece; the danger from France was not in a truculent pro-Germanism, there were no illusions about Ribbentrop's designs. " I am convinced ", wrote the right wing de Kerilis, " that Ribbentrop's game consists in ' neutralizing ' France with a view to a great offensive in Eastern Europe next spring. . . . While Poland is attacked we will be told every morning that Germany loves us and will love us for ever. What will France do, especially if at the same time Italy is ready to pounce on Tunis, Corsica and Nice? " Daladier left no doubt about the measure of French alarm, and on 5th December proclaimed France's determination " to ensure respect by any means for the absolute integrity of all territories flying the national flag ", and further, announced his intention to visit Corsica and Tunis at the beginning of January. If Mussolini had calculated on French dissensions and weakness he was soon to be undeceived. Overnight her finances were put in order, her ranks closed, and Bonnet's clear assertion that France would not surrender an inch of territory to Italy and that " any attempt to achieve such ambitions can only lead to an armed conflict " aroused far more enthusiasm than all his elaborate apologies for Ribbentrop. For with sure insight the Quai d'Orsay recognized that underlying all the crude stage effects Mussolini was asserting his one consistent and implacable ambition to dominate the Mediterranean.

At this critical moment Chamberlain faltered. The

Italian Press had already given it out that there was influential sympathy in Britain for Italy's claim on Tunis; as if to give substance to this contention, he stated baldly, replying to a question in Parliament, that no treaty or pact with France contained any specific requirement that Great Britain should render military assistance to her should Italy embark on warlike operations against France or her possessions. This deplorable lapse caused "immense satisfaction" in Rome and corresponding anxiety in Paris, and although Halifax's influence was no doubt at work in securing Chamberlain's prompt avowal at the Foreign Press Association dinner the next evening that "our relations with France are so close as to pass beyond mere legal obligations, since they are founded on identity of interest", the damage had been done, and the discreet British hopes of mediation in Rome receded. On 22nd December Mussolini formally denounced Laval's notorious agreement of January 1935, which had in fact effected the barter of Abyssinia, as "null and void"; France bluntly rejected his denunciation. At the beginning of January Daladier made his much heralded tour of French possessions in the Mediterranean. Everywhere he met with the utmost enthusiasm and was in a strong position to make clear to the British Ministers when they were once more entertained at Paris on their way to Rome that they could carry with them no French mandate for appeasing Mussolini. Not merely was Britain thus debarred from mediating between France and Italy, but the tone of Goebbels' outrageous propaganda seemed to undermine all prospects of Mussolini probing Germany's intentions on behalf of Britain, which was the second major objective of the visit.

. . . .

In what J. L. Garvin aptly termed "these execrable circumstances" Halifax once more accompanied Chamberlain to test and apply appeasement. "The mission is vindicated", Garvin added, "because in dealing with a bedevilled situation there is no present chance of improving it through Berlin or Tokyo or by any means whatever except the possible moderation and mediation of Signor Mussolini. Within certain limits he is a balance-holder and arbiter in Europe." This hyperbole, however, could not conceal the fact that there was little left but diplomatic small change in which appeasement could be traded and that the Duce had, to say the least, unorthodox ideas on what constituted mediation or moderation. On arrival in Rome Chamberlain and Halifax were met by Mussolini, Ciano and Grandi; the Fascist hierarchy, dressed in its most flamboyant uniforms, provided a striking contrast to the representatives of " decadent democracy " in their sober mufti, and the whole antithesis of Fascist and democratic diplomacy was summed up in the difference between the tall austere figure of Halifax, top hat in hand, and his opposite number, the swaggering Ciano with his smart military cap set at a jaunty angle.

The most notable feature of this lavish hospitality, however, was the one element which Fascist organization could neither organize nor arrange—the spontaneous welcome of Italian crowds for men whom they realized had sacrificed so much in the overriding cause of peace. During his stay in Rome Halifax was asked about the meaning and origin of his name. " It is declined the same as Pax," he replied; if that was a contemptible answer to full-blooded Fascists, it was readily appreciated by the Italian masses. The demonstrations were no less impressive than those which had been accorded to Chamberlain by the people of Munich, and if Chamberlain was at fault in identifying this popularity with the detailed implications of his policy, Halifax in Rome was able to gauge for himself the strength of this craving for peace which no Dictator sensitive to popular moods could afford to ignore. On the evening of their arrival they had an hour and a half's discussion with the Duce and Ciano, followed up by a State banquet in which Mussolini and Chamberlain gave each other fulsome credit for their respective contributions to Munich. Chamberlain invoked " friendship with all and enmity with none ", the Duce " peace with justice ", which was interpreted by Gayda as meaning that Italian claims on France were based on documentary rights as well as on essential political and moral reasons. The next day, 12th January, King Victor Emmanuel received the two British Ministers and entertained them and Mussolini to lunch. Then after attending that inevitable symbol of Fascist showmanship, a Youth display at the Toro Mussolini, Chamberlain and Halifax had a prolonged discussion with the Duce at Palazzo

Venezia. In the evening the formal welcome culminated in a gala performance at the opera attended by the four statesmen and the cream of Roman Society.

But for Halifax the occasion charged with the deepest meaning must have been his and Chamberlain's reception the next morning at the Vatican by the aged Pius XI, the Pope who in his youth had lived in Oxford and formed abiding friendships with Oxford men, and who on his elevation to the throne of St. Peter had shown a keen solicitude for the architects of Malines. Now desperately ill, with the pretensions and traditions of the Roman Church ruthlessly challenged by the new Paganism, his life seemed to hang solely on the strength of his spiritual resistance to tyranny. As Papal Nuncio in Warsaw during the struggle against the Bolsheviks, his mind had at first inclined to accept the Nazi claim to lead a crusade against the Red peril, but in the end he had realized that the more immediate menace to the Christian order in Europe was from the Nazis themselves. When Hitler paid his triumphal visit to Rome in the summer of 1938 the Pope ostentatiously left for his country retreat at Castel Gandolfo. Only three weeks before the British Ministers' visit, in a Christmas address to the College of Cardinals, he had denounced " the recent apotheosis of a cross hostile to the Cross of Christ, prepared in this very city of Rome ". It is surely no exaggeration to suggest that this first and last encounter with Pius XI, whose religious status he revered and whose spiritual and political judgment were obviously those of a man standing on the brink of the eternal, must have quickened Halifax's sense of danger in the moral neutrality implied by appeasement. While at the Vatican, he was able also to have a comprehensive exchange of view with Cardinal Pacelli, then Secretary of State, who three months later was to be acclaimed as Pius XII and who, although of a less dominant and robust personality than his predecessor and more influenced by diplomatic nicety, confirmed the impression that the Roman Church was anxious for closer relations with the British Government if only to reinforce its protests against Mussolini's various violations of the Lateran Pact.

At the end of the day, after further conversations, the usual colourless communiqué was issued simultaneously by the Foreign Ministry and the British Embassy, speaking of the " greatest cordiality " and a " frank and full exchange of views ". Mussolini's substantive claims on France had appreciably been narrowed to a question of rights in Tunisia, Jibuti and the Suez Canal, but the savage extravagance of the Press campaign had in no way abated. Moreover, while Chamberlain and Halifax stressed the great store they set by the explicit Italian pledge to maintain the *status quo* in the Mediterranean, and intimated firmly that the dispute with France was a matter for the French and Italian Governments to solve between themselves, although Britain would not be unmoved by any direct threat to France, the German Press proceeded to fan the flames of Italian " intransigence ". The only tangible outcome of the visit was that instead of a compliant Italy steering Hitler into the paths of Pax Britannica, Mussolini was himself favourably placed to press his Mediterranean demands with increased vigour encouraged by Germany's uncompromising support.

As for the Spanish war, which was in its last death agonies, Halifax at once proceeded from Rome to Geneva in order to attend the Council's equivocal deliberations on the subject. Alvarez del Vayo, who was also there to make one last desperate plea for the Republicans, has described in his book *Freedom's Battle* a significant talk with him from which he gathered that when the British guests discreetly drew Mussolini's attention to the ill effects produced on British public opinion by the decisive part played by Italian divisions in the Catalan offensive, the Duce had brazenly replied " that matter has already been settled. Franco has won and there is no point in pursuing the question further." This rebuff, and the fact that he saw fit to communicate it to del Vayo, may be taken as yet another incident in the general hardening of his attitude towards Axis diplomacy. Desperate as was the plight of the Republicans, Halifax's mediation might have been forthcoming if Negrin had shown greater flexibility and frankness. Not until after the fall of Barcelona, which involved the complete isolation of the Central Zone, was he ready to reduce his thirteen points to three. By now he was compelled to operate from France, but French support was waning. The supply of arms from Russia had ceased altogether with the collapse in Aragon, and at last he reduced his terms to one—a request for a general amnesty.

Although it seemed out of the question that Franco with

decisive victory in his grasp would consider negotiation, Halifax regarded Negrin's offer as reasonable, and conversations began at once. From the sound assumption that the British Government's primary concern was to bring the Spanish war to an end before Europe was convulsed in another crisis of Nazi origin Negrin rashly concluded that by withholding the details of his negotiations with Halifax from his military chiefs and threatening to continue the war throughout the summer he could secure more active British support. But Halifax was as well informed as Negrin about the tragic position in the Central Zone, and with Negrin's failure to take up his original offer there was nothing left for him but to watch separatist and ideological conflicts, famine and war weariness, clinch Franco's complete victory.

In those last dark days the British role, whether in tentatively sponsoring Colonel Cassado and the Defence junta, or openly aiding Franco to secure Minorca, or in the ultimate recognition of Franco, Halifax sought comfort for the last time in the classic quietism of Walpole. It was not only that the Government, he told an audience in Sunderland on 13th March, " have kept this country from the horrors of war, though that surely is nothing for which we need apologize; it is rather that with no Spanish blood on our hands we might be better able to lend special help in allaying some of the bitterness and repairing some of the damage of that most unhappy conflict ". Two days later the last of Hitler's legions were in Prague; the spirit of Munich, the doctrine of non-intervention and the framework of appeasement were alike shattered.

CHAPTER XXXIV

FORWARD FROM PRAGUE

THE Rome visit had, for all its " cordiality ", shed no light on the overriding problem of German intentions. Immediately after Munich, Funk, the Nazi Finance Minister, set out on a grandiose tour of Eastern Europe. The centre of Nazi penetration was Rumania, but when Carol paid his state visit to London in November 1938 he found no ready appreciation of the implications of Germany's economic plight; on the contrary, Chamberlain, Sir Horace Wilson, and the leading spirits of the Federation of British Industries were obsessed with the idea that diplomacy should be bent to secure a comprehensive economic settlement with the Nazis. In consultation with Henderson plans were at once advanced for Oliver Stanley, President of the Board of Trade, and R. S. Hudson, Secretary to the Department of Overseas Trade, to visit Berlin. Apart from one truculent outburst by Hudson that if the German Government continued to exploit unfair subsidy methods in her Eastern European trade policy " we would beat her at her own game ", the general trend of British appeasement policy after Munich was to subordinate diplomatic advantage to economic convenience. Had not Hitler made his last territorial demand on Europe? Was not his primary objective his need to consolidate his gains?

In Halifax's mind the touchstone to test Hitler's sincerity and prove his value as an investment was the question of the Czech Guarantee. Imperceptibly he was adopting the same attitude towards Hitler that Eden had taken up a year before with Mussolini, and in the process he was encountering much the same opposition, but in seeking to take his stand on Czech Sovereignty and the " Spirit of Munich " he was on much stronger ground than Eden had been on Austrian independence and settlement in Spain. Hitler, however, was more circumspect than the Italian Dictator. Colonel Beck, the Polish Foreign Minister, who had visited him at Berchtesgaden on 12th January at his express invitation, had reported to the French Ambassador in Warsaw that " he did not give me the impression of a man who was preparing to start a crusade against anybody ". In his annual Reichstag speech on 30th January Hitler gratuitously extolled friendship with Poland as " one of the reassuring factors in the political life of Europe ", and he went out of his way to predict " a long period of peace ", but although the speech in terms of Hitlerian jargon was restrained, none of his menacing pretensions were abandoned or even modified. Munich now appeared in the guise of self-defence against the attempt of a third party to interfere. " I need not assure you," Hitler added, " that in the future, too, we shall not tolerate any attempt by the Western Powers to interfere in affairs which solely concern us for the purpose of preventing natural and reasonable solutions."

Those sensitive to the nuances of public speeches could detect that Chamberlain and Halifax in their reactions to Hitler's address were not speaking to quite the same brief. Chamberlain was the unqualified optimist, and repeated Beck's formula. " I very definitely got the impression," he said, " that it was not the speech of a man who was preparing to throw Europe into another crisis. It seemed to me that there were many passages in the speech which indicated the necessity of peace for Germany as well as for other countries." Halifax did not pitch his expectation so high. " Herr Hitler has predicted," he observed, " a long period of peace. No one hopes more devoutly than I do that this prediction will be fulfilled. It is not my business to discuss the extent to which the difficulties of Germany, or of any other country, might be reduced by action that it is within the power of a single country to take. But I know that so long as the world remains an armed camp the present difficulties will in greater or less degree persist for all."

The contrast is more pointed if it is linked with Hitler's sudden dismissal, a few days before his speech, of Schacht and of his confidant, Wiedemann. It was widely stressed that Schacht's departure meant unbridled inflation and a new era of economic and therefore political extremism, while Wiedemann's banishment to San Francisco was interpreted as yet another blow for moderate influences in Germany. It was in order to resolve these doubts that Halifax at last secured the Cabinet's consent to sound the Wilhelmstrasse on its intentions about maintaining the Czech frontiers; and while at Geneva he prevailed on Bonnet to make a parallel *démarche*. The French sent their note in on 8th February; by the 24th Coulondre, in response to an urgent request for information from Bonnet, reported No reply. Chamberlain still refused to be deflected from his easy optimism. He assured an audience at Blackburn on the 22nd that trade had improved when Hitler by his statement about his hopes of peace had " eased international tension ", and that that fact, together with other indications, encouraged him to think that trade might develop in 1939 " unhampered by political anxieties ". Nothing would conduce more greatly to the establishment of world peace than Anglo-German collaboration.

The next day in the House of Lords Halifax was at pains to repudiate " attempts in some quarters " to qualify the Prime Minister's assurance of solidarity with France, which was not accompanied by any mental reservation whatever. " It is clear and unmistakable," he added pointedly, " and can be illustrated by the homely comparison with the signs at danger-points on the highway, ' Halt: major road ahead '." While there was no party or statesman who would contemplate aggressive war, equally unfounded were suggestions that the British and French will to peace proved weakness, cowardice and lack of resolution. " The people of France and Britain, with bitter experiences in common, condemn war as an instrument of policy and they wish to set themselves alongside all other Governments who will join in that abjuration." This last statement, which was soon to be charged with dynamic meaning, was a further definite stage in his retreat from the orthodox appeasement position and was based, no doubt, on a shrewd estimate of what was implied by the Wilhelmstrasse's delay in acknowledging his *démarche*.

At last, on 2nd March, the German reply reached London and Paris. In what Coulondre aptly termed " its comparatively veiled form, which does not, however, exclude certain brutal or perfidious thrusts ", the Nazis committed themselves in writing to the view that the conditions foreseen in the Munich Agreement for an international guarantee had in no way been fulfilled. They thereby shamelessly confessed the failure of the Vienna Award which Hitler and Mussolini had, without consulting the French or British Governments, imposed on the Czechs in settlement of Hungarian and Polish claims and then duly proclaimed as a triumph of benevolent Axis arbitration. " The position thus taken," as Coulondre pointed out, " allows the Government of the Reich to refuse its guarantee, and consequently leaves the door open for it eventually to reconsider the entire question." But in addition, the Note[1] challenged not only the expediency but also the rights of " an extension of this guarantee obligation to the Western Powers " which would be an element " liable to increase unreasonable tendencies as has already been the case ". " The German Government is perfectly aware that, all things considered, the general evolution of that part of Europe falls primarily into the sphere of the Reich's most vital interests, and that not only from the historical point of view, but also from the geographical and, above all, the economic angle."

We do not know what Henderson's comment was, but Coulondre left his Government in no doubt. " Translated into clear language," he said, " this phrase means that the Western Powers have no longer any right to interest themselves in Central European affairs. . . . At first sight this document is therefore anything but reassuring as to the immediate intentions of Hitler's policy towards Czechoslovakia." There can be little doubt but that Halifax, having digested its contents, shared Coulondre's misgivings, but it was a considerable achievement on his part to have drawn Hitler by ordinary diplomatic process into revealing so much of his thoughts and plans. The exponents of further appeasement both in London and Paris were thus forewarned; yet it was just this moment when reports were crowding in from every capital in Europe that a Hitler putsch was imminent that they chose for launching what was aptly termed in Italy " a pacifist offensive ". Hoare, for instance, ascended into cloud cuckoo land with an ecstatic vision of " a golden age ". Five men in Europe, he declared, the three Dictators and the Prime Ministers of England and France, if they worked with a singleness of purpose and a unity of action to that end might in an incredibly short space of time transform the whole history of the world. Now was the greatest oppor-

[1] No. 51 in French Yellow Book.

tunity ever offered to the leaders of the world to discover the road to peace.

More sober in its language but more disturbing in its implications was an inspired statement released to the Press on the same day which suggested that " the international outlook had distinctly improved ", that " Europe was settling down ", and that the Government was therefore contemplating the possibility of a general limitation of armament. The *Evening Standard* actually went so far as to name the source of this inspiration. " Bursting optimism ", proclaimed its leading article, " breaks through the clouds. It comes direct from the Foreign Office and it is founded on a solid array of facts." The *Daily Mail* in its post-mortem on Prague repeated the allegation by expressing its dismay at " the blindness of the British Foreign Office to what was impending. . . . The skies were blue—until the bolt came. And no Department was more astonished than the Foreign Office." But in fact that Foreign Office's astonishment was directed solely at those who had the temerity to put out such scandalous official soporifics in face of the serious view Halifax was known to take of the situation. The authority, of course, was not Halifax and his officials but the so-called Prime Minister's department operating from 10 Downing Street under Sir Horace Wilson's direction independently of the Foreign Office. The motive behind the statement and Hoare's speech seems to have been an attempt to resuscitate the Inner Cabinet, which for all its omnipotence during the September crisis had no formal authority and had subsequently lapsed. After the first enthusiasm for Munich had died away the Cabinet had shown a marked unwillingness to allow its powers over foreign policy to be put into commission again; nor had Halifax given any signs that he regarded as a precedent procedure which had so effectively encroached upon the functions of his department and the status of his office.

Now on the eve of Hitler's fateful putsch to stifle the last liberties of the Czechs and to convert the Munich Agreement into yet another scrap of paper, the prophets and publicists overreached themselves. Whatever their purpose, whether to isolate or compromise Halifax and the Foreign Office, or to protect the delegates of the British Federation of Industries negotiating a comprehensive commercial agreement at Dusseldorf from the wrath to come, when the blow fell they were at once the victims of their own propaganda. By preparing the public for a new era of peace they merely intensified the surprise and revulsion felt at Hitler's coup. There was a surge of political and moral opinion comparable to that over Abyssinia which had rocked the Government and swept Hoare from office. At first Chamberlain tried to ride the storm by ignoring it. While Hitler's troops were pouring over the Munich frontiers, he informed Parliament, in the dialect of appeasement, that Czechoslovakia had " become disentegrated ", that " a state consisting of Czechs, Slovaks, as well as minorities of other nationalities " was liable to " possibilities of change ", and that " I have so often heard charges of breach of faith bandied about which did not seem to me to be founded upon sufficient premises, that I do not wish to associate myself to-day with any charges of that character ". But the words died on his lips; he succeeded in appeasing neither an ambitious Hitler nor a restless Parliament. Indeed, Chamberlain's equivocal reaction to the new Nazi aggression on a non-German race had the two immediate effects of encouraging Hitler to increase the tempo of his Drang nach Osten, and of causing the most severe crisis within the Conservative Party since the inception of the National Government.

. . . .

In this grave hour of decision all Halifax's qualities of ripe judgment and firm character were enhanced, and to him must be given the primary credit for ensuring that further Nazi aggression in Europe without war would be impossible. The rape of Czechoslovakia enabled Halifax both to mould a Grand Alliance and save a Government. By his words and actions in that crucial third week of March 1939, more formative if less dramatic than the last days of August when the Polish crisis moved to the inevitable arbitrament of war, he emerged as the most powerful man in England. The period of his unqualified ascendancy lasted until the beginning of July when the difficulties inherent throughout in bringing Soviet Russia into the so-called Peace Front were widely attributed, for want of any other obvious motive, to Halifax's High Churchmanship and alleged anti-Bolshevik phobias.

Chamberlain's statement to Parliament of 15th March was not to be his last word on the subject, he had been scheduled beforehand to make a big speech in Birmingham on the 17th; throughout the 16th there was a growing volume of informal criticism among Conservative M.P.s of Chamberlain's apparently stubborn refusal to be deflected from his appeasement course. It was argued that unless he had some stronger pronouncement to make about the future of British policy towards Germany his personal position as Prime Minister would be in danger. Linked up with this comment was anxiety on the issue of conscription to which Chamberlain still hesitated to commit himself. Halifax, on the other hand, was known to be firmly advocating a modified conscription scheme and to have influential backing for it. To meet the emergency and to give effect to the plea for national unity, a theme which Halifax had preached with far more frequency and earnestness than any other member of the Administration, it was widely held that nothing less than the reconstruction of the Government would suffice. The Inner Cabinet as such had collapsed, but Simon as Chancellor of the Exchequer still spoke for a group of Chamberlain's senior colleagues who looked with dismay on any drastic alteration in the balance of political forces at home as the price of a complete withdrawal from appeasement. Simon, too, still nursed ambitions of succeeding Chamberlain as the first "Liberal" Prime Minister of the "National" Coalition. His only chance of reaching the summit depended on the strength of his influence over Chamberlain and of Chamberlain's over the Government. The only concession he and his friends in the Cabinet would consider was the establishment of a Council of State representing all parties to develop an agreed foreign policy which the Government of the day would then execute.

Halifax, however, boldly advocated the formation of an entirely new National Government which would comprise the leaders of all parties and include Churchill and Eden, with both of whom he maintained close contact at this critical time.[1] "He does not visualize a Coalition Government in the usual sense of the term," wrote the Political Correspondent of *The Star* on 17th March, "but a Govern-

[1] Indeed the first formal suggestion that the Government should be put upon a wider basis had come in a speech from Eden during the debate following Chamberlain's statement of 15th March. The speech was sympathetically received, but only began to attract serious attention when it was known that Halifax was in sympathy with Eden's proposal.

ment of co-operation for the one purpose of formulating an agreed policy and supporting that policy by suitable defence measures. When that dual purpose has been achieved the political parties would resume their respective positions." He no doubt sincerely hoped that the obvious advantages in such a frank and open arrangement would overcome the Labour Party's overriding objection to any terms of collaboration with a Government led by Chamberlain. The tragedy of Chamberlain's leadership was that he allowed his deference and loyalty to his senior colleagues to outweigh his personal readiness to overhaul the Administration. History may well record that Chamberlain's forbidding manner completely belied and rendered futile generous motives. However, for all practical purposes, as *The Star's* Political Correspondent admitted, " if Lord Halifax's proposal is to succeed, a new Prime Minister must be found ". The question then arose and was widely canvassed whether Halifax himself might head such a Government.

During the next three months the idea of the Halifax Coalition was never far removed from practical politics, and while the storm clouds of impending conflict over Danzig and Poland gathered it was merged in discussion over his acceptability as the leader of a War Cabinet. Not all the speculation was Lobby or Fleet Street gossip; Sir Arthur Salter in his powerful treatise on *Security*, published during the spring of 1939, echoed the views of an influential body of political moderates when he wrote: " In present circumstances, therefore, a National combination would perhaps, if the present Prime Minister resigned, be more practicable under Lord Halifax than any other. That he is in the Lords is no insuperable obstacle. The needs of the country must override every technical consideration, and if necessary an Act of Parliament could give him a place in the Commons." After stressing close resemblance in personal qualities to Edward Grey, his Indian record, his age—" more than a decade's advantage of one kind over Mr. Eden, and of the opposite kind over Mr. Chamberlain "—he went on to discuss doubts " whether his personal force is sufficient, whether he has a tough enough fibre in his will . . . for a particular objective he has a less concentrated strength than Mr. Chamberlain. Partly, however, for this very reason he is less compromised by his association with Mr. Chamberlain's

LOST CAUSE

Bonnet, French Foreign Minister, Halifax and Maisky, Soviet Ambassador in London, meet for the last time at Geneva. January, 1939

earlier policy and less handicapped in any attempt to secure the co-operation of the Left."

Salter envisaged that a Ministry of all the talents of which Halifax was the head, " stiffened by the inclusion of Mr. Churchill as Minister of Defence, including Mr. Eden and also the ablest of the Labour leaders (in particular Mr. Morrison), and possibly associating Mr. Chamberlain and Mr. Lloyd George as Ministers without Portfolio " would best serve the country at this time. Salter, a friend and confidant of Halifax's from undergraduate days, may well have helped to mould his views on the scope of and need for reconstruction; but of one thing there can be absolute certainty, Halifax never countenanced active lobbying on his own behalf; no man in our time, with the possible exception of Austen Chamberlain, has advanced so near to the highest office and done so little to advance himself. His personal position he strictly subordinated to the demands of foreign policy, which allowed no respite, and as a result the whole question of a political realignment was stored away until the actual outbreak of war.

In the meanwhile Halifax, by the measure of his own efforts, carried the Prime Minister, the Government and the country with him in a Diplomatic Revolution, or rather Restoration; for the essence of his achievement, which culminated in the " unprecedented " guarantees to Poland, Rumania and Greece, was that it was an attempt to revive Britain's historic and traditional role, the Balance of Power. For all the reassuring apologies it was the policy of appeasement that involved a diplomatic journey through uncharted seas. This was one paradox which had helped to confuse the public mind, it was to be substituted by another. By promoting the Peace Front, Halifax at once rallied many who saw in it the triumph of the Geneva principle of collective security; but if the method of unilateral and advance guarantee was novel the resistance to Hitler which Halifax evoked was in its broad essentials identical with that which succeeded in despatching the Kaiser to Doorn and Napoleon to St. Helena. It was the diplomacy not of the League of Nations but of the Grand Alliance.

Halifax first of all summoned the suave German Ambassador, Dr. von Dirksen, late on the Wednesday night and " spoke his mind with considerable candour, expressing much more strongly than had been possible in the British Note delivered in Berlin on Wednesday morning the sense of outrage which is felt in Britain against the latest German conquest ".[1] There followed a brief tussle between Halifax and Chamberlain over the recall of Sir Nevile Henderson, who had telegraphed to his chief, " His Majesty's Government will doubtless consider what attitude to adopt towards a Government which has shown itself incapable of observing an agreement not six months old ". Chamberlain, however, was at first reluctant to order Henderson's recall, and wanted time for reaching a decision, but before leaving for Birmingham a formula had been found, which Roosevelt had used to show American disgust at the Jewish pogroms, whereby the Ambassador was to be brought back for consultations which would keep him in London indefinitely. This constituted a substantial victory for Halifax, who had insisted on the importance of removing the impression which Ribbentrop was known to be fostering that Britain was really indifferent to a German campaign of conquest in Eastern Europe. At the same time Stanley's and Hudson's visit to Berlin was " postponed ". On the 17th Halifax saw Corbin, who conveyed somewhat meagre instructions from Bonnet—beyond the need for France and Britain to take concerted action in Berlin there was no suggestion for the future. Vansittart, however, was in touch with Maisky, while Halifax gave Kennedy, the American Ambassador, an outline of Chamberlain's Birmingham speech which, although it was unrepentant in its defence of Munich, contained a sufficiency of strength to quell the incipient revolt of his followers.

While Chamberlain was speaking, Halifax was poring over grave reports from the Rumanian Ambassador, Tilea, who told of far-reaching economic demands made on the eve of the invasion of Czechoslovakia by Wohlthat, who was head of a German economic mission then in Bucharest. Wohlthat was pressing Rumania to close down all existing industries and revert solely to agriculture and to grant Germany a complete monopoly over all Rumania's exports, particularly grain and oil. There were at first grounds for believing that Rumania had surrendered, and that Hitler had won out of hand what many shrewd judges estimated was the real motive behind his putsch on Prague, namely the

[1] *Daily Telegraph*, 17th March 1939.

replenishment of his overburdened oil supplies, but King Carol conveyed to Halifax his intention to fight rather than submit to any attack on Rumanian territory or independence, and Tilea confirmed that at a Brown Council, which had included Army Chiefs, Wohlthat's demands had been decisively rejected. On the morning of the 18th it seemed that Rumania would be overrun. Chamberlain hurried back from Birmingham for an emergency Cabinet meeting that night. Halifax had prolonged exchanges of view with the French, American and Soviet Ambassadors and—a sure sign of the gravity of the position—there were meetings of the Defence Ministers and discussion with the Dominions High Commissioners. During the day Hitler's reply, rejecting the British Note of protest as illegal and immoral, was received.

. . . .

The immediate threat to Rumania brought to a head the problem of applying the policy that was to take the place of appeasement. " The Londoner's Diary " in the *Evening Standard* (which has often contained contributions from Beaverbrook himself) gave a very shrewd and well-informed survey of the position. After pointing out that the Cabinet agreed that Britain and France had to decide at once at what point they meant to resist Nazi aggression and that the only hope of peace would be to make that decision known to Hitler as soon as it was reached, " the Londoner " continued, " there are two main schools of thought as to where the modern ' ne plus ultra ' line should be drawn. One led by Sir John Simon argues that it is useless to try to stop Hitler short of the Near East. Resistance would be made on a line drawn from Turkey, through Syria and Palestine down to Egypt. Lord Halifax and the bulk of Conservative opinion outside the Government favour a policy which would be in effect the adoption of a plan put forward by King Carol for joint action. They favour drawing the line from Poland to Rumania, Greece and Turkey."

Carol's plan, which had found favour with Halifax, was in effect a promise that he could rally Poland, Bulgaria and the Balkan Entente (Rumania, Greece, Turkey and Jugoslavia) in resistance to any further move by Hitler, if Britain, France and Russia would add their support. But this grandiose project was lost in the rapid and baffling sequence of events, not only because Hitler's " sickening technique " of threats and self-pity were duly transferred from Bucharest to Warsaw after the Rumanian Government had accepted a modified economic arrangement with Germany, but also because the Cabinet was unable to reach, or rather execute, a clear-cut decision as between the view-points of Simon and Halifax. Chamberlain himself reflected this spirit of compromise when, a fortnight later, he announced the guarantee to Poland which for all its momentous implications was a tardy and uninspiring conclusion to so many ambitious proposals for the protection of Europe from wanton aggression. The schismatic influences within the Cabinet helped to undermine the Russian proposal made on 18th March for a Six Power Conference to be held in an Eastern European capital, preferably Bucharest, and to bring together the Foreign Ministers of Britain, Russia, France, Poland, Rumania and Turkey; and following the fateful Cabinet meeting Halifax was obliged to inform Maisky that the proposal was considered " premature ". The Government, unwilling in any case to submit to Russian leadership in a Coalition, satisfied itself by preparing a Four Power Declaration pledging the signatories to consult in the event of further aggression. France accepted at once, but Poland was not ready to provoke Hitler with a Declaration which stood across his ambitions but ruled out advance military commitments to resist them.

How far Halifax ever believed in the Declaration we cannot tell, but by the time Russia accepted it he was known to be ready to consider a conference comparable in scope to that proposed by Moscow. But on the very day that Russian and British diplomacy seemed to converge towards complete agreement Hitler struck again not in the Balkans as anticipated, but in the Baltic, this time forcing the Lithuanian Government, under threat of invasion and aerial bombardment, to surrender the Memelland. Memel had always been one of post-war Europe's danger-spots, but now when the expected coup occurred its full significance was lost. It appeared as nothing more than an incident in the larger Czech crisis, but it was more than that. It linked Baltic and Balkan security; it gave momentum to Moscow's thesis that the guarantees to Poland or Rumania could not be divorced from Russian protection for Lithuania, Latvia and Esthonia.

The price of Russia underwriting Balkan independence would have to be a drastic revision of Baltic neutrality. On the day that Hoare was bleating of a conference which in effect meant adding Stalin's name to the delegates of Munich, Stalin delivered one of his rare speeches; the occasion was the eighteenth Congress of the Communist Party, and it would have been better for public enlightenment if more space in the papers had been devoted to Stalin's realism and rather less to Hoare's fantasies. Among the tasks of the Party was "to be cautious and not allow our country to be drawn into conflicts by warmongers who are accustomed to have others pull the chestnuts out of the fire for them". The Poles were no less suspicious, and there were powerful influences at Warsaw that preferred even a German conquest to Soviet "assistance"; but if these crippling factors operated from the outset against an effective Peace Front in Europe, so also did the persistent activity of inveterate appeasers at home.

Yet in spite of all the frustration and intrigue, strategical uncertainties and political sharp practice surrounding him, Halifax was the only member of the Government who seemed to reach out into the conscience of the nation and summon up the greatness that the hour demanded. As one American commentator put it, "not only Chamberlain himself, but all the John Bulls throughout the land, who had supported his policy of appeasement . . . all these ordinary common decent conservative British men and women exclaimed with one voice, 'This can't go on.' But somehow Halifax, not Chamberlain, became their real voice. For he possesses that *grandezza del animio* to which men respond when their true self is stirred." His speech to the Lords on 20th March bears splendid witness to his eloquence and conviction. Under his searching moral scrutiny, the whole sordid fabrication of Slovak nationalism and Czech oppression was laid bare. "Indeed," he justly concluded, "if I may sum up my own thought in these various explanations, I could wish that instead of the communications and explanations which have been issued and which carry scant conviction, German superior force had been frankly acknowledged as the supreme arbiter that in fact it was."

The operative sentence in Chamberlain's Birmingham speech had been no more than a rhetorical question, "Is this the end of an old adventure or is it the beginning of a new? " Halifax supplied the emphatic answer. He admitted that Germany must from some points of view be more interested in Czechoslovakia and South Eastern Europe than Britain and that it was a natural field for the expansion of German trade. " But apart from the fact that changes in any part of Europe produce profound effects elsewhere, the position is entirely changed when we are confronted with the arbitrary suppression of an independent sovereign State by force, and by the violation of what I must regard as the elementary rules of international conduct." American opinion found this sudden burst of moral indignation rather difficult to digest. For many Americans Czechoslovakia was sold " up the river " when Chamberlain went to Munich, and they would have concurred with Coulondre's verdict in his despatch to Bonnet three days before the occupation of Prague that the Munich Agreements were for the Nazi rulers nothing but a means of disarming Czechoslovakia before annexing it. But looked at historically the difference in emphasis was not one of principle but of timing. Coulondre was arguing in retrospect, and in any case was careful to add that " it would be going rather too far " to assert that the Führer had conceived the occupation of Prague in the previous September.

The fact that Halifax was wise after the event did not on that account impair the force and depth of his wisdom. Hitler had committed the unforgivable sin of being untrue to his own philosophy. In September he had invoked the principle of self-determination, " one on which the British Empire itself has been erected and one to which accordingly . . . we felt obliged to give weight in considering Herr Hitler's claim. That principle has now been rudely contradicted by a sequence of acts which denies the very right on which the German attitude of six months ago was based; and whatever may have been the truth about the treatment of 250,000 Germans it is impossible for me to believe that it could only be remedied by the subjugation of 8,000,000 Czechs." Halifax was not misled by this philosophical deceit. A new international technique prevailed—" wars without declarations of war. Pressure exercised under threat of immediate employment of force. Intervention in the internal struggles of other States. Countries are now faced with the encouragement of separatism, not in the interest of separatist or minority interests, but in the imperial interests of Germany." Hence the events in Czechoslovakia required His Majesty's Government and every free people to " rethink their attitude towards them ". For Halifax the process involved a new readiness to acknowledge the philosophy of collective security in its struggle against the rival claims of isolationism; " if and when," he argued, " it becomes plain to States that there is no apparent guarantee against successive attacks directed in turn on all who might seem to stand in the way of ambitious schemes of domination, then at once the scale tips the other way (i.e. against isolationism), and in all quarters there is likely to be found immediately a very much greater readiness to consider whether the acceptance of wider mutual obligations, in the cause of mutual support, is not dictated, if for no other reason than the necessity of self-defence."

But perhaps his final peroration will live longest in his memory. In the hour of humiliation and despair he sent a message which helped to wipe out the meaning of so much that was tinselled and even tainted in the triumphs of appeasement. Here was the authentic language of liberty addressed to a people who had known freedom and were going into captivity, but dreamt that they might yet be free. " It is not possible as yet fully to appraise the consequences of German action. History records many attempts to impose a domination on Europe, but all these attempts have, sooner or later, terminated in disaster for those who made them. It has never in the long run proved possible to stamp out the spirit of free peoples. If history is any guide, the German people may yet regret the action that has been taken in their name against the people of Czechoslovakia. Twenty years ago that people of Czechoslovakia recovered their liberties with the support and encouragement of the greater part of the world. They have now been deprived of them by violence. In the course of their long history this will not be the first time that this tenacious, valiant, and industrious people have lost their independence, but they have never lost that which is the foundation of independence—the love of liberty. Meanwhile, just as after the last war the world watched the emergence of the Czech nation, so it will watch to-day their efforts to preserve intact their cultural identity, and more important, their spiritual freedom under the last and most cruel blow of which they have been the victims."

The days, however, in which Britain merely watched the agonies of Europe were numbered. Soon Halifax was travelling the same dark journey that Grey before him had made towards the unpredictable ordeals of world war. But with his speech of 20th March there was no longer any doubt but that the old inhibitions were gone; there might be disappointments and set-backs, but Halifax was from henceforward ready to take up without quibble or mental reservation the supreme challenge of Nazism to the spiritual and moral integrity of mankind. Halifax's nature and experience were such that the only war supportable to him was a Holy War. If diplomacy could not teach Hitler to keep the peace, Halifax had found the inner assurance he needed that the resultant war would in fact be a crusade. This speech therefore may be regarded as something more than a mere formal Government statement, it was rather a personal confession of faith long dormant but now fully roused.

CHAPTER XXXV

PEACE FRONTS

THE momentous decision to guarantee Poland was only reached after three prolonged Cabinet meetings; it had been hastened by a sudden Nazi Press offensive directed against Warsaw and identical in its violence with those which had preceded the seizure of Prague and Memel. Halifax in his statement to the Lords referred to " certain circumstances " which seemed to suggest " the possibility of dangerous developments in the relations between Germany and Poland ". While the Cabinet was meeting, the German Foreign Office had been at pains to state that there was not a word of truth in reports that Germany had handed Poland a twenty-four hour ultimatum. " The question of Danzig has been discussed between us on and off for some time," it was added, " but there has been no specific development." That such a denial, however, was thought necessary was not without significance, and in itself served only to draw attention to Hitler's avowed resolve to effect the return of Danzig to the Reich together with a German Corridor passing through the Polish Corridor. The Government has often been accused of taking a panic measure, and, as a result, of failing to consult Russia, who alone could give military substance to the British guarantee to Poland whether it was unilateral or, as after Colonel Beck's visit to London on 3rd April, reciprocal. But two immediate reactions, from *The Times* and from Hitler himself, help to modify this criticism.

The Times in its leading article on 1st April showed clearly that the devotees of appeasement were still far from discouraged and were ready to challenge the Foreign Office. It stressed first that Chamberlain's statement involved no blind acceptance of the *status quo,* " on the contrary, his repeated references to free negotiation imply that he thinks that these are problems in which adjustments are still necessary "; secondly that the " relative strengths of nations will always, and rightly, be an important consideration in diplomacy ", that Germany is " admittedly bound to be the most powerful Continental State " and finally that the new obligation did not bind Great Britain " to defend every inch of the present frontiers of Poland. The key word in the declaration is not integrity but ' independence '. The independence of every negotiating State is what matters." There could hardly have been a more flagrant incitement to Hitler to make Danzig a second Sudetenland.

Halifax saw fit to authorize yet another Foreign Office disclaimer which expressed surprise that " attempts should have been made to minimize the Prime Minister's statement in the House of Commons. The statement is regarded as of outstanding importance, the meaning of which is perfectly clear and logical. No doubt is felt in official quarters that in present conditions the Polish Government will wish to keep His Majesty's Government fully informed, although the latter do not seek in any way to influence the Polish Government in the conduct of their relations with the German Government." In other words, unless the Polish Government agreed to a distinction between independence and integrity, which was the perfect formula for German infiltration into Danzig, there would be no such suggestion from Britain. This prompt disavowal was necessary if only to set at rest the dismay in Warsaw. As Halifax subsequently admitted, the guarantee to Poland was given without regard to the ultimate Soviet attitude; it served an immediate purpose, as with the " May crisis " of 1938, by deflecting Hitler from direct assault and forcing him back into diplomatic manœuvre. Hitler's reaction was an ominous speech at Wilhelmshaven delivered behind bullet-proof glass, during which, with accustomed cunning, he addressed himself to the cautious Stalin by pointing out that " whoever declares himself prepared to pull the chestnuts out of the fire for the Great Powers must expect to burn his fingers ". But before Halifax could begin to think of the ways and means of persuading Stalin to the contrary, Mussolini, not to be outdone in the scramble for forbidden fruit, marched into Albania. With symbolic thoroughness, the self-styled " Sword of Islam " used his weapon to strike down a Moslem people, and in order that Christian sensibilities should not go unscathed, chose Good Friday for his exploit. Chamberlain was on holiday when this latest and in many ways most sordid and contemptible of the pre-war aggressions took place, and incurred some criticism for not unduly hurrying himself to return.

Halifax thus found himself with a wider discretion than usual, which he exploited to good advantage. Particularly satisfying was his interview on Easter Eve with the Italian Chargé d'Affaires, Crolla, on the delicate question of Corfu. Crolla raised the subject by drawing Halifax's attention to reports that the English Sunday Press would the next day be making various suggestions about a possible British occupation of Corfu. While the Italian Government would certainly not threaten Greek independence, such occupation by Britain would " create the most dangerous reactions." " I at once told Signor Crolla that he could dismiss from his mind, and his Government could dismiss from theirs, the idea that the British Government had any intention of occupying Corfu. That was not the sort of thing we did, but the British Government, I said, would certainly take a very grave view if anybody else occupied it."[1] According to M. Simopoulos, the Greek Minister in London, Halifax's full retort was that acts of aggression on a Good Friday were not in the British tradition! The whole incident, however, is a good illustration of Fascist diplomatic technique and of the only kind of reaction to it calculated to produce positive results.

After further searching enquiries on Easter Sunday morning Halifax secured a personal message from Mussolini, subsequently transmitted to Athens, in which he spoke of Italy's intention to base her relations with Greece on " a cordial and solid friendship ", and " to respect in the most absolute manner the territorial and insular integrity of Greece ". None the less the Albanian coup provided Halifax with the pretext for following up the Polish guarantee with similar pledges to Greece and Rumania. The Greek guarantee had been generally expected, but although conversations between London and Bucharest were already in progress the inclusion of Rumania in the new Peace Front came as rather a surprise to many, and seems to have been brought about on French insistence and information. For all Carol's ambitious projects, Rumania merely rein-

[1] Government statement in the House of Lords on 13th April.

forced Polish objections to any arrangement involving the presence of Soviet troops on their soil. However, the conversations with Poland, Turkey and Soviet Russia were actively pursued.

During the second half of April and throughout May and June, Halifax was engaged in solving as complex a diplomatic riddle as has ever been presented to a British Foreign Secretary. In the first place, he was opposed to a German campaign of extreme subtlety which probed by means of a barrage of verbal abuse all possible points of weakness in the British, French and Polish will to resist. This campaign was effectively launched by Hitler in a speech to the Reichstag on 28th April when he made his first public claim for the return of the Free City to the Reich and offered in exchange a twenty-five year non-aggression Pact.[1] At the same time he tore up the famous German-Polish Agreement of 1934 which had originally done so much to consolidate his position but which had now served its purpose. In addition he denounced the Anglo-German Naval Agreements. This hard brick was thrown in a wrapping of tissue-paper sentiments about his respect for England and her contribution to the world's culture. The appealing cry of " encirclement ", perhaps the most insidious of the Nazi hymns of hate, was raised with renewed emphasis, and Halifax was at great pains to eliminate the slightest excuse for its successful propagation either in Germany or in England. As he himself confessed, " one of the difficulties of the present position is that when His Majesty's Government offer negotiation they are accused of weakness, and when they show a disposition to defend their interests or the principles upon which international society, as we think, depends, they are accused of aggressive designs ".[2]

His last supreme effort to invoke the principle of negotiation with Germany was made on 8th June during a Lords' debate on foreign policy. The Peace Front had been strengthened by an excellent agreement with Turkey which laid the foundations of subsequent alliance, Anglo-Portuguese solidarity had just been proclaimed, but the

[1] German proposals to this effect had, in fact, been presented by Germany to the Polish Government less than a week after the occupation of Prague.

[2] In the House of Lords on 19th April 1939.

cornerstone to the new confederation of the Powers was still not in place. Over-optimistic reports of an imminent Pact with Russia had now given way to dark and sinister forebodings. Halifax chose this moment of perilous uncertainty, with Hitler on the brink of reversing his whole lifework and of inviting Stalin to collaborate with him in a fourth partition of Poland, to stress " the really dangerous element in the present situation, which is that the German people as a whole should drift to the conclusion that Great Britain had abandoned all desire to reach an understanding with Germany, and that any further attempt at such a thing must be once for all written off as hopeless ".

This speech was widely interpreted as a return to " appeasement ", but a close scrutiny of his carefully weighed words does not justify such a sweeping interpretation. It would be a shrewder estimate to say that he was primarily concerned with appeasing the appeasers, ensuring that he carried with him a united Government ready to underwrite the Polish guarantee in the hour of trial, and avoiding repetition of the Cabinet splits that so nearly shipwrecked Grey's patient diplomacy in July 1914. Even though the political outcry made necessary an explanatory statement four days later, and in spite of an ambiguous reference to " rival claims adjusted on a basis that might secure lasting Peace " and more than a hint that Britain was ready to take up the role of honest broker, there was no mistaking that Halifax still regarded war as the only alternative to negotiation. But that the speech was liable to misinterpretation in view of the Government's known record and the influences surrounding it can hardly be denied. It took no account of the remorseless but unavoidable fact that you cannot freely negotiate with a Government that has seized and retained its power by eliminating free negotiation as an instrument of public policy.

If he seriously hoped to create conditions for subsequent *détente* he was rudely rebuffed. *Diplomatische Korrespondenz* said simply, " not words but deeds will be Germany's answer to England ", while Goebbels' *Angriff* declared that the time had passed when the world believed the solemn protestations of British statesmen. In Rome his speech was represented as a mere tactical manœuvre dictated by the manifold difficulties of the situation and the slow progress of the negotiations with Russia. Gayda was perplexed and Ansaldo incredulous. Whatever Halifax's immediate purpose, it was strangled at birth, but if he temporarily lost ground with a mobilized public opinion, he soon more than made up for the reverse by his magnificent address to Chatham House and the nation on 29th June. In that hour he made world history and gave utterance to the will of a resurgent and united Commonwealth. An audience as politically representative and diverse as it would well be possible to pack in one room was roused to a pitch of vocal enthusiasm which in itself conveyed a tonic inspiration to the listening millions in their homes. Yet the secret of Halifax's triumph was not in oratorical technique, there could have been no greater contrast imaginable between Halifax's even tones, his mental detachment and moral sincerity than Hitler's manipulated hysterics. Yet in this antithesis was Halifax's victory, for being neither more nor less than himself, he spoke for England with a completeness to which no inflated egoism could aspire.

Politically Halifax's Chatham House speech ruled out the possibility of any further retreat; from henceforward appeasement was no longer an openly avowed aspiration but a furtive intrigue. Nowhere more fully than in Berlin and Rome was the pregnant meaning of his language understood; only the incredible stupidity of Ribbentrop could interpret Halifax's speech as bluff. The whole fantastic fraud of *Lebensraum* was exposed with ruthless cogency, encirclement's authorship held up to the light. "We are told that our motives are to isolate Germany within a ring of hostile States, to stifle her national outlets, to cramp and throttle the very existence of a great nation. What are the facts? They are simple and everybody knows them. Germany is isolating herself, and is doing it most successfully and most completely. She is isolating herself from other countries economically by her policy of autarky; she is isolating herself politically by a policy that causes constant anxiety to other nations, and culturally by her policy of racialism . . . it depends on the German Government, and on the German Government alone, whether this process of isolation continues or not, for any day it can be ended by a policy of co-operation. It is well that this should be stated plainly so that there may be no misunderstanding here or elsewhere." The principles of British Colonial administration were amply defended from German calumnies.

He was speaking at a moment not only when Germany and Italy were rattling the sabre with renewed zeal and entering into formal military alliance, but also when the Japanese, thwarted by Chiang Kai Shek's heroic resistance, were turning openly against what they rightly regarded as the focal centres of resistance to their New Order in East Asia—the Western Concessions. The specific crisis centred round the Tientsin Concession. The British Government refused to surrender to the local district court four Chinese alleged by the Japanese authorities to be implicated in the murder of another Chinese. The Japanese reprisal was out of all proportion to the issue at stake and bespoke wider designs. Tientsin was blockaded on 14th June, British citizens stripped and searched; but beyond these threats and humiliations was the shrewd hope that Britain's preoccupations in Europe would make it impossible for her to defend her interests in China, that by disrupting the currency by which Chinese foreign trade is largely financed the whole structure of the Open Door and equality of commercial opportunity in China would be overthrown and substituted by a closed East Asian economy designed to reinforce the Japanese armies and markets. The militarists in Tokyo no doubt calculated that if they could make the British position in China untenable the other Western Powers would soon abandon their holdings in the Far East. Tientsin was only the most flagrant in a whole series of provocations in the Japanese design to whittle away all foreign rights and interests. Halifax showed considerable resilience in handling this difficult question, which of necessity reacted on British relations both with Germany and Russia; he was ready to encourage the Japanese Foreign Office's reluctance to avow the wider aims of the military chauvinists, while at the same time maintaining the closest contact with France and America, thereby shrewdly refusing to admit the purely bilateral nature of the crisis.

The full force of his indignation was reserved, however, for his Chatham House speech. "I can say at once," he declared, and his words fitted Japan no less closely than Germany, "that Great Britain is not prepared to yield either to calumnies or to force. For every insult that is offered to our people, every rude challenge that is made to what we value and are determined to defend, only unites us, only increases our determination and strengthens our loyalty to those others who share our feelings and our aspirations." European and Asiatic dictators were alike solemnly warned. " British policy rests on twin foundations of purpose. One is determined to resist force. The other is our recognition of the world's desire to get on with the constructive work of building peace. If we could once be satisfied that the intentions of others were the same as our own, and that we all really wanted peaceful solutions—then, I say here definitely, we could discuss the problems that are to-day causing the world anxiety. . . . But this is not the position which we face to-day. The threat of military force is holding the world to ransom, and our immediate task is – and here I end as I began—to resist aggression. I would emphasize that to-night with all the strength at my command, so that nobody may misunderstand it. And if we are ever to succeed in removing misunderstanding and reaching a settlement which the world can trust, it must be upon some basis more substantial than verbal undertakings. It has been said that deeds, not words, are necessary. That also is our view."

. . . .

The buoyant temper of the Chatham House speech helped to offset the disappointments and delays in the negotiations with Russia. Halifax has been called upon to take more than his fair share of the blame for a momentous diplomatic reverse which made war inevitable. It is unfortunate for his personal reputation, although no doubt in the national interest for the duration of this incalculable war, that the demand for a White Paper on the abortive Anglo-French negotiations with Russia has not been met. The project was apparently abandoned at the request of the Ouai d'Orsay. Shortly after the outbreak of the Russo-Finnish war it was confidently reported that Halifax might decide to make a statement in the House of Lords " fully and frankly " explaining the circumstances of the breakdown, but he did not, and he has as a result been widely caricatured as the pious but none the less evil genius of the Soviet talks. It became almost a cliché to imply that he allowed his religious convictions to stand in the way of either full or frank discussion with blood-red Bolshevists. But this glib interpretation of his role is not borne out by available evidence, and ignores the fact that in the whole attempt to approach Stalin he was from the outset swimming against the diplomatic stream.

There was one notable omission from Hitler's Reichstag speech of 28th April which Coulondre aptly termed as " for the defence rather than an indictment ", there was for the first time no anti-Bolshevik tirade, indeed no reference to Russia at all. The significance of this extraordinary hiatus was brilliantly set out by Coulondre in a despatch on 7th May which enclosed a résumé of a conversation with one of Hitler's close associates. This informant supplied the key to German machinations. " The Poles," he was reported as saying, " fancy that they can be insolent to us, as they feel strong in the support of France and Britain, and believe that they can count upon the material assistance of Russia. They are mistaken in their calculations: just as Hitler did not consider himself in a position to settle the question of Austria and Czechoslovakia without Italy's consent, he now would not dream of settling the German-Polish difference without Russia. . . . In any case, we will arrange this matter in such a way that you will have neither reason nor even intention to intervene. It will not be in a month nor even in two months' time. Time is needed for preparation." Hitler was not at once openly committed to this conspiracy against the basic ideology of National Socialism, but the influences urging him towards rapprochement were powerful and persuasive. Himmler and Ribbentrop urged that France and Britain would never fight for Danzig, and that news of a pact with Russia would clinch the matter in favour of another bloodless victory. The Army chiefs saw in it release from the dreaded war on two fronts, while big industrialists envisaged Soviet Russia in the role of a totalitarian America.

When Halifax arrived in Geneva towards the end of May for what was to be the last forlorn meeting of the League Council, he received abundant information that Germany was working with accustomed thoroughness for agreement with Russia. The British Cabinet had been adamant in its refusal to consider the Soviet plea for a tripartite Pact and universal obligations, and obstinately required Russia to subscribe to unilateral guarantees to Poland and Rumania on the British model. If Halifax condoned this attitude during the first month he certainly revised his opinions at Geneva. Gordon Lennox, in a despatch to the *Daily Telegraph*,[1] described the " growing impression " that he was " prepared to urge most strongly on his Cabinet colleagues . . . that they should propose to Moscow an Anglo-Soviet agreement based on mutual aid against aggression ". " Contacts here," he added, " increase the conviction that if an Anglo-Soviet Pact is to be concluded at all it will have to be done in the next few days, and on realistic and straightforward lines."

In addition to German activity, and to Russian resentment at the unfounded optimism of British Press reports, Halifax discovered two other dangerous symptoms. Suspicions of a divergence of view between Daladier and Bonnet were confirmed. In Paris Halifax and Daladier reached agreement on the broad principle for a Three Power Pact, but in Geneva Bonnet was busy informing Maisky that there were no new French proposals. The attitude of the Quai d'Orsay was wholly supine, unready to incur risk or take initiative. Hardly less serious was the effect on Turkey of the deadlock with Russia. " The attitude of Turkey," commented Gordon Lennox, " is a further argument which will strengthen the hand of Lord Halifax should he determine to press the British Cabinet in the sense I have indicated. Turkey has regarded Anglo-Soviet agreement as a foregone conclusion, the essential counterpart of the Anglo-Turkish mutual assistance pact. It should be remembered that no treaty has yet been signed between London and Angora. I have good reason to believe that the signature may be indefinitely delayed if the Anglo-Soviet Pact fails to materialize."

On 19th May Chamberlain confessed in the House of Commons that he could not help feeling there was " a sort of veil, a sort of wall between the two Governments which it is extremely difficult to penetrate ", yet by the 27th the British and French Ambassadors had been instructed by their Governments to agree to discuss a triple pact. That Halifax instigated this *volte-face,* carried the day with both Governments and thereby saved the negotiations from complete collapse can hardly be questioned. Certainly the Kremlin

[1] 23rd May 1939.

entertained no doubts about the genuineness of his desire for agreement or the extent of his contribution to it, and proceeded at once to put out informal suggestions that he should come and take personal charge of the negotiations in Moscow.

His failure to respond has been the subject of perhaps the widest criticism. " If Lord Halifax had gone to Moscow ", wrote D. N. Pritt, most loyal of Stalin's British advocates, " the negotiations would probably have had so smooth a course that they would have succeeded. He did not go."[1] Setting aside this weighty compliment from a political adversary, if Halifax had been really convinced that his presence in Moscow would have made success " probable " it is highly unlikely that the pressure of any interests at home or abroad could have stopped him. Even if Chamberlain did spend his week-ends with men of pronounced anti-Bolshevist views, such as Sir Francis Lindley, Halifax's position in the country was far too strong to admit of any Cabinet prohibition. The fate of the Administration at this time, as Wickham Steed has justly observed, was in the hollow of his hand. At the annual meeting of All Souls —itself a virtual Inner Cabinet—Sir Arthur Salter was said vehemently to have pleaded with him that if only he would meet Stalin face to face he could save the peace of Europe, and Halifax to have replied no less earnestly that he was wondering whether to go but had grave misgivings whether any useful purpose would be served if he did. Two months later when he discussed the question, he recalled the Washington Naval Conference of 1921. In spite of Britain being represented by Balfour and of the most careful diplomatic preparation, it took three months to reach agreement. " In the present case I understand M. Molotov is obliged at every stage to consult his Government, and the same would have applied to any British representative, whether in the Cabinet or out of the Cabinet, who had been on our behalf conducting the negotiations for His Majesty's Government in Moscow."

The second stage in Halifax's approach to Russia was reached in the middle of June with the decision to send out William Strang of the Foreign Office. This move was widely welcomed at first, but when the days passed and frustration seemed to be the only outcome of intensive labours there

[1] *Light on Moscow*, page 83.

were indignant references to the deplorable policy of sending a " third-rate official " to treat with a first-class Power. But this invective was more rhetorical than accurate. Strang is an official, but as far as his record and experience are concerned neither third nor even second rate. He had a record of distinguished service in Moscow, had accompanied Eden there in 1935, he was the only Foreign Office man to assist Chamberlain on all three of his trips to Germany during the September crisis, and he was with Chamberlain and Halifax for the Paris conversations in November 1938. If the Kremlin meant business and was not merely playing the same insincere game which its propaganda accused Britain and France of doing, Strang was just the man for them, for he was in closest touch with the most recent trends of British diplomacy and with the requisite expertise to narrow down technical differences. Nor were instructions and comments wanting from Halifax; but do what he would, he and his experts could find no definition satisfactory to the Kremlin to cover the circumstances in which Britain would come to Russian aid.

Even more elusive was the formula that would meet the problem of " indirect attack ". Here indeed was the crux of the problem. Molotov kept on expressing the fear that the Baltic States might " be powerless to defend their neutrality ", by which he meant he was afraid they might prefer German occupation to Soviet protection. Hitler, too, might not need to invade these territories; Nazi influence from outside might be strong enough to constitute a serious threat to Russia's vital interests in the Baltic, which Halifax never hesitated to recognize. What he was not prepared for Britain to condone was that in order to forestall the menace of German indirect aggression Russia should herself violate the neutrality of the Baltic States. He was acutely conscious of the bearing Baltic neutrality had upon the destiny of Danzig, which Hitler had deliberately made the test case in his war of nerves. Ribbentrop's cynical opportunism was, quite apart from moral promptings, never even practical politics for Halifax.

The dramatic irony of Russia's position was one from which the watchful Stalin was pleased to derive the maximum profit and satisfaction. At Munich Hitler had made the elimination of Russia from Europe a condition of peace, and the Democracies had willingly concurred; now Whitehall and the Wilhelmstrasse were allied in their anxiety to reinstate the Soviet pariah. In such circumstances the temptation, always attractive to the Slav mind, to indulge in negotiation for its own sake, to put up his price against both bidders, was not seriously resisted. The first warning came with the sudden dismissal in May of Maxim Litvinov, the brilliant Soviet Foreign Minister. Halifax once asked who was responsible for the historic phrase " collective security ", the answer, unfortunately, was " Litvinov ", and his departure from the scene meant not only the dismissal of the one Soviet leader who had travelled beyond the Russian frontiers and gained an international reputation and experience, but also the death-blow to his policy. Russia from now on officially placed her confidence in the traditional and bourgeois military alliance.

To meet these new conditions Halifax agreed as a last resort to the Soviet request to institute military conversations in advance of a political agreement. Admittedly, it was not a very formidable military mission that set out in leisurely style from London late in the summer, but the measure of the risk in sending it out at all was soon to be gauged when it was discovered on arrival that a German special mission had made considerable headway in negotiations covering Russia's occupation of strategic bases in the Baltic and, it was rumoured, even more ambitious spheres of influence. The British officers did not have a chance of laying before the Russians any important Staff secrets; their French colleagues, however, were less fortunate. So, to the accompaniment of petty deceit, all Halifax's patient and scrupulous instructions were swept aside and the masters of the Kremlin carried through the most portentous diplomatic coup of the century. In some respects, however, the reverse was so overwhelming as to defeat itself. Hitler had secured himself against the threat of war on two fronts, but if his grand design was nothing less than the downfall of the British Empire by way of Moscow he might still find, as Napoleon did before him, that in the long run the conquest of Britain would involve the conquest of Russia.

Such reflections, however, could not compensate for the immediate shock and frustration. The knowledge that the guarantee to Poland, with the ambiguous test case of the Free City, was nothing like so obvious a moral issue as

Belgium in 1914; the persistent interference of appeasers in City and Government and even Court circles, Germany's unprecedented political and diplomatic technique and ideological distortions, made Halifax's task more uncertain and onerous than even Grey's had been. Yet by sheer steadfastness of mind and will he was able to withstand all the influences that sought to wear him down.

CHAPTER XXXVI

THE LIGHTS GO OUT

" ' DANZIG is not worth a European war '—this seems to be the catchword of German propaganda. Here great hopes are based on this phrase and on the echo which it might awaken abroad. That is the reason why it is maintained that there will be no war on account of Danzig, though it is at the same time claimed that the question will have to be settled sooner or later in a manner in conformity with the wishes of the Reich." Thus wrote Coulondre to Bonnet on 9th May, and the echo he mentioned had already been taken up in Printing House Square. We have seen that the immediate purpose of the Polish guarantee in diverting Hitler from direct action had been served; the second phase of Halifax's diplomacy is essentially the story of how he broke the conspiracy Coulondre so acutely foresaw. His success was largely attained by the double process of restraining the Poles, while at the same time leaving Hitler with no semblance of doubt or excuse that Great Britain would fulfil her pledged word to them. He reported, for instance, to Henderson in June that while disavowing all intention of encircling Germany he had told Dirksen firmly during an interview at the Foreign Office that " it seemed to us quite plain that the German Chancellor had broken the china in Europe and it was only he who could put it together again ".

Nevertheless to Sir Howard Kennard, the British Ambassador in Warsaw, a fortnight later, on 30th June, he wired a caveat which was to be the keynote of all his subsequent advice to Poland. " It would seem ", he wrote, " that Hitler is laying his plans very astutely so as to present the Polish Government with a *fait accompli* in Danzig, to which it would be difficult for them to react without appearing in the role of aggressors. I feel that the moment has come where consultation between the Polish, British and French Governments is necessary in order that the plans of the three

Governments may be co-ordinated in time. It is in the view of His Majesty's Government essential that these plans shall be so devised as to ensure that Hitler shall not be able to manage matters as to manœuvre the Polish Government into the position of aggressors." His pertinacity in stressing and developing this argument for Warsaw's benefit did much to ensure that when Hitler launched his war Nazi aggression was revealed to the whole world in its wanton nakedness.

But perhaps his most signal victory was his enhanced influence over the Prime Minister. No longer did Sir Horace Wilson enjoy a virtual monopoly, as during the Czech crisis, over the drafting of Chamberlain's speeches and letters to Hitler; Chamberlain was now fully restored to his official advisers. A good example of the new dispensation followed shortly upon Halifax's suggestion that the British, French and Polish Governments should consult and co-ordinate their plans in order to counteract the extensive military preparations that were taking place in Danzig. There was no immediate response from Warsaw, meanwhile the local situation in Danzig was rapidly becoming critical. To meet it Chamberlain made a formal statement on 10th July reviewing the British attitude, the language and the tone of which were firmer than any previous utterance of his in face of potential Nazi aggression. The argument that Danzig was predominantly a German city was at last put into proper perspective. Justice was done to Poland's strategic rights and economic necessity. " Moreover, there is no question of any oppression of the German population in Danzig." Chamberlain had at last closed the door against all Hitler's devices to isolate the forcible attainment of a particular Nazi objective from a general European war. In recalling a month later its " precise ", " clear " and " carefully weighed " terms Halifax added significantly, and not perhaps without a faint trace of relish, that it was a statement " which, in some quarters there may be surprise to learn, I had some hand in drafting ".

The effect of this well-timed display of explicit firmness seems to have thrown German diplomacy into temporary confusion. In Berlin, Coulondre reported that Chamberlain's declaration " unpleasantly surprised those who, like Herr von Ribbentrop, wished to cast doubts upon the possibility of armed intervention by Great Britain in the event of a

German-Polish conflict ". Indeed it may even have slightly weakened the Führer's confidence in the vindictive but non-combatant Foreign Minister who more than anyone else in Germany had been responsible for raising the Danzig issue next after Memel; for Hitler complained that Ribbentrop had been concealing vital information from him about Britain's war potential. In pressing home Chamberlain's statement at this vital moment the emphasis that Halifax was trying to impose on the Wilhelmstrasse seems to have been more resolutely made by Coulondre than by Henderson. When Weizsäcker complained to both Ambassadors separately about public warnings only making it more difficult for Hitler to heed them, Henderson reported to Halifax that personally he appreciated the force of this hint in favour of private communications and confined himself to the rejoinder that one of the main causes for anxiety in England was the belief that disagreeable facts were withheld from Hitler. Coulondre, with greater finesse, neatly refuted Weizsäcker's complaint about " the endless repetition of public declaration indulged in by the British Government " by remarking that the Prime Minister's speech was very cool and very objective and that to his knowledge it was the first time that he had defined the British Government's attitude concerning Danzig.

But it was in Danzig itself that the most encouraging developments were to be observed. Förster, the local Nazi leader, following an interview with Hitler, stated that " nothing will be done on the German side to provoke a conflict " and that the Danzig question could " wait if necessary until next year or even longer ". In addition he specifically invited the mediation of the resourceful League High Commissioner, Burckhardt. Halifax immediately seized on this somewhat clumsy Nazi attempt to secure a line of diplomatic retreat once more to urge caution on Warsaw. " Whatever may be the import of this German move," he wired to Kennard, " position of Polish Government cannot be worsened in any respect by doing their utmost to make a success of procedure proposed by Gauleiter to High Commissioner."

The *détente* lasted until early in August, when there were two grave developments. Germany formally intervened in a dispute which had hitherto been confined to negotiation between the Polish Government and the Danzig Senate. At the same time there was a noticeable tendency to drop the local Danzig issue in favour of questions affecting the existence of the Polish State as a whole. In both respects German policy was following lines laid down in the Sudeten crisis; an even more interesting parallel was Hitler's search for a " mediator " who might perhaps play the role of Runciman, and his choice of Burckhardt, whose record at Danzig seemed to commend him as a man of sympathetic temper but whose status was sufficiently " democratic " to draw the British and French. Accordingly on 11th August, in spite of some previous opposition from Ribbentrop, who perhaps sensed a threat to his personal ascendancy, Hitler interviewed Burckhardt at Berchtesgaden. Halifax was shrewd enough to realize, however, that Burckhardt's position to effect a genuine settlement, if such was Hitler's intention, was very much stronger than ever Runciman's was, and he did not hesitate to commend him to Beck. " In dealing with local Danzig issues ", he wrote to Kennard on the 15th, " I would beg M. Beck to work through the intermediary of the High Commissioner, or at all events after consultation with him, rather than direct with the Senate." While Burckhardt was with Hitler, Ribbentrop and Ciano were in conclave at Salzburg and the preparations laid for another *deus ex machina* act by Mussolini.

In the prevailing confusion which Hitler did his best to intensify, Halifax still refused to accept war as the inevitable outcome, there was still margin for reasoned hope. " I have the impression ", he told Kennard in the same message," that Herr Hitler is still undecided, and anxious to avoid war and to hold his hand if he can do so without losing face." A week later, on the 22nd, Ribbentrop was in Moscow, and an astonished world confronted with a Pact which had obviously been the outcome of prolonged preparation. There was, however, no undue dismay in Downing Street, only renewed resolve. Chamberlain's letter to Hitler, written and despatched on the day of the Pact, was an heroic effort to meet the menace of the Führer's mental exhilaration following his supreme diplomatic coup, but for all its statesmanlike promptitude and clarity the last hope of negotiation seemed to have been deliberately snuffed out by Hitler. Henderson found him at first " excitable and uncompromising ", then in a second conversation " calmer but wholly uncompromising ", Britain, he maintained, was " determined to destroy and exterminate Germany. He was, he said, fifty years old; he preferred war now to when he would be fifty-five or sixty." His written reply was no less destructive, the only substantial point he made being that if effect was given to the precautionary military measures Chamberlain had mentioned he would at once order the mobilization of all the German forces.

There was reliable information to show that the onslaught on Poland was scheduled to begin on the night of August 25th-26th. Yet for one more week the agony was prolonged. The very bulk of the material available to us helps to conceal the parts played by Halifax in this last strange *détente*. Hitler took the first initiative in summoning Henderson and Coulondre on the 25th, but his mood and motives were hardly those of a man who seriously intended to switch over from the processes of war to those of sweet reason and peace. To Henderson he spoke in the jargon of a demi-god. He described himself to him as a man of great decisions, " and in this case also he will be capable of being great in his action. He accepts the British Empire and is ready to pledge himself personally for its continued existence . . . the Führer repeats that he is a man of *ad infinitum* decisions by which he himself is bound and that this is his last offer. Immediately after solution of the German-Polish question he would approach the British Government with an offer." Translated into less prophetic and ambiguous language Hitler's last offer was the promise to make an offer (unspecified) after Poland had been conquered. To Coulondre he adopted an entirely different tone, speaking as man to man. " I want to state once again: I wish to avoid war with your country. I will not attack France, but if she joins in the conflict, I will see it through to the bitter end."

Of all the possible explanations for Hitler's action, the most plausible seems to be that he was bent upon making a last desperate attempt to separate France from Britain. He was well aware how deeply disturbed Bonnet and Daladier were by the military limitations of the Entente. The dispute about the British contribution to the French armies had been going on ever since Chamberlain and Halifax had attempted to shelve it during their visit to Paris in November 1938 by referring it back to the General Staffs. British conscription was now, on the edge of the abyss, seen in Paris for what it was, little more than a symbol and a gesture. All the immediate help Belisha could promise was six divisions. Furthermore, Hitler calculated that the meaning of the Russian Pact would make an even deeper impression on the Quai d'Orsay than on Whitehall. Bonnet was dissuaded from openly requesting the Poles to cede Danzig and the Corridor to the Germans only by the overriding opinion of French Army chiefs who professed to see no reason for postponing the war. Hitler's " peace offer " was characteristic in its timing and deception, but that the ruse was thwarted and that the spectre of aggression returned to plague its author was very largely due to the resource, sincerity and strength of Halifax's diplomacy.

. . . .

Although Chamberlain was in no sense backward in assuming supreme responsibility, the most noticeable contrast between this and the Munich crisis was the dominance of Halifax, a fact certainly recognized by the crowds gathered outside Whitehall who during the last days of peace never failed to single him out for specially warm applause. On the 26th August, two days after Parliament had reassembled, it was, significantly, Halifax and not Chamberlain who broadcast from 10 Downing Street to the world. His words, naturally, recalled Chamberlain's message to the nation two days before Munich, but only in the circumstances of their delivery, not the force of their argument. The new era of equivocal understatement was over. " It is not the British way to go back on obligations. We mean to fulfil the obligations which we have assumed." As these words of measured defiance sped across the earth, there was a sense almost of relief that Great Britain had at last taken her stand. Millions in America heard his broadcast which made a particularly deep impression there. " The speech was news," declared Raymond Gram Swing, " because Halifax showed no sign of wavering."

On the evening of the 25th, under pressure of imminent aggression, Halifax and Raczynski, the Polish Ambassador in London, signed the long-delayed agreement of Mutual Assistance. This step was taken without reference to Hitler's peace feeler, and it seemed as though it would involve too brusque a challenge to totalitarian prestige for Hitler to delay military action any longer; his Army chiefs, fearing that the dry weather in Poland might break and irreparably damage their blitzkrieg, were chafing at each day's delay. His retort was to stop just short of war, to announce the appointment of Förster, the local Nazi leader, as head of the Danzig State, and at the same time to complete German military concentrations on the Polish frontier.

The whole of Halifax's effort during the next two days was bent upon engaging Hitler in some form of direct negotiation with Warsaw. To this end he put before the Polish Government the suggestion of a corps of neutral observers who would enter upon their duties as soon as it was found possible for the negotiations to begin. More ambitious was his further proposal that the Poles should consent to discuss exchange of populations. For a brief moment a gleam of hope lit up the Chancellories of Europe that Hitler was seriously anxious to negotiate with the Poles on this issue, and Halifax was urged by Henderson to make the most of the opportunity. But when it is realized that Hitler's only comment which could be said to bear any relation to the question was a truculent reference to his determination " to abolish Macedonian conditions on Germany's Eastern frontier ", it will be seen just how flimsy was the material at Halifax's disposal. " It is true ", he wired to Kennard on the 26th, " this would afford no immediate safeguard as it is a remedy that would take some time to apply, but it would be a pledge that the Polish Government recognize the difficulty and are genuinely seeking means to overcome it, and it would give Polish Government some definite and new point on which to open up negotiations. If action is to be taken by the Polish Government in this sense it ought to be done immediately." Two days later he assured the Poles that in the British reply to Hitler " a clear distinction " had been drawn between " the method of reaching agreement on German-Polish differences and the nature of the solution to be arrived at. As to the method, we wish to express our clear view that direct discussion on equal terms between the parties is the proper means."

The outcome of all this correspondence with Warsaw was that the British Government was able to confront Hitler in its reply, which Henderson presented to him on the 28th, with " the definite assurance from the Polish Government that they are prepared to enter into discussions ". It was an assurance which got beneath Hitler's guard and which it was equally difficult for him to accept or reject out of hand. Henderson underlined its import; he told Hitler that the choice before him was " the unilateral solution, which would mean war as regards Poland, or British friendship ". At first he hedged, his army was ready and eager for battle and he was not prepared to answer at once whether he would negotiate direct with Poland. On the afternoon of the 29th Halifax and Chamberlain reiterated the British position. " Everything," Halifax declared, " turns upon the manner in which the immediate differences between Germany and Poland can be handled and the nature of the proposals which might be made for any settlement. For we have made it plain that our obligations to Poland, cast into formal shape by the agreement signed on August 25th, will be carried out."

At 7.15 that evening Henderson received Hitler's fateful answer: the German Government was prepared to accept the British proposal for direct German-Polish negotiation, but counted on the arrival of the Polish plenipotentiary by 30th August. Henderson at once observed that this latter demand sounded like an ultimatum, and in spite of Hitler's and Ribbentrop's heated disavowal and a concluding paragraph to the effect that the German Government would immediately draw up proposals for a solution acceptable to themselves and would, if possible, place these at the disposal of the British Government before the arrival of the Polish negotiator, the whole procedure was essentially a sordid repetition of Godesberg. At four o'clock on the morning of the 30th, Henderson, on instructions from Halifax, informed the German Government that it would be " unreasonable to expect the British Government to produce a Polish representative in Berlin " by the 30th and that " the German Government must not expect this ".

Throughout the 30th and 31st Halifax strove heroically for the double objective of peace and the united action and moral integrity of the Allies in the event of war. He held the scales equally between German duplicity and Polish intransigence. He did not hesitate on the 30th to warn Berlin of reports " that Germans have committed acts of sabotage which would justify the sternest measures ", and to add an hour afterwards, "We understand that German Government are insisting that a Polish representative with full powers must come to Berlin to receive German proposals. We cannot advise Polish Government to comply with this procedure, which is wholly unreasonable. Could you not suggest to German Government," he continued, "that they adopt the normal procedure, when their proposals are ready, of inviting the Polish Ambassador to call and handing proposals to him for transmission to Warsaw and inviting suggestions as to conduct of negotiations?" He could claim that when Henderson handed in at midnight the British reply to the German letter accepting direct negotiation in principle, nothing that was diplomatically possible had been left undone to guide Germany into the paths of peace. In effect, Halifax's pertinacity now compelled the Nazi wolf to rip off his sheep's clothing. Ribbentrop's barbarous behaviour in producing Germany's sixteen point proposals, reading them out aloud to Henderson in German at top speed, then withholding them from him on the grounds that it was now "too late" to do anything more about them as the Polish representative had not arrived by midnight, was in itself a tribute to the skill and precision of British diplomacy which forced him to adopt such pitiful and revealing chicanery.

Throughout the 31st Halifax, in a last desperate effort to meet the German demands, studiously ignored Henderson's damning evidence. Even after the Nazis had broadcast their sixteen points and pronounced them rejected by Poland Halifax was still "earnestly hoping" Beck would modify his instructions to his Ambassador in Berlin which forbade him to receive a document from the German Government for transmission to Warsaw. Not until the next morning after Hitler had released the lightning of his war on Poland and the world, was Halifax aware that Lipski, the Polish Ambassador in Berlin, had seen Ribbentrop shortly before the German proposals were broadcast, but that he had been unable to get in touch with his Government as the Nazis had cut him off from all means of communication with Warsaw.[1]

[1] "Moreover, the fact cannot be overstressed, that on August 31st, as early as 1 p.m., the Polish Ambassador in Berlin requested Herr von Ribbentrop to see him in order to inform him of the consent by Poland to conversations being opened. It was not until 7.45 p.m. that M. Lipski was received by the Minister for Foreign Affairs, who confined himself to taking note of his communication, without informing him as to the contents of the German plan or even making mention of it in any way."—Coulondre to Bonnet, 2nd September 1939.

" Herr Hitler is trying," commented Léon Noël, French Ambassador in Warsaw, in the early hours of 1st September, " by this broadcast to escape from the diplomatic negotiation in which, contrary to his methods, he got involved by Great Britain." Four hours later his armies released him by crossing the frontiers of Poland.

The House of Lords can have heard few more damning indictments of perjured intrigue than Halifax's cool and unemotional report of 1st September. " The rulers of Germany," he declared, " appear to have conceived of a negotiation between themselves and Poland as nothing more than the summoning of a Polish plenipotentiary to Berlin at twenty-four hours notice, to discuss terms not previously communicated to them; and I am bound to say that such a position, with the examples of the Austrian Chancellor and the President of Czechoslovakia before them, was not one which I think the Polish Government could readily be expected to accept. And thus, in those circumstances when the German Chancellor issued this morning a statement that ' the Polish State has refused the peaceful settlement of relations which I desire '—My Lords," said Halifax quietly and deliberately, looking up from his papers, " of those issues and of those doings the world will judge." Halifax on 1st September spoke with an air of finality. " It is thus," he said, " that we reach the end of all the efforts and the hopes of these last weeks. . . . It has been a source of great satisfaction to us to know that Signor Mussolini also was using all his influence in an endeavour, up to the last moment, to save the peace. Our conscience, I think we can say, is clear."

But the ordeal by diplomacy was not yet ended. On 31st August Mussolini had suddenly offered, if France and England would accept, to invite Germany to a conference on 5th September " during which present difficulties arising out of the Versailles Treaty would be examined ". Throughout 1st September there were distracting exchanges of view between London and Paris as to the form of the Allied reply. In order to avoid any appearance of dissension at such a critical moment Halifax at first wisely left the French to reply to Mussolini as they saw fit, but when on 2nd September Ciano made contact with Bonnet and Halifax direct by telephone saying he believed it was still

CHURCHILL'S COLLEAGUE

possible to take up the subject of a conference, some form of agreed decision from the Allies was imperative. An attempt was made to convey the impression that Italy's mediation was last minute altruism, but it would be a shrewder estimate to suggest that ever since Ciano's and Ribbentrop's meeting at Salzburg in the middle of August Axis diplomacy had stored carefully in reserve the expedient of a second and more comprehensive Munich. Given the same balance of political power as had operated in London and Paris in September 1938, the ruse might have succeeded. As it was, Bonnet and the French Government clutched at the straw with an eagerness which must have encouraged the Dictators in their persistent attempts to divide the Democracies. Even in Westminster the utmost confusion prevailed, and when after several delays Chamberlain made his statement that evening and announced after thirty-six hours of German aggression on Poland neither war nor even an ultimatum, the temper of the Commons reached breaking-point.

Parliament can never have known so drastic an emotional revolution as had taken place between 28th September 1938 and 2nd September 1939. Instead of the hysterical longing for peace was a fierce resolve, brooking no denial, to resist an intolerable tyranny. " Speak for England! " cried the Conservative Amery when on behalf of the Labour Opposition Arthur Greenwood rose to make his inspired reply and to urge even war itself as preferable to uncertainty. Greenwood himself aptly summed up for me the political atmosphere of that day of rumour and suspense. " If someone," he said, " had come along and told me ' Jo Stalin has gone to Rome and is kissing the Pope's toe ', I should have believed him! "

But if Greenwood spoke for England, Halifax no less surely acted for her. " Lord Halifax," Corbin informed Bonnet early in the afternoon of 2nd September, " deems it impossible to allow the present situation to continue any longer. That was why, as early as last night, he had suggested that our representatives in Berlin should, without further delay, inform the Government of the Reich of the obligations under which both our Governments would be free to consider themselves in a state of war with Germany if satisfaction was not given, or if no answer had reached them within a few hours. Lord Halifax would make a declaration that France and England consider themselves from now on as being in a state of war with the Reich." When Halifax spoke with Ciano by telephone he confirmed that Britain had as yet delivered no ultimatum to Germany, but added that in his opinion to halt the German troops on their positions would be insufficient and that the occupied territories would have to be evacuated. Ciano replied at once that in his opinion there was little possibility of obtaining this from the Germans.

Shortly after five o'clock Halifax informed Bonnet that the Cabinet had formally decided that a favourable reply to the proposed conference could only be given upon one preliminary condition; " that is that the German troops are withdrawn from the territory which they occupy ". By seven o'clock Mussolini himself decided, in view of Halifax's attitude, to take no further action. None the less Bonnet held back the French reply for two more hours, then confirmed that the French note of 1st September was not an ultimatum and that he was prepared to wait until noon on Sunday, 3rd September, for the German reply. " However, the French Government deems, like the British Government, that the conference cannot open under auspices of force, and that, in order that the plan might be successfully realized, it is advisable that the German armies should evacuate the territory occupied in Poland."

But the time for Bonnet's equivocation and finesse was over. André Maurois, in his poignant book *Why France Fell,* reveals that at nine o'clock on the morning of 3rd September Halifax called Bonnet by telephone and said to him: " I am aware of the reasons that prevent you from sending your ultimatum before noon, but we have not made the same promise to Count Ciano and we are obliged to send ours this morning. The House of Commons convenes at noon, and if the Prime Minister appears there without having fulfilled his promises to Poland he may be overthrown by a unanimous movement of indignation." Thus it came about that Parliament and the people heard of Britain's ultimatum only when it had expired and France did not go to war until seven hours afterwards.

. . . .

It was not given to Halifax to play Grey's dramatic role.

Here was no situation in which the very support of Parliament for war hung on the Foreign Secretary's interpretation of unknown events, here was no short and sharp crisis taking the people by surprise, no sense of " gay adventure " in the impending conflict. Rather, war in 1939 came as the anti-climax to three years of the most ruthless and complicated diplomatic struggle that this nation had ever known. For months the strategy, the tactics and the menace of Hitler had been discussed, until war itself alone could simplify the endless argument. In such an atmosphere of recurring tension Halifax's diplomacy could never achieve in public estimation the epic and Olympian quality attributed to Grey. In addition, although Halifax was undoubtedly at the helm throughout the Polish crisis, it was Chamberlain's conversion to the doctrine of resistance, the collapse of all that Chamberlain had striven for during the period of his personal ascendancy, that made the most obvious appeal to the public mind. The balance of power within the Inner Cabinet, the underlying conflict between the Foreign Office and Sir Horace Wilson, these things were secondary in popular estimation to the martyrdom of Chamberlain. Yet as that acute free-lance Parliamentarian, Josiah Wedgwood, observed, and he is a merciless critic of his contemporaries, " we must indeed go far back in history to find a match for the diplomacy of Great Britain under Lord Halifax from November 1938 to August 1939 ".

Unprecedented national unity had been achieved without concession to the popular clamour for a Pact with Russia, and even more remarkable, without any change in the personnel of the most bitterly criticized Administration in living memory. The advantages of standing firm over Russia were soon apparent. By refusing to barter away the independence of the Baltic States he was able to give convincing evidence that his policy was not primarily aimed at encircling Germany but upholding the rights of all States from aggression everywhere. He was, as a result, able to extract the maximum advantage from the revulsion felt by all neutral governments, great and small, at Hitler's shameless cynicism. An attitude of official reserve, for instance, could not conceal the dismay felt in Madrid where the militant Falangist newspaper, *Arriba,* of otherwise Anglophobe tendencies, reacted to the new situation by singling out Halifax's broadcast of 26th August for special praise. " Seldom ", it significantly stated, " has a British Minister expressed himself in terms so measured and so noble as Lord Halifax has done."

Halifax's policy of negotiating with Japan, giving way on the local issues, standing firm on the wider demands, was abundantly justified. To engage Britain in the Tokyo Conference when the advantage seemed to be stacked so heavily in favour of Japan required political courage; to reject out of hand, as he did her pretensions over Chinese currency and silver deposits in Tientsin only a fortnight before the outbreak of war with Germany, seemed to verge on rashness. His policy constituted a grave check to Japan's hope of controlling the trade of North China, and now Germany's Pact with Moscow undermined the political meaning of the Anti-Comintern Pact at the very moment that Japan needed to exploit it against the Democracies. Moreover, Russia as well as Germany was released from the danger of war on two fronts. Stalin was now free to take whatever action he liked in the Far East.

Not the least satisfactory feature in Japan's discomfiture was the co-ordination of British and American diplomatic pressure. The Foreign Office had been slow to avail itself of Roosevelt's benign influence, and the Far East had been a fruitful source of misunderstanding; but when at the end of July Roosevelt denounced America's trade agreement with Japan, involving over fifty per cent of essential Japanese raw material, militarists in Tokyo could not fail to link it up with British firmness as part of one formidable operation. Washington had from the outset shown a lively appreciation of Halifax as Foreign Secretary, and throughout all the vicissitudes of appeasement and the Peace Front his motives were far more sympathetically understood by a shrewd American Government than by the public on either side of the Atlantic. The career of the mercurial Joseph Kennedy as American Ambassador to London roughly coincided with Halifax's at the Foreign Office, and his respect for the Foreign Secretary amounted almost to veneration. " He is," he once asserted, " the most noble figure in public life I have encountered, almost a saint."

Of all Halifax's appointments, quite the most timely and inspired was his decision in May 1939 to send Lothian to

Washington. There was plenty of criticism at the time, Lothian was particularly identified with the philosophy of appeasement, but with his capacity to see below the surface of things Halifax realized that Lothian's personality, and above all his unique experience of American people and outlook, would transcend all difficulties and make his mission an outstanding episode in Anglo-American relations. Indeed, measured in terms of its effects on the destiny of democracy, the Lothian appointment was Halifax's supreme achievement. Lothian's mind, intellectually subtle, religious, non-partisan, was set in the same mould as Halifax's; both were attracted by the broader vision of the philosophy behind politics. Perhaps Lothian was keenly stimulated by the exercise of power, although that may have been because he had not been vouchsafed Halifax's ample share of it, and was, until called to Washington, in a sense a frustrated man. The friendship and affinity of these two men during the thirty years that they were grappling with the same problems of Imperial and foreign policy, bridged, as no formal relationship could, the gulf between Washington and London. But more than that, Lothian by his despatches was with unconscious but splendid thoroughness training his sponsor and chief to become his successor. It was to prove an initiation unique in the annals of British diplomacy.

CHAPTER XXXVII

HAZARDS OF WAR

It would be premature and presumptuous to enter into any detailed narrative or assessment of Halifax's war record. While the struggle lasts, military strategy dominates the conduct of foreign affairs, and censorship dominates both. On the assumption that new wine can be carried in old bottles, Britain was led into war by the Government who had initiated and then abandoned appeasement. The new policy had failed to produce new men; now having failed to secure peace either by appeasement or its opposite, the same men, although reinforced by Churchill and Eden, remained in office to do battle. The Opposition leaders were at once invited by Chamberlain to join the Government, but after two years of embittered party strife the offer was easier for the Prime Minister to make than for the Socialists and Liberals to accept, nor was the emergency such as to rule out the possible usefulness of organized political opposition. Chamberlain then fell back on a preconceived plan of a War Cabinet of six which was to include—at long last—Winston Churchill in the sovereign guise of Minister of Defence; but even that proposal could not apparently stand up against the usual political pressures, and a compromise Cabinet emerged with Churchill as First Lord and the other two Service Ministers, Kingsley Wood for Air and Belisha for War, sharing the strategic sovereignty with him and helping to bring the total membership up to nine. In spite, however, of all these " safeguards " Churchill seems to have dominated the councils of that Cabinet just as surely as if he had been given the powers originally meant for him, and before many months were out Belisha and Kingsley Wood had found the pace too hot for them.

Halifax remained untouched by all these shufflings and reshufflings of his colleagues; in the various speeches he rarely committed himself to any considered military opinion and was extremely reticent even about his own department.

The catastrophic destruction of Poland, followed by the period of apparent lull throughout the winter which was broken only by the Soviet aggression on Finland, did not allow of much diplomatic initiative. The Maginot mentality seems to have paralysed the deliberations of the inchoate Supreme War Council which Halifax occasionally attended. Chamberlain and Daladier confined themselves to generalities and only the negative suspicions of Darlan or the creative energy of Churchill marred the soothing complacence of its official proceedings.

On the diplomatic front the bare fact was that we were at war with too few allies and too many neutrals, and without spectacular military success there was little Halifax could do to enlarge the coalition or circumvent neutrality. His first diplomatic duty was to help in rebutting Hitler's inevitable peace offensive following the annihilation of Poland. Flushed with easy victory, Hitler neither conceived nor carried through his peace campaign with his accustomed guile, and apart from the warnings of Lloyd George, whose Polish antipathies went back to Versailles and whose strategic experience and insight could not be ignored, there was singularly little reaction. Halifax's chief contribution to the discussion was to stress that resistance to Nazism was not confined to its breaches of faith with Governments. In a broadcast to the world on the purpose of the struggle he stressed that " when the challenge in the sphere of international relations is sharpened, as to-day in Germany, by the denial to man and woman of elementary human rights, the challenge is at once extended to something instinctive and profound in the universal conscience of mankind. We are therefore fighting to maintain the rule of law and the quality of mercy in dealings between man and man and in the great society of civilized States." The concept, so admirably expressed by Dorothy Thompson, that the war was basically a civil war, a fight to bring the Germans back into the European and Christian family of which they are indispensable members and to which they have made so many historic contributions, was never far removed from Halifax's best thought on the subject.

Perhaps his most notable and mature reflections are to be found in an address he delivered in February 1940 to Oxford University in his capacity as Chancellor. Speaking to a crowded meeting at the Sheldonian he put forward the view that the real conflict underlying the war was not between age and youth, but between youth and youth. Beyond asserting that there was " something sinister " in the acceptance by the growing generations in different countries, of standards of conduct in sharp contradiction to one another and that it constituted " a terrifying challenge to the very foundation of human thought and action " he did not develop in coherent detail what was in itself a somewhat trite proposition. Nevertheless *The Times* in reprinting the address at once seized on this paragraph to give it the title " A Conflict of Youth ", but the Oxford University Press edition, which termed it " The Challenge to Liberty ", more accurately conveyed its message. Under that heading there is much that will endure in his bold defence of British values, his clear recognition of the menace of Nazi nihilism, " primitive nonsense " in theory, " a crime against humanity " in practice. In such a titanic conflict the immolation of opposing youth is but an incident, and on his own reckoning there would indeed be " something sinister " if British youth failed to rise to arms in defence of the British way of life or to comprehend what it was defending. The dangerous feature of this war is not the conflict between youth—it is in the nature of things that young men should fight the wars—but the absorption of all civilian life, both sexes, every age and category of the country in the processes of self-slaughter. But for all that, Halifax's thesis that the " future of humanity must not be left in the hands of those who would imprison and enslave it " at once justifies and ennobles even wholesale sacrifice.

The only major diplomatic victory for the Allies in the early phases of the war was the Tripartite Treaty with Turkey for which Chamberlain and Halifax had laboured indefatigably throughout the summer. Much was made of Italian neutrality and many economic concessions were devised, but for all the protestations and expectations following Germany's Pact with Russia, Mussolini continued to work in closest collusion with Hitler; just before he took the final plunge and engaged prostrate France in war Mussolini was formally warned by Russia that " nothing but disgrace and defeat awaited such an attempt ". " Nearly all the world shares the view ", the statement continued, " that the present Italian Government is distinguished by the most shameful,

AMBASSADOR TO WASHINGTON

Lord and Lady Halifax walking up the stairs past a large portrait of King George V on taking up Residence in their new home, the British Embassy in Massachusetts Avenue

degenerate, corrupt and opportunist characteristics." But even the most choice Soviet invective did not disturb the underlying fact that Russia and Italy were at one in friendship and usefulness to the Reich.

The Russo-Finnish war was more than a distracting incident, it brought Halifax face to face with the problem of neutral rights, obligations and commitments, and by complicating the general situation helped to conceal Hitler's real strategic aims. Halifax certainly had the Russian attack in Finland in perspective in regarding it as a direct consequence of German policy and in refusing to be drawn into any violent and unprofitable anti-Soviet position. The sting in the criticism that Allied aid to Finland had been " too little and too late " rested in the rigid refusal of Sweden and Norway to allow British and French troops to pass through their territories. Nothing could have been more reasonable or timely than Halifax's warning to the neutrals. " We do our best," he pleaded in December 1939, " to apply the policy with restraint and consideration. We try to alleviate hardships to neutral trade, and nothing that we have done on the sea has brought into peril a single life of any neutral citizen." Germany had shown no such humanity and discrimination. " Her policy clearly threatens both the liberties of neutral countries and the fundamental principles on which their life, just as much as our own, is founded. It is in that light that we have a right to ask neutrals to judge the actions which are forced upon us through the methods by which the German Government makes war." When all the facts are available, history will surely acquit Halifax of any negligence in his applying all possible political pressure.

Reynaud, superseding the over-cautious Daladier as Prime Minister in France, at once attempted to launch a French diplomatic offensive in the Balkans which Halifax supported with alacrity. Britain's Ambassadors to Turkey, Greece, Rumania, Hungary, Bulgaria and Jugoslavia were recalled for a conference at the Foreign Office under Halifax's chairmanship. That such deliberations were in fact scheduled to coincide with the German onslaught on Norway and Denmark is a tribute more to Nazi stealth than British Intelligence work. The immediate prelude to the Norwegian fiasco was, then, a detailed review of a possible drive by Hitler to the East. Even more inauspicious was the unhappy wrangle over the *Altmark* incident in which Halifax was compelled to counteract German pressure with energetic protests. When the storm broke, Halifax reacted with the requisite vigour. Speaking virtually impromptu at a luncheon on the day after the invasion, he stressed that Britain or France could at any moment during the past six months have occupied any port or base in Norway that they chose; " and this kind of thing, I venture to think, is liable to happen if neutral States are not prepared to ask in time for the help that they often ask for when it is all too late to render it effectively ".

Beverley Baxter, a shrewd and well-informed judge of political " form ", found Halifax's reputation in the ascendant during the early phase of the Battle for Norway. He noted that he was developing into a " benevolent autocrat " at the Foreign Office, that his voice carried much weight in the War Cabinet and that he was said to be " the champion of aggressive action ", stating his opinions with " firmness and clarity ". Dr. Koht, the Norwegian Foreign Minister, has himself testified to Halifax's buoyancy at that time. " Lord Halifax was not a talkative man," he writes, " but his impressive, warm-hearted personality sometimes said much more than words could do. He was filled with noble eagerness to help our country, and it was a relief to listen to his quiet, warm voice expressing absolute confidence in victory."[1] How far Halifax's aggressive spirit, clarity and firmness resisted the abandonment of the original Allied plan to recapture Trondheim is still only a matter for conjecture; what is certain is that the decision exercised a disastrous influence on the course of the whole campaign, and the only aerodrome in South Norway, the lack of which Hoare bemoaned in the fateful post-mortem debate a month later, was irretrievably lost to the Allies.

. . . .

But Hitler's conquest of Norway was to have a consequence even he could not have foreseen. During the brief breathing-space between the British withdrawal from Scandinavia and the German onslaught upon the Low Countries, under the very shadow of new invasions, Parliament in the course of one feverish debate closed an era in British political history. The Conservative domination set up at the Carlton

[1] *Norway—Neutral and Invaded.*

Club in 1922, and with two brief exceptions of minority Socialism enjoying uninterrupted power for the next seventeen years, was swept away on the evening of 8th May, 1940. The smoothness of the processes which brought the Churchill Government into power, the overwhelming cataclysm of the next six weeks, have tended to submerge their dramatic contrast and even their meaning. Captain Margesson, the omnipotent and omniscient Government Chief Whip, apparently advised Chamberlain that there was no danger of a serious Conservative revolt over Norway, and Chamberlain on the first day of the debate accordingly confined himself to a routine and superficial defence of the Government's policy, a second best effort to meet a secondary occasion. Two formidable assaults by Sir Roger Keyes, who pledged the whole weight of his experience and conviction on the Trondheim offensive, and by L. S. Amery, who in a desperate attempt to stir the Government from complacency invoked Cromwell's exhortation to the Long Parliament—" In the name of God go ", pierced the Administration's outer defences; but when on the next day the Labour Party decided to make the issue a vote of confidence, many experienced judges believed that with customary obtuseness they had misread the position and that their action would merely force a group of potentially dissident Conservatives back into the fold.

That the Labour tactic confounded these critics was immediately due to Chamberlain's fatal appeal to his " friends " in the House after Herbert Morrison had deliberately widened the scope of the debate to cover not merely Norway but the whole conduct of the war. Although Lloyd George was not in the House when Chamberlain made his intervention, it gave him the opening he required for one of the most devastating political attacks of even his fighting life. All the pent-up bitterness of years was contained in his demand that the best service Chamberlain could do to the State was to give up his Seals of Office. The strained silence of the House after Lloyd George sat down testified more eloquently than any demonstration would have done to the sense that a great taboo had been violated, that there was release at last from frustration. The Government apologists, Hoare in the Commons, Hankey in the Lords, spoke like desperately tired men.

When Halifax wound up the debate in the Lords it was abundantly clear that the Administration was in danger. His insistence on the collective responsibility of the Cabinet for all decisions taken instinctively recalled his attitude to the crumbling Coalition eighteen years before. "We all have one purpose," he added with sublime detachment. "If it was at any time thought to be the case that other men could do the job better, certainly no member of the Government, so far as I am aware, would be unwilling to be relieved of responsibility that can bring no personal satisfaction, but only a burden that at times must be wellnigh insupportable." When Churchill was at last called upon to save the Government from the wrath to come he was in a desperate dilemma. The obvious exponent of more vigorous national action, he had now to act as the supreme apologist for negative compromise. A peculiar spirit of irony which seemed resolved always to distort and confine Churchill's splendid genius operated once again in this the most critical moment of his career. His speech winding up the Norwegian debate was in cold print a Parliamentary masterpiece, but in the electric atmosphere of the Commons M.P.s were in no mood to appreciate his technique. For one reason and another his special pleading made no appeal to the Labour Opposition, and there were one or two unfortunate incidents, which were trivial enough in themselves but which in the heat of battle were exaggerated far beyond their real importance. In the feverish discussion in the Lobbies immediately after the vote which had reduced the Government's majority to a mere 81, it was generally conceded that no broadening of the Administration under Chamberlain's command would meet the case, but there was a distinct tendency to mark down Churchill's claims, to recall his past rather than enhance his future. His closest supporters were cautious in promoting his interests.

Almost inevitably Halifax's name emerged as the natural compromise leader under whom all differences could be resolved, and if he had seen fit to adopt the tactics of even a normally ambitious statesman he might have manœuvred himself into the highest office. Churchill could, of course, have imposed the ultimate sanction of refusing to serve under him, but such considerations never arose. Lord Camrose, who enjoyed Neville Chamberlain's close confidence at the time, has described how Chamberlain when the firm insistence of the Opposition made his resignation inevitable "sought the views of Lord Halifax, who from his position in the Conservative Party, might have claimed some say in the future of the leadership. Halifax had agreed immediately that there was only one possible successor, said he would be happy to serve under Churchill." Halifax's cool altruism was not the least factor in effecting a political transition which not merely baffled the pretensions and propaganda of Dictatorship but in one of the darkest hours of recorded history secured a glorious reprieve for Democracy. Six more weeks of the tentative technique of the Chamberlain Administration and the Allied cause might have been engulfed in total defeat. The dispensation of Dunkirk was not the only escape from peril.

At 6.30 in the morning of 11th May Halifax was receiving the Dutch and Belgian Ambassadors to hear their melancholy reports; it required a stern sense of public duty to insist upon or even to condone a change in the Premiership under such dire conditions. As far as Halifax's personal relationships were concerned he was on equally cordial terms with Churchill as he had been with Chamberlain; differences over India had not impinged upon the two men's genuine respect for each other. There is no reason to think that the undoubted resistance among Chamberlain's colleagues which had impelled Chamberlain against his better judgment to keep Churchill out of the Government until the actual outbreak of hostilities had Halifax's approval; nor again was the change in the political bias from Right to Left-Centre one which would normally disturb Halifax's equilibrium. In fact, the composition of the Churchill Cabinet was more in accord with Halifax's political outlook than its predecessor. None the less it was not long before Halifax found his position in the new Government somewhat exposed; the symptoms of fatal illness soon forced Chamberlain to retire from the political front line. There was a growing volume of comment and criticism that Churchill had been compelled to form his Cabinet in terms of a mere balance of party forces, and that he intended at the first convenient opportunity to effect a more comprehensive reconstruction on national lines. Further scrutiny revealed that Halifax was the only survivor of appeasement.

• • • • • • • •

With astonishing facility a public which had not thought it blasphemy to couple Chamberlain with Christ now eagerly approved a slim new testament entitled *Guilty Men.* Halifax was among the dramatis personae, although the anonymous authors failed to give him a speaking part or press home any indictment against him. But invective is no less damaging for being tendentious; Halifax was the principal victim of this inevitable if haphazard urge to avenge the unpreparedness of Britain, the defencelessness of Dunkirk. In a hue and cry ranging from Middleton Murry to the *Daily Mirror* Halifax was pursued until his very blamelessness became a crime, until even Beverley Baxter was compelled to ask whether he would go down to history as a great man or merely as a good one—a distinction which according to Baxter's glib philosophy was the difference between meaning well and doing well, but which in cruder but more realistic terms involved not so much Halifax's achievements as his prospects. He described how he and several other M.P.s had in 1938 " made a book " on the succession to Chamberlain, from which Halifax emerged as " 6 to 4 favourite " while Churchill was well down the list as a 40 to 1 outsider. " In the meantime," he concluded, " if another book were made on the succession to Mr. Churchill you would now be able to back Lord Halifax at what are technically known as most attractive odds."

A good example of the animosity aroused against Halifax was the battery of criticism and sarcasm to which he was subjected when it was announced that the rooms in the Foreign Office were being redecorated and made into an apartment for the Foreign Secretary. At the beginning of the war Halifax closed his house at Eaton Square and went to live in a suite at the Dorchester, and one incidental effect of the move was to convert that hotel into what might perhaps be termed the " sounding board of Democracy ". Although there was something incongruous in Halifax making his abode in such an atmosphere of sophisticated luxury, social columnists, while he was still in favour, confined themselves to noting approvingly that he had changed his place of worship and was attending the Grosvenor Chapel in South Audley Street several times a week; but the comment on his projected move to the Foreign Office, which was, it would have seemed, extremely sensible procedure and which was in fact made at the express request of Churchill, who required his Foreign Secretary to be immediately available for conference at all times of the day and night, now merely reflected the measure of his fall from grace. " It is gratifying to learn ", wrote A. J. Cummings, " that Lord Halifax is now comfortably ensconced in his new residential quarters—complete with three bathrooms—at the Foreign Office. It would be still more gratifying to learn that somebody else had taken his place there—somebody able and willing to take the right line of approach to Moscow."

Over and above Halifax's general association with appeasement the prolonged frustration of British diplomacy at the Kremlin was perhaps the most potent source of grievance against Halifax. That he had willingly consented to Stafford Cripps' appointment as Ambassador to Russia was overlooked, but instead it was darkly hinted that obstacles to Cripps achieving a glorious reconciliation with Stalin were due mainly to the prejudiced piety of his Chief at the Foreign Office. But in fact the arch appeaser was Stalin himself, and the Russian brand of that policy was even more ambiguous and baffling than its British counterpart had been. During November the scope of the British offer which Cripps had been instructed to put before Stalin for the improvement of Anglo-Soviet relations was suddenly revealed. Apparently Halifax had categorically proposed the *de facto* recognition of Russia's Baltic annexation, an undertaking by the British Government to accept Russia as an equal at the Peace Conference resulting from the war, and in the meanwhile Britain was to take no part in any attack on Russia. All that was asked for in return was a Soviet guarantee of a general attitude of benevolent neutrality.

In rejecting this dramatic bid to short-circuit Hitler's strategy, the *News Chronicle* Diplomatic Correspondent added that it was understood that one of the conditions imposed by the Russians on the negotiations was that any agreement arrived at on the basis of the British plan should remain secret, and he proceeded to ask whether the British indiscretion after waiting in vain for three weeks and three days for a reply from Moscow was yet another " incident in the unfortunate series of misjudgments which have poisoned the relations between Moscow and London for the past eighteen months ". But it is pertinent to suggest that the only value of this still obscure diplomatic initiative rested in the measure of Stalin's readiness to avow it in public.

Rapprochement with Russia and Halifax's popularity were further compromised by a calculated approach to Tokyo to secure some temporary respite in the Far East, a process which culminated during October in the closure of China's military life-line, the Burma Road. It was at once assumed that the arch instigator of this forlorn attempt to appease Japan was Halifax; but the evidence is that, on the contrary, he strongly opposed the experiment as being one which in the light of previous experience would not achieve the immediate results required of it and would from a long-term point of view only increase our diplomatic liabilities, and that Churchill, purely on grounds of military expediency, overruled him. It is greatly to the credit of Kingsley Martin, whose political advocacy was by no means in line with Halifax's, that he specifically corrected this misapprehension in the *New Statesman.* " The decision to close the Burma Road ", he wrote on 12th October, " was Mr. Churchill's own decision, and the decision to open it is also his—Lord Halifax fought against the closing of the road and Mr. Churchill took full responsibility when he announced it."

When in July Halifax made a direct reply over the wireless to one of Hitler's blackmailing orations there was some vigorous politics in his speech, as when he described Mussolini, " flushed by his triumphs over a France whom he has not fought ", in the role of " master of a Mediterranean which he has not conquered ", but his main emphasis was upon Nazism as the challenge of anti-Christ which " it is our duty as Christians to fight with all our power ". The nation was, in fact, regaled not with foreign policy but with a sermon. A few days previously Lord Gort had spoken in similar terms, and there was a widespread reaction that when a Foreign Secretary and a Commander-in-Chief took it upon themselves to expound religious precepts, they were in fact covering up deficiencies in the departments for which they were primarily responsible. It was felt that Halifax's comment on the meaning of prayer and Gort's views on national regeneration would have come better from the Archbishops. Instead the Archbishops changed roles with the soldiers and statesmen and Erastianism prevailed at Lambeth and Bishopthorpe. Neither Halifax and Gort nor the Arch-

GOOD NEIGHBOURS

The U.S. Secretary of the Navy Frank Knox greets Lord and Lady Halifax after the new British Ambassador had left the "Potomac" following his dramatic conference with President Roosevelt at sea. Halifax arrived on the new British warship George V after a secret dash across the Atlantic

bishops enhanced their prestige by this tendency to stray from the context of their duties.

By November rumours of an imminent and drastic Cabinet reshuffle were revived, and were based largely on the assumption that Halifax, unable to see eye to eye with Churchill, worn out by his prolonged labours and anxious for a rest, was about to retire. These reports were so boldly featured that it became necessary for the Ministry of Information to issue a formal denial of them as being " entirely without foundation ", while Gordon Lennox was at pains to point out that Halifax enjoyed the full confidence of the Prime Minister. In the same month Chamberlain died, and in paying tribute and recalling his last farewell to his former Chief Halifax mentioned appeasement and significantly stressed the ill-preparedness not only of Britain but also of France impelling Chamberlain to realize " while he was working for peace how great was the value of time gained even if it amounted to no more ".

This problem of French weakness continued to haunt Halifax's diplomacy to the end, and his appeals to Pétain's honour were not calculated to produce any more solid results than the " decisions " of the Supreme War Council to evoke community of action after the war. All his work, it seemed, was moving towards final frustration. Heroic Greece alone was in active resistance to Nazi designs on the European continent. British diplomacy, along with all other accepted checks and balances, Halifax's ethic and technique, must all surely be swept away or crushed beneath the juggernaut of German strength.

CHAPTER XXXVIII

CHURCHILL'S AMBASSADOR

It was at this fateful moment when Halifax's whole career seemed to be setting in dismal twilight that Lothian's sudden death only a few hours after an epic speech composed by him had been delivered on his behalf, startled the world and snapped the strongest link in Anglo-American co-operation. Roosevelt, who had just secured re-election as President for a third term of four years by as masterly an exhibition of political tactics and strategy as has ever been witnessed in the annals of American democracy, was shrewdly moving from a period of passivity into one of fulfilment and Lothian had just returned after a brief period of leave to Washington full of instructions from the Cabinet, but he was worn out, he could predict the future, he could not live to mould it. There was at once eager speculation as to how Churchill would meet the unforeseen catastrophe which is, it seems, the ineluctable condition of all politics. The first refusal was appropriately given to Lloyd George, but the victor of 1914-18, in spite of his incredible resilience and energy, wisely declined a post of such rigorous implications. When it was known that Lloyd George had definitely refused, informed commentators almost inevitably turned to Halifax. There were, of course, other candidates mentioned, including the Duke of Windsor, Anthony Eden, Sir Archibald Sinclair, Sir Robert Vansittart and Lord Eustace Percy, but from the outset there seemed to be no serious doubt but that Churchill would select his Foreign Secretary and principal colleague. There were obvious reasons for doing so.

The broad strategy of the war, as well as Lothian in the guise of John the Baptist, had created a unique position in the British Embassy at Washington to which only a man who had been in constant touch with and largely responsible for British policy could hope to do justice. The choice was, in fact, virtually confined to the War Cabinet, and in that

Cabinet Halifax alone could take up the strands easily and meet the overwhelming demand for continuity in the representation in America. Furthermore, no one in the Government had been so long in office. Halifax was, in terms of mere efficiency, approaching the end of human endurance; for nineteen years he had, with only the briefest interruption, been subjected to a remorseless administrative grind. If any man needed a change of political air it was, above all, Halifax. If when the news of his appointment was made known there was an underlying impression in the public mind that from the strictly personal view-point he was being awarded a consolation prize, there was no less a lively appreciation that in breaking new ground he would be refreshing himself and thereby enlarging the scope of his contribution to the State.

Halifax in his tribute to Lothian as man and Ambassador unwittingly defined his own qualifications to succeed him. " His perspective was seldom at fault, so that he naturally faced any problem in its right relation to the whole setting. . . . Being almost completely natural and wholly devoid of insincerity, he was naturally at ease with all people and all people were at ease with him." There are many illusions about Halifax, but perhaps the most damaging and deceptive is that he is aloof and formal in his personal relationships, pious to the point of frigidity. The doctrine " We are not amused " has been all too frequently applied to him, but Halifax is both amused and amusing. Indeed his personal charm and persuasiveness are such that political adversaries justly regard them as a menace! The attractiveness of his personality does not easily lend itself to the mass adulation required by modern high-powered propaganda, and although Halifax's capacity for informal friendships was indeed a priceless asset for his duties in America, this attribute of his was largely hidden from public view, and the American reaction to his appointment was not enthusiastic.

The idea that Churchill was sending to America a representative of an old and discredited British order to interpret a New Deal for Britain and for Europe was widely canvassed; but there was at the same time the realization that, to quote the *New York Times,* " there is no more determined enemy of Hitler and all he stands for than this gentle, great-hearted Englishman. If Lord Halifax had not been bent on winning the war and ridding mankind of the greatest menace of modern times, we can be sure that Churchill would not have sent him." What Churchill had done was, in fact, to raise the status of the Embassy in Washington to that of a Cabinet post. It was already, with salary and expenses allowance amounting to £16,000 a year, at the summit of the diplomatic hierarchy. The mission of Halifax to Washington was the first British response to the doctrine so successfully sponsored by the Nazis that an Ambassador's mission is more than that of a diplomat. Not only were two Ministers of outstanding ability appointed, Neville Butler who had served under Lothian, and Sir Gerald Campbell who was transferred from Canada, to reinforce the new Ambassador on the "career" work, but Churchill in the farewell Pilgrims' luncheon was at pains to point out that Halifax still retained his place in the War Cabinet and was merely seconded for special duty.

By this imaginative decision Churchill has undoubtedly insured and enhanced Halifax's political influence for the future. Politically Halifax has not been pensioned off, but deliberately retained among the four or five probables for the Premiership in succession to Churchill. At the moment such a consideration seems to be merest fantasy. Never in the history of British politics has a leader enjoyed such an unqualified personal ascendancy as Churchill. It is a terrifying popularity of which at times even he seems to be a little afraid. Like the elder Pitt, he can always appeal beyond Parliament to the people, but that is an asset to be held in reserve; at Westminster, although the loyalty to Churchill is by now complete, it must not be regarded as permanent or unqualified. As far as the alignment of party groups is concerned he leads a somewhat uneasy and unnatural alliance. There is, of course, nothing in it from which Hitler can derive the slightest encouragement; opposition to Nazism resolves all discords, and by assuming leadership of the Conservative Party Churchill effectively stified any political prospects of a British Vichy. But neither Socialists nor the large Conservative majority which underwrote appeasement can be wholly relied upon to follow Churchill into the paths of peacemaking. Churchill has himself testified to the inevitable descent from platitude to controversy, but this is not wholly due to the exigencies of war but to unresolved claims and controversies between the party groups which make up the Churchill Coalition.

Once again Halifax has escaped from what is potentially a delicate and compromising political situation. " It may well be argued ", commented *The Times,* " in support of his going at this moment that his greatest value to this country will be shown in the days that are still to come, when victory is finally assured and all our resources of leadership will be needed to secure a just and lasting settlement. Those days may be far distant; it is possible that Lord Halifax may have returned from his mission before they arrive; it is by no means inconceivable that for the time being he may be able to hasten this better from Washington than from London." The reshuffle resulting from Halifax's appointment brought Eden automatically back to the Foreign Office after a period of glittering success as War Minister. The only surprise was the transfer of Margesson from his pivotal position as Chief Whip to the War Office, a move which has materially affected the discipline and cohesion of Conservatism.

. . . .

The high drama of Halifax's departure from England and arrival in America, Churchill's farewell and Roosevelt's greeting, the historic maiden voyage of the giant battleship *King George V* was not only the consummation of his own resplendent career but also authentic showmanship. At last the Democracies had paid due tribute to symbolism. Here was a pageant of power and goodwill the details of which as they were flashed across the world were an inspiring contrast to the whole elaborate sham of Hitler's ceremonial. Churchill's " fervent hope that he may prosper in a mission as momentous as any that the Monarch has entrusted to an Englishman in the lifetime of the oldest of us here " set the tone of the popular attitude to Halifax's royal progress. Any lingering doubt about Churchill's confidence in the new Ambassador was decisively set at rest. " In Edward Halifax," said Churchill in a memorable eulogy, " we have a man of light and leading, whose company is a treat and whose friendship it is an honour to enjoy. I have often disagreed with him in the twenty years I have known him in the rough and tumble of British politics, but I have always respected him and his actions because I know that courage and fidelity are the essence of his being, and that, whether as a soldier with his regiment in the last war or as the ruler of, and trustee for 400,000,000 in India, he has never swerved from the path of duty as he saw it shining out before him ", and then a typically endearing and exhilarating Churchillian thrust, " as a man of deep but unparaded and unaffected religious convictions and as for many years an ardent lover of the chase he has known how to get the best out of both worlds ".

The War Cabinet was present in force at the station to see him off; Mr. and Mrs. Churchill, Roosevelt's friend and special envoy in England, Harry Hopkins, accompanied Lord and Lady Halifax to the north. The journey across the Atlantic in the mighty new battleship was comparatively uneventful, and the form of his arrival took the American Press, which prides itself on its sources of information and on its capacity to anticipate news, completely by surprise. Even while the *King George V* steamed slowly and carefully through the fog past the great naval base at Norfolk Virginia towards Annapolis no clear information was available about the precise plans of arrival. Then came the astonishing news that Roosevelt, wearing fur cap and fur-lined coat to protect him against the worst blizzard of the winter, risking slippery ice-covered roads, and ignoring warnings of mist, storm and gale, had driven from the White House and boarded the Presidential yacht *Potomac*. He was accompanied by the Republican Colonel Frank Knox, Secretary of the Navy, Admiral Stark, Chief of naval operations, and his military and naval aides. The *Potomac* disappeared into the haze, and several miles off shore Lord and Lady Halifax were transferred to her; when she arrived at Annapolis Roosevelt was seen dining with Halifax on his left and Lady Halifax on his right. So protocol and precedent were set aside, so Anglo-American friendship knew its finest hour.

If America is the home of sensation, here was a sensation which required no overstatement to arouse the eager interest and generous emotions of the American people. From the exacting ordeal of his initiation with the omnipotent and hard-boiled reporters of the American Press Halifax emerged triumphant. There could surely be no higher tribute to his resilient personality nor better augury for the future progress of his mission than this success with the most searching and remorseless cross-examiners in the world. He struck the right note from the outset, when he greeted the rain-soaked reporters at Annapolis with the apology " I'm sorry you have waited so long on a night like this ". To guide him in the mysteries of " Public Relations " Halifax had brought with him Charles Peake of the Foreign Office, who had served him with almost excessive zeal throughout his Foreign Secretaryship. Peake assiduously watched over Halifax's contacts with the Press in London and Geneva, and must accordingly take some share of responsibility for the needless distortions and barriers which separated his Chief from British newspapermen. An American journalist in London was reported in the *Evening Standard* as saying, " If in Washington Charles is as successful in establishing personal contacts between Lord Halifax and the newshounds as he has been in preventing it in London he will be doing a swell job."

All the evidence would suggest that this indispensable " swell job " has been done. Halifax has already had several Press receptions, and at each he has shown readiness to speak with complete frankness, to express a full-blooded personal view-point on big strategic questions, a surprising aptitude for impromptu reply; in a word, a capacity for supplying genuine news. Glen Parry of the *New York Sun* summed up the general sentiment when he asserted that the British Envoy " revealed himself as being as able a conductor of relations with the Press as any man in Washington, which, considering the Chief Executive's talents in that direction, is no weak statement ". Similarly the Washington Correspondent of *United Press* asserted that he " had shown himself as ready as President Roosevelt to toss diplomatic niceties and stuffy formalities from the window ". This signal praise was in some ways a natural reaction from the widespread " opposition " estimates of the man and his work which held the field before his arrival in America.

Not that it was roses all the way, not all the tact and discretion in the world will guarantee escape from attack in a land where so many regard criticism of all executive action as a solemn duty and a priceless heritage. Thus Halifax soon found himself embroiled with suspicious Isolationists because of an inoffensive courtesy visit to Sol Bloom and Senator Walter George, Government leaders in Congress and

Senate respectively. Isolationist Congressmen, in desperate search for material with which to stem the steady advance of the Lease and Lend Bill, pounced on Halifax's " extraordinarily unusual " procedure. Dark hints were dropped that he was lobbying for support, demands were made that Congress should be fully informed. Bloom was provoked into retorting " Lord Halifax called at my office. He didn't sneak in. The Press knew about it. We had a nice talk, the principal subject of which was the exhibit of Magna Carta during the World's Fair." Halifax had also asked apparently about the timing of the Lease and Lend Bill. That was the secret Congress was trying to uncover, " and it is the kind of secret I want the world to know about ", Bloom added. It was probably as a result of this incident that Halifax decided to postpone his first major speech to the Pilgrims until the Lease and Lend Bill was brought safely to the Statute book. There was resentment even at what was termed the " barrage of secrecy " surrounding the Roosevelt-Halifax meeting, and Roosevelt was obliged to explain at his Press Conference that war risks were involved.

In all his public statements, however, Halifax has shown acute perception of the general temper of the people. His very first words were, " the more quickly your generous help can be effected, the sooner we will be able to break this Nazi power that is trying to enslave Europe and the world ", and he has never relaxed the pressure of this message. Within twelve hours of his arrival he was in conclave with Cordell Hull, a man of similar temperament and moral outlook to himself, who has during the past three years been in a position to form a full and fair assessment of his record at the Foreign Office. His eagerly awaited speech to the Pilgrims was undoubtedly his most ambitious and comprehensive analysis of Britain's peace aims, and it was a sufficiently powerful vindication of British statesmanship to thwart the manœuvres of the Isolationists who hoped that a non-committal Halifax would provide damaging evidence of a perfidious Albion. The inherent liberality of his vision is to be seen in his emphasis on " our aim to promote the common interests in the greatest possible interchange of goods and services. Problems invoking common needs can only be solved by common action." Perhaps it is fitting that we should take leave of him as he identifies himself with this

IN CONFERENCE

Halifax enters at once on his momentous duties in America by conferring at the State Department in Washington with the Secretary of State, Cordell Hull. January, 1941.

splendid but none the less substantial vision of democratic co-operation.

. . . .

He is working in America not simply as a respected emissary of a friendly foreign Power but as the trusted entrepreneur between two men who at a supreme crisis in human affairs have by monumental words and heroic action restored men to a new and higher faith in freedom. It has been suggested that Halifax's career has run the full circle, and that he is repeating in the West the same mission of fulfilment as he accomplished in the East, but the analogy between Irwin the Viceroy and Halifax the Ambassador should not be pressed too far. There were in India obvious limitations to his possible initiative, but in America there is almost boundless scope. "I have always taken the view," said Churchill when he proposed Halifax's health at the farewell Pilgrims' luncheon, "that the fortunes of mankind in its tremendous journey are principally decided for good or ill—but mainly for good, for the path is upward—by its greatest men and its greatest episodes." In this mysterious interplay of personality and events from which Roosevelt and Churchill emerge as two of the most formative leaders in history, Halifax is given at once the chance and the capacity to unite their ideals and assimilate their inspiration.

Now that he has been called to this pivotal position, his period as Foreign Secretary should not be regarded as an irrelevant or retrograde phase in his career; it was in a sense a period of preparation. Like Salisbury before him, and he is in many ways a genuine Cecilian, he readily embraced the concept of a Britain inherently detached from, yet interested in Europe, using a diplomacy weighted and adjusted by armed power but made more acceptable to insular tradition by lack of commitments. But with America's entry into the last war and departure from the League, and with the general political, economic and social upheavals in Europe in the period of so-called peace, Pax Britannica was no longer a European reality. Britain had, in fact, ceased to be the fulcrum in the Balance of Power; she was of herself no more than one of the acting and counteracting forces. Thus in terms of strategic action, the British Navy is one force, and German population, industry and organization operating as Nazi militarism are the other, and embody the problem of irresistible force meeting the immovable object.

In Halifax's attitude to Munich is to be found a genuine attempt to circumvent by diplomacy this unprecedented dilemma by a remembrance of a vanished past. There was bluff at Munich, but Hitler was not responsible for it; the deepest deception lay in Chamberlain's and Halifax's implicit belief that the concert of Europe could still be made to play a recognizable tune. Chamberlain kept up the pretence even to recalling Disraeli and reiterating the Peace with Honour motif. The only analogy was that Hitler, like his master Bismarck, was prepared—though grudgingly perhaps—to give us the illusion of being arbiters, knowing well where the balance of effective force lay. The blame for this disastrous misconception is not really to be attributed to any one man; it has been distributed evenly over the popular sentiment and opinion of the British Commonwealth.

Yet here is perhaps the deepest reason why, to quote Keith Feiling, the strain of Halifax's speeches over the past six years have not been " of the confident morning but of the weary midnight watch ". But even in the midst of bloody ordeal and unpredictable hazards a new Pax Britannica begins to take shape, and to this great Renaissance are dedicated the service, the faith and the talent of Edward Halifax.

INDEX